ASSESSING WRITING

ASSESSING WRITING

A Critical Sourcebook

EDITED BY

Brian Huot
Kent State University

Peggy O'Neill
Loyola College in Maryland

BEDFORD / ST. MARTIN'S   Boston • New York

NCTE National Council of
Teachers of English

Urbana, Illinois

For Bedford/St. Martin's

Executive Editor: Leasa Burton
Editorial Assistant: Sarah Guariglia
Production Supervisor: Andrew Ensor
Executive Marketing Manager: Jenna Bookin Barry
Project Management: DeMasi Design and Publishing Services
Text Design: Anna Palchik
Cover Design: Donna Lee Dennison
Composition: LinMark Design
Printing and Binding: RR Donnelley & Sons Company

President: Joan E. Feinberg
Editorial Director: Denise B. Wydra
Editor in Chief: Karen S. Henry
Director of Marketing: Karen Melton Soeltz
Director of Editing, Design, and Production: Marcia Cohen
Assistant Director of Editing, Design, and Production: Elise S. Kaiser
Manager, Publishing Services: Emily Berleth

NCTE Stock No. 02077
Published in cooperation with the
National Council of Teachers of English
1111 W. Kenyon Road
Urbana, Illinois 61801-1096
www.ncte.org

Library of Congress Control Number: 2007933786

Manufactured in the United States of America.

3 2 1 0 9
f e d c

For information, write: Bedford/St. Martin's, 75 Arlington Street,
Boston, MA 02116   (617-399-4000)

ISBN-10: 0-312-47596-9
ISBN-13: 978-0-312-47596-3

ACKNOWLEDGMENTS
Acknowledgments and copyrights are continued at the back of the book on pages
474–75, which constitute an extension of the copyright page.

CONTENTS

*assessment culture in which teachers talk with each other about their
students and teaching.*

ASSESSING WRITING

An Introduction to Writing Assessment Theory and Practice

Now, more than ever, writing assessment is a critical activity in our profession — for accrediting agencies, policymakers, and government organizations demanding evidence of learning from educational institutions. While the demand for assessment often comes from those outside the writing assessment field, assessment is still a critical component when teaching writing, creating curricula, and developing programs.

Increasingly, to be considered an effective writing teacher — not to mention an effective writing program director — one must be able to respond to the varied writing assessment needs of students, faculty, and institutions. However, many practicing composition teachers and administrators lack formal assessment preparation, and many writing teachers and writing program administrators view assessment as a punitive force for students, faculty, and progressive forms of instruction. While assessment fears are justified, a powerful discourse like assessment can be harnessed for positive and productive writing instruction and administration. Many conversations about assessment seem to assume formal, standardized activities, such as placement or exit testing, but it is important to remember that assessment is a critical component of writing: Writers self-assess and frequently seek evaluative input from readers throughout their writing processes. Although this volume does not focus on the assessment writers do as they write, it does remind us that assessment activities are not hostile to writing. On the contrary, they contribute to success (Huot 2002).

The purpose of this collection of articles is to help both practicing professionals and graduate students understand the theory and practice of writing assessment. We focus on assessment that functions outside a single course — that is, placement, exit testing, and program evaluation. While we realize the significance of response and classroom evaluation and see it as closely connected to large-scale assessment, we have excluded articles about it in this volume due to space constraints. Portfolios, for example, could be the topic of a stand-alone volume, but readers should view portfolios as part of the wider field, not as isolated or distinct from other methods and not as separate from assessment theory.

The readings collected here reflect a field of writing assessment that encompasses ideas, issues, and research from a range of scholars in college writing assessment, K–12 teachers and researchers, and educational measurement theory and practice. For example, we include a piece by Roberta Camp, who was an employee of the Educational Testing Service (ETS). Camp's research on portfolios in the late 1970s and early 1980s was a precursor to a wealth of portfolio activity in composition and education. While it is common for college assessment scholarship to represent ETS and other educational measurement scholars in opposition to the models, theories, and practices best suited to theoretically and pedagogically informed assessment practices (Lynne, White, Yancey, and others), we see theories from educational measurement, especially validity theory, as a strong platform for advocating newer, more progressive forms of writing assessment. In addition to Camp, this volume includes work from those like Pamela Moss, who are not primarily associated with college composition but instead specialize in education and educational measurement.

To illustrate how theories from outside college writing assessment can be valuable and how this volume projects a specific vision of writing assessment, we look at dual historic threads since the 1940s. The first thread reviews the role of reliability in the development of holistic scoring of student writing; the second looks at the development of validity as a psychometric concept. For us, these two threads come together to produce a rich understanding of writing assessment as a field.

Writing assessment has had reliability problems since at least the 1912 study by Daniel Starch and Edward Elliot, which reported that teachers could not agree on grades for the same student essays. Reliability in this sense referred to consistency of scoring across readers, which later became known as interrater reliability. By the beginning of the 1940s, the College Entrance Examination Board (CEEB), looking at the great success it had had piloting the Scholastic Aptitude Test (SAT) for the college admission for special populations of students, was seeking ways to expand the use of the SAT. When America went to war in late 1941, however, the death knell for essay testing at the CEEB sounded. The CEEB immediately, and permanently, suspended essay testing, because the then-new SAT could produce admission data for students more quickly, allowing them to start college sooner. This would contribute to America's war effort because colleges like Princeton accelerated instruction for students who had deferred military service and who upon graduation would be called to active service (Elliot 100). The backlash from English teachers was strong and vociferous, causing John Stalnaker, chief CEEB officer, to note:

> The type of test so highly valued by teachers of English, which requires the candidate to write a theme or essay, is not a worthwhile testing device. Whether or not the writing of essays as a means of teaching writing deserves the place it has in the secondary school curriculum may be equally questioned. Eventually, it is hoped, sufficient evidence may be accumulated to outlaw forever "the write a theme on . . ." type of examination. (Fuess 158)

English teachers' protest over the termination of essay testing forced the CEEB to develop the English Composition Test (ECT), which was read and scored by teachers at their home institutions. Test developers found the requirement amusing considering the labor involved (see O'Neill et al.'s discussion of the labor involved in writing assessment), though it might also be taken as a sign of the commitment teachers had to the direct assessment of student writing (Elliot).

At any rate, the ECT compounded the ongoing problems with the ability of test developers to furnish a testing environment that yielded consistent scores from different readers for the same papers (interrater reliability). Throughout the 1950s, test developers, most employed by ETS, worked to develop methods that would ensure agreement among raters. Ultimately, this work failed, inspiring the ETS to discontinue the ECT and create tests of usage and mechanics[1] to assess student writing (Elliot; Yancey).

During the 1960s, test developers made two important breakthroughs. First, in 1961, Diederich, French, and Carlton published a study in which 53 raters scored 300 papers on a nine-point scale. Although the vast majority of papers (over 94 percent) received at least seven different scores, the researchers used factor analysis to analyze and determine the main influences on the raters' scores. These five main factors—Ideas, Form, Flavor (style), Mechanics, and Wording—became the basis of what would become analytic scoring, a system in which raters read and scored student writing according to their evaluations of essays' five factors. Scores could be weighted depending on the assessment's purpose. A decade or so later, a team led by Richard Lloyd-Jones revised analytic scoring using categories germane to the writing task to create what came to be known as primary trait scoring, which was used in early writing assessment for the National Assessment of Educational Progress (NAEP).

The second important breakthrough of test development came in 1966, when Godshalk, Swineford, and Coffman published a study detailing a set of procedures in an ETS research bulletin. These procedures, which would become known as holistic scoring, assigned texts single scores based on a set of criteria, or rubric, through which readers were trained to agree. By the mid-1960s, ETS researchers had developed the procedures to begin the modern era in writing assessment, in which writing assessment contained actual student writing that was read and scored at reliable rates.[2] By the mid-1970s, direct writing assessment was a common practice in education and composition and a subject for the scholarly literature (Cooper and Odell).

While educational measurement test developers—largely from ETS—had seemingly solved the reliability problem for writing within a psychometric framework that demands "reliability be a necessary but insufficient condition for validity" (Cherry and Meyer 110), validity theorists headed by Lee J. Cronbach had begun to repudiate the positivist basis for validity in educational and psychological tests. Since the creation of educational and psychological measurement and testing in the later nineteenth and early twentieth centuries, validity had been considered the most important aspect of assessment (Angoff; Ittenbach, Esters, and Wainer; Mayrhauser). Nonetheless, very little scholarship about validity appeared during the first half or so of the twentieth century (Angoff). Odd as it might seem, test validity was often seen as something best left to test authors because those authors would have the most information and deepest understanding of how well a test or measure might work. The lack of scholarship in validity for the burgeoning field of assessment, which was dominated by intelligence testing,[3] was also influenced by the development of psychometrics, the statistical apparatus for measurement, as well as by the largely positivist paradigm within which most social science operated during the first half of the twentieth century.

J. P. Guilford's essay on validity in 1946 is the most substantive scholarship on validity in testing from the first part of the twentieth century and the best summary of the way in which validity was conceived and used. For Guilford, "a test is valid for anything with which it correlates" (429). This definition reflects both the acontextual nature of much positivist philosophy as well as the psychometric orientation for the social science and testing of that era. As Cronbach notes, validity's definition at this time as the degree to which a test measures what it purports to measure focuses on the test's accuracy: Did the test do what it said it would, and how well did it do it? Subsequent notions that stipulated "a test is valid if it serves the purpose for which it is used, raised a question about worth" (Cronbach, 1988, 5). This shift in focus from accuracy and truth (positivism is, after all, based on a Platonic search for truth) to the value or meaning of a measure began the long road away from a positivist orientation for validity to one based on a measure's value. Whether we focus on the work of Samuel Messick or Cronbach or the most recent *Standards for Educational and Psychological Testing* authored jointly in 1999[4] by the American Educational Research Association, the American Psychological Association, and the National Council on Measurement in Education, validity as it is currently understood is about validating decisions based on an assessment. Cronbach sums up this position and the logic that guides it in his memorable statement about validity and interpretation:

> To call Test A or Test B invalid is illogical. Particular interpretations are what we validate. To say "the evidence to date is consistent with the interpretation" makes far better sense than saying "the test has construct validity." Validation is a lengthy, even endless process. ("Construct Validation . . ." 151)

The shift in focus for validity from the test itself to the decisions and interpretations we make based on the test marks a movement away from a positivist orientation that looks for an ideal reality or "true score" and recognizes the contingent nature of human experience and value. This shift in focus from the test itself to the decisions made based on a test also moves away from the form of the examination to the examination's use. In other words, we cannot assume, assert, or even argue that one form of assessment is more valid than another, because validation is a local, contingent process. It is also, as Cronbach notes, an ongoing process in which every use of an assessment implies a series of inquiries into the assessment's accuracy, appropriateness, and consequences for learners and the learning environment. This local, contingent, fluid nature of validity and validity inquiry also marks a movement away from a fixed, positivist notion of truth to a more postmodern notion of reality as something in which value is constructed by individuals and groups to reflect the ongoing, changing nature of human experience. This localized positioning for validity works to deconstruct unequal power relationships in which a central authority is in control and in which European, middle-class, male, heterosexual values are held above all others.

In short, once the CEEB decided to switch to the cheaper, quicker, more reliable SAT, English teachers lobbied for reliable writing assessment that included students' writing. While the ETS was working toward new, reliable writing assessments that would eventually produce holistic, analytic, and primary trait scoring, educational measurement theorists headed by Cronbach and later joined by Messick would work to develop theories and practices for validity that reflect the importance and weight of decisions made on data generated from tests and exams.

Writing-assessment procedures have advanced beyond holistic, analytic, and primary trait scoring. Many new procedures work toward having readers make decisions (like the basis for validity) rather than score pieces of writing. Reliability is still an important part of writing assessment because without consistency in judgment, decisions about students' writing would have more to do with who read the piece of writing than with who wrote it. On the other hand, current understanding positions reliability within the overall umbrella of validity, so each use of a writing assessment includes a check on the consistency of decision making among judges, when multiple judges are used for the same decision. We see and present in this volume a field of writing assessment that draws together the issues of reliability and validity reviewed previously with the insistence on using student writing or student decision making (self-directed placement asks students to decide which courses they would like to be placed in) as the basis for making decisions about students. Exploring the accuracy, appropriateness, and consequences of decision making based on assessment should be a part of writing assessment. The articles presented here introduce this view.

Depending on a host of factors, the field of writing assessment can be constructed in various ways. As a result, we faced the challenge of how to construct this volume, and with which articles. In the end, after much discussion, negotiation, and reviewer feedback, we settled on three sections: (1) Foundations, (2) Models, and (3) Issues. This structure recognizes that there is varied important and necessary work in writing assessment and that people who will be using this volume will have different needs. For example, some readers will look for models for writing assessments, while others will look for basic, foundational knowledge of writing-assessment history, practice, and theory. While these three sections overlap to some degree, each presents a unique version of the field in which an understanding of foundational issues is as important as a range of assessment options or forays into specific issues.

We chose "Foundations" as one of our volume's sections after using categories like "Theory" and "History." While it is important that compositionists know both writing theory and history, we see this knowledge as foundational to other work. "Foundations," as we call them, span such subjects as fundamental research comparing analytic, holistic, and primary trait scoring (Veal and Hudson); theoretical work on holistic scoring (White), reliability (Cherry and Meyer; Moss, 1994; Williamson), and validity (Huot; Moss, 1998); and the history of writing assessment (Camp; Yancey). This section functions as an abbreviated introduction to the field and, with our bibliography, should provide interested writing teachers and program administrators an introduction to the most important historical and theoretical issues in writing assessment.

If the "Foundations" section recognizes the need for a theoretical and historical introduction to the field of writing assessment, the "Models" section reminds us that assessment is something you do. Writing assessment is an activity — a practice — as well as a theoretically rich scholarly field. Our article selection for this section is hardly comprehensive. In fact, we left out several model programs we are fond of, including work by SusanMarie Harrington; David Blakesley; Lisa Johnson-Shull and Diane Kelley-Riley, contributors to *Beyond Outcomes* edited by Rich Haswell, a volume we recommend to any anyone looking for models;[5] and many others. (See *Assessing Writing across the Curriculum* and the *Outcomes Book* edited by SusanMarie Harrington, Keith Rhodes, Ruth Overman Fischer, and Rita Malenczyk for other great models for writing assessment.) For this section of the volume, we selected articles to represent models that are varied as well as influential. For example, William L. Smith was one of the first to really move beyond holistic scoring with his set of procedures, which produced decisions directly with greater accuracy and a higher degree of interrater reliability. Smith's work also furnishes a strong model for validating a writing assessment program. For example, Hester et al. adapted Smith's procedures for writing assessment and validation over a 6-year period. Haswell and Wyche-Smith provided one of the first procedures to move beyond holistic scoring and having each paper read twice. Durst, Roemer, and Schultz reported on a model for exit testing that includes teams of teachers reading student portfolios. Royer and Gilles's work on placement moved the decision to the student. Their work has been highly influential, and we recommend their edited collection. Haswell and McLeod modeled various strategies for reporting on writing across the curriculum assessment. Michael Carter's piece provides a clear introduction to outcomes assessment for writing across a curriculum and can be easily adapted to any writing program. This piece should be especially useful for the many writing teachers and program administrators responding to calls for outcomes assessment.

Together, the models in this volume offer a solid introduction to, and resource for, various kinds of writing assessment. These models should be useful for readers who want to understand how theories like reliability and validity function in practice as well as demonstrate site-based, context-sensitive, rhetorically informed, and accessible assessments that meet local needs. The assessment programs described in this section are designed not as models to be mimicked but rather are samples of how writing assessments can be tailored to specific purposes, programs, and institutions.

The choice of "Issues" as our last volume section—and our article choices for it—illustrate how the field of writing assessment has changed over the past several years. In 1990, Brian published a bibliographic essay in *Review of Educational Research* in which he determined the three main research areas in writing assessment to be topic selection and task development, text and writing quality, and influences on raters. Through the 1990s, however, researchers' attention shifted, or rather expanded, to include many topics beyond technical concerns of procedures and practices. Our "Issues" section attempts to capture this wide range of topics, from the ways in which teachers construct student writing (Freedman) to the machine scoring of student essays (Williamson). While we could devote an entire volume to the issues now being addressed in writing assessment, the purpose of this section is to provide a strong introduction to such important issues as programmatic and extracurricular influences (Hamp-Lyons and Condon), gender (Haswell and Haswell), race (Ball), politics and power (Huot and Williamson), teaching and assessing English as a second language (Hamp-Lyons), and the tensions inherent in many assessment programs. This section identifies some of the key issues we need to attend to, not just in designing and implementing writing assessments but in reading and evaluating the results of assessments. By helping readers frame questions and articulate concerns that may relate to specific assessment decisions, this section can also serve as a starting place for critical issues when discussing writing assessments with institutional administrators or testing staff. Certainly, we cannot cover all issues, but we hope to give readers a sense of many of the issues being addressed and the wide range of issues writing assessment touches. In addition to the articles that appear in each section, we include an annotation in the table of contents for each article, as well as an additional readings section at the end of the book.

Choosing articles and sections for this volume has been quite an adventure. This version is quite different from the one we sent out for review. The original, well over 700 pages, was pared to less than half the selections. Only one original section remains. We learned much from our reviewers, who made suggestions about articles and challenged our conceptions of this book. We could not have done the job we were finally able to do without the expert help of Linda Adler-Kassner, Eastern Michigan University; Chris Anson, North Carolina State University; Norbert Elliot, New Jersey Institute of Technology; Anne Herrington, University of Massachusetts, Amherst; William Smith, Oregon Health & Science University, *emeritus*; and two anonymous reviewers. In some ways, this project was like a puzzle: "Pick X number of readings on your area of expertise that make a statement about the area within X number of pages." As with all puzzles, we learned a lot and eventually arrived at a spot in which the pieces seemed to fit. We hope they fit for you, our readers. What is even clearer to us now than when we first started is that a sourcebook on writing assessment for those who teach writing and administer writing programs at the college level is an important and needed resource. We are grateful to Bedford / St. Martin's for giving us the opportunity and support to produce such a volume and for assigning Leasa Burton to work with us. She and her assistant, Sarah Guariglia, have been insightful and supportive in too many ways for us to mention. This volume would not be as good without their help. We would also like to recognize and thank Joan Feinberg, Denise Wydra, Karen Henry, and Emily Berleth.

Brian Huot, Hudson, Ohio
Peggy O'Neill, Baltimore, Maryland

NOTES

1. These tests of usage and mechanics used to assess writing ability and later generations like the COMPASS test, an untimed editing test delivered on computer, were called indirect writing assessment, a term we refuse to use because we believe writing assessment must include students actually writing.

2. These rates of reliability were often not high enough in a strict psychometric sense for the scores produced to stand by themselves (Camp, P. Cooper). The Godshalk study, for example, included scores from multiple-choice tests as well as holistically scored essays.

3. For a discussion of the history of intelligence testing and its connection to the history of writing assessment, see the history chapter in the forthcoming volume *The Handbook of College Writing Assessment*, by Peggy O'Neill, Cindy Moore, and Brian Huot (under contract with Utah State University Press).

4. This version of the *Standards* was the fifth to be produced since the 1950s. It is updated every 10 years or so to reflect the professional standards for educational and psychological testing.

5. See the Additional Readings section at the end of this volume for the bibliographic information of this work and others mentioned which are not included in the book's contents.

WORKS CITED

American Educational Research Association, American Psychological Association, and National Council on Measurement in Education. *Standards for Educational and Psychological Testing*. Washington, DC: American Educational Research Association. 1999.

Angoff, William H. "Validity: An Evolving Concept." *Test Validity*. Eds. Howard Wainer and Henry I. Braun. Hillsdale, NJ: Lawrence Erlbaum, 1988. 19–32.

Cherry, Roger, and Paul Meyer. "Reliability Issues in Holistic Assessment." *Validating Holistic Scoring for Writing Assessment: Theoretical and Empirical Foundations*. Eds. Michael Williamson and Brian Huot. Cresskill, NJ: Hampton P, 1993. 109–41.

Cooper, Charles, and Lee Odell, eds. *Evaluating Writing: Describing, Measuring, and Judging*. Urbana, IL: NCTE, 1977.

Cooper, P. *The Assessment of Writing Ability: A Review of Research*. Princeton, NJ: Educational Testing Service, 1984. GREB No. 82–15R.

Cronbach, Lee J. "Construct Validation after 30 Years." *Intelligence Measurement, Theory, and Public Policy: Proceedings of a Symposium in Honor of L. G. Humphreys*. Ed. R. L. Linn. Urbana and Chicago, IL: U of Illinois P, 1989. 147–71.

———. "Five Perspectives on Validity Argument." *Test Validity*. Eds. H. Wainer and H. I. Braun. Hillsdale, NJ: Lawrence Erlbaum, 1988. 3–17.

Diederich, Paul, B. John W. French, and Sydell T. Carlton. *Factors in Judgments of Writing Quality*. Princeton, NJ: Educational Testing Service, 1961. RB No. 61–15 ED 002 172.

Elliot, Norbert. *On a Scale: A Social History of Writing Assessment in America*. New York: Peter Lang, 2005.

Fuess, Claude. *The College Board: Its First 50 Years*. New York: College Entrance Examination Board, 1967.

Godshalk, Fred I., Frances Swineford, and William E. Coffman. *The Measurement of Writing Ability*. Princeton, NJ: Educational Testing Service, 1966. CEEB RM No. 6.

Huot, Brian. "The Literature of Direct Writing Assessment: Major Concerns and Prevailing Trends." *Review of Educational Research* 60 (1990): 237–63.

————. *(Re)Articulating Writing Assessment for Teaching and Learning*. Logan: Utah State UP, 2002.

Ittenbach, Richard F., Irvin G. Esters, and Howard Wainer. "The History of Test Development." *Contemporary Intellectual Assessment: Theories, Tests, and Issues*. Eds. Dawn P. Flanagan, Judy L. Genshaft, and Patti L. Harrison. New York: Guilford, 1997. 17–31.

Lloyd-Jones, Richard. "Primary Trait Scoring." *Evaluating Writing: Describing, Measuring, and Judging*. Eds. Charles R. Cooper and Lee Odell. Urbana, IL: NCTE, 1977.

Lynne, Patricia. *Coming to Terms: A Theory of Writing Assessment*. Logan: Utah State UP, 2004.

Mayrhauser Von, Richard T. "The Mental Testing Community and Validity: A Prehistory." *Evolving Perspectives on the History of Psychology*. Eds. Wade E. Pickren and Donald A. Dewsbury. Washington, DC: American Psychological Association, 2005. 303–21.

Messick, Samuel. "Meaning and Values in Test Validation: The Science and Ethics of Assessment." *Educational Researcher* 18.2 (1989): 5–11.

O'Neill, Peggy, Ellen Schendel, Michael Williamson, and Brian Huot. "Assessment as Labor and the Labor of Assessment." *Labor, Writing Technologies, and the Shaping of Composition in the Academy*. Eds. Pamela Takayoshi and Patricia Sullivan. Cresskill, NJ: Hampton P, 2007. 75–96.

Starch Daniel, and Edward Elliott. "Reliability of the Grading of High School Work in English." *School Review* 20 (1912): 442–57.

White, Edward M. *Teaching and Assessing Writing, 2nd Ed*. San Francisco: Jossey-Bass, 1994.

Yancey, Kathleen Blake. "Looking Back as We Look Forward: Historicizing Writing Assessment." *College Composition and Communication* 1999 (50): 483–503.

PART ONE

Foundations

1   *Direct and Indirect Measures for Large-Scale Evaluation of Writing*

L. RAMON VEAL AND SALLY ANN HUDSON

As a result of the competency based education movement, efforts have been made to specify performance objectives and develop applied performance assessments. A performance objective frequently identified as a requirement for high school graduation is the "ability to select, organize, and compose written material in the context of academic problems, everyday tasks, and employment activities" (Georgia State Board of Education Policy 30–700). This ability is best tested, according to many professionals, directly through actual writing (NCTE, 1979; ETS, 1978; CEEB, 1979), and at least 23 states now rely on writing samples for all or part of their statewide writing assessments (Spandel & Stiggins, 1980). As an alternative, approximations of this ability can be tested indirectly with objective tests. These "skills related to writing," such as choosing the correctly spelled word from a list, selecting the appropriate punctuation for an unpunctuated sentence, or picking out the best organized paragraph from among several offered, can all be assessed reliably (Spandel & Stiggins, 1980; Godshalk et al., 1966; Coffman, 1971; Breland & Gaynor, 1979). Determining which approach or what combination of approaches to use is therefore a primary question for large-scale assessments of writing.

The results presented in this report provide data for comparison of the potential validity, reliability, and costs of several direct and indirect measures of writing. The direct measures include holistic, analytic, primary trait, and mechanics counts scoring of actual writing samples. The indirect measures include the language arts items of the following objective tests: *California Achievement Test, Iowa Test of Basic Skills, Tests of Achievement and Proficiency,* and *Writing Proficiency Test.*

Twenty-four high schools in 18 Georgia school systems were included in this study. As a group, they comprise approximately 10% of the total number of Georgia high schools. They represent a range of geographical areas (north, middle, and south Georgia), achievement levels (based on whether the school

---

From *Research in the Teaching of English* 17 (1983): 290–96.

had more or less than 60% of its students achieving 17 of 20 objectives in the language arts section of the state criterion referenced test), and system sizes (either a one high school system or a system with two or more high schools).

English teachers from the 24 schools served as planning committee members and raters of writing samples. Approximately 100 tenth grade students from each high school were randomly selected for testing. Each participating school received two tests: one writing sample that could be scored holistically, analytically, or by mechanics counts and either an objective test or a second writing sample to be scored for primary traits. Tests were distributed so that each test would be given in each geographic area, achievement level range, and school size.

Based on the reported experience of the Educational Testing Service (1978) and other agencies such as the Clearinghouse for Applied Performance Testing (1980), holistic ratings were selected as the main or most widely representative score. Initially, inter-rater reliability for the holistic ratings (the ones to be compared with other scoring methods) was therefore an important issue. Data in Table 1–1 show a range from .69 to .76, close to similar holistic reliabilities. Since three direct measures and four indirect measures were compared to the holistic scores, results are reported from seven different groups. These results are shown in Table 1–2. Clearly, analytic ratings correspond most closely to holistic ratings (.64), and the scores of the *Iowa Test of Basic Skills* from the indirect measures come closest (.70) to the holistic ratings.

TABLE 1–1   Inter-rater Reliability for Holistic Ratings by Comparison Group

Correlation Between Holistic Raters	Analytic Group	Mechanics Count Group	Primary Trait Group	TAP Grp	CAT Grp	ITBS Grp.	Writing Profic. Group
A & B	.74	.69	.73	.71	.76	.74	.70
N=	344	352	302	233	257	255	276

All correlations are significant at the .01 level.

TABLE 1–2   Correlations Between Holistic Ratings and Other Measures

Scoring Method	Analytic	Mechanics Count	Primary Trait	TAP	CAT	ITBS	Writ. Prof.
Holistic	.64	−.25 (est)	.19	.42	.40	.70	.57
N=	342	354	302	233	257	255	276

All correlations are significant at the .01 level.

The .64 correlation between holistic ratings and overall or total analytic ratings cover sub-scores on the analytical scale. As Table 1–3 indicates, holistic score correlations with analytic sub-scores parallel the overall .64 correlation. They are as follows: content, .62; style, .58; and mechanics, .57. Overall agreement between the two analytic raters is .90. The raters agree only slightly more on the content sub-score (.82) than on style (.76) or mechanics (.80).

Negative correlations were obtained for holistic scores and scores for the mechanics count, as Table 1–4 indicates. The negative relationship results from the fact that holistic ratings assign high scores for the best papers while the mechanics count assigns the highest scores to the papers with the most errors. In this case, significant correlations which are reported as negative can really reflect common or positive associations. For instance, the low moderate correlations (−.31, −.23, −.30, −.25, −.29) indicate at least a minor association between papers rated holistically and by mechanics counts of punctuation, capitalization, awkward construction, agreement, and word choice. There are no reliability estimates to report.

The correlation between the two primary trait raters for each paper turned out to be .72, very close to the level of agreement for the holistic ratings, .69 through .76.

Holistic ratings were compared to indirect measures (objective tests) as well as other direct measures. Reliability coefficients for indirect measures

TABLE 1–3   Correlations of Holistic Ratings and Analytic Sub-score Ratings

Scoring Method	Content	Analytic Style	(N=344) Mechanics	Total
Holistic (N=342)	.62	.58	.57	.64
Means	26.00	12.66	25.81	64.33
Range	10–40	5–20	10–40	25–100

All correlations are significant at the .01 level.

TABLE 1–4   Correlations Between Holistic Ratings and the Component Scores of the Mechanics Counts

Scoring Method	Spelling	Punctuation	Capitalization	Fragments	Runons	Awk. Cons.	Agreements	Word Choice
Holistic (N=352)	−.05	−.31*	−.23*	−.12	−.13	−.30*	−.25*	−.29*
Means (errors per 100 words)	2.4	2.7	.7	.5	.9	.9	.7	1.2

*Significant at the .01 level.

(Cronbach Alphas) are listed in Table 1–5. For total tests, these coefficients seem high enough, but, except for the ITBS, sub-scores are mixed and only moderate at best.

Many significant correlations emerged from the trial of these four tests, as Table 1–6 reports. The *Iowa Test of Basic Skills* showed the strongest correlation with the holistic ratings, .50s and .60s. The lowest correlations came with the *California Achievement Test*. Second and third place, in terms of correlation, went to the *Writing Proficiency Test* and the *Tests of Achievement and Proficiency*, respectively.

Even though the main comparisons were between holistic ratings and seven other measures, several other relationships were checked (see Table 1–7). Analytic ratings correlated with four other measures as follows: mechanics

TABLE 1–5   Reliability Coefficients* for Indirect Measures

Tests & Test Category	Spell-ing	Capi-tali-ztn.	Punc-tua-tion	Usage	Sent. Strc.	Para-graph	Essay	Letter	Total
ITBS	.08	.71	.73	.90	–	.74	–	.88	.89
TAP	.47	.83	.64	.53	.51	−.02	.50	.57	.83
CAT	.53	.31	.59	.31	.47	.46	–	–	.59
WRT PRF	.47	.22	.12	.50	.18	.85	.69	.76	.80

*Cronbach Alphas

TABLE 1–6   Correlations Between Holistic Ratings and Objective Test Scores

Tests & Test Categories	Spell-ing	Capi-tali-ztn.	Punc-tua-tion	Usage	Sent. Strc.	Para-graph	Essay	Letter	Total
Hol. vs									
ITBS (N=258)	.52	.60	.65	.65	–	.48	–	.54	.70
TAP (N=242)	.29	.23	.36	.42	.16*	.29	.24	.29	.42
CAT (N=270)	−.06*	−.20	.35	.29	.37	−.09*	–	–	.40
WRIT PROF (N=285)	.43	.44	.45	.51	.43	.47	.23	.35	.57

*Not significant at .01 level; all others are.

TABLE 1–7 Correlations Among the Scoring Methods Checked Other Than
Those Checked Primarily With Holistic Ratings

Scoring Methods	Mechanics Count	Primary Trait	ITBS	Writing Proficiency
Analytic	−.33	.19	.83	.01*
	(N=308)	(N=109)	(N=29)	(N=285)
Mechanics		−.03*	−.67	−.05*
Count		(N=109)	(N=29)	(N=285)

*Not significant at the .01 level; all others are.

count, −.33 (really a positive connection); primary trait, .19 (statistically significant but still low); *Iowa Test of Basic Skills*, .83 (paralleling the ITBS–holistic relationship but a relatively small N, 29); and *Writing Proficiency*, .01 (virtually no connection). And, in addition to the −.33 analytic/mechanics count relationship, the mechanics counts further correlated with primary trait scores, −.03 (virtually nothing); ITBS, −.67 (actually a positive association but still a low N); and *Writing Proficiency*, −.05 (again nothing).

Based on actual expenditures from this project, costs for scoring individual student papers were calculated. Scoring costs may differ depending on how raters are paid, e.g., stipends only for non-school days, release days only for substitute pay on school days, or either method in combination with travel expenses. Table 1–8 details the estimated per student cost for each method of reimbursement and each scoring measure for writing samples. For each measure, releasing teachers from school allows the least expensive scoring while paying both stipends and travel incurs the greatest expense. Objective tests scored by computer averaged $.53 per student.

In general, the results of this project support the findings of previous researchers (Breland & Gaynor, 1979; Spandel & Stiggins, 1980). Holistic scoring does indeed require less time and money, making it the most economical of the direct measures. Analytic scoring does correlate highly with holistic ratings and does provide more detailed analysis of some holistic ratings. Primary trait and mechanics count scoring, because of lower correlations and higher cost figures, may more appropriately remain the tools of the researcher

TABLE 1–8 Scoring Costs Per Student for Each Direct Measure of Writing

	Holistic	Analytic	Primary Trait	Mechanics Counts
Stipends Only	$.72	$2.37	$1.07	$1.06
Released Days Only	$.39	$1.29	$.58	$.58
Stipends and Travel	$1.55	$5.07	$2.29	$2.27
Released Days and Travel	$1.22	$3.99	$1.80	$1.79

concerned with more specific contexts and features of writing. Among objective tests used here, the *Iowa Test of Basic Skills* appears to be most highly correlated with a direct measure of writing ability. The smaller cost of selecting and using an objective test as an indirect measure of writing may be advantageous if users are primarily interested in testing only mechanical skills related to writing.

If a large scale summative assessment of writing is what is needed, then in light of validity, reliability, and cost considerations, recommendations from this study call for a holistically rated writing sample as a measure of minimum competence because of its face validity, proven reliability (.69 through .76), and economy ($.39 to $1.55 per paper). A backup system whereby certain of the holistically rated papers are also rated analytically to give detailed feedback like that provided in regular English classes is also suggested. Since at least one of the indirect measures, the *Iowa Test of Basic Skills*, correlated rather highly (.70) with the holistic ratings, and since it is similar to analytic ratings with which it correlates .83, a carefully chosen objective measure might substitute for this analytic backup.

The consideration of the user at this point becomes whether the cost or the face validity of a direct assessment of writing is more critical. (See Breland & Gaynor, 1979.) The selection of an appropriate measure will depend on the scope and purposes of the writing assessment as well as the resources available.

Language arts items for the following tests were used:
California Achievement Test, Level 17C, McGraw-Hill, 1977.
Iowa Test of Basic Skills, Level 14, Houghton Mifflin, 1978, with the *Adult Performance Level Test*, American College Testing Program, 1978.
Tests of Achievement and Proficiency, Level 16, Houghton Mifflin, 1978.
Writing Proficiency Test, McGraw-Hill, 1979.

REFERENCES

Breland, H., & Gaynor, J. L. A comparison of direct and indirect assessments of writing skill. *Journal of Educational Measurement*, 1979, *16*, 119–128.
Clearinghouse for Applied Performance Testing. *Writing assessment for the 1980's*. Proceedings of a National Conference on the Assessment of Writing, Boulder, Colorado, June, 1980.
Coffman, W. E. Essay examination. In R. L. Thorndike (Ed.), *Educational measurement*. Washington, D.C.: American Council on Education, 1971.
College Entrance Examination Board. *The English composition test with essay*. Princeton: Educational Testing Service, 1979.
Educational Testing Service. *Focus 5: The concern for writing*. Princeton: Educational Testing Service, 1978.
Godshalk, F. I., Swineford, F., & Coffman, W. Z. *The measurement of writing ability*. New York: College Entrance Examination Board, 1966.
Grommon, A. *Reviews of selected published tests in the English language arts*. Urbana, Illinois: National Council of Teachers of English, 1976.
National Council of Teachers of English. *Standards for basic skills writing programs*. Urbana, Illinois: National Council of Teachers of English, March, 1979.
Spandel, V. & Stiggins, R. J. *Direct measures of writing skill: Issues and applications*. Portland: Clearinghouse for Applied Performance Testing, 1980.

2   *Holisticism*

EDWARD M. WHITE

To proceed holistically is to see things as units, as complete, as *wholes*, and to do so is to oppose the dominant tendency of our time, the analytic spirit, which breaks things down into constituent parts in order to see how they work. Analytic reductionism assumes that knowledge of the parts will lead to understanding of the whole, a theory which works very well with machinery or other objects, but less well with art forms or life forms. A table leg is much the same whether attached to the table or not; my leg or that of Michelangelo's *David* changes meaning drastically when detached. Holisticism argues against reductionism and denies that the whole is only the sum of its parts.

The advent of holisticism in the scoring of student papers is one interesting and practical manifestation of this spirit. Holisticism in English seems related to several movements in the field, such as process research in composition and poststructural literary criticism, which reject the reductionism implied by product analysis and formalism. The three movements in the profession have developed along parallel paths during the last fifteen years, each of them stressing the rediscovery of the functioning human being behind texts and each of them rejecting ways of thinking about texts that are now seen as reductionist. Thus holisticism, with its emphasis on evaluation and response to student writing as a unit without sub-scores or separable aspects, presents itself in opposition to multiple-choice testing on the one hand and analytic approaches to writing on the other. It is the most obvious example in the field of English of the attempt to evoke and evaluate wholes rather than parts.

It is a little hard to believe that just eleven years ago, when I first became responsible for a large-scale testing program, the only systematic work in essay scoring was being done in just two locations: at the National Assessment of Educational Progress in Denver and at the Educational Testing Service in Princeton. The concept of holistic scoring was almost unknown in the field of

From *College Composition and Communication* 35 (1985): 400–409.

English, and the term, now so familiar, elicited titters or wisecracks from the uninformed. The change has been so rapid that it is well to pause to review what has occurred and think about why. Rosentene Purnell reported in *CCC* (December 1982) on a survey the CCCC Committee on Testing had taken of English departments. Not only did almost 90% state that they used holistic scoring, but nowhere did either Purnell or the responding parties feel the need to define the term by more than a parenthetical reminder. In one decade, in a notoriously conservative and slow-moving profession, a new concept in testing and (hence) in teaching writing has triumphed while no one was watching.

My purpose here is to chronicle the development of holisticism in English testing, define the term and others associated with it with some care, and suggest the central reasons for its use. Finally, I will set out some of the problems and disadvantages of this powerful and generally positive approach to student writing. As with any other complex and handy concept, holistic scoring is frequently misunderstood, misused, and misinterpreted. Since this advance in measurement has had, and continues to have, important uses in writing research, in teaching, and in program evaluation, holisticism needs to be better understood and its advantages and disadvantages need to be seen clearly.

The early development of what we now call holistic scoring took place wholly under the auspices of the Educational Testing Service, and ETS deserves considerable credit for sponsoring the research and developing the techniques which have led to the present state of the art. The problem of developing valid, reliable, and economical measures of writing ability has been a particularly difficult and thorny one for ETS, and we have all profited from the results of the prolonged internal debate this problem has produced. On one side were those who pointed to the well-established unreliability of essay scores and who saw the cost of scoring writing samples as prohibitive; for them, multiple-choice testing, with its established reliability and economy, was the preferred, sometimes the only, way to measure writing ability. On the other side were those who argued that a valid measure of writing needs to include writing. These latter gained strength from a College Board study entitled *The Measurement of Writing Ability* (1966), which neatly straddled the issue, concluding that a mass of correlational data showed that the best test of writing ability would include both multiple-choice and written portions. But the most compelling arguments raised by those holding this position and by their academic supporters were based on educational and holistic grounds. Testing shapes curriculum, they said, and multiple-choice usage tests were leading some teachers to doubt the importance of writing in the schools as well as defeating those who were teaching literature and creativity. Writing combines very many skills and cognitive activities, only some of which could be readily measured by machine-scored tests, and so vital a combination could only be well evaluated as a whole. While the reliability of multiple-choice tests was (and remains) higher than that of more direct measures, the validity of indirect testing in this field was open to serious question: only a few statisticians were fully convinced that such tests in fact measured writing ability.

Despite the persuasive arguments in favor of including writing on tests of writing ability, multiple-choice testing of usage (sometimes, erroneously, called objective testing, as if machine-scored tests had been created with no human participation) remained the dominant form of testing for some time. It remains dominant in the schools today, though not in the university. In order for the direct measurement of writing ability to become an accepted component of writing testing, it had to meet the two criteria of reliability and economy, without losing its face validity as a legitimate test of writing skill.

While financial considerations generally follow educational policy, anyone involved with measurement needs to be concerned directly with the importance of economy in testing. No matter how valuable we may find some kinds of testing, if they cost too much they will not be used. Thus, it was an important step to demonstrate that the holistic scoring of writing samples could take place quickly enough to be practical; a single score for a piece of writing meant a single decision by a grader, and such decisions could be made with sufficient speed to make direct measurement of writing cost effective. The significance of this fact is not yet well understood. Since the cost of scoring writing samples is always considerably higher than the cost of running answer sheets through a computer, many people conclude that essay testing as a whole is more expensive than multiple-choice testing. However, when we consider the cost of test development, a major hidden cost in all testing, expenses tend to even out. Development of multiple-choice tests, if properly done, is enormously expensive and time-consuming. Although essay test development requires considerable committee work, pretesting, and revision, it is far cheaper and quicker. If, in addition, we consider the costs of new forms of a test as well as those of the initial administration, as we are forced to do by increasingly detailed truth-in-testing legislation, essay resting can be highly cost effective. If we add to the equation the benefits of direct measurement of writing to the teachers, the curriculum, and the learning of students (a calculus less convincing to many of those controlling educational funding), essay testing becomes economical indeed. The evolution of holistic scoring thus made direct measurement of writing ability an economically feasible alternative to multiple-choice testing even for the accounting office; until its reliability could be demonstrated, however, it could not be widely used.

Early studies at ETS by Paul Diederich, the principal (almost the only) scholar in the field a generation ago, tended to confirm the unreliability of essay testing as it was then customarily conducted. (He summarizes much of that research in *Measuring Growth in English* [Urbana, IL: National Council of Teachers of English, 1974].) When he distributed a quantity of student writing to a large group of readers, with no directions or criteria for scoring, all papers received all possible scores. He went on to categorize the scoring criteria the readers seemed to be using, grouping them into five categories according to what different readers valued: the scores of readers who seemed to judge papers according to their structure, say, had a low correlation with those of readers whose basic criterion was style. The problem with this general impression scoring was clear: a paper's score depended on the accident of who wound up as reader, rather than on its quality, however that quality was defined.

Reliability in scoring is a complex subject, with many shapes and forms. No test, of course, is wholly reliable, since student performance will change from test to test for reasons that have little or nothing to do with the test. Scoring reliability is only one part of this complicated problem, but it is the part most directly controlled by those in charge of the test. Since reliability is in a sense a technical term to describe fairness, or simple consistency, good testing practice aims for the highest reliability that can be reached. While economy is important, it means nothing without reliability; unfair and inconsistent scores are meaningless, and meaningless scores, however cheaply obtained, are not worth anything at all.

The problem, then, was to develop a method of scoring papers that retained the economy of a single, general impression score, with its underlying view that writing should be evaluated as a whole, and added to it substantial reliability of scoring. At this point, a general confusion of terminology entered the field, a confusion which remains. The general impression scoring which Diederich used in his experiments, without any guides or controls, is sometimes called "general impression scoring" and sometimes called "holistic." Many of the objections to and arguments against holistic scoring are, in fact, arguments against the unreliability of the general impression scoring that Diederich tested. I will here call that system "general impression scoring," reserving the other term for the later and more reliable form; I hope that others in the field will do the same, in the interests of clear discussion.

Two developments from general impression scoring, with very similar outcomes, have led to the present generally accepted form of holistic scoring. At the National Assessment of Educational Progress, committees developed what came to be called "Primary Trait" (P-T) scoring, while committees at ETS, particularly those working on the Advanced Placement Program, developed what they and most others now call "holistic" scoring. While the names look very different, and while some proponents argue strongly that one is much better than the other, in fact there is very little difference between them; "primary trait" scoring merely defines with greater precision and exclusiveness the criteria to be used in the holistic scoring. Both groups were engaged in developing a series of techniques to increase the reliability of scoring by defining the kinds of skills tapped by different kinds of topics. In fact both groups retained the single overall score and evolved similar procedures; the subsequent experience of dozens of essay readings has confirmed the good sense and statistical significance of these improvements in reliability. The result is what is now generally called "holistic" essay scoring.

Holistic scoring is able to achieve acceptably high reliability by adding a series of constraints to the economically efficient practice of general impression scoring. Basic to all of these constraints is a carefully developed and precise writing assignment (sometimes called a "prompt"), followed by an attempt to reduce unnecessary variability in the scoring process. Six procedures and practices have been developed for scoring, and where all six are observed with sensitivity and care, high reliability of scoring has been achieved with no appreciable sacrifice of economy.

1. *Controlled Essay Reading.* All those scoring the papers are brought together to read at the same time and place, with the same working hours and breaks. The controlled reading not only eliminates all kinds of extraneous variables from the scoring process but establishes a positive social situation which, under the right condition, becomes an indirect and powerful in-service training workshop. The establishment of a sense of community is important for the success of the reading, since it is that particular interpretive community (as Stanley Fish might term it) that determines and enforces the standards of measurement.

2. *Scoring Criteria Guide* (called by ETS a "rubric"). This direct statement of descriptors for papers at different points on the scoring scale is developed by those leading the controlled essay reading before the readers gather. After reading many student papers (sometimes many hundreds), these experienced readers will develop a sense of the distinctions between papers on the continuum from the worst to the best. The Scoring Guide sets down the characteristics (or "traits" in P-T scoring) which define the points on the scoring scale. Often, the test design committee will prepare a tentative scoring guide that expresses the specifications and intentions of the question, and, since such a plan usually emerges out of pre-testing a topic, this early guide is usually very helpful. But the final scoring guide needs to reflect the reality of the actual test group.

3. *Sample Papers* (sometimes called "anchor papers"). While the scoring guide is an abstract description of points on the scale, these papers are examples of these points. Chosen by the leaders of the reading in order to illustrate and make real the scoring guide, these papers are given unmarked to readers for scoring during the training session. Not until all readers are in close agreement on the scores of these sample papers, and on what characteristics have determined the score, can a reliable reading begin. The goal is not only to obtain agreement on the scores of sample papers and on the usefulness of the scoring guide but to help the readers internalize the scoring scale by combining description with example. If this "calibration" of the readers is done with sensitivity and toleration of some differences of view, the readers will agree to agree to common standards for the sake of the test; sufficient time in the training session is essential for reliable scoring and will be more than repaid by readers who score accurately and quickly, needing only occasional reference to the scoring guide or the sample papers after calibration.

4. *Checks on the Reading in Progress.* Readers are customarily grouped by tables seating five or six (never more than seven) with an experienced Table Leader responsible for consistent scoring at the table. The Table Leader does not originate scores; his or her task is to circulate from reader to reader at the table, checking scores so that all readers will continue scoring at the same level. This guards against individual readers drifting down or up from original standards. If more than one table of readers is at work, a "Chief Reader" or "Question Leader" performs the same function for the various tables. At a long reading, there will be occasional additional training sessions, with more sample papers for all readers to score. Sometimes a sample paper from early in the reading will be renumbered as a new sample for scoring, in order to guard against a scoring drift which might be unfair to papers read late (or early) in the reading. Readers who understand and are sympathetic to the process, and realize that the goal is a reliable, fair reading,

will cooperate with these procedures, as long as they are carried on with sensitivity and good humor.

5. *Multiple Independent Scoring.* Two readers from two different tables in the reading score each essay; the first score is concealed so that the second scoring is independent. The two scores should be added together to create a full-range distribution of scores. A one-point difference is allowable; two-point differences are read a third time in order to resolve the discrepancy. An excellent reading on a six-point scale will have 5% or fewer discrepant scores; an average reading will have 7–10% of its scores more than one point apart. Unless there is more than one reading for each essay, there is no way to evaluate the reliability of the reading or of individual readers.

6. *Evaluation and Record Keeping.* Since a reliable reading requires reliable readers, a continuing program will keep records of the scoring done by readers, with particular attention to their consistency in observing the established criteria. The most reliable scorers form the cadre around which future essay readings may be built.

There is some uncertainty at this time as to just how reliable controlled essay readings may be. Unfortunately, statisticians have reached no agreement about ways to measure comparative reliability of readings, and there are many different ways of computing reading reliability. Reports of reliabilities in the .90 range occur from time to time (as, for example, in the opening chapter of Charles Cooper and Lee Odell, *Evaluating Writing* [Urbana, Illinois: The National Council of Teachers of English, 1977]), but it is rarely clear how these numbers are derived. The statistical report published each year by the California State University English Equivalency Examination includes a narrative of the methodology and shows just how the reliability statistics have been developed; if more reports of testing programs did the same, we might begin to move toward a more consistent way of comparing the accuracy of essay readings. In general, it appears that carefully controlled essay readings do yield reasonably reliable scores, though a close reading of the data reported by many such readings suggests that overstatement of reliability is common.

The present state of the art, then, shows substantial progress over the last decade. Holistic scorings have become routine across the nation, and many of them exhibit the six procedures which yield the most reliable results. The results have in general satisfied reasonable demands for both economy and reliability and have led the way to restoring the role of writing in testing and (since we test that which we hold to be important) in the curriculum. The development of holisticism in scoring of writing tests has helped the profession to resist the forces of pseudo-objectivism (as in workbooks or multiple-choice tests) and analytic reductionism (with its emphasis on the supposedly immutable laws of usage and grammar) in English classrooms and testing rooms. Those of us who have been involved in these matters have considerable cause for self-congratulation.

And yet we are perhaps a little too prone to self-congratulation, considering the misuses and abuses that have been committed in the name of holistic scoring. It is important to remind ourselves what such scoring can not be expected to do, and to temper our enthusiasm and that of our colleagues.

In the first place, we need to realize that holistic scoring is only a means of rank-ordering papers according to the criteria established in the scoring guide. While efficient, economical, and reliable rank-ordering is a great deal more than we had, it is only, well, rank-ordering. That is, a holistic score is like a percentile rating; it has meaning only in reference to the group that was tested. This means on the one hand that the usefulness of holistic scores is limited, and on the other that we cannot take a holistic score as if it were an absolute value. While each of these implications appears obvious, since they derive from the limits of rank-ordering, they are not at all well understood.

The most important limitation of the holistic score is that it gives no meaningful diagnostic information beyond the comparative ranking it represents. Even if we assume the score to be reliable, we cannot tell much that we might want to know about the student. For example, a low score might represent an inability to control sentence structure, a major spelling incapacity, a total misreading of the question, or a misguided attempt to be whimsical or creative. A high score might mean a correct but boring response or a genuinely creative piece of prose. All we have is a single score, where we might wish to have a profile.

The second limit on the value of the holistic score emerges from its connection to its particular test group; it cannot represent an absolute value in itself. A second-stage operation is needed to give meaning to the ranking. This means that every time a holistic scoring is completed, those responsible for reporting scores need to make a fresh decision about where cutting levels should be. Suppose last year a score of seven or above was needed by an entering student to enter regular freshman composition. This year the question is harder, or easier, the freshman class is stronger, or weaker, and so the score of seven is likely to represent a different level of achievement. Perhaps the cutting score should be six, or eight? It is an unfortunate fact that most users of holistic scores act as if the ranking has some absolute meaning, when it does not. No two essay questions make exactly the same demands upon students; no two groups of students have exactly the same range of writing abilities. The additional step of deciding the meaning of a particular test's ranking of students cannot be avoided by those responsible for reporting and using holistic scores.

The third important limitation of holistic scores is also common to all test scores: reliabilities are customarily overestimated and the inescapable inaccuracy of scores tends to be ignored. All tests yield only approximations of ability levels, and even the most highly developed multiple-choice tests (which have almost perfect scoring reliability) report a wide band of possible error. For example, despite the efforts of ETS and the College Board to point out that the standard error of measurement of each part of the Scholastic Aptitude Test is thirty points in each direction, and that scores on the SAT should be seen as a band rather than a point, almost everyone ignores the caution. Ten points more or less on the SAT can mean the difference between admission or rejection at far too many colleges. In a similar way, those who use holistic scores tend to ignore the fact that most papers, if rescored by the same readers at the same reading, would probably receive different scores.

In a careful reliability study reported by the California State University English Equivalency Examination (*Comparison and Contrast* [Long Beach, CA: The California State University, 1977], pp. 51–56), 699 student examinations containing two essays each were rescored a year later under similar but not identical conditions. Each of the two essays was scored independently by two readers using a six-point scale (thus yielding a score range from 0–24) on each occasion. The reading a year later produced scores that were identical to the first in 20.7% of the cases; 58% of the scores (including the first 20.7%) varied by one point or less, 82.7% (including the 58%) by two points or less, 92% (including the 82.7%) by three points or less. This is, overall, a very good record for one of the most rigorously controlled and well-funded essay readings in the country. But it does show that most of the essay scores will change slightly upon rereading, and that some scores will change a great deal.

The inability of holistic scores to give diagnostic information has led to a not very successful development of analytic scoring, an attempt to gain a series of separate scores for separate sub-skills from the student writing sample. In theory, analytic scoring should provide the diagnostic information that holistic scoring fails to provide, and in the process yield a desirable increase in information from the writing sample. In practice, three major problems have so far demonstrated the limitations of analytic scoring: there is as yet no agreement (except among the uninformed) about what, if any, separable sub-skills exist in writing; it is extremely difficult to obtain reliable analytic scores, since there is so little professional consensus about sub-skills; analytic scoring tends to be quite complicated for readers, which leads to slow scoring, which in turn leads to high cost. Since analytic scoring solves neither the reliability nor the cost problems, it is not a likely candidate to replace holistic scoring. The theory of analytic scoring also assumes that writing can be seen and evaluated as a sum of its parts, and so stands in opposition to holisticism; in ways parallel to multiple-choice testing, analytic scoring imagines a model of writing that is neatly sequential and comfortably segmented. As with machine-scored tests, analytical essay scoring offers some valuable adjunct measures of some kinds of skills, but not a useful or valid measurement of writing. Its promise of producing diagnostic information has not yet been demonstrated successfully with large numbers of papers.

Thus we are left with holistic scoring, with all its limitations, as the most successful method of scoring writing in quantity that is now available. Let me be quite explicit. I am not citing the limitations of holistic scores in order to attack this major advance in the measurement of writing ability. I enthusiastically endorse holistic scoring because it has made the direct testing of writing practical and relatively reliable, because it brings together English teachers to talk about the goals of writing instruction, and because it embodies a concept of writing that is responsible in the widest sense. Nonetheless, I think we need to be fully aware of the limitations of holistic scoring if we are to use it responsibly and to protect the direct testing of writing from those who would undermine it in the name of efficiency. Those who misunderstand or misuse holistic scores, however well motivated, are not supporting the teaching of writing or the testing of writing, since they open the whole procedure to justified attack.

I would like to single out for particular attention one abuse of the holistic scoring process that occurs when the leaders of an essay reading are not well informed about the theory behind the procedure. These leaders, the Table Leaders and Chief Readers, have a heavy responsibility: their task is to ensure a reliable essay reading, while, at the same time, they must respect the professionalism and good will and individuality of the readers who are grading the papers. The best of these fine teachers are able to work so well with readers that group standards emerge from informed and willing assent. These leaders have an almost magical mixture of firmness in their own standards and a willingness to listen to others who just might be even more right than they are. When readers feel comfortable enough with the question, the scoring guide, the process, and the people in charge, the grading of endless papers becomes a purposeful, even pleasant endeavor, despite the inevitable boredom of the work. Readers will be eager to return to well-run essay readings, and take away from the experience much that is valuable to their teaching. After many hours of scoring papers to intelligent criteria, seeing student writing holistically, it is not easy to return to the idiosyncratic, arbitrary, and mechanical response to student work that is standard practice for many of those teaching writing classes. The best of these readings even lead the participants (indirectly) to reconsider their teaching practices through the social interaction of colleagues working together to achieve a common goal. Indeed, the best holistic scoring sessions have a summer-vacation tone to them, sometimes including joyful after-hours memories not easy to come by in our mature years.

But when the readers feel intimidated or coerced by insensitive leaders, or harassed by an uncomfortable or autocratic working environment, the whole situation becomes destructive to personal and professional relations. The worst of these readings allow the leaders to exercise an awkward kind of bureaucratic power instead of academic leadership, and such readings set up an adversary relationship between exploited readers and their employers. Anyone who has been part of such a sad experience will be reluctant to repeat it and is likely to blame holistic grading itself for the corrupt version of it that took place. Like many aspects of human experience (which we normally respond to holistically), the difference between a fine and a terrible essay reading is made up of a series of minor yet symbolic acts and omissions which add up to a major difference in tone and result.

In a curious way, to consider holistic readings, as I have been doing, in all their necessary details, is to demonstrate the importance, indeed the necessity, of holisticism for clear understanding of complex matters. Once again, the whole is considerably greater than its parts, and too much attention to the parts is likely to obscure the meaning of the whole. The great claim of holisticism in the scoring of student papers is not that it has finally achieved perfection in testing; clearly this measurement is still in its infancy, as a series of new studies is making clear. We do not know enough about how readers make their judgments in holistic readings, and skeptical researchers with dark suspicions about penmanship and sheer length are continuing to challenge the assumption that readers are making responsibly holistic judgments. The research on this form of measurement has far to go, and we will be hearing from statisticians, psychologists, and various kinds of (usually analytic) thinkers for at least another decade.

Holisticism, however, is important for reasons beyond measurements, for reasons that return us to the nature of writing and to the importance of the study of English itself. It is in our writing that we see ourselves thinking, and we ask our students to write so that they can think more clearly, learn more quickly, and develop more fully. Writing, like reading, is an exercise for the whole mind, including its most creative and imaginative faculties. The rapid growth of holisticism in grading reflects this view of reading and writing as activities not describable through an inventory of their parts, and it serves as a direct expression of it: by maintaining that writing must be seen as a whole, and that the evaluating of writing cannot be split into a sequence of objective activities, holisticism reinforces the vision of reading and writing as intensely human activities involving the full self.

Holisticism is the form that humanism takes when confronted with analytic reductionism. Holisticism says that the human spirit and its most significant form of expression (writing) must be seen and understood not in parts, but as a whole, face to face as it were, almost sacramentally. Even the meanest bit of halting prose, even the most down-trodden of our fellow creatures, deserves to be taken as a living and vital unit of meaning, an artistic and human whole, not merely as a collection of scraps and parts.

3

Reliability Issues in Holistic Assessment

ROGER D. CHERRY AND PAUL R. MEYER

In the last 15 years, holistic evaluation of written texts has become widely used as a means of assessing writing abilities. In a typical evaluation scheme, writing samples are collected and scored in accordance with a rating scale by two or more trained raters. A substantial — and growing — literature proposes guidelines for constructing and administering writing tasks and for conducting rating sessions (e.g., Davis, Scriven, & Thomas, 1987; Hoetker & Brossell, 1986; Myers, 1980; Ruth & Murphy, 1984, 1988; Spandel & Stiggins, 1981; White, 1985).

Despite the prevalence of direct assessment practices, the reliability of scores obtained through those practices has not been adequately understood. The literature on writing research and assessment reveals a good deal of confusion about the nature of reliability in general and about the relationship between reliability and validity in particular. Moreover, the field has experienced widespread methodological confusion about computing, interpreting, and reporting reliability coefficients that result from direct assessments of writing. This chapter addresses these theoretical and practical issues under the following headings:

- Reliability as a Psychometric Construct
- The Reliability of Holistic Scoring: Instrument Reliability vs. Interrater Reliability
- Problems with Reliability in Writing Research and Evaluation
- Estimating and Reporting Instrument and Interrater Reliability Coefficients
- Needed Research on Reliability

The basic argument of the chapter is that our profession needs to come to a better understanding of reliability, particularly the relationship between reliability

From *Validating Holistic Scoring for Writing Assessment: Theoretical and Empirical Foundations*, eds. M. M. Williamson and B. A. Huot (Cresskill, NJ: Hampton Press, 1993): 109–41.

and validity. The profession also needs to standardize the statistical methods used for calculating and reporting the reliability of holistic scores. We offer the remarks that follow as a first step toward addressing these needs.

Although we have tried to make the chapter as accessible as possible, it examines the technical aspects of several issues in some detail. The technical discussions are essential because they form the basis for the specific claims and recommendations we make concerning reliability. Understanding why some current holistic assessment practices are problematic or why high inter-rater reliabilities do not guarantee reliable assessments requires some knowledge of both the theoretical assumptions and the computational formulas on which reliability statistics are based.

Reliability as a Psychometric Construct

Reliability and validity are two of the most basic concepts in measurement theory. *Reliability* refers to how consistently a test measures whatever it measures. *Validity* addresses the question of whether the test measures what it is designed to measure. In order for a test to be a valid measure of a trait such as writing ability, it must be both reliable and valid: It must yield consistent results, and it must actually measure writing ability. A test cannot be valid unless it is reliable, but the opposite is not true; a test can be reliable but still not be valid. *Thus, reliability is a necessary but not a sufficient condition for validity.*

Both reliability and validity are theoretical constructs developed by psychometricians to describe certain properties of test scores and the confidence with which decisions might be based on those scores. Technically speaking, reliability is a property not of particular tests but of the scores derived from those tests. (Although, for economy of expression, we will often speak of "the reliability of a test," it is important to keep in mind that reliability refers to the consistency of information provided by test scores rather than to a property of a given test.) The applicability and proper use of reliability coefficients in various situations is closely tied to the assumptions and limitations of reliability and validity as psychometric constructs.

According to Jackson and Ferguson (1941), "the term reliability was first introduced into mental test theory by Spearman in 1904" (p. 9). Since that time, reliability has been a central problem in measurement and evaluation (Stanley, 1971). Generally speaking, reliability is not as complex and therefore not as problematic as validity. Psychometricians have achieved greater agreement on the nature of reliability and methods of determining whether a test is reliable than on these issues for validity. Three concepts are central to understanding contemporary treatments of reliability: measurement error, analysis of variance, and the contextual nature of reliability.

Like all things human, measurement is not a perfect business. All measurement, whether of physical characteristics or of psychological traits, involves some degree of error. Repeated measurements of even a relatively stable phenomenon will not yield precisely the same results each time. In classical testing and measurement theory, an individual's score on a particular test is considered to be an inexact estimate of his or her "true score." The "true score" is a hypothetical construct that refers to what a given measurement would be if our knowledge were perfect and complete and we could devise perfect tests. In contrast, an individual's *observed score* is considered to be made up of two components: a *true score* and some degree of *error*.

$$\text{observed score} = \text{true score} + \text{error} \qquad (1)$$

Modern psychometricians have used a statistical procedure called analysis of variance to analyze measurement error and define reliability. Analysis of variance, as its name suggests, is used to analyze patterns of variation in a set of data. By identifying and measuring independent "sources" of variation, analysis of variance can determine the extent to which particular factors in a testing situation influence the resulting test scores. Analysis of variance defines measurement error as variation that cannot be attributed to a particular source. In the same way that observed scores are conceived in terms of true score and error, variance is broken into true variance and error variance:

$$\text{total variance} = \text{true variance} + \text{error variance} \qquad (2)$$

As Sax (1974) pointed out, when we try to measure student knowledge or ability, variance and measurement error have three main sources:

1. Characteristics of the students,
2. Characteristics of the test, and
3. Conditions affecting test administration and scoring. (p. 196)

Students. We know that students do not perform with perfect consistency from one writing task to another. Even if students were given the same writing task on different occasions, we would expect their performance on a given day to differ at least somewhat from their performance on another day. The necessary implication of this difference is that although a writing sample may reflect a student's writing ability, it cannot do so perfectly. The inherent inconsistency of student performance lessens our ability to rely on a single writing sample to make judgments about a student's writing ability. In statistical terms, variability in student performance contributes to the error in measurements of writing ability.

Tests. We also know that all essay prompts are not equal. Some writing tasks are easier for students of a certain age or students with particular kinds of knowledge or experience; other writing tasks are more difficult for these same groups. Some tests of writing ability require students to write narratives; others require students to synthesize information. Differences in the way writing tests measure writing ability make it more difficult to assess writing ability consistently. Thus, the writing test itself contributes to the error in measurements of writing ability.

Test Administration and Scoring.   Finally, we know that the rating of writing samples is not perfectly reliable. The way raters are trained influences the way they make judgments about a set of writing samples. Similarly, raters' personal values influence their judgments. Even if a rater were to be given the same writing sample at two different times during the same rating session, he or she might score the text differently. Much of the variability in the scores assigned to writing samples is due to idiosyncratic features of rating sessions and individual raters. Test administration and scoring are major contributors to measurement error in holistic assessments.

Common sense and statistical theory both tell us that when we attempt to measure writing ability holistically, we must consider the three sources of error discussed above. This fact was recognized by Godshalk, Swineford, and Coffman (1966), who used analysis of variance to identify the influence of "students," "topics," and "readings" on holistic judgments.

The reliability of a testing instrument is a function of the magnitude of measurement error associated with that instrument. When analysis of variance is used to quantify measurement error, it provides a way of defining and quantifying reliability. According to Thorndike (1951),

> The numerical value of the reliability coefficient of a test corresponds exactly to the proportion of the variance in test scores, which is due to true differences between individuals in the quality being evaluated by the test. A test is unreliable in proportion as it has error variance. (p. 567)

In other words, reliability is, by definition, the ratio of true variance to total variance. This ratio can be expressed in two ways:

$$\text{reliability} = \frac{\text{true variance}}{\text{total variance}} = \frac{\text{total variance} - \text{error variance}}{\text{total variance}} \qquad (3)$$

Equation (3) is the basis of all reliability formulas. In general terms, the higher the proportion of variance due to error, the more likely individual performance on the measure will vary across repeated testing; low reliability means that the testing instrument will not provide consistent information about individual performance. Measurement error and predictability have an inverse relationship to one another: A greater degree of error means that individual performance on the test is less predictable. Quantifying reliability is a matter of determining how true variance and error variance should be defined and measured in particular assessment situations.

Because they represent a ratio of true variance to total variance, reliability coefficients range between 0 and 1. A reliability of 0 would indicate that a test was entirely unreliable because all of the variance in scores on the test could be attributed to measurement error. A reliability of 1 would indicate that the true score and the test score were identical because there was no measurement error. In practice, reliability coefficients are greater than 0 and less than 1.

THE RELIABILITY OF HOLISTIC ASSESSMENT: INTERRATER RELIABILITY VS. INSTRUMENT RELIABILITY

Procedures for estimating reliability were developed when "objective" tests began to gain currency in American education (ca. 1930–1950). Because classical testing and measurement dealt with "objective" tests consisting of items with right and wrong answers (e.g., Gulliksen, 1936; Valentine, 1932; Vernon, 1940), reliability generally has been regarded as a unitary construct. For "objective" tests, scoring is not problematic, and reliability is a question of whether the test produces consistent results on different occasions. For essay testing, reliability is more complicated. In addition to test consistency, evaluators must also be concerned with the consistency of student performance and with the scoring of raters who will never achieve perfect agreement. Thus, the reliability of essay testing is multidimensional rather than one-dimensional.

Unfortunately, writing researchers and evaluators generally have not recognized the complexity of reliability. Perhaps following their predecessors in classical testing and measurement theory, those who discuss the reliability of holistic scoring typically have assumed that reliability is one-dimensional. With few exceptions (e.g., Breland, Camp, Jones, Morris, & Rock, 1987; Godshalk et al., 1966), reliability has been considered synonymous with *interrater reliability*, the reliability with which raters assign scores to written texts. Yet interrater reliability treats only part of one of the three sources of assessment error, that due to scoring. Neglected almost entirely has been instrument reliability, the reliability of the writing assessment as a whole. Instrument reliability is concerned with the consistency of assessments across successive administrations of a test. It necessarily takes into account all three sources of error — students, test, and scoring.

Although the instrument reliability of essay testing corresponds most closely with the notion of reliability assumed in classical testing and measurement theory, this dimension of reliability has been grossly neglected in writing research and evaluation. Despite the fact that instrument reliability rather than interrater reliability provides a basis for making inferences about writing ability, most researchers and evaluators have been more concerned with interrater reliability. To an extent, their concern has been justified because rater judgments can be a major source of error and of low reliability in measurements that involve human judgment. Despite what some advocates of holistic assessment suggest, however, interrater reliability alone cannot establish holistic assessment as a reliable or valid procedure. Focusing only on interrater reliability has resulted in a truncated notion of the reliability of holistic scoring as an assessment procedure.

Interrater reliability tells only part of the story with respect to the reliability of holistic scoring. By describing the consistency with which raters assign scores to written texts, interrater reliability indicates how likely it is that a group of texts would be rated the same way in a second rating. It addresses the question of whether, within the assessment context, raters can reliably judge the quality of writing samples. Interrater reliability, however, says nothing about the reliability of the assessment as a whole.

Instrument reliability, on the other hand, evaluates the consistency of both the writing prompt and the rating of writing samples across successive assessments. Whereas interrater reliability describes how consistently raters judge the *writing quality* of writing samples, instrument reliability addresses the reliability of judgments of *writing ability* made on the basis of those samples. Because most holistic assessments purport to measure writing ability (rather than the quality of a writing sample or the consistency of the raters), instrument reliability should be of greater concern to evaluators than interrater reliability.

The study reported by Godshalk et al. (1966) is one of the few to distinguish between interrater and instrument reliability. Godshalk et al. reported coefficients for both a "reliability of reading" (interrater reliability) and a "reliability of total essay score" (instrument reliability). They explained that their interrater reliability of .921 "means that if a second group of 25 readers as competent as the first group were chosen and the papers were read again, it might be expected that the two sets of total scores would produce a correlation of approximately .921" (p. 12). The "reliability of total essay score" (reported as .841) is an estimate of the reliability of the testing instrument itself, which in this case consisted of a total of five different "essays" produced by each writer. The authors suggested that their overall instrument reliability was "an estimate of the correlation to be expected if the students were to write five more essays on five new topics and if these essays were read by 25 new readers" (pp. 12–13). It is possible to quibble with some of the assumptions underlying this last statement (e.g., Godshalk et al. assume that any writing sample would be an equally good measure of writing ability and that all raters are equally competent), but the examples provide good basic definitions of the concepts of interrater and instrument reliability.

As Godshalk et al. recognized, interrater reliability accounts for only one source of measurement error, that deriving from raters. Regardless of how consistently raters assign scores to written texts, if the writing prompt (the test) is faulty or if examinees do not respond consistently to it, the holistic scores will not reliably reflect writing ability. In order to obtain accurate estimates of the reliability of holistic assessment, all three sources of measurement error — student, test, and scoring procedure — must be taken into account.

Interrater reliability stands in relation to instrument reliability as reliability stands in relation to validity. Just as reliability is a necessary but not sufficient condition for validity, *interrater reliability is a necessary but not sufficient condition for instrument reliability*. As such, interrater reliability provides an upper bound for instrument reliability.

As Stanley and Hopkins (1972) pointed out in a general treatment of essay testing, "agreement in marking the essay test is higher than the reliability of the test itself" (p. 204). This is not a statistical result but a logical consequence of the fact that the total error in a testing situation must be greater than or equal to the error associated with any of its components. Interrater reliability would be equal to instrument reliability only if students responded like automata to writing tasks, performing with identical skill on different occasions without regard to the task. Because students inevitably respond differently on different days and perform differently on different writing tasks, instrument reliability is always lower than interrater reliability, often substantially lower.

PROBLEMS WITH RELIABILITY IN WRITING RESEARCH AND EVALUATION

Several problems have plagued the treatment of reliability in writing research and evaluation. As we have noted, one problem has been that discussions of "reliability" have typically been limited to interrater reliability. In addition, a number of writing researchers have been confused about the difference between interrater reliability and instrument reliability, about the relationship between the two types of reliability, and about how different types of reliability coefficients can be used in decision making.[1]

A second, but related, problem has been confusion over the notions of reliability and validity in influential studies of writing assessment.

A third problem has been a lack of agreement on appropriate statistics for calculating and reporting interrater reliabilities. A wide variety of coefficients has been reported in the composition research and testing literature, with no discussion of, or apparent consensus on, which statistics are appropriate for which circumstances. In many cases, interrater reliability coefficients have been reported without identification of the particular statistic that has been calculated or of the procedures used to calculate it.

A fourth problem is that a number of procedures typically employed in holistic rating sessions are highly problematic with respect to reliability. For example, the practice of calculating and reporting interrater reliability coefficients based on a "sample rating" involving more ratings per text than are actually obtained during a rating session often results in erroneous reports of interrater reliability. A more serious problem is the common procedure of "resolving" discrepancies between two raters by obtaining a third rating, a practice that results in inflated and misleading interrater reliability coefficients. Each of these problems is considered in some detail below.

Reliability and Validity

The relationship between the reliability and validity of essay tests of writing ability has rarely been discussed explicitly, let alone adequately. In fact, one of the more troublesome tendencies in the assessment literature has been the conflation of the two concepts.

Consider, for example, the study conducted by Godshalk et al. (1966). Several times in this report the authors discussed reliability and validity as if the two concepts were interchangeable. When discussing objective and essay tests of writing ability, the authors reported that

> In spite of the growing evidence that the objective and semi-objective English composition questions were *valid*, teachers and administrators in schools and colleges kept insisting that candidates for admission to college ought to be required to demonstrate their writing skill directly. In 1953 experimentation was begun on a two-hour General Composition Test, but Pearson (1955) reported that it had proved no more *reliable* than the shorter essay examinations used in earlier years. (p. 3; emphasis added)

Of course, if the General Composition test was not reliable, it could not be valid. Thus, technically speaking, there is nothing wrong with this discussion. But because reliability appears to be the sole criterion for judging validity, the passage can be read as implying that reliability and validity are interchangeable constructs. A clearer statement might have suggested that the General Composition Test had been judged not to be valid *because* it was not sufficiently reliable.

Consider another passage from the report, one in which the authors pose the central question of the study:

> The testing problem . . . may be stated as follows: How *valid* is the English Composition Test as a measure of each student's ability to write? At the time the study was designed, it was known that the *unreliability* of essay tests came from two major sources: the difference in quality of student writing from one topic to another, and the differences among readers in what they consider the characteristics of good writing. (p. 4; emphasis added)

The second source of unreliability mentioned here — "differences among readers in what they consider the characteristics of good writing" — is indeed a problem of interrater reliability. But the first source — "differences in quality of student writing from one topic to another" — is a problem not only of reliability but also of validity. Variation in performance from one topic to another results in part from natural variation in human performance (human beings cannot perfectly replicate any action or performance) and in part from differences in the writing topics. Different writing topics generally make different demands on writers and assume different kinds and degrees of background knowledge. Differences across topics are more a question of construct validity than of reliability.

Consider a final passage from the Godshalk et al. study:

> During the 1940s, when serious efforts were being made to improve the *reliability* of reading of essays, attempts were made to train readers in making a detailed analysis of each essay. . . . It looked as if the efforts to improve reading reliability had been going in the wrong direction. The solution, it seemed, was in subjecting each paper to the judgment of a number of different readers. The consensus would constitute a *valid* measure of writing, assuming, of course, that the readers were competent. (p. 4; emphasis added)

An unjustifiable assumption underlies the reasoning in this passage. The unstated assumption that all writing topics are equally valid tests of writing ability leads the authors to confound validity and scoring reliability and to suggest that the two are interchangeable, if not synonymous. This oversimplification and misrepresentation of the problem of validity in holistic assessment—reducing it to scoring reliability—is a problem not only with Godshalk et al. but with others as well (e.g., Anderson, 1960; White, 1985).

To be fair to Godshalk et al., we would have to acknowledge that their apparent assumption that a reliably scored writing sample would be a valid measure of writing ability is based on an understanding of writing ability that was current in 1966. Godshalk et al. assumed that writing ability is monolithic and manifests itself in some uniform way whenever it is tested. If this were true, their assumption that scoring reliability established validity would have some merit. But if we have learned anything about writing in the 25 years since the Godshalk et al. study, it is that writing is complex and multidimensional. The multidimensionality of writing ability requires us to maintain a distinction between reliability and validity in holistic assessment of writing.

Another source of confusion is that instrument reliability and criterion-related validity are closely related when applied to writing assessment. The only way to determine instrument reliability is to compare student performance on different writing tasks. A common method of determining validity is to correlate student performance on one task with performance on other tasks and with other measures of the same ability. But even though the methods for estimating instrument reliability and criterion-related validity are similar, the two constructs are distinct theoretically.

Instrument reliability makes a claim about what would happen if the same assessment were to be done again in the same way, with the same distribution of students, the same method of assessment, and the same general kinds of topics, but with different topics, students, and raters. Criterion-related validity, on the other hand, makes qualified, contextual claims about the validity of a test by correlating performance on a test with other measures of writing ability: objective tests, performance in a writing course, or other essay scores, for example.

Both instrument reliability and criterion-related validity are context-bound. Instrument reliability cannot be generalized to other assessment situations that do not correspond to the original one in terms of the students, the test itself, and the assessment procedures. Claims of criterion-related validity are similarly limited. The predictive validity of a test, for example, is no better than the validity of the tests with which it correlates. One of the major criticisms of standardized tests such as the SAT, GRE, and LSAT is that they mostly predict performance on one another.

Instrument reliability and criterion-related validity are similar in that they are both concerned with the kinds of generalizations that can be drawn from a given assessment. As Cronbach, Rajaratnam, and Gleser (1963) explained, when assessment is considered from the point of view of generalizability theory, the theory of "reliability" and the theory of "validity" coalesce; the analysis of generalizability indicates how validly one can interpret a measure as representative of a certain set of possible measures. (p. 157)

What this means in a practical sense is that instrument reliability approaches a common-sense notion of validity. By describing how consistently an assessment instrument measures the performance of a particular group of students on a particular kind of writing task scored in a particular way, instrument reliability comes close to describing how valid the assessment is within the given constraints. In any case, instrument reliability tells us much more about the validity of an assessment procedure than does interrater reliability.

The Reporting of Interrater Reliability Statistics

Two major problems occur with the reporting of interrater reliability statistics in writing research and evaluation: (a) a number of different methods of calculating interrater reliability have been employed, and these different procedures do not yield values that can be compared across studies, and (b) reports of interrater reliability coefficients frequently do not indicate which calculations were used to arrive at a given statistic.

Psychometricians have not achieved a great deal of consensus on how to compute and report the reliability of human judgments, in part because their theoretical understanding of reliability has changed over time and in part because of differences of opinion about the most appropriate formulas for computing interrater reliability coefficients. Between 1948 and 1977, for example, at least 15 formulas for interobserver or interrater *agreement* were proposed. Similarly, between 1950 and 1975, six different coefficients of interobserver or interrater *reliability* were proposed and debated in over 30 scholarly papers (Berk, 1979). The composition literature has reflected the inconsistency of the psychometricians in computing and reporting reliability statistics. At least eight different statistics—and probably more—have been used to compute the interrater reliability (or agreement) of holistic scoring:

- straight percentage of agreement
- Scott's *pi*
- Pearson correlation coefficient
- average intercorrelation
- tetrachoric correlation
- Spearman-Brown formula
- intraclass correlation
- Cronbach's alpha

This wide array of interrater reliability formulas in the composition literature prompted Coffman (1971a) to lament, "Much of the literature on rating reliability of essay examinations is difficult to assess because of the great variety of procedures that have been used to estimate reliability" (p. 277; see also Coffman, 1971b; Coffman & Kurfman, 1968). Coffman has a gift for litotes.

The problem with these various indices is that reliability figures based on different formulas are not comparable. There is simply no way to compare one researcher's findings based on a straight percentage of agreement with another researcher's findings based on Cronbach's alpha.

Worse than the wide variety of statistics that have been employed to calculate and report interrater reliability are the many cases in which reliability statistics are not even identified. It is not uncommon, for example, for a researcher or evaluator to claim simply that "interrater reliability was .90." Unless ".90" is identified as the result of a particular calculation and as the reliability of a single rater judgment or a composite of rater judgments, it is impossible to attach any significance to the figure or to compare it to other interrater reliability coefficients.

Fortunately, in the 1970s psychometricians applying generalizability theory to classical concepts of reliability came close to agreeing on how to think about reliability and reliability formulas. The recommendations we offer later for estimating interrater and instrument reliability derive from that emergent consensus.

Procedures Used During Holistic Scoring Sessions

The procedures used for rating texts holistically can directly affect the reliability of the scores that result. It is well known that careful training of raters can improve interrater reliabilities. In most scoring sessions, raters review and judge a number of sample texts, discuss the criteria that inform their judgments, and gradually move toward greater agreement about how to score the papers. Using two or more raters to score papers and conducting careful training sessions are both sound ways to increase the interrater reliability of holistic assessments.

A problem that occurs with some regularity, however, is that investigators will select a small subsample of texts to be rated by a large number of raters in a "trial" or preliminary rating designed to establish a theoretical interrater reliability. The difficulty is that interrater reliability calculated on the basis of this "trial" session will not reflect the reliability of judgments that are made on the basis of ratings obtained during the actual scoring. Because the more times a text is rated, the more reliable will be its composite score, reliabilities can be artificially inflated by conducting a "trial" rating with more ratings than are obtained during actual scoring. In order for an interrater reliability coefficient to be legitimate, that coefficient must be calculated on the basis of data obtained during the session itself (cf. Tinsley & Weiss, 1975, p. 373).

A much more serious problem in holistic scoring is the practice of "resolving" differences between two raters by seeking a third rating, a procedure we call the *tertium quid method*.[2] The tertium quid procedure is usually invoked when two holistic scores assigned to a given text are more than one point apart on the scale used. Several evaluators (e.g., Myers, 1980; White, 1985) recommend such a procedure, which can take any of several forms. In one version of the procedure, the third party is asked to rate the essay in question and the third score is substituted for one of the original scores. In another version, the third party is asked to choose one of the two previously assigned scores. In the first case, a text assigned scores of 2 and 4, for example, could be assigned a 2 and a 3 or a 3 and a 4. In the second case, the text would be assigned scores of 2 and 2 or 4 and 4. In the system advocated by Myers, the adjudicator "reads the paper a third time and changes one of the original scores, moving the total of the paper up or down" (1980, p. 41). (Note that this advice does not describe what to do when the adjudicator of a 2 and a 4 wants to give the paper a 3. In this case, does the composite score move up or down?)

The motivation behind the tertium quid procedure is admirable when the concern is to make sounder decisions about people's lives. After all, if two doctors disagree about whether a patient needs major surgery, the wise patient goes to a third doctor. However, in such a case, the third doctor doesn't force the odd doctor out to recant his/her opinion. In some cases, the odd doctor out will have made the correct diagnosis.

The tertium quid procedure usually involves three steps.

1. When two ratings of a text disagree by more than one point, a third rating is obtained.

2. The "bad" rating of the three is thrown out.

3. Interrater reliabilities are calculated on the basis of the new set of paired ratings.

The first step is unnecessary. From the point of view of reliability theory, which treats all rater judgments as a combination of true score and error, there is no sound reason to treat a text that receives scores of 2 and 4 differently from one that receives two 3s. Both have an average score of 3 and a summed score of 6. Because there is no a priori reason for thinking that the error in a 2–4 pair of ratings is concentrated in one of the two ratings, rather than residing in both, there is no justification for changing one of the original ratings.

The second step — throwing out a rating — is totally unjustifiable from the point of view of statistics. There is no legitimate way of distinguishing between "good" ratings and "bad" ratings in holistic scoring. In situations in which three ratings are obtained, statistical theory says that the best estimate of the true value (in this case, of writing ability) is the average of the three ratings.

The third step — calculating reliabilities on the basis of the "revised" ratings — is even worse than the second. Adjudication procedures such as the tertium quid method violate the most basic assumptions on which reliability formulas are based: that scoring error is distributed randomly, that each rating is equally likely to be erroneous, and that individual scores are independently determined. When a particular text is singled out for special treatment (for example, when a text is identified as having scores that need to be "resolved" through a third reading), the assumptions on which reliability coefficients are based are seriously compromised. *If pairs of ratings that do not agree are altered through adjudication and if a reliability coefficient is computed with the new numbers as if the numbers had occurred without intervention, the resulting coefficient will be vastly inflated and largely meaningless.*

In fact, calculating interrater reliabilities on the basis of modified ratings constitutes a kind of fraud since such a calculation is guaranteed to result in an inflated and false report of interrater reliabilities. Calculating interrater reliabilities in this way is like a defense contractor calculating the accuracy of its missiles after throwing out data for projectiles that missed their targets by more than 100 feet. It is precisely the big misses that most contribute to low reliability. Because calculating reliabilities using data resulting from the tertium quid procedure is inaccurate and misleading, the practice should be discontinued altogether in writing research and evaluation.

Interrater reliability formulas are quite sensitive to the manipulation of data through tertium quid methods, even in cases in which a relatively low percentage of scores is affected. The example shown in Table 3–1 demonstrates the results of the worst possible tertium quid procedure—one that

TABLE 3–1   Sample Data for Showing the Effect of Tertium Quid Adjudication

Test	Rater 1	Rater 2	Tertium Quid
1	1	2	
2	2	2	
3	2	2	
4	4	3	
5	4	1	4
6	2	2	
7	2	2	
8	2	2	
9	3	2	
10	4	3	
11	4	3	
12	3	2	
13	2	2	
14	2	3	
15	1	3	3
16	3	3	
17	3	3	
18	4	3	
19	4	4	
20	4	4	
21	2	3	
22	3	3	
23	2	1	
24	3	3	
25	4	4	
26	2	1	
27	3	3	
28	2	4	2
29	4	4	
30	2	1	
31	3	3	

forces the adjudicator to choose one of two discrepant scores and repeat it. In this example, less than 10% of the scores have been adjudicated using the tertium quid method (a percentage that may be a little higher than normal according to Myers).

If the tertium quid scores are ignored, the interrater reliability coefficient for the summed scores is .63 (using formula 3b, which is discussed in a later section). If the tertium quid score is substituted for the dissimilar score in each of the three cases that have been "adjudicated," the reliability coefficient jumps to .88. Did the reliability of the assessment as a whole actually improve that much? Of course not. Calculating the interrater reliability of the complete set of scores above using a one-way analysis of variance model for situations involving unequal numbers of judgments per subject (Ebel, 1951, p. 412) results in an interrater reliability of .59 for the summed scores.[3]

The important point is that the adjudications do not significantly change the "real" reliability of the scoring session. The gain of .25 (from .63 to .88) resulting from the tertium quid procedure is entirely bogus. Substituting tertium quid scores for even a small fraction of disparate pairs can have a profound (and obviously misleading) effect on interrater reliability coefficients that are calculated for a set of holistic scores. To insure that interrater reliability figures truly reflect the reliability of holistic scoring sessions, researchers and evaluators should choose one of the following options:

- *Option 1.* Do not use the tertium quid adjudication procedure. Use the original scores and report reliabilities based on those scores.

- *Option 2.* If there is a compelling reason to use tertium quid methods to adjudicate disagreements, calculate and report the reliability of the data prior to adjudication, or use a formula such as Ebel's (1951) that takes into account all the ratings.

Each of these options will result in lower reported reliabilities. But those reliabilities will be accurate and meaningful.

ESTIMATING AND REPORTING INSTRUMENT AND INTERRATER RELIABILITY COEFFICIENTS

Estimating Instrument Reliability

Most treatments of reliability focus on "objective" tests rather than on essay testing or direct measurement of writing abilities. These discussions assume that such tests consist of a number of items that collectively cover the domain being tested. It will be helpful to review the methods used to determine the reliability of "objective" tests for two reasons: (a) understanding the procedures used for estimating the reliability of "objective" tests can contribute to a better understanding of the nature of instrument reliability and (b) we must eventually ask whether the methods used for "objective" tests can or should be adapted for tests of writing ability.

Estimating the Reliability of "Objective" Tests

Four methods have been most commonly used for determining the instrument reliability of "objective" tests: (a) comparison of equivalent test forms, (b) division of a test into equivalent halves, (c) repeated administration of a single test form, and (d) analysis of individual items to determine error variance. The first three methods rely on the calculation of correlation coefficients, the fourth on analysis of variance.

Equivalent forms.   With this method of establishing instrument reliability, test makers create at least two different forms of a test, administer the test forms to the same group of subjects or to comparable groups, and then compare the scores yielded by the two forms. (See Thorndike [1951] for a discussion of issues involved in determining "equivalence.") Coefficients of correlation are used to compare the scores resulting from the two test forms. The correlation coefficient is interpreted as an indication of the reliability of the test; it represents a measure of the likelihood that the test will produce consistent results across successive administrations. A typical equivalent forms procedure for establishing the reliability of an arithmetic test, for example, would involve constructing two or more exams (or forms) with different problems but ones judged to be testing the same kinds of knowledge and to be of comparable difficulty.

Equivalent halves.   This "poor person's alternative" to using equivalent forms is often referred to as the "split-halves" method. When lack of time or resources prohibits development of equivalent forms of a test, an acceptable alternative is to divide the items on the test into equivalent halves. Scores on the two halves are then compared by calculating a coefficient of correlation. As with the equivalent forms method, this correlation coefficient is interpreted as a reliability coefficient.

Repeated administration.   Some abilities or traits are defined so narrowly that it does not make sense to develop equivalent tests to measure them. It would not seem useful, for example, to develop different tests in order to measure people's weight. In such cases as these it is more reasonable to administer the same test on two or more occasions. Scores from the different administrations are then correlated and the resulting coefficient interpreted as a reliability coefficient.

Analysis of variance methods.   Analysis of variance techniques can also be used to estimate the instrument reliability of a test (Hoyt, 1941). When applied to a group of subjects with scores on individual items in a test, analysis of variance breaks the variance into separate components attributable to subjects, items, and error. True variance is due to real differences across subjects being tested and to differences in items on the test. Error variance is error due to chance and/or poor test questions. The ratio of true variance to error variance is, by definition, the instrument reliability of the test. The relia-bility coefficients developed by Kuder and Richardson (1937) are based on analysis of variance principles.

Determining the Instrument Reliability of Essay Tests

Correlation and analysis of variance techniques have been widely used for es-timating the instrument reliability of "objective" tests, tests that consist of multiple items. But how should we estimate the instrument reliability of essay tests of writing ability, tests that typically consist of a single "item" to which examinees respond — that is, a writing prompt?

Three of the four methods used for establishing the reliability of objective tests are not readily applicable to essay testing. Both the equivalent forms and equivalent halves methods would require writing prompts different enough in content to avoid a practice effect but virtually identical in the demands they place on writers. This kind of equivalence is possible for tests of arithmetic but very difficult to achieve for essay tests of writing abilities.

Some research has examined how students respond to writing topics (e.g., Brossell, 1983, 1986; Brossell & Ash, 1984; Ruth & Murphy, 1984, 1988). Hoetker and Brossell (1986) showed that it was possible to vary the rhetorical specificity of a single topic without affecting student performance. But we have not yet established procedures for creating truly equivalent writing tests — tests that would be different in content but identical in the demands they place on writers. Perhaps future research will allow equivalent halves testing to establish instrument reliability. What is needed are pairs of topics that are so similar that it does not matter which one a student writes about (which was the case in Hoetker and Brossell's study) but different enough so that a student could write about both topics without having the writing of the first paper affect the writing of the second.

Trying to establish instrument reliability by having students write twice in response to the same prompt — the procedure of repeated measures — has similar problems with respect to the practice effect. If the second test is ad-ministered soon after the first, student performance on the first test will affect the second. If, on the other hand, the second administration is postponed un-til subjects have "forgotten" the first test, their writing abilities may well have changed and, in an important sense, they may no longer be the same people.

Largely because of these difficulties, writing researchers and evaluators have turned to analysis of variance as a way of addressing the question of in-strument reliability. Thorndike (1951) suggested that "the analysis of vari-ance approach ... appears useful for obtaining reliability estimates from items or trials which are scored with a range of scores, and not merely as 'passed' or 'failed'" (p. 591). This method, however, requires at least two independent tests of writing. Instead of trying to create "equivalent" writing tasks, examiners sample different dimensions or domains of writing ability and correlate performances on these different domains in order to assess the instrument reliability of particular writing prompts. Scores on different tests can be correlated using one of several forms of the intraclass correlation, which we discuss in greater detail below.

Godshalk et al. (1966) and Breland et al. (1987) estimated the instrument reliability of writing prompts in this manner by correlating students' performance on one writing task with their performance on others. The instrument reliabilities Godshalk et al. reported for five writing prompts (p. 16) ranged from .435 to .592 (based on five readings of each essay). Breland et al. (p. 27) estimated that a single essay exam like those in their study would have an instrument reliability of .42 (if rated once) and .63 (if rated four times).

These two studies provide the best available estimates of the instrument reliability of essay tests of writing ability. Unfortunately, the results of these studies cannot be generalized to other writing topics or other assessment situations. Even if evaluators used one of the Breland topics in an assessment, for example, the same instrument reliability could not be assumed unless two things were true: (a) the assessment procedures (including training and raters) were indistinguishable from Breland's and (b) the examinees were indistinguishable from those in the Breland study by range of writing abilities and average writing ability.

At present, the only way to determine the instrument reliability of a given essay test of writing is for individual researchers or evaluators to obtain multiple writing samples from a representative group of subjects and intercorrelate them. The problem, of course, is the expense and time required to establish the instrument reliability of a writing test using these procedures. Most research or assessment teams are not likely to have the necessary resources at their disposal. Nevertheless, a hard fact remains: If researchers and evaluators continue to use holistic assessment without addressing issues of instrument reliability, they will do so without knowing how reliably they are assessing writing ability.

Estimating Interrater Reliability

For most "objective" tests, interrater reliability is not an issue because true/false or multiple-choice items leave no room for disagreement among scorers or raters (at least in terms of scoring itself). A particular response either agrees with the "right" answer identified by the test maker(s) or it doesn't. With essay tests of writing ability, interrater reliability has been recognized as a critical issue for many years (Coffman 1971b; Coffman & Kurfman 1968; Finlayson, 1951; Follman & Anderson, 1967; Hartog, Ballard, Gurrey, Harnley, & Smith, 1941; Huddelston, 1954; Stalnaker, 1936; Stalnaker & Stalnaker, 1934; Starch & Elliott, 1912; Traxler & Anderson, 1935; Vernon & Millican, 1954). Because there is no single "right" response to the testing instrument and because scoring depends on human judgment, it is inevitable that scorers (or raters) will not agree with one another 100% of the time.

Of the several methods of determining interrater reliability, a particular class of statistical formulas, the intraclass correlation, seems especially appropriate for holistic scoring. Tinsley and Weiss (1975) consider the intraclass correlation "the best measure of interrater reliability available for ordinal and interval level measurement" (p. 373; see also Algina, 1978; Bartko, 1976; Haggard, 1958). The intraclass correlation is based theoretically on analysis of variance, and the rationale for interpreting intraclass correlations as reliability coefficients derives from generalizability theory (Cardinet, Tourneur, & Allal, 1976; Cronbach, Gleser, Nanda, & Rajaratnam, 1972; Cronbach, Ikeda, & Avner, 1964; Cronbach et al., 1963; Gleser, Cronbach, & Rajaratnam, 1965; Rentz, 1980).[4]

According to Berk (1979), "the intraclass correlation expresses the classical theory of measurement error relationship between true and observed variance" (p. 463). The most general form of the intraclass correlation is the simple ratio of true to total variance, which we presented earlier as equation (3) and reproduce here in an equivalent but slightly different form (following Ebel, 1951, p. 409):

$$\text{reliability} = \frac{\text{true variance}}{\text{true variance} + \text{error variance}} \tag{4}$$

A whole family of intraclass correlations has been developed, but all derive from equation (4).

Shrout and Fleiss (1979) discuss three pairs of the intraclass correlation, each of which is based on a different analysis of variance model. The formulas differ in how they define particular components of variance as true variance or error. In some versions of the formula, variance due to differences in mean scores awarded by raters is defined as part of the error term; in others, it is defined as part of the true variance. These differences are important for interrater reliability because definitions of true and error variance depend on how rating sessions are conducted and on the kinds of decisions evaluators intend to make.

The appropriate form of the intraclass correlation depends on a number of contextual factors associated with the assessment: (a) whether individual or composite ratings are the measure of interest, (b) whether all raters rate all texts, and (c) whether ratings are considered relative or absolute.

Below we discuss three typical holistic assessment situations. For each situation, two different forms of the intraclass correlation are introduced. The first formula in each pair (i.e., 1a, 2a, and 3a) is the appropriate equation for determining the reliability of a single rating. The second formula in each pair (i.e., 1b, 2b, and 3b) is appropriate for determining the reliability of a judgment based on summing or averaging scores across two or more raters.[5]

In most situations, researchers and evaluators make decisions based on composite scores and should calculate reliability accordingly. For example, if two ratings have been given to each text and the evaluator is using the summed score for placement purposes, calculating the reliability of the summed scores would be appropriate. In contrast, if a single score of "failing" on an exit exam would prevent a student from passing, then, in terms of reliability, a single score would be serving as the basis for judgment and the reliability of a single score, rather than a composite score, should be calculated and reported.

The three situations described below differ along two lines: (a) whether all raters rate all texts and (b) whether scores will be considered relative or absolute. Situation One describes the very common case in which, instead of scoring all the texts, individual raters score only a fraction of them. In Situations Two and Three, individual raters rate all texts available for scoring. The distinction between Situations Two and Three rests on whether scores are considered relative or absolute. In Situation Two, scores are considered absolute or criterion-referenced; in Situation Three, scores are considered relative.

Assessment Situation One.   The evaluators have a large number of texts to rate and a pool of more than two raters. Each rater rates a portion, but not all, of the texts. For example, six raters might each rate one-third of the texts. The appropriate intraclass formulas in this case are as follows:[6]

Formula 1a (reliability of single rating):

$$r = \frac{MSp - MSwp}{MSp + (k - 1)\, MSwp}$$

r = reliability coefficient
MSp = between persons mean square
MSwp = within persons mean square
k = number of raters

Formula 1b (reliability of summed or averaged ratings):

$$\frac{MSp - MSwp}{MSp}$$

Formulas 1a and 1b are based on a one-way, random effects analysis of variance model (see Cho, 1981).[7] When individual raters do not rate all essays, "raters" cannot be treated as an independent variable; thus, the model is "one-way," with "students" as the only independent variable. Because student writing abilities are assumed to be distributed normally, the student effect is considered random. The formulas based on the one-way random effects model take into account the fact that each rater does not rate every essay, a fact that lowers the interrater reliability of the assessment, although often by only a small amount.[8] The example below illustrates the relationships among texts, raters, and ratings in Situation One:

Text	Rater	Rating	Rater	Rating
1	R3	1	R5	1
2	R1	2	R4	4
3	R5	3	R1	3
4	R2	3	R6	4

Formula 1a (reliability of a single rating) = .59
Formula 1b (reliability of a composite rating) = .75

Formula 1a or 1b *must* be used when individual raters do not rate all texts in a given scoring session, regardless of whether ratings are considered relative or absolute. In Assessment Situations Two and Three, each rater rates all of the texts available in a given scoring session. The distinction between the two situations rests on whether ratings are absolute or relative. In Situation Two, scores are absolute; in Situation Three, they are relative.

Assessment Situation Two.   Each rater rates every essay. In addition, ratings are considered objective or criterion-referenced rather than relative. The raters are not simply assigning relative ratings on a scale of, for example, 1 to 6. Instead, the rating categories are tied to some outside criterion. An example would be a placement situation in which raters are trained to think of a score of 1 as meaning that a student should be placed in a remedial class, a score of 2 as meaning that a student should be placed in regular class, and a score of 3 as meaning a student should be exempt from Freshman English.[9] The appropriate intraclass formulas for Situation Two are the following:

Formula 2a (reliability of single rating):

$$r = \frac{MSp - MSe}{MSp + (k - 1)\, MSe + k/n\, (MSr - MSe)}$$

$\quad r$ = reliability coefficient
MSp = between persons mean square
$\ MSr$ = between raters mean square
MSe = error mean square
$\quad k$ = number of raters
$\quad n$ = number of persons

Formula 2b (reliability of summed or averaged scores):

$$r = \frac{MSp - MSe}{MSp + 1/n\, (MSn - MSe)}$$

Formulas 2a and 2b are based on a two-way random effects analysis of variance model. Because all raters rate all texts, "raters" constitutes an independent variable as well as "students"; thus, the model is "two-way." "Students" is treated as a random effect as in Situation One: "raters" is treated as a random effect as well because scores are criterion-referenced. Because differences between raters' mean scores have an objective meaning, variance due to differences in rater means is included in the error term of intraclass formulas 2a and 2b.[10]

The example below uses the same hypothetical data as used for Situation One. This time, however, the columns in the table for ratings correspond to particular raters, making it possible to account for the systematic effect of raters on the scoring.

Text	Rater A	Rater B
1	1	1
2	2	4
3	3	3
4	3	4

Intraclass formula 2a (reliability of a single rating) = .65
Intraclass formula 2b (reliability of a composite rating) = .76

Because scores are considered objective in Situation Two, differences in raters' mean scores must be taken into account. Between-rater variance has been factored into the error term of the intraclass formulas, resulting in lower estimates of interrater reliability than will result using the same data in Situation Three. In fact, formula 2 treats rater disagreement more strictly than does formula 3, and because it considers any differences between raters' scores as error, formula 2 can be thought of as an agreement formula (Shrout & Fleiss, 1979, p. 425).[11]

Assessment Situation Three.   Each rater rates every text. In addition, ratings are considered relative rather than objective. Each rater simply evaluates the relative quality of the writing samples. An example would be a case in which a researcher wanted to identify groups with different levels of writing ability. The ratings are not tied to an outside criterion but are considered relative within the group of texts to be assessed. The appropriate forms of the intraclass formula in this situation would be the following:

Formula 3a (reliability of single rating):

$$r = \frac{MSp - MSe}{MSp + (k - 1)\,MSe}$$

r = reliability coefficient
MSp = between persons mean square
MSe = error mean square
k = number of raters

Formula 3b (reliability of summed or averaged scores):

$$r = \frac{MSp - MSe}{MSp}$$

Formulas 3a and 3b are based on a two-way mixed effects analysis of variance model. As does the model for Situation Two, this model includes both "students" and "raters" as independent variables. "Students" is again considered a random effect, but because scores are relative rather than objective, "raters" is treated as a fixed effect. This means that the difference in average scores between two raters (or among three or more raters) is attributed to raters consistently applying slightly different standards of judgment rather than to error, and the difference in average scores is therefore considered true variance. Because the student effect is random and the rater effect is fixed, this model is described as "mixed."

The example below uses the same hypothetical data as used for Situations One and Two:

Text	Rater A	Rater B
1	1	1
2	2	4
3	3	3
4	3	4

Intraclass formula 3a (reliability of a single rating) = .69
Intraclass formula 3b (reliability of a composite rating) = .81

Because they consider raters' scores to be relative, Formulas 3a and 3b treat between-rater variance as true variance, which results in higher inter-rater reliability estimates than the inclusion of between-rater variance in the error term (as in Situation Two). When all raters rate all texts and scores are relative, differences among raters' mean scores are of no consequence because the differences cancel out when scores are added or averaged. It makes no difference, for example, if one rater's scores average 3 and another rater's scores average 4 as long as their judgments are consistent relative to one another.

Versions 1 to 3 of the intraclass formula are progressively less "restrictive," and coefficients will generally be higher for Situation Three than for Situation Two and in turn higher for Situation Two than for Situation One.[12] With the exception of formula 3b, which is equivalent to Cronbach's alpha, the different versions of the intraclass correlation are not easily obtained through standard statistical packages such as SAS and SPSS, but the formulas can be calculated from an analysis of variance table. An extensive knowledge of ANOVA theory and procedures is not necessary for computing the formulas; Cho (1981) provides a clear description of the necessary procedures.[13]

Needed Research on Reliability

Further research will be needed to answer a number of questions concerning the reliability of holistic assessment. Among the questions we consider most important are these: What standards should be expected for the reliability of holistic ratings? Specifically, how high should interrater reliability figures be? Should different standards apply for different assessment purposes? For example, should one standard be employed for research and another for educational decision making? For educational decision making, should different standards apply, for example, for placement testing as opposed to proficiency testing?

How High Should Interrater and Instrument Reliability Coefficients Be?

As we suggested above, it is difficult to provide definitive expectations for interrater reliability coefficients, in part because the wide range of statistics used to calculate them reduces our ability to compare the interrater reliability figures reported in various studies.

Berk (1979) suggested that "coefficients in the .80s are indicative of a high level of agreement" (p. 467), and it does seem clear from a number of studies that interrater reliability coefficients in the .80s or .90s can be reached with careful training and monitoring of raters. In our view, however, about the best that can be said about high interrater reliabilities is that they are better than low ones. It is essential to keep in mind that high interrater reliabilities do not insure that the testing procedure as a whole is reliable. The more important concept to consider is instrument reliability.

Godshalk et al. (1966) reported an instrument reliability of .841. This figure represented the reliability of composite scores formed by summing five scores for each of five essays by each student in the study (i.e., 25 pieces of information for each subject). The instrument reliability of a single writing task in the Godshalk study was about .5.

Psychometricians generally strive for instrument reliabilities of over .8 for tests that are used to make important judgments about individuals. When a test with a reliability of .5 is used to discriminate between students at the 50th and 75th percentiles of a group, over one-third (36.8%) of those at the 50th percentile would seem to be better than those at the 75th percentile on a second testing (Sax, 1974, p. 194). What this means, of course, is that those who rely on holistic assessments of writing ability should be concerned about whether a single writing sample provides enough information to make reasonable and fair judgments about individual students.

If most holistic assessment tasks have an instrument reliability comparable to that of the tasks in the Godshalk and Breland studies (i.e., in the range of .5 to .6 for a single writing sample scored twice), then the true instrument reliability of such tests may be too low for making important decisions about individuals. There is reason to believe that the Godshalk et al. and Breland et al. studies were conducted under very favorable conditions and that studies conducted in more typical circumstances would likely result in testing instruments with even lower reliabilities.

Kelly (1927) suggested that instrument reliabilities of .5 were fine for making decisions about the behavior of groups, but he recommended instrument reliabilities of at least .94 for making decisions about individuals. Breland et al. projected achieving such a level of reliability would have required nine writing samples and somewhere between four and an infinite number of ratings of each one (p. 27). Kelly's standards would probably be considered a bit strict today, and indications are that .94 is not a realistic number for writing assessment. But most psychometricians would be very uncomfortable about using a test with an instrument reliability of only .5 for making decisions about individuals.

Should Different Standards Apply for Different Assessment Purposes?

Reliabilities should be high enough to justify whatever decisions are being made on the basis of the scores. This is not a simple numerical answer, but it is the only good answer. Evaluators need to be concerned about the reliability of their decisions in proportion to the impact their decisions will have on individuals. Common sense and good judgment must come into play in such situations. The more significantly a decision will affect an individual's life, the more the evaluator needs to be concerned with instrument reliability.

For research decisions for which the goal is to differentiate between or among groups, instrument reliabilities of .5 are generally considered high enough. In addition, placement decisions, although they affect people's lives, are probably not as critical as other types of educational decisions. In contrast, exit exams that determine whether a student graduates from high school or college, writing exams that determine whether a student can take advanced coursework or whether someone with a teacher's certificate will be allowed to teach — these are serious assessment decisions for which instrument reliability is critical. Anyone making such decisions based on a single writing sample for which the reliability is probably no more than .5 is on shaky ground at best.

How high should instrument reliabilities be, then? In our view, a definitive answer to this question is not possible at this time. We need additional research on instrument reliability in different assessment situations before we begin to answer the question with any confidence. Our hope is that researchers and evaluators will begin to recognize the importance of instrument reliability and that such research will be forthcoming.

What Can Be Done to Achieve Higher Instrument Reliabilities?

As we mentioned above, the procedures for determining the instrument reliability of direct writing assessments are time-consuming and costly. Although it may not be feasible for individual researchers and evaluators to undertake the necessary testing, they must still be concerned about instrument reliability and do everything in their power to achieve instrument reliabilities that are as high as possible.

A number of procedures will contribute to a higher instrument reliability. First, important decisions should be based on more than one piece of information. The more independent pieces of information used in making a decision, the more reliable the decision will be. A writing sample and an objective test can be used, as Breland et al. suggested. Or two or more writing samples can be elicited. Or a writing sample and a course grade can be used.

Second, great care should be taken in the development of writing topics and in the training of raters. The three main sources of error in the assessment of writing are the student, the test, and the assessment situation. Thorough development and testing of writing topics will help to improve instrument reliability. Careful rater training will result in higher interrater reliability and reduce error from this component. Evaluators may not have much control over student performance, but they should attempt to make the testing situation as favorable for students as possible by providing manageable topics and well-trained raters.

Finally, evaluators should develop procedures for appeal and review so that incorrect placements or assessments can be identified and corrected.

Conclusion

Reliability should not be regarded as a fixed, monolithic attribute of a particular testing instrument. Strictly speaking, "reliability" refers not to a characteristic (or set of characteristics) of a particular test but to the confidence that test users can place in scores yielded by the test as a basis for making certain kinds of decisions. For essay tests of writing ability, reliability is multidimensional, consisting of components associated with the test, the student, and the assessment situation. An essay test of writing ability can be said to be reliable only for a certain population for a certain purpose.

Reliability is a necessary but not sufficient condition for validity. Holistic scoring must be reliable, but reliable testing is not necessarily valid testing. For a complete understanding of the reliability of holistic assessment, we must distinguish between scoring reliability and instrument reliability. We must employ rating methods that ensure high agreement among raters, but we must also gauge the extent to which our assessment instruments yield comparable results across successive testing occasions. We must keep in mind that reliable scoring is not necessarily reliable testing.

As research on holistic scoring progresses and as writing assessments become more refined, our profession must begin to use common formulas for computing and reporting interrater and instrument reliability. In our view, much research remains to be done to provide answers to the questions still surrounding the reliability of essay tests of writing ability. We consider it imperative, however, that this research be conducted and reported using common procedures and statistics. Researchers and evaluators must begin to provide explicit, detailed descriptions of the methods and computational formulas used to arrive at estimates of interrater and instrument reliability. Only then can results be compared across studies and only then can the research community move toward informed, intelligent answers to important questions that still remain about the direct measurement of writing skills.

NOTES

1. Even some who attempt to distinguish between interrater and instrument reliability fail to maintain the distinction or to discuss it clearly. The treatment of this issue by Lauer and Asher (1988, pp. 138–39) is problematic in this respect.

2. "Tertium quid" is a term derived from medieval dialectic. It refers to a situation in which two disputants have reached a deadlock and a third party is called in to decide on a particular point in favor of one of the disputants so that the debate can proceed.

3. This figure is lower than the original estimation of .63 in part because Ebel uses a more restrictive interrater reliability formula than is possible when all raters rate all texts.

4. Analysis of variance is most commonly used as a statistical test of hypotheses regarding group differences. Generalizability theory applies similar statistical calculations somewhat differently. Instead of analyzing group differences, generalizability theory focuses on the magnitude of variance components in order to determine the ratio of true variance to error variance in a set of measurements or observations.

5. The reliability of composite scores is the same regardless of whether they are formed by summing or averaging.

6. The formulas given for these situations are appropriate only if one writing sample per student is elicited. The analysis of variance model gets more complicated if multiple writing samples are considered, although the same general principles discussed here apply.

7. Glass and Stanley (1970) provide a good explanation of the distinctions among random, fixed, and mixed effects analysis of variance models.

8. Strictly speaking, the model posited for Situation One assumes that each writing sample is rated by a different set of raters chosen randomly from a larger pool, i.e., no samples share a common set of raters, except by chance. In a typical holistic rating session, raters rate a large number of texts, and many texts are likely to share a common set of raters because texts are grouped into packets that move intact from one rater to another. This circumstance represents a mild violation of the assumptions of the analysis of variance model on which the formula for Situation One is based, but Cronbach et al. (1963) argue that "the absence of true random sampling from a pool of items or judges is unfortunate but no more so than in the ubiquitous studies that make statistical inferences from persons who are not chosen in a strictly random fashion" (p. 160). Thus, because the discrepancy is minor, the model and reliability formulas for Situation One are appropriate for cases in which individual raters do not rate all texts.

9. Other examples might include some forms of analytic scoring, primary trait scoring, or performative assessment (Faigley, Cherry, Jolliffe, & Skinner, 1985). The formulas presented for Situation Two might also be appropriate for many types of text analysis commonly used in writing research (e.g., asking readers to identify particular text features or to determine when text features should be considered cues to other phenomena).

10. A number of statisticians have discussed the circumstances in which it is appropriate to treat between-rater variance as true variance (Cronbach, 1951; Cronbach et al., 1963; Ebel, 1951; Shrout & Fleiss, 1979; Tinsley & Weiss, 1975). Ebel's (1951, 411ff.) discussion is accurate and detailed but somewhat confusing. Berk's (1979, p. 466) treatment of the issue is clearer and easier to follow.

11. The terms *reliability* and *agreement* are often used interchangeably in treatments of holistic scoring and other types of judgments that raters are called upon to make about written texts. Although the two notions are related, they should be distinguished both conceptually and computationally. Space does not permit a full treatment of this issue here. Lawlis and Lu (1972), Tinsley and Weiss (1975), and Berk (1979) provide helpful discussions of this issue.

12. It is important to note, however, that when assessments are conducted with writing topics that have been thoroughly tested and with raters who have been carefully trained, the differences among various forms of the intraclass correlation may be much less pronounced than in the examples above. In some cases, even though it would not be appropriate to calculate all versions of the formula, the different intraclass coefficients might yield very similar results. Careful testing of topics and training of raters helps to reduce random variation between ratings and between-rater variance, the most important potential sources of lower interrater reliabilities when formulas 1 and 2 of the intraclass correlation are appropriate.

13. It is not difficult to write a computer program using Cho (1981) as a guide. A source listing of such a program in C and in BASIC is available free of charge by sending a stamped, self-addressed envelope to Paul Meyer, Department of English, Box 3E, New Mexico State University, Las Cruces, NM 88003.

REFERENCES

Algina, J. (1978). Comment on Bartko's "On various intraclass correlation reliability coefficients." *Psychological Bulletin, 85,* 135–138.

Anderson, C. C. (1960). The new STEP essay test as a measure of composition ability. *Educational and Psychological Measurement, 20,* 95–102.

Bartko, J. J. (1976). On various intraclass correlation reliability coefficients. *Psychological Bulletin, 83,* 762–765.

Berk, R. A. (1979). Generalizability of behavioral observations: A clarification of interobserver agreement and interobserver reliability. *American Journal of Mental Deficiency, 83,* 460–472.

Breland, H. M., Camp, R., Jones, R. J., Morris, M. M., & Rock, D. A. (1987). *Assessing writing skill.* New York: College Entrance Examination Board.

Brossell, G. (1983). Rhetorical specification in essay examination topics. *College English, 45,* 165–173.

Brossell, G. (1986). Current research and unanswered questions in writing assessment. In K. Greenberg, H. Weiner, & R. Donovan (Eds.), *Writing assessment: Issues and strategies* (pp. 168–182). New York: Longman.

Brossell, G., & Ash, B. H. (1984). An experiment with the wording of essay topics. *College Composition and Communication, 35,* 423–425.

Cardinet, J., Tourneur, Y., & Allal, L. (1976). The symmetry of generalizability theory: Applications to educational measurement. *Journal of Educational Measurement, 13,* 119–135.

Cho, D.W. (1981). Inter-rater reliability: Intraclass correlation coefficients. *Educational and Psychological Measurement, 41,* 223–226.

Coffman, W. E. (1971a). Essay examinations. In R. L. Thorndike (Ed.), *Educational measurement.* Washington, DC: American Council on Education.

Coffman, W. E. (1971b). On the reliability of ratings of essay examinations in English. *Research in the Teaching of English, 5,* 24–36.

Coffman, W. E., & Kurfman, D. (1968). A comparison of two methods of reading essay examinations. *American Educational Research Journal, 5,* 99–107.

Cronbach, L. J. (1951). Coefficient alpha and the internal structure of tests. *Psychometrika, 16,* 297–334.

Cronbach, L. J., Gleser, G. C., Nanda, H., & Rajaratnam, N. (1972). *The dependability of behavioral measurements.* New York: John Wiley.

Cronbach, L. J., Ikeda, M., & Avner, R. A. (1964). Intraclass correlation as an approximation to the coefficient of generalizability. *Psychological Reports, 15,* 727–736.

Cronbach, L. J., Rajaratnam, N., & Gleser, G. C. (1963). Theory of generalizability: A liberalization of reliability theory. *The British Journal of Statistical Psychology, 16,* 137–163.

Davis, B. G., Scriven, M., & Thomas, S. (1987). *The evaluation of composition instruction* (2nd ed). New York: Teachers College Press.

Ebel, R. L. (1951). Estimation of the reliability of ratings. *Psychometrika, 16,* 407–424.

Faigley, L., Cherry, R. D., Jolliffe, D. A., & Skinner, A. M. (1985). *Assessing writers' knowledge and processes of composing.* Norwood, NJ: Ablex.

Finlayson, D. S. (1951). The reliability of the marking of essays. *The British Journal of Educational Psychology, 21,* 126–134.

Follman, J. C., & Anderson, J. A. (1967). An investigation of the reliability of five procedures for grading English themes. *Research in the Teaching of English, 1,* 190–200.

Glass, G. V., & Stanley, J.C. (1970). *Statistical methods in education and psychology.* Englewood Cliffs, NJ: Prentice-Hall.

Gleser, G. C., Cronbach, L. J., & Rajaratnam, N. (1965). Generalizability of scores influenced by multiple sources of variance. *Psychometrika, 30,* 395–418.

Godshalk, F. I., Swineford, F., & Coffman, W. E. (1966). *The measurement of writing ability* (Research Monograph No. 6). New York: College Entrance Examination Board.

Gulliksen, H. (1936). The content reliability of a test. *Psychometrika, 1,* 189–194.

Haggard, E. A. (1958). *Intraclass correlation and the analysis of variance.* New York: Dryden Press.

Hartog, P., Ballard, P. B., Gurrey, P., Harnley, H. R., & Smith, C. E. (1941). *The marking of English essays.* London: Macmillan. (International Institute Examinations Enquiry, Britain).

Hoetker, J., & Brossell, G. (1986). A procedure for writing content-fair essay examination topics for large-scale writing assessments. *College Composition and Communication, 37,* 328–335.

Hoyt, C. (1941). Test reliability estimated by analysis of variance. *Psychometrika, 6,* 153–160.

Huddelston, E. M. (1954). Measurement of writing ability at the college-entrance level: Objective vs. subjective testing techniques. *Journal of Experimental Education, 22,* 165–213.

Jackson, R. W. B., & Ferguson, G. A. (1941). *Studies on the reliability of tests*. Toronto: University of Toronto Press. (Department of Educational Research, Bulletin 12).

Kelly, T. L. (1927). *Interpretation of educational measurements*. Yonkers-on-Hudson, NY: World Book Co.

Kuder, G. F., & Richardson, M. W. (1937). The theory of the estimation of test reliability. *Psychometrika, 2*, 151–160.

Lauer, J., & Asher, J. W. (1988). *Composition research: Empirical designs*. New York: Oxford.

Lawlis, G. F., & Lu, E. (1972). Judgment of counseling process: Reliability, agreement, and error. *Psychological Bulletin, 78*, 17–20.

Myers, M. (1980). *Procedures for writing assessment and holistic scoring*. Urbana, IL: National Council of Teachers of English.

Rentz, R. R. (1980). Rules of thumb for estimating reliability coefficients using generalizability theory. *Educational and Psychological Measurement, 40*, 575–592.

Ruth, L., & Murphy, S. (1984). Designing topics for writing assessment: Problems and meaning. *College Composition and Communication, 35*, 410–422.

Ruth, L., & Murphy, S. (1988). *Designing writing tasks for the assessment of writing*. Norwood, NJ: Ablex.

Sax, G. (1974). *Principles of educational measurement and evaluation*. Belmont, CA: Wadsworth.

Shrout, P. E., & Fleiss, J. L. (1979). Intraclass correlations: Uses in assessing rater reliability. *Psychological Bulletin, 86*, 420–428.

Spandel, V., & Stiggins, R. J. (1981). *Direct measures of writing skill: Issues and applications* (Revised ed.). Portland, OR: Northwest Regional Educational Laboratory.

Stalnaker, J. M. (1936). The measurement of the ability to write. In W. S. Gray (Ed.), *Tests and measurements in higher education*. Chicago: University of Chicago Press.

Stalnaker, J. M., & Stalnaker, R. C. (1934). Reliable reading of essay tests. *School Review, 42*, 599–605.

Stanley, J. C. (1971). Reliability. In R. L. Thorndike (Ed.), *Educational measurement*. Washington, DC: American Council on Education.

Stanley, J. C. & Hopkins, K. D. (1972). *Educational and psychological measurement and evaluation*. Englewood Cliffs, NJ: Prentice-Hall.

Starch, D., & Elliott, E. C. (1912). Reliability of the grading of high-school work in English. *School Review, 20*, 442–457.

Thorndike, R. L. (1951). Reliability. In E. F. Lundquist (Ed.), *Educational measurement* (pp. 560–620). Washington: American Council on Education.

Tinsley, E. A., & Weiss, D. J. (1975). Interrater reliability and agreement of subjective judgments. *Journal of Counseling Psychology, 22*, 358–376.

Traxler, A. E., & Anderson, H. A. (1935). The reliability of an essay test in English. *School Review, 43*, 534–539.

Valentine, C. W. (1932). *The reliability of examinations*. London: University of London Press.

Vernon, P. E. (1940). *The measurement of abilities*. London: University of London Press.

Vernon, P. E., & Millican, G. D. (1954). A further study of the reliability of English essays. *The British Journal of Statistical Psychology, 7*, 65–74.

White, E. M. (1985). *Teaching and assessing writing: Recent advances in understanding, evaluating, and improving student performance*. San Francisco, CA: Jossey-Bass.

4

The Worship of Efficiency: Untangling Theoretical and Practical Considerations in Writing Assessment

MICHAEL WILLIAMSON

AMERICAN EDUCATION AND THE EMERGENCE OF EFFICIENCY

Since the end of the nineteenth century, efficiency has been a dominant theme in American education. While the central focus of schooling in America has always been the preparation of good citizens, the common school movement, which began in the 1830s and 40s, introduced schools as publicly funded instruments of government policy, subject to government regulation (Spring, 1986). The subsequent reform of schooling, signaled by John Dewey's work just prior to the end of that century, represents a complete change—from the traditional, predominantly religious functions of schooling in colonial and early American society to a schooling devoted to a broader set of social and economic functions. Ultimately, the concern for providing a universal, common education, which grew out of these two reform movements, fostered the need for efficiency defined in two ways: in terms of the public funds expended on schooling: and in terms of the human products of education in the work force.

Witte, Trachsel, and Walters (1986), citing Horace Mann (1845), note that education prior to 1845 was largely oriented toward providing students with "religious knowledge and virtue" (p. 15). The content of reading and writing lessons in American schools during colonial times was predominantly moralistic (Applebee, 1974; Spring, 1986; Witte, Trachsel, & Walters, 1986); its dominant purpose was to provide access to reading and comprehension of the Bible. Later, when American schools in the nineteenth century provided basic religious and moral education, they were also intended to prepare the social elite for college admission, with a college education assuring passage through the gateway to participation in leadership roles in American society.

Changes in the functions of schools resulted, of course, in changes in school curricula. In English studies for instance, as Applebee (1974) notes, there was a call for a common curriculum for both college bound students

From *Assessing Writing 1* (1994): 147–74.

and students who would be ending their education with high school, in what today are known as academic and vocational tracks. The success of the educational reformers' ideas was no doubt connected to the demographic changes occurring in America at the same time, a movement of the population from rural to urban settings and a rising middle-class developing in the cities (Gutek, 1972). Their success is reflected in the fact that the percentage of 14- to 17-year-olds in high school rose from the end of the nineteenth century such that by 1940, two thirds of that population was enrolled in high school (Spring, 1986). Legislation designed to prevent abuse of child labor passed in the early part of the twentieth century undoubtedly provided additional encouragement for people in this age group to stay in school.

Spring (1986) notes that the guiding principle emerging in the development of the twentieth century high school was the need to prepare workers for their appropriate place in the work force. (See also Ohmann, 1976.) One explanation of the increasing percentage of 14- to 17-year-olds remaining in school may be the increasing skill required by American industry. (This particular trend seems to be continuing, with larger numbers of students now going onto some form of training beyond high school.) In terms of the schools themselves, Spring notes,

> The nineteenth century American high school was primarily academic, whereas the twentieth century high school offered academic, general, and vocational studies. These changes in curriculum reflected the more general attempt to have schools serve the needs of the economic system (Spring, 1986, p. 194).

The turn of the century also saw the emergence of a scientific perspective on educational research and school administration. Looking toward the positivist orientation in the natural and emerging social sciences, educators began to see their role as part of providing for "selection and training of human capital" in a "scientifically controlled society" in which merit would determine the future of the individual more than his or her social or economic status (Spring, 1986, p. 222). In this context, Spring sees efficiency emerging as one of the single most important aspects of management in American education.

Efficiency here appears to be related to the value returned on investment for public money, human resources, and human raw materials invested in the public schools. These would seem to involve a concern, as Spring suggests, for three kinds of efficiency:

1. the efficient use of taxes collected to fund the schools;
2. the efficient work of teachers and administrators; and
3. the efficient achievement of students.

Clearly, this definition of efficiency is no different from those commonly used in business and industry. In fact, even today most contemporary school reformers refer to one or more of these categories as important targets for their proposed reform efforts.

Competing Models of Education

It is important to note that the educational reform movements of the last 150 years have left us with competing models of education that persist to this day. The study of literacy is no different in that regard. The controversy over whole language approaches to English language arts (Atwell, 1987) and the controversy over grammar instruction (Hartwell, 1985; Kolln, 1981) can be understood as a reflection of a deeper controversy over the basic goals of literacy education. The most general level of discussion about this matter in the study and teaching of writing has been the continuing controversy over *basic skills* (Myers, 1981). I suspect that most writing researchers and teachers see the matter as settled. However, the sophisticated views of writing and rhetoric that have allowed them to push forward to newer, richer definitions of writing and the teaching and learning of writing have not yet reached any sizable number of state and federal legislators nor have they entered the definition of literacy and literacy education for any sizable segment of the American population.

Shedd and Bacharach (1991) suggest that the competing goals of education have led to several very different conceptualizations of the nature of professionalism in teaching and the methods by which the schools should be managed. Their extensive empirical and scholarly research on the nature of professionalism in teaching (Shedd & Bacharach, 1991) led them to describe three competing models of educational management that exist today.

- The *factory management model*, an older approach, uses the relationship between industrial workers and managers as a model for the management of teachers by administrators and school boards.

- The *bureaucratic management model*, probably the dominant model in large urban and suburban school districts, exists when teachers are given broad policy guidelines to interpret and are expected to teach within those guidelines.

- The *craft management model* seems to be an emergent model that is based on the assumption that the work of teachers cannot be clearly defined. Teachers are given broad latitude to establish their own policies and goals within a framework bounded by the needs of the various stakeholders in education, including parents, administrators, government officials, and even other teachers.

Shedd and Bacharach (1991) suggest that the *bureaucratic management model* has begun to supersede the *factory management model* as the dominant organization pattern for managing the work of teachers. The assumptions of *factory management model* are as follows:

- The purpose of a public school system is to provide students with training in a common, basic set of academic skills.

- Training is a relatively straightforward process. The situations that teachers face can be anticipated, and appropriate behaviors for handling those situations can be specified in advance.

- Except for age differences, students are a relatively homogenous group. Differences in their needs and abilities within age groups are minimal or irrelevant.

- Funds for education, like all resources, are in short supply and their provision needs to be carefully monitored to maximize their efficient use (p. 52).

In this model, the work of teachers is narrowly circumscribed in terms of specific skills that are to be taught, such as literacy and mathematics. Since this approach to school organization seems to emerge from the more traditional approaches to education of the early nineteenth century, proponents of the factory model often include morality as one of the basics that have to be taught to children, although it too is narrowly circumscribed.

On the other hand, in the *bureaucratic management model* teachers are given broad curricular and policy guidelines to interpret. This model is based on the following assumptions:

- The purpose of a public school system is to provide students with whatever education and services they need in order to pursue further education or employment once they leave the system, given their individual abilities.

- The public can be expected to provide the money needed to support such educational services, provided a school system can make a rational case for them.

- If different students have different abilities and future career prospects, and different programs are needed to reflect those differences, it is necessary to identify those differences and therefore place particular students in appropriate programs, classes, or levels of a curriculum. Specialized expertise is needed to identify student differences and decide how such services should be designed and delivered, but the delivery processes themselves are well understood. Those processes can therefore be reduced to established diagnostic and delivery routines that all teachers can readily follow (p. 55).

The underlying assumption of the value of individual merit that entered American education at the end of the nineteenth century is quite evident in this model, as well as some of the discoveries of scientific inquiry into education, such as the uses of assessment for placement in special curricula and the need for specialized expertise in identifying student differences. It is the use of assessment and the specification of the need for specialized expertise that is one of the foundations of approaches to assessment in contemporary American education.

Some important differences emerge in a comparison of the two competing models. While the factory model assumes that education is not problematic and that teaching and learning involve a set of commonly agreed upon skills, the bureaucratic model acknowledges that education involves a complex set of decisions for each student, reflecting the developments that emerged in the twentieth century. More importantly, the bureaucratic model suggests that there is a need for fairness in treatment, and that such fairness entails differentiation and specialization. If traditional models of education depend upon a person's birthright to identify socioeconomic leadership, then the newer, bureaucratic approach implies that individual traits and characteristics determine the rights and needs of each person, and assessment provides the vehicle for establishing these needs. However, since fair treatment is the essential issue, assessment procedures also need to demonstrate that they provide a fair grounding for decisions about inclusions or exclusions in particular educational programs, given that the decision to include or exclude a person from a program is likely to determine his or her social and economic role in society.

The positivist science of psychometrics that developed in the late nineteenth century connected to this shift in education began to provide assessment tools believed to be objective and fair because they were seen as independent of the bias of the human decisions of individual teachers (Williamson, 1993). The assessment procedures developed by psychometricians and used in education beginning in the early 20th century were also considered to provide a more cost-efficient approach to assessment than the written examinations in use at that time. Thus, the cycle of educational reform moved from the oral recitation assessment procedures of the 18th and early 19th centuries to the written examinations of the last half of the 19th century, and then onto the use of multiple choice items in the 20th.

An interesting paradox emerges here. In traditional educational practices, the individual either learns or fails to learn the common skills and morality taught in the curriculum. Learning is seen to take place as a result of teaching. If the individual fails to learn when material is taught, he or she is at fault for failure to attend or some inability to learn. Failure to learn is, in and of itself, proof of ability. Since the schools are clearly designed to achieve differential goals for students that in fact simply reinforce social distinctions among individuals and socioeconomic groups, failure is not seen as problematic. It just reflects perceptions of the existing social order. In contrast, the ideal of the bureaucratic model, born in the notion of a meritocracy that emerged at the beginning of this century (Spring, 1986), is based upon a view of education that uses differential curricula to bring all students to one common set of social outcomes, while continuing to foster differential abilities for groups of students. The common outcomes are considered to be related to basic mathematics and literacy skills, as well as other knowledge that is considered necessary to function in the American political and economic system. The differential outcomes are related to identifying and preparing students for their socioeconomic roles in working, middle, or upper socioeconomic groupings (Pattison, 1982). Thus, individual merit begins to compete with birthright as the basis for selection for differing programs. Furthermore, assessment, which must necessarily be perceived as fair assessment, attempts to replace birthright as the index of selection for identifying students for development as socioeconomic and cultural leaders. The continuing importance of independent admissions tests confirms the continuing dominance of this basic goal for higher education (through such examinations as the SAT for college admission and the Graduate Record Examination, Medical College Admission Test, and Law School Admission Test for graduate and professional school admission).

However, it is important to note that the economic forces working within the context of socioeconomic class structures will still work to reinforce the existing socioeconomic structure. Students from wealthy families are more able to provide learning resources, such as access to books and computers, than students from poor families. Furthermore, schools are modeled on the normative behavior and mores of middle-class and upper middle-class culture (Becker, 1970; Heath, 1983). Thus, wealthier students are more likely to have the cultural and material resources to perform well in school and less likely to drop out or perform poorly than students from working class or poor families (Heath, 1983). While this process tends to perpetuate existing social and cultural institutions, it also ensures that graduates at each succeeding level of schooling are fewer in number than at the previous level.

In a further paradox, proponents of the religious morality of traditional schooling are now calling for the removal of moral education from schools because the apparently secular nature of contemporary American morality in the bureaucratic schools appears as a threat to their religious beliefs. This apparent threat has led to an increasing number of pupils leaving public education for Christian schools in the last few years, a further testimonial to the effective dominance of the bureaucratic model in American education. This development complements the increasing numbers of private schools that began to emerge in the 1950s, resulting from the integration of African Americans and other people of color into the public schools.

However, both the factory and bureaucratic approaches to schooling share an underlying commonality which leads to a drive for more efficient education. In the factory model, as education is not problematic, extensive funding should not be required for its support. School boards in many rural school districts reflect this orientation in their general hostility toward the rise in teachers' salaries and in other educational costs, particularly at a time when economic conditions have been unfavorable for the kinds of agricultural and industrial enterprises common in those areas of the United States. At the same time, in the bureaucratic model dominant in wealthier urban and suburban districts, rational cases to voters for continued and increasing funding for education must address efficiency as a concern, since efficiency reflects the definition of rational argument in the larger culture. American business operates on the basic premise that efficiency maximizes profits, while American government operates on the premise that efficiency maximizes the number of opportunities which can be provided by limited government resources. Furthermore, both models assume public funding for schools, which, of necessity, gives rise to a concern for efficient use of taxpayers' money.

This analysis of the context for the development of assessment in American education is a necessary preliminary to understanding that practical considerations, such as efficiency and fairness, have often been more important than theoretical issues. The rising importance of assessment in the schools emerged in a social context that privileged efficiency in educational practice due to the need to educate large numbers of students in increasingly differentiated and specialized ways. The ideals underlying perceptions about the social structure led to a concern for fairness. While the system itself promoted efficiency due to economic pressures, the democratic ideals of the culture itself also had an influence. As decisions based upon assessments took on greater importance in the lives of students and their families, they insisted on greater assurance that the assessments were fair processes for decision making.

From here then, it is necessary to turn to the development of the assessment procedures themselves. I will attempt to demonstrate how these two practical issues, efficiency and fairness, influenced the development of educational assessment in general before analyzing the specific case of writing assessment.

Historical Changes in Assessment Procedures in the Schools

Witte, Trachsel, and Walters (1986) and Lunsford (1986) note that oral examinations were the most common form of assessment used in the United States in the first half of the nineteenth century. Student assessment involved a visiting examiner in oral interviews with and recitation by students (Anastasi, 1976). These assessments also involved reading aloud and translation of passages from classical languages. However, in 1845, as Witte, Trachsel, and Walters note, the Boston Public Schools began to use writing as a form of assessment because it was considered more efficient than the short oral examinations of individual students used until that time (see also Spring, 1986).

Anastasi (1976) notes that Horace Mann's arguments for changing from oral examinations to written examinations include the following reasons:

> The written examinations, Mann noted, put all students in a uniform situation, permitted a wider coverage of content, reduced the chance element in question choice, and eliminated the possibility of favoritism on the examiner's part (p. 16).

As Anastasi notes, these reasons mirror the later arguments for changing from written examinations to multiple choice examinations, which then became the most common form of admissions and achievement testing in American education.

One of the other goals for assessment also emerged in the common school movement of the 1830s and 40s. Since the notion of the common school involved delivery of a common set of learning experiences to all students, the examinations which were used to evaluate achievement became a form of audit for individual teachers' and whole schools' successes in delivering the curriculum. Traveling external examiners had been utilized prior to the advent of the common schools, as Lunsford (1986) notes. However, the common school movement and the change from oral to written examinations created the foundation for the serious development of extensive and organized uses of achievement testing for both student and teacher evaluation which was to follow, because it provided artifacts to a central authority that could analyze them from a variety of perspectives. As with all developments in education, nothing disappears entirely. The traveling external examiner remains common in the assessment procedures used by many state departments of education and other school and college accreditation agencies today.[1]

Universal Education, Bureaucracy, and Assessment: A Practical Matter

Another of the notable differences between the two approaches to educational management that I have been discussing is that the bureaucratic model provides an important new role for assessment. In the factory model, assessment is not complex since the skills that the schools teach are straightforward and differences among pupils are minimal. There is a need for assessment if only to insure that the schools are properly discharging their responsibilities.

The need for assessment in the bureaucratic model is reflected in the first and last of its assumptions, as cited by Shedd and Bacharach (1991), because they imply the need to identify students with exceptional needs and to place them into "appropriate programs." Moreover, assessment can provide the rationale for the money necessary to maintain a variety of programs, as well as contribute to the reasonableness of the request for money by demonstrating that education is being conducted efficiently. In both models, however, assessment is a matter secondary to the actual process of education, which involves moving students through curricula. Furthermore, the bureaucratic model seems to assume that assessment is the function of a separate set of professionals, for example, the school psychologist as opposed to the teacher. Of course, this separation between teacher and examiner is older than the common school movement itself. Thus, it was a natural development for psychometricians, as external examiners, to assume greater control of educational assessment as the technology for that assessment became more complex.

Modern assessment in education emerged at the turn of the century in a context characterized by a concern for identification of students who needed extra help to benefit from instruction. The first real developments were in France, where Binet and Simon (Anastasi, 1976; Binet & Simon, 1908) developed the prototype for ability assessment of school children and employed it in the Parisian schools at the very end of the nineteenth century. Their approach to the assessment of students experiencing difficulties in school, which still influences American education today, was based in an intensive interview with and observation of individuals, using visual, oral, and literacy materials as well as psychomotor manipulatives. Two critical features of the standardized interview developed by Binet and Simon, which continue in such tests today, are that they

1. involve multiple tasks, including both literacy and performance tasks to asses the child's ability, and

2. involve tasks that require both convergent and divergent thinking on the part of the student.

These assessment procedures are not efficient measurement devices since they require the time and efforts of one examiner working with a single student for a period typically involving several hours, including the tasks of test administration, test scoring, and evaluation of results. It is worth noting, however, that these assessment procedures reflect the general concern for efficiency that emerged at the time because the underlying assumption seems to be that education is made less efficient when special needs students are not provided with extra help.

The difference between the definition of efficiency here that competes with the definition of efficiency that emerged in America is evident. In Binet and Simon's model, efficiency seems to refer only to the efficiency of the child as a learner. Thus, it is a learner-centered model, albeit a nineteenth century one. In this view, the school is obligated to provide those experiences necessary for exceptional children to be able to benefit from schooling. In the modern bureaucratic model, however, the scope and complexity of locating each child fairly in an appropriate education track requires considerably more streamlined procedures than a standardized interview. The work of Binet and Simon was adapted to American schools by the psychometric research group at Stanford University (see Terman, 1916). Nearly 100 years later, the standardized interview seems to remain one of the single most important aspects of labeling and prescribing instruction for American children with special needs, including both the gifted and talented as well as the physically and intellectually challenged. In some states their use is mandated by selection procedures for assignment to special needs classes. Usually, such tests are employed as part of a larger set of procedures for developing the individualized curriculum adjustments that the student will experience.

The most important point to note here, however, is that their use is extremely limited. The schools only utilize these relatively inefficient procedures when mandated by outside agencies or when attempting to solve particularly difficult problems posed by students with special needs and abilities. Thus, the child-centered role of assessment has not provided any real challenge to system-centered assessment, which focuses on a very different view of learners and, hence, assessment as well.

Technological Developments for More Efficient Approaches to Assessment

American educators seem to have chosen the system-centered assessment that exists today and the child-centered assessment of Binet and Simon. However, the choice was not a foregone conclusion. Pearson (1986) suggested that we might be looking at a very different school system in America if the basic orientation of Binet and Simon's view of assessment had become the dominant one. However, the growing needs of a system that has had to educate increasing numbers of students and two important technological innovations intervened to foster the development of systemic assessment oriented toward sorting and selection of students. At the same time, standardized interview procedures were subsumed by the psychometric theory they helped to develop, a body of theory that enabled the development of large scale assessment, due to the technological innovations of the multiple choice item and computer scoring.

The first of these important technological innovations in assessment and a great step forward in terms of efficiency, the multiple choice item, was developed by Arthur Otis in a graduate class at Stanford taught by Lewis Terman (Anastasi, 1976), one of the original psychometricians who adapted the Binet and Simon examination procedure to American education. The multiple choice item was an important innovation in educational and psychological assessment because it allowed for a highly efficient approach to administration and scoring. It was also considered a fairer approach to assessment because it led to more reliable scores as it removed the causes of certain types of errors not associated with the actual performance of the examinee. In particular, it removed the apparent error involved with teachers' differential evaluations of the same student's performance by reducing the decision about whether the examinee had given a right or a wrong answer to a clerical decision, thus replacing teacher judgment with the predictable answers preselected by the psychometric scientist responsible for test construction.

Here, efficiency has additional theoretical support. Positivism requires of a science that it be independent of the observer. As I have noted elsewhere, all measurement science requires that instrumentation for observation of the human being, the scientific apparatus of the psychologist, must be free of the potential bias introduced by a human being. Educational and psychological tests are not different, in this matter, than the instruments of the physicist. Thus, the very characteristics of the multiple choice item that make it efficient are also theoretically pleasing because they make them independent of teachers' judgments of pupils, which are considered subjective (Williamson, 1993).

Anastasi (1976) also notes that the multiple choice item designed by Otis and incorporated into the Army Alpha intelligence test as America entered World War I provided a highly efficient method for culling potential officers and trainees for skilled war work from the mass of one and one half million recruits who had to be trained quickly and sent to Europe. Refinements to this technology have emerged in the subsequent extensive applications to achievement and ability testing in American schools and colleges. Thus, it was the strategic needs of the war that provided the impetus for the extensive development and use of this new technology.

The second technological boost for multiple choice format assessment emerged from the advent of computer scoring of an important technological innovation contributing to the dominance of large scale assessment procedures. Computer scoring virtually eliminates the clerical error in scoring multiple choice items, removing scoring error as a practical consideration in test reliability. Furthermore, compared to hand scoring of multiple choice tests, computer scoring enables more rapid assessment of larger numbers of subjects.

Unfortunately, the technology has not been very successful in developing item formats that are capable of emphasizing divergent kinds of knowledge with any accuracy, a form of knowledge important in written examinations and standardized interviews. But, multiple choice tests are very efficient since a single examiner can administer such a test to a large number of students. Furthermore, even when these tests are scored by hand, scoring can be completed more rapidly and with greater precision compared to the judging of written examinations or the administration and scoring of standardized interviews. Thus, they seem both more efficient and more fair than written examinations or standardized interviews. Of course, the advent of computer scoring increased both the speed and precision of multiple choice tests because computer grading is very rapid and removes any possible human error in marking the answers on a test. Even though human error might intervene if the computer is instructed to mark an incorrect answer as correct in a multiple choice test, all examinees would be subject to the error and such errors are considered minor in the framework of large scale assessment, when compared to the subjectivity of teachers' markings of written examinations.

The dominance of computer scored, standardized tests in American education reflects the importance of efficiency more clearly than any other technological innovation in assessment. Assessment in this context would seem to allow for the convergence of a variety of data in the process of deciding to label a child handicapped or gifted. Indeed, the process of labeling and prescribing special curricula for special needs children does involve input from classroom teachers and the psychologists who administer standardized interviews, in addition to parents and other relevant school administrators. However, such procedures are only utilized in special cases, where students' failure in school suggests emotional adjustment to school and academic ability or lack of ability that would prevent them from profiting from normal instruction in one or more subjects. For the most part, students are assessed, labeled, and placed in school curricula on the basis of their scores on succeeding standardized tests. And, while sufficient questions have been raised about both the theory and practice of large scale assessment to lead to some regulation, these tests remain one of the single most important indicators of a child's future.

The Growth of Educational Assessment

The factory management model seems to have provided the initial impetus for the development of assessment of achievement and ability in education. Since the nature of the skills that students are expected to learn is straightforward and unproblematic to describe, assessment was not a complex undertaking. The problem was to develop an assessment technology that could be used fairly and efficiently. However, these assumptions emerge during the same period that saw the emergence of concerns about the subjectivity of teachers' grades. Thus, the climate for the emergence of objective assessment was set by the assumptions about teaching and learning as well as by a definition of teaching as a profession. Unfortunately, the theoretical definitions of the literacy skills to be assessed, like the definitions of other academic skills, were limited in their range and scope when compared to the views of literacy that are common among English teachers and researchers today.

Since written tests were considered too subjective and, like standardized interviews, are labor intensive, they were seen as too costly and unfair. Thus, multiple choice tests emerged as a clear winner in the search for efficiency and fairness. Subsequently, the emphasis in validation research has been to show that the primary virtues of assessment procedures are their reliability, or fairness, and their efficiency.

The paper and pencil ability and achievement tests that have emerged as primary sorting devices in American education involve only a single, limited form of data. They represent highly efficient measures of what students have learned or what they are capable of learning and are pervasive throughout all levels of education, from the readiness measures administered in the early grades to the SAT for college admissions, as well as the Graduate Record Examination, Law School Admission Test, and the Medical College Admission Test. Educational doors continue to be opened and closed to students based upon their scores on standardized tests. Of course, we need to judge each of these tests on its own merits in terms of the context of its construction, administration, and use in a particular setting, since the validity of a test is now viewed not as a property of a test so much as a function of the particular use of a test (Messick, 1989). Furthermore, admissions tests in particular have typically been used in conjunction with other data when colleges or graduate and professional schools arrive at decisions about acceptance or denial of an applicant. Thus, an actual decision may be based upon a variety of evidence, a matter that must be considered in judging the validity of any assessment procedure.

The concern for recognizing individual merit, regardless of social birthright, and the promise of positivist empiricism, introduced into education, were a part of context that led to growing concerns about the subjectivity of teachers' grades in classrooms and of judges' summative evaluation of written examination. These concerns also involved questions about the fairness of the examinations themselves, including the test administration and scoring procedures. Furthermore, educators came under increasing scrutiny, as the public and private sectors began to call for an accounting of the use of public funds spent on educating children. In this historical context, mass testing based in multiple choice formats emerged as an inexpensive means of evaluating the achievement of both the schools and individual pupils. Because they were standardized, they removed several sources of error not related to the actual performance of an examinee on the test. Hence, they are more reliable than the written examinations common at the time. Thus, they were perceived to be a fairer means of sorting students than written examinations. Furthermore, because they could be norm referenced, they could be used as an index to compare the ability or achievement of individual students, whole classrooms, and whole schools to an appropriate reference group. Thus, the tests could provide several types of information for all of the stakeholders in public education. Individual information about the child was available for the students themselves, as well as for parents, teachers, and administrators responsible for making decisions about the child's future. Administrators and school boards could use the same information to monitor the success of individual teachers or of whole schools. Finally, school districts could be monitored by the state regulators, while states could be monitored by federal regulators.

Rereading the literature on educational and psychological measurement from the period in American education in which multiple choice assessment emerged is an interesting undertaking. The debate over competing values is interesting and reflects the debate that continues today. The democratic impulse to find the fairest approach to evaluating student performance and ability is counterbalanced by the concerns of educators about the impact of multiple choice testing on teaching and learning. The archives of the Educational Testing Service contain agendas, minutes, and notes from conferences and meetings that rehearse all aspects of the dispute, even as it continues today. Even so, proponents of continuing the use of writing in school assessment seemed shocked when multiple choice testing was adopted. As I read through the literature in both published and unpublished forms, I am struck by the fact that theoretical arguments for multiple choice testing did not seem to account for their universal adoption in educational assessment.

Rather, the concern for efficiency in assessment procedures seems to have been the more important factor in adoptions, in educational and psychological assessment in general, and writing assessment in particular; efficiency has governed both the theoretical and practical developments in assessment. My reading of the literature on writing assessment suggests that the debate over writing assessment has been cast in terms of a need for efficiency, which in turn reflects the dominating concern for efficiency in American education as a whole, as my analysis here attempts to demonstrate. Unfortunately, the sense of a need for efficiency implicit in most of the work in writing assessment is rarely stated explicitly enough for a thorough examination of its effects on the development of assessment procedures themselves or the subsequent debate on the efficacy of particular approaches to assessment. However, the choice to favor more efficient assessment procedures reflects a preference in assessment techniques that lies outside the scope of assessment theory itself and reflects, I think, an important aspect of American social and cultural history. In particular, efficiency has become the single most important force directing American education because of the pressure to provide some form of education for all citizens. However, proponents of more efficient writing assessment techniques have also cast the debate over efficiency in terms of fairness and have related the need for fairness to the reliability of measures of academic ability (White, 1993).

Thus, efficiency and fairness become the dominant issues facing researchers and teachers of writing as they attempt further theoretical developments in the study and teaching of writing. Also important in this matter are the regulatory and gatekeeping functions of assessment in the American schools. Accountability involves a concern for both what is taught and how efficiently it is taught. Accountability also involves a concern that each child is treated fairly by the system. So far, multiple choice assessment programs appear to have been the most persuasive in this regard to stakeholders in education since these stakeholders continue to support their use, at the least by refraining from challenging the widespread use of multiple choice, large scale assessment procedures.

The Case for Writing Assessment

As Moss (1994a, 1994b, 1992) has pointed out, reliability is not the single or even the most important aspect of an assessment procedure. In measurement theory in most sciences, two instruments or measures of unequal reliability can estimate with equal accuracy. The more reliable measure involves greater precision in its estimation, while the comparatively less reliable measure represented has equal accuracy, albeit with less precision. It is important to note, however, that each instrument must involve multiple data points.

All things being equal, any assessment specialist would favor the more reliable measure because it is more efficient and probably requires fewer data points to achieve greater accuracy than the comparatively less reliable measure. However, it is possible to conceive of a situation in which the more reliable measure is not as accurate (valid) when compared to a less reliable measure. The comparatively greater reliability of the first test then provides a less adequate assessment when compared to the second, comparatively less reliable test.

Translating these hypothetical examples to writing assessment, the case of the more reliable, but less valid test, compared to the less reliable but more valid test, represents the case that has been argued for a number of years by proponents of direct writing assessment. They have argued that multiple choice tests of writing ability are more reliable, but less valid, when compared to direct assessment procedures like holistic scoring or primary trait scoring (Cooper, 1977; Greenberg, Wiener, & Donovan, 1986). Unfortunately, the controversy, from both sides, has been based in a monolithic view of reliability as opposed to an understanding of reliability as only a single aspect of the validity of that procedure (Cherry & Meyer, 1993). Furthermore, as explained earlier, reliability has recently been explicitly recast as a measure of the fairness to the examinee (White, 1993). If we understand the second example I presented as the comparison of two writing placement procedures, the more reliable procedure would really result in less "fair" placement in a writing course compared to the less reliable procedure. Furthermore, in the first example, the less reliable, but more valid test would be as "fair" as the more reliable test because the accuracy of the estimation is the same for both procedures.

An analogy to firearms marksmanship might help make the issues explicit in this discussion of precision (reliability) and accuracy (validity). Novice shooters are taught to achieve precision first, that is, the ability to hit the same spot on the target. The sights of the firearm are then adjusted to hit the bullseye once the strikes on the target are consistently grouped. In this analogy, a test would be constructed first in terms of its reliability and then adjusted for its validity. Unfortunately, constructing an accurate test is not as simple as learning to shoot a firearm. In fact, an assessment procedure is a constellation of interlocking and interactive properties. Small changes in one property can have a profound effect on other properties. Therefore the properties of a test that establish its reliability do not necessarily contribute to its validity. In fact, I have argued elsewhere that item analysis procedures which make a test more homogeneous may actually detract from its validity (Williamson, 1993). Thus, comparatively high reliability is neither a necessary nor a sufficient condition for establishing the validity of a measure. It is one aspect of a test that has to be weighed in conjunction with many other aspects of the validity of that test, as Moss (1994a; 1994b) and Cherry and Meyer (1993) have argued.

The problem with conflicts over reliability and validity are nearly as old as psychometric science itself. One famous acknowledgement of the distinction between reliable measures and valid ones and the relative importance of reliability and validity was clearly stated quite early in the early development of measurement theory by Torgerson (1958, p. 8):

> The concepts of theoretical interest (in psychology and education) tend to lack empirical meaning, whereas the corresponding concepts with precise empirical meaning often lack theoretical importance (cited in Lord & Novick, 1968).

This seems to me a compelling representation of the current situation in writing assessment. The greater the reliability of an assessment procedure, the less interesting a description it provides of writing.

Moreover, an understanding of the relationship between reliability and efficiency seems to be at the center of many decisions about mass testing. For instance, Godshalk, Swineford, and Coffman (1966), in one of the earliest studies of the relationship between indirect and direct measures of writing conducted for the College Entrance Examination Board by the Educational Testing Service, concluded that a multiple choice test of knowledge of grammar provided a better prediction of summed scores on several short essays than was provided by a single, holistically scored writing sample. Given the expense and difficulty of scoring even a short writing sample, the Board chose to use a multiple choice format. Essentially, this decision was made on the basis of the relative efficiencies of the two measures.

Proponents of holistic scoring began to address the apparent limits of direct measures within the context set by the Godshalk, Swineford, and Coffman study. They failed to note, however, that the study was most likely conceived as a basis for policy decisions by the College Board about the English Composition Test of the SAT test battery, as opposed to a study of the validity of either holistic scoring or multiple choice tests as measures of writing ability. The study clearly demonstrated, for the College Board and ETS, that the more cost effective procedure was more desirable since more accurate statistical predictions of criterion scores were achieved by the relatively more efficient multiple choice format compared to a holistically scored essay. The results of the study led the College Board to direct their test development contractor, Educational Testing Service, to offer the English Composition Test using a multiple choice format exclusively, a practice which was continued for some time. However, the operational definition of writing ability that was used as a criterion involved several 20-minute essays. Of course, the College Board did not hope to find resources to fund that amount of writing from each examinee, much less judge it. Today, we can look back on such a definition of literacy as an entirely too limited view of this socially and psychologically complex practice of human beings. However, given the limited aims of the College Board testing program and their resources, such a criterion may not seem unreasonable.

The College Board and ETS have continued to experiment with direct writing assessment from time to time, as they are continuing to do today. Additionally, extensive research conducted by teams of researchers at the Educational Testing Service under the leadership of Hunter Breland has focused on exhaustive study of the relationship between the Test of Standard Written English, a multiple choice format part of the SAT Verbal examination, and direct writing assessment (Breland, Camp, Jones, Morris, & Rock, 1987; Breland & Gaynor, 1979). Notably, the TSWE will be dropped from the SAT battery in the next year. The English Composition Test has also undergone some significant changes in recent years.

ETS, for better or worse, often tends to set the standard for educational assessment acting as a corporation that contracts with various agencies, like the College Board, to set up assessment procedures. They have helped to steer theoretical developments in psychometrics through the work of assessment scientists employed at ETS, such as Frederick Lord and Samuel Messick. While the work of ETS is typically involved with the development of large scale, nationally administered and normed testing procedures, it was the work of ETS test development specialists with such assessments as the foreign service written examinations that led, in part, to the development of holistic scoring. Furthermore, ETS scientists were also responsible for the development of holistic scoring, despite the experience of early workers in writing assessment such as White and Cooper, who saw ETS as one of the primary impediments to their efforts (Cooper, 1977; White, 1993).

Since the very first use of multiple choice formats for school ability and achievement tests, educators have been concerned about their impact on curriculum and instruction. English teachers were no exceptions. Details of the concerns raised by English teachers and English teacher educators have been documented quite thoroughly elsewhere (Cooper, 1977; Taylor, 1990; Williamson, 1993). In this historical context, holistic scoring emerged as the leading challenger to multiple choice tests. Of course, holistic scoring itself was created by test development specialists at ETS who needed to have a procedure for assessing writing for clients who believed that they needed to see actual writing by examinees as part of their assessment procedures and who were not particularly concerned with efficiency. Since, practically speaking, large scale assessment precluded the use of writing, smaller clients such as the State Department, interested in the foreign service officer's selection examination, probably remained the sole users of writing in writing assessment at ETS for a long time.

Proponents of holistic scoring conducted their own studies to challenge the notion that multiple choice tests are more efficient than holistically scored essays. Veal and Hudson (1983), for instance, suggest that the Georgia state writing assessment provided an equally reliable and cost effective use of direct assessment, when compared to multiple choice assessments. Despite the problems with costs, New Jersey and California developed large scale writing assessment programs. Cooper (1977) asserts that holistic scoring can be conducted with reliabilities equal to those commonly found with multiple choice tests. However, because proponents of holistic scoring have allowed the agenda for discussion of writing assessment to be set by their opposition, efficiency continued as the dominant concern in writing assessment (Williamson, 1993).

How to Cope with Efficient Measures

In the case of college writing assessment procedures, placement into or exit from writing courses is consistently made on the basis of a single data point, a score on a multiple choice test, for example, or a score on a 45-minute to one-hour holistically scored essay. Thus, the historical emphasis on efficiency has continued to favor reliability over validity. Here, as elsewhere, the emphasis on reliability has had a highly deleterious effect on pedagogy, since most researchers or teachers of writing would see such a presumed definition of writing as extremely limited. Furthermore, since the most reliable measures seem to suggest that students lack knowledge about the basic facts of language, courses have often been structured around mastery of the "basics" of language mechanics without providing students with any opportunity to learn to write. This situation seems especially problematic when reflected against the assessment procedures used in the schools. The proliferation of multiple choice tests has probably led teachers to emphasize knowledge of grammar in English/language arts classes, although these same pupils do not seem to have mastered very much in school, when retested for college admission or placement with either direct or indirect writing assessment procedures. It's unlikely that the problem here lies with the students or their teachers. The problem results from the use of a limited definition of writing used in the development of the highly reliable tests of writing that sacrifice their validity (Williamson, 1993). In this formula, underlying knowledge about facts of language is assumed to equate with the ability to compose in writing. Unfortunately, knowledge of grammatical conventions is only one kind of knowledge involved in composing stylistically effective sentences, and is even more limited in the composing of a whole piece of discourse.

Teachers, for the most part, work in a situation where multiple constituencies dictate the content of their work (Shedd & Bacharach, 1991). Thus, one can hardly blame them for emphasizing the content of the tests their students take, when their students' success or failure on those tests will be used as part of evaluating their competence, as it has been since the use of oral examinations by external examiners. This situation is precisely what Popham (1988) means when he suggests that assessment inevitably drives curriculum. In this case it may be for the worst.

The Current Scene in Writing Assessment

It is the primary goal of the American educational system—universal, compulsory education through twelfth grade—that is the chief force behind the need for efficiency. Furthermore, the emerging belief that a college education provides a ticket to success for workers in the American economy has combined with this basic goal to necessitate gatekeeping assessment procedures on a large scale, hence large scale assessment. American culture, which views itself as fostering an upwardly mobile society, has looked to education as one important means of fueling aspirations for moving up the socioeconomic ladder. Horatio Alger may have provided the inspiration for some visions of successful upward mobility, a move from poor to rich based upon personal courage and skill. However, education, when available, has more often been seen as providing opportunities for success. A college education, in particular, has been the focus of individuals who aspire for upward mobility through education.

Historically, the movement toward universal education provided the framework leading to the sense of a need for compulsory education in citizenship for all Americans. The belief in the need for education to permit rational involvement in democracy included the belief that literacy is a necessary skill for such participation. Despite this Jeffersonian belief in the importance of literacy, and despite the institution of composition as an undergraduate course at Harvard near the end of the last century, writing assessment remained a quiet educational backwater in American education until the explosion in college applications resulting from the veterans returning with government-sponsored benefits after World War II. It was this explosion that created a sense of the need to teach literacy skills in college, skills that were earlier presumed to have been learned in high school. This influx also fostered a need for more efficient sorting of applicants to college for admission and placement. It was in this historical context that the work of Godshalk, Swineford, and Coffman (1966) was conducted, and large scale writing assessment became predominantly multiple choice in format.

Since that time, a number of approaches to large scale writing assessment involving the use of direct assessment have been explored. The statewide assessments in New Jersey, Florida, and California are three such examples which use assessment procedures that were defined as early as the 1960s and 70s. However, the limits of large scale assessment in writing have been a continuing source of discomfort for many teachers of writing (Taylor, 1990), largely because those assessments have been designed with a concern for reliability as opposed to theoretical validity (Williamson, 1993). In sum, efficiency was also at the root of the development of direct writing assessment. Most locally developed college placement tests and large scale, state mandated writing proficiency examinations depend largely upon short, impromptu writing tasks in which the student writes only to the teacher as examiner. The number of essays that have to be written and scored and the concern for interrater reliability obscured our understanding that writing is a highly contextualized social act and that it creates texts that are read by readers who bring highly individualized and often divergent responses to any piece of writing.

Here I don't mean to minimize the efforts of such ardent proponents of direct writing assessment as Charles Cooper and Lee Odell (1977), Paul Diederich (1974), and Ed White (1985) who often seemed to feel as if they were struggling with a many headed hydra in their attempt to get any sort of written test by examinees included in large scale assessment (White, 1993). At the same time I acknowledge my debt to their work, however, I must raise the basic issue in this article. This concern for efficiency and fairness, the issues with which the early writing assessment specialists wrestled, has undermined the necessary next steps in developing approaches to writing assessment with even greater validity. How might a different approach to education lead to a different approach to assessment?

It is to this final piece of the puzzle, how might the future appear, that I now turn.

Craft Workshop Approach to Teaching

Shedd and Bacharach (1991) articulate a model of educational management that is more consistent with contemporary approaches to the teaching of writing, the *craft workshop model*. In this model, teachers are given what is known as *operational autonomy* (Anglin, 1979; Bailyn, 1985). In this model, teaching is considered to be a craft whose application cannot be understood by those "without direct and ongoing contact with students"; it is not possible for administrators, parents, or legislators to "specify *how* a teacher ought to teach in a given situation." As is currently the case with some college writing programs, "school systems should define teachers' responsibilities in terms of expected outcomes . . . to plan, adjust, execute, and evaluate their work with students according to their own judgment" (Shedd & Bacharach, 1991, p. 57).

Readers of Schon (1991) will immediately recognize the parallels between the reflective practitioner and the craft workshop model teacher suggested for teacher professionalism in the Shedd and Bacharach model. What is important here is that the teacher be allowed to assume responsibility for both instruction and evaluation. This means that assessment will be used by both student and teacher, and that the development of assessment is an integral part of the professional responsibility of the teacher. Shedd and Bacharach see teacher self evaluation as one of the crucial aspects of professionalism in teaching. Schon also sees the reflective stance, one that involves self assessment, to be an important aspect for the continued personal growth of teachers and for their continuing development of professional competence and commitment.

In the factory and bureaucratic models, teaching and learning are assumed to be sufficiently well understood that they can be assessed with validity. However, in the craft model, teaching and learning are assumed to be highly contextualized processes involving the abilities of individual students in classes and their particular learning needs and goals as defined by themselves and their teachers. Such a view of teaching as a profession is consistent with the views of most researchers and teachers of literacy as they define the nature of literacy and appropriate pedagogies for teaching and learning of literacy (Taylor, 1990). Furthermore, the role of assessment in the craft model is consistent with the view of these researchers and teachers as well.

Taylor (1990) has suggested that literacy can be taught without testing. Clearly, she equates testing with the earlier approaches to efficient assessment in education that I have been describing. In her model, testing is a form of assessment that is independent of the teacher's activity in teaching. However, at the very heart of her approach to pedagogy lie various forms of teaching and learning in which assessment, in a more general sense, is an integral part of the relationship between teacher and student. The pedagogical model she presents seems to be a variation of the whole language approach to literacy education initially fostered by Atwell (1987) and Graves (1983). In this model, the teacher approaches her students' learning as a researcher into the acquisition of language and literacy of each student, as well as a researcher of the classroom learning community and of the teacher's own pedagogy. Pedagogy and assessment then involve helping each student to acquire greater facility with a broad variety of literacies.

The descriptions of students' activities and the products of their work represent the "data" that the teacher as researcher uses for ongoing assessment of students' learning. Such data is multifaceted, when compared with either a multiple choice test of writing or a holistically graded essay. These highly varied and inconsistent sets of data can be seen as not just a valid indicator, but as the only *true* indicator of a child's achievement in school because it is each child's learning. Thus, it is not reliable in that it reflects the daily ups and downs of a child's learning. It is, however, valid because in its variety of data points, it presents an accurate picture of the work the child has undertaken and the teacher's role in that work. Thus, psychometrically speaking, it is a highly unreliable picture that provides a highly valid representation of what the child knows.

Taylor formalizes the implicit connection between assessment and teaching in the portrait she paints of teaching without testing. As teachers, at the moment we begin to think about teaching literacy to any group of students, we necessarily begin to think about how to construct our teaching to meet their needs. Assessment begins in the attempt to understand students' needs and continues with our constant alterations in our pedagogical strategies to meet those changing needs, precisely what Shedd and Bacharach make explicit in their definition of the teacher as professional in a craft workshop model, also precisely what Schon means by the reflective practitioner. Such assessment is not efficient, nor need that be a consideration, since assessment is an ongoing and integral part of teaching, validated by our willingness to understand that we need to keep assessing each student as long as we are teaching him or her.

However, one question that emerges here may have more to do with how we are to understand the future of assessment as a regulatory aspect of teaching and learning. In other words, how can we address the constraints imposed on us by parents, administrators, taxpayers, and other stakeholders in education who never really enter the classroom? It is not unreasonable for a parent to ask for information about his or her children's learning. It is not unreasonable for parents and other stakeholders to inquire about the level of expertise of a teacher. Nor is it unreasonable for legislators to ask us how they can help us to teach more effectively. One answer is posed by Moss (1994b) who suggests that different forms of assessment will continue to be used to address the needs of different stakeholders. Thus, she sees large scale assessment as likely to be with us for some time to come, since accountability in education is not a new concept, just a new package. At the same time, English teachers and researchers are becoming more successful in communicating the importance of literacy, seen as multiple literacies, to students and parents and to school boards and administrators.

Moss (1994b) is probably quite correct. Large scale assessment will continue to be an important part of the demands of policy makers. However, English teachers can help the immediate stakeholders — such as parents, school board, and school administrators — more uncomfortable with the meaning of those efficient forms of assessment by continuing to educate stakeholders about their limitations. Policy makers will require a more organized effort. Still, parents, administrators, school boards, and legislators need to see that their stance is one that is not helpful in the first place. They need to begin with questions. What did my child learn this year? How would you characterize your teaching this year? What can we do to help? But, this perspective depends upon these groups as seeing teaching differently. They need to see that teachers are professionals operating in a highly complex context and that teachers have to represent the context for them, first to pose, and then to understand the answer to their questions.

Ultimately, I suspect that the growing recognition of the ethnic diversity of American culture now occurring will help to foreground the fact that American culture involves a variety of literacies. As apparently competing literacies from different social and ethnic groups of Americans come into the mainstream, the mainstream will inevitably be enriched. As Spanish becomes the native language of a greater majority of Americans, the language of both Spanish-speaking and English-speaking Americans will be enriched. Viewed diachronically, language tends to change historically by blending divergent sources. Thus, the very rich variety of American culture should help us to see the complexity of literacy. This richer view of literacy and the language of our home cultures should help us to see that the more limited views of literacy supported by efficient large scale assessment are not viable. It may also help stakeholders in education to see that efficient assessment blurs many of the complexities of learning and teaching language and literacy in the English classroom.

Of course, assessment becomes much more difficult if we accept the craft workshop model. Implicit in this statement is the fact that we will need to begin to trust teachers in ways that we have not trusted them since their judgments were seen as subjective. When teachers provide a broad description of children's work as evidence of their success or failure, we can begin to engage in a much more focused discussion of both the achievement of our students, as well as our teaching and learning goals. If we choose to begin the discussion of students' achievement and teachers' competence at this level, I believe that we will find *less* rather than *more* difficulty understanding both.

I recognize that this prediction lacks any concrete details of what an assessment might look like. However, I only set for myself the task of attempting to understand the foundations of writing assessment. The rush to declare portfolio assessment or naturalistic assessment as a suitable alternative to large scale assessment may cause us to fail, if we are forced to continue to define efficiency and fairness in the limited terms that have dominated us so far. It is far better to think long and hard about Binet and Simon's student-centered functions of assessment and about Taylor's naturalistic assessment in terms of what they could promote in the teaching and learning of language and literacy in English language arts. It is better to help others understand that valid assessment in the teaching of writing only emerges from an explicit pedagogical or institutional context. This conclusion is the result of understanding that validity involves the actual use of assessment and is not limited to the assessment itself. It is better to think long and hard about parents', school boards', and policy makers' needs for information in more complex and local terms, privileging the richness of a variety of information from the smallest communities of writing classrooms that can be represented for the particular level of decision making that is necessary at the time. This conclusion would likely be the result of teachers being accorded the status of professionals as defined in the craft workshop model.

Ultimately, we have to ask ourselves whose best interests are served by assessment. Representing our work and our students' work in terms of single data points seems only to fuel the controversy. Does the decline in SAT scores mean that students in 1994 are less able than students of earlier generations? Do students write more poorly than they used to? I suspect the predisposition to see things as better or worse may, in fact, precede the inspection of such data as SAT scores. But had we the opportunity to examine exhibits of students' learning from earlier times, we might be much more likely to find that the basic functions of literacy have so changed that such comparisons are absurd, that conclusions made on the basis of large scale assessment are specious.

If Pearson (1986) is correct about our making a wrong turn when we abandoned Binet and Simon's orientation toward assessment, I think that we were also wrong when we began to distrust teachers' judgments. In so doing, we have defined teaching as less than a profession, as Shedd and Bacharach note, while saddling ourselves with work, particularly for teachers in the public schools, involving highly complex and rapid decision making about our students during the course of our teaching. All of these small decisions ultimately add up to the directions we create for our students. I like Taylor's vision of assessment, one that acknowledges the complexity and variety within each of our classrooms and that attempts to preserve it by integrating assessment with teaching. But, do we have the courage to trust ourselves, and will the other stakeholders in our work accord us the privilege of true professionalism? That, it seems to me, is the first step.

NOTE

   1. I have documented the theoretical basis for educational assessment in the positivism of psychometric theory, as well as its historical emergence elsewhere (Williamson, 1993). In the context of this article, it is important to note only that Anastasi, one of the most important psychometricians of the last 50 years, cites the same basic rationale underlying the continuing developments in educational assessment, arguments about 150 years old.

REFERENCES

Anastasi, A. (1976). *Psychological testing* (4th ed.) New York: Macmillan.
Anglin, L. W. (1979, May). Teacher roles and alternative school organizations. *The Educational Forum*, 439–452.
Applebee, A. (1974). *Tradition and reform in the teaching of English*. Urbana, IL: National Council of Teachers of English.
Atwell, N. (1987). *In the middle: Writing, reading, and learning with adolescents*. Portsmouth, NH: Boyton-Cook/Heinemann.
Bailyn, L. (1985). Autonomy in the industrial R&D lab. *Human Resource Management, 24,* 129–146.
Becker, H. (1970). *Sociological work*. Chicago: Aldine.
Binet, A., & Simon, T. (1908). Le development de l'intelligence chez les enfants. *Annee psychologique, 14,* 1–94.
Breland, H. M., Camp, R., Jones, R. J., Morris, M. M., & Rock, D. A. (1987). *Assessing writing skill: College Entrance Examination Board research monograph no. 11*. New York: The College Entrance Examination Board.
Breland, H. M., & Gaynor, J. L. (1979). A comparison of direct and indirect assessment of writing skill. *Journal of Education Measurement, 15,* 119–128.
Cherry, R. D., & Meyer, P. R. (1993). Reliability issues in holistic assessment. In M. M. Williamson & B. A. Huot (Eds.), *Validating holistic scoring for writing assessment* (pp. 109–141). Cresskill, NJ: Hampton.
Cooper, C. R. (1977). Holistic evaluation in writing. In C. R. Cooper & L. Odell (Eds.), *Evaluating writing: Measuring, describing, judging* (pp. 3–32). Urbana, IL: National Council of Teachers of English.
Cooper, C. R., & Odell, L. (1977). *Evaluating writing: Measuring, describing, judging*. Urbana, IL: National Council of Teachers of English.
Diederich, P. B. (1974). *Measuring growth in English*. Urbana, IL: National Council of Teachers of English.
Godshalk, F. I., Swineford, F., & Coffman, W. E. (1966). *The measurement of writing ability: College Entrance Examination Board* (Research Monograph No. 6). New York: The College Entrance Examination Board.
Graves, D. H. (1983). *Writing: Teachers and children at work*. Exeter, NH: Heinemann.
Greenberg, K. L., Wiener, H. S., & Donovan, R. A. (1986). Preface. In K. L. Greenberg, H. S. Wiener, & R. A. Donovan (Eds.), *Writing assessment: Issues and strategies* (pp. xi–xxi). New York: Longman.
Gutek, G. L. (1972). *A history of the western educational experience*. Prospect Heights, IL: Waveland.
Hartwell, P. (1985). Grammar, grammars and the teaching of grammar. *College English, 47,* 105–127.

Heath, S. B. (1983). *Ways with words: Language, life, and work in communities and classrooms.* New York: Cambridge University Press.

Hirsch, E. D. Jr. (1988). *Cultural literacy: What every American needs to know.* New York: Vintage.

Kolln, M. (1981). Closing the books on alchemy. *College Composition and Communication, 32,* 139–151.

Lord, F. M., & Novick, M. R. (1968). *Statistical theories of mental test scores.* Reading, MA: Addison-Wesley.

Lunsford, A. A. (1986). The past — and future — of writing assessment. In K. L. Greenberg, H. S. Wiener, & R. A. Donovan (Eds.), *Writing assessment: Issues and strategies* (pp. 1–12). New York: Longman.

Mann, H. (1845). Boston grammar and writing schools. *The Common School Journal, 7,* 321–368.

Messick, S. (1989). Validity. In R. Linn (Ed.), *Educational measurement* (3rd ed., pp. 13–103). New York: American Council on Education.

Moss, P. A. (1994a). Can there be validity without reliability? *Educational Researcher, 23*(2), 5–12.

Moss, P. A. (1994b). Validity in high stakes writing assessment. *Assessing writing, 1*(1), 109–128.

Moss, P. A. (1992). Shifting conceptions of validity in educational measurement: Implications for performance assessment. *Review of Educational Research, 62,* 229–258.

Myers, M. (1981). The politics of minimum competency. In Charles R. Cooper (Ed.). *The nature and measurement of competency in English* (pp. 165–174). Urbana, IL: National Council of Teachers of English.

Ohmann, R. (1976). *English in America: A radical view of the profession.* New York: Oxford University Press.

Pattison, R. (1982). *On literacy: The politics of the word from Homer to the age of the rock.* New York: Oxford University.

Pearson, P. D. (1986, March). Invited speech at the Conference on English Education Luncheon at the Spring Meeting of the National Council of Teachers of English. Phoenix, AZ.

Popham, J. W. (1988). *Educational evaluation* (2nd ed.). Englewood Cliffs, NJ: Prentice Hall.

Schon, D. A. (1991). *Educating the reflective practitioner.* San Francisco: Jossey-Bass.

Shedd, J. B., & Bacharach, S. B. (1991). *Tangled hierarchies: Teachers as professionals and the management of the schools.* San Francisco: Jossey-Bass.

Spring, J. (1986). *The American school, 1642–1985.* New York: Longman.

Taylor, D. (1990). Teaching without testing. *English Education, 22,* 4–74.

Terman, L. M. (1916). *The measurement of intelligence: An explanation of and a complete guide to the use of the Stanford revision and extension of the Binet-Simon Intelligence Scale.* New York: Houghton Mifflin.

Torgerson, W. S. (1958). *Theory and methods of scaling.* London: The Institute of Physics.

Veal, L. R., & Hudson, S. A. (1983). Direct and indirect measures for large-scale evaluation of writing. *Research in the Teaching of English, 17,* 243–261.

White, E. (1993). Holistic scoring: Past triumphs, future challenges. In M. M. Williamson & B. A. Huot (Eds.). *Validating holistic scoring for writing assessment* (pp. 79–108). Cresskill, NJ: Hampton.

White, E. (1985). *Teaching and assessing writing.* San Francisco: Jossey-Bass.

Williamson, M. M. (1993). An introduction to holistic scoring: The social, historical, and theoretical context for writing assessment. In M. M. Williamson & B. A. Huot (Eds.), *Validating holistic scoring for writing assessment* (pp. 1–44). Cresskill, NJ: Hampton.

Witte, S. P., Trachsel, M., & Walters, K. (1986). Literacy and direct assessment of writing: A diachronic perspective. In K. L. Greenberg, H. S. Wiener, & R. A. Donovan (Eds.), *Writing assessment: Issues and strategies* (pp. 13–34). New York: Longman.

5 *Can There Be Validity Without Reliability?*

PAMELA A. MOSS

Reliability has traditionally been taken for granted as a necessary but insufficient condition for validity in assessment use. My purpose in this article is to illuminate and challenge this presumption by exploring a dialectic between psychometric and hermeneutic approaches to drawing and warranting interpretations of human products or performances. Reliability, as it is typically defined and operationalized in the measurement literature (e.g., American Educational Research Association [AERA], American Psychological Association, & National Council on Measurement in Education, 1985; Feldt & Brennan, 1989), privileges standardized forms of assessment. By considering hermeneutic alternatives for serving the important epistemological and ethical purposes that reliability serves, we expand the range of viable high-stakes assessment practices to include those that honor the purposes that students bring to their work and the contextualized judgments of teachers.

— *EDUCATIONAL RESEARCH*, VOL. 23, NO. 2, PP. 5–12.

Some time ago, I submitted to a journal a manuscript in which my coauthors and I argued for the value of teachers' contextualized judgments in making consequential decisions about individual students and educational programs. Drawing on epistemological strategies typically used by qualitative or interpretive researchers, we offered an example of how teachers' narrative evaluations of their students' collected work, which varied in substance from student to student and classroom to classroom, might be warranted and used for accountability purposes. We based our argument for the value of this sort of contextualized assessment on the unique quality of information it might provide when used in conjunction with more standardized forms of assessment and on the educational benefits it might have for teachers and

From *Educational Researcher* 23.4 (1994): 5–12.

students. We warranted the narrative evaluation, in part, in critical dialogue among readers about the multidimensional evidence contained in students' folders and, in part, in documentation of evidence allowing subsequent readers of the report to "audit" or confirm the conclusions for themselves.

Reviewer B thought our manuscript was a "superb and important article" and gave it her "highest endorsement." Reviewer A thought the manuscript should not be published in its current form because we had "confused the purpose of assessment with that of instruction" and had "failed to establish reliability" (in this case, adequate consistency among independent readings). She commented that our argument showed a lack of understanding of the essential function of reliability, not only in service of validity, but also "for fairness to the student to prevent the subjectivity and potential bias of an individual teacher." The editor, faced with the dilemma of divergent opinions, wrote that he would be willing to publish an article based on the manuscript if it dealt effectively with the concerns of Reviewer A. He commented, diplomatically, that he feared our position "might be misread as a rejection of a fundamental measurement principle." He noted that "any measurement should have adequate reliability for its purposes, otherwise it is not good measurement, regardless of its positive features."

There is an instructive irony embedded in this anecdote. The process by which a working decision was reached regarding our manuscript was based in an epistemology that more closely resembled the one we had proposed than the one against which our manuscript was evaluated. The editor's decision was not grounded in the consistency among independent readings, which diverged substantially; rather, he made a thoughtful judgment based upon a careful reading of both sets of comments and his own evaluation of the manuscript. I am confident that he was concerned with the validity and fairness of his decision. Of course, I didn't agree with his initial decision, but our dialogue continued through the mail, and the paper improved (and was published) as we strengthened our argument in response to his concerns. I am also confident that both the readers of the journal and I were well served by the written dialogue that accompanied what, for me, was a "high-stakes" decision.

My purpose in this article is to illuminate and challenge the presumption that reliability, as it's typically defined and operationalized in the professional measurement literature (e. g., AERA et al., 1985; Feldt & Brennan, 1989), is essential to sound assessment practice; in doing this, I give particular attention to the context of accountability in public education. I explore a dialectic between two diverse approaches to drawing and warranting interpretations of human products and performances — one based in psychometrics and one in hermeneutics. This task, I believe, honors Messick's (1989) proposed "Singerian" mode of inquiry in validity research, where one inquiring system is observed in terms of another inquiring system "to elucidate the distinctive technical and value assumptions underlying each system application and to integrate the scientific and ethical implications of the inquiry" (p. 32). My point is not to overturn a traditional criterion but rather to suggest that it be treated as only one of several possible strategies of serving important epistemological and ethical purposes. The choice among reliability and its alternatives has consequences for stakeholders in the educational system. That choice should be not be taken for granted or treated as nonproblematic.

CONCERNS WITH THE TRADITIONAL VIEW OF RELIABILITY

"Without reliability, there is no validity." Many of us who develop and use educational assessments were taught to take this maxim for granted as a fundamental principle of sound measurement. *The Standards for Educational and Psychological Testing* (AERA et al., 1985), along with most major measurement texts (e.g., Crocker & Algina, 1986; Cronbach, 1990), present reliability as a necessary, albeit insufficient, condition for validity. Theoretically, reliability is defined as "the degree to which test scores are free from errors of measurement. . . . Measurement errors reduce the reliability (and therefore the generalizability) of the score obtained for a person from a single measurement" (AERA et al., 1985, p. 19). Typically, reliability is operationalized by examining consistency, quantitatively defined, among independent observations or sets of observations that are intended as interchangeable—consistency among independent evaluations or readings of a performance, consistency among performances in response to independent tasks, and so on. In fact, Feldt and Brennan (1989) describe the "essence" of reliability analysis as the "quantification of the consistency and inconsistency in examinee performance" (p. 105). In this article, I focus primarily on issues of reliability or generalizability across tasks (products or performances by the person or persons about whom conclusions are drawn) and across readers (interpreters or evaluators of those performances).

Less standardized forms of assessment, such as performance assessments, present serious problems for reliability, in terms of generalizability across readers and tasks as well as across other facets of measurement. These less standardized assessments typically permit students substantial latitude in interpreting, responding to, and perhaps designing tasks; they result in fewer independent responses, each of which is more complex, reflecting integration of multiple skills and knowledge; and they require expert judgment for evaluation. Empirical studies of reliability or generalizability with performance assessments are quite consistent in their conclusions that (a) reader reliability, defined as consistency of evaluation across readers on a given task, can reach acceptable levels when carefully trained readers evaluate responses to one task at a time and (b) adequate task or "score" reliability, defined as consistency in performances across tasks intended to address the same capabilities, is far more difficult to achieve (e.g., Breland, Camp, Jones, Morris, & Rock, 1987; Dunbar, Koretz, & Hoover, 1991; Shavelson, Baxter, & Gao, 1993). In the case of portfolios, where the tasks may vary substantially from student to student and where multiple tasks may be evaluated simultaneously, inter-reader reliability may drop below acceptable levels for consequential decisions about individuals or programs (Koretz, McCaffrey, Klein, Bell, & Stecher, 1992; Nystrand, Cohen, & Martinez, 1993).[1]

Validity researchers in performance assessment, building on the pioneering work of Messick (1964, 1975, 1980, 1989) and Cronbach (1980, 1988) that expanded the definition of validity to include consideration of social consequences, have stressed the importance of *balancing* concerns about reliability, replicability, or generalizability with additional criteria such as "authenticity" (Newmann, 1990), "directness" (Frederiksen & Collins, 1989), or "cognitive complexity" (Linn, Baker, & Dunbar, 1991). This balancing of often competing concerns has resulted in the sanctioning of lower levels of reliability, as long as "acceptable levels are achieved for particular purposes of assessment" (Linn et al., 1991, p. 11; see Messick, 1992, and Moss, 1992, for a review). Where acceptable levels have not been reached, recommendations for enhancing reliability without increasing the number of tasks or readers beyond cost-efficient levels have typically involved (a) increasing the specification of tasks or scoring procedures, thereby resulting in increased standardization, and (b), in the case of portfolios, disaggregating the contents so that tasks may be scored, independently, one task at a time. Wiley and Haertel (1996) offer a promising means of addressing task reliability without the constraining assumption of homogeneity of tasks. As part of a comprehensive assessment development process, they suggest carefully analyzing assessment tasks to describe the capabilities required for performance, scoring tasks separately for the relevant capabilities, and examining reliability within capability across tasks to which the capability applies. While this supports the use of complex and authentic tasks that may naturally vary in terms of the capabilities elicited, it still requires detailed specification of measurement intents, performance records, and scoring criteria. So although growing attention to the consequences of assessment use in validity research provides theoretical support for the move toward less standardized assessment, continued reliance on reliability, defined as quantification of consistency among independent observations, requires a significant level of standardization.

Given the growing body of evidence about the impact of high-stakes assessment on educational practice (Corbett & Wilson, 1991; Johnston, Weiss, & Afflerbach, 1990; Smith, 1991), this privileging of standardization is problematic. As Resnick and Resnick (1992) conclude, to the extent that assessment results "are made visible and have consequences" (p. 55), efforts to improve performance on a given assessment "seem to drive out most other educational concerns" (p. 58). There are certain intellectual activities that standardized assessments can neither document nor promote; these include encouraging students to find their own purposes for reading and writing, encouraging teachers to make informed instructional decisions consistent with the needs of individual students, and encouraging students and teachers to collaborate in developing criteria and standards to evaluate their work. A growing number of educators are calling for alternative approaches to assessment that support collaborative inquiry and foreground the development of purpose and meaning over skills and content in the intellectual work of students (Greene, 1992; Willinsky, 1990) and teachers (Darling-Hammond, 1989; Lieberman, 1992). If Resnick and Resnick (1992) are correct in their conclusion that what isn't assessed tends to disappear from the curriculum, then we need to find ways to document the validity of assessments that support a wider range of valued educational goals. And, as Wolf, Bixby, Glenn, and Gardner (1991) have suggested, we need to "revise our notions of high-agreement reliability as a cardinal symptom of a useful and viable approach to scoring student performance" and "seek other sorts of evidence that responsible judgment is unfolding" (p. 63).

Unquestionably, reliability serves an important purpose. Underlying our concerns about reliability are both epistemological and ethical issues. These include the extent to which we can generalize to the construct of interest from particular samples of behavior evaluated by particular readers and the extent to which those generalizations are fair. These are, however, alternative means of serving those purposes. The decision about which strategy to use should depend upon the aims and consequences of the assessment in question. In the sections that follow, I explore the potential of a hermeneutic approach to drawing and warranting interpretations of human products or performances.[2] Although the focus here is on reliability (consistency among independent measures intended as interchangeable), it should be clear that reliability is an aspect of construct validity (consonance among multiple lines of evidence supporting the intended interpretation over alternative interpretations). And as assessment becomes less standardized, distinctions between reliability and validity blur.

A HERMENEUTIC APPROACH TO INTERPRETATION

Hermeneutics characterizes a general approach to the interpretation of meaning reflected in any human product, expression, or action, often referred to as a text or "text analog." Although hermeneutics is not a unitary tradition, most hermeneutic philosophers share a holistic and integrative approach to interpretation of human phenomena that seeks to understand the whole in light of its parts, repeatedly testing interpretations against the available evidence until each of the parts can be accounted for in a coherent interpretation of the whole. (Edited volumes by Bleicher, 1980, and Ormiston and Schrift, 1990, provide excerpts from the works of the major philosophers in the hermeneutic tradition.) Recently, a number of philosophers of science have suggested that this "hermeneutic circle" of initial interpretation, validation, and revised interpretation characterizes much that occurs in the natural as well as the social sciences (Bernstein, 1983; Diesing, 1991; Kuhn, 1986).

Hermeneutic writings are often categorized into three major perspectives reflecting differences in the relative "authority" they give to text, context, and reader in building an interpretation (Bleicher, 1980; Ormiston & Schrift, 1990; Rabinow & Sullivan, 1987; Warnke, 1987). One perspective, reflected in the writings of Schleiermacher, Dilthey, Betti, and, more recently Hirsch, treats "hermeneutical theory" as a methodology intended to produce relatively objective or correct interpretations that reflect the original intent of the author while bracketing the preconceptions of the reader. Here, the hermeneutic circle is conceived of in terms of a dialectical relationship between the parts of the text and the whole. A second perspective, "hermeneutic philosophy," which is reflected in the writings of Heidegger and Gadamer, recognizes that the reader's preconceptions, "enabling" prejudices, or foreknowledge are inevitable and valuable in interpreting a text. In fact, they make understanding possible. Here, the hermeneutic circle is viewed as including a dialectic between reader and text to develop practically relevant knowledge. A third perspective, often called "critical" or "depth hermeneutics," reflected in the writings of Habermas and Apel, highlights the importance of considering social dynamics that may distort meaning. Here the hermeneutic circle expands to include a critique of ideology from the ideal perspective of an unconstrained communication — one in which all parties concerned (including researcher and researched) approach each other as equals. These differing perspectives provide alternative resolutions to concerns about such issues as subjectivity, objectivity, and generalizability that psychometricians have confronted in building *their* interpretations.

COMPARING HERMENEUTIC AND PSYCHOMETRIC APPROACHES

Major differences between hermeneutic and psychometric approaches to validity research can be characterized largely in terms of how each treats the relationships between the parts of an assessment (individual products or performances) and the whole (entire collection of available evidence) and how human judgment is used to arrive at a well-warranted conclusion.

In a typical psychometric approach to assessment, each performance is scored independently by readers who have no additional knowledge about the student or about the judgments of other readers. Inferences about achievement, competence, or growth are based upon composite scores, aggregated from independent observations across readers and performances, and references to relevant criteria or norm groups. These scores, whose interpretability and validity rest largely on previous research, are provided to users with guidelines for interpretation. Users are typically (and appropriately) advised to consider scores in light of other information about the individual, although mainstream validity theory provides little guidance about how to combine such information to reach a well-warranted conclusion — a task to which hermeneutic analysis is well suited.

A hermeneutic approach to assessment would involve holistic, integrative interpretations of collected performances that seek to understand the whole in light of its parts, that privilege readers who are most knowledgeable about the context in which the assessment occurs, and that ground those interpretations not only in the textual and contextual evidence available, but also in a rational debate among the community of interpreters. Here, the interpretation might be warranted by criteria like a reader's extensive knowledge of the learning context; multiple and varied sources of evidence; an ethic of disciplined, collaborative inquiry that encourages challenges and revisions to initial interpretations; and the transparency of the trail of evidence leading to the interpretations, which allows users to evaluate the conclusions for themselves.

ILLUSTRATIONS OF MORE HERMENEUTIC APPROACHES TO ASSESSMENT

In higher education, we have a number of models of high-stakes assessments that are not standardized. For instance, consider how we confer graduate degrees, grant tenure, or, as my introductory paragraphs illustrated, make decisions about which articles will be published and which will not. As an extended example, consider what, based on my experience, appears to be a typical process for making decisions about hiring faculty colleagues. Candidates submit portfolios of their work and evaluations by others. While there may be some minimal standardization (e.g., three representative publications, teaching evaluations, and a letter articulating their programs of research and teaching), candidates are expected to compile evidence that they believe best represents the substance and quality of their work. Search committee members are selected because of their areas of expertise and affiliation — to cover the knowledge and political bases that a thoughtful decision requires. They are not trained to agree on a common set of criteria and standards; rather, it is expected that all will bring expertise to bear in evaluating candidates' credentials. Candidates' portfolios, interviews, and presentations are not parceled out to be evaluated independently by different committee members. Rather, each member examines all the evidence available to reach and support an integrative judgment about the qualifications of the candidates. These judgments are not aggregated to arrive at a set of scores; rather, they are brought to the table for a sometimes contentious discussion. Disagreement is taken seriously and positions are sometimes changed as different perspectives are brought to bear on the evidence. The final decision represents a consensus or compromise based on that discussion. An ethic of fairness typically pervades these discussions, as credentials are viewed and reviewed to make sure no qualified candidates have been overlooked. The recommendation, rationale, and supporting evidence are passed on for review to other levels of the system, typically including executive committees, administrators, and affirmative action committees. Taken together, these procedures serve to warrant the validity and fairness of the decision. Would we really believe the process more fair and valid if we followed more traditional assessment techniques of evaluating the parts independently and aggregating the scores?

These models are not unheard of in K–12 education. Edited volumes by Berlak et al. (1992) and Perrone (1991) describe successful examples of more contextualized and dialogic forms of assessment. For instance, at the Walden School in Racine, Wisconsin, students prepare papers or exhibits that are evaluated by a committee of teachers, parents, other students, and members of the community. At the Prospect School in North Bennington, Vermont, teachers meet regularly to discuss progress of individual students or curriculum issues, in much the same way that physicians conduct case conferences. In pilot projects in England, committees of teachers, supervisors, and others at the school level engage in periodic audits of the individual portfolios, and committees at higher levels of the system review the procedures of the school level committees to ensure that appropriate standards are being followed. (Elsewhere, my colleagues and I have provided an extended illustration; Moss et al., 1992.)

While the above examples focus primarily on individual assessment, other examples more directly address the problems of providing system level information in more dialogic and contextualized forms. In Pittsburgh, Pennsylvania, the Arts PROPEL project has involved committees of teachers in designing a districtwide portfolio assessment system and has invited educators from outside the district to audit the portfolio evaluation process (LeMahieu, Eresh, & Wallace, 1992). At the Brooklyn New School in New York City, the staff has developed a "learner-centered accountability system" in which a comprehensive set of structures and processes have been set up to support opportunities for guided student choice, collaborative learning and inquiry among teachers and administrators, active involvement of students and their families in educational decisions, and regular involvement by educators and researchers from outside the school in formative evaluation activities (Darling-Hammond & Snyder, 1992). These examples of assessment are all consistent with what Darling-Hammond and Snyder call a professional model of accountability, which seeks evidence that teachers are engaging in collaborative inquiry to make knowledge-based decisions that respond to individual students' needs.

YES, BUT WHAT ABOUT GENERALIZABILITY AND FAIRNESS?

Regardless of whether one is using a hermeneutic or psychometric approach to drawing and evaluating interpretations and decisions, the activity involves inference from observable parts to an unobservable whole that is implicit in the purpose and intent of the assessment. The question is whether those generalizations are best made by limiting human judgment to single performances, the results of which are then aggregated and compared with performance standards, or by expanding the role of human judgment to development integrative interpretations based on all the relevant evidence.

With a psychometric approach, generalizability is warranted in quantitative measures of consistency across independent observations (across tasks, readers, and so on). As I argued above, the nature of the warrant privileges more standardized forms of assessment. When operationalized in this way, inadequate consistency puts the validity of the assessment use in jeopardy. While consistency or consensus supports the validity of the interpretations in both psychometric and hermeneutic approaches, the difference rests in how it is addressed. Here I will consider the way generalizations may be constructed and warranted from more hermeneutic perspectives and how this, in turn, expands possibilities for assessment.

Generalization Across Tasks

With respect to generalization across tasks, the goal of a more hermeneutic approach is to construct a coherent interpretation of the collected performances, continually revising initial interpretations until they account for all of the available evidence. Inconsistency in students' performance across tasks does not invalidate the assessment. Rather, it becomes an empirical puzzle to be solved by searching for a more comprehensive or elaborated interpretation that explains the inconsistency or articulates the need for additional evidence. A well-documented report describes the evidence available to other readers so that they may judge its adequacy for themselves in supporting the desired generalization. Moreover, when the interpretation informs a subsequent action, such as a revised pedagogical strategy, the success of the action becomes another warrant of the validity of the working interpretation. This is consistent with the characterization of the hermeneutic circle by Packer and Addison (1989) as a dialectic between problem and solution that furthers the concern of the reader.

In terms of task selection, hermeneutic approaches to assessment can allow students and others being assessed substantial latitude in selecting the products by which they will be represented — a latitude that need not be constrained by concerns about quantitative measures of consistency across tasks. As my hiring illustration suggested, permitting those assessed to choose products that best represent their strengths and interests may, in some circumstances, enhance not only validity but also fairness. With psychometric approaches to assessment, fairness in task selection has typically been addressed by requiring that all subjects respond to equivalent tasks, which have been investigated for bias against various groups of concern (Cole & Moss, 1989). Neither approach ensures fairness: With the psychometric approach, we may present students with tasks for which there is differential familiarity, and with the hermeneutic approach, students may not be prepared to choose the products that best represent their capabilities. However, both approaches to fairness in task selection are defensible and deserve discussion.

Generalization Across Readers

With respect to generalization across readers, a more hermeneutic approach to assessment would warrant interpretations in a critical dialogue among readers that challenged initial interpretations while privileging interpretations from readers most knowledgeable about the context of assessment. Initial disagreement among readers would not invalidate the assessment; rather, it would provide an impetus for dialogue, debate, and enriched understanding informed by multiple perspectives as interpretations are refined and as decisions or actions are justified. And again, if well documented, it would allow users of the assessment information, including students, parents, and others affected by the results, to become part of the dialogue by evaluating (and challenging) the conclusions for themselves.

Concerns about the objectivity (and hence the fairness) of such a process have been thoughtfully addressed by qualitative researchers from both hermeneutic and postpositivist empirical traditions of research. Phillips (1990), a persuasive defender of postpositivist empirical research, citing Scriven's (1972) distinction between quantitative and qualitative senses of objectivity, notes that consensus or agreement among independent observations is no guarantor of objectivity. Rather, he defines objectivity, procedurally, as acceptance of a critical tradition: "The community of inquirers must be a critical community, where dissent and reasoned disputation (and sustained efforts to overthrow even the most favored of viewpoints) are welcomed as being central to the process of inquiry" (pp. 30–31). Moreover, he notes, objectivity is no guarantor of "truth":

> A critical community might never reach agreement over, say, two viable alternative views, but if both of these views have been subjected to critical scrutiny, then both would have to be regarded as objective. . . . And even if agreement is reached, it can still happen that the objective view reached within such a community will turn out to be wrong — this is the cross that all of us living in the new nonfoundationalist age have to learn to bear! (p. 31)

This dialogic perspective on the role of the critical community of interpreters in an age where no knowledge is viewed as certain is consistent with the recent writing of Cronbach (1988, 1989) and Messick (1989) on the philosophy of validity. It is also consistent with the writing of hermeneutic philosophers. Here, however, a comparison among the hermeneutic perspectives that I described earlier reflects instructive differences in the role of the readers' preconceptions and the role of the power dynamics within the social context when interpretations are formed. Proponents of hermeneutic philosophy and depth hermeneutics would question the possibility of "objective" knowledge that required readers to bracket their preconceptions. Bernstein (1983), citing Gadamer, argues that we cannot bracket all our prejudices because there is no knowledge or understanding without prejudice (foreknowledge). (Imagine trying to interpret a response written in an unknown foreign language.) The point is to discriminate between blind and enabling prejudices by critically testing them in the course of inquiry.

In a very real sense, attention to reliability actually works against critical dialogue, at least at one phase of inquiry. It leads to procedures that attempt to exclude, to the extent possible, the values and contextualized knowledge of the reader and that foreclose on dialogue among readers about the specific performances being evaluated. A hermeneutic approach to assessment encourages such dialogue at all phases of the assessment. As Bernstein (1983) argues, the absence of a sure foundation against which to test knowledge claims does not condemn us to relativism: Themes in the work of Gadamer, Habermas, and others writing in the hermeneutic and critical traditions look to "dialogue, conversation, undistorted communication, communal judgment, and the type of rational wooing that can take place when individuals confront each other as equals" (p. 223).

If interpretations are warranted through critical dialogue, then the question of who participates in the dialogue becomes an issue of power, as proponents of critical or depth hermeneutics would remind us. In articulating criteria for valid assessment in the service of accountability purposes, a number of assessment specialists have explicitly advised against using the judgments of classroom teachers (e.g., Mehrens, 1992; Resnick & Resnick, 1992). Resnick and Resnick, for instance, assert:

> A principal requirement of accountability and program evaluation tests is that they permit detached and impartial judgments of students' performance, that is, judgments by individuals other than the students' own teachers, using assessment instruments not of the teachers' devising. . . . Like accountability tests, selection and certification tests must be impartial. The public function of certification would not be met if teachers were to grade the performance of their own students. (pp. 48–50)

In contrast, other educators raise concerns about the absence of teachers' voices in mechanisms of accountability that affect them and their students (e.g., Darling-Hammond & Snyder, 1992; Erickson, 1986; Lieberman, 1992). Erickson, for instance, laments the fact that teachers' accounts of their own practices typically have no place in the discourse of schooling. He notes that in other professions, including medicine, law, and social work, "it is routine for practitioners to characterize their own practice, both for purposes of basic clinical research and for the evaluation of their services" (p. 157) and that "the lack of these opportunities [for teachers] is indicative of the relative powerlessness of the profession outside the walls of the classroom" (p. 157). Similar concerns have been raised about the role of students in assessments that have consequences in their lives (e.g., Greene, 1992; Willinsky, 1990).

From a psychometric perspective, the call for "detached and impartial" high-stakes assessment reflects a profound concern for fairness to individual students and protection of stakeholders' interests by providing accurate information. From a hermeneutic perspective, however, it can be criticized as arbitrarily authoritarian and counterproductive, because it silences the voices of those who are most knowledgeable about the context and most directly affected by the results. Quantitative definitions of reliability locate the authority for determining meaning with the assessment developers. In contrast, Gadamer (cited in Bernstein, 1983) argues that the point of philosophical hermeneutics is to correct "the peculiar falsehood of modern consciousness: the idolatry of scientific method and of the anonymous authority of the sciences" (p. 40) and to vindicate "the noblest task of the citizen — decision-making according to one's own responsibility — instead of conceding that task to the expert" (p. 40).

Of course, the validity of any consequential interpretation, including the extent to which it is free from inappropriate or "disabling" prejudices, must be carefully warranted through critical, evidence-based review and dialogue. The process proposed is not dissimilar from the way decisions are made and warranted in the law (see Ricoeur, 1981). Again, neither a psychometric nor a hermeneutic approach guarantees fairness; however, a consideration of the assumptions and consequences associated with both approaches leads to a better informed choice.

IMPLICATIONS

I now return to my title, "Can there be validity without reliability?" When reliability is defined as consistency among *independent* measures intended as *interchangeable*, the answer is, yes. Should there be? Here, the answer is, it depends on the context and purposes for assessment. My argument shares much with Mishler's (1990) views on reliability as a means of warranting knowledge claims:

> Reformulating validation as the social discourse through which trustworthiness is established elides such familiar shibboleths as reliability, falsifiability, and objectivity. These criteria are neither trivial nor irrelevant, but they must be understood as particular ways of warranting validity claims rather than as universal, abstract guarantors of truth. They are rhetorical strategies . . . that fit only one model of science. (p. 420)

Like Mishler, I am not advocating the abandonment of reliability. Rather, I am advocating that we consider it one alternative for serving important epistemological and ethical purposes — an alternative that should always be justified in critical dialogue and in confrontation with other possible means of warranting knowledge claims. As Messick (1989) has advised, such confrontations between epistemologies illuminate assumptions, consequences, and the values implied therein. Ultimately, the purpose of educational assessment is to improve teaching and learning. If reliability is put on the table for discussion, if it becomes an option rather than a requirement, then the possibilities for designing assessment and accountability systems that reflect a full range of valued educational goals become greatly expanded.

I believe the dialogue I have proposed here is not only timely but urgent. We are at a crossroads in education: There is a crisis mentality accompanied by a flurry of activity to design assessment and accountability systems that both document and promote desired educational change. Current conceptions of reliability and validity in educational measurement constrain the kinds of assessment practices that are likely to find favor, and these in turn constrain educational opportunities for teachers and students. A more hermeneutic approach to assessment would lend theoretical support to new directions in assessment and accountability that honor the purposes and lived experiences of students and the professional, collaborative judgments of teachers. Exploring the dialectic between hermeneutics and psychometrics should provoke and inform a much needed debate among those who develop and use assessments about why particular methods of validity inquiry are privileged and what the effects of that privileging are on the community.

Epilogue

My friend and collaborator, Roberta Herter, who is a veteran English teacher in a large urban school district, tells the story of "Cory," one of her former 10th-grade students. Cory's experience puts a human face on the "detached and impartial" nature of psychometrically sound standardized assessments and illustrates the potential consequences of devaluing more contextualized and dialogic approaches to assessment:

> When he first took the competency exam mandated by the district in 1989, the writing proficiency component required Cory to produce a paragraph of at least five sentences about his experience with friendship. Using the language of the prompt to guide his opening sentence, Cory responded to the test prompt by relating a story about influencing friends to quit smoking while attempting to maintain his relationship with them. The eight sentences he wrote responded to the prompt as if they had been rehearsed, practiced in classroom exercises in preparation for the exam, conforming to the minimum response required to pass the test. The anonymous readers of his exam both rated him a 3.5 on a 5.0 holistic scale, a sufficient score to pass the paragraph portion of the exam.
>
> Cory failed the exam, however, because he did not pass the multiple choice portion of the writing test. Even though his writing demonstrated that he could apply mechanics appropriately, he also needed to demonstrate that he could recognize errors such as misplaced punctuation marks and lack of subject-verb agreement in decontextualized sentences. The decontextualized editing tasks required of the multiple choice portion of the exam failed him.
>
> When contrasted with the lively writing from his folder, work collected over a semester, the writing test distorted and underestimated Cory's capabilities. He wrote on racism, Malcolm X, teen pregnancy, drugs, issues important to him and the community in which he lives. He stood out among his peers as a good writer — a thoughtful, intelligent student who put his writing to real purposes — letters to pen friends, the eulogy he wrote and delivered at his uncle's funeral, and plays on current issues of interest to his classmates read and performed in class.
>
> His versatility as a writer, demonstrated by his ability to write for a variety of audiences in appropriate registers, set him apart from many of his peers who had not achieved Cory's degree of competence. Where Cory's test profile painted a picture of a formulaic writer who could not recognize errors in English usage, his folder showed evidence of a purposeful writer capable of producing controlled and coherent prose. His letters, raps, library reports for science and history, his journal documenting his personal growth and changing attitudes were powerful indicators of his potential for success both in and out of school. In an interview on his own learning he defined education as something ultimately, "you have to do for yourself." He showed himself to be a responsible student, a reflective, critical thinker, conscious of the choices afforded him by the school he attended.

Cory's failure on the exam consigned him to a reading competency class and a class in writing improvement, a low-track English elective where students who fail the exam label themselves LD or learning disabled. Both of these tracked classes were designed to prepare students to pass the test so they might receive an endorsed diploma at graduation — classifying them as having achieved minimum competency in basic skills of reading, writing, and math, or reducing the value of their diploma to a certificate of attendance. But Cory didn't wait to take the test again; he dropped out of day school in his senior year. (adapted from Moss & Herter, 1993)

NOTES

1. Dunbar, Koretz, and Hoover (1991), in a review of empirical research on performance assessment, describe reliability estimates based on the average of coefficients reported for each of nine studies, adjusted via the Spearman Brown formula to reflect an assessment based on a single reader and sample of performance. For the seven studies that took place after 1984, reader reliability ranged from .59 to .91 and task or "score" reliability ranged from .27 to .60. Koretz (1993), describing inter-reader reliability on portfolios from Vermont's statewide assessment, reports that correlations between readers ranged from .33 to .43, with raters assigning the same score between about 50% and 60% of the time.

2. Other articles have suggested the use of qualitative methods for validity research with less standardized forms of assessment. See, for example, Hipps (1992), Johnston (1992), and Moss et al. (1992). Hermeneutics provides a philosophical underpinning largely consistent with these authors' methodological suggestions. Cherryholmes (1988) suggests that other research discourses, including phenomenology, critical theory, interpretive analytics, and deconstructionism can each contribute, in different ways, to validity research. Mishler (1990) and Johnston (1989) echo similar themes.

REFERENCES

American Educational Research Association, American Psychological Association, & National Council on Measurement in Education. (1985). *Standards for educational and psychological testing.* Washington, DC: Authors.

Berlak, H., Newmann, F. M., Adams, E., Archbald, D. A., Burgess, T., Raven, J., & Romberg, T. A. (1992). *Toward a new science of educational testing and assessment.* Albany: State University of New York Press.

Bernstein, R. J. (1983). *Beyond objectivism and relativism: Science, hermeneutics, and praxis.* Philadelphia: University of Pennsylvania Press.

Bleicher, J. (1980). *Contemporary hermeneutics: Hermeneutics as method, philosophy, and critique.* London: Routledge and Kegan Paul.

Breland, H. M., Camp, R., Jones, R. J., Morris, M. M., & Rock, D. A. (1987). *Assessing writing skill* (Research Monograph No. 11). New York: College Entrance Examination Board.

Cherryholmes, C. H. (1988). Construct validity and discourses of research. *American Journal of Education, 96,* 421–457.

Cole, N. S., & Moss, P. A. (1989). Bias in test use. In R. L. Linn (Ed.), *Educational measurement* (3rd ed., pp. 201–219). Washington, DC: The American Council on Education and the National Council on Measurement in Education.

Corbett, H. D., & Wilson, B. L. (1991). *Testing, reform, and rebellion.* Norwood, NJ: Ablex.

Crocker, L., & Algina, J. (1986). *Introduction to classical and modern test theory.* Fort Worth, TX: Holt, Rinehart, & Winston.

Cronbach, L. J. (1980). Validity on parole: How can we go straight? *New directions for testing and measurement: Measuring achievement, progress over a decade,* no. 5 (pp. 99–108). San Francisco: Jossey-Bass.

Cronbach, L. J. (1988). Five perspectives on validity argument. In H. Wainer (Ed.), *Test validity.* Hillsdale, NJ: Erlbaum.

Cronbach, L. J. (1989). Construct validation after thirty years. In R. L. Linn (Ed.), *Intelligence: Measurement, theory and public policy.* Urbana: University of Illinois Press.

Cronbach, L. J. (1990). *Essentials of psychological testing* (5th ed.). New York: Harper & Row.

Darling-Hammond, L. (1989). Accountability for professional practice. *Teachers College Record, 91,* 59–80.

Darling-Hammond, L., & Snyder, J. (1992). Reframing accountability: Creating learner-centered schools. In A. Lieberman (Ed.), *The changing contexts of teaching* (91st Yearbook of the National Society for the Study of Education). Chicago: University of Chicago Press.

Diesing, P. (1991). *How does social science work? Reflections on practice.* Pittsburgh: University of Pittsburgh Press.

Dunbar, S. B., Koretz, D. M., & Hoover, H. D. (1991). Quality control in the development and use of performance assessments. *Applied Measurement in Education, 4,* 289–303.

Erickson, F. (1986). Qualitative methods in research on teaching. In M. C. Wittrock (Ed.), *Handbook of research on teaching* (pp. 119–161). New York: Macmillan.

Feldt, L. S., & Brennan, R. L. (1989). Reliability. In R. L. Linn (Ed.), *Educational measurement* (3rd ed.). Washington, DC: The American Council on Education and the National Council on Measurement in Education.

Frederiksen, J. R., & Collins, A. (1989). A systems approach to educational testing. *Educational Researcher, 18*(9), 27–32.

Greene, M. (1992). Evaluation and dignity. *Quarterly of the National Writing Project, 14,* 10–13.

Hipps, J. A. (1992, April). *New frameworks for judging alternative assessments.* Paper presented at the Annual Meeting of the American Educational Research Association, San Francisco.

Johnston, P. (1989). Constructive evaluation and the improvement of teaching and learning. *Teachers College Record, 90,* 509–528.

Johnston, P. H. (1992). *Constructive evaluation of literate activity.* New York: Longman.

Johnston, P. H., Weiss, P., & Afflerbach, P. (1990). *Teachers' evaluation of the teaching and learning in literacy and literature* (Report Series 3.4). Albany: State University of New York at Albany, Center for the Learning and Teaching of Literature.

Koretz, D. (1993). New report on Vermont Portfolio Project documents challenges. *National Council on Measurement in Education Quarterly Newsletter, 1*(4), 1–2.

Koretz, D., McCaffrey, D., Klein, S., Bell, R., & Stecher, B. (1992). *The reliability of scores from the 1992 Vermont Portfolio Assessment Program: Interim report.* Santa Monica, CA: Rand Institute on Education and Training, National Center for Research on Evaluation, Standards, and Student Testing.

Kuhn, T. S. (1986). *The essential tension: Selected studies in scientific tradition and change.* Chicago: The University of Chicago Press.

LeMahieu, P. G., Eresh, J. T., & Wallace, R. C., Jr. (1992). Using student portfolios for public accounting. *The School Administrator, 49*(11), 8–15.

Lieberman, A. (1992). The meaning of scholarly activity and the building of community. *Educational Researcher, 21*(6), 5–12.

Linn, R. L., Baker, E. L., & Dunbar, S. B. (1991). Complex, performance-based assessment: Expectations and validation criteria. *Educational Researcher, 20*(8), 5–21.

Mehrens, W. A. (1992). Using performance assessment for accountability purposes. *Educational Measurement: Issues and Practice, 11*(1), 3–20.

Messick, S. (1964). Personality measurement and college performance. In *Proceedings of the 1963 Invitational Conference on Testing Problems* (pp. 110–129). Princeton, NJ: Educational Testing Service.

Messick, S. (1975). The standard problem: Meaning and values in measurement and evaluation. *American Psychologist, 30,* 955–966.

Messick, S. (1980). Test validity and the ethics of assessment. *American Psychologist, 35,* 1012–1027.

Messick, S. (1989). Validity. In R. L. Linn (Ed.), *Educational measurement* (3rd ed., pp. 13–103). Washington, DC: The American Council on Education and the National Council on Measurement in Education.

Messick, S. (1992, April). *The interplay of evidence and consequences in the validation of performance assessments.* Paper presented at the Annual Meeting of the National Council on Measurement in Education, San Francisco.

Mishler, E. G. (1990). Validation in inquiry-guided research. *Harvard Educational Review, 60,* 415–442.

Moss, P. A. (1992). Shifting conceptions of validity in educational measurement: Implications for performance assessment. *Review of Educational Research, 62,* 229–258.

Moss, P. A., Beck, J. S., Ebbs, C., Herter, R., Hatson, B., Muchmore, J., Steele, D., & Taylor, C. (1992). Portfolios, accountability, and an interpretive approach to validity. *Educational Measurement: Issues and Practice, 3*(11), 1–11.

Moss, P. A., & Herter, R. (1993). Assessment, accountability, and authority in urban schools. *The Long Term View, 1*(4), 68–75.

Newmann, F. M. (1990). Higher order thinking in teaching social studies: A rationale for the assessment of classroom thoughtfulness. *Journal of Curriculum Studies, 22*(1), 41–56.

Nystrand, M., Cohen, A. S., & Martinez, N. M. (1993). Addressing reliability problems in the portfolio assessment of college writing. *Educational Assessment, 1*(1), 53–70.

Ormiston, G. L., & Schrift, A. D. (Eds.). (1990). *The hermeneutic tradition: From Ast to Ricoeur.* Albany: State University of New York Press.

Packer, M. J., & Addison, R. B. (1989). *Entering the circle: Hermeneutic investigation in psychology.* Albany: State University of New York Press.

Perrone, V. (Ed.). (1991). *Expanding student assessment.* Washington, DC: Association for Supervision and Curriculum Development.

Phillips, D. C. (1990). Subjectivity and objectivity: An objective inquiry. In E. W. Eisner & A. Peshkin (Eds.), *Qualitative inquiry in education: The continuing debate* (pp. 19–37). New York: Teachers College Press.

Rabinow, P., & Sullivan, W. M. (Eds.). (1987). *Interpretive social science: A second look.* Berkeley: University of California Press.

Resnick, L. B., & Resnick, D. (1992). Assessing the thinking curriculum: New tools for educational reform. In B. Gifford & M. C. O'Connor (Eds.), *Cognitive approaches to assessment.* Boston: Kluwer-Nijhoff.

Ricoeur, P. (1981). The model of the text: Meaningful action considered as a text. In R. Bicoeur (J. B. Thompson, Ed. and Trans.), *Hermeneutics and the human sciences.* New York: Cambridge University Press.

Scriven, M. (1972). Objectivity and subjectivity in educational research. In L. G. Thomas (Ed.), *Philosophical redirection of educational research* (71st Yearbook of the National Society for the Study of Education, Part 1). Chicago: The University of Chicago Press.

Shavelson, R. J., Baxter, G. P., & Gao, X. (1993). Sampling variability of performance assessments. *Journal of Educational Measurement, 30*, 215–232.

Smith, M. L. (1991). Put to the test: The effects of external testing on teachers. *Educational Researcher, 20*(5), 8–11.

Warnke, G. (1987). *Gadamer: Hermeneutics, tradition, and reason.* Stanford, CA: Stanford University Press.

Wiley, D. E., & Haertel, E. H. (1996). Extended assessment tasks: Purposes, definitions, scoring, and accuracy. In R. Mitchell & M. Kane (Eds.), *Implementing performance assessment: Promises, problems, and challenges.* Washington, DC: Pelavin Associates.

Willinsky, J. (1990). *The new literacy: Redefining reading and writing in the schools.* New York: Routledge.

Wolf, D., Bixby, J., Glenn, J., III, & Gardner, H. (1991). To use their minds well: Investigating new forms of student assessment. *Review of Research in Education, 17*, 31–74.

6

Portfolios as a Substitute for Proficiency Examinations

PETER ELBOW AND PAT BELANOFF

We were troubled by the proficiency examination we found at Stony Brook. We believe proficiency examinations undermine good teaching by sending the wrong message about the writing process: that proficient writing means having a serious topic sprung on you (with no chance for reading, reflection, or discussion) and writing one draft (with no chance for sharing or feedback or revising). Besides, an exam can't give a valid picture of a student's proficiency in writing: we need at least two or three samples of her writing — in two or three genres at two or three sittings.[1]

After four semesters of small scale experimentation, and in coordination with a new University writing requirement, we gave up the proficiency exam and made portfolios official in the 40-plus sections of our required Writing 101 course. The new requirement says that every student must get a C or higher in 101 or else take it again. The portfolio system says that no student can *get* that C unless her portfolio has been judged worth a C not only by her teacher but also by at least one other teacher who does not know her.

A portfolio system might take different forms. Here is how our version works at the moment. Every 101 student must now develop — out of all the writing done during the semester — a portfolio of three revised papers: (a) a narrative, descriptive, or expressive piece; (b) an essay of any sort (so long as it is in the discourse of the academic community — i.e., not a personal, digressive, *essai* as by Montaigne); (c) an analysis of a prose text. With each of these papers students must submit a brief informal cover sheet which explores their writing process in that paper and acknowledges any help they have received. The portfolio must also contain a fourth piece: an in-class essay done without benefit of feedback.

Every 101 teacher is a member of a portfolio group. Experienced teachers create their own small groups. New teachers are in a large group — constituted by the Teaching Practicum that all new teachers take.

From *College Composition and Communication* 37 (1986): 336–39.

At mid-semester *all* teachers meet to discuss sample papers and agree on some verdicts: a "calibration" session. Then teachers meet in their smaller groups and distribute their students' mid-semester "dry run" papers to each other for readings. (We've learned that students need an outside reading of one or two of their portfolio essays at mid-semester — in order to get used to the system and be warned of the standards.) The judgment is a simple binary Yes or No — worth a C or not. Readers make no comments on the papers (except for light checkmarks at unambiguous mistakes in mechanics — especially if a paper fails for that reason). A brief comment by the reader who is not the student's teacher is paper-clipped only to failing papers — usually only a few sentences. It is not the reader's job to diagnose or teach — only to judge. It is the teacher's job to interpret these comments to the student when that is necessary. (We're trying to keep the portfolio system from being much of an extra burden on teachers. Strong portfolios can be read quickly — sometimes just skimmed.)

If the teacher agrees with the verdict, the process is finished — and this is what happens with most papers. But if the teacher disagrees, she can ask for a second reading from another reader. If that second reading is the same, the teacher may feel that she should change her view and go along with those two outside readers, but she is free to seek a third reading to validate her original perception. However, the stakes are not high at mid-semester; a failure doesn't count. Teachers tend to prefer stern verdicts at mid-semester to keep students from being lulled into false security.

This collaborative evaluating process is repeated at the end of the semester — but with full portfolios: a calibration meeting for all teachers on sample portfolios; small groups for first, second, and occasionally third readings; yes/no judgments on whole portfolios (not separate verdicts on each paper): no comments except on failed portfolios. This time, of course, the gun is loaded: it's the end of the semester and a student who fails her portfolio must repeat the course. However, if the two readers agree that the failure stems from *only one* paper, the student may revise that paper and resubmit the portfolio.

By giving students more time and more chance for help, and by letting them choose their best writing, the system is a way to ask for *better* writing and push *more* students to provide it. Sometimes 50% of the mid-semester "dry run" papers fail, but at semester's end fewer than 10% of the portfolios fail — and that goes down to less than 5% after some are rewritten.

This may sound like trying to raise standards and passing rates at the same time, but evaluation by portfolio gets away from the traditional norm-referenced model of evaluation which has given us most of our gut-level assumptions about testing. The goal in traditional evaluation is to rank or differentiate students into as many different "grades" as possible; it is a tradition of "measuring" minds; the ideal end product is population distributed along a bell-shaped curve (as in IQ or SAT scores). The portfolio process uses a very different model of evaluation — criterion-referenced or mastery-based or competence-based — which assumes that the ideal end product is a population of students who have *all* finally passed because they have all been given enough time and help to do what we ask of them.[2]

The portfolio system makes some teachers feel a bit uncomfortable — especially the first time they use it. But it helps teachers too, and has a number of other benefits. Most important, it encourages good teaching and a sound writing process. A proficiency exam rewards playing it safe and plastic, five-paragraph essays; portfolio papers won't pass with a required C unless they show some genuine thought and investment. The portfolio encourages revising, peer feedback, and collaboration among students. (As for cheating: teachers do not submit a portfolio unless they are confident it is the student's own work; students may not change topics at the last minute in revising papers.)

The portfolio system throws the teacher somewhat into the role of *coach* or *editor* because the crucial decision as to whether the student is eligible to get a C (or must repeat the course) depends on someone other than the teacher. The teacher becomes someone who can *help* the student overcome an obstacle posed by a third party and is thus less likely to be seen by students as merely "the enemy." Thus the portfolio system leads teachers to make comments like this:

> I like this piece. It works for me. But I think some of my pleasure comes from knowing how hard you've worked and how much progress you've made. It helps me to have read some of your earlier drafts and gotten to know you and your concerns. I fear your piece won't work so well for a reader who is a stranger to you.

In effect this sets up the "good-cop/bad-cop" game ("I'd like to give you a break but my buddy is a mean son of a bitch"). But the portfolio also sets up the "cop-handcuffed-to-the-prisoner" game: an insecure teacher is liable to feel her student's failure as a reflection on her — and may even be tempted to give *too* much help. Most teachers have gotten burnt once: "I'm sorry, but I seem to have misled you. Your portfolio didn't pass." (Even after going back for third and fourth readings.) Thus teachers learn to say, "I think this is good work, I like it, I would give it at least a C. But we'll have to see what portfolio readers think."

We like what this does to the use of grades in a writing course. Teachers retain *almost* complete power over grades. (They can give any grade to an individual paper; they can give any course grade to students who pass the portfolio; they can give any grade below a C to students who do not pass it.) But the portfolio system anchors that crucial "C" line to negotiation by the community. And the system makes teachers less likely to put grades on weekly papers, more likely to concentrate all their energies on useful comments. Students often ignore comments when there is a grade; teachers often write better comments when not having to justify a grade.

The portfolio system encourages collaboration among teachers. When teachers work in isolation they often drift into believing that they use standards made in heaven — that they *know* what A and F mean. (It's painful to give grades when you experience the full sense of indeterminacy involved.)

Yet of course there is enormous inconsistency among the grades of isolated teachers, so *students* often drift in the opposite direction — into complete skepticism or even cynicism about the possibility of evaluation or even judgment at all. They often feel that *all* evaluations or judgments are nothing but accidents of teachers' personalities. Such students think that getting good grades is nothing but psyching out idiosyncracies — figuring out what particular teachers "like" or "want."

Our profession lacks any firm, theoretical, discipline-wide basis for deciding the right interpretation or evaluation of a text. The only way to bring a bit of trustworthiness to grading is to get teachers negotiating together in a community to make some collaborative judgments. That the portfolio promotes collaboration and works against isolation may be, in the end, its main advantage.

These collaborative discussions of sample papers are interesting. One faction may give powerful arguments for failing the sample paper; someone even says, "How can anyone who considers himself a literate professional possibly give this paper a C?" But another group gives strong arguments in its favor, and the blurter discovers that the defenders of the paper are not just the flakey wimps he suspected but also include a colleague he respects as more perceptive and learned than himself.

Hurtful words are sometimes spoken, e.g., "It's not the paper that flunks, it's the assignment!" Yet over the semesters we have come to treasure these difficult moments. As one of us said just the other day when the heat was rising in the room: "We're sorry you are having a hard time, but *we're* having a ball!" It's a relief for us to see all this disparity of judgment out on the floor *as interaction between people* — as heads butting against other heads. Normally, the disparity is locked inside solitary heads, visible only to students who compare notes and to administrators looking at different teachers' grade sheets. When a newcomer complains, "Why do you encourage all this chaos and disagreement?" it's fun to be able to reply, "We're not making it, we're just getting it out from under the rug."

On most samples there is a decisive majority or even consensus. But when teachers remain divided, it's important for us to intervene, get a quick vote to show where the numbers lie (sometimes the discussion can fool you), and say, "Fine. We're split. Here's a picture of where our community disagrees; here is a paper that will pass in some groups and fail in others; nevertheless this picture can give you some guidance when you go off to make your individual verdicts. We're gradually giving each other a sense of our standards as a community." For even though it is the *disagreement* that is most obvious at such moments, *we*, from where we sit, see such discussions producing much more *agreement* in grading and community standards than we used to have when all teachers graded alone.[3]

NOTES

1. Charles Cooper, *The Nature and Measurement of Competency in English* (Urbana, IL: National Council of Teachers of English, 1981).

2. See D. C. McClelland, "Testing for Competence Rather than for 'Intelligence,'" *American Psychologist 28* (January, 1973), 1–14. Also Gerald Grant and Wendy Kohli, "Contributing to Learning by Assessing Student Performance," in *On Competence,* ed. Gerald Grant and Associates (San Francisco: Jossey-Bass, 1979), pp. 138–59. Also Peter Elbow on the effects of competence-based curricula on teachers: "Trying to Teach While Thinking About the End," in *Embracing Contraries* (New York: Oxford University Press, 1986).

3. We have written two essays which describe the system more fully: (1) "Using Portfolios to Judge Writing Proficiency at SUNY Stony Brook," in *New Methods in College Writing Programs,* ed. Paul Connolly and Teresa Vilardi (New York: Modern Language Association, 1986); (2) "Using Portfolios to Increase Collaboration and Community in a Writing Program," *WPA: Journal of Writing Program Administration, 9* (Spring, 1986). For an interesting account of another use of portfolios for grading (but not as a substitute for proficiency examinations), see Christopher Burnham's "Portfolio Evaluation: Room to Breathe and Grow" in the new collection, *Training the Teacher of College Composition,* ed. Charles Bridges (Urbana, IL: National Council of Teachers of English, 1986).

7 Changing the Model for the Direct Assessment of Writing

ROBERTA CAMP[1]

INTRODUCTION

Research and practice in writing and writing instruction have led us in recent years to look at writing as a rich and multifaceted activity deeply immersed in the context that surrounds it. As a community of educators and researchers interested in writing, we understand more thoroughly than we once did that the tasks of writing vary with purpose, audience, and context (Hairston, 1982). We think of writing, like reading, as a meaning-making activity requiring the orchestration of skills and strategies, and we see that each mode of purpose for writing draws on different skills and strategies, and different linguistic abilities and cognitive operations (Applebee, 1986; Durst, 1987; Freedman & Pringle, 1981; Langer & Applebee, 1987; Odell, 1981; Penrose, 1989; Pringle & Freedman, 1985).

In addition, we now see that this meaning-making activity occurs over time and involves processes that are recursive, that are used differently by different writers, and that vary with knowledge of the topic, the context for writing, and personal and cultural history (Applebee, 1986; Flower & Hayes, 1981; O'Conner, 1989). We know now, too, that writers switch among processes and strategies as they generate text, depending on their perception of goals for the writing and their plans for addressing them, and that writers' awareness of the strategies they use is important to their performance in writing (Bereiter & Scardamalia, 1987; Flower & Hayes, 1980; Thompson, 1985). Further, we recognize that many of the processes and strategies for writing involve interaction with texts — and therefore the skills and strategies of reading — and with a social and communicative context (Bruffee, 1986; Carter, 1990; Faigley,

From *Validating Holistic Scoring for Writing Assessment: Theoretical and Empirical Foundations*, ed. M. M. Williamson and B. A. Huot (Cresskill, NJ: Hampton Press, 1993): 45–78.

1986; Freedman, Dyson, Flower, & Chafe, 1987; Johnston, 1987; Macrorie, 1976; Moffett, 1968; Smith, 1982; Valencia, McGinley, & Pearson, 1990).

This complex view of writing is not easily reconciled with traditional approaches to assessment. The magnitude of the differences in perspective are prefigured in the conflicts about writing assessment in recent decades, especially in the long-standing controversies surrounding the two most common forms of writing assessment — multiple-choice tests and holistically scored writing samples. Although workable compromises have frequently been found for dealing with the issues behind these controversies, the issues have never been resolved to the complete satisfaction of all parties concerned. With the development of more complex views of writing, there is reason to expect that the issues driving the earlier controversies will resurface in terms that are far more challenging (see Johnston, 1987).

To set out more clearly the issues to be confronted in writing assessment and the possible resolutions of those issues, this chapter will first present a historical and theoretical perspective. The discussion will begin with a reflection on the history of writing assessment in recent decades, then go on to examine the current status of existing models for writing assessment. It will next outline recent shifts in measurement theory that indicate the need for assessments compatible with our new and more complex views of writing. The final section of the chapter will present a description of resources that can help to guide us in the development of new models for writing assessment. The chapter will close with a summary of characteristics likely to be incorporated in such models.

TRADITIONAL FORMATS FOR WRITING ASSESSMENT

The prevailing formats for large-scale writing assessments in the last decades, at least until very recently, have been the multiple-choice test and the impromptu writing sample, and in many cases a combination of the two. The combination in particular has represented for many, including developers of smaller-scale assessments, a compromise accommodating both traditional psychometric expectations for reliability and the concern for validity expressed by teachers of writing and others convinced that judgments about writing ability should be based on writing performance (Breland, Camp, Jones, Morris, & Rock, 1987; Coffman, 1971; Conlon, 1986; Diederich, 1974; Spandel & Stiggins, 1980; White, 1986). It seems worthwhile here to examine the issues that lie behind that compromise.

The History: Balancing the Requirements of Reliability and Validity

The multiple-choice test, with its machine-scorable items, provides evidence taken from multiple data points representing relatively discrete components of the writing task each measured separately. The number and the discreteness of the items yield high test reliability and make possible the construction of multiple versions of the test that are parallel in difficulty and in the characteristics of the tasks presented. Although human judgment is involved in the development and selection of test items, the multiple-choice test is unaffected by the subjectivity of human scoring. It has been seen as reliable, efficient, and economical.

From the perspective of traditional psychometrics, in which high test reliability is a prerequisite for validity, the multiple-choice writing test has also been seen as a valid measure. The claims for its validity have rested on its coverage of skills necessary to writing and on correlations between test scores and course grades — or, more recently, between test scores and performance on samples of writing, including writing generated under classroom conditions (Breland et al., 1987; Breland & Gaynor, 1979; Godshalk, Swineford, & Coffman, 1966). By and large these claims have been more convincing to statistically oriented members of the measurement community than to teachers of writing, who have pointed to the limitations of testing component skills separately and to the narrowness of the range of skills that can be tested in multiple-choice format (see Faigley, Cherry, Jolliffe, & Skinner, 1985).

The claims for the validity of using multiple-choice tests to determine writing competence are not entirely without foundation. Most students who do well on carefully designed and relatively comprehensive multiple-choice tests of grammar, sentence structure, and usage are likely to perform well in response to well-designed prompts for writing, as the correlational studies indicate. It may be that students who have relatively good control over such aspects of writing as mechanics, usage, grammar, and syntax can more easily generate text within relatively short periods of time (Bereiter & Scardamalia, 1987; Scardamalia & Bereiter, 1985). Or perhaps the breadth and depth of experience with reading and writing that help students to recognize conventional expectations for language use also provide them in most instances with the more global skills they need to generate good prose. Whatever the explanation, under most circumstances and for most test takers, performance on a series of independent multiple-choice questions corresponds fairly well with performance on a writing sample (Breland & Gaynor, 1979).

Yet the validity of the multiple-choice test as a measure of writing ability has never been completely certain. Although Breland and Gaynor (1979) felt they had demonstrated, on the basis of correlational studies, that indirect, multiple-choice measures of writing tap skills similar to those called for by writing samples, later studies reflecting greater sensitivity to cognitive processes have come to different conclusions. Ward, Frederiksen, and Carlson (1980), looking at free-response and machine-scorable versions of items testing the ability to generate hypotheses, pointed out that multiple-choice items which depend on the test takers' ability to recognize possible solutions may be a sufficient basis for predicting performance in actually generating solutions, as indicated by correlational studies, but they do not necessarily measure constructs identical with those measured by open-ended, free-response formats. Similarly, and more to the point here, a study of direct and indirect measures of writing for first- and second-language users of English, while finding the expected correlations between performance on indirect and direct assessments of writing, found in the factor analyses that the two formats were not measuring identical skills (Carlson, Bridgeman, Camp, & Waanders, 1985).

In addition, theoretical considerations suggest limitations in the validity of multiple-choice tests of writing. As concepts of writing ability began to focus on performance beyond the sentence level, it became increasingly clear that multiple-choice tests do not sample the full range of knowledge and skills involved in writing (Cooper, 1977; Gere, 1980; Lloyd-Jones, 1977; Odell, 1981). Nor do they sample writing skills in a manner that is consistent with either the theoretical constructs for writing—what we currently understand writing to be—or with practices to be encouraged in the teaching of writing (Odell, 1981).

Furthermore, increased awareness of the differences in the operational grammars of working-class and middle-class children and of speakers of black English and standard English (Cole & Moss, 1989, citing Bernstein, 1975, Heath, 1982, and M. D. Linn, 1975) and of basic writers (Bartholomae, 1980; Beaugrande, 1982; Shaughnessy, 1977) suggests that the cognitive tasks presented by multiple-choice items may be substantially different for nontraditional students and for students familiar with the standard dialect. If this difference proves to be more than theoretical for students whose language experience lies outside the cultural mainstream, the multiple-choice test may be less valid as an indicator of writing ability for such students than it is for mainstream students. To the extent that multiple-choice tests emphasize grammar and usage, they may also be less valid as measures of these students' writing ability than assessments tapping a more comprehensive range of writing skills and abilities.

In many respects, the holistically scored writing sample fares better than the multiple-choice test with respect to validity. As a performance measure drawing on the broader range of skills and strategies necessary for actually generating a piece of writing, the writing sample has frequently been seen as a more valid form of assessment. It allows students to demonstrate skills not tapped by the multiple-choice test and more compatible with the current theoretical construct for writing and with desirable practice in writing instruction. It has therefore been seen by some writing assessment practitioners as a stand-alone format for more valid assessment, especially when more than one writing sample is used, and by others as essential to the validity of writing assessments based on the combination of multiple-choice tests and writing samples.

However, concerns about the relatively low reliability of the writing sample have persisted, especially in the measurement community (Breland et al., 1987; Conlon, 1986), and with some justification. Some of the factors contributing to this low reliability arise from the complex and generative nature of the task of writing. Performance in response to a single prompt for writing, which involves the complexities of understanding and interpreting a task and generating text in response to it, varies far more from one occasion to another and from one prompt to another than does performance on a multiple-choice test made up of a relatively large number of discrete tasks, each of which typically requires little more than recognizing errors or choosing among alternative phrasings. Awareness of these sources of variation in the test taker's performance and of similar sources of variation in raters' perceptions of writing has led even strong advocates of direct assessment to recognize the limits of a single sample of writing (Cooper, 1977; Greenberg & Witte, 1988; Odell, 1981). Even with the high interrater reliabilities now possible in well-run holistic scoring sessions drawing on the expertise of experienced raters, the estimated test reliability for a single essay scored twice is insufficient to fully justify the use of a single essay as the sole basis for important judgments about students' academic careers (see Breland et al., 1987, Table 5.4, p. 27).

Thus the compromise has persisted. Multiple-choice tests of writing offer reliability, efficiency, economy, some contribution to validity, and a convenient basis for statistical comparisons from one test to another, even though they measure only a limited number of subskills for writing, and measure them only indirectly. The impromptu writing sample provides a demonstration of the writer's handling of both subskills for writing and the larger-order skills involved in actually composing text: generating and developing ideas, organizing, establishing connections within the text, and finding a tone and rhetorical stance appropriate to the topic and audience. In addition, use of the writing sample in assessment sends a clear message that writing performance is important, and that grammar and usage are not sufficient proxies for actual writing (Conlon, 1986).

What We Have Learned from Our Experience with Direct Assessment

In the last decades, our collective experience with writing assessments based on the combination of the multiple-choice test and impromptu writing sample has led to genuine advances in knowledge and practice. In recent years, as we have become increasingly aware of the complexities of performance in writing and increasingly skeptical of multiple-choice formats, we have focused proportionally greater attention on direct assessment based on the writing sample. The efforts of researchers and test designers have brought increased awareness of the procedures necessary to enhance the reliability and validity of direct assessment (Lucas & Carlson, 1989). They have also enhanced our understanding of the performance required of writers not only in assessments but in other, more typical situations for academic writing (Faigley et al., 1985; Ruth & Murphy, 1988).

We can estimate how much we have learned from our experience with writing assessment, particularly direct assessment based on the writing sample, by looking at the sizable and rapidly growing bibliography on writing assessment. Within that bibliography we find, in addition to the early formulations of issues for direct assessment (Cooper, 1981; Cooper & Odell, 1977), works that describe and examine the practices and procedures of prompt design and holistic evaluation (i.e., Brossell, 1983; Freedman, 1981; Hoetker, 1982; Ruth &

Murphy, 1988; White, 1985), increasingly sophisticated treatments of the history and issues of writing assessment (i.e., Greenberg, Weiner, & Donovan, 1986), and historical retrospectives looking at the last decades as a basis for future directions in writing assessment (i.e., Faigley et al., 1985; Keech-Lucas, 1988a, 1988b). Some of these efforts, especially those focusing on the cognitive processes of writers responding to topics and of raters evaluating writers' performance, have contributed to our reconceptualizations of the skills and strategies involved in writing in both test and nontest situations.

We have also made a number of changes in assessment practice for the purpose of improving the measurement properties of holistically scored writing samples. We attempt to minimize or compensate for those factors most likely to create variation in writing performance from one occasion to another. We try to present prompts that are immediately accessible to all test takers — whatever their individual interests, knowledge, or cultural experience — and that can be dealt with in the limited time available for writing. We avoid topics that are likely to evoke emotional responses on the part of the writer or the rater of the paper. We ask that test takers all write under comparable conditions, with the same time allotment and in an environment free of distraction or interruption.

In the interest of reliable and equitable assessment, we have in effect streamlined the writing experience and removed from it the particulars of context in which it typically occurs. We have created within the constraints of the testing situation the circumstances for a limited performance in writing that we expect will correspond to other writing experiences — a simulated, universalized performance that we use to predict performance on a number of other occasions and in a variety of other circumstances for writing.

We have further increased the reliability of the writing sample and the usefulness of the information it provides by attending to the ways in which we conduct evaluation sessions and report the results. We use controlled procedures in the evaluation of writing samples; we develop shared sets of standards for the scoring of papers; and we ask that papers be scored anonymously and independently by individuals with broad experience of student writing and few eccentricities in judging its quality. We publish examples of writing accompanied by analyses that make public — for teachers, students, and the community — the criteria that inform the raters' holistic judgments.

Altogether, we have made significant changes, in both research and practice. Yet in many respects we have not, until recently, recognized the assumptions about writing implied in the traditional model for assessment — indeed, in any model that depends on a single impromptu writing sample for much of its validity. As Faigley et al. (1985) have observed in the case of writing assessment in general, "practice has far outrun theory" (p. 205). We are now able to see more clearly the assumptions underlying traditional approaches to writing assessment in part because we are moving away from them. With the clarity of hindsight, we are now able as well to examine their implications.

New Views of Writing and the Assumptions Behind Traditional Formats for Assessment

From the perspective of our new understanding of writing and writing processes, the assumptions about writing underlying the traditional model for writing assessment become more apparent; so, too, do the model's limitations. Whereas we once regarded a piece of writing in a single mode or for a single purpose to be a sufficient sample, we now see it as insufficient to represent the variety of modes and purposes for writing (Emig, 1982; Greenberg & Witte, 1988). The timed, controlled conditions for writing that once seemed the means to ensure equal opportunity to all test takers now seem unnatural limits that preclude use of the processes, among them interactions with others, that we now understand to be part of most writing (Polin, 1980). The prompts that we so carefully designed for equal accessibility are now seen to cut off the opening explorations of a topic in which writers find a way into it that engages their interests and allows them to use their knowledge and skills to best advantage. Our reluctance to evoke emotional responses even seems at times to have precluded the kind of personal engagement that is at the heart of really good student writing. Ironically, many of the efforts we made to enhance the reliability of the writing sample — especially those aimed at streamlining and universalizing the writing experience — appear now to limit the value of the assessment (Keech-Lucas, 1988b).

Questions About the Validity of the Impromptu Writing Sample

From this perspective, the traditional formats for writing assessment, including the writing sample, seem insufficient. The skills measured by multiple-choice tests of writing seem more remote than ever from the skills required for complex performances in writing. More critically, however, the streamlined performance represented by the single impromptu writing sample, which corresponds to only a small portion of what we now understand to be involved in writing, no longer seems a strong basis for validity. Performance on the writing sample no longer appears to be an adequate representation of the accepted theoretical construct for writing; nor does it seem an adequate representation of students' likely experiences with writing, past or future, or with the skills and strategies called upon in those experiences. In addition, the view of writing encouraged by the assessment does not reflect the instructional goals required by our new and more complex views of writing.

The implication, when we take all of these observations into account, is that the changes in our views of writing amount to a shift in the construct to be measured in writing assessment. It is no longer possible to claim that "an adequate essay test of writing ability is valid by definition" (Eley, 1955, p. 11) or to trust in the belief that "good writing is good writing." What we are experiencing, in fact, is a mismatch between the complexities of the conceptual framework for writing that we find in current research and practice and the simpler construct implied by traditional approaches to writing assessment, including the writing sample. Very likely we are also seeing the signs of a growing incompatibility between our views of writing and the constraints necessary to satisfy the requirements of traditional psychometrics — in particular, of reliability and validity narrowly defined.

Perhaps we can better understand the full extent of our dilemma by seeing it in schematic terms. First, let us go back to the multiple-choice test, the writing sample, and the relationship between them in the traditional model for assessment. As indicated earlier, the multiple-choice test draws on discrete skills required to recognize correct and incorrect or better and worse language use presented in the context of multiple, largely unrelated, and quite brief examples of writing. The inclusion in the multiple-choice test of a relatively large number of such items addressing a variety of skills at the sentence and sometimes intersentence level was once thought a sufficient basis for content validity; in this view, the items were seen as sampling fully if indirectly the universe of skills necessary for writing. With our more complex and enlarged views of writing, however, the domain sampled by the multiple-choice test appears far more constricted. We now see the multiple-choice test as drawing on relatively low-level skills (such as recognition of agreement or lack of agreement between subject and verb or between pronoun and antecedent), which we are now likely to understand as subskills or component skills necessary for writing performance.

From our new perspective, we see the writing sample as drawing on a variety of skills and strategies related to one another, many of them beyond the scope of the multiple-choice test, with any particular writing sample from any particular student drawing on some but not all of the skills tapped by a particular multiple-choice test. For example, a prompt calling for narrative writing based on personal experience may not require the writer to deal with parallelism in sentence structure. Or a particular writer responding to such a prompt may choose a rhetorical strategy that does not involve writing sentences calling for parallelism.

In schematic terms, we might see the domains covered by the writing sample and by the multiple-choice test as circles that are partially overlapping but not concentric (see Figure 7–1).

FIGURE 7–1   Relationship of Domains Covered by the Multiple-Choice Test of Writing and the Writing Sample

Multiple-Choice Test

Writing Sample

In earlier views of writing and assessment in which the multiple-choice test and the writing sample were assumed to be measuring the same skills, the circle for the domain sampled in the multiple-choice test might have been seen—if we had examined our assumptions carefully—as more or less congruent with the circle for the writing sample. The two formats would have been understood to be measuring roughly the same construct, defined generally as writing ability. We now see the circles as overlapping but not congruent, and the formats as measuring some but not all of the same skills. Further, we are more aware of the differences in skills required for performance on the two kinds of tests; we make a stronger distinction between the skills required to recognize correct and incorrect language use and those required to generate text in response to a prompt.

Getting the Picture on Validity: The Mismatch Between the Model for Assessment and Current Concepts of Writing

Now let us place this model for assessment within the conceptual framework for literacy suggested by Valencia, McGinley, and Pearson (1990, p. 129) in their discussion of the need for forms of literacy assessment that reflect our current understanding of literacy and learning. In this framework, reading and writing are seen as holistic processes drawing on a number of specific but related subskills, such as decoding or comprehension skills for reading and understanding of grammar or principles of organization for writing. The holistic process of reading and writing, in turn, are perceived as serving and shaped by particular functions and goals in the life of the individual using them. Thus, for example, if a person writes on one occasion primarily to gain clarity or insight about a difficult issue and on another to communicate what is already known, it is likely that the processes and strategies the person uses will vary across the two occasions (see Figure 7–2).

FIGURE 7–2   Valencia et al.: Dimensions of Reading and Writing

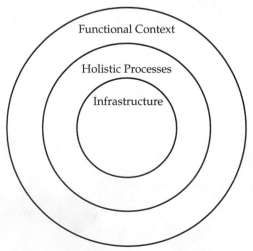

The relationship between subskills and holistic processes is represented in the Valencia et al. framework by two concentric circles, the inner circle representing subskills (described as "the infrastructure for reading and writing") and the surrounding circle representing the holistic processes of reading and writing. A third concentric circle surrounds the other two, representing the ways in which context informs holistic processes as they are shaped to serve particular functions in the life of the reader or writer.

If we focus only on writing for the moment (with apologies to Valencia et al.) and superimpose our figure for writing assessment on the framework, we can place the multiple-choice test entirely within the innermost circle of discrete subskills. Without altering the relationship of the writing sample to the multiple-choice test, we can place the writing sample within the circle representing holistic processes and overlapping into the innermost circle representing subskills for writing (see Figure 7–3).

The relationship of the area of the writing sample circle to the area of the two inner circles fits with what we know from research, from discourse theory, and from experience with prompt design and analysis of student writing samples. It reflects our current awareness that the skills and strategies needed in writing for one mode or purpose are not necessarily those needed in writing for another (Greenberg & Witte, 1988; Pringle & Freedman, 1985). It corresponds to what we know about the knowledge of text structure and discourse type required by each mode or purpose for writing — that each mode or purpose requires different knowledge (Pringle & Freedman, 1985; Scardamalia & Bereiter, 1985). It even allows us to see that the skills and strategies required may differ from any one writing task to another, or from one writer to another, depending on how familiar the writer is with content related to the topic and on how the writer redefines the task in the course of writing.

FIGURE 7–3   Relationship of Domains Covered by the Multiple-Choice Test of Writing and Writing Sample to Dimensions of Writing

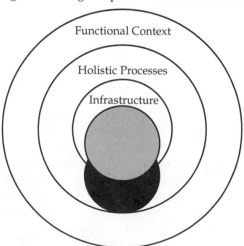

In this respect, the figure is consistent with observations such as those reported by Breland et al. (1987). In the Breland study, in which the same groups of first-year college students wrote on six topics, the writing samples showed evidence of students using different rhetorical strategies and cognitive processes for each of the topics, and even for the same topic. For example, the topic that asked for persuasive writing on an issue involving trends over time called on repeated use of both comparative structures and the vocabulary of comparison, neither of which was evoked to any great extent in the other five topics, and the organizational structure for narrative papers varied with the course of events described. The differences in performance across purposes and topics were observed by researchers and by readers scoring the papers; they were also reflected in the factor analysis (see Breland et al., 1987, pp. 19–22 and 40–47).

We can also see from Figure 7–3 that even if we focus only on writing independent of reading, the traditional formats for assessment address only a portion of the subskills and strategies represented in our new construct for writing. An assessment addressing all of the construct would be represented by a series of circles (and possibly other shapes) covering the whole of both the subskills and holistic processes circles — or, in nonschematic terms, by a variety of assessments, including multiple samples of writing generated for a variety of modes and purposes and written under both test and nontest conditions.

Whereas we might once have seen the results of performance on the multiple-choice test or the writing sample or both as a basis for generalizing to all other performance in writing, we are now reluctant to do so. The arguments for the predictive validity of these two formats for writing assessment, arguments based on correlations between scores derived from the assessments and statistical indicators of performance in other contexts, now seem beside the point; they do not take into account what we know to be important about writing. Again we see in the figure the disjuncture between the assumptions and methods of the traditional model for assessment and our new concepts of writing.

The limitations of the traditional formats for writing assessment become even more striking if we look in Figure 7–3 at the relationship of the circles representing the multiple-choice test and the writing sample to the third and outermost of the concentric circles from the Valencia et al. framework, the one representing processes related to the communicative contexts for writing. If we understand this outermost circle to include ways in which contexts for writing enrich and inform the processes for writing, we see represented in it the most substantial of the challenges to traditional views of assessment. We can see in this graphic representation what we have lost by streamlining and universalizing writing performance to fit the constraints of test conditions. We discover that we have excluded from the assessment many of the experiences and resources that motivate and shape writing (see Johnston, 1985), especially for novice writers and for writers who do not easily see themselves as participants in the academic discourse community.

The figure tells us that by cutting off performance in writing from social and communicative contexts, both multiple-choice test and writing sample formats eliminate the collaborative exploration and problem solving that enable many student writers to engage with issues, to identify their own perspectives, and to discover and shape a topic appropriate to that perspective. These formats also eliminate the opportunity for the writer to draw on private explorations of particular interests and knowledge in personal and expressive writing, unless the topic of the prompt happens to coincide with one the writer has already begun to explore. Also absent from performance in either format are opportunities to try out strategies and reshape ideas orally before committing them finally to paper. The model for assessment represented in the multiple-choice and writing sample formats thus deprives many student writers of the advantages that come with writing for genuine communicative purposes and contexts.

The loss of communicative purpose and context is likely to be most damaging for students who are relatively unfamiliar with the mainstream culture and the discourse of academic settings. We have become increasingly aware in recent years of the discomfort experienced by these students when they are asked to write in settings in which the implicit expectations for discourse are unfamiliar to them (see Heath, 1983; Rafoth & Rubin, 1988; Rose, 1989; Taylor, 1989). With our greater understanding of the interaction between cognitive and social dimensions of expertise in writing, we have also become more attentive to the differences between the strategies used by these writers and those used by writers familiar with academic discourse. If students with less expertise fall back on more general strategies for writing, and if these general strategies are related to cultural expectations for discourse, as seems to be the case (Carter, 1990), then students from nonmainstream cultures may be especially disadvantaged by the lack of social and instructional context in traditional formats and conditions for assessment (see Johnston, 1987).

Yet the figure does not tell the whole story. In addition to the limitations made visible in Figure 7–3, a further limitation becomes apparent when we match our current concepts of writing with the construct implied in and the information provided by traditional formats for writing assessment. Neither the multiple-choice test nor the impromptu writing sample provides a basis in the assessment for obtaining information about metacognitive aspects of writing, information that is essential to instruction and to the writer's development (Bereiter & Scardamalia, 1987; Campione & Brown, 1990; Scardamalia & Bereiter, 1985). Neither yields information about the ways in which writers monitor the processes and strategies they use in writing performance. The impromptu writing sample draws on only the most constrained of the processes and strategies available to writers in other situations, and it provides no opportunity for writers to demonstrate the ways in which they modify processes and strategies in relation to their understanding of the goals and conditions for writing.

TAKING STOCK: THE CURRENT STATUS OF WRITING ASSESSMENT

Altogether then, the views of writing evident in research and increasingly evident in instruction pose serious challenges to traditional approaches to writing assessment and to the assumptions behind them. The multiple-choice test and the writing sample seem clearly insufficient for measuring writing ability as we now understand it. More significantly, the concept of writing implied in the two formats and in combinations of them no longer approximates the concepts for writing evident in research and forward-looking instruction.

What does this state of affairs mean for writing assessments? Are we to conclude that neither multiple-choice tests nor writing samples can ever be used in a writing assessment without risk to its validity? That what we have learned in the last decades about enhancing the measurement value of direct assessment is somehow worthless? That our careful attention to the characteristics of writing tasks or to the procedures for scoring has been wasted? Not at all. The achievements of writing assessment in recent decades are real. No responsible educator would want to see a return to evaluations of writing based on the private idiosyncrasies of the individual evaluator (see Keech-Lucas, 1988b). Nor would we want to see assessment based on any of the shared, but largely unexamined, assumptions about literacy and learning evident in previous eras of writing assessment (see Witte, Trachsel, & Walters, 1986). But the advances we have made do not answer the challenges we now face.

There is considerable work to be done. To facilitate that work, we need to develop a conceptual framework for writing assessment that reflects our current understanding of writing. Within that framework we need to examine the limitations of the traditional formats for assessment so that we understand what our assessments can tell us and what they cannot tell us about student ability. If we determine, as we have already in many instances, that our new views of writing are too complex to be served well by any single approach to assessment, then we will need to think about the ways in which different formats for assessment—including some yet to be developed—can provide us with information about different aspects of writers' skills, processes, and strategies. We will then be able to explore possible ways in which the different kinds of information obtained from different formats can be used to serve different assessment purposes. In addition, we will be able to think about ways in which information from different assessments can be combined to create more comprehensive descriptions of writers' knowledge and abilities.

Such a conceptual framework for writing assessment will also help us to estimate the value of new approaches to assessment, to understand which aspects of writers' knowledge and abilities they address, and what kinds of inferences they can be expected to support. As new approaches are developed in both large-scale and classroom-based assessments, they can be placed within the conceptual framework. Their purpose and value in promoting the comprehensive understanding necessary to teaching and learning, as well as to institutional decisions and research, can then be determined. In addition, where aspects of the writer's experience in writing or development as a writer are not addressed by available approaches to assessment, we can identify the need for further information and perhaps the possible means by which we might obtain it.

Thinking about such a conceptual framework for writing assessment and about the approaches to assessment that might fall within it require a substantial change in our understanding of the issues in educational assessment. If it is true that the limitations of the two most prevalent formats for writing assessment reflect an incompatibility between complex views of writing and the requirements of traditional views of measurement, as has been suggested here, then a new perspective on educational measurement is essential for richer and more comprehensive approaches to writing assessment. In fact, if assessments are to be created that truly reflect our new understanding of writing and writing processes, we will need, in addition to new methodology, nothing less than a redefinition of the very purposes and roles of assessment within our educational institutions.

New Views of the Meaning and Functions of Assessment

Many of the concerns about the limitations and effects of assessment that are felt by educators and researchers focusing on writing are shared by educators and researchers in other fields, including educational measurement. Indeed, some of the same intellectual and societal concerns are at work across academic disciplines and research communities. In particular, the recent developments in cognitive psychology that have stimulated new perspectives on writing have brought new views of intellectual behavior and learning to all of education, including the field of assessment. Similarly, the emphasis in the educational reform literature of the last decade on students as active learners and on teachers as professionals has affected researchers and practitioners across the entire educational community, including those involved in assessment. In addition, the sense of social responsibility that stimulates our attempts in the field of writing to better understand and serve the needs of minority populations is shared by educators in other academic disciplines and in the assessment community. It may well be time, therefore, to survey the changes in perspective evident in current thinking about assessment and to incorporate these perspectives in our attempts to shape new approaches to the assessment of writing.

New Views of Validity

Within the educational assessment community in recent years, considerable attention has been given to the concept of validity. As a result, validity is now seen as a single, unified concept in which the construct to be measured is central to all other considerations (Cole & Moss, 1989; Cronbach, 1988; Messick, 1989a, 1989b; Moss, 1992). At one time the validity of a test might have been discussed in terms of one or more kinds of validity, each seen as independent of and more or less equal in value to the others: content validity, construct validity, criterion-related validity (including predictive and concurrent validity), and face validity. In the last two decades, however, validity has been increasingly seen as taking on a central focus: the inferences about a test taker that are derived from performance on a test. (See Moss, 1992, for a comprehensive review and analysis of emerging perspectives on validity.) Investigations of validity involve the ongoing evaluation of such inferences on the basis of evidence derived from multiple considerations. The investigations may draw on the methodologies associated with the earlier approaches to validity, but to be consistent with current views, they must consider validity in integrated and comprehensive terms and always in relation to the theoretical construct — what the assessment is intended to measure. In addition, the evidence for validity must be examined in relation to the social consequences for the inferences made about test takers and the actions taken on the basis of those inferences (Cole & Moss, 1989; Messick, 1989a, 1989b; Moss, 1992).

Thus, the investigation of validity is seen as including far more than traditional content validity studies, which were essentially examinations of the coverage of the subject represented by the test's content, and also as more than the comparisons of performances within and across tests that have characterized many studies of predictive validity. Most important, however, is that all evidence for validity is to be interpreted in relation to the theoretical construct, the purpose for the assessment, and therefore the inferences derived from it, and the social consequences.

What this view suggests for writing assessment is that our concerns about validity are legitimate. The mismatch between the current theoretical constructs for writing and the construct implied by traditional formats for assessment casts serious doubt on the validity of traditional approaches to writing assessment. Furthermore, that doubt is not entirely relieved by the familiar arguments for the content validity of the multiple-choice writing test as a broad sampling of writing subskills or for criterion validity as indicated by correlational studies showing a high degree of correspondence between performance on multiple-choice tests and writing samples. In addition, our concerns about the possible deleterious effects of conventional writing assessment formats on students outside the mainstream of academic culture no longer appear peripheral; they are central to validity, especially if those effects derive from misrepresentation of the construct of writing.

Current thinking about validity suggests that problems with a test's validity, especially those likely to be associated with adverse social consequences, be investigated by looking at the ways in which the construct to be measured is represented in the test. In the case of writing, we should think about whether our assessments adequately represent writing as we understand it. If an assessment fails to include important and relevant dimensions or facets of the construct — as we have said traditional writing assessments do — it is said to suffer from "construct underrepresentation." If the assessment is easier or more difficult for some test takers than for others for reasons irrelevant to the construct—as we suspect may be the case with our traditional writing assessment formats—then it is said to exhibit "construct-irrelevant variance" (Messick, 1989a). Similarly, if the information derived from an assessment is more valid for some groups of the test-taking population than for others—if it exhibits "differential validity"—the assessment can be said to show test bias (Cole & Moss, 1989).

These criteria for validity can be quite useful as we investigate traditional formats for writing assessment and search for new ones. What they suggest is that our assessments, and the inferences about writers' abilities we derive from them, must take into account both the current construct for writing in its entirety and the possible distortions in our estimates of writers' abilities that derive from limitations in our formats for assessment.

Also useful to our investigations of existing and experimental formats for assessment is a shift in methods used for construct validation (Messick, 1989a). The historical development associated with emerging views of validity is moving the field away from a primary emphasis on patterns of relationships, such as the correlational studies of predictive validity so often used to justify multiple-choice tests of writing, toward methods more likely to be supportive of complex performances in writing. Studies of predictive validity are still seen as contributing to investigations of construct validity, but there is considerably more interest in insights to be derived from studies of the processes underlying performance on the assessment and studies of test takers' performances over time and across groups and settings.

Following upon the new definitions of validity in which all considerations are related to the construct, the inferences made, and the social consequences of those inferences, a further expansion of the concept of validity has recently become evident—one that has far-reaching implications, especially if we combine it with our emerging sense of the new constructs for writing. Pointing out the unfortunate effects of indirect assessments on teaching and learning, Frederiksen and Collins (1989) suggest that our notions of validity be expanded to include the effects of an assessment on the educational system in which it occurs. For an assessment to demonstrate "systemic validity," they argue, it must support instruction and learning that foster development of the cognitive skills the assessment is intended to measure.

In this view, indirect assessments, despite their purported economy, efficiency, and objectivity, are seen as extracting a high price in terms of such effects on teaching and learning as the emphasis on isolated, low-level skills and the displacement of skills and strategies necessary to higher-order thinking, problem solving, and metacognitive awareness. Direct assessments, however, have the advantage from this perspective of being based on performances that can address the intended cognitive skills directly and incorporate not only the product to be created but the process of creating it. They also provide a basis for developing awareness among teachers and learners of the characteristics important to good performances and products. The processes involved in creating the assessment, especially if they occur within the educational institution they serve, provide opportunities for teachers and learners to become aware of the expectations and criteria for performance.

This expansion of the concept of validity to include system effects has a number of implications for writing assessment. It means, first of all, that in many respects the struggle to establish the legitimacy of direct assessment has been won. Thus, the procedures associated with the direct assessment of writing are seen from this perspective as exemplary for assessments in other areas of the curriculum (Frederiksen & Collins, 1989; Linn, Baker, & Dunbar, 1991). The setting of representative tasks, the identification of criteria and standards for judging performance on the tasks, the development of libraries of sample performances illustrating how the scoring criteria have been applied, and the involvement of all parties to the assessment, including classroom teachers and eventually students, have the effect of emphasizing the skills and strategies the assessment is intended to address. In short, the procedures involved in direct assessments of writing are seen as having great potential for enhancing systemic validity.

Moreover, the concept of systemic validity can help us find direction for the writing assessments of the future. If we take from systemic validity the sense of assessment as a set of contextualized experiences and procedures, many of them already familiar to us from direct assessments of writing, and if we combine that sense with our understanding of the recently expanded constructs for writing, we can begin to address the challenges for assessment that we now experience. We can envision richer approaches to writing assessment, approaches that reflect the current construct for writing, that are more closely integrated with instruction, and more immediately useful to teachers and students.

Broader Concepts of Assessments and What They Should Measure

Within the educational assessment research community there have been indications in the last several years of dissatisfaction with the limited perspective on human intelligence underlying traditional standardized tests and implied by the psychometric methods that support them (N. Frederiksen, 1984, 1986). Increased attention to the cognitive processes involved in taking tests has brought increased awareness of the limitations of test and item formats in both multiple-choice and essay tests. Multiple-choice tests are seen as unsuitable for the measurement of higher-order skills, and essay exams as too far removed from those real-life situations in which the test taker will eventually need to use the skills tested. In addition, most test-taking situations, with their controlled, timed, strictly monitored settings and their expectations for "right answers," are seen as restricting the use of cognitive processes because they allow little opportunity to reformulate a problem or develop an original solution and virtually no opportunity to deal with the kinds of ill-structured problems we encounter in real life (N. Frederiksen, 1986).

Clearly, such criticisms of prevailing test formats echo those so often raised for traditional approaches to writing assessment. In fact, much of this argument is consistent with the discussion earlier in this chapter of the limitations of multiple-choice and writing sample formats for writing assessment. Two suggestions associated with this argument seem especially applicable to the current challenges for writing assessment. One such suggestion is that conventional tests be supplemented with simulations of real-life problems that allow for some of the open-endedness characteristic of responses to real-life situations, but "with enough structure and standardization to make data interpretable" (N. Frederiksen, 1986, p. 446). The second is that simulated performances and scoring systems be developed that yield qualitative descriptions of the strategies and processes evident in the test takers' responses rather than a single-score report (N. Frederiksen, 1986).

Cognitive Psychology Perspectives on Measurement

The influence of cognitive psychology is clearly evident in the perspectives on validity and assessment already described. But to fully understand the implications of cognitive psychology for measurement, and for writing assessment in particular, we need to look more directly at its influence on measurement theory.

One of the ways in which cognitive psychology influences educational measurement is through the methods it provides for examining the constructs measured by tests (Snow & Lohman, 1989). Focusing on the skills, processes, and strategies used in responding to assessment tasks, the methods of cognitive psychology aim to identify more precisely what a task or set of tasks measures than do the correlational studies and factor analyses of more traditional psychometrics. They also attempt to make distinctions among the component behaviors that contribute to successful or unsuccessful performance. As suggested earlier in the discussion on new views of validity, the methodology provided by cognitive psychology thus addresses issues of construct validity in ways that are more supportive of rich and complex forms of writing assessment than we were earlier methodologies.

Research in cognitive psychology also leads to a more detailed understanding of learning and of the ways in which instruction — and assessment — can promote learning (Snow, 1989). Combined with closer examination of the constructs measured by assessment and increased awareness of the issues of context, this research is beginning to help us identify more precisely the limitations of existing assessments and the likely characteristics of more promising approaches. Particularly relevant to writing assessment are studies using information-processing models to examine performance. Studies investigating how and how well individuals process information, or how they use controlled and automated modes of processing and shift between them, for example, will eventually inform the development of models for assessment, including writing assessment, that are truly helpful to learning and informative to instruction.

Not surprisingly, the perspectives on learning and performance developed by cognitive psychologists have led to increased awareness of the shortcomings of the psychometric models underlying most standardized tests.

From a cognitive perspective, conventional psychometric approaches are deficient because they lack a theory of learning (Snow & Lohman, 1989). The result is that tests and test items have no inherent psychological justification in terms of the processes they evoke in the test taker. Purely psychometric models are therefore seen as incapable of addressing the meaning of test performance except in terms of statistical properties. To the extent that conventional psychometric models de facto imply a view of learning, it is learning as the aggregation of discrete skills and knowledge, a view inconsistent with recent research in cognitive psychology (Mislevy, 1993; Shepard, 1991; Wolf, Bixby, Glenn, & Gardner, 1991).

A further criticism of conventional test theory from this perspective is that it does not take into account the differences among test takers that affect their performance (see Snow & Lohman, 1989). The individuals taking tests use different strategies on different tests and even on the items within a test, depending, among other things, on ability level, level of expertise with the tasks presented, and test taking or learning style. Yet these differences are not reflected in test scores because they are not captured by psychometric models of the test-taking experience. In this sense, test scores appear to indicate differences among test takers along a single dimension, while the real differences may need to be described in terms of multiple dimensions (Snow & Lohman, 1989). Without some differentiation among these dimensions and an indication of the extent to which each is represented in the score, the meaning of the score cannot be understood in terms that are genuinely useful to learners and to the institutions that serve them.

To address the shortcomings of conventional test theory and create the foundations for new approaches to assessment, a number of researchers in educational measurement have begun to lay the groundwork for a theory of measurement "more suited to the new constructs" (Snow, 1989, p. 8), one that "can provide a theoretical basis for developing new assessment methods" (N. Frederiksen, 1990, p. ix) and can "link testing with the cognitive process of learning" (Mislevy, 1993). That theory will support a greater variety of assessment approaches than does traditional test theory, because it will recognize a variety of purposes for assessment, among them the need to provide information directly useful for instruction and learning, and because it will recognize multiple goals for instruction and learning (Snow, 1989). It is likely to be a theory far more supportive of assessment compatible with our current construct for writing than traditional psychometric models have been.

Some researchers keenly aware of the role that processes and strategies play in learning have already begun to develop new models for assessment as well as the research base necessary to support them. One such model, dynamic assessment, focuses on how students actually learn and how well they are able to use resources made available to them (Campione & Brown, 1990). The purpose of this model is to "assess as directly as possible the psychological processes involved in task performance" (p. 142), thereby providing a more accurate basis for predicting future academic performance than standardized tests. The method in dynamic assessment, which combines instruction with assessment, is to provide a small-scale cooperative learning environment in which instructional support is supplied as needed by the learner, and to estimate the learner's potential levels of performance by taking into account the extent and kind of support supplied. This approach appears to be especially useful in estimating the capabilities of students who have not had the advantages of rich environments for learning. The data from the research on this approach indicate that "estimates of [students'] initial response to instruction and of their ability to make use of newly acquired resources are powerful tools" (p. 167) in determining which students are likely to do well and which are likely to experience difficulties.

The Call for Contextualized Assessment

The movement toward new theories of measurement is complemented by a movement within curriculum and school reform toward alternative models for assessment (Berlak et al., 1992; Gardner, 1988; Glaser, 1988; Haney & Madaus, 1989; Mitchell, 1989; Resnick & Resnick, 1985; Stiggins, 1988; Wiggins, 1989). In many of these alternative models, assessment is based on the performance of complex and meaningful tasks that are related to real-world contexts and are themselves valuable to learning (Archbald & Newmann, 1988; Gitomer, 1993; Mitchell, 1992; Wiggins, 1989). The performances draw on knowledge and skills integrated within the context of purposeful problem solving, which is accomplished in collaboration with others and within a relatively extended and flexible time frame. The tasks are challenging, but support is provided as needed, enabling all performers to demonstrate some degree of success.

The performances central to these models of assessment are likely to culminate in production of discourse or artifacts that yield evidence of achievement, but the products are not the exclusive focus for evaluation. The evaluation involves informed judgment on the part of knowledgeable witnesses to the performance (teachers, for example) who attend to the essentials of performance, including the strategies and processes used to bring it about. Evaluative judgments are expressed in the form of scoring systems built on multiple indicators of achievement or indicators of achievement described in multiple facets. The criteria informing the judgments are public, shared, and eventually internalized by performers and evaluators alike. The tasks for the assessment are consistent with individual and institutional goals for learning, and the purpose of assessment is to enable learners to discover and demonstrate what they can do and what they might work on in the future.

Possible models for contextualized assessment are being explored, as are the issues involved in their implementation, in discussions and projects extending across academic disciplines and educational institutions. Some of these assessments are built around hands-on, problem-solving projects, as in the science projects developed by the National Assessment of Educational Progress and the Connecticut Assessment of Educational Progress, in the New York science and mathematics assessments, and in the science and mathematics projects in the British Assessment Performance Unit. Others, especially in reading and writing, but also in other areas of the curriculum, involve students in the creation of portfolios. A number of schools, school districts, states, and college writing programs from Juneau, Alaska to Fort Worth, Texas and from California to Vermont are developing portfolio assessments (see Belanoff & Dickson, 1991; Murphy & Smith, 1991; Tierney, Carter, & Desai, 1991; Yancey, 1992).

Such models have strong potential for addressing the limitations of traditional approaches to literacy assessment, including those identified in this chapter. They represent a movement toward assessments that are "ecological" in the ways described by Keech-Lucas (1988a, 1988b): They have a positive effect on the learning environment, they take into account the whole environment of the learner, and they increase the amount, quality, and usefulness of the information provided to teachers and students. These models also point toward assessment which exhibits the qualities that Valencia et al. indicate as necessary for richer forms of literacy assessment — assessment that is "continuous, multidimensional, collaborative, knowledge-based, and authentic" (1990, p. 144). Equally important is that the use of such models reflects significant transformations in the expectations for assessment held by the institutions that use them, transformations consistent with current discussions of school reform and restructuring (Berlak et al., 1992; Camp, 1992b; Darling-Hammond & Ascher, 1991; Newmann, 1991).

MOVING TOWARD NEW MODELS FOR WRITING ASSESSMENT

The challenges involved in developing models of assessment compatible with our new understanding of writing will not be met easily or quickly. Clearly, though, we are not alone in our effort. Educators and designers of assessments in other academic disciplines face many of the same challenges, and researchers in educational measurement are engaged with many of the same issues. It may be helpful to consider briefly the resources we have available to us, both in the research literature on measurement and in our previous experience with writing assessment.

Resources for a New Conceptual Framework for Writing Assessment

The work of several of the researchers already cited in this chapter can provide us with guidelines for new approaches to assessment. Frederiksen and Collins describe several "Principles for the Design of Systemically Valid Testing" (1989, p. 30). Snow identifies three major "Issues for Assessment Development" (1989, pp. 10–11). Archbald and Newmann identify critical issues for alternative assessments (1988, p. vi), as well as criteria for the tasks presented (1988, pp. 2–4). Wiggins describes "Criteria of Authenticity" for contextualized assessment (1989, pp. 711–712). Linn, Baker, and Dunbar (1991) identify a set of criteria to be applied in evaluating complex, performance-based assessments. Valencia et al. indicate "Important Attributes of Classroom and Individual Assessment" (1990, pp. 2–4), and Keech-Lucas describes criteria for ecological validity in writing assessment (1988b, p. 5). Although these various sets of criteria arise out of different perspectives, they are remarkably similar in the issues they address. They constitute the beginnings of a literature to which we can refer in our efforts to shape writing assessments compatible with the construct of writing as we currently understand it.

The principles behind such established psychometric concerns as reliability and validity can also inform us in our design and evaluation of new approaches to assessment, although they need to be understood and applied in new ways. Principles of fairness, equity, and generalizability still pertain to assessments based on complex performance in writing; the challenge now is to apply them in ways that lead far beyond the narrow focus on score reliability and the constricted definitions of validity that characterized earlier discussions of the measurement properties of writing assessments (see Gitomer, 1993; Linn, Baker, & Dunbar, 1991; Moss, 1992). We will need to think and observe carefully, for example, to determine whether the writing performance required for our new assessments are equally appropriate for students drawing on different cultural and linguistic experiences. Similarly, we will need to consider which kinds of performances are central to students' learning about writing, what kinds of information can legitimately be derived from those performances, and what generalizations about students' ability and development can be made on the basis of the information derived. Although we do not yet have methodologies that tell us how to apply these principles, the principles themselves can help guide us until the methodologies are developed.

A further resource in our attempt to create richer forms of assessment lies in the research that has been done on the processes and strategies involved in writing. The work of researchers such as Flower and Hayes, Beaugrande, and Scardamalia and Bereiter, for example, will help us to develop models for assessment that inform both teachers and student writers about the ways in which the writers' processes and strategies contribute or fail to contribute to the success of the writing performance. In moving toward these assessments, we will be building on and enlarging the scope of research like that of Ruth and Murphy, which has focused on analysis of the demands of writing tasks used in assessments.

Other aspects of our earlier experience with direct assessments of writing are also likely to help us move toward the design and evaluation of more complex performances in writing. Lucas and Carlson (1989), in creating a prototype for alternative assessment strategies, described the procedures of development, evaluation, and analysis familiar from direct assessment as providing "some systematic control," yet permitting writers and evaluators of the writing to accommodate performance on more open-ended tasks (pp. 14–16). These procedures move through several stages drawing on the expertise of individuals experienced in the teaching and assessment of writing. The first stages involve identifying the competencies to be assessed and the expectations for performance, translating them into specifications for the tasks to be presented, and developing the tasks. Later stages involve trying out the tasks, evaluating them, exploring preliminary scoring systems, and further refining tasks and scoring systems. The final stages focus on training readers, scoring the samples resulting from the performances, conducting statistical and qualitative analyses to establish reliability, validity, and generalizability, and examining the assessments' feasibility, cost effectiveness, and social consequences.

Procedures such as these suggest an orderly and responsible approach to developing and trying out new assessments of writing, including assessments that draw on performances considerably more complex than those evoked by traditional approaches. With some adaptation, such procedures can also allow the developers and users of the assessment to focus attention on the skills and strategies addressed as well as the performances themselves. What is more, if the procedures are carried out through activities that involve teachers in the development and refinement of the assessment design, the evaluation of student performances and products, and the examination of the effects of the assessment on teaching and learning, and if they result in the articulation of criteria and standards for performance and the selection of performances illustrating those criteria and standards, then they can also become in themselves a means of promoting the kinds of learning addressed in the assessment (Camp, 1992b). In short, they can help to establish the assessment's systemic validity (see Frederiksen & Collins, 1989).

It is no accident, then, that the procedures associated with the direct assessment of writing are seen as exemplary for models of assessment designed to foster desirable instruction and learning within educational systems. Very likely, these procedures will inform us in our exploration of new approaches to writing assessment, especially if we use what we have learned from them to press beyond the constraints of current forms of assessment.

Probable Characteristics of New Models for Writing Assessment

Attempts to describe a new conceptual framework for writing assessment or the probable new forms for assessment seem premature, as do attempts to describe the range of possibilities for new forms of writing assessment. Nevertheless, if we survey both the needs that lead us to search for new approaches to assessment and the exploratory activity evident in classrooms, schools, school districts, and state departments of education, we can get a sense of some possible approaches and — more to the point — of the qualities we might hope to find in writing assessment compatible with our current understanding of writing and writing instruction.

The most obvious examples of forward-looking writing assessment are provided by assessments using portfolios. In terms of both their potential for accommodating the new constructs for writing and the intensity of current exploration, portfolio approaches to writing assessment seem especially promising. Portfolios can provide evidence of complex and varied performance in writing, of writing generated in a rich instruction and social contexts, of the processes and strategies that students use, and of their awareness of those processes (Camp, 1990, 1992b; Camp & Levine, 1991; Mitchell, 1992; Paulson, Paulson, & Meyer, 1991; Wolf, 1989). The procedures associated with portfolio design, implementation, and evaluation provide valuable opportunities for discussion of the skills and abilities that the portfolios are intended to measure and of the criteria and standards used to evaluate performances; through these opportunities they become a stimulus for teachers' professional development (Belanoff & Elbow, 1986; Camp, 1990, 1992a, 1992b; Murphy & Smith, 1990). If portfolios are designed to engage students to reflect on their work in writing, they can also help them to learn to evaluate their writing and to assume increased responsibility for their own learning (Camp, 1990, 1992b, 1993; Camp & Levine, 1991; Howard, 1990; Paulson et al., 1991; Reif, 1990; Wolf, 1989).

Other assessment approaches closely related and complementary to portfolios are being explored in a number of school assessments, school sites, and research projects. Some of them involve extended classroom projects integrating instruction and assessment and emphasizing the use of writing as a tool for exploring ideas or techniques, or for solving problems (see Levine, 1992). A few such projects have already been developed with an explicit connection to writing (Central Park East High School in New York City, Arts PROPEL imaginative writing projects and the Syllabus Examination Program in Pittsburgh, the College Outcomes Examination Program for the New Jersey colleges); they suggest an approach to writing assessment that may be well worth exploring, especially since comparable projects are being developed in other areas of the curriculum (see *Arts PROPEL: An Introductory Handbook*, 1992; Lesh & Lamon, 1992; Mitchell, 1992).

Despite the limitations of our experience with assessments based on alternatives to the traditional formats, some tendencies seem likely on the basis of our collective experience to date, the current constructs for writing, and the current developments in measurement as they have been described in this chapter. These tendencies suggest a number of characteristics we might expect to see in future writing assessments:

- Use of a variety of assessment approaches with different methods and formats serving different purposes and educational contexts

- Samples of writing performances and products generated on multiple occasions, for multiple purposes, and under various circumstances — including circumstances typical for classroom writing and over extended periods of time

- Increased attention to the cognitive processes involved in writing, with awareness of the connections between the processes used and the skills, abilities, and strategies available to the writer

- Opportunities for writers to reflect on the processes and strategies they use in single and multiple pieces of writing and over extended periods of time

- Increased attention to the knowledge required and cognitive processes involved in evaluating writing products and performances

- Increased attention to the procedures involved in developing and conducting writing assessments, with particular interest in the opportunities they provide for teachers' professional development, for curriculum development, and for examination of institutional goals for learning

- Formats for reporting on writing performance that are more informative to teachers and student writers than are single numerical scores, including profiles and qualitative descriptions about the processes and strategies evident in writing performance

- Caution in generalizing from single performances in writing to performances that call for substantially different knowledge, skills, and strategies, that make different resources available to the writer, or that draw on different kinds of linguistic or cultural experience

- Assessments that take into account the evolving abilities of writers and the evolving needs of the educational systems within which assessment occurs

NOTE

1. The author would like to thank Drew Gitomer, Pamela Moss, and Sandra Murphy for their reviews of earlier versions of this chapter. The views expressed are those of the author.

REFERENCES

Applebee, A. N. (1986). Problems in process approaches: Toward a reconceptualization of process instruction. In A. Petrosky & D. Bartholomae (Eds.), *The teaching of writing. 85th Yearbook of the National Society for the Study of Education* (Part II, pp. 95–113). Chicago: University of Chicago Press.

Archbald, D. A., & Newmann, F. M. (1988). *Beyond standardized testing*. Paper published by the National Center on Effective Secondary Schools, School of Education, University of Wisconsin-Madison.

Arts PROPEL: An Introductory Handbook. (1992). Princeton, NJ: Educational Testing Service.

Bartholomae, D. (1980). The study of error. *College Composition and Communication, 31*, 253–269.

Beaugrande, R. de. (1982). Psychology and composition: Past, present, future. In M. Nystrand (Ed.), *What writers know: The language, process, and structure of written discourse* (pp. 211–267). New York: Academic Press.

Belanoff, P., & Dickson, M. (Eds.). (1991). *Portfolios: Process and product*. Portsmouth, NH: Heinemann Boynton/Cook.

Belanoff, P., & Elbow, P. (1986). Using portfolios to increase collaboration and community in a writing program. *Writing Program Administration, 9*, 27–40.

Bereiter, C., & Scardamalia, M. (1987). *The psychology of written composition*. Hillsdale, NJ: Erlbaum.

Berlak, H., Newmann, F. M., Adams, E., Archbald, D. A. Burgess, T., Raven, J., & Romberg, T. A. (1992). *Toward a new science of educational testing and assessment*. Albany, NY: State University of New York Press.

Breland, H. M., Camp, R., Jones, R. J., Morris, M. M., & Rock, D. A. (1987). *Assessing writing skill* (Research Monograph No. 11). New York: College Entrance Examination Board.

Breland, H. M., & Gaynor, J. L. (1979). A comparison of direct and indirect assessments of writing skill. *Journal of Educational Measurement, 16*, 119–128.

Brossell, G. (1983). Rhetorical specification in essay examination topics. *College English, 45*, 165–173.

Bruffee, K. A. (1986). Social construction, language, and the authority of knowledge: A bibliographical essay. *College English, 48*, 773–790.

Camp, R. (1990). Thinking together about portfolios. *The Quarterly of the National Writing Project and the Center for the Study of Writing, 12*(2), 8–14, 27.

Camp, R. (1992a). Portfolio reflections in middle and secondary school classrooms. In K. Yancey (Eds.), *Portfolios in the writing classroom: An introduction* (pp. 61–79). Urbana, IL: National Council of Teachers of English.

Camp, R. (1992b). Assessment in the context of schools and school change. In H. H. Marshall (Ed.), *Redefining student learning: Roots of educational change* (pp. 241–263). Norwood, NJ: Ablex.

Camp, R. (1993). The place of portfolios in our changing views of writing assessment. In R. Bennett & W. Ward (Eds.), *Construction versus choice in cognitive measurement* (pp. 183–212). Hillsdale, NJ: Erlbaum.

Camp, R., & Levine, D. (1991). Portfolios evolving: Background and variations in sixth- through twelfth-grade portfolios. In P. Belanoff & M. Dickson (Eds.), *Portfolios: Process and product* (pp. 194–205). Portsmouth, NH: Heinemann Boynton/Cook.

Campione, J. C., & Brown, A. L. (1990). Guided learning and transfer: Implications for approaches to assessment. In N. Frederiksen, R. Glaser, A. Lesgold, & M. G. Shafto (Eds.), *Diagnostic monitoring of skill and knowledge acquisition* (pp. 141–172). Hillsdale, NJ: Erlbaum.

Carlson, S. B., Bridgeman, B., Camp, R., & Waanders, J. (1985). *Relationship of admission test scores to writing performance of native and non-native speakers of English* (TOEFL Research Report No. 19). Princeton, NJ: Educational Testing Service.

Carter, M. (1990). The idea of expertise: An exploration of cognitive and social dimensions of writing. *College Composition and Communication, 41,* 265–286.

Coffman, W. (1971). Essay examinations. In R. L. Thorndike (Eds.), *Educational measurement* (2nd ed., pp. 271–302). Washington, DC: American Council on Education.

Cole, N., & Moss, P. (1989). Bias in test use. In R. Linn (Ed.), *Educational measurement* (3rd ed., pp. 201–219). New York: Macmillan.

Conlon, G. (1986). "Objective" measures of writing ability. In K. Greenberg, H. S. Weiner, & R. A. Donovan (Eds.), *Writing assessment: Issues and strategies* (pp. 109–125). New York: Longman.

Cooper, C. (1977). Holistic evaluation of writing. In C. Cooper & L. Odell (Eds.), *Evaluating writing: Describing, measuring, judging* (pp. 3–31). Urbana, IL: National Council of Teachers of English.

Cooper, C. (Ed.), (1981). *The nature and measurement of competency in English.* Urbana, IL: National Council of Teachers of English.

Cooper, C., & Odell, L. (Eds.), (1977). *Evaluating writing: Describing, measuring, judging.* Urbana, IL: National Council of Teachers of English.

Cronbach, L. J. (1988). Five perspectives on validity argument. In H. Wainer & H. I. Braun (Eds.), *Test validity* (pp. 3–17). Hillsdale, NJ: Erlbaum.

Darling-Hammond, L., & Ascher, C. (1991). *Creating accountability in big city school systems.* New York: ERIC Clearinghouse on Urban Education and the National Center for Restructuring Education, Schools, and Teaching, Teachers College, Columbia.

Diederich, P. (1974). *Measuring growth in English.* Urbana, IL: National Council of Teachers of English.

Durst, R. K. (1987). Cognitive and linguistic demands of analytic writing. *Research in the Teaching of English, 21*(4), 347–376.

Eley, E. G. (1955). Should the General Composition Test be continued? The test satisfices an education need. *College Board Review, 25,* 10–13.

Emig, J. (1982). Inquiry paradigms and writing. *College Composition and Communication, 33,* 64–75.

Faigley, L. (1986). Competing theories of process: A critique and a proposal. *College English, 48,* 527–542.

Faigley, L., Cherry, R., Jolliffe, D., & Skinner, A. (1985). *Assessing writers' knowledge and processes of composing.* Norwood, NJ: Ablex.

Flower, L., & Hayes, J. R.(1980). The dynamics of composing: Making plans and juggling constraints. In L. W. Gregg & E. R. Steinberg (Eds.), *Cognitive process in writing* (pp. 31–50). Hillsdale, NJ: Erlbaum.

Flower, L., & Hayes, J. R. (1981). A cognitive process theory of writing. *College Composition and Communication, 32,* 365–387.

Frederiksen, J. R., & Collins, A. (1989). A systems approach to educational testing. *Educational Researcher, 18,* 27–32.

Frederiksen, N. (1984). The real test bias: Influences of testing on teaching and learning. *American Psychologist, 39,* 193–202.

Frederiksen, N. (1986). Toward a broader conception of human intelligence. *American Psychologist, 41,* 445–452.

Frederiksen, N. (1990). Introduction. In N. Frederiksen, R. Glaser, A. Lesgold, & M. G. Shafto (Eds.), *Diagnostic monitoring of skill and knowledge acquisition* (pp. ix–xvii). Hillsdale, NJ: Erlbaum.

Freedman, A., & Pringle, I. (1981). *Why students can't write arguments.* Unpublished manuscript, Carleton University, Linguistics Department, Ottawa, Canada.

Freedman, S. W. (1981). Influences on evaluators of expository essays: Beyond the text. *Research in the Teaching of English, 15,* 245–255.

Freedman, S. W., Dyson, A. H., Flower, L., & Chafe, W. (1987). *Research in writing: Past, present, and future* (Tech. Rep. No. 1). Berkeley: University of California, Center for the Study of Writing.

Gardner, H. (1988). *Assessment in context: The alternative to standardized testing.* Paper prepared for the National Commission on Testing and Public Policy, Berkeley, CA.

Gere, A. (1980). Written composition: Toward a theory of evaluation. *College English, 42,* 44–58.

Gitomer, D. H. (1993). Performance assessment and educational measurement. In R. Bennett & W. Ward (Eds.), *Construction versus choice in cognitive measurement.* Hillsdale, NJ: Erlbaum.

Glaser, R. (1988). Cognitive and environmental perspectives on assessing achievement. In E. Freeman (Ed.), *Assessment in the service of learning: Proceedings of the ETS Invitational Conference* (pp. 37–43). Princeton, NJ: Educational Testing Service.

Godshalk, F., Swineford, F., & Coffman, W. (1966). *The measurement of writing ability* (Research Monograph No. 6). New York: College Entrance Examination Board.

Greenberg, K. L., Weiner, H. S., & Donovan, R. A. (Eds.), (1986). *Writing assessment: Issues and strategies.* New York: Longman.

Greenberg, K., & Witte, S. (1988). Validity issues in direct writing assessment. *Notes from the National Testing Network in Writing, 8,* 13–14.

Hairston, M. (1982). The winds of change: Thomas Kuhn and the revolution in the teaching of writing. *College Composition and Communication, 33*(1), 76–88.

Haney, W., & Madaus, G. (1989). Standardized testing: Harmful to education health. *Phi Delta Kappan, 70,* 683–687.

Heath, S. B. (1983). *Ways with words: Language, life, and work in communities and classrooms.* Cambridge, MA: Cambridge University Press.

Hoetker, J. (1982). Essay examination topics and student writing. *College Composition and Communication, 33,* 377–392.

Howard, K. (1990). Making the writing portfolio real. *The Quarterly of the National Writing Project and the Center for the Study of Writing, 12*(2), 4–7, 27.

Johnston, P. (1987). Assessing the process and the process of assessment in the language arts. In J. Squire (Ed.), *The dynamics of language learning: Research in reading and English* (pp. 335–357). Urbana, IL: National Council of Teachers of English/ERIC.

Keech-Lucas, C. (1988a). Toward ecological evaluation. *The Quarterly of the National Writing Project and the Center for the Study of Writing, 10*(1), 1–17.

Keech-Lucas, C. (1988b). Toward ecological evaluation: Part Two. *The Quarterly of the National Writing Project and the Center for the Study of Writing, 10*(2), 4–10.

Langer, J. A., & Applebee, A. N. (1987). *How writing shapes thinking: A study of teaching and learning.* Urbana, IL: National Council of Teachers of English.

Lesh, R., & Lamon, S. J. (Eds.), (1992). *Assessment of authentic performance in school mathematics.* Washington, DC: AAAS Press.

Levine, D. S. (1992). The four P's of context-based assessment: Evaluating literacy across the curriculum. In C. Hedley, P. Antonacci, & D. Feldman (Eds.), *Literacy across the curriculum.* Norwood, NJ: Ablex.

Linn, R. L., Baker, E.L., & Dunbar, S. B. (1991). Complex, performance-based assessment: Expectations and validation criteria. *Educational Researcher, 20,* 5–21.

Lloyd-Jones, R. (1977). Primary trait scoring. In C. Cooper & L. Odell (Eds.), *Evaluating writing: Describing, measuring, judging* (pp. 33–55). Urbana, IL: National Council of Teachers of English.

Lucas, C., & Carlson, S. B. (1989). *Prototype of alternative assessment strategies for new teachers of English.* San Francisco, CA: Report to the California New Teacher Project.

Macrorie, K. (1976). *Telling writing.* Rochelle Park, NJ: Hayden.

Messick, S. (1989a). Meaning and values in test validation: The science and ethics of assessment. *Educational Researcher, 18,* 5–14.

Messick, S. (1989b). Validity. In R. Linn (Ed.), *Educational measurement* (3rd ed., pp. 13–104). New York: Macmillan.

Mislevy, R. J. (1993). Foundations for a new test theory. In N. Fredriksen, R. J. Mislevy, & I. Bejar (Eds.), *Test theory for a new generation of tests* (pp. 19–40). Hillsdale, NJ: Erlbaum.

Mitchell, R. (1989). *A sampler of authentic assessment: What it is and what it looks like.* Paper prepared for the California Assessment Program Conference, Sacramento, CA.

Mitchell, R. (1992). *Testing for learning.* New York: Free Press.

Moffett, J. (1968). *Teaching the universe of discourse.* Boston: Houghton Mifflin.

Moss, P. A. (1992). Shifting conceptions of validity in educational measurement: Implications for performance assessment. *Review of Educational Research, 62*(3), 229–258.

Murphy, S., & Smith, M. A. (1990). Talking about portfolios. *The Quarterly of the National Writing Project and the Center for the Study of Writing, 12*(2), 1–3, 24–27.

Murphy, S., & Smith, M. A. (1991). *Writing portfolios: A bridge from teaching to assessment.* Markam, Ontario, Canada: Pippin.

Newmann, F. (1991). Linking restructuring to authentic student achievement. *Phi Delta Kappan, 72*(6), 458–463.

O'Connor, M. C. (1989). Aspects of differential performance by minorities on standardized tests: Linguistic and sociocultural factors. In B. Gifford (Ed.), *Test policy and test performance: Education, language and culture* (pp. 129–181). Boston: Kluwer.

Odell, L. (1981). Defining and assessing competence in writing. In C. Cooper (Ed.), *The nature and measurement of competency in English* (pp. 95–138). Urbana, IL: National Council of Teachers of English.

Paulson, F. L., Paulson, P. P., & Meyer, C. A. (1991). What makes a portfolio a portfolio? *Educational Leadership, 48*(5), 60–63.

Penrose, A. M. (1989). *Strategic differences in composing: Consequences for learning through writing* (Tech. Rep. No. 31). Berkeley: University of California, Center for the Study of Writing.

Polin, L. (1980). *Specifying the writing domain for assessment: Recommendations to the practitioner* (CSE Rep. No. 135). Los Angeles, CA: Center for the Study of Evaluation.

Pringle, I., & Freedman, A. (1985). *A comparative study of writing abilities in two modes at the grade 5, 8, and 12 levels.* Toronto, Canada: Ontario Ministry of Education.

Rafoth, B. A., & Rubin, D. L. (Eds.), (1988). *The social construction of written communication.* Norwood, NJ: Ablex.

Reif, L. (1990). Finding the value in evaluation: Self-assessment in a middle-school classroom. *Educational Leadership, 47*(6), 24–29.

Resnick, D. P., & Resnick, L. B. (1985). Standards, curriculum, and performance: A historical and comparative perspective. *Educational Researcher, 14*(4), 5–20.

Rose, M. (1989). *Lives on the boundary: The struggles and achievements of America's underprepared.* New York: Free Press.

Ruth, L., & Murphy, S. (1988). *Designing writing tasks for the assessment of writing.* Norwood, NJ: Ablex.

Scardamalia, M., & Bereiter, C. (1985). Research on written composition. In M. Wittrock (Ed.), *Handbook of research on teaching* (3rd ed., pp. 708–803). New York: Macmillan.

Shaughnessy, M. (1977). *Errors and expectations: A guide for the teacher of basic writing.* New York: Oxford University Press.

Shepard, L. A. (1991). Psychometricians' beliefs about learning. *Educational Researcher, 20,* 2–16.

Smith, F. (1982). *Writing and the writer.* New York: Holt, Rinehart & Winston.

Snow, R. E. (1989). Toward assessment of cognitive and conative structures in learning. *Educational Researcher, 18,* 8–14.

Snow, R. E., & Lohman, D. F. (1989). Implications of cognitive psychology for educational measurement. In R. Linn (Ed.), *Educational measurement* (3rd ed., pp. 263–331). Washington, DC: American Council on Education.

Spandel, V., & Stiggins, R. J. (1980). *Direct measures of writing skill: Issues and applications.* Portland: Northwest Regional Educational Laboratory, Clearinghouse for Applied Performance Testing.

Stiggins, R. J. (1988). Revitalizing classroom assessment: The highest instructional priority. *Phi Delta Kappan, 69*(5), 184–193.

Taylor, D. (1989). The many keys to literacy. *Phi Delta Kappan, 70,* 184–193.

Thompson, E. H. (1985). Self-assessment and the mastery of writing. In J. Beard & S. McNaff (Eds.), *Testing in the English language arts: Uses and abuses.* Rochester, MI: Michigan Council of Teachers of English.

Tierney, R. J., Carter, M. A., & Desai, L. E. (1991). *Portfolio assessment in the reading-writing classroom.* Norwood, MA: Christopher Gordon.

Valencia, S., McGinley, W., & Pearson, P. D. (1990). Assessing literacy in the middle school. In G. Duffy (Ed.), *Reading in the middle school* (2nd ed., pp. 124–141). Newark, DE: International Reading Association.

Ward, W. C., Frederiksen, N., & Carlson, S. B. (1980). Construct validity of free-response and machine-scorable forms of a test. *Journal of Educational Measurement, 17,* 11–29.

White, E. (1985). *Teaching and assessing writing.* San Francisco: Jossey-Bass.

White, E. (1986). Pitfalls in the testing of writing. In K. L. Greenberg, H. S. Weiner, & R. A. Donovan (Eds.), *Writing assessment: Issues and strategies* (pp. 53–78). New York: Longman.

Wiggins, G. (1989). A true test: Toward more authentic and equitable assessment. *Phi Delta Kappan, 70,* 703–713.

Witte, S., Trachsel, M., & Walters, K. (1986). Literacy and the direct assessment of writing: A diachronic perspective. In K. Greenberg, H. S. Weiner, & R. A. Donovan (Eds.), *Writing assessment: Issues and strategies* (pp. 109–125). New York: Longman.

Wolf, D. P. (1989). Portfolio assessment: Sampling student work. *Educational Leadership, 46,* 35–39.

Wolf, D., Bixby, J., Glenn, J., & Gardner, H. (1991). To use their minds well: Investigating new forms of student assessment. In G. Grant (Ed.), *Review of Research in Education, 17,* 31–73.

Yancey, K. B. (Ed.), (1992). *Portfolios in the writing classroom: An introduction.* Urbana, IL: National Council of Teachers of English.

8

Looking Back as We Look Forward: Historicizing Writing Assessment

KATHLEEN BLAKE YANCEY

Even if by another name, writing assessment has always been at the center of work in writing: and it surely was there in 1950 when CCCC began. It wasn't called *assessment* then, of course; that language came later. During the first of what I'll identify as three waves in writing assessment, it was called *testing*, and it permeated the entire institution of composition—the contexts surrounding writing classes as well as the classes themselves, from the admission tests students completed to determine who would enroll in "sub-freshman English" and who in the "regular" course, to the grades that were awarded within the classroom, to the exit and proficiency tests that marked the single way out of many a composition program. Ironically, assessment in composition studies in those early days wasn't just routine: it was ubiquitous—and invisible.

Like composition studies itself, however, writing assessment has changed during the past half century. One way to historicize those changes is to think of them as occurring in overlapping waves, with one wave feeding into another but without completely displacing waves that came before. The trends marked by these waves, then, are just that: trends that constitute a general forward movement, at least chronologically, but a movement that is composed of both kinds of waves, those that move forward, those that don't. The metaphor of waves is useful conceptually, precisely because it allows us to mark past non-discrete patterns whose outlines and effects become clearer over time and upon reflection—and whose observation allows us in turn to think in an informed way about issues that might contribute to future waves.

An Overview

During the first wave (1950–1970), writing assessment took the form of objective tests; during the second (1970–1986), it took the form of the holistically scored essay; and during the current wave, the third (1986–present), it has taken the form of portfolio assessment and of programmatic assessment. This

From *College Composition and Communication* 50 (1999): 483–503.

is the common history of writing assessment: the one located in method. But as Kenneth Burke suggests, other lenses permit other views; particularly when brought together, they allow us to understand differently and more fully. We could also historicize writing assessment, for instance, by thinking of it in terms of the twin defining concepts: validity and reliability. Seen through this conceptual lens, as Brian Huot suggests, writing assessment's recent history is the story of back-and-forth shifts between these concepts, with first one dominating the field, then another, now both. A related approach constructs the history of writing assessment as the struggle between and among scholars and testing practitioners and faculty, those who speak the terms validity and reliability quite differently: the old *expert*; the new *non-expert*. From this perspective, the last 50 years of writing assessment can be narrativized as the teacher-layperson (often successfully) challenging the (psychometric) expert, developing and then applying both expertise and theory located not in psychometrics, but in rhetoric, in reading and hermeneutics, and, increasingly, in writing practice.

Still another way to trace the history of writing assessment is through its movement into the classroom; multiple choice tests standing outside of and apart from the classroom have become the portfolios composed within. And finally, writing assessment can be historicized through the lens of the self. Which self does any writing assessment permit? As important, given that "tests create that which they purport to measure" (Hanson 294), which self does an assessment construct? Portfolio assessment, with its multiple discourses and its reflective text, has highlighted this second question, certainly, but it's a question to be put to any writing assessment seeking to serve education.

Significantly, these lenses don't just frame the past; they point to the future, specifically to three issues. First, the role that the self should play in any assessment is a central concern for educators. It is the self that we want to teach, that we hope will learn, but that we are often loath to evaluate. What is the role of the person/al in any writing assessment? A second future concern has to do with programmatic assessment: how can we use this kind of assessment — which is quite different than the individual assessment that has focused most of our attention for 50 years — to help students? A third concern focuses on what assessment activities can teach us: it's only recently that assessment was seen as a knowledge-making endeavor. Which raises a good question: what (else) might we learn from writing assessment? And how would we learn? Underlying these concerns is a particular construct of writing assessment itself: as rhetorical act that is both humane and ethical.

In itself, that understanding of writing assessment is perhaps the most significant change in the last 50 years.

A Context for a History of Writing Assessment: Spheres of Influence

During the first wave of writing assessment, dating from around 1950 to 1970, writing assessment was young, complex, conflicted. It was a critical time in that most of the issues that currently define the field were identified. Consequently, in our practices today, in the questions that continue to tease out some of our best thinking, we can trace the outlines of yesterday's concerns.

Much of the lore about the early days in writing assessment is accurate. It's true that "objective" tests, particularly multiple choice tests of usage, vocabulary, and grammar, dominated practice. It's true that most testing concerns focused on sites ancillary to the classroom: typically, on the placement exercise used to "place" students into "appropriate" writing courses. And, in general, it's true that in the early days of CCCC, classrooms were defined, at least in part, by what we could call a *technology of testing* — not only by means of the tests that moved students in and out of classrooms, but also by way of contemporaneous efforts to bring "our work" — i.e., the reading and grading of student work — into line with testing theory. The early issues of *CCC* speak of these practices and aspirations convincingly: in summaries of CCCC workshops where the usefulness of objective tests is explained to the lay teacher, for instance, and in endorsements of *national* grading standards.

What's at least as interesting is a specific account of why these issues gained attention, why testing didn't include writing samples more often, why people who knew well how to read and value texts would turn to test theory when it came time to read and evaluate student texts. One contextual factor was demographic: the numbers and kinds of students that were beginning to attend school in the early 50s, students that seemed more and different than students we'd seen before. Consequently, there were genuine questions as to what to do with these students: where to put them, how and what to teach them, and how to be sure that they learned what they needed.[1] In theory, those three tasks — (1) where to put students and (2) how and what to teach them and (3) how to be sure that they learned what they needed — belonged to all educators. In practice, the tasks initially divided themselves into two clearly demarcated spheres of influence that characterize the first wave of writing assessment: the process of *deciding what to teach* the students belonged to educators, those who would become new compositionists; the process of *moving students about*, to testing specialists.

During the second two waves of writing assessment in composition studies — those of holistically scored essay tests, and next portfolios and program assessments — the two spheres merge and overlap, with administrators and then faculty taking on institutional and epistemological responsibilities for testing previously claimed by testing experts, and in the process developing a new expertise and a new discipline: *writing assessment*.

This history is also that story.

METHODS AND SAMPLING: TWO SIDES OF THE SAME (ASSESSMENT) COIN

From the perspective of method, changes in writing assessment appear straightforward and familiar: from first-wave "objective" measures like multiple choice tests, largely of grammar and usage, to second-wave holistically scored essay tests to third-wave portfolios. Put another way, first-wave evaluation relied on an "indirect" measure — a test of something assumed to be related to the behavior, but not the behavior itself (e.g., items like comma usage questions and pronoun reference corrections). Within twenty years, during the second wave, we began employing a "direct" measure — a sample of the behavior that we seek to examine, in this case a text that the student composes. Once the direct measure becomes accepted and even routinized as the measure of choice, the "one essay" model is soon replaced by a set of texts, so that: a single draft becomes two drafts; two drafts become two drafts accompanied by some authorial commentary; two drafts plus commentary become an undetermined number of multiple final drafts accompanied by "reflection," and the set of texts becomes the new: *portfolio assessment*. As important as the *method* of assessing writing in this account is the *sampling* technique. The question "How shall we evaluate writing?" concerns itself not only with methodology, but also with behavior: which behavior should we examine? Sampling was critical, in part because sampling was (and is) the stuff of everyday classroom life: day in and day out, faculty assign, read, and evaluate student texts. In this sense, *teaching writing is itself an exercise in direct measure*. Accordingly, (1) teachers saw the difference between what they taught in their classes — *writing* — and what was evaluated — *selection of homonyms* and *sentence completion exercises*; (2) they thought that difference mattered; and (3) they continued to address this disjunction rhetorically, *as though the testing enterprise could be altered* — first on their own campuses; also at composition studies conferences like CCCC, later and concurrently at testing-focused conferences like the National Testing Network in Writing and the NCTE conferences on portfolio assessment; and concurrently in articles and books.

Still, it took over 20 years for this critique to make an impact, over 20 years for the second wave to occur. It's fair to ask, then: if compositionists saw this disjunction between classroom practice and testing practice early on, why did it take over two decades to shift from one sampling technique to another, from one methodology to another? And the waves are overlapping, not discreet: why is it that even today, 50 years later, multiple choice tests continue to be routinely used in many assessment exercises (Murphy)[2]? The responses to these questions, phrased themselves as four general questions, are inter-related, each of them located in or deriving from the methods and sampling issues:

- What roles have validity and reliability played in writing assessment?
- Who is authorized and who has the appropriate expertise to make the best judgment about writing assessment issues?
- Who is best suited to orchestrate these questions, design an assessment based on the answers, and implement that design? In other words, who will wield this power?
- What, after all, is the overall purpose of writing assessment in an educational situation?

Each one of these questions points to one understanding of writing assessment; each one identifies a dimension of writing assessment still in contest.

VALIDITY AND RELIABILITY: THE PENDULUM SWINGING

Writing assessment is commonly understood as an exercise in balancing the twin concepts of validity and reliability. Validity means that you are measuring what you intend to measure, reliability that you can measure it consistently. While both features are desirable in any writing evaluation, advocates of each tend to play them off against each other. Accordingly, which one should dominate, assuming only one could be favored, has generated considerable discussion — and change.

During the first wave, reliability prevailed; we see this, first, in the kinds of assessments that were commonly employed, and second, by the rationale for using them. That such tests were common is confirmed by various survey data. One survey in 1952, for example, included over 100 responding institutions and provided an all-too-common portrait: 90% of the responding institutions administered placement tests to entering freshman, 84% of those tests were standardized, and most of those tests were created by external experts (Sasser 13). Similarly, the same survey reported that nearly half of the reporting institutions (44%) also included a test at the *conclusion* of the course, a "follow up retest," with half of the schools folding that test score into the course grade. From placement to exit, then, objective testing defined the borders of many first-year composition courses, and in doing so, it also influenced what went on inside.

Such testing was theorized persuasively. Perhaps the most articulate theorist for this perspective was Paul Diederich, the ETS researcher whose *Measuring Growth in English* was the first monograph to address the specifics of postsecondary writing assessment. As unofficial representative of the testing community, Diederich — at nearly every CCCC during the 1950s and within the pages of *CCC* — repeatedly explained the value of the reliable measure, taking as his primary exemplar the prototypic placement test:

> The best test to use at the college entrance level to pick out good, average, and poor writers is not a writing test at all but a long, unspeeded reading test. That will usually yield a correlation of about .65 with good teachers' estimates of the writing ability of their own students in excellent private schools, in which a great deal of writing is required. Next best is a good objective test of writing ability; it will usually yield a correlation of about .60 with such judgments. A long way down from that is a single two-hour essay, even when it is graded twice independently by expert College Board readers. It will usually correlate .45 to .50 with such estimates. Furthermore, if you test the same students twice — in the junior and again in the senior year — the two reading tests will correlate about .85 with one another, while the two essays will correlate only about .45 with each other. Thus the reading test will not only pick out good and poor writers each year better than the essay but it will also pick out the same one both years, while the essay tends to pick out different ones. (qtd. in Valentine 90)

The logic here, admittedly, is compelling in its own way. If you want to predict how students will perform and if you want to do this in a fair, consistent, and efficient way, you go the route of objective testing — because even to generate the most favorable conditions with an essay, which of course are considerably less than those of the standardized test, you have to use *expert College Board readers* (an impossibility for the average campus), and even then the texts don't *correlate* well *with one another*. Teachers' *estimates* are just that: they cannot compete with *correlations*. Properly understood, then, the placement exercise is an exercise in numbers, not words.

Not that Diederich and other testing specialists didn't consider the essay test (which, in fact, Diederich's monograph both touts and complicates). It's just that from both psychometric and administrative perspectives, the testing task as they construct it is almost insurmountingly difficult because it is error-prone, inefficient, and expensive. You'd need, they say, "*Six two-hour papers, each written in a separate testing session*," read by "*Four well-selected and trained readers, who will read and grade each paper independently*," a process that costs "$100 per student" (qtd. in Valentine 91). What it all comes down to is twofold: (prohibitive) cost, of course, but also "the inevitable margin of testing error," a *margin* that is a given in a testing context, but that can be minimized. According to this view of placement (and testing more generally), what we need to do is to rely on "reliability of measurement"; "it is only when we use highly reliable tests that we come close to coming up with scores for an individual that are just measures of his ability — that don't seriously over-value him or under-value him" (Valentine 91).

The first wave of writing assessment is dominated by a single question: not the question we might expect — "What is the best or most valid measure of writing?" — but a question tied to testing theory, to institutional need, to cost, and ultimately to efficiency (Williamson) — "Which measure can do the best and fairest job of prediction with the least amount of work and the lowest cost?"

The answer: the reliable test.

THE DISCOURSE OF A *WRITING* ASSESSMENT: TABLES TURNED

But what about validity? This question, raised often enough by faculty, dominated the second wave of writing assessment. Faculty teaching in new open admissions schools and elsewhere saw new and other kinds of students; and an obvious discrepancy between what they did with their students in class and what students were then asked to do on tests (White, *Teaching and Assessing Writing*). Their concern with validity was also motivated by the fact that by the 1970s, faculty had begun to identify themselves as compositionists. They *knew more* about writing: about writing process, about teaching writing process, about writing courses and what they might look like, about what composition studies might be. Given what we were learning, it made increasingly less sense to use tests whose chief virtues were reliability and efficiency. The shift to what did seem obvious — the essay test — had to be orchestrated, however, and it was, by two rhetorical moves, both of which worked inside psychometric concepts to alter assessment practice: first, to make validity (and not reliability) the testing feature of choice; and second, to undermine the concept of correlation as a criterion for evaluating tests.

Edward White took the first approach. As a faculty member who became an administrator — the first director of the California State University (CSU) Freshman English Equivalency Examination Program — he understood the three variables that had to be accounted for in order to make essay testing feasible:

> While some . . . chancellors, regents, and the like are impervious to argument, most are not; many of those who employ multiple-choice tests as the only measure of writing ability are properly defensive of their stance but will include actual writing samples if they can be shown that writing tests can be *properly constructed, reliably scored, and economically handled.* (*Teaching* xiv, my italics)

Which is exactly what White and others — Richard Lloyd Jones, Karen Greenberg, Lee Odell, and Charles Cooper, to name but a few — set out to do: devise a *writing* test that could meet the standard stipulated by the testing experts. To do that, they had to solve the reliability dilemma: they had to assure that essay tests would perform the same task as the objective tests. Administrators like White thus borrowed from the Advanced Placement Program at ETS their now-familiar "testing technology." Called holistic writing assessment, the AP assessment, unlike the ETS-driven placement tests, was a classroom-implemented curriculum culminating in a final essay test that met adequate psychometric reliability standards through several quite explicit procedures: (1) using writing "prompts" that directed students; (2) selecting "anchor" papers and scoring guides that directed teacher-readers who rated; and (3) devising methods of calculating "acceptable" agreement.[3] By importing these procedures, test-makers like White could determine both what acceptable reliability for an essay test should be and, perhaps more important, how to get it.[4] The AP testing technology, then, marks the second wave of writing assessment by making a more valid, classroom-like writing assessment possible.

At the same time that administrators and faculty were showing how a more valid measure could also meet an acceptable standard of reliability — and therefore how testing could be more congruent with classroom practice — other administrators and faculty were demonstrating in the language of testing why the reliable-only test was particularly *incongruent*. In 1978, for instance, Rexford Brown made this case not only by appealing to the context of assessment, but also by connecting that test to the context of the larger world:

> *Of course* these [objective] tests correlate with writing ability and predict academic success; but the number of cars or television sets or bathrooms in one's family also correlate with this writing ability, and parental education is one of the best predictors there is. All existing objective tests of "writing" are very similar to I.Q. tests; even the very best of them test only reading, proofreading, editing, logic, and guessing skills. They cannot distinguish between proofreading errors and process errors, reading problems and scribal stutter, failure to consider audience or lack of interest in materials manufactured by someone else. (3)[5]

The *correlations* here correlate with more than predictive ability: they are themselves a measure of affluence, of *the number of cars or television sets or bathrooms in one's family*, and of another variable, *parental education*. Are these, Brown implicitly queries, the items we seek to test? Moreover, given the discrepancy between the items on the test and what we in our classrooms teach, what could such *scores* based on such items really *mean*, anyway? Meaning is, after all, located in more and other than correlations: it is intellectual and rhetorical substance.

By working both within and against the psychometric paradigm, then, faculty and administrators moved us during the second wave of writing assessment closer to classroom practice.

THE THIRD WAVE: NEW ASSESSMENT AS POLITICS OF LOCATION

During the second wave of writing assessment, not all faculty, and not all institutions, were carried along: many of both continued the objective measures of the first wave, particularly when they engaged in placement assessments, and many continue these practices today. The first wave, in other words, hasn't disappeared. And yet, at the same time, waves feed into other waves: just as the first wave fed into the second wave, the second wave itself began to make room for the third, again because classroom assumptions and practices could be translated into an assessment scheme. Put simply: if one text increases the validity of a test, how much more so two or three texts? In responding to this question, Gordon Brossell forecast the preferred technology of the third wave, the portfolio:

> We know that for a valid test of writing performance, multiple writing samples written on different occasions and in various rhetorical modes are preferable to single samples drawn from an isolated writing instance. But given the sizable and growing populations of test takers and the increasing costs associated with administering tests to them, the problems of collecting and scoring multiple writing samples are formidable. Until we find ways to reduce testing costs and to improve the validity of the assessments, the whole enterprise is not likely to serve any purposes higher than routine sorting and certifying. (179)

As Writing Program Administrators, Peter Elbow and Pat Belanoff in the mid-1980s found a purpose *higher than routine sorting* when they directed a first-year composition program that — like the programs of the 1950s — required an exit exam. Dissatisfied with its form (it was a second-wave essay test), Elbow and Belanoff used classroom materials to create a writing assessment embodying Brossell's description: *multiple writing samples written on different occasions and in various rhetorical modes*. Or, a *portfolio*.

This model of writing assessment, with its different genres and multiple texts and classroom writing environment, seemed more valid still. But built into the model was another new feature, a reliability based not on statistics, but on reading and interpretation and negotiation. Rather than use an elaborated holistic scale (with a 1–6 scoring range, for instance), theirs required a simple dichotomous (if still holistic) decision: pass or fail. The "raters" were the classroom teachers themselves. They were not *trained* to agree, as in the holistic scoring model, but rather released to read, to negotiate among themselves, "hammering out an agreeable compromise" (Elbow, *Portfolios* xxi). Elbow called this a "communal assessment" and argued that it was both more realistic and productive:

> The more we grade with others, the more attuned we become to community standards and the more likely we are to award grades fairly to all. Even though we know, for example, that we are passing a paper because of the quality of its language, we can become aware that the rest of the group would fail it for faulty thinking, and we can then recognize that all of us need to rethink and perhaps adjust our standards. And the greatest benefit of all comes when we return to our classrooms enriched by new ways of commenting on student texts which have come to us during discussions with our colleagues. (xxi)

In the late 1980s and into the 1990s, other portfolio systems developed, notably the portfolio-based basic writing program at Purdue University, the exemption program at Miami University, the placement program at the University of Michigan, and the rising junior portfolio at Washington State University. Simultaneously, individual faculty began using writing portfolios, sometimes as a means of formal assessment, sometimes as a way of learning. All of these portfolio assessments expressed a direct connection to classroom practice.

The Elbow-Belanoff model, however, was the first to raise several interesting, still-unresolved questions challenging both theory and practice in writing assessment. First, this model quite deliberately conflated two different processes — *grading*, typically a non-systematic classroom evaluative procedure, and the more psychometrically oriented operation called *scoring* (which involves the technology of scoring described above). Consequently, psychometric reliability isn't entirely ignored, nor is its historical concern for fairness — Elbow and Belanoff stipulate that *award[ing] grades fairly to all* is a prime objective. But the mechanisms of classic reliability are supplanted by different understandings and larger concerns: (1) about how raters can be led to agree (through "negotiation" rather than training); and (2) about the value of such agreement (desirable, but not required nor expected). Second, faculty are readers, not raters. As readers, they are guided rather than directed by anchor papers and scoring guides; and they are asked to read portfolios with the understanding that readers necessarily will value texts and textual features differently, that they will disagree, that they should *negotiate*. In sum, we see in this model a shift from a desire for the uniform replication of scoring practice to an assumed negotiation and acceptance of different readings. It's only through the articulation of difference and negotiation, Elbow and Belanoff say, that *community standards* are developed, and through these standards that fairer grades can be derived. Moreover, they claim, this process enables us to refine responding skills that can be taken back to the classroom. This model of assessment, then, functions three ways: (1) as a sorting mechanism (pass-fail); (2) as a check on practice; (3) as a means of faculty development.[6]

It's worth noting that this model of assessment — one that emphasizes validity at the same time it re-contextualizes reliability — emerged from a different context than the one primarily responsible for shaping earlier assessments. During the first and second waves of writing assessment, the common reference point against and from which reform occurred was the placement exercise, which is conducted as an extra-curricular exercise, one prior to college matriculation. By contrast, *in early iterations of programmatic portfolio assessment, the initial reference point is curriculum-based,* occurring (like the AP exams) at the *end of a course* — where it's difficult to ignore the program you've just delivered, to bifurcate that program from a high-stakes assessment marking the students you've just taught in that program.[7] Or: like other disciplines, writing assessment functions out of a politics of location.

Faculty experience with portfolios has raised three other, also-unresolved theoretical issues related to portfolios and to assessment more generally: (1) the nature of reading processes and their relationship to assessment; (2) the role of scoring procedures in an assessment; and (3) what writing assessments can teach us when they are located in practice.

Precisely because portfolios are "messy" — that is, they are composed of multiple kinds of texts, and different students compose quite different portfolios, even in the same setting and for the same purposes, which in turn can make evaluating them difficult — they invite several questions. Certainly, portfolios should be read: but how? Initially, it was assumed that faculty would read portfolios similarly (Hamp-Lyons and Condon), but this given has been contradicted experientially. More specifically, several recorded communal "readings" have suggested at least two quite different portfolio reading processes — one, a linear process; and a second, "hypertexual" — and these different processes have called into question *how any text is read* in an assessment context unconstrained by the technology of holistic scoring (Allen et al., "Outside"). A second issue focuses on the propriety of portfolio scoring; like Elbow and Belanoff, others have questioned whether or not portfolios should be scored at all. A perhaps more interesting and related question has to do with whether a single holistic score is appropriate given the complexity of the materials being evaluated (e.g., Broad). A third issue inquires into the nature of collaborative scoring — a later version of communal scoring — and the value of including a mix of perspectives from various "stakeholders," for instance, a set of outsider and insider readers, or a set of administrative, faculty, and external reviewers (Allen et al., "Outside," *Situating*; Broad). A fourth issue focuses on what can be learned about our own practices from portfolios; exemplifying this aspect is Richard Larson's review of curriculum as it is evidenced in a set of working folders.

Together, these concerns illustrate a new function identified for writing assessment during the third wave: creating knowledge about assessment, of course, but also about our own practices. When writing assessment is located within practice, its validity is enhanced, to be sure. But equally important, it reflects back to us that practice, the assumptions undergirding it, the discrepancy between what it is that we say we value and what we enact. It helps us understand, critique, and enhance our own practice, in other words, because of its location — in practice — and because it makes that practice visible and thus accessible to change.

EXPERTS AND AMATEURS

Another way of understanding writing assessment in the last 50 years is to observe that expertise in writing assessment has been redefined and created anew. During the first wave, testing specialists dominated the field, articulating in a testing jargon why (testing) things are. To create the second wave, a new, hybrid expertise developed: one influenced by testing concepts like validity and reliability, but one also influenced by pedagogical knowledge, composing process research, and rhetorical study. Simply put, we had a clearer sense of what we were doing in class, we began to administer programs, and so we began looking for ways to accommodate the assessment needs of our institutions to our own classroom practices. To do that, we, like Sylvia Holladay, began to develop our own expertise, an expertise located in two disciplines — *writing* and *assessment*. Likewise, we began to develop the disciplinary machinery that would support and disseminate such expertise: organizations like the National Testing Network in Writing; and books like Charles Cooper's and Lee Odell's NCTE edited collection *Evaluating Writing*, the Faigley et al. *Assessing Writers' Knowledge and Processes of Composing*, and the Williamson and Huot edited volume *Validating Holistic Scoring for Writing Assessment*.

In the third wave, another shift regarding expertise is under way; this one appears to be bimodal. On the one hand, as indicated in documents like the *CCCC Bibliography*, the CCCC Position Statement on Writing Assessment, and the CCCC program proposal forms, composition studies recognize writing assessment as a field; we have a journal devoted exclusively to the discipline, *Assessing Writing*; and graduates of programs in rhetoric and composition contribute to their own programs as well as to the composition studies literature (books like *New Directions in Portfolio Assessment* and *Assessing Writing across the Curriculum*; articles in *WPA: Writing Program Administration* and the *Journal of Teaching Writing*, as well as in *CCC*).

On the other hand, there still continues reluctance at best, and aversion at worst, to writing assessment. Sometimes it appears in resistance to grading practices (see Tchudi); sometimes it's identified as the villain when a major educational disenfranchising event occurs (as with the current eradication of many basic writing programs); often it's evidenced in a generalized faculty reluctance to take on the tasks entailed in any assessment. And sometimes, discomfort at least is articulated quite clearly when faculty practicing assessment presume to something quite different, a *deliberately non-expert status*, as Elbow and Belanoff suggest:

> First, we note that we are not assessment specialists. We have not mastered the technical dimensions of psychometrics. That doesn't mean we don't respect the field; we agree with Ed White that one of the greatest

needs is for practitioners and theorists like us to talk to psychometricians. But we don't feel comfortable doing that so long as they continue to worship numbers as the bottom line. We think teaching is more important than assessment. (21)

Still associated with number-crunching and reductionism, assessment expertise is, at least sometimes, foiled against a teaching grounded in humanism. Ironically, it's expertise rooted twice, in teaching knowledge and in assessment non-expertise; they seem to work together. At the same time, other new experts — theorists like Huot and theorist-practitioners like Michael Allen and Jeff Sommers and Gail Stygall — understand writing assessment itself as the grounds for that same humanism. They argue that the humanistic endeavor requires a student-informed and -informing assessment and the expertise that can create it.

Faculty experience with portfolios as an assessment technology has focused our attention from yet another perspective: that of practice. The effect of this practice has been to suggest new understandings about the kinds of expertise that might inform our assessment practices, with the specific effects of democratizing, localizing, and grounding expertise of three kinds: student expertise, reader expertise, and theorist expertise.

- First, *student expertise*. Through the reflective texts in portfolios,[8] students are asked to demonstrate a kind of expertise about their own work; their "secondary" reflective texts are used as confirming evidence of student achievement as documented in a primary text (Yancey, *Reflection*). Writing well is thus coming to mean twofold: writing well and being an expert on one's writing.

- Second, *reader expertise*. Assessment specialists are looking more carefully at what they are calling "expert" readers, based on a second-wave holistic model that Bill Smith used at Pittsburgh and was later adapted for portfolio assessment by Washington State (Haswell and Wyche-Smith). In this model, readers are expert in a local sense — authoritative about the relationship between a student and a specific course, one that the teacher-reader has very recently taught. Conceived of this way, reliability is not a function of agreement, directed or otherwise, among raters so much as it is a function of rater experience with particular curricula.

- Third, *theoretical expertise* that grows out of and is integrated with practice. The practical work in assessment undertaken during the third wave has created a body of rich data permitting theories of writing assessment to emerge. The theories are developing in two ways: as elaborations and new applications of assessment theory generally (Huot); and as readings of practice suggest (Broad; Allen; Allen et al., "Outside").

ORCHESTRATING ASSESSMENT: POLITICS OF LOCATION, PLURAL

Closely related to the issue of expertise is that of power. During the first wave of writing assessment, faculty seemed content to allow testing specialists to direct the tests while they directed classroom activities: a kind of specialization of effort mimicked what appeared as a co-distribution of power. During the second wave of writing assessment, faculty began to see writing assessment as something that wasn't tangential to the classroom, but important in its own right, as Daniel Fader suggests: "... writing assessment is to be taken seriously because its first purpose is to determine quality of thought rather than precision of form. As our students, our readers, and our network of co-operating teachers have told us, it matters because it tries to test something that matters so much" (83). Assessment within the classroom thus took on increased emphasis and importance. Two examples — one focused on the role of error and another on response to student texts — illustrate how assessment concerns begin to move inside the classroom, become transformed in that context, and generate new questions for assessment specialists and compositionists alike.

During the first wave of writing assessment, error (by means of test items) outside the classroom determines which classroom a student enters: error has an ontological status of its own. During the second wave, error comes inside the classroom: taken together, errors weave a pattern amenable to teacher observation and intervention (Shaughnessy). Still understood as mistakes, they become clues allowing a teacher to plot where to start and what to do. During the third wave, pattern of error is its own discourse: errors work together to create unconventional readings that evidence their own uncommon logic (Hull and Rose). Originally an external marker of deficit, error thus moves into the classroom and becomes its own legitimate text, a means of knowing for both student and teacher.

A similar kind of movement occurs with response to student writing. During the first wave of writing assessment, considerable comment is provided on how important response is in helping students: the early pages of *CCC* speak to this near-universal concern eloquently. But assessment as a discipline, located outside the classroom, includes no provision for response: it's a null set. During the second wave, we see the first formal study of response, conducted by Nancy Sommers in 1981. Located not outside the classroom but inside, Sommers' study is based in and oriented toward recommending good classroom practice. During the third wave of writing assessment, modes of response and their functions — when to praise, how to help students move toward reflective writing, and how students interpret our comments to them — have become a central concern (Daiker; Anson; Chandler). A current debate: should preferred response always be non-directive (Straub and Lunsford), or should it be situated (Smagorinsky)? As significant, response is theorized newly, not as an evaluative end, but rather as an inventive moment in composing. It's a text in its own right, another place to continue what Joseph Harris calls the opportunity for writers to "change not only their phrasings but their minds when given a chance to talk about their work with other people" (68). Moving inward now — into the classroom and then into and within composing itself — writing assessment becomes social act.

As social act, writing assessment exerts enormous influence, both explicitly and implicitly, often in ways we, both faculty and students, do not fully appreciate. Certainly, writing assessment has been used historically to exclude entire groups of people: White makes the point that a primary motivation for holistic scoring was explicitly political, to enlarge and diversify the student body. Portfolios, for many, developed from similar impulses, as Catharine Lucas notes: portfolios provide for what she calls "'reflective evaluation,' a kind of formative feedback the *learners give themselves*" (2). Through this technology, then, "students' own evaluative acuity is allowed to develop" (10). That is the hope. As others make clear, the hope is not yet realized. Two of the early portfolio models no longer exist: the Elbow/Belanoff model is now defunct, a victim of politics; the University of Michigan portfolio program is rumored to be in demise along with its Composition Board; many other models oppress more than make possible, as Sandra Murphy and Barbara Grant detail. Beyond portfolio as technology, scholars continue to look, with depressingly frugal effect, for assessments more congruent with other epistemologies, like that of feminism (Holdstein); with other rhetorics, like that of African Americans (Ball); with other composing technologies, like that of hypertext (Yancey, "Portfolio").

How these issues play out — and how we compositionists alleviate or exacerbate them — is a central and largely unexamined question for assessment, as Pamela Moss explains, one ideally suited to program assessment. This kind of assessment provides another lens through which to understand our practices and their effects, so that we might, ultimately and in a reflective way, take on the central question that doesn't seem to surface often enough: whose needs does this writing assessment serve? (Johnston). In detailing such a program assessment, Moss focuses on the power of naming and of forming that assessment wields: how, she asks, do students and others come to *understand themselves* as a result of our interpretations, our representations, our assessments? How does such an interpretation impact students' "access to material resources and [how does it] locate them within social relations of power" (119)? Moss argues that in taking up these questions, it is insufficient merely to interview and survey students. "Rather, it is important to study the actual discourse that occurs around the products and practices of testing — to see how those whose lives a testing program impacts are using the representations (interpretations) it produces" (119). Writing assessment here, then, is rhetorical: positioned as shaper of students and as means of understanding the effects of such shaping.

WRITING ASSESSMENT AND THE SELF: A REFLECTING LENS

As Lester Faigley and James Berlin have suggested, education ultimately and always is about identity formation, and this is no less true for writing assessment than for any other discipline. What we are about, in a phrase, is formation of the *self*: and writing assessment, because it wields so much power, plays a crucial role in what self, or selves, will be permitted — in our classrooms; in our tests; ultimately, in our culture. The self also provides a lens through which we can look backward and forward at once, to inquire as to how it was constructed during the three waves of writing assessment as well as how it may be constructed in the fourth.

During the first wave of writing assessment, the *tested self* of course took very narrow forms. In multiple choice tests, the self is a passive, forced-choice response to an external expert's understanding of language conventions. Agency is neither desired nor allowed. During the second wave, the self becomes a producer — of a holistically scored essay — and thus an agent who creates text. Still, there is less agency there than it appears. The text that is created is conventionally and substantively determined — some might say overdetermined — by an expert who constrains what is possible, by creating the prompt, designing the scoring guide used to evaluate the text, training the readers who do the scoring. Given these constraints, the authorship of such a text is likely to be a static, single-voiced self who can only anticipate and fulfill the expert's expectations, indeed whose task is to do just that (Sullivan). At best, agency is limited; a self-in-writing is permitted, but it is a very limited self, with very circumscribed agency. The text does not admit alternative discourses conceptually or pragmatically: it's text as correct answer.

During the third wave of writing assessment, the self emerges, and it's often multiple, created both through diverse texts and through the reflective text that accompanies those texts. And yet many are uncomfortable with this model of assessment, as Charles Schuster argues. He takes issue particularly with the reflective text since it invites portfolio readers to "fictionalize" authors:

> In effect, fictionalizing student authors moves readers away from normed criteria, replacing careful evaluation with reader response. . . . Presumptions concerning personality, intention, behavior, and the like skew readings or turn assessment into novel reading. . . . Such fictionalizing serves a useful purpose within a classroom. . . . Writing assessment, however, demands that we exclusively evaluate what the student has produced on the page in the portfolio. Fictionalizing in this context can only obscure judgment. (319)

Others, however, aren't so sure, some pointing out that such fictionalizing occurs even within singular texts (Faigley; Sullivan), and others that such "narrativizing tendencies" are inevitable (Schultz, Durst, Roemer):

> This narrativizing tendency constitutes one of our primary ways of understanding, one of our primary ways of making sense of the world, and is an essential strategy in comprehension. As far as portfolio evaluation is concerned, rather than say that narrativizing is right or wrong, perhaps we should start by admitting its inevitability, and by advising teachers to be aware of this tendency and not overvalue the stories we create. (130)

The questions raised within this portfolio assessment, then, take us back to reliability and link it to the personal: how *do* we read, particularly this kind of text; what do we *reward* when we read; and what (different) role(s) should the answers to these questions play in both classroom and external assessment? Or: where and when does the self belong, and why?

A final point: the self is constructed quite explicitly through reflection, it's true. But the self is constructed as well through multiple school discourses — academic writing, writing connected to service learning, writing within disciplines, writing for the workplace, writing for the public. Each of these rhetorical tasks assumes a somewhat different self: how are these selves represented — or even evoked — in writing assessment? Or: how *could* they be represented in writing assessment, particularly one that is linked to democracy?

THE ROLE OF CCCC: WRITING ASSESSMENT WITHIN COMPOSITION STUDIES

Through its conferences and within the pages of its journal, as the many citations here attest, the Conference on College Composition and Communication has provided the place where postsecondary writing assessment has developed as a discipline. Reading through 50 years of volumes impresses one with the sophistication of the issues raised, the commitment of compositionists to their students, the frustration that easier answers were not to be had. In addition to numerous articles of various kinds — theoretical, pedagogical, and research — the pages of *CCC* include writing assessment's disciplinary consolidation, as we see in ever-longer, ever-more-complete and rhetorically informed bibliographies — in 1952, in 1979, and in 1992. It was likewise within the pages of *CCC* where the first comprehensive statement about writing assessment was published, The Position Statement on Writing Assessment, which moves from what we know to include *what that means*: what we can and must do because of what we know. Because literacy is social, this statement claims, assessment must be specific, purposeful, contextual, ethical. And because it is social, we — students, faculty, administrators, legislators — all have rights and responsibilities.

Which is not to say that the story of writing assessment is a narrative of uninterrupted progress; it's rather a narrative of incomplete and uncompleted waves; the early wave, governed by the objective measure; the second wave, which saw the move to the more valid holistically scored essay; the third wave, where portfolios contextualized our students' work and invited us to consider how we read, how we interpret, how we evaluate. At the same time, energies are currently accumulating as though to gather a fourth wave. Perhaps this next wave will focus on program assessment as epistemelogical and ideological work; perhaps it will focus more on individual assessment as interpretive act; perhaps it will take on the challenges posed by non-canonical texts (email, hypertext, multi-generic writings); perhaps it will address the kinds of expertise and ways that they can construct and be represented in writing assessment; perhaps it will include topics that are only now forming.

What is certain is that writing assessment is now construed as a rhetorical act: as its own agent with responsibilities to all its participants. What's also certain is that practice has located assessment, even during the first wave, and that practice has motivated successive waves of development, permitting a kind of theorizing that is congruent with a composition studies that is art and practice. Grounded in such practice, then, writing assessment is becoming more reflective about that practice and the practices to which it connects, uncovering assumptions we bring to texts and that we create as we read texts, understanding our work in the light of what others do, apprehending that what we do is social and thus entails both ideological and ethical dimensions that themselves are increasingly very much a part of both theory and practice.

Acknowledgments: Thanks to Russell Durst, to Cynthia Lewiecki-Wilson, and to a third anonymous reviewer for their clarifying and productive remarks on this essay.

NOTES

1. Of course, how and what to teach them — that is, what the content of the English course should be — was also a frequent topic in the early days.

2. Even as I write this, there is a call on the listserv WPA-L inquiring into how multiple choice tests can assist in placement.

3. As I suggest later in this paper, the fact that this is a classroom based program is significant.

4. And White demonstrates: "the actual reliability of the essay test therefore lies between the lower limit of .68 and the upper limit of .89; in practice, this means that any two readers of the test, working independently on a six-point scale, agreed (or differed by no more than one point) approximately 95 percent of the time" (*Teaching* 27).

5. Ironically, what Brown recommends seems considerably less progressive: "Use computers. Have people mark off T-units in the essays so you can gather information about number of words per T-unit, number of clauses per T-unit, number of words per clause, number of adjective clauses, number of noun clauses, and so on — information about embedding, in short, which ties you directly to indices of syntactic maturity" (5).

6. Assessment — or the specter thereof — has sparked many a faculty development program. See, for instance, Toby Fulwiler and Art Young's account of the way the WAC program at Michigan Tech began, in their introduction to *Assessing Writing across the Curriculum.*

7. The first books on writing portfolios all concern themselves with portfolio practice as it occurs in classrooms or just after. See Belanoff and Dickson, and Yancey, *Portfolios.*

8. Reflection is increasingly a part of nonportfolio placement exercises: at Coe College, for instance, at Morehead State, and at Grand Valley State College. And these practices show how waves overlap in still other ways, here in a second-wave essay format enriched by a third-wave reflective text. For more on self-assessment in placement, see Royer and Gilles's "Directed Self-Placement."

WORKS CITED

Allen, Michael. "Valuing Differences: Portnet's First Year." *Assessing Writing* 2 (1995): 67–91.

Allen, Michael, William Condon, Marcia Dickson, Cheryl Forbes, George Meece, and Kathleen Yancey. "Portfolios, WAC, Email and Assessment: An Inquiry on Portnet." *Situating Portfolios: Four Perspectives.* Ed. Kathleen Blake Yancey and Irwin Weiser. Logan: Utah State UP, 1997. 370–84.

Allen, Michael, Jane Frick, Jeff Sommers, and Kathleen Yancey. "Outside Review of Writing Portfolios: An On-Line Evaluation." *WPA* 20.3 (1997): 64–88.

Anson, Chris. "Response Styles and Ways of Knowing." *Writing and Response: Theory, Practice, Research.* Ed. Chris Anson. Urbana: NCTE, 1989. 332–67.

Ball, Arnetha. "Expanding the Dialogue on Culture as a Critical Component when Assessing Writing." *Assessing Writing* 4 (1997): 169–203.

Belanoff, Pat, and Marcia Dickson, eds. *Portfolios: Process and Product.* Portsmouth: Boynton, 1991.

Berlin, James. *Writing Instruction in Nineteenth-Century American Colleges.* Carbondale: Southern Illinois UP, 1984.

Broad, Robert. "Reciprocal Authority in Communal Writing Assessment: Constructing Textual Value in a New Politics of Inquiry." *Assessing Writing* 4(1997): 133–69.

Brossell, Gordon. "Current Research and Unanswered Questions in Writing Assessment." Greenberg et al. 168–83.

Brown, R. "What We Know Now and How We Could Know More about Writing Ability in America." *Journal of Basic Writing 1.4* (1978): 1–6.

CCCC Committee on Assessment. "Writing Assessment: A Position Statement." *CCC*: 46 (1994): 430–37.

Chandler, Jean. "Positive Control." *CCC 48* (1997): 273–274.

Cooper, Charles and Lee Odell, eds. *Evaluating Writing: Describing, Judging, Measuring.* Urbana: NCTE, 1989.

Daiker, Donald. "Learning to Praise." *Writing and Response: Theory, Practice, and Research.* Ed. Chris Anson. Urbana: NCTE, 1989. 103–14.

Elbow, Peter. Introduction. Belenoff and Dickson ix–xxiv.

Elbow, Peter and Pat Belanoff. "Reflections on an Explosion: Portfolios in the 90s and Beyond." *Situating Portfolios: Four Perspectives.* Ed. Kathleen Yancey and Irwin Weiser. Logan: Utah State UP, 1997. 21–34.

Fader, Daniel. "Writing Samples and Virtues." Greenberg et al. 79–92.

Faigley, Lester. "Judging Writing, Judging Selves." *CCC 40* (1989): 395–412.

Faigley, Lester, Roger Cherry, David Jolliffe, and Anna Skinner. *Assessing Writers' Knowledge and Processes of Composing.* Norwood: Ablex, 1985.

Fulwiler, Toby and Art Young. "Preface — The WAC Archives Revisited." *Assessing Writing Across the Curriculum: Diverse Approaches and Practices.* Eds. Kathleen Blake Yancey and Brian Huot. Greenwich: Ablex, 1997. 1–7.

Greenberg, Karen, Harvey Wiener, and Richard Donovan, eds. *Writing Assessment: Issues and Strategies.* New York, Longman, 1993.

Hamp-Lyons, Liz and William Condon. "Questioning Assumptions about Portfolio-Based Assessment." *CCC 44* (1993): 176–90.

Hanson, F. A. *Testing Testing: Social Consequences of the Examined Life.* Berkeley: U of California P, 1993.

Harris, Joseph. *A Teaching Subject: Composition Since 1966.* Upper Saddle River: Prentice, 1997.

Haswell, Richard and Susan Wyche-Smith. "Adventuring Into Writing Assessments." *CCC 45* (1994): 220–36.

Holdstein, Deborah. "Gender, Feminism, and Institution-Wide Assessment Programs." *Assessment of Writing: Politics, Policies, Practices.* Eds. Edward White, William Lutz, and Sandra Kamusikiri. New York: MLA, 1996. 204–26.

Holladay, Sylvia, guest ed. *Teaching English in the Two-Year College 20.4* (1993). Special Issue on Writing Assessment.

Hull, Glynda, and Mike Rose. "This Wooden Shack Place: The Logic of an Unconventional Reading." *CCC 41* (1990): 287–98.

Huot, Brian. "Toward a New Theory of Writing Assessment." *CCC 47* (1996): 549–67.

Johnston, Peter. "Theoretical Consistencies in Reading, Writing, Literature, and Teaching." NCTE, Baltimore, 1989.

Larson, Richard. "Using Portfolios in the Assessment of Writing in the Academic Disciplines." Belanoff and Dickson 137–51.

Lucas, Catharine. "Introduction: Writing Portfolios — Changes and Challenges." *Portfolios in the Writing Classroom: An Introduction.* Ed. Kathleen Yancey. Urbana: NCTE, 1992. 1–12.

Moss, Pamela. "Response: Testing the Test of the Test." *Assessing Writing 5* (1998): 111–23.

Murphy, Sandra, and the CCCC Committee on Writing Assessment. "Survey of Postsecondary Placement Practices." Unpublished ms, 1994.

Murphy, Sandra, and Barbara Grant. "Portfolio Approaches to Assessment: Breakthrough or More of the Same?" *Assessment of Writing: Politics, Policies, Practices.* Eds. Edward White, William Lutz, and Sandra Kamusikiri. New York: MLA, 1996. 284–301.

Royer, Daniel J., and Roger Gilles. "Directed Self-Placement: An Attitude of Orientation." *CCC 50* (1998): 54–70.

Sasser, E. "Some Aspects of Freshman English." *CCC 3.3* (1952): 12–14.

Schultz, Lucy, Russel Durst, and Marjorie Roemer. "Stories of Reading: Inside and Outside the Texts of Portfolios." *Assessing Writing 4* (1997): 121–33.

Schuster, Charles. "Climbing the Slippery Slope of Writing Assessment: The Programmatic Use of Writing Portfolios." *New Directions in Portfolio Assessment: Reflective Practice, Critical Theory, and Large-Scale Scoring.* Eds. Laurel Black, Donald Daiker, Jeffrey Sommers, and Gail Stygall. Portsmouth: Boynton, 1994. 314–25.

Shaughnessy, Mina. *Errors and Expectations.* New York: Oxford UP, 1977.

Smagorinsky, Peter. "Response to Writers, Not Writing: A Review of Twelve Readers Reading." *Assessing Writing 3*: 211–21.

Sommers, Nancy. "Revision Strategies of Student Writers and Adult Experienced Writers." *CCC 31* (1981): 378–88.

Straub, Richard, and Ronald Lunsford. *Twelve Readers Reading*. Creskill: Hampton, 1995.

Sullivan, Francis. "Calling Writers' Bluffs: The Social Production of Writing Ability in University Placement Testing." *Assessing Writing 4* (1997): 53–81.

Tchudi, Stephen, ed. *Alternatives to Grading Student Writing*. Urbana: NCTE, 1997.

Valentine, John. "The College Entrance Examination Board." *CCC 12* (1961): 88–92.

White, Edward. "Pitfalls in the Testing of Writing." Greenberg et al. 53–79.

———. "Holistic Scoring: Past Triumphs, Future Challenges." *Validating Holistic Scoring for Writing Assessment*. Ed. Michael Williamson and Brian Huot. Creskill: Hampton, 1993. 79–108.

———. *Teaching and Assessing Writing*. San Francisco: Jossey-Bass, 1985.

Williamson, Michael, and Brian Huot, eds. *Validating Holistic Scoring*. Norwood: Ablex, 1992.

Williamson, Michael. "The Worship of Efficiency: Untangling Practical and Theoretical Considerations in Writing Assessment." *Assessing Writing 1* (1994): 147–74.

Yancey, Kathleen Blake. *Portfolios in the Writing Classroom: An Introduction*. Urbana: NCTE, 1992.

———. *Reflection in the Writing Classroom*. Logan: Utah State UP, 1998.

———. "Portfolio, Electronic, and the Links Between." *Computers and Composition 13* (1996): 129–35.

Yancey, Kathleen Blake, and Brian Huot, eds. *WAC Program Assessment*. Norwood: Ablex, 1997.

9

Testing the Test of the Test: A Response to "Multiple Inquiry in the Validation of Writing Tests"

PAMELA A. MOSS

Within the first few pages of his article, Professor Haswell raises a number of critical issues to be considered in evaluating a writing test and the larger program of which it is part:

> What (fallible) humans run [the program] for what (debatable) ends and (more or less) how well, and how do the (vulnerable) people who are labeled by it feel (they think) about the process? . . . How well do [the test's] labels match up with performance of people in the world outside the test? . . . What is the value system that underlies it? . . . How long before the historical motives for the original construction change, or how long before the labels drift out of use, attached as they are to people who are also changing? . . . And, most crucially, what *are* the uses that are made of this labeling, by the people who constructed the test, by the people who run the apparatus, by the institutions that use the labels, by the people who acquire the labels? (p. 92)

These issues highlight testing as a social practice with social origins and social consequences, not just for the person assessed, but for all stakeholders in the assessment process. The article moves on to argue for the value of "multi-method" research, citing program evaluation theorists who call not just for multiple methods but for methods that span disciplinary perspectives, including, for instance, ethnographic, historical, and biographical investigations. Multiple methods of inquiry, Haswell suggests enable validity research

> to be of use to a variety of stakeholders, to be sensitive to the presence of conflicting perspectives, to seek convergent findings among studies with different biases, and to probe a social context that is complex, fluid, and provisional. (p. 89)

These are all important points for validity researchers to take into account. The article then turns to an extended example intended to illustrate "the potential" of this multiple inquiry approach to validation. It is here, in my judgment,

From *Assessing Writing* 5 (1998): 111–22.

that the article falls somewhat short of both what the introduction promises and what thorough practice in validity research requires. The first concern, taken alone, is not yet a criticism of the research itself: most programs of validity research, operating with limited resources, fall short of the ideals articulated in validity theory. It is, however, a criticism of the extent to which the example serves as an illustration of the potential of the multiple inquiry approach. It would have been useful to read more about Professor Haswell's research "wishlist," or at least to hear more of his concerns about the limitations of the current research. In this response, then, I will point to some possibilities for additional research in the spirit of the important questions he raises, drawing on scholars that represent a variety of theories of inquiry. The second, more critical, concern with the extended example is that it remains silent about certain issues and practices that are, in my judgment, crucial to a strong program of validity research. It is important to note that these "silences" to which I refer may simply reflect choices of what to include in the limited space of a journal article rather than gaps in the research actually undertaken. To complement the advice Professor Haswell provides, I will point to theories and practices in the mainstream literature on validity in educational measurement (e.g., Cronbach, 1988, 1989; Messick, 1989, 1994; Shepard, 1993, 1997; and *The Standards for Educational and Psychological Testing*, 1985) to which this article does not refer. This literature not only supports many of Professor Haswell's points about multiple methods, but it also provides a coherent conceptual framework to guide research design that speaks directly to the particular issues associated with test evaluation. Where the mainstream literature in validity theory (and program evaluation) falls short, in my judgment, at least in practical emphasis if not in intent, is in encouraging a kind of critical reflection about its own taken-for-granted theories and practices (e.g., Bourdieu & Wacquant, 1992; Kogler, 1996) — the kind of critical reflection that appears to underlie Professor Haswell's introductory questions. To find practices that support this kind of critical reflection, it is useful to look beyond the literature in program evaluation and educational measurement, to the work of theorists who locate their writing in alternative traditions of social science.

And so, in responding to this piece, first, I'll highlight those places where validity theory in educational measurement, in fact, supports and extends many of the recommendations that Professor Haswell makes in the introductory sections, focusing primarily on the work of Cronbach (1988, 1989), Messick (1989, 1994), Shepard (1993, 1997), and the authors of the *Standards for Educational and Psychological Testing* (APA, AERA, and NCME, 1999). Following that, I'll consider the extended example in light of the theories and practices proposed in the mainstream validity literature, pointing in particular to areas where the research can (and, I believe, should) be extended. I have chosen not to respond at the level of detail of particular studies or types of evidence, but rather to consider the big picture — the quality of validity argument that is built when the evidence presented here is comprehensively considered. Finally, I'll consider the extended example in light of Professor Haswell's important question about the values that underlie the assessment system.

LOCATING THE PRINCIPLES OF MULTIPLE INQUIRY WITHIN VALIDITY THEORY IN EDUCATIONAL MEASUREMENT

Professor Haswell paints a picture of the field of college writing assessment that appears seriously isolated from the larger educational assessment community. He characterizes the field as relying, at least until recently, on "traditional methods of test evaluation (e.g., item analysis, inter-rater reliability, test-retest correlations)" (msp. 7) and single method investigations. In order to address these shortcomings, he points readers to literature on program evaluation. To the extent that this characterization is true of research in college writing assessment, it is crucial to distinguish it from the theory and practice of validity research in educational measurement more generally, where there is strong support (and concrete advice) for most of the principles Professor Haswell articulates in the introduction.

Within educational and psychological measurement, validity has never been defined in a way that would consider item analysis, inter-rater reliability, and test-retest correlations sufficient evidence.[1] The literature on validity theory in educational measurement is multimethod and has been for many years. [See Messick (1989), Moss (1992, 1995), and Shepard (1993) for a historical perspective.] Moreover, as I suggested above, the work of theorists like Cronbach, Messick, Shepard, and the authors of the *Standards* offer conceptual frameworks for guiding validity research, varying somewhat from theorist to theorist, which directly address the specific issues associated with test evaluation.

As represented in the educational measurement literature, validity research is designed around an explicit understanding of the purpose(s) the test will serve and of the kinds of interpretations that are intended to be drawn. Thus, validity research involves attention both to the meaning of test scores or other test results as well as to their effects (Shepard, 1993). A "strong" program of research requires an explicit conceptual framework or theoretical rationale, testable hypotheses or questions deduced from it, and multiple lines of relevant evidence to test the hypotheses (Cronbach, 1989). Although validity research is always designed in light of the intended interpretation and use of the test, most theorists suggest general categories of evidence to consider in any testing situation. Messick (1989), for instance, suggests we can:

- appraise the relevance and representativeness of the test content in relation to the content of the domain about which inferences are to be drawn, . . .

- examine relationships among responses to the tasks, items, or parts of the test — that is, the internal structure of test responses, . . .

- survey relationships of the test scores with other measures and background variables — that is, the test's external structure, . . .

- directly probe the ways in which individuals cope with the items or tasks, in an effort to illuminate the processes underlying item response and task performance, . . .

- investigate uniformities and differences in these test processes and structures over time or across groups and settings — that is the generalizability of test interpretation and use, . . .

- see if the test scores display appropriate variations as a function of instructional and other interventions, . . . [and]

- appraise the value implications and social consequences of interpreting and using the test scores. (p. 6)

Validity research is most efficiently guided by the testing of "plausible rival hypotheses" which suggest credible alternative explanations or meanings for the test score that are challenged and refuted by the evidence collected. Does the test require capabilities that are irrelevant to the intended interpretation? Does it result in performances that under-represent or provide a narrower interpretation than what is intended?

Shephard (1993) suggests that "validity evaluations be organized in response to the question: 'What does the testing practice claim to do?'" (p. 429). Related guiding questions include: "What are the arguments for and against the intended aims of the test? And what does the test do in the system other than what it claims, for good or bad?" (p. 429). These questions entail evidence both about the soundness of the test-based interpretations and decisions as well as the effects of test use. It requires examining the *intended* interpretations and effects (uses), as well as those that are unintended.

To evaluate the potential consequences of a test use, Messick suggests pitting the proposed use against alternative assessment techniques and alternative means of serving the same purpose, including the generalized alternative of not assessing at all. Cronbach (1988, 1989) suggests using stakeholders' interests as well as evaluators' concerns to generate a list of potential questions and then prioritizing the questions based on (a) prior uncertainty about the issue; (b) information to be yielded by a feasible study compared to how much uncertainty will remain; (c) cost of the investigation in terms of time and dollars; and (d) leverage for achieving consensus about the use of the test in the relevant audience. Shepard (1993) suggests using the intended purposes of assessment to generate rival hypotheses about unintended consequences and prioritizing questions in light of the seriousness of consequences for individuals and programs. In the work of these theorists, the kind of general advice outlined here is regularly accompanied by concrete examples of validity research in specific contexts. [Shepard's (1993) cases of validity research provide a particularly useful and accessible view of how evidence from studies can be integrated into a comprehensive validity argument.]

And so the literature on validity in educational assessment not only supports but offers specific guidance on a number of the important issues Professor Haswell raises in this article including an emphasis on how tests are used, on meeting the needs of different stakeholders, on the importance of cross-checking or triangulation, and on the importance of probing a complex social context.

EXAMINING THE EXTENDED EXAMPLE FROM THE PERSPECTIVE OF VALIDITY THEORY IN EDUCATIONAL MEASUREMENT

Professor Haswell begins the extended example with a list of the purposes the writing (assessment) program is intended to serve:

to place students in writing courses, to support a WAC initiative, to support a general-education reform of the undergraduate curriculum, to send a message to prospective employers of degree-holders, to help fulfill a mandate for outcomes assessment from the state higher education coordinating board, and to serve as a form of writing instruction itself." (p. 96)

There are many distinct purposes here, each of which brings a partially different set of contingencies (and primary stakeholders) to validity research. For this paper, I'll focus on the purpose of placing students in writing courses. Professor Haswell describes a number of different ways, organized by the interests of different stakeholders, in which evidence has been gathered and used to support the validity of the assessment for this purpose. These include:

a. comparing placement tests' results with

- students'perceptions of the their accuracy before and after instruction,

- students' enrollment patterns,

- teachers' perceptions of their accuracy after students are placed in their courses, and

- subsequent measures of students' writing capability, including course outcomes and outcomes on the portfolio later administered by the writing program;

b. examining the consistency of ratings and the processes in which raters engage;

c. considering "formal equivalency tests" (msp. 21) for the on-demand writing tasks;

d. comparing performance of different groups, including

- native and non-native English speakers,

- transfer and non-transfer students, and

- students who elected to take the second placement exam at different stages in their education;

e. comparing performance of students who elected different course options;

f. examining frequency distributions of students' performance in light of what is expected; and

g. considering other evidence with respect to cost, participation, and satisfaction across teachers and departments, differences in performance by department, support of the program by administrators and policy makers, and student subscription for the examination program.

These are all sources of evidence that can be useful in evaluating a placement program. However, when considered in light of the more comprehensive programs of validity research outlined in the previous section, there are some serious gaps in the evidence as presented in this article.

Missing from this list of activities is any evidence of what the test scores actually mean in terms of students' writing capabilities and whether this meaning is coherent with other aspects of the program. It is not clear to me what the substantive goals of the program are — what counts as good writing — or what theoretical rationale underlies the placement of students into different courses. What substantive and rhetorical demands do the on-demand writing tasks place on students? What specific criteria do readers use to evaluate the on-demand writing assessments or the contents of the junior portfolio? What is the nature and range of types of writing that are included in the junior portfolio? When teachers of other courses evaluate papers as "acceptable" for inclusion in the junior portfolio, what criteria do they use? How does that differ across departments and teachers? How coherent are the visions of writing reflected in these different assessments and in the goals of the program?

In addition to the meaning of the scores, it's important to consider the meaningfulness of the placement decisions. What are the goals of the different courses into which students are placed and what kinds of learning activities are available to students in these courses? How coherent are course goals and activities with the assessment of students' needs that underlies the placement decision? What do students actually learn as a result of participating in these classes? To what extent is that consistent with the assumptions that are made as students are placed into those classes? Certainly, empirical evidence about the relationship between test scores and other outcome measures is relevant information, but in the absence of evidence about the meaning of test scores and the nature of instruction, it is not possible to fully understand (or document) the reason for this relationship. As I suggested above, a sound program of validity research begins with a clear statement of both the purpose and the intended interpretation or meaning of test scores and then examines, through logical analysis, the coherence of tests with that understanding. In the case of a placement exam, logical analysis of coherence must also encompass an understanding of the different courses as well as the outcome measures used to evaluate success in those courses.

Beyond the essential activity of evaluating the coherence among the various products of the writing program, it is useful to examine the processes in which the various participants engage in terms of their consistency with theoretical expectations. Here, the article does refer to studies of readers' processes through think-aloud protocols — a very useful activity. Consideration of the processes of other stakeholders, and their understanding reflected therein, would also inform validity research. What about the processes that students go through as they complete the assessments or that teachers use as they consider the appropriateness of the students' placement, make instructional decisions, and implement those decisions in class? To what extent are these consistent with the expectations of the program? What unintended consequences are apparent and are these consequences beneficial or detrimental? These kinds of process studies are admittedly costly and time consuming but extremely useful if resources permit.

Another concern to raise about the extended example relates to how the perspectives of different stakeholders are elicited and used to improve the program. Professor Haswell argues, and I agree, that one of the primary benefits of multiple method inquiry is to "give voice to different perspectives" (msp. 8): "any one validation measure tends to privilege the perspectives of certain people and suppress the perspectives of others" (msp. 7). This is, indeed, one of the most important roles that multiple inquiry can play. Studies that elicit different perspectives enable stakeholders to engage in critical reflection on their own perspectives so that they can be reaffirmed with a new self-consciousness or enabled to evolve. While the extended example contains a number of opportunities for different voices to be raised, there are places where the potential may not be fully realized. In some cases it appears that the perspectives of various stakeholders were either assumed or based on the author's recollection of meetings or other personal experience. And, in some cases, even where different perspectives were systematically documented, it appears that validity evidence was not used to illuminate biases of those responsible for the writing program, but rather to persuade the stakeholders that they should see things differently:[2] to persuade students to enroll in the courses into which they were placed (p. 99) and to take the junior exam on time (p. 99), to persuade teachers to accept and support the system which places students in their classes (p. 99), to persuade raters to avoid circumnavigating criteria to work toward a more cohesive community (p. 101), and so on.

I don't mean to suggest that these are necessarily inappropriate uses of validity information. Indeed, one of the purposes of validity research is to enable stakeholders to make more informed decisions. However, there appears to be a lost opportunity here. Given the goal of challenging biases through multiple inquiry, it is premature to dismiss alternative perspectives without fully understanding what they are and why they are held. Why do ESL students feel "doomed to failure" (p. 98) and why are they enrolling in courses at other colleges (p. 99)? Can the writing program be modified to better meet their needs? What "unique methods of evaluation" (p. 103) are raters using and what can be learned from those practices to improve the system? Why do upper division teachers feel that "some of their worse writers were exempted as freshmen" (p. 100)? Are they attending to different criteria of what counts as good writing than what the writing program supports? Again, how might the writing program be improved in light of their concerns?

MOVING BEYOND CONVENTIONAL PRACTICE TOWARD CRITICAL REFLECTION ON THAT PRACTICE

In closing, I'd like to move beyond what might be expected of a conventional program of validity research and consider the extended example in light of the questions about underlying values and consequences raised at the beginning of the article. Here, in a sense, the inquiry lens is turned back on researchers and program developers themselves as stakeholders, encouraging critical reflection about their own theories and practices. Within the educational measurement community, Messick (1989) opened the door to this kind of reflection by suggesting that we evaluate one inquiring system in terms of another to probe the methodological and value assumptions underlying each system. Concrete illustrations of practices that promote such critical reflection are hard to find in the educational measurement literature and I have turned to the work of researchers informed by hermeneutic, critical, feminist, and poststructuralist perspectives [see Moss, 1996; Moss, Schultz, & Collins, 1998]. Here, I'll simply offer a few possibilities for research practices and issues to consider that might encourage this kind of critical reflection.

One important set of questions focuses on the consequences of the writing program for how its stakeholders — students, teachers, administrators, and so on — come to understand themselves and others, as writers, as constructors of knowledge, and as members of the educational and broader communities in which they participate. Luke (1995) argues for the importance of investigating the extent to which the interpretations "we" (teachers and researchers) produce become "part of the taken-for-granted definitions and categories by which members of communities define themselves and others" (p. 9) and how this, in turn, impacts their access to material resources and locates them within social relations of power. These questions cannot be fully addressed through the interview and survey techniques to which we are accustomed. By eliciting information in that way, we lose our ability to understand the ways in which stakeholders might represent themselves, absent our concepts and categories, or the way in which our categories may simply mean something different to them. Further, in many cases these "understandings" are tacit, beneath conscious awareness, and they cannot be provoked through self-reflection alone. Rather, it is important to study the actual discourse that occurs around the products and practices of testing — to see how those whose lives a testing program impacts are using the representations (interpretations) it produces. Useful resources for engaging in this sort of critical discourse analysis include Gee (1996) and Luke (1995). As we (teachers and researchers) come to understand the consequences of our actions for how people understand themselves, our own tacit understandings — the values implicit in our practices — are also illuminated.

Another set of useful questions might interrogate the goals of the writing program and the vision of writing reflected therein. Willard (1996) raises concerns about what Gee (1996) calls the essayist model of good writing in the academy which undervalues more personal kinds of academic writing as reflected, for instance, in the work of anthropologist Ruth Behar (1995). To what extent is the writing program complicit in simply reproducing a narrow model of academic writing (and the understanding of knowledge it entails) without providing opportunity for the values implicit in the model to be illuminated and self-consciously considered? Here the perspectives of outsiders — those not acculturated to the values of the writing program — become particularly important. Inviting readers who are known to hold different perspectives to evaluate portfolios and to articulate the criteria they are using to arrive at their judgments of quality can be a productive way to illuminate taken-for-granted perspectives of those within the program (Hoy, 1994; Kogler, 1996). Lather (1993) pushes the potential role of multiple perspectives even further with her "transgressive" validity criteria. She suggests proliferating multiple interpretations of a phenomena from multiple perspectives so as to high-light the arbitrariness of any single interpretation. Here, one might also under-take a genealogical analysis (Foucault, 1977; Dreyfus & Rabinow, 1982) of the practices through which a certain form of writing came to be privileged. Con-sider, for instance, Gere's (1997) historical investigation of women's literary groups that contrasts their writing practices, and the values that underlie them, with those developing in the (male-dominated) academy.

While the suggestions I've just made are well beyond what might be ex-pected in a conventional program of validity research, they are consistent with the principles Professor Haswell puts forth and, I believe, a productive means of growth for an educational community. Activities like these enable what Bourdieu calls "epistemic reflexivity," which is achieved by subjecting the beliefs and practices of researchers to the same critical analysis as those of the researched: "What has to be constantly scrutinized and neutralized . . . is the collective scientific unconscious embedded in the theories, problems, and . . . categories of scholarly judgment" (Bourdieu & Wacquant, 1992, p. 40). The courageous act of opening the details of a program of research to critical public review, as Professor Haswell has done in this article, is yet another means of encouraging this kind of critical reflection. It not only enhances the program that is the focus of the evaluation effort, but more importantly en-hances the practice of evaluation itself.

NOTES

1. The earliest versions of the testing standards (APA, 1954; AERA & NCMUE, 1955) offered four approaches to validity research — content, concurrent, predictive, and construct. The first re-quired examining the logical relationship between a test and the content domain about which in-ferences are drawn, the second and third (later subsumed under "criterion") required examining the empirical relationship between the test and some criterion of interest, and the fourth, con-struct validity, involved "indirect validating procedures" (note the plural) when no content do-main or criterion measure was adequate to represent the degree to which the test measures what it was intended to measure. As early as the subsequent edition of the *Standards* (1966), the authors were emphasizing the importance of multiple methods for all validity research: "only rarely is just one of them important in a particular situation. A complete study of a test would normally in-volve all types . . ." (APA, 1966, in Messick, 1989, p. 18). Since then it has been argued that no con-tent domain or criterion measure is ever sufficient to establish the validity of a test-based interpretation, and so the multi-method approach of construct validity should guide all validity research.

2. It is the following kinds of statements that caused me to raise this concern: "Upper divi-sion teachers often aver that some of their worse writers were exempted as freshmen, a belief that these figures document as largely a myth" (p. 100). "From the vantage of students who place into basic courses, the benefit may be hard to see. But that student opinion is subject to change, and it will take more than one inquiry to see it" (p. 97). "Some WSU administrators would like to believe that as a group transfer students write worse than non-transfer students, but here the evidence suggests that this is not the case, not at least with native speakers" (p. 98). "Think aloud protocols of raters reading full portfolios found them following unique and sometimes eccentric methods of evaluation, not so much deviating from the criteria and method that raters were trained for as cir-cumnavigating parts of it. Yet subsequent training sessions found them eager to work toward a more cohesive rating community" (p. 103). "It would be a productive act of advising to show these freshman the performance distributions above, which demonstrate transfer NNS [non-native speaker] students performing much worse than NNS students who had undertaken the ESL se-quences of writing courses at Washington State" (p. 98). "There is a natural tendency for teachers to resist placement procedures *per se*. It is difficult to convince them they can't bring along any stu-dent who ends up in this section." (p. 99)

REFERENCES

AERA, APA, and NCME (1999). *Standards for educational and psychological testing*. Washington, DC: Authors.

Behar, R. (1995). Writing in my father's name. A diary of Translated Woman's first year. In R. Behar & D. A. Gordon (Eds.). *Women writing culture* (pp. 65–84). Berkeley: University of California Press.

Bourdieu, P. & Wacquant, L. J. D. (1992). *An invitation to reflexive sociology*. Chicago: University of Chicago Press.

Cronbach, L. J. (1988). Five perspectives on validity argument. In H. Wainer (Ed.). *Test validity*. Hillsdale, NJ: Lawrence Erlbaum Associates, Inc.

Cronbach, L. J. (1989). Construct validation after thirty years. In R. L. Linn (Ed.). *Intelligence: Measurement, theory and public policy* (pp. 147–171). Urbana, IL: University of Illinois Press.

Dreyfus, H. L. & Rabinow, P. (1982). *Michel Foucault: Beyond structuralism and hermeneutics* (2nd ed.). Chicago: University of Chicago Press.

Foucault, M. (1977). *Discipline and punish* (A. Sheridan, Trans.). New York: Vintage Books.

Gee, J. P. (1996). *Social linguistics and literacies: Ideology in discourses* (2nd ed.). London: Taylor and Francis.

Gere, A. R. (1997). *Intimate practices: Literacy and cultural work in U.S. women's clubs, 1880–1920*. Urbana, IL: University of Illinois Press.

Hoy, D. C. (1994). Critical theory and critical history. In D. C. Hoy & T. McCarthy, *Critical theory* (pp. 101–214). Oxford: Blackwell.

Kogler, H. H. (1996). *The power of dialogue* (P. Hendrickson, Trans.). Cambridge, MA: The MIT Press.

Lather, P. (1993). Fertile obsession: Validity after poststructuralism. *Sociological Quarterly, 32* (4), 673–693.

Luke, A. (1995). Text and discourse in education: An introduction to critical discourse analysis. *Review of Research in Education, 21,* 3–48.

Messick, S. (1989). Validity. *Educational measurement* (3rd ed.). Washington, DC: The American Council on Education and the National Council on Measurement in Education.

Messick, S. (1994). The interplay of evidence and consequences in the validation of performance assessments. *Educational Researcher, 23* (2), 13–24.

Moss, P. A. (1992). Shifting conceptions of validity in educational measurement: Implications for performance assessment. *Review of Educational Research, 62* (3), 229–258.

Moss, P. A. (1995). Themes and variations in validity theory. *Educational Measurement: Issues and Practice, 14* (2), 5–13.

Moss, P. A. (1996). Enlarging the dialogue in educational measurement: Voices from interpretive research traditions. *Educational Researchers, 25* (1), 20–28, 43.

Moss, P. A., Schultz, A. M., & Collins, K. M. (1998). An integrative approach to portfolio evaluation for teacher licensure. *Journal for Personnel Evaluation in Education, 12*(2), 139–161.

Shepard, L. A. (1993). Evaluating test validity. *Review of Research in Education, 19*, 405–450.

Shepard, L. A. (1997). The centrality of test use and consequences for test validity. *Educational Measurement: Issues and Practice, 16*(2), 5–8, 13, 24.

Willard, M. K. (1996). *Interanimating voices: Theorizing the turn toward reflective writing in the academy*. Paper presented at the annual meeting of the Modern Language Association, Washington, DC.

10 Toward a New Theory of Writing Assessment

BRIAN HUOT

Many composition teachers and scholars feel frustrated by, cut off from, or otherwise uninterested in the subject of writing assessment—especially assessment that takes place outside of the classroom for purposes of placement, exit, or program evaluation. This distrust and estrangement are understandable, given the highly technical aspects of much discourse about writing assessment. For the most part, writing assessment has been developed, constructed, and privatized by the measurement community as a technological apparatus whose inner workings are known only to those with specialized knowledge. Consequently, English professionals have been made to feel inadequate and naive by considerations of technical concepts like validity and reliability. At the same time, teachers have remained skeptical (and rightly so) of assessment practices that do not reflect the values important to an understanding of how people learn to read and write. It does not take a measurement specialist to realize that many writing assessment procedures have missed the mark in examining students' writing ability.

At the core of this inability to communicate are basic theoretical differences between the measurement and composition communities (White, "Language"). Writing assessment procedures, as they have been traditionally constructed, are designed to produce reliable (that is, consistent) numerical scores of individual student papers from independent judges. Traditional writing assessment practices are based upon classical test theory, with roots in a positivist epistemology that assumes "that there exists a reality out there, driven by immutable natural laws" (Guba 19). The assumption is that student ability in writing, as in anything else, is a fixed, consistent, and acontextual human trait. Our ability to measure such a trait would need to recognize these consistencies and could be built upon psychometrics, a statistical apparatus devised for use in the social sciences.

Within such a paradigm, for example, the scores students receive on a writing test like the National Assessment of Educational Progress are an accu-

From *College Composition and Communication* 47 (1996): 549–66.

rate measure of the writing ability of the nation's students.[1] The results represent students' ability to write and can be compared from school to school and year to year. In such large scale assessment, individual matters of context and rhetoric are to be overcome in favor of producing a "true" measure of student ability whose validity can only be established through technical and statistical rigor. These beliefs and assumptions put enormous faith in the technology of testing, things like the development of scoring guidelines or rubrics, the training of raters, the scores papers receive, and the statistical calculation of interrater reliability. It is through this psychometric technology that we can isolate the "reality" — in this case student writing ability — which a positivist epistemology assumes is "out there." Table 10–1 provides a summary of the procedures used in traditional writing assessment, the purpose of these procedures and the assumptions upon which they are based.

Currently, new ideas in measurement theory are being supported by the same theoretical movements in the social construction of knowledge that are used to explore and explain written communication in a postmodern age. At the heart of the movement in measurement theory toward considerations of context and individuality is the evolution of theories of validity (see Moss, "Shifting," for a good overview). Since the 1980s, validity has come to be defined as more than the traditional notion that a test measures what it purports to measure. Several validity scholars, prominent among them Samuel Messick and Lee Cronbach, have been revising their views for nearly 20 years.

For Messick, validity is "an integrated evaluative judgment of the degree to which empirical evidence and theoretical rationales support the adequacy

TABLE 10–1   Traditional Writing Assessment Procedures, Purposes, and Assumptions

Procedure	Purpose	Assumption
Scoring Guideline	Recognize features of writing quality	Writing quality can be defined and determined
Rater Training	Foster agreement on independent rater scores	One set of features of student writing for which raters should agree
Scores on Papers	Fix degree of writing quality for comparing writing ability and making decisions on that ability	Student ability to write can be coded and communicated numerically
Interrater Reliability	Calculate the degree of agreement between independent raters	Consistency and standardization to be maintained across time and location
Validity	Determine the assessment measures what it purports to measure	An assessment's value is limited to distinct goals and properties in the instrument itself

and appropriateness of inferences and actions based on test scores of other modes of assessment" (5). In this definition there are two striking differences from traditional notions of validity. First of all, Messick includes multiple theoretical as well as empirical considerations. In other words, in writing assessment, the validity of a test must include a recognizable and supportable theoretical foundation as well as empirical data from students' work. To be valid, writing assessment would need input from the scholarly literature about the teaching and learning of writing. Second, a test's validity also includes its use. A test, for example, which is used for purposes outside a relevant theoretical foundation for the teaching of writing would be an invalid measure of writing ability. Cronbach's stance is similar. For Cronbach validity "must link concepts, evidence, social and personal consequences and values" (4). Under these terms, many current procedures now in use could be seriously challeneged as invalid. Both of these newer definitions of validity question current-traditional preoccupations with the technical aspects of writing assessment procedures. Cronbach contends that we will need to link together assessment procedures with what we know about writing pedagogy and the impact of assessment procedures with what we know about writing pedagogy and the impact of assessment procedures on teaching and learning. Both these new notions of validity look beyond the assessment measures themselves and demand that a valid procedure for assessing writing must have positive impact and consequences for the teaching and learning of writing.

Few important or long lasting changes can occur in the way we assess student writing outside of the classroom unless we attempt to change the theory which drives our practices and attitudes toward assessment. At present, assessment procedures which attempt to fix objectively a student's ability to write are based upon an outdated theory supported by an irrelevant epistemology. Emergent ideas about measurement define teaching, learning, and assessment in new ways, ways which are compatible with our own developing theories about literacy, though for the most part they have yet to filter down to the assessment of student writing. The result has been a stalemate for writing assessment. Although we have been able to move from single-sample impromptu essays to portfolios in less than 20 years, we are still primarily concerned with constructing scoring guidelines and achieving high rates of interrater reliability.

This essay explores our ability to construct a theory of writing assessment based upon our understandings about the nature of language, written communication, and its teaching. The bases for this theoretical exploration are current practices at universities that have been using assessment procedures unsupported by conventional writing assessment's reliance on the positivist, epistemological foundations of classical test theory. Instead, these new procedures recognize the importance of context, rhetoric, and other characteristics integral to a specific purpose and institution. The procedures are site-based, practical, and have been developed and controlled locally. They were created by faculty and administrators at individual institutions to solve specific assessment needs and to address particular problems. Individually, these procedures for assessing writing provide solutions for specific institutions. It is my hope to connect these procedures through their common sets of beliefs and assumptions in order to create the possibility of a theoretical umbrella. This theorizing can help other institutions create their own procedures that solve local assessment problems and recognize the importance of context, rhetoric, teaching, and learning. By themselves, each of these institutions has had to develop and create its own wheel; together, they can aid others to understand the nature of their assessment needs and to provide solutions that link together the concerns of a variety of "stakeholders."[2]

EXAMINING AND UNDERSTANDING NEW PROCEDURES

One of the most common forms of writing assessment employed by many institutions is the placement of students into various writing courses offered by a specific college or university. Traditionally, schools have used holistic scoring procedures to place students, adapting specific numerical scores, usually the combined or sum scores of two raters, to indicate placement for a particular class. Some of the earliest and most interesting procedures developed outside the traditional theoretical umbrella for writing assessment involve placement. This makes sense because current traditional placement procedures require the additional steps necessary to code rater decisions numerically and to apply these numbers to specific courses. Research indicates that traditional procedures might be even more indirect, since talk-aloud protocols of raters using holistic methods for placement demonstrate that often raters first decide on student placement into a class and then locate the appropriate numerical score that reflects their decision (Huot; Pula and Huot). Newer placement programs end this indirection by having raters make placement decisions directly.

One of the first and most rigorously documented of the new placement programs was developed by William L. Smith at the University of Pittsburgh. His method involved using instructors to place students in specific classes based upon the writing ability necessary for success in the courses those instructors actually taught. This method of placing students proved to be more cost-efficient and effective than conventional scoring methods (Smith). Such a placement program circumvents many of the problems found in current placement testing. Raters are hired in groups of two to represent each of the courses in which students can be placed. These pairs of raters are chosen because their most immediate and extensive teaching experience is in a specific course. A rater either decides that a student belongs in her class or passes the paper on to the rater for the class in which she thinks the student belongs. Using standard holistic scoring methods to verify this contextual placement scoring procedure, Smith found that students were placed into courses with greater teacher satisfaction and without the need for rubrics, training sessions, quantification, and interrater reliability.

Recently, this method has been under revision as the curriculum it supports is also revised (Harris). This revision is in keeping with the local nature of this and other emergent writing assessment methods. Unlike traditional methods that centralize rating guidelines or other features of an assessment scheme, these site-based procedures can and should be constantly revised to meet the developing needs of an institution. It might be best to think of the Smith method for placement as a prototype, since it requires a very stable pool of raters that teach specific courses on a consistent basis. In keeping with the purpose of this essay, Smith's or other procedures that have been developed outside of a psychometric framework are less important for the utilization of the procedures themselves and more for their ability to define a set of principles capable of solving particular assessment problems, developed and revised according to local assessment needs.

Another placement procedure dubbed a two-tier process has been developed at Washington State University in which student essays are read by a single reader who makes one decision about whether or not students should enter the most heavily enrolled first-year composition course (Haswell and Wyche-Smith). Students not so placed by the first-tier reader have their essays read in mutual consultation by a second tier of raters, experts in all courses in the curriculum. In this method, 60 % of all students are placed into a course on the first reading.

Pedagogically, these contextualized forms of placement assessment are sound because teachers make placement decisions based upon what they know about writing and the curriculum of the courses they teach. Placement of students in various levels of composition instruction is primarily a teaching decision. Smith analyzed the talk-aloud protocols of his raters and found that they made placement decisions upon whether or not they could "see" a particular student in their classrooms. Judith Pula and I report similar findings from interviewing raters reading placement essays in holistic scoring sessions. Raters reported making placement decisions not upon the established scoring guidelines on a numerical rubric but rather on the "teachability" of students. The context for reading student writing appears to guide raters regardless of rubrics or training found in many assessment practices (Huot; Pula and Huot).

While the first two procedures I've discussed have to do with placement, the others involve exit exams and program assessment. Michael Allen discusses his and his colleagues' experience with reading portfolios from various institutions. Allen found that readers who knew the context and institutional guidelines of the school at which the portfolios were written could achieve an acceptable rate of interrater reliability by just discussing the essays on-line over the internet, without any need for scoring guidelines or training sessions. Allen theorizes that readers are able "to put on the hat" of other institutions because they are experts in reading student writing and teaching student writers. Borrowing a term Bill Condon used in his keynote at the Scottsdale Conference on "Portfolios, WAC and Program Assessment," Allen offers the notion of "shared evaluation" to describe the experience of reading portfolios together. Such an evaluation would include:

1. A tentative score based on an evaluator's reading of a student text

2. An openness of evaluators to other evaluators' perspectives

3. A rapid exchange of discursive analysis of the student text

4. And examination of assessment issues that may arise from the exchange of evaluators' perspectives (84)

While Allen discusses the results and implications of reading program portfolios with a group of teachers across the country, Durst, Roemer, and Schultz write about using portfolios read by a team of teachers as an exit exam at the University of Cincinnati to determine whether or not students should move from one course to another. What makes their system different is that these "trios," as the three-teacher teams are called, not only read each others' portfolios but discuss that work to make "internal struggles [about value and judgment] outward and visible" (286). This system revolves around the notion that talk is integral to understanding the value of a given student portfolio. While White (*Teaching*) and Elbow and Belanoff have noted that bringing teachers together to talk about standards and values was one of the most important aspects of writing assessment, Durst, Roemer, and Schultz make the conversation between teachers the center of their portfolio exit scheme. They assert that their system for exit examination has benefits beyond the accurate assessment of student writing: "portfolio negotiations can serve as an important means of faculty development, can help ease anxieties about grading and passing judgment on students' work, and can provide a forum for teachers and administrators to rethink the goals of a freshman English program" (287). This public discussion of student work not only furnishes a workable method to determine the exit of particular students but also provides real benefits for the teachers and curriculum at a specific institution as newer conceptions of validity advocate (Cronbach; Messick; Moss, "Shifting").

While each of the methods we have examined have distinctions predicated upon the context of their role(s) for a specific institution or purpose, they also share assumptions about the importance of situating assessment methods and rater judgment within a particular rhetorical, linguistic, and pedagogical context. The focus of each of these programs is inward toward the needs of students, teachers, and programs rather than outward toward standardized norms or generalizable criteria. In sharp contrast to the acontextual assumptions of traditional procedures, these developing methods depend on specific assessment situations and contexts. Table 10–2 on page 166 summarizes the procedures and purposes of these emergent assessment methods.

IMPACT ON RELIABILITY

All of these procedures either bypass or make moot the most important feature of current traditional writing assessment: the agreement of independent readers, or interrater reliability. Although Smith's procedures involve raters reading independently (without discussion or collaboration), rater agreement, by itself, is not crucial because all raters are not equally good judges for

TABLE 10–2   New, Emergent Writing Assessment Procedures, Purposes, and Assumptions

Procedure	Purpose	Assumptions
Raters from specific courses place students into their courses	Writing placement	Placement is a teaching decision based on specific curricular knowledge
One rater reads all essays and places 60% of all students; other 40% placed by expert team of consultants	Writing placement	Placement largely a screening process; teachers recognize students in primary course
Rater groups discuss portfolios for exit or specific level of achievement	Exit and program assessment	Discussion and multiple interpretation necessary for high stakes decisions about students or programs
Validity	Determine accuracy of assessment and impact of process on teaching and learning for a specific site and its mission and goals	Value of an assessment can only be known and accountable in a specific context

all courses. Those decisions by the teachers of the course are privileged, since they are made by the experts for that course and that educational decision. In current traditional writing assessment agreement is "a necessary but not a sufficient condition for validity" (Cherry and Meyer 110). In other words, without a sufficient level of agreement between raters a writing assessment procedure cannot be valid. For this reason, reliability has historically dominated the literature on writing assessment, and it was only after procedures such as scoring guidelines and rating training could guarantee agreement between raters that the reading and scoring of student writing (direct writing assessment) became psychometrically viable. Before that, only indirect measures that consist of multiple choice tests of usage and mechanics could be supported by classical test theory.

While the need for reliability is theoretically mandated within classical test theory, it has been supported on practical and ethical grounds in composition by those who see it as a means of ensuring fairness to students. Edward White provides a good summary of this position: "Reliability is a simple way of talking about fairness to test takers, and if we are not interested in fairness, we have no business giving tests or using test results" ("Holistic" 93). Logically, then, the same procedures which ensure consistency should also provide fairness. However, this is not the case. We should understand that in writing assessment interrater reliability means consistency among raters and nothing else. "Reliability refers to how consistently a test measures whatever it measures . . . a test can be reliable but not be valid" (Cherry and Meyer 110). For example, I could decide to measure student writing by counting the number of words in each essay (in fact a computer could count the words). This method could achieve perfect interrater reliability, since it is possible that two independent judges would count the same number of words for each paper. While reliable, we could hardly consider my method to be a fair evaluation of student writing. Consistency is only one aspect of fairness. In order for an assessment instrument to be fair, we must know something about the nature of the judgment.[3] Procedures that involve teachers in development and discussion and reflect clearly defined and negotiated local standards should provide for fair and responsible judgments of student writing. Translating reliability into fairness is not only inaccurate, it is dangerous because it equates statistical consistency with value about the nature of the judgments being made.

One of the possible reasons we have historically needed methods to ensure rater agreement stems from the stripping away of context, common in conventional writing assessment procedures to obtain objective and consistent scores. This absence of context distorts the ability of individuals who rely on it to make meaning. For example, the most famous study involving the inability of raters to agree on scores for the same papers was conducted by Paul Diederich, John French, and Sydell Carlton. Three hundred papers were distributed to 53 readers representing six different fields. Readers were given no sense of where the papers came from or the purpose of the reading. Given this lack of contextual cues, it is not surprising that 90% of the papers got at least seven different scores on a nine-point scale. The absence of context in traditional writing assessment procedures could be responsible for the lack of agreement among raters which these procedures are, ironically, supposed to supply. The traditional response to raters' inability to agree has been to impose an artificial context, consisting of scoring guidelines and rater training in an attempt to "calibrate" human judges as one might adjust a mechanical tool, instrument or machine. White (*Teaching*) and other early advocates of holistic and other current traditional procedures for evaluating writing likened these scoring sessions to the creation of a discourse community of readers. However, Pula and Huot's study of the influence of teacher experience, training, and personal background on raters outlines the existence of two discourse communities in a holistic scoring sessions, one the immediate group of raters and the other a community whose membership depends upon disciplinary, experiential, and social ties. It seems practically and theoretically sound that we design schemes for assessment on the second discourse community instead of attempting to superimpose one just for assessment purposes.

This inability of raters to agree in contextually stripped environments has fueled the overwhelming emphasis on reliability in writing assessment. Michael Williamson examines the connection between reliability and validity in writing reliability by looking at the ways more reliable measures like multiple choice exams are actually less valid ways to evaluate student writing. Looking at validity and reliability historically, Williamson concludes that "the properties of a test which establish its reliability do not necessarily contribute to its validity" (162). Williamson goes on to challenge the traditional notion that reliability is a precondition for validity: "Thus, comparatively high reliability is neither a necessary nor a sufficient condition for establishing the validity of a measure" (162).

While Williamson contends that reliability should be just one aspect of judging the worthwhile nature of an assessment, Pamela Moss asks the question in her title, "Can There be Validity Without Reliability?" Moss asserts that reliability in the psychometric sense "requires a significant level of standardization [and that] this privileging of standardization is problematic" (6). Moss goes on to explore what assessment procedures look like within a hermeneutic framework. She uses the example of a faculty search in which members of a committee read an entire dossier of material from prospective candidates and make hiring decisions only after a full discussion with other members of the committee. In a more recent article, Moss ("Enlarging") explores the value of drawing on the work and procedures from interpretive research traditions to increase an understanding of the importance of context in assessment. Within an interpretive tradition, reliability becomes not interchangeable consistency but rather a critical standard with which communities of knowledgeable stakeholders make important and valid decisions. Interpretive research traditions like hermeneutics support the emerging procedures in writing evaluation because they "privilege interpretations from readers most knowledgeable about the context of assessment" ("Can" 9). An interpretive framework supports the linguistic context within which all writing assessment should take place because it acknowledges the indeterminacy of meaning and the importance of individual and communal interpretations and values.

Interpretive research traditions hold special significance for the assessment of student writing, since reading and writing are essentially interpretive acts. It is a truism in current ideas about literacy that context is a critical component in the ability of people to transact meaning with written language. In composition pedagogy we have been concerned with creating meaningful contexts for students to write in. A theory of assessment that recognizes the importance of context should also be concerned with creating assessment procedures that establish meaningful contexts within which teachers read and assess. Building a context in which writing can be drafted, read, and evaluated is a step toward the creation of assessment procedures based on recognizable characteristics of language use. Assessment procedures which ignore or attempt to overcome context distort the communicative situation. Michael Halliday asserts that "any account of language which fails to build in the situation as an essential ingredient is likely to be artificial and unrewarding" (29). Halliday's contention that "language functions in contexts of situations and is relatable to those contexts" (32) is part of a consensus among scholars in sociolinguistics (Labov), pragmatics (Levinson), discourse analysis (Brown and Yule), and text linguistics (de Beaugrande and Dressler) about the preeminence of context in language use.

CREATING NEW ASSESSMENTS OF WRITING

Research on the nature of raters' decisions (Barritt, Stock, and Clark; Pula and Huot) indicate the powerful tension teachers feel between their roles as reader and rater in an assessment environment. An appropriate way to harness this tension is to base assessment practices within specific contexts, so that raters are forced to make practical, pedagogical, programmatic, and interpretive judgments without having to define writing quality or other abstract values which end up tapping influences beyond the raters or test administrators' control. As Smith along with Haswell and Wyche-Smith have illustrated with placement readers; Durst, Roemer, and Schultz with exit raters; and Allen with program assessment, we can harness the expertise and ability of raters within the place they know, live, work, and read. Assessment practices need to be based upon the notion that we are attempting to assess a writer's ability to communicate within a particular context and to a specific audience who needs to read this writing as part of a clearly defined communicative event.

It follows logically and theoretically that rather than base assessment decisions on the abstract and inaccurate notion of writing quality as a fixed entity,[4] a notion which is driven by a positivist view of reality, we should define each evaluative situation and judge students upon their ability to accomplish a specific communicative task, much like the basic tenets of primary trait scoring. However, instead of just basing the scores upon rhetorical principles, I propose that we design the complete assessment procedure upon the purpose and context of the specific writing ability to be described and evaluated. The three major means for assessing writing—holistic, analytic, and primary trait—are largely text-based procedures which merely manipulate the numerically-based scoring guidelines. These procedures would be replaced by contextually and rhetorically defined testing environments. The type of scoring would be identified by the genre of the text to be written, the discipline within which it was produced, and the type of decisions the raters are attempting to make.

In business writing, for example, students might be required to condense extensive documents into a few paragraphs for an executive summary. Students in the natural or physical sciences might be given the data obtained through research procedures and be required to present such information in a recognizable format, complete with applications. In environmental writing, where speed and the ability to synthesize technical information for a lay audience is crucial, students might be given a prompt they have never seen and be asked to produce text in a relatively short period of time. Instead of current methods, we would have placement testing in which varying purposes, contexts, and criteria would be linked together to create procedures built upon the rhetorical, linguistic, practical, and pedagogical demands of reading and writing in a specific context. Current debates, for example, about the use of single-samples or portfolios (Purves, "Apologia"; White, "Apologia" and "Response") would be moot, since the number and type of writing samples and the method for producing the texts would depend upon the specific assessment context. The criteria for judgment would be built into a method and purpose for assessment and would be available, along with successful examples of such writing to the student writers. Not only do these proposed methods for assessing writing reject scoring guidelines, rater training for agreement, calculations of interrater reliability, and the other technologies of testing, but they also connect the context, genre, and discipline of the writing with those making evaluative decisions and the criteria they use to judge this writing. When we begin to base writing evaluation on the context of a specific rhetorical situation adjudged by experts from within a particular area, we can eliminate the guessing students now go through in preparing for such examinations as well as the abstract debates and considerations about the best procedures for a wide variety of assessment purposes.

TOWARD A THEORY OF WRITING ASSESSMENT

The proposed writing assessments we have discussed and other procedures like them exist outside the "old" theoretical tenets of classical test theory.[5] Instead of generalizability, technical rigor, and large scale measures that minimize context and aim for a standardization of writing quality, these new procedures emphasize the context of the texts being read, the position of the readers, and the local, practical standards teachers and other stakeholders establish for written communication. There is a clear link between the judgments being made and the outcome of these judgments that is neither hidden nor shaded by reference to numerical scores, guidelines, or statistical calculations of validity or reliability. These site-based, locally-driven procedures for evaluating student writing have their roots in the methods and beliefs held by the teachers who teach the courses students are entering or exiting or the program under review. In this light, there is a much clearer connection between the way writing is taught and the way it is evaluated. For the last two or three decades writing pedagogy has moved toward process-oriented and context-specific approaches that focus on students' individual cognitive energies and their socially positioned identities as members of culturally bound groups. On the contrary, writing assessment has remained a contextless activity emphasizing standardization and an ideal version of writing quality.

These emergent methods can be viewed under a new theoretical umbrella, one supported by evolving conceptions of validity that include the consequences of the tests and a linking of instruction and practical purposes with the concept of measuring students' ability to engage in a specific literacy event or events. These procedures also have their bases in theories of language and literacy that recognize the importance of context and the individual in constructing acceptable written communication. These methods are sensitive to the importance of interpretation inherent in reader response and psycholinguistic theories of reading. Although it is premature to attempt any full-blown discussion of the criteria for newer conceptions of writing assessment, Figure 10–1 on page 171 provides a set of preliminary principles extrapolated from our consideration and discussion of these new assessment

FIGURE 10–1   Principles for a New Theory and Practice of Writing Assessment

---

SITE-BASED
An assessment for writing is developed in response to a need that occurs at a specific site. Procedures are based upon the resources and concerns of an institution, department, program or agency and its administrators, faculty, students, or other constituents.

LOCALLY-CONTROLLED
The individual institution or agency is responsible for managing, revising, updating, and validating the assessment procedures that should be carefully reviewed according to clearly outlined goals and guidelines on a regular basis to safeguard the concerns of all those affected by the assessment process.

CONTEXT-SENSITIVE
The procedures should honor the instructional goals and objectives as well as the cultural and social environment of the institution or agency and its students, teachers, and other stakeholders. It is important to establish and maintain the contextual integrity necessary for the authentic reading and writing of textual communication.

RHETORICALLY-BASED
All writing assignments, scoring criteria, writing environments, and reading procedures should adhere to recognizable and supportable rhetorical principles integral to the thoughtful expression and reflective interpretation of texts.

ACCESSIBILITY
All procedures and rationales for the creation of writing assignments, scoring criteria, and reading procedures, as well as samples of student work and rater judgment should be available to those whose work is being evaluated.

---

procedures and their connection to current theories of measurement, language, and composition pedagogy.

Developing writing assessment procedures upon an epistemological basis that honors local standards, includes a specific context for both the composing and reading of student writing, and allows for the communal interpretation of written communication is an important first step in furnishing a new theoretical umbrella for assessing student writing. However, it is only a first step. We must also develop procedures with which to document and validate such assessment. These validation procedures must be sensitive to the local and contextual nature of the assessment being done. While traditional writing assessment methods rely on statistical validation and standardization that are important to the beliefs and assumptions that fuel them, emergent procedures will need to employ more qualitative and ethnographic validation procedures — like interviews, observations, and thick descriptions to understand the role an assessment plays within a specific program or institution. We can also study course outcomes to examine specific assessments based upon specific curricula. Smith's validation procedures at the University of Pittsburgh and Haswell's at Washington State can probably serve as models for documenting emerging procedures.

These local procedures can be connected beyond a specific context by public displays of student work and locally developed standards. Harold Berlak proposes that the use of samples from several locations be submitted to a larger board of reviewers who represent individual localities and that this larger board conduct regular reviews of student work and individual assessment programs. Pamela Moss ("Validity in High Stakes") outlines a model in which representative samples of student work and localized assessment procedures work can be reviewed by outside agencies. Allen's study furnishes a model for a "board" of expert readers from across the country to examine specific assessment programs, including samples of student work and the local judgments given that work. His use of electronic communication points out the vast potential the Internet and World Wide Web have in providing the linkage and access necessary to connect site-based, locally-controlled assessment programs from various locations. As Moss cautions, we have only begun to revise a very established measurement mechanism, and there is much we still need to learn about how to set up, validate, and connect local assessment procedures.

Inherent in a new conception of writing assessment is the strict limitation of what it can and cannot do. For example, large scale testing, which strives to define writing quality for a huge population of students, will have far less value than it now holds because context and population size will be part of a theoretical constraint on evaluation procedures, much in the same way most composition courses now impose some sort of enrollment cap. Instead, local results can be sampled and combined to replace current procedures that presently attempt to assess thousands of students across rhetorical and contextual boundaries. While Moss ("Enlarging") and others offer the interpretive tradition as one possible way of supporting assessment procedures, it is important to remember that various epistemological stances are not neutral or innocent. For writing assessment, it is difficult to see the value in maintaining procedures based on a positivist epistemolology. These new assessment schemes are context-rich and rely upon raters knowing as much as possible about the papers, the students, the purpose of the evaluation, the consequences of their decisions, and the decisions of fellow raters. Within these procedures, the sacred cow of writing assessment, interrater reliability, becomes irrelevant because agreement on blind readings is no longer a crucial element for an accurate or valid evaluative decision. Instead, our attention is directed toward creating an assessment environment for reading and writing that is sensitive to the purpose and criteria for successful communication in which student ability in writing becomes part of a community's search for value and meaning within a shared context.

It is important to note that all of the procedures I have highlighted as depending upon an emergent theory of assessment that recognize context and local control were developed at the college level. Even state-mandated portfolio systems, like those in Kentucky and Vermont, continue to be standardized in order to provide for acceptable rates of interrater reliability. It is imperative that we at the college level continue our experimentation and expand our theorizing to create a strong platform for new writing assessment theory and practice, so that we can see the emergence of rhetorical and contextual writing assessment for all students. We need to begin thinking of writing evaluation in new ways, not so much as the ability to judge accurately a piece of writing or a particular writer but to be able to describe the promise and limitations of a writer working within a particular rhetorical and linguistic context.

As much as these new procedures for writing assessment make practical and theoretical sense to those of us who teach and research written communication, they will not be widely developed or implemented without much work and struggle, without an increased emphasis on writing assessment within the teaching of writing at all levels. Composition's justifiable distrust of writing assessment has given those outside of the discipline power to assess our students. The ability to assess is the ability to determine and control what is valuable. Standardized forms of assessment locate the power for making decisions about students with a central authority. Harold Berlak labels the educational policies of the Reagan-Bush era "incoherent" because while policy makers called for increased local control of schools, they also instituted massive standardized testing, rendering any kind of local decision-making superfluous. Changing the foundation which directs the way student writing is assessed involves altering the power relations between students and teachers and teachers and administrators. It can also change what we will come to value as literacy in and outside of school.

At this point, the door is open for real and lasting changes in writing assessment procedures. We who teach and research written communication need to become active in assessment issues and active developers of these new, emergent practices. In the past, current writing assessment procedures were largely developed by ETS and other testing companies outside of a community of English or composition teachers and were based upon a set of assumptions and beliefs irrelevant to written communication. Unlike the past, it is time for us to go through the door and take charge of how our students are to be evaluated. It is time to build and maintain writing assessment theories and practices which are consonant with our teaching and research.

NOTES

1. It is important to note that only a certain, "trend" sample of NAEP'S writing assessment claims to measure writing ability from year to year.

2. An assessment term that refers to all those who are affected by the measurement process, typically students, teachers administrators, and parents. See Guba and Lincoln for a full treatment of the term and concept.

3. Current traditional procedures do not make the content of the scoring guideline an explicit part of the validation process. The unfortunate result is that some "acceptable" assessments of student writing have problematic scoring criteria. For example, George Englehard Jr., Belita Gordon and Stephen Gabrielson report on having assessed the writing of over 125,000 students in which rater judgment was largely based on language conventions. While such assessment practices furnish the illusion of having evaluated student writing, in reality we have learned little more than what a multiple choice test might provide.

4. While I arrive at this idea theoretically, Alan Purves, in "Reflections on Research and Assessment in Written Composition," details the breakdown of writing quality as a concept in a study undertaken by the International Association of Educational Achievement on student writing in fourteen countries.

5. This movement away from psychometric procedures has been under way for some time (Barrit, Stock, and Clark; Carini; Faigley, Cherry, Jolliffe, and Skinner). There are many institutions employing similar, locally-developed procedures. SUNY Stony Brook, for example, has students write placement essays as part of a two-hour class on writing. The essay is read and judged by two teachers, one of which taught that group of students (Robertson). At the University of Louisville, teachers have met in groups to discuss and evaluate student portfolios as part of an evaluation of general education. We have adapted Smith's scheme to read high school portfolios for placement, and the English Department piloted a program last year in which teachers' portfolios were read collaboratively as part of an institutional evaluation of individual departments.

WORKS CITED

Allen, Michael. "Valuing Differences: Portnet's First Year." *Assessing Writing* 2 (1995): 67–90.
Barritt, Loren, Patricia L. Stock, and Francelia Clark. "Researching Practice: Evaluating Assessment Essays." *CCC 38* (1986): 315–27.
de Beaugrande, Robert, and Wolfgang Dressler. *Introduction to Text Linguistics*. New York: Longman, 1981.
Berlak, Harold. "Toward the Development of a New Science of Educational Testing and Assessment." *Toward a New Science of Educational Testing and Assessment*. Ed. Harold Berlak et al. Albany, New York: State U of New York P, 1992, 181–206.
Brown, George and Gillian Yule. *Discourse Analysis*. New York: Cambridge UP, 1983.
Carini, Patricia F. *Observation and Description: An Alternative Methodology for the Investigation of Human Phenomenon*. Grand Forks, North Dakota Study Group on Evaluation, 1975.
Cherry, Roger and Paul Meyer. "Reliability Issues in Holistic Assessment." Williamson and Huot 109–41.
Cronbach, Lee J. "Five Perspectives on Validity Argument." *Test Validity*. Ed. Harold Wainer. Hillside: Erlbaum, 1988. 3–17.
Diederich, Paul, John W. French, and Sydell T. Carlton. *Factors in Judgments of Writing Quality*. Princeton: Educational Testing Service, 1961. RB No. 61–15. ERIC ED 002 172.
Durst, Russel K., Marjorie Roemer, and Lucille Schultz. "Portfolio Negotiations: Acts in Speech." *New Directions in Portfolio Assessment*. Ed. Laurel Black, Donald A. Daiker, Jeffrey Sommers, and Gail Stygail. Portsmouth, NH: Boynton/Cook, 1994. 286–300.
Elbow, Peter, and Patricia Belanoff. "State University of New York at Stony Brook Portfolio-based Evaluation Program." *Portfolios: Process and Product*. Ed. Pat Belanoff and Marcia Dickson. Portsmouth, NH: Boynton/Cook, 1991. 3–16.
Englehard, George Jr., Belita Gordon, and Stephen Gabrielson. "The Influences of Mode of Discourse, Experiential Demand, and Gender on the Quality of Student Writing." *Research in the Teaching of English 26* (1992): 315–36.
Faigley, Lester, Roger Cherry, David A. Jolliffe, and Anna M. Skinner. *Assessing Writers' Knowledge and Processes of Composing*. Norwood: Ablex, 1985.
Guba, Egon G. "The Alternative Paradigm Dialog." *The Paradigm Dialog*. Ed. Egon G. Guba. Newbury Park: Sage, 1990. 17–27.
Guba, Egon G., and Lincoln, Yvonna S. *Fourth Generation Evaluation*. Newbury Park: Sage, 1989.
Halliday, Michael. *Language as Social Semiotic*. Baltimore: Arnold, 1978.
Harris, Joseph. Personal Correspondence, June, 1996.
Haswell, Richard, and Susan Wyche-Smith. "A Two-Tiered Raging Procedure for Placement Essays." *Assessment in Practice: Putting Principles to Work on College Campuses*. Ed. Trudy Banta. San Francisco: Jossey-Bass, 1995. 204–07.
Huot, Brian. "The Influence of Holistic Scoring Procedures on Reading and Rating Student Essays." Williamson and Huot 206–36.
Labov, William, ed. *Locating Language in Time and Space*. New York: Academic, 1980.
Levinson, Stephen C. *Pragmatics*. New York: Cambridge UP, 1983.
Messick, Samuel. "Meaning and Values in Test Validation: The Science and Ethics of Assessment." *Educational Researcher 18.2* (1989): 5–11.
Moss, Pamela A. "Can There be Validity Without Reliability?" *Educational Researcher 23.2* (1994): 5–12.
———. "Enlarging the Dialogue in Educational Measurement: Voices From Interpretive Research Traditions." *Educational Researcher 25.1* (1996): 20–28.

———. "Shifting Conceptions of Validity in Educational Measurement: Implications for Perform-ance Assessment." *Review of Educational Research 62* (1992): 229–58.

———. "Validity in High Stakes Writing Assessment: Problems and Possibilities." *Assessing Writ-ing* (1994): 109–28.

Pula, Judith J., and Brian Huot "A Model of Background Influences on Holistic Raters." Williamson and Huot. 237–65.

Purves, Alan C. "Apologia Not Accepted." *CCC 46* (1995): 549–50.

———. "Reflections on Research and Assessment in Written Composition." *Research in the Teach-ing of English 26* (1992): 108–22.

Robertson, Alice. "Teach, Not Test: A Look at a New Writing Placement Procedure." *WPA, 18* (1994): 56–63.

Smith, William L. "Assessing the Reliability and Adequacy of Using Holistic Scoring of Essays as a College Composition Placement Program Technique." Williamson and Huot. 142–205.

White, Edward M. "Apologia for the Timed Impromptu Essay Test." *CCC 46* (1995): 30–45.

———. "Holistic Scoring: Past Triumphs and Future Challenges." Williamson and Huot 79–108.

———. "Language and Reality in Writing Assessment." *CCC 40* (1990): 187–200.

———. "Response to Alan Purves," *CCC 46* (1995): 550–51.

———. *Teaching and Assessing Writing*. 2nd Ed. San Francisco: Jossey-Bass, 1994.

Williamson, Michael M. "The Worship of Efficiency: Untangling Theoretical and Practical Consid-erations in Writing Assessment." *Assessing Writing 1* (1994): 147–74.

Williamson, Michael M., and Brian Huot, eds. *Validating Holistic Scoring for Writing Assessment: The-oretical & Empirical Foundations*. Cresskill, NJ: Hampton, 1993.

PART TWO

Models

11

The Importance of Teacher Knowledge in College Composition Placement Testing

WILLIAM L. SMITH

Direct assessment of student writing has, over the past decade, become the dominant method for evaluating students' writing performance and abilities. This method requires students to write an essay which is then read and evaluated using what is generically called "holistic" reading, i.e., a relatively fast reading resulting in a single score based on the reader's gestalt impression. However, the generic term masks some very specific differences in the purposes of the assessment and the methods used, and it is, therefore, highly probable that research on one purpose/method may not be applicable to other purposes/methods.

There are two very different purposes for direct assessment. The first, the one almost exclusively reported in the literature, is to assess the quality of written compositions with no direct impact on the writer. That is, regardless of the results, the writers are not affected in grade-in-course, progress in curriculum, or placement into or out of a course. Quite commonly, the results of such assessment are used to draw conclusions about writing ability (e.g., research on instructional methods or large-scale descriptive studies such as the National Assessment of Educational Progress studies), but these conclusions apply only to groups of writers, not individuals. Such assessment would more precisely be called "assessment of writer-groups through direct assessment of text."

The second purpose is to assess the essays with a direct impact on the writer. That is, the real purpose is not to assess the text but to assess the writer in order to make a decision about that writer. This purpose underlies all placement testing, either into courses (e.g., pre-enrollment placement into diversified college composition courses) or out of courses (commonly called "exit exams"). This purpose would more precisely be called "assessment of individual writers/students through direct assessment."

Within this purpose, the scale and technique used to derive the final score will depend upon the constituency being served. If that constituency is broad,

From *Reading Empirical Research Studies: The Rhetoric of Research,* ed. R. J. Hayes (Hillsdale, NJ: Lawrence Erlbaum, 1992), 289–316.

for example several schools or colleges, each with different curricula and/or pedagogy, the scale may have any number of points and can be derived in at least three ways: 1) it may be the sum of raters' ratings, 2) it may be the average of the raters' ratings, or 3) it may be the modal, or more frequent, rating. Each school or college would then establish local cut-off points for each course placement.

However, when the constituency is one school or college, the scale can be tailored to local needs. The scale can be curriculum derived, each scale point (or set of scale points) representing a specific course. The real purpose of the assessment is to use the student's text as a window into that student so as to place the student into the course which best matches her needs and abilities. The technique used must produce a final score which refers to a course. Summing or averaging raters' scores is sometimes used, but the most common procedure is to use modal scores. When the primary raters (usually two) agree, that is the modal score. If these raters disagree and the split-resolver agrees with one rater, then that is the modal score. When the primary raters disagree by more than one scale point, quite commonly the split-resolver's score becomes the final score. (From discussions with colleagues at other universities, we have found that none use more than three readers to determine a modal final score.)

Although there is a considerable body of literature on direct assessment, little is devoted to placement resting (e.g., Smith et al., 1980; Alexander and Swartz, 1982). Even the best works on testing in composition (e.g., White, 1985) devote little space to this type of testing. Furthermore, no research has been done on the relationships between the two purposes of direct assessment. No one has compared, using the same texts, how the two purposes affect final ratings or the distribution of ratings. Therefore, I will limit my interpretations to only placement testing within a local constituency, the University of Pittsburgh. And, thus, some information about the University of Pittsburgh composition program and courses must be presented to frame my discussion.

THE UNIVERSITY OF PITTSBURGH COMPOSITION PROGRAM AND COURSES

The composition program is based on four concepts (or dimensions): that writing is an effort to make meaning, that writing is closely related to reading, that to make meaning a writer must develop a sense of authority, and that students gradually come to that sense of authority. Consequently, in all of our courses, the students respond to a sequence of assignments on a central topic (see Coles, 1981, Bartholomae, 1983, and Bartholomae and Petrosky, 1987 for more detailed exposition of the bases of the program). It is also important to note that we do not consider composition courses to be "service" courses. That is, they are not intended, specifically, to train students to write for other courses. Consequently, we, for example, do not have students write research papers, nor are they required to write papers in the various modes (narrative, exposition, etc.).

Because our students have varied abilities along these dimensions, the composition program consists of three courses, each addressing a particular range of ability. Course A is designed for students who have serious writing problems which indicate problems with reading and appropriating a text they have read. These students' essays lack development of ideas, lack coherence, are not well organized, and do not address the issue. Commonly, these students either inadequately summarize the given passage or make general statements about the issue. But they do not interrelate the passage and their own ideas. These students also typically have patterns of surface level errors caused by their inability to read and proofread. However, error alone is not a good predictor of placement in Course A.

Course B is designed for students who have significant problems with writing (e.g., development of ideas, coherence, and organization), but these problems are not related to their ability to read the given passage. Instead, they indicate a lack of sense of text and a lack of authority. Surface level error commonly exists in their tests also, error and error patterns caused by their lack of a sense of text. If asked whether they read their own texts as they read other texts, they will say they don't, and if pressed for reasons, will say that their own writing doesn't merit such reading.

Course C is designed for students who have the ability to read and make meaning but need more experience in developing their abilities, particularly in dealing with problematic texts and in using writing as a means for working their way through complex problems. Our research has shown that the students placed into Course C actually make more surface level errors than the students placed in the other courses, but these errors are not caused by a lack of sense of text. Rather, they are either "typos" or result from risk-taking.

Some students are exempted from composition courses because the writing ability they demonstrate on the placement test suggests that these courses would not be of significant value. Thus, when we conduct our placement ratings, we use a four point nominal scale: Course A, Course B, Course C, and Exempt.

One might assume that these four alternatives might be treated as points of an ordinal scale, with Exempt representing the best outcome, followed by Course C, Course B, and Course A in that order. However, this assumption is not necessarily correct because the students placed into Course A do not subsequently take Course B. Instead, they move to Course C. In effect, then, Courses A and B are parallel but serve different student needs (see Figure 11–1).

FIGURE 11–1   Pattern of Movement from Course to Course

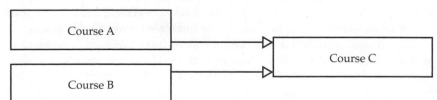

PROBLEMS IN PLACEMENT TESTING

It is generally agreed that in all direct assessment, including local constituency placement testing, raters must be highly reliable, i.e., give the same ratings to the same essays. There are two common methods for increasing reliability. The first, and most common, is to train or "calibrate" the raters in practice sessions so that they come to agreement prior to rating the essays (see Myers, 1980, and White, 1985, for methods). It is generally agreed that the minimum acceptable level of agreement is .70 (Cooper, 1977). The other method, one particular to local constituency placement testing, is to use raters who have taught the range of courses and thus are perceptive to the kinds of students typical of each course. This creates what might be called a local discourse community calibration (cf. Follman and Anderson, 1967) concerning homogeneity versus heterogeneity of raters [academic experiential backgrounds] as sources of reliability and unreliability. To increase that reliability, the raters participate in practice sessions, typically before each rating session.

Practical experience tells us that even two highly trained readers commonly disagree about the relative quality of a text. This is especially true if we believe that students' texts are a form of literature — that is, if the purpose of writing is to make meaning (cf. Bartholomae, 1983, and many others). This is a crucial point in the research presented below, for the curriculum and the pedagogy driving each of our composition courses are built on this belief. However, disagreements about *quality* do not necessarily mean disagreements about placement because the raters focus on the writer, not the quality, per se, of the text. Disagreements about placement, then, may be quite different than disagreements about quality.

Because errors do happen in the placement rating, double-checks are commonly used. For example, during the first week of each term, classroom teachers have their students write an essay which is evaluated to determine whether any students should be moved to a different course. But even with elaborate double-checks, schools must find methods to determine the reliability of their own raters for two reasons: 1) to determine whether the raters need additional or better or different training, and 2) to provide public evidence that students are not subject to capricious placement. The obvious, and most common, method to assess the reliability of raters is to compare the raters' ratings. However, this method does not adequately determine reliability in local constituency testing because there is one factor that makes such testing different from other forms of direct assessment: each scale point is specifically related to the local curriculum, i.e., there is one scale point for each course, and the purpose of testing is to place each student into the course which best fits his or her needs. Thus, the scale used cannot be considered interval because the intervals between scale points, the courses, are unknown (and may be unknowable). It is really either a nominal (or an ordinal) scale. Further, even if the curriculum is based on careful analysis of the needs and abilities of the local population, not all students will fit neatly into the courses. Invariably, some will be "between courses."

THE STUDY

In earlier research on rater reliability (Smith, 1993), I found evidence that when one pair of raters disagreed about the placement of a student, a second pair or raters was likely to disagree in the same way. I had thought it reasonable that some students could show characteristics of two distinct courses, but that might not be the real reason for the judgment split. The split might be related to the raters, not the writer. Therefore, I reanalyzed the data, looking at the raters' backgrounds. I discovered that one other possible reason might be the course that the rater had most recently taught. It is important to remember here that all of the raters in the pool are teachers of composition courses and that they are placing students, not just rating essays. Furthermore, in order to teach Course B, one must have successfully taught Course C, and to teach Course A, one must have successfully taught Course B. Thus, the Course B raters would have knowledge of Courses B and C, and the Course A teacher would have knowledge of all three courses, but that knowledge might be several years old. My reanalysis of the data showed that almost all of the disagreements between the raters happened when the raters had most recently taught different courses. One of the most striking features of these differences was that most of them involved two raters, each of whom judged that the student didn't belong in the course that he or she was most familiar with. For example, a rater most familiar with Course A judged that the student belonged in Course B while a rater most familiar with Course B judged that the same student belonged in Course A.

While I was conducting the first study, I also collected some Think-Aloud Protocols (TAPs) on raters while they were rating, and those data led me to a new perspective. The TAP data showed that when raters were reading an essay which they would place into the course they had most recently taught, their comments were not just about the essay. They also made specific comments about the writer as a student. They would say such things as "This student is one of those who never talks in class," or "This student will make significant progress in the first few weeks." When reading an essay they would place into some other course, there were no statements about the writer as student, only comments about the text or the writer as writer. The writer-as-student comments indicated that the raters had a privileged sense of the students in the course they had most recently taught, and this might alter their placement decisions.

Thus, it seemed that I might have missed the real point. The raters' expertise, the expertise which comes from working with their students, might be more powerful than any training session in which they are told about the various courses and read essays prototypic of those courses. I call this expertise "Most Recent Course Taught" expertise. In effect, I was speculating that a rater's expertise is linked to the course that rater has most recently taught because those are the students most recently encountered. This is not unlikely. If, for example, fourth grade teachers were asked to grade-rate essays written by students from a wide range of grades, they would make the most errors on the grades farthest from their own grade. Their expert-vision would be greatest when the students were near the fourth grade. Thus, it might be the case that raters are less able to make expert judgments when reading essays written by students who don't belong in their course. Therefore, I conducted the following experiment to test the theory that agreement among rater-sets differs according to the course-taught expertise of the raters. Specifically, I was testing the hypothesis that raters who have most recently taught the same course will agree with each other, whereas there would be lower agreement when the raters have most recently taught different courses.

PROCEDURE

For this experiment, I selected essays from a previous placement rating session (a month previous) which had been rated by rater sets composed of specific combinations of raters with particular Most Recent Course Taught (hereafter "RCT") experience (see Figure 11–2). I could not use all possible combinations of rater-sets and their decisions because that would have overloaded the placement session and, thus, might adversely affect placement decisions. I excluded all "D" (Exempt) ratings because D is not a course and thus there could be no "course-taught expertise." I randomly selected eight essays from within the six high frequency combinations (see Figure 11–2). These high frequency combinations included cases in which both raters accepted students into the course they were most familiar with, e.g., AA in Figure 11–2 indicates that the student was assigned to Course A by two raters most familiar with Course A, and cases in which both raters were rejecting students from

FIGURE 11–2   Essays Selected for the Second Study (8 essays per study)

Rating	RS1, by Course Taught
AA	Both ratings given by Course A rater (i.e., "accept into course")
AB	"A" rating given by Course B rater "B" rating given by Course A rater (i.e., both "reject from course")
BB	Both ratings given by Course B rater (i.e., "accept into course")
BC	"B" rating given by Course C rater "C" rating given by Course B rater (i.e., both "reject from course")
CC	Both ratings given by Course C rater (i.e., "accept into course")
AC	"A" rating given by Course C rater "C" rating given by Course A rater (i.e., both "reject from course")

the course they were most familiar with, e.g., AB in Figure 11–2 indicates that the student was assigned to Course B by the rater most familiar with Course A and to Course A by the rater most familiar with Course B. Other combinations than those shown in Figure 11–2 were possible but relatively infrequent. Figure 11–2, then, defines the categories of the essays used in the study.

The raters for this study were randomly selected from the raters working in the placement session, with the constraint that four had most recently taught Course A; four, Course B; and four, Course C. I will refer to the original rater as R1 and the rater in this study as R2. Each rater-set read a total of 48 essays, 8 from each of the six categories of ratings (e.g., AA, AB, etc.). Thus, each R2 read eight essays previously rated by an R1 set of raters with the same RCT patterns and forty essays previously rated by R1 raters with different RCT patterns. The target essays were randomly placed into the stacks of essays the raters were to read. Original versions were used so that the raters would not know that these essays had been previously rated.

RESULTS AND DISCUSSION

When given essays which the two Course A raters in R1 had rated AA (i.e., accepted), only the Courses C R2 raters disagreed (see Table 11–1). In seven

TABLE 11–1   Ratings Given by Individual RS2 Raters

Essay Rating (RS1 rating)	RS2 Rater (by RCT)	Rating Given by RS2 Raters			
		A	B	C	D
AA	A	32	0	0	0
	B	32	0	0	0
	C	25	7	0	0
BB	A	0	25	7	0
	B	0	32	0	0
	C	2	30	0	0
CC	A	0	3	24	5
	B	0	0	32	0
	C	0	0	32	0
AB	A	0	32	0	0
	B	30	2	0	0
	C	19	13	0	0
BC	A	0	12	20	0
	B	0	1	31	0
	C	1	31	0	0
AC	A	0	15	17	0
	B	5	21	6	0
	C	17	15	0	0

cases, a Course C rater produced a B rating. When given essays which the two Course B raters in R1 had rated BB (i.e., accepted), only the Course A and the Course C R2 raters disagreed. Course A raters produced seven C decisions, and Course C raters produced two A ratings. When given essays which the two Course C raters in R1 had rated CC (i.e., accepted), only the Course A R2 raters disagreed, producing three B ratings and five D ratings. Theses data indicate that the Course B raters never disagreed with R1 on any non-split and that when Course A and Course C raters disagreed with R1, they never placed the student into their own course. Although we have been careful not to assume a priori that the courses are ordered with Course A on the bottom, Course C on the top, and Course B between them (see Figure 11–1), the pattern of rater judgments suggests that the raters were treating the courses as if this ordering assumption were true. In the following discussion, we will show how the rater's judgments are consistent with the ordering assumption. If the raters do treat the courses as ordered, then, when Course B raters "reject" students, they must either place them above or below, and this creates agreement with the R1 raters. Thus, it would be expected that they would disagree less on prototypic essays (although they might give a Course C student a D rating). When Course A or Course C raters "reject" students, there is more "room" for placement. Course A raters select from three ratings above their course. When Course A raters disagreed on a student rated B by R1, they couldn't select A because they had already rejected the student from their course. Thus they had to select C. (Selecting D would be unlikely because the essay would not have the right characteristics for exemption.) When they disagreed on a student rated C by RS1, they could, and did, produce B, C, and D ratings. The pattern here is that a disagreement will be "one course off," i.e., a course contiguous to the course determined by R1. Similarly, when Course C raters "reject," they have two courses below theirs, and all of their disagreements were also one course off. It should be noted, however, that disagreements were far less common than agreements. Twelve raters read each of the twenty-four non-split essays, yet there were only 24 disagreements. Thus, they agreed on 91.6% of the cases.

Splits Produced by R1

Split decisions offer a more taxing test of the course-taught expertise theory. If the theory is right, then when two R1 raters disagree (i.e., produce a split vote), the matched R1 raters should agree with that decision. All split-vote essays selected for this study share one commonality: the raters never "accepted" the students into their own courses (see Figure 11–2). Thus, for the R1 AB split, the A was given by a Course B rater and the B by a Course A rater. The theory would predict that R2 Course A raters would not "accept."

When given an AB split, the R2 Course A raters always rejected as did the Course C raters. The Course B raters rejected in 93.75% of the cases. When Course A raters rejected a student, they always placed the student in Course B. Thus, since A was not possible, B is the only remaining possibility because their prior experience teaching Course C allowed them to deduce that the student didn't belong in C. The Courses C raters had more "room" for a decision. A rejected student could be placed into either A or B, and these raters were clearly not in accord with each other on which placement to select. Nineteen of the thirty-two decisions (59.38%) were for A, thirteen (40.62%) were for B. Thus, it seems that the Course C raters, when given an essay which has characteristics of both Course A and Course B, very nearly flip a coin. This confirms the course-taught-expertise theory, for since Course C raters had not taught Course A or Course B, they did not have expert vision when making their decisions.

When given a BC split, the same phenomenon occurs. The raters from all three courses always reject the students. Course B raters always give a C because that is the only alternative for a student who isn't B but is higher. (They could have given a D, but the students apparently didn't have the right characteristics for exemption, or the raters were being conservative. Whatever the reason, none of the raters gave these students a D rating.) The Course C raters always rejected, and since the students were not at the C level, they would have to be either A or B. B is the more probable choice (R1 had already determined that) and thus the Course C raters produced a B rating in all but one case. The Course A raters rejected the students, and thus had to select between B and C as ratings. They favored the C rating, giving this rating in twenty of the thirty-two cases (62.50%). Thus, the data from the BC split are almost exactly the same as the data from the AB split. This confirms that the original split decision was probably well deserved.

The one macro-split tested in this study, AC split, the split that provoked this experiment, provides a somewhat different picture. The most notable difference is that it elicited every possible combination of votes (assuming D was not a possibility).

The AC split data, like the AB and BC split data, reveal that Course A and Course C raters never accepted a student. However, these raters had equal dispersion in their decisions. The course A raters gave 15 Bs and 17 Cs; the Course C raters gave 17 As and 15 Bs. If Courses A, B, and C really were unordered, one might expect the AC split data to look like the AB and BC split data, but it did not. The AB students and the BC students were "rejected" by all three rater groups. In contrast, in nearly two-thirds of the cases, the Course B raters *accepted* these students. What is clear about the AC students is that they are neither A nor C. Not once did a Course A or Course C rater accept an AC student. One might suspect that the AC students were really BB students who had been misclassified by the R1 raters. However, this does not appear to be the case. Table 11-1 shows that although Course B raters accepted AC students in nearly two-thirds of the cases, they accepted BB students in all cases. Further, Table 11-1 also shows that although Course A and Course C raters classified AC students as B in 30 out of 64 cases, they classified BB students as B in 55 out of 64 cases. Thus, although the AC students resemble the BB students more than they resemble any other group, they do not appear to be fully typical of that group. To confirm this observation, I had an additional rater-set, composed of two Course B raters, rate the eight AC essays. These raters rated B in 10 out of 16 cases, or just under two-thirds of the time, confirming the earlier observation.

Perhaps the most compelling result in this study is the exceptionally high "accept/reject" agreement (99%) among the raters with common RCTs (see Table 11–2). This led me to reconsider the standard method used for placement rating. The standard method specifies that the essays be randomly assigned to raters, regardless of the course they have most recently taught or ever taught, and that those raters place students into the appropriate course (i.e., make full-scale decisions). The new method I devised specified that raters determine only whether a student should be accepted into or rejected from the course they have most recently taught. The new method relies, therefore, on the "expert" opinion of each rater, that rater's expertise having been gained by teaching the students. Furthermore, the method does not require raters to make judgements based on the full scale, a scale which includes courses they have not taught. They are only concerned with "accepting" into their course or "rejecting" from it.

The "expert" rating model predicts that acceptance implies rejection, i.e., that acceptance into Course X by a rater whose RCT is Course X implies rejection from Course Z by rater whose RCT is Z. To test this assumption, I selected twelve essays which had been accepted by raters in each of the three courses, Courses A, B, and C, and had those essays re-rated by raters from the other courses. Not one of the 36 essays were accepted. Thus, I could conclude

TABLE 11–2 Acceptance and Rejection from Rater's Own Course: A Comparison of RS1 Raters and RS2 Raters

		RS2 RCT = A	
		Accept	Reject
RS1 RCT = A	Accept	32	0
	Reject	0	64
		RS2 RCT = B	
		Accept	Reject
RS1 RCT = B	Accept	32	0
	Reject	2	62
		RS2 RCT = C	
		Accept	Reject
RS1 RCT = C	Accept	32	0
	Reject	0	64
		RS2 ALL	
		Accept	Reject
RS1 ALL	Accept	96	0
	Reject	2	190

that the raters were highly reliable. They knew whether an essay fit into their course, and, as these data show, they knew when it didn't.

However, the expert model does not predict that rejection implies acceptance, for it is possible that a student doesn't belong in any extant course. To test this aspect of the model, I selected 63 essays which had been rejected by raters of contiguous courses and had them rated by two other raters of those courses. Of these, only one was accepted by another rater. Thus, out of 126 ratings, there was a 99.2% agreement rate. One essay, an essay which a Course B rater had rejected-high and a Course C rater had rejected-low (thus, by inference, that student could not belong in A or D), was put through 13 iterations. That is, it was read by 13 Course B raters and by 13 Course C raters. That essay was never accepted. Although they never agreed on the final placement (and thus would seem unreliable using standard reliability measures), in fact, they always agreed and were perfectly reliable. We just don't have a placement slot for such students; they are reliably between scale points.

Thus, it appears to me that our standard methods of examining reliability — of determining reliability by asking how often raters agree on a scale-point — misses the point. The scales we use are made up by us. In the case of placement, the scale is often determined by the number of course placements. In other types of testing, that scale, whether it has 4 or 12 points, is still concocted by us. To assume that there are only 4 or 12 categories of students or texts seems untenable. Some students (or essays), regardless of the number of points on the scale, will not fit neatly into that scale.

CONCLUSIONS AND IMPLICATIONS

The results from this study, especially when combined with the results from the previous study, permit two conclusions. First, the method we use to determine reliability is inappropriate, certainly in placement testing and probably in all direct assessment ("holistic") testing. To assume that only agreement (giving the same score) between raters indicates reliability does not take into account either the artificial nature of the scales we use or that good raters can legitimately disagree. Second, the role of expertise — in the case of placement testing, course-taught expertise — has not been adequately utilized. Raters can, with high reliability, determine who belongs in their courses and who does not belong (i.e., "accept" and "reject"), but they do not appear to be as reliable when making decisions about who belongs in other courses.

The results from the studies have three immediate implications. The first is that what might be considered a lack of rater reliability may, in reality, be high reliability. We simply use the wrong approach when determining reliability and thus assume that the raters are not reliable. This research implies that disagreement among raters, which is normal, is not something which must be avoided if we are to be credible. However, this research doesn't tell us whether this is true in all types of direct assessment. I would not generalize to non-local placement testing because that constituency is much broader and the scale points cannot be defined in terms of specific courses. Furthermore, the raters involved in such testing probably do not have the same sense of the immediate impact their decisions will have on students. Thus, when an essay is problematic, these raters would not be swayed toward a particular decision just because, for instance, they think that, when in doubt, it is better to require one course than to exempt from all courses.

The second implication concerns local placement and exit-exam testing where the scale points refer to courses and, thus, there can be no between-point placement. If a student fits into neither course, some additional measure (e.g., a second piece of writing, a portfolio, or an indirect measure of writing ability) may be necessary because split-resolving seems to be problematic. Additional research on these students is necessary, examining both their performance in the course and the teachers' perceptions of the adequacy of the placement (see Smith, 1993, for some preliminary evidence about teacher perception).

In particular, two lines of research seem appropriate. The macro-split texts contain symptoms of quite diverse needs and abilities, and the split-resolvers (who consistently place such students in the course between the primary ratings) seem to sense this dissonance and resolve it by a default to the middle. Since it appears the rate-set method allows us to locate such students, it is possible to track these students to determine how they perform and the degree to which the "default to the middle" puts them "at risk." These essays could also be analyzed to determine whether there are common causes for the diverse ratings. If such causes are found, they might provide insights into how raters read. Furthermore, the essays could be rewritten (much like Freedman, 1979, rewrote essays) and re-rated to determine whether, and how, particular changes evoke different ratings.

The third implication concerns the use of split-resolvers. Since split-resolution by a third rater can be problematic, it might be worthwhile to investigate the use of rater-conferencing to come to agreement. For local placement testing, the key issues would be whether conferencing requires significantly more time (cost being the underlying issue) and whether the conference method produces better results. Determining the latter would require several years of research, for students would have to be tracked at least through the sequence of composition courses.

There is another implication which concerns the courses offered to meet the needs of the population. By using the rater-set method for determining reliability, one gains considerable new information about the fit of the curriculum to the students. If, for instance, a large number of students are reliably "between courses," then there is clear justification for either creating new courses to fit those students' needs or revamping existing courses. This method seems more useful for department heads or writing program administrators who want to make an empirically motivated claim for altering the courses or the structure of the sequence of courses, or for adding or deleting courses.

The results may also have implications for a commonly used scaling method in all types of direct assessment where essays are rated by two raters on a 1 to N scale, but the ratings are summed so that the scale is actually 2 to 2N. One consequence of this method is that essays which have quite different ratings become the same when summed. For example, an essay given ratings of 2 and 4 would be considered the same as an essay given ratings of 3 and 3. The raters in this research denied this equation.

At one level, this research shows that highly trained, well qualified raters can disagree reliably. That, in itself, is of considerable importance. At another level, this research indicates how little we know about placement testing (and about how much we are willing to believe without hard evidence), about the way readers make decisions about students (not about texts, but about the writers of those texts), about the fit between our testing procedures and the courses into which we place students, and about our methods for evaluating how well our courses match and meet the needs of the populations we serve. Clearly, we need to know much more about the effects of placement, especially about the students who receive micro- and macro-split votes, before we can make any legitimate public statements about the reliability or validity of our placement testing.

While the expert-rater method may not transfer to all testing situations, the theory behind it should. Basically, that theory has three points:

1. Rating scales are limited and, thus, not all essays or writers can fit neatly into them. There are bound to be essays which fall between the scale points. I call this the "space-between points" hypothesis. This, by necessity, leads to lower inter-rater reliability, unless the raters have a protocol which tells them what to do with those essays (e.g., when in doubt, select the higher rating). But that seems like artificial reliability.

2. The more points on the rating scale, the more likely that the essays will fit within a point. Conversely, if a scale has only two points (e.g., pass/fail), it is also likely that most of the essays will fit within a point. The problem, therefore, is determining the number of points. This decision cannot be just statistically motivated, especially when the decision has a direct impact on the writer. And this leads to the third point.

3. The greater the number of scale-points, the greater the difficulty for the raters, and the greater the number of scale-points, the greater the likelihood of error and low inter-rater reliability. It is very difficult to keep 6 scale points in mind while reading. But it's much easier to keep just one in mind, especially when one has expertise on that point. Thus, it is possible that we could increase the reliability and the validity of our rating by revising the standard rating method so that each rater is responsible for only one scale point.

MODELS OF SCALES AND DECISION-MAKING

The two types of holistic assessment discussed in the introduction, the No-Direct-Impact on writers (NDI) and the Direct-Impact on writers (DI), share an important feature: For both types, the raters create their range for each scale-point (i.e., the range of essays which would fall within a scale-point) on the basis of their experience with a set of essays. For NDI raters, the data-base would be the calibration essays (the "range-finders"). For the DI raters, the data-base would be the essays/students the teacher/rater has encountered in her course.

The theory underlying NDI testing is that the scale-points are contiguous, that the scale is either interval or ordinal, and that all raters have the same scale-point ranges. (This theory also seems prevalent in DI ratings.) Schematically, this theory looks like this:

Rater 1	Scale-point A	Scale-point B	Scale-point C	Scale-point D
Rater 2	Scale-point A	Scale-point B	Scale-point C	Scale-point D

If this were the case, then there would be no disagreements. Every essay would have to fall within a scale-point and every rater would make the same decision. But disagreements do exist. I have not seen one piece of research where rater agreement was perfect. Thus, it must be the case that either the raters do not have exactly the same scale-point ranges or that the scale-points are not contiguous and the distance between the scale-points is not known.

Contiguous	Scale-point A	Scale-point B	Scale-point C	Scale-point D
Non-contiguous	Scale-point A	Scale-point B	Scale-point C	Scale-point D

The "between points" would be the grey areas in which raters are pressed to make a fuzzy decision. And it would be the essays in these grey areas that would produce low intra-rater reliability.

It seems reasonable to assume that neither any group of NDI raters nor any group of DI raters would have exactly the same ranges. Thus, two raters, of either type, might have scale-point ranges which look this:

Rater 1	Scale-point A	Scale-point B	Scale-point C	Scale-point D
Rater 2	Scale-point A	Scale-point B	Scale-point C	Scale-point D

Consequently, given five essays (E1 through E5) near scale-point B on the continuum, the two raters would agree on only three, E1 (both would say "A"), E3 (both would say "B"), and E5 (both would say "C").

	E1	E2	E3	E4	E5	

Rater 1	Scale-point A	Scale-point B	Scale-point C	Scale-point D
Rater 2	Scale-point A	Scale-point B	Scale-point C	Scale-point D

However, on E2, Rater 1 would say "B" whereas Rater 2 would say "A," and on E4, Rater 1 would say "C" whereas Rater 2 would say "B." And this is for only one scale-point. The number of disagreements would be compounded by the number of scale-points.

The problem is compounded when the raters' scale-point ranges are non-contiguous and are of different sizes. In the example below, only E3 would produce two B ratings. For Rater 1, E1 and E5 would be clear decisions (A and C), but for Rater 2, those essays would require fuzzy decisions. Conversely, for Rater 2, E2 and E6 are clear decisions, but they are fuzzy for Rater 1. E4 requires a fuzzy decision by both raters. Thus, for these six essays, agreement could range from 17% (agree on one essay) to 100% (agree on all six). Clearly, the problem of inter-rater reliability is compounded when the raters' scale-point ranges are both non-contiguous and of different sizes.

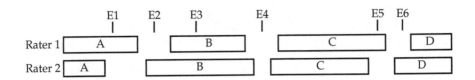

In all of these models, there is an assumption that the scale-points are ordinal. If we alter that assumption, the models change. All assessment is based on someone making a decision about "where to place" (or "what grade to give"). The decision is proscribed by the scale (e.g., A to F grades) as well as the assumption that the scale is linear, ordinal, or nominal. There are also assumptions about the discreteness of the scale-points (whether the boundaries are sharp or fuzzy).

Schematically, the three courses in Pitt's composition program (A, B, and C) can be portrayed as follows, assuming that they are not ordinal.

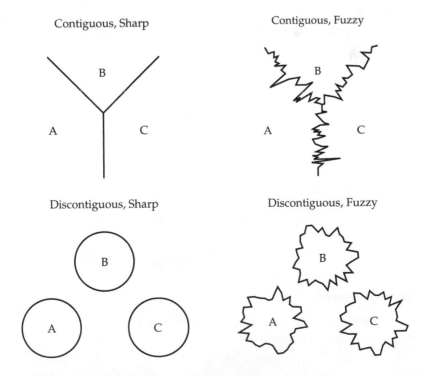

These four models can be tested using the placement data. The Non-Contiguous, Sharp model accounts for all of the non-split data and for the micro-splits. The AB and BC splits would be as shown below.

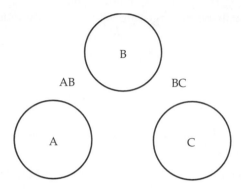

However, the macro-split (AC) data does not fit this model, for while those essays were always rejected by both Course A and Course C raters, they were often accepted by Course B raters. In effect, the Course A and C raters said "Definitely not in my course" while the Course B raters said "Maybe in my course."

If the model is revised to accommodate the sharp and fuzzy boundaries, all of the data fit, and the resulting diagram (below) becomes more ordinal, thus closer to what we assume about our students and our courses, i.e., that Course A students are less well prepared than Course B students, who are less well prepared than Course C students.

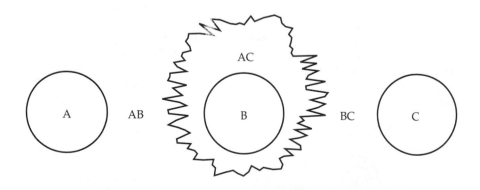

A DECISION MODEL

If the data concerning the decisions raters made are combined with the TAP data, a process decision model emerges.

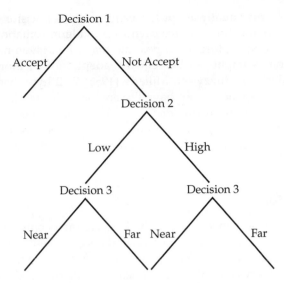

The TAP data showed that the first decision was whether or not to "accept" the student into the rater's own course. If "not accept," the second decision was "high" or "low" and the third was "how high or low." The data from the research shows that the raters have 100% accuracy on both Decision 1 and Decision 2, but they become "fuzzy" on Decision 3. They can't always tell "near" from "far."

The fuzziness of the near-far decision, in our placement system, can be partially explained by the course-taught expertise of the raters. Those Course C raters who have not taught Courses A and B would not have the privileged knowledge needed for making the distinction between A and B, except, perhaps, when it is a very clear call, i.e., the student is prototypic of the course. The Course A raters have taught Courses B and C, but not recently. Thus, they must rely on remote memory of those students. Even the Course B raters, whose only near-far decision would be Course C/Exempt, had trouble making that distinction.

This explanation, of course, begs a question: How do raters who are teaching two of the courses respond? Our composition program, in nearly all cases, prevents studying this question because our policy is to have teachers teach only one course, i.e., to have only one preparation. Thus, this research must be done elsewhere.

The decision-making model was based, in part, on the TAP data on our raters. I know of no similar data on placement raters at other universities, but if we assume that placement raters at other universities have taught the relevant courses, those raters would provide the best test of the tree, especially if they are required to make full-scale placement decisions. If their tree is similar, then their decisions become fuzzier as they move away from their most recent course(s) taught.

In large scale, no-direct impact assessments, where the raters are "calibrated" to all scale-points and must make full-scale decisions, the assumption is that the raters are equally adept (expert) in making decisions on all scale-points. Here again, there is no research to provide information concerning this assumption, but it does seem possible that when given more than five scale-points, raters might not be "equally adept," for memory limitations might make decisions fuzzy (cf. Miller's [1956] 7±2 hypothesis). It is also possible that raters who do not have the analog to course-taught expertise might be most adept in making decisions on the one scale-point and, thus, become fuzzier at distant points. Testing this hypothesis would not be difficult, and it might help explain the disagreements which are common in all testing.

THE EXPERT MODEL

The advantage of the expert rater method, where raters only "accept" or "reject" (or "reject high" and "reject low") is that disagreement is altered because agreement is not based on whether the raters agree on specific courses. Thus, the problem of "between-points" disappears. Furthermore, the data indicate that the scale-points surrounding the "accept" space are sharp. For example, for "A," "B," "C," and "D" raters, the spaces would look like this:

Expert on "A"	Accept		Reject-High	
Expert on "B"	Reject-Low	Accept	Reject-High	
Expert on "C"	Reject-Low		Accept	Reject-High
Expert on "D"	Reject-Low			Accept

However, the problem of raters not having the same ranges within their "accept" space still exists. As the figure below illustrates, even if two "B" raters did not have the same exact scale-point ranges, the potential for agreement is increased. (The black areas indicate areas of agreement; the cross-hashed areas indicate areas of disagreement.) But even the areas of disagreement between two raters with the same RCT can be resolved by agreement because the expert-rater model specifies that any essay Rejected-Low must be read by a rater whose RCT is that "lower" area and any essay Rejected-High must be read by a rater whose RCT is that "higher" area. Thus, an essay which Rater 1 had Accepted and Rater 2 had Rejected-Low would be then read by a Course A rater. It is highly probable that this rater would Reject-High, for in order to Accept that rater would have to have a very high top end on her range, an unlikely possibility. Thus, even in cases where there is disagreement between two raters with the same RCT, there will be appropriate final resolution.

Since the data from the second study showed that raters had the greatest trouble when the student was not from the raters' own course or from a contiguous course, the expert method radically alters the number of times the

Rater 1	Reject-Low	Accept	Reject-High

Rater 2	Reject-Low	Accept	Reject-High

raters agreed with the R1 raters and with the other R2 raters. For the non-split essays, there was total agreement. On the essays rated AA by R1 (that is, "accept-accept" by the R1 Course A raters), the R2 Course A raters also always accepted them and the Course B and Course C raters always rejected them. (Compare to Course B raters: 32 A ratings; Course C raters: 25 A and 7 B ratings.) On the essays rated BB by the R1 Course B raters (i.e., "accept-accept"), the R2 Course A raters always rejected-high, the Course B raters always accepted, and the Course C raters always rejected-low. (Compare to Course A raters: 25 B and 7 C ratings; Course B raters: 32 B ratings; Course C raters: 2 A ratings and 30 B ratings.) On the essays rated CC by R1 Course C raters ("accept-accept"), the R1 Course A and B raters always rejected-high, and the Course C raters always accepted. (Compare to Course A raters: 3 D, 24 C, and 5 D ratings; Course B raters: 32 C ratings; Course C: 32 C ratings.)

The splits provide even stronger evidence. On the essays rated AB by R1 (i.e., "reject-low" by the Course B rater and "reject-high" by the Course A rater), Course A R2 raters always rejected-high, and Course C raters always rejected-low. All but two of the Course B raters also rejected-low (two accepted). Thus, there was 97.9% agreement. (Compare to Course A raters: 32 B ratings; Course B raters: 30 A and 2 B ratings; Course C raters: 19 A and 13 B ratings.) On the essays rated BC by R1 ("reject-low" by Course C raters and "reject-high" by Course B raters), Course A and Course B raters in R2 always rejected-high, and the Course C raters always rejected-low. Thus, there was 100% agreement. (Compare to Course A raters: 12 B ratings and 20 C ratings; Course B raters: 32 C ratings; Course C raters: 1 A and 31 B ratings.) On the essays rated AC by R1 ("reject-low" by Course C raters; "reject-high" by Course A raters), Course C raters in R2 always rejected-low and the Course A raters always rejected-high. The Course B raters spread their ratings over all three categories, but most (65.6%) returned a B rating. (Compare to Course A raters: 15 B and 17 C ratings; Course B raters: 5 A and 21 B, and 6 C ratings; Course C raters: 17 A and 15 B ratings.)

Thus, what would be considerable disagreement if the raters had to determine which course the students belonged in became very high agreement when the raters made only the "accept-reject" decision.

The "space-between" hypothesis is testable, and it may even be possible to measure the space. For example, if no essay is ever rejected-low by a "B" rater and also never rejected-high by an "A" rater, then there would be no space between scale-points A and B. But if some essays are rejected-low and rejected-high, then that space would exist, and the space size could be calculated.

The data from the two experiments clearly shows that such space exists. If that space is real, i.e., if it is not just caused by raters having different scale-point ranges, then other measures, such as final grades, should corroborate it. We have found that the final grades of students who are "B/C" (in the space between Course B and Course C) are different from those who are either "B/B" or "C/C." Since we have no "B/C" course, all such students must be placed into either Course B and Course C. If placed into Course B, they received higher grades than the B/B students, and if placed into Course C, they received lower grades than the C/C students.

Obviously, my research on expert placement method is not sufficient to draw firm conclusions. It has to be tested at other institutions to determine whether the results are just artifact of the training and courses at Pitt. And we need to test the method in other types of testing. We need to know, for instance, whether this method is too expensive to be feasible. My data shows that it actually is cheaper because the raters can work at higher speeds. The method has cut rating time by about thirty to forty percent, but this may be an artifact of the training (seminars and teaching the courses) of our raters. We also need to know the optimal number of scale-points a reader can handle. I have seen no research on that.

The "comfort" raters feel in their decisions is also an issue that has not been addressed. Anyone who has done holistic rating has had the feeling of being under the gun to conform to the group, has had to make "coin-flip" decisions (raters often put a "+" or "−" next to such decisions), and, in the case of placement testing, has worried about the effect of the decision on the student. It stands to reason that when raters are comfortable, they will perform better, more efficiently and more effectively. Although I have no large data set on rater comfort, my conversations with raters who have worked with both our old and new methods indicate that they much prefer the new. They have stated that 1) they felt less pressure when rejecting because they knew that other raters, with different course expertise, would read the essay; 2) they felt they were making more defensible decisions; and 3) they had greater freedom in the way they read the essays. This diversity in the way of reading is confirmed by the TAP data. When raters made an initial, tentative decision to accept (i.e., to place into their course), their subsequent way of reading varied more than when the initial decision was to reject. They were more likely to skip to the last paragraph or sample-read through the essay. When the initial decision was to reject, they usually read the essay linearly.

A POTENTIAL PROBLEM WITH THE EXPERT MODEL

Since my experience with raters suggests that "having taught" training is more powerful than "calibration" training (the TAP data most clearly showed this), the potential problem is that there could be a shift in the "having taught" training because we place the between-course student (I call them Tweeners) in the higher course. Thus, the teachers of the higher course might develop a "lower threshold" for decision making. In effect, we would have a shift in the scale-point range. Students who are currently rejected because they are Tweeners would be accepted into the higher course and a new set of

Tweeners would evolve. It will take several years of research to determine whether this problem exists, but it can be done.

For the past several years, I have included previously rated essays (from previous years and for previous rating sessions within the year) in the stacks of essays the raters read. The data have shown that, using the old placement procedure — where the raters were required to make a four-way decision — a very small percentage of the non-split essays (i.e., the two primary raters agreed) were placed into a different course on that second reading, but a somewhat larger percentage of the split-vote essays were placed differently. However, I have no idea whether these "good reliability" results were facts or artifacts. Given what I found in the two studies, the raters during the second year/session may have just repeated the errors made the previous year/session. Thus, my conclusion back then, that "between year/session" reliability was adequate, may be quite inappropriate or even dead wrong. This is, of course, extremely important, for placement must not depend on the session or year. I have always assumed that if the reliability were high, I could claim that our placement procedure is valid. Yet if that reliability is just a compounded error — which may be caused by the methods used to determine who rates each essay and to determine the kinds of decisions raters may make — then validity cannot exist.

REFERENCES

Alexander, J. & Swartz, F. (1982). The dynamics of computer assisted writing sample measurements at Ferris State College. Paper presented at the annual meeting of the Michigan Council of Teachers of English, East Lansing, MI, October 29–31. (ERIC Document Reproduction Services No. ED 233 344).

Bartholomae, D. (1983). Writing assignments: where writing begins. In P. L. Stock (Ed.), *Fforum: Essays on Theory and Practice in the Teaching of Writing*, Upper Montclair, NJ: Boynton/Cook, pp. 300–312.

Bartholomae, D., & Petrosky, A. (1987). *Ways of Reading: An Anthology for Writers*. New York: Bedford/St. Martin's Press.

Cohen, A. M. (1973). Assessing college student's ability to write compositions. *Research in the Teaching of English, 7,* 356–371.

Coles, W. E., Jr. (1981). *Composing II: Writing as a Self-Creating Process*. Rochelle Park, NJ: Hayden Book Company.

Cooper, C. R. (1977). Holistic evaluation in writing. In Cooper & Odell (Eds.), *Evaluating Writing: Describing, Measuring, Judging*. Urbana: National Council of Teachers of English.

Follman, J. C., & Anderson, J. A. (1967). An investigation of the reliability of five procedures for grading English themes. *Research in the Teaching of English, 1,* 190–200.

Freedman, S. W. (1979). How characteristics of student essays influence teachers' evaluation. *Journal of Educational Psychology, 71,* 328–338.

Hillocks, G. (1986). *Research on Written Composition*. Urbana: ERIC Clearinghouse on Reading and Communication Skills.

Hughes, D. C., Kelling, B., & Tuck, B. F. (1980). Essay marking and the context problems. *Educational Research, 22,* 147–148.

Miller, G. A. (1956). The magic number seven, plus or minus two. *Psychological Review, 69,* 81–97.

Myers, M. (1980). *A Procedure for Writing Assessment and Holistic Scoring*. Urbana: National Council of Teachers of English.

Smith, L. S., Winters, L., Quellmalz, E. W., & Baker, E. L. (1980). Characteristics of students writing competence: an investigation of alternative score systems. (Research Report No. 134). Los Angeles: Center for the study of Evaluation. (ERIC Document Reproduction Services No. ED 217 074).

Smith, W. L. (1993). Assessing the reliability and adequacy of placement using holistic scoring of essays as a college composition placement test. In M. M. Williamson & B. A. Huot (Eds.), *Validating Holistic Scoring for Writing Assessment: Theoretical and Empirical Foundations* (pp. 142–205). Cresskill, NJ: Hampton Press.

Smith, W. L., Hull, G. A., Land, R. E., Moore, M. T., Ball, C., Dunham, D. E., Hickey, L. S., & Ruzich, C. W. (1985). Some effects of varying the structure of a topic on college students' writing. *Written Communication, 2,* 73–89.

White, E. M. (1975–81). *Comparison and Contrast: The California State University and College Freshman English Equivalency Examination.* Long Beach: English Council of the California State Universities & Colleges. (ERIC Document Reproduction Services No. ED 227 510).

White, E. M. (1985). *Teaching and Assessing Writing.* San Francisco: Jossey-Bass.

Author's Comment — William L. Smith

All composition teachers and researchers constantly confront two problems: Our willingness to believe our lore rather than to seriously question it, and our tendency to adopt rather than adapt methods and premises from other disciplines. These two problems have plagued me for many years.

When I became the Director of Testing for the University of Pittsburgh's Composition Program, I inherited a method for placing students. That method was a standard method, one used in many universities. It seemed to work, so there had been no impetus to examine it, let alone change it. The incoming students were placed into our courses efficiently and with what appeared to be a tolerable numbers of errors. Perhaps this alone explains that there is almost no literature on placement testing.

But something about the system nagged the backburners of my brain. So, I began what has become a long series of research projects, most focusing on why students are misplaced, then later on how they are placed, that is, on how raters make decisions. My article in this chapter presents a small series of studies, but these studies are the culmination of many previous studies, the product of years of wandering down blind alleys as well as into light.

In order to understand how I came to the present research (or, as a dear colleague said, how I came to the painfully obvious), let me trace some history.

If error exists in placement, that error must be caused by something or a combination of somethings. The most obvious choices are 1) the writing prompts, 2) the conditions under which students write, 3) the writers not writing essays which adequately represent them, 4) the raters not making good decisions, 5) an inadequate rating scale, and 6) me. I include "me" because I make decisions such as whom to hire as raters, because I design the rating procedure, and because I design the studies and analyze the data.

Our first study focused on the writing prompts. We found that, given what we teach in our composition courses, those prompts were the most effective, so the prompts, by themselves weren't the cause of errors.

The second study looked at the conditions, e.g., whether writing the essay in a large group produced different results that writing in a small group, whether the two-hour time limit was a factor, whether "warm-up" exercises alter students' writing, and whether a difference resulted when there was a real teacher in the room — one who made preliminary comments about how we teach, how we read, and what we expect. The results showed that group size and time were not factors, and "warm-ups" and teacher presence made only slight differences — primarily with students who are weaker writers. But the differences were not consistently positive. Thus, the conditions might be a factor, but not a very powerful one.

The research on the writers indicated that they were a factor, but not one that I could control. For example, we found that some writers, especially males, were often distracted. For many, the trip to campus to take the placement tests (in math, foreign language, and composition) and to sit through "orientation" sessions was the first trip to our campus. Thus, encountering the new setting and new people was a distraction. More than one student has come to the composition test quite drunk — they had discovered that beer is readily available and their parents and high school peers were no longer restraining forces.

The "error rate" in placement has always been measured by the number of students we move to new courses during the first week of class. (This is the case at most universities.) During that first week, the instructors in all composition courses have their students write an essay which is read as a check on placement. If a teacher thinks a student is clearly misplaced, the essay is read by senior faculty and we make any appropriate adjustments. Of course, this double check itself introduces more than one variable. Students who don't like where they are placed may try harder on the first-week essay, but students who like their placement may not. Teachers may not identify many students as potential misplacements because they don't want to have many students transferring out because that would mean others would be transferred in — and that creates extra work. Furthermore, a few students don't even bother to attend the first few classes. I presume they are extending their vacations. Thus, the first-week essay provides only marginal evidence about how many students we misplace. I have long suspected that this measure seriously under-estimates the error rate.

Because I didn't, and still don't, trust this measure of error, I had to find a different measure. That research cost me three years, but I found that — to no teacher's surprise — the best measure is the teacher's perception of the goodness of placement. However, we also found that this perception must be obtained within a rather narrow band of time. If the teacher is asked too early (before the third week of class), she doesn't have sufficient evidence to make the decision. If she is asked too late (after mid-term), the response correlates almost exactly with the final grade and, thus, it is not a perception of placement. As is often the case with research, what you looked at reveals unexpected, and often more interesting information.

Since the errors in placement could not, with any consistency, be attributed to the prompts, to the conditions, or to the students, that left the raters, the scale, and me. And these are the foci of the research for this chapter.

What I really found is that the raters are extremely good, but the rating system didn't allow them to be that good. Since I chose the rating system, the problem was me because I adopted straight from the literature without questioning it. There was nothing wrong with the scale; it is dictated by our curriculum. But my ways of interpreting the rater's ratings — i.e., their use of the scale — were also adopted straight from measurement and evaluation paradigms. For example, I accepted the standard methods for "inter-rater reliability." I did not adapt them to the very special conditions of writing.

The bottom line, then, of my research up to now is quite simple. 1) Don't accept anything until you've tested it for several years, don't "believe" before testing. 2) Don't adopt methods or paradigms until they are tested in two ways. First, test them with whatever common sense you have. As a teacher, I knew that writers do not fit into a bell curve, but that is the assumption underlying some of the statistical methods I used. Second, test them with discipline-relevant assumptions and research. Rating essays is more than a bit like grading: the more evidence one has the more likely one is to make an appropriate decision. It should not shock anyone that teachers — who know the student, the human, as well as they know student's writing — do not give the same "grades" as raters who don't know the student.

And 3) I have hardly begun to tap into the more interesting problems, such as the social construction of teachers (e.g., all that affects how they teach and grade and rate essays), the cognitive process involved in making what seems to be simple decisions, or the ways we can use what we know about readers/raters to make our teaching more effective and our students better writers.

12   *Adventuring into Writing Assessment*

RICHARD HASWELL AND
SUSAN WYCHE-SMITH

Accoring to Peter Ewell, teachers should begin thinking of formal assessment "as a condition of doing business" (75). According to Patricia Stock and Jay L. Robinson, writing teachers had better begin taking part in formal assessment "as an act of self-defense" (97). The clash between these two pieces of advice is intriguing. Should the involvement of teachers in the new writing assessment be passive ("a condition") or reactive ("self-defense"), entrepreneurial ("doing business") or military ("self-defense")? It can be all, of course. The clash itself reflects pretty accurately the contradictory feelings of many writing teachers when they hear of plans for assessment at their institution. They feel at once helpless and angry, at once caught in a war whose objectives are not their own and squeezed by a monopoly whose methods are not their own.

The two of us know the feeling. But strangely enough, our own recent involvement in institutional writing assessment proved the feeling wrong—or if not wrong, misconceived. We certainly started off with that sense of being embattled customers. Our institution, a land-grant university, had committed itself to a program of multilevel assessment several years ago. Suddenly the first deadline laid down by the faculty senate was just nine months off. There was a university committee in charge of creating and implementing the new assessment package, but only one member of the composition faculty had ever served on it. So far, the people most affected—the rest of the composition faculty, including the directors of composition and the campus writing lab—had heard about crucial steps in the process only after the fact. Already two assessment instruments had been piloted, entry placement and rising-junior exams, with outdated procedures and no intrinsic connections to one another. The two exams generated one-shot impromptu writings, pilot ratings of which showed a concordance among readers far below recommended levels. Yet there was little doubt that these exams, however flawed, would soon be approved and implemented.

It seems we had joined a scenario taking place at colleges and universities across the nation. Composition faculty find themselves ancillary to the political

---

From *College Composition and Communication* 45 (1994): 220–36.

reform movements promoting assessment within their own institutions. They blink an eye, and suddenly some victor is nailing a manifesto right on their classroom door, directly affecting their programs and the lives of their students. The only recourse seems frustrated acceptance or angry protest. But, as we have said, this is not how our story turned out. We discovered, perhaps mostly by luck, that the real site of writing assessment is not so much a battle zone or a contested economic sphere of influence as a territory open for venture, and that writing teachers will do well neither to accept passively nor to react angrily — but simply to act.

In short, we have a story to tell and some advice to give, both contrary to folklore and folk remedies. Our story is not a repeat of "teachers victimized by administrative interests." We will not tell of efforts coming too late to avert educational disaster. Just the opposite. We want to recount a success story, about how a writing faculty reclaimed their university's writing assessment program. Nor does our story end with the offer of an assessment package, ready for others to use. Again, just the opposite. Our moral is that writing teachers should be leery of assessment tools made by others, that they should, and can, make their own. Finally, our story does not take the shape of a bestseller. If it did so, it would probably promote the latest craze, say, some version of a portfolio system for placement. Our adventure into assessment was *sui generis*, as we believe all such ventures should be.

The push for educational assessment is not new. But the present atmosphere, of openness to faculty initiatives in writing assessment, is new and not yet well appreciated. This is why we believe the following narrative will be valuable, though as a travellers' account with some travellers' advice rather than as an itinerary. This also may explain why a small corpus of similar (and uniquely valuable) accounts has lately appeared (e.g., Condon and Hamp-Lyons; Anson and Brown; Roemer, Schultz, and Durst).

THE WAITING CALL

Our first discovery was that *they* were waiting for *us*. Initially, we were content to have others design the examinations. Absorbed in our own projects, implementing new courses and rehabilitating old ones, we gave little thought to the work taking place at the university level. Our involvement began with the pilot for the placement exam. We saw the results first hand, since it was tested in composition courses and the readers were drawn from English department faculty and graduate students. We also saw that the placement test would directly impact the courses we taught and supervised, and would do so soon, since it was the part of the assessment scheduled for earliest implementation. Our uneasiness grew when we began to talk together. Little things that had disturbed us individually seemed more serious when shared. One of us taught a seminar in writing evaluation and was familiar with the standard literature on assessment; the other had served as a reader for ETS and for senior-level writing examinations at another university. We knew what we didn't like about traditional assessment, and we saw taking shape at our own university exactly that. We acted first in self-defense.

Yet perhaps that act involved less conscious strategy than traveller's luck. For instance, because we were not part of the official team, we allowed ourselves to dream. We felt neither committed to a clean slate nor yoked to previous work, but free to keep and free to junk. Here is some of the dream. If there had to be an examination, we imagined, it should reflect the content of our courses. If there were to be two examinations, entry and junior level, they should be linked, providing a way to evaluate not only individual student development but the lower-division writing program as a whole. If teaching assistants were to be primary readers, at least for the placement exam, the rating system should use their expertise as teachers rather than just their obedience to holistic rubric. And if we were to implement such a beast, we also would want the means to assess *it*, to gather reactions from students and teachers as well as our state and university officials. We didn't want it to cost students a lot of money, or to be labor intensive (we all had other things to do). And we wanted an assessment program that integrated with our university's recent ambitious and innovative program to improve general education for its undergraduates.

Having imagined an ideal which appealed even to us (two people who detest tests), we protested. We wrote memos and visited offices. Thereupon came our first surprise. People listened. People who counted, like the Vice Provost for Instruction. We discovered the first truth about institutional assessment of writing: No one feels competent to do it. There was no cabal surreptitiously administering their own agenda behind our backs. There was an administration, delighted to find two writing teachers who said they had an innovative plan, and eager to get a problematic task out of their own amateur hands. (We didn't tell anybody that we felt like amateurs ourselves.) They gave us the opportunity not only to redesign and run new pilots but to administer the real thing.

So we inherited the commitment and the yoke. With the placement test, from inspiration to implementation, we had little more than six months. But what we lacked in time we had gained in trust. The university committee — captivated with the sound of a "cutting-edge" assessment — put us in charge of a new testing subcommittee containing several other university officials who either liked our ideas or could provide logistical support. These last turned out to be crucial; their knowledge about summer orientation, registration, fees, data reporting, budget, and university policy shaped the assessment from the start, precluding any later need to reshape and then gather approval from scattered offices. These members also provided us with a vocal group of supporters when our plan finally went to the university committee for permission to implement.

In retrospect, we see four rules of thumb that we believe will help writing faculty at any campus get an initial hearing and find their way through the labyrinth of practical and political demands. The first we have just discussed:

1. Assume that administrators are eager to let English faculty create the institution's writing assessment.

The other three pertain to the process:

2. Let the local scene shape the examination, not the other way around.

3. Take inspiration but not necessarily orders from the most recent literature on assessment.
4. For help in constructing the assessment test, rely most on the people who will maintain it.

Though obvious, these premises were originally disregarded at our institution. Our assessment program would have been largely imported from other institutions, with rating methods reflecting the best designs of a decade or more ago. There would have been little connection among the two examination (placement and junior-level) and the curriculum they supposedly supported. Worst of all, the program would have been alien to the people faced with the real challenge: to keep it going year after year (maintenance is the Achilles heel of assessment innovation: see White, 1990).

We do not offer these four guidelines, however, as, theorems. We will not argue that they will generate one kind of writing assessment (better) rather than another (worse). As we describe our local content, the literature we found most inspirational, and the people who were involved with our assessment program, we merely hope to show how faculty at other institutions can map out their own assessments. Our main hope is that teachers will sally forth, appropriate the new pressure on their institutions to implement large-scale assessment, and convert that power to drive a program that serves their own instructional ideals.

THE LOCAL SCENE

In the rest of this article, we will focus on our construction of the placement exam (the junior-level exam is still in the making; see Haswell, Johnson-Shull, and Wyche-Smith). Especially with placement, local context should be the major shaping force. After all, students walk into an "entry" exam right off the street of the local scene. Just as national standardized advance-placement tests are justly criticized for slighting regional groups, so institutional placement tests should be constructed around regional groups. But "constructed around" misconstrues our experience: we discovered less that we had to find an exam to fit local conditions and more that local conditions helped build the exam for us. The distinction is important and worth illustrating.

To our campus come students primarily from public schools in the Pacific Northwest. We are a residential university in rural location, with comparatively few nontraditional students. For the most part, we can assume that our students already have basic writing skills. The "basic writers" described by Mina Shaughnessy, Mike Rose, and other researchers who have worked at large urban campuses have little to do with the "basic writers" in our program. At the other end of the spectrum, we knew some students did not need freshman composition in any form, and that the exam could be used as evidence for exemption and advanced credit. Our placement exam would have to sort our stronger and weaker students based on differences in the quality of their high school training.

From earlier piloting of the exam, we had inherited a complication as well as a means to help answer this need. There was a new Writing Tutorial course, English 102, already on the books, and ready to accept freshmen. This one-credit, pass/fail course was to serve students within but at the bottom margin of competency, students who were not basic writers but still "at risk." English 102, taken concurrently with the core course, would provide extra instructional support in the form of conferencing and small group work with tutors in the campus writing center. The placement examination would have to distinguish these marginal students from competent writers on the one hand and from basic writers on the other.

Another given was the core course, English 101. In the last three years it had been revamped to focus on academic writing, with emphasis on critical thinking and college-level reading and library skills, not to mention computer literacy. It had also acquired a multicultural slant with its integration into the new general-education requirements. English 101 was conceived as a mainstream course for the great majority of freshmen. There they would face instructors, almost exclusively graduate teaching assistants, all using the same multicultural reader and giving three common assignments: responses to readings, critiques of cultural events on campus, and essays requiring secondary sources. The placement exam would have to enable us to judge whether students were ready for such a course.

English 101 also had another special feature, which added certain placement parameters. The course applied a midsemester and final portfolio system modelled loosely after the one developed by Peter Elbow and Pat Belanoff at Stony Brook. Students could not earn credit without passing the final portfolio, as judged by readers other than their teacher. Also, the midsemester portfolio would determine which 102 students could have the option of exiting their tutorials. The placement exam would have to forecast the likelihood of students succeeding within this portfolio system.

Finally, 101 had been reinterpreted by the new core curriculum as one step in a series of undergraduate writing requirements: passing the course would qualify students to take the junior-level portfolio exam, which would admit them to upper-division writing courses in their major. The exam placing students within that sequence had to link up with later exams to facilitate assessment of the new core.

Our "basic writing" course, English 100, has its own distinct character. Instead of the more usual remedial course, it is an opportunity for underprepared students to work on assignments like those in English 101 — but at a slower pace with greater opportunity for peer and instructor conferencing. Because the course is graded pass/fail, it offers an easier transition into college-level writing. But because its credits do not apply toward general undergraduate requirements, it also doubles the time students spend in composition courses. The placement exam would have to set writing tasks easy enough to give marginal students a fair shake yet difficult enough to identify 100 students with high validity.

The largest minority group would be ESL students, most of them from Pacific-rim countries. We had a three-course ESL sequence, English 103/104/

105, all preceding English 101. Students placed in any of these could, on the advice of their instructor, move to the core course when they seemed prepared. But these students face the same problem as their peers in English 100: the additional credit hours of work do not satisfy university writing requirements. Eventually all would have to pass English 101. Students would not be placed in these ESL courses by any specialized testing (e.g., via TOFFL scores), but by the same exam taken by first-language writers. The placement exam would have to give ESL writers a fair chance to show their true skills in English-language essay composing.

Two other local conditions, not academic but logistical, helped shape the exam. First, nearly 60% of our incoming freshmen would arrive on campus during the summer for one of six two-day orientation sessions. Because the university promised that students could preregister for fall classes during these orientations, tests would have to be administered on the first day and results ready the following morning for advisors. Most of the remaining freshmen (over 700) would take the exam during fall registration week and would need the same quick response. The exam would be given three more times during the academic year — a total of ten times. The exam had to be manipulable for multiple sessions and readable within a 24-hour turnaround time.

The second logistical problem followed from the first. We needed to maintain a small group of readers, test administrators, and clerical staff throughout the academic year. Especially during the summer, we would have no guarantee that the same readers would always be available. We already knew that the readers — with the exception of test administrators — would be graduate teaching assistants. We needed a relatively simple rating and administering system, one that would not require repeated training to maintain reliability and validity from session to session.

At first these constraints seemed just that: constraints. Faced with local situations equally eccentric, many writing administrators shut their eyes and hope boilerplate exams will place their students with not too much ill fit and ill will. We discovered, however, that our local constraints exerted a liberating and even creative force. For instance, we strove for topics that would be open enough to allow both first-language and second-language writers scope for their talents, and at the same time challenging enough to distinguish the most accomplished writers. In keeping with our English 101 design, we also sought topics that would encourage multiperspectival thinking. To link with the core writing sequence, we set the rhetorical task at a developmental level meant to show the limitations of freshmen and the advancement of juniors and seniors. We invented a frame-and-slot design for the rhetorical task, allowing permutation of prompts, so that frequent sessions could be administered without concern for security. We devised rating and recordkeeping procedures that permitted a seven-slot placement within a 24-hour turnaround. Here the literature on assessment, to which we now turn, taught an invaluable, and similar, lesson; like the local conditions, it seemed formidable and constraining at first, but proved liberating.

THE SCHOLARLY BACKGROUND

It is a serious mistake to think that a local context sets current problems to which solutions will be found in the literature of past assessment. On that false assumption, teachers who fear the technical specialization of the literature (or only discover how poor the bibliographical access to it is) will soon despair and turn to readymade exams. Teachers who persist will find that solutions reported for one locale only occasionally match the problems of another, or that the solution promoted in one report will be questioned in four others. This does not mean, however, that the literature on writing assessment is useless in constructing local tests. It means its uses go far beyond solving problems, most often freeing test-constructors creatively with options and insights rather than binding them with set answers. It should not intimidate, it should intimate. We recommend reading as much of it as possible during the gestation of the exam, and feeling fortunate that it is plentiful.

It also is quite readable. While some articles are written by educators with statistical training — and *can* be intimidating to the uninitiated — a surprisingly large majority are by composition teachers and humanities administrators and are perfectly accessible. And once into this material, teachers will find multiple uses for it. For us it had a circular relationship to exam-building. Sometimes the literature gave us ideas for the exam, sometimes our work on the exam gave us new interpretation of the literature. In a word, our encounter with the literature was adventitious. So much so that the only honest account will take a form that may be called, with only slight exaggeration, picaresque. We will end, however, by trying to pack together the varied ways that assessment literature can help rather than hinder someone tailoring a new exam for a new context.

The literature first reinforced for us an already known fact, that different placement-test methods place students differently. This is true of different kinds of tests — direct and indirect (Smith et al.) — and also of different rating procedures — general impression, holistic, analytic scale, trait measurement, paired comparisons (Winters; Haswell, 1989). We needed a constant reminder of this truth as we were designing our exam, because different outcomes would only become apparent later through laborious empirical comparison.

Also early on, the literature reinforced some of our biases. For example, we were not about to incorporate indirect testing of writing into our placement system, although we sensed some pressure from our university to do so (e.g., to use SAT scores or high-school grades). Although SAT scores are still used exclusively by more than a third of the nation's colleges for writing placement (Wiener), repeated study suggests that they can only predict success at similar tests. The same is true of high-school grades, which predict college grades better than they do college writing performance. It is also known that indirect testing disadvantages minority writers (White and Thomas; Cohen et al.). Here the literature gave us ammunition to defend a position we already held.

It also clarified — materialized, so to speak — our cloudy intuitions about rating methods. The most common rating procedure today, of course, is still the holistic, where typically an essay is rated independently by two readers, both trained to apply an evaluative rubric, with a third independent reader ready to resolve discrepancies. Our first-hand experience with holistic rating had aroused a somewhat unreasoned dislike. So we were pleased to discover in the most current literature a growing indictment of the holistic as a valid placement procedure (e.g., Lucas, 1982; Charney; Gorman et al.; Scharton; Huot; Belanoff). Better, the literature provided reasons. The primary one is that holistic scoring is product centered. It compares one student's writing sample, *as a product*, to an ideal performance, as described in the rubric of subskills. Focus on product comparison may be appropriate for assessing a program's outcomes, but not for guessing which course will best improve an individual's skills. There the focus should be less what the student did or did not do in an examination essay and more what the student shows promise of doing.

Assessment literature is abundantly successful at explaining past mistakes. A good placement decision, for instance, requires close and knowledgeable reading between the lines, if not in a majority then still in a significant number of cases. But the literature documents the ways in which the holistic procedure actually mitigates against such careful reading. Where it has achieved high reliability, it has done so only with rapid and, to be honest, unsophisticated readings. This explains the history of discrepancies between novice and experienced scoring (Baker and Quellmalz; Breland and Jones; Ruth and Murphy). It also explains why holistic assessment has worked less validly with impromptu writing, where readers are unduly influenced by such surface features as length, handwriting, mechanical mistakes, and unevenness. It also may be why ESL writing has fared so poorly in holistic readings: ESL writing often betrays problematic mismatches between surface deficiencies and content proficiencies (Johns). We were especially impressed with the evidence that holistic procedures seem harsher in placing students when compared to analytic methods (Quellmalz).

At this point, in our search for an alternative, a number of scattered points in the literature came together in a subterranean way, where it is hard now to distinguish spark from fuel. We began formulating a more open method of assessment, closest perhaps to ones described at Michigan State (Barritt et al.) and at the University of Pittsburgh (Smith). In contrast to holistic norm-referencing, it would strive for diagnosis. While the holistic forces a comparison of an actual student piece with an ideal and therefore highlights the negative, our diagnostic reading would force a prediction of a student writer's potential given several different future paths of instruction, and therefore would highlight the positive in the form of "growth points" in the writing (Boomer). The emphasis would be less on scoring reliability and more on what we later found called "instructional validity," where a test elicits a response that can be matched with the writer's past and future coursework (Feldhusen et al.). In that conflict between reliability and validity which lurks under the surface of all assessment accounts, we would put our money on validity.

But how much money would that take? At first glance, a diagnostic procedure looked impossibly expensive. Instead of paying modestly for a large number of novice raters trained to apply a scoring rubric independently and fast, we would have to pay well for a few seasoned teachers (our experienced graduate teachers), who would need time to see through difficult essays, perhaps even to confer about the one course most likely to help problem writers. In fact, since the raters' diagnostic intuition would have to be based on extensive knowledge of how various students have fared in specialized courses, then they would have to be those very people — teachers and administrators — who knew the most about the courses. Here the assessment literature gave no explicit advice. But, as if through the back door, we remembered a fact about rater reliability reported by numerous studies, namely that disagreement occurs on only a fraction of the essays in a typical run (usually from 10% to 25%). The majority are quickly and reliably placed, and only a few recalcitrant pieces require thorough analysis.

We decided to experiment with a two-stage reading procedure, even though the literature provided no precedent. In the first stage, our relatively inexperienced instructors would read essays only to pick out obvious English 101 placements. These essays — read blind to the writer's gender and ESL status to avoid well-documented areas of bias — would each be given a single perusal of perhaps less than a minute. All doubtful essays would be turned over to more experienced instructors and the administrators of the courses under consideration (the basic course, the one-hour writing lab course, and the ESL courses) for as much study and discussion as needed. Our novel division between clear and grey pieces illustrates the way a test-maker's eccentric bents, the past experience of others, and the local curricular needs can sometimes mysteriously synthesize. We amalgamated, for instance, our distaste for the holistic, Edward A. Morante's argument that the grey area of placement most strongly demands specialized methods (60), and our inheritance of the new English 102 tutorial course. During pilot readings, we realized that our new rating procedure satisfied us as teachers, allowed us to pay the readers a professional wage, and kept expenses within the fee for the examination.

Looking back, we see that the literature encouraged us to begin our thinking with the rating procedure. That seemed strange. But it was better to let constraints involving raters, time, budget, and curriculum first shape the exam, since it was the more malleable. So we again considered the exam, this time in light of the system we had chosen for rating its products. Just as we had negotiated the dilemma between reliability and validity in rating, we now had to negotiate dilemmas well known in test construction. There are basically two. First, in direct tests of essay writing, a sample of just one mode of writing is less valid than a sample of two or more, and indeed one sample taken at one sitting (with several modes or without), is less valid than two or more taken at different times (the classic proof is presented in Braddock et al.; for a recent confirmation, see Breland et al.). For us the dilemma was that a multimodal, multisample assessment would not fit our pragmatic constraints. Students arriving on campus in summer for a two-day orientation or in fall for rush and residual registration were too rushed and distracted for arduous testing, and our brief turnaround time for reporting results forbade complex samples. We could only envy schools with space to handle placement portfolios. We had to go with impromptu, single-mode essay of less than two hours duration.

The second dilemma had to do with constructing that very kind of essay exam to suit our aims and our students. As we have said, it would have to be complex enough to serve later for upper-division testing, to fit the first-year curricular emphasis on college-level style, and to distinguish between basic, intermediate, and exemptable competency levels. On the other hand, it would have to be simple enough to keep many kinds of students—not only basic and ESL writers but certain personality types—from suffering the worst effects of pressured, impromptu writing assignments (Livingston; Bernhardt; Brooks; Peyton et al.; Johns; for a summary, see Ruth and Murphy).

If the assessment literature taught us any foolproof lesson, it was to give up hope of escaping these two dilemmas with one radical innovation, overturning decades of trial in higher education. Instead the message was to rely on an ensemble of partial adjustments to the conventional format. We decided to write rhetorical tasks that were fairly sophisticated, trusting the counterintuitive research finding that simpler prompts, or prompts best liked by students, are not necessarily the more diagnostic (Brossell and Ash; Hoetker et al.). We would, however, make students study the prompt before they began writing, by handing out the prompt sheet first and then distributing bluebooks fifteen minutes later. Instead of jumping into their essay within a few minutes of reading the assignment, students would be almost forced to compose themselves and comprehend the task beforehand (late in the game we were delighted to find Patricia Stock and Jay L. Robinson recommending just such a strategy, though their students worked on brainstorming techniques with teachers for the interim period [107]). And while we would make the rhetorical task intellectually demanding, we would take special pains to write clear directions (Caroll and Murphy). Since ambivalence in audience specification often distracts exam-writers (Fitzgerald; Lucas, 1988; Plasse; Raforth), we decided to explain outright that they should address not some hypothetical readers, such as the editors of a student newspaper, but indeed their actual readers, college teachers using the essay to decide placement. And we would clarify the question of criteria, which students often misconceive to their disadvantage (Fitzgerald, Millward) by listing the few main ones that readers would focus on.

Finally, we would try to counter the known negative effects of impromptu writing on writers. First, we would familiarize the readers with the ways timed writing impacts prior knowledge, test apprehension, cultural background, personality type, and composing habit. Since the readers would not be constrained by the product-bound rubric of the holistic procedure, they could diagnose through such effects as unfinished or hastily finished essays, misinterpreted topics, and ragged surface features. Second, all students who placed in the basic course would be allowed a retest. In our reading we had noticed that the issue of retesting emerges in a highly contradictory fashion. Our profession has documented the psychological damage sometimes done to students who fail impromptu exams (Freedman and Robinson; Clark; Millward), yet the rare placement procedures that have allowed a retest usually have done so begrudgingly. We decided to honor the assessment truth that certain individuals need more than one sample to show their true capabilities. We would not sit back and wait for the few action-minded and disgruntled students to plead their case, but would actively encourage all English 100 placers to try again.

In such ways we mapped out our particular exam from the Baedecker of assessment literature — from experimental studies, theoretical position papers, statistical analyses, historical accounts of failures, and reproductions of actual exams. The literature also provided something less concrete but perhaps more influential. The temptation is to call it a philosophy, but it was more a pervasive sense of the land acquired through experience, a kind of old-timer's advice. For us it is summed up in Patricia Bizzell's caution that writing examinations can easily become a "counter-agenda for teaching" (67). Over and over the literature reminded us that as teachers of the courses most affected, we should make sure our exam did not belie our best hopes for them. If, as Stock and Robinson put it so forthrightly, testing simply makes "explicit the values inherent in the set of expectations that assessors bring to the act of evaluation" (100), then we would try to manifest values held by teachers. If administrators, institution overseers, and indeed the general public liked the test and its results, so much the better, but we would not put their particular values first. This is why we elected, for instance, to favor valid student diagnosis over rater reliability (that mainstay of direct-writing test critique), declined to write prompts with a low FOG index, and challenged test-takers with quotations that required sophisticated thinking and an ability to grapple with academic style. Put another way, or rather following another line of reasoning, if placement tests quickly remake curricula in their image, encouraging high-school teachers to teach to the test that their students will soon take (Loofbourrow), then we would make ours as instructional as we could.

In retrospect, our picaresque trek through the land of assessment (there is no official tour) was characterized almost entirely by our freedom to react and act as we pleased, and hardly at all by our ceding to foreign laws and customs. We found our options increased, our sensitivity to salient issues shifted, our inklings explained, our direction unchanged but our route shortened, our awareness of dangers expanded and sharpened, our convictions strengthened. Some of the ideas we chanced on were new to us, but instead of feeling obliged to follow where they led, we combined them with ideas of our own or used them to find new paths of our own. Some of the evidence argued against our plans, but while sometimes we altered our course, sometimes we carried on, knowing that our situation was unique and therefore unprecedented in certain ways. Some of the sources we stumbled on repelled us, but rather than discourage us, they warned of avenues which had turned into cul de sacs for others and encouraged us to search for new routes. Overall, our experience with the literature bore out the encouraging truth for the second generation, that there are advantages to arriving late.

THE PEOPLE

Perhaps the most effective decision we made early on was to involve in our discussions those colleagues who would provide support for the examination. Looking back, we see this was smart for two reasons: A task of this magnitude cannot be done by just one or two people, and once implemented, it becomes a permanent responsibility that needs to be handed off periodically, particularly when housed in an academic department rather than a testing office. Before we became involved, the people responsible for design and implementation seemed distant from those who would ultimately maintain the exam and be most affected by it. We wanted to take a different approach, though at first this was less a conscious strategy than a desperate lurch to organize the exam. We called together our colleagues — the Director of the Writing Lab, the administrators of the undergraduate composition program, and several writing teachers — for a series of conversations concerning our courses, our students, our past problems with placement, and our doubts about the earlier pilot tests. From these first discussions, we started piecing together a picture of both our program and the students who *successfully* inhabited it — a picture that better represented the perspectives we shared as a community.

We also began to identify those students who found their way to the margins: nontraditional students who chose the "bottom rung" of English 100 because they were overly anxious about their writing skills; students who failed English 101 because they needed more assistance than their teachers could provide; students whose high school grades were better than the preparation they had received; and students whose ESL background landed them in inappropriate courses. We discussed individual cases and explored ways that an exam could guide us toward the best possible placement. Because of their familiarity with such students, our teachers played a crucial role in the process. These discussions, along with the professional literature, began to give our examination its agenda and its final shape.

With the piloting of the examination in sections of our writing courses, we entered the second round of discussions. We wanted to know what characterized the responses of students in English 100 and 101 and, especially, to identify the kinds of problems that marked students whom the pilot placed in the new tutorial course. Once again, the collective experience of participating teachers helped us refine our rubric. By the end of that semester, we had a diagnostic description of our courses, sample essays from students at various levels, and an outline of our analyses of these essays — all distilled into a handbook to be used for training future raters. Though the discussions took time, they resulted in tough decisions being made together, generated language for prompts and for the rater's handbook, and gave us a core of supporters. This last point is especially important. Not just one or two but several people would be able to answer questions in the rush of implementing the new program. Several people were also qualified to administer the exam and the rating sessions and, later, as team members called in sick or went on sabbatical, could step into leading roles. Similarly, our rating procedure, with its two tiers of readers, provided a system of advancement and rotation to train new readers each year while maintaining a pool of more experienced readers as guides. And because the format we chose for the ratings depends on dialogue, the conversations needed to keep the program running smoothly would continue as part of its normal administration.

DOWN THE ROAD

Travellers' tales, if honest, are partly cautionary tales. Writing teachers willing to take assessment into their own hands should be aware of two inevitable consequences. First, authoring of an examination obligates subsequent examination of the exam. To the degree that the test is innovative, and especially at the points of originality, follow-up studies are essential. This will be both time-consuming and rewarding. During the year our placement examination has been in place, while others were expressing their satisfaction, we spent much of our time investigating the validity of our rating system, the effects of actual placements as seen through the eyes of students and their teachers, and the reliability of the prompts (the literature tells us prompts are never fully predictable; see Ruth and Murphy, and for an especially insightful case study, see Johns). That is another story, but we will extract from it a last piece of travellers' advice. Just as it helps if the people who created the exam give it, so it helps if the people who created and give the exam conduct the follow-up studies.

The second consequence is more pleasant. It especially pertains to teachers who have kept their distance from assessment from fear that it will take time away from their true work, teaching. In fact, involvement in original assessment projects expands participation in teaching. Our own involvement has given us, for instance, access to conversations from which we otherwise would have been excluded: conversations about general education, upper-division writing courses across the curriculum, and the articulation between our institution, its branch campuses, and regional high schools and community colleges. We may still detest tests, but we do not regret the time devoted to designing one we detest a little less strenuously. And we see now that our excursion into the land of assessment has brought us roundabout to what we like to do best, not only to teach but also to talk and work profitably with others who are committed to teaching.

Acknowledgments: An adventure of this size could not be undertaken alone, so we would like to thank some of our more important fellow travellers at Washington State University: Don Bushaw, Vice Provost for Instruction, and Richard Law, Director of General Education, for making our trip part of their larger expedition for curricular reform; Robin Magnuson, the Director of WSU's Writing Lab, for offering suggestions on design, assisting on the pilot project and now taking the driver's seat; Lisa Johnson-Shull, designer and co-ordinator of the new English 102 tutorials (and respondent to this article) for keeping her feet planted on Terra Firma and reminding us from time to time that we need to do the same; and, finally, John Tarnai, Associate Director of Social and Economic Sciences Research Center, for always finding time to explain the labyrinths of statistical analysis.

WORKS CITED

Anson, Chris M., and Robert L. Brown, Jr. "Large-Scale Portfolio Assessment." Belanoff and Dixon 248–69.

Baker, Eva L., and Edys Quellmalz. *Results of Pilot Studies: Effects of Variations in Writing Task Stimuli on the Analysis of Student Writing Performance.* Studies in Measurement and Methodology No. 2: Effects of Topic Familiarity. EDRS No. ED213728, 1979.

Barritt, Loren, Patricia L. Stock, and Francelia Clark. "Researching Practice: Evaluating Assessment Essays." *CCC* 37 (1986): 315–27.

Belanoff, Pat. "The Myths of Assessment." *Journal of Basic Writing* 10 (1991): 54–67.

Belanoff, Pat, and Marcia Dickson, eds. *Portfolios: Process and Product.* Portsmouth: Boynton/Cook, 1991.

Bernhardt, Stephen A. "Text Revisions by Basic Writers: From Impromptu First Draft to Take-Home Revision." *Research in the Teaching of English* 22 (1988): 266–80.

Bizzell, Patricia. "Composing Processes: An Overview." *The Teaching of Writing,* 85th Yearbook of the National Society for the Study of Education (Part II). Ed. Anthony R. Petrosky and David Bartholomae. Chicago: National Society for the Study of Education. 1986. 49–70.

Boomer, Garth. "Assessment of Writing." *Directions and Misdirections in English Evaluation.* Ed. Peter J. A. Evans. Toronto: Canadian Council of Teachers of English, 1985. 63–64.

Braddock, Richard, Richard Lloyd-Jones, and Lowell Schoer. *Research in Written Composition.* Champaign: NCTE, 1963.

Breland, Hunter M., et al. *Assessing Writing Skill.* Research Monograph No. 11. New York: College Entrance Examination Board, 1987.

—— and Roberta J. Jones. "Perceptions of Writing Skills." *Written Communication* 1 (1984): 101–19.

Brooks, Elaine. *Interviews with Students and Colleagues: What Can We Learn?* EDRS No. ED314958, 1989.

Brossell, Gordon, and Barbara Hoetker Ash. "An Experiment with the Wording of Essay Topics." *CCC* 35 (1984): 423–25.

Carroll, Karen, and Sandra Murphy. *A Study of the Construction of the Meanings of a Writing Prompt by Its Authors, the Student Writers, and the Raters.* EDRS No. ED230576, 1982.

Charney, Davida. "The Validity of Using Holistic Scoring to Evaluate Writing: A Critical Overview." *Research in the Teaching of English* 18 (1984): 65–81.

Clark, Michael. "Evaluating Writing in an Academic Setting." *Fforum Essays on Theory and Practice in the Teaching of Writing.* Ed. Patricia Stock. Upper Montclair: Boynton/Cook, 1983. 59–79.

Cohen, Elaine, et al. *Approaches to Predicting Student Success: Findings and Recommendations from a Study of California Community Colleges.* EDRS No. ED310808, 1989.

Condon, William, and Liz Hamp-Lyons. "Introducing a Portfolio-Based Writing Assessment." Belanoff and Dickson 231–47.

Elbow, Peter, and Pat Belanoff. "Portfolios as a Substitute for Proficiency Examination." *College Communication and Composition* 37 (Oct. 1986): 336–39.

Ewell, Peter. "To Capture the Ineffable: New Forms of Assessment in Higher Education." *Review of Research in Higher Education* 17 (1991): 75–125.

Feldhusen, John F., Kevin Hynes, and Carole A. Ames. "Is a Lack of Instructional Validity Contributing to the Decline of Achievement Test Scores?" *The Test Score Decline: Meaning and Issues.* Ed. Lawrence Lipsitz. Englewood Cliffs: Educational Technology Publications, 1977. 87–96.

Fitzgerald, Kathryn. "Rhetorical Implications of School Discourse for Writing Placement." *Journal of Basic Writing* 7 (1988): 61–72.

Freedman, Sara Warshauer, and William S. Robinson. "Testing Proficiency in Writing at San Francisco State University." *CCC* 33 (1982): 393–98.

Gorman, Thomas P., Alan C. Purves, and R. E. Degenhart. *The IEA Study of Written Composition I: The International Writing Tasks and Scoring Scales*. Vol. 5 of *International Studies in Educational Achievement*. Oxford: Pergamon, 1988.

Haswell, Richard. *Contrasting Ways to Appraise Improvement in a Writing Course: Paired Comparison and Holistic*. EDRS No. ED294315, 1989.

Haswell, Richard, Lisa Johnson-Shull, and Susan Wyche-Smith. "Shooting Niagara: Making Portfolio Assessment Serve Instruction at a State University." Conference on New Directions in Portfolio Assessment. Miami OH, October 1992.

Hoetker, James, Gordon Brossell, and Barbara Hoetker Ash. *Creating Essay Examination Topics*. Tallahassee: Florida State Department of Education, 1981.

Huot, Brian. "Reliability, Validity, and Holistic Scoring: What We Know and What We Need to Know." *CCC* 41 (1990): 201–13.

Johns, Ann M. "Interpreting an English Competency Examination: The Frustrations of an ESL Science Student." *Written Communication* 8 (1991): 379–401.

Livingston, Samuel. *The Effects of Time Limits on the Quality of Student-Written Essays*. EDRS No. ED286936, 1980.

Loofbourrow, Peggy T. *Composition in the Context of CAP: A Case Study of the Interplay Between Assessment and School Life*. Berkeley: National Center for the Study of Writing and Literacy, 1992.

Lucas, Catherine Keech. "Toward Ecological Evaluation." *The Quarterly* 10 (1988) no. 1: 1–3, 12–17; no. 2: 4–10.

———. "Unexpected Direction of Change in Writing Performance." *Properties of Writing Tasks: A Study of Alternative Procedures for Holistic Writing Assessment*. Ed. Leo Ruth. EDRS No. ED230576, 1982. 473–568.

Millward, Jody. "Placement and Pedagogy: UC Santa Barbara's Preparatory Program." *Journal of Basic Writing* 9 (1990): 99–113.

Morante, Edward A. "A Primer on Placement Testing." *Issues in Student Assessment*, New Directions for Community Colleges No. 59. Ed. Dorothy Bray and Marcia J. Belcher. San Francisco: Jossey-Bass, 1987. 55–63.

Peyton, Joy Kreeft, et al. "The Influence of Writing Task on ESL Students' Written Production." *Research in the Teaching of English* 24 (1990): 142–71.

Plassee, Lorraine A. *The Influence of Audience on the Assessment of Student Writing*. EDRS No. ED229760, 1982.

Quellmalz, Edys S. "Designing Writing Assessments: Balancing Fairness, Utility, and Cost." *Educational Evaluation and Policy Analysis* 6 (1984): 63–72.

Raforth, Bennett A. "Audience and Information." *Research in the Teaching of English* 23 (1989): 273–90.

Roemer, Marjorie, Lucille M. Schultz, and Russel K. Durst. "Portfolios and the Process of Change." *CCC* 42 (1991): 455–69.

Ruth, Leo, and Sandra Murphy. *Designing Tasks for the Assessment of Writing*. Norwood, NJ: Ablex, 1988.

Scharton, Maurice. "Models of Competence: Responses to a Scenario Writing Assignment." *Research in the Teaching of English* 23 (1989): 163–80.

Smith, Laura, et al. *Characteristics of Student Writing Competence: An Investigation of Alternative Scoring Systems*. Los Angeles: University of California, Los Angeles Center for the Study of Evaluation, 1980.

Smith, William L. "Teachers Informing Placement Testing: A New Method Based on Teacher Expertise." Conference on College Composition and Communication. Cincinnati, April 1992.

Stock, Patricia, and Jay L. Robinson. "Taking on Testing: Teachers as Tester-Researchers." *English Education* 19 (1987): 93–121.

White, Edward. "The Damage of Innovations Set Adrift." *Bulletin of the American Association for Higher Education* 43 (1990): 3–5.

White, Edward, and Leon Thomas. "Racial Minorities and Writing Skills Assessment in the California State University and Colleges." *College English* 43 (1981): 276–83.

Wiener, Harvey S. "Evaluating Assessment Programs in Basic Skills." *Journal of Developmental Education* 13 (Winter 1989): 24–26.

Winters, Lynn. *The Effects of Differing Response Criteria on the Assessment of Writing Competence*. EDRS No. ED212659, 1982.

13   *Portfolio Negotiations: Acts in Speech*

RUSSEL K. DURST, MARJORIE ROEMER,
AND LUCILLE M. SCHULTZ

When we evaluate student writing, we consider diverse and at times
contradictory evidence, reducing multiple factors such as voice, elaboration,
organization, coherence, diction, and usage to arrive at a single, unequivocal
judgment of the student's work. Sometimes our internal struggle with conflicting claims is intense, but this struggle is usually a silent one. We pause over the
page, and then we write the verdict. However, in our version of portfolio scoring at the University of Cincinnati, which emphasizes group discussion of student work, we seek to make these internal struggles outward and visible. In
debating the merits of particular papers to arrive at pass/fail judgments, we
engage in speech-acts, performing our judgments in open discussion, subjecting out decisions to debate and possible revision. These discussions reflect
something of J. L. Austin's category of the performative, where "the issuing of
the utterance is the performing of an action" (6). What we seek to do in these
discussion groups is to make our actions, normally carried out in isolation, into
language that is open to interrogation, not merely in terms of true or false, or
right or wrong, as if the judgment reflected a description of the paper's absolute value, but in terms of evaluations to be contested. Our portfolio process
thus makes writing evaluation a more multivocal project and at least reminds
us of the complexity of considerations that the letter grade or pass/fail judgment represents.

The idea of talk, of discussion about students' written work, is central to
our notion of the value of portfolio assessment. From the time we first considered adopting this form of assessment in our Freshman English Program in
1987, to our early pilot studies familiarizing ourselves with portfolios, to our
1989 decision to adopt them program-wide, we have seen portfolios as providing invaluable opportunities for teachers to get together and discuss student writing. In our program, these discussions have centered around such
key issues as establishing criteria for evaluation, gauging signs of writing development, and examining questions of dialect interference and control of

From *New Directions in Portfolio Assessment*, ed. Laurel Black, Donald A. Diaker, Jeffrey
Sommers, and Gail Stygall (Portsmouth, NH: Boynton/Cook, 1994), 286–300.

standard English. Discussion is particularly important in portfolio assessment because portfolio evaluation, as we are coming to understand it, is a fluid form of assessment that requires negotiation not calibration, a form of assessment that moves away from absolute judgments about writing into more shaded, nuanced understandings of difference.

In 1991, we published an essay in *College Composition and Communication* entitled "Portfolios and the Process of Change," which looked at the challenges and benefits of implementing portfolio evaluation in a large freshman English program. In this [section], we move into "second stage" research, examining what happens once the system is up and running. In particular, we look closely at the kinds of discussion and negotiation that take place around student writing in portfolio norming sessions. We examine, first, a conversation among new teaching assistants and their practicum teacher about the difficulties of juggling what Peter Elbow refers to as the conflicting roles of coach and judge. We next examine a discussion by experienced instructors and a program administrator on the complexities of determining evaluation standards. These discussions illustrate ways in which, for both beginning and experienced instructors, portfolio negotiations can serve as an important means of faculty development, can help ease anxieties about grading and passing judgment on students' work, and can provide a forum for teachers and administrators to re-think the goals of a freshman English program.

A brief description of our portfolio system and how it fits into the Freshman English Program will provide a context for the examination of portfolio discussions that follows. Ours is a large program in which approximately three thousand students annually go through a year-long, three-quarter course sequence. The program employs about sixty FE instructors, a diverse group including teaching assistants, adjuncts, and tenure-track faculty. We, the program administrators, decided to adopt portfolios, replacing a long-established, sit-down exit exam at the end of the sequence. We did so because portfolios put the emphasis where we felt it belonged, on students' writing development over time. With portfolios, as opposed to a timed exit exam, students are judged on their best work, on a number of different pieces of writing, on writing produced within a context of the course, not writing tacked on at the end. The portfolio system is much more consistent with our philosophy and our curriculum than was the exit exam, fitting our emphasis on process, multiple drafting, the development of self-reflective powers, and encouraging students to take more responsibility for their own growth as writers. In addition, we felt that portfolio evaluation had the potential to empower teachers, and we wanted very much to decentralize our program, giving teachers more of a say in determining standards as well as more opportunities to meet and discuss writing.

Under our portfolio system, every student taking the first quarter composition course keeps a portfolio consisting of clean copies of four essays, chosen from the five essays required for the class. Teachers form trios, exchange portfolios within their trios, and give a pass/fail evaluation to each other's student portfolios. They do so at midterm for diagnostic purposes and at the end of the quarter to determine which students will actually pass or fail the course. Before the mid- and end-of-quarter evaluations, teachers meet in groups of about twenty for norming sessions facilitated by one of the program directors. They read a range of anchor portfolios in advance, then discuss at the meeting whether they would pass or fail the portfolios and the reasons for their judgments. Both these norming sessions and the trio meetings provide opportunities for lively and at times intense discussion of critical issues in writing evaluation. What follows are two mediations on conversations that occurred at norming sessions.

CONVERSATION ONE: MARJORIE'S GROUP

"But I Thought We Were Teaching Process," or Teaching TAs to Give Grades

This first conversation (actually pieces of two conversations) emerges from work with a group of nineteen teaching assistants. They are teaching English 101 for the first time and so are just being initiated into the mysteries of becoming authority figures in the classroom and the awful responsibility of giving grades; for this reason, they are a particularly striking group to study. In our earliest phase of the development of portfolios, we emphasized the process of developing this kind of assessment as an institutional practice. We said then: "We learned that because the portfolio system depends on negotiations and adjustments, it is a system that will always be subject to further negotiation and adjustment." Now, a year later, we have more experience with some of the forms these negotiations take.

Early on, Peter Elbow provided us with a useful way to describe a central conflict for every teacher of writing, the tension between the dual roles of being both coach and judge. Portfolios allow us, as Elbow said, a way to look at that double function and, in some measure, to clarify the division. As classroom teacher, we coach; as portfolio team member, we judge. But nothing in our lives is that simple (not these days, anyway). These categories, like all categories, leak. Our coaching always rests on certain kinds of judgments we have made, and our judging is the judging of teachers. It is part of our work as coaches, part of our pedagogic function.

The TAs were grappling with the issue of standard-setting and gatekeeping for the first time, and their responses are dramatic. As a group, the practicum class had responded eagerly to our early pep-talks about process writing and generative strategies. They were stimulating their students to gather "telling facts" and "fabulous realities"; they were "looping" and "brainstorming," "collaborating" and encouraging "feedback," and then came October 23, the day of our midterm norming session. Here's an excerpt from the discussion that followed examination of one piece of student writing:

> GRAHAM: In this paper they use some ridiculous word choices. . . .
>
> MARTHA: Engfish.
>
> ALISON: . . . not exactly.

GRAHAM: It looks like they went wild with a thesaurus, but he did have a certain number of details that helped it move along. The presence of the details made me doubt whether it was a fail.

CASSY: I passed it in the vote, but I have an enormous criticism that the resolution doesn't follow what the thesis proposes.

SAMUEL: Well, wait a minute. I was drawn to this paper for two reasons, because of its details, which I emphasize in class. Its malapropisms are correctable. It's correctable. Somebody could work on it.

BETSY: But this is a final, revised version.

BERNIE: For me, this is a much clearer fail than the other. This person isn't paying attention, is flinging the language around like a bag of seeds.

FLORENCE: It's really out of control.

By the end of the hour, Karen Slaper, our graduate assistant and the observer/recorder at every norming session, made the following observations. (She has given each participant a number.)

#6 and 8 look troubled — hands drawn over mouths, wrinkled brows

#14 is rubbing head

#17 is obviously upset, says: *If this paper fails, I have twenty-five failed students right now.*

#11 says: *This session was sobering; now I have to think about what to tell my students.*

#5 says: *I thought we were teaching process; now all we're talking about is product.*

A few days later I asked the TAs to write some responses to these sessions. Here are two such answers:

#1

It scared me. Then I realized I had better enlighten my students quick. Took in "Gold" and the Florida trip papers — passed them around — we went over each one and decided what we liked/didn't like about them. Then what was wrong, mechanically-speaking. Had lively discussion, with most students understanding the drawbacks of each paper — regarding form — content — grammar — "flow" — etc. (only abstractly, I don't much use technical terms). Told them some would be failing at midterm — not to think that would keep them from ultimately passing the course — emphasized the course is a developmental one — they can't be expected to perform perfectly with only two papers. Afraid my encouragement is too gushy — they're so tender — but I told them college was tough — professors would not accept error in "real" classes — they must write effectively to move on successfully. (Success is a word that usually perks up their ears.)

#2

I felt reassured with the norming class; I found that I was on the same wave length as the majority of instructors in the group. I became concerned about my students, though, when I realized that my portfolio group may recommend passing an essay which I really feel should not pass. I don't think it's to a student's benefit to pass work which doesn't bode well for his/her progress in other courses. I'm concerned I may feel myself in disagreement with my portfolio group and still be inclined to follow my instincts. Attitude entrenchment.

Perhaps norming session might be useful earlier in the course? My impression was that many in the practicum felt upset because they felt they may have misled the students about their progress up to that time (having already dealt with essay one).

There are many themes we could trace in these responses to what one of the TAs called the "norming shock." There is concern in the last one about loss of teacher autonomy, a very real concern for teachers; there is the usual paranoia of the freshman English program about what "real" teachers in "real" classes will demand and about how well we can prepare students for these demands to come; but most of all there is the jolting move from coach to judge, from process to product. The trauma of this experience seems largely unavoidable, and better faced head-on as a group than left to private terrors and individual nightmares. It is hard to combine the desire (and need) to reassure, to encourage, to stimulate, with that other responsibility, to establish and assert standards. For me, both roles are a part of the job and both are integral to our roles as instructors (and sometimes as coaches and judges of other people's instruction).

While this October 23 meeting was a little bit hairy, in the end I think it was very useful. Some TAs thought we should have done more of this work together earlier in the quarter, but I'm not really sure of that. I think it was reasonable early on for the TAs to experience the excitement of their ability to encourage, to inspire, to liberate their students' writing and that the atmosphere of these classrooms promoting fluency made for a very rich beginning of the course. The process of learning to teach, like the process of learning to write, can't start with evaluation. Four weeks into the quarter, this first time around, was time enough for us to begin thinking together about where all this writing would have to take us if the freshmen were to be successful in the tenth week.

So, we survived the midterm, and in the tenth week of the quarter we began our portfolio norming. The following conversation is part of a transcript from the second norming session, held at the end of the quarter. We have been looking at a very difficult portfolio by a student we will call Marvin. Marvin's portfolio was difficult in part because his in-class essay seemed much stronger than his take-home writing. This student's work was chosen as an anchor portfolio because of its problematic status, and it has engendered much disagreement and some very strong feeling. (Two papers from the portfolio appear in the appendix at the end of this chapter.)

In the transcript we will see Betsy has just said, "What about asking students whether they think they are ready to go on to 102 (that is, to pass this 101 class)? Can they become part of the process in this way; is there room for negotiation?" Garth saves me (momentarily) by offering his response to that question. Then I "answer."

GARTH: I think there is because I had a student who . . . um . . . she . . . I . . . I . . . she is one of the cases where I just could not figure out what was going on . . . um . . . her papers were always underdeveloped. They looked like they . . . the paper had been rolled into the typewriter and something had been banged out and brought in, okay. Whether or not that was true, I don't know. But she avoided coming to see me for her conference at midterm time. And she waited around, she disappeared. I kept telling . . . generally a blanket statement to the class . . . come see me, come see me, because if you haven't received your midterm grade you may want to see it, okay. Then she comes to me . . . I got another paper like this and I just put on it "see me." You know, I was tired of talking about the whole thing. She came and I told her, look you were failing at the midterm, you know, I don't know. Her fourth paper was better and it looked like she was going to make some improvement. But I just stopped and said, do you think that you're ready to go on to 102? And she said, no. And I said, okay. I said, you're going to be in 101 next quarter, and there's not much . . . I said, I could, you know, go to bat for you for this and try to get the graders to change their mind, but if they've already failed you and you haven't made any development; if they failed you at the midterm and you've haven't changed much since the midterm I can almost guarantee that you're going to fail the class. And she said, that's fine, I understand.

MARJORIE: What if she hadn't said that?

GARTH: If she hadn't said that then I would have tried to have persuaded her that it would have been better for her to repeat the class.

MARJORIE: I guess, I don't know the answer to your question, Betsy. And, I mean, I certainly don't want to pretend there are no gray areas and there is no room for negotiation. What I'd like to suggest is that we want as a group to get fairly clear standards, as clear as we can get. We want to have those portfolio teams fail the papers that look as though they are not securely in control of the language. If you are in a team, and your other reader . . . this is your portfolio and you feel very strongly that it would serve the student well to go forward and your other . . . I mean that's what happened with this one actually; this portfolio was sent to me; . . . what would you do? what do you think? . . . so, I mean, clearly this was a problematic portfolio and one around which a certain amount of negotiation could take place. So, I think it's important, at least for the original reading of the portfolio group to have standards. If there is some reason why we feel that this is a borderline case and it should go this way instead of that way, then I think that has to be negotiated out, and I think teachers' judgment counts. I think you have hunches and intuitions, but I also think that it's very important to send a pretty clear message to students that is not sentimentalized, you know, that is not some kind of liberal guilt thing, but that is really: look, here are the standards for success in this field and we're going to uphold them and press to see that you have a chance at speaking in this conversation.

As you can see, I miss part of the original question, and, in fact, answer a slightly different question — one about negotiation, but not directly about students' participation in the process. Perhaps the confusion and the complication of this exchange is some indication of just how many sorts of negotiations are going on here at once. We, as a group, are negotiating standards together; we are trying to square those with some sense of "programmatic" or "departmental" standards, and we are negotiating with our students, trying to engage them in the process of framing acceptance of the standards that inform our community. This moment on the tape captures with embarrassing clarity the inexactitude of our calibrations. We are trying very hard to be fair and to be helpful. We want to do what we think will help students, but we are not always sure, either individually or as a group, what that is. We have to read between the lines, to "concretize" the text of a student's progress as best we can. What story of emerging skill do these essays tell us? Why do we each read the story differently? These are reader-response issues. I would like to suggest that while our readings are never identical, they can be mutually illuminating. I can learn from your reading and you can learn from mine. Just as in the study of other texts, the reading of a group can be richer and more nuanced than the reading with which each person began the discussion.

Some years ago I participated with a group of lecturers from the University of California at Santa Barbara in a project that we called the videocell. We videotaped our classes, viewed and discussed them together and then made a tape of clips from our classes and bits of discussion about the clips. One of my freshman classes knew about the project and asked to see the final, composite tape. I showed it, and they got to see a group of teachers talking about teaching, disagreeing sometimes, negotiating. My class loved it, and at the final class meeting when we were evaluating our class together, many of them referred to the video to clarify what they thought the course was all about. I had the distinct impression that they had learned more about the course from the video than from the course itself. Perhaps work like this around portfolio evaluations will need to be done more and more in classes to bring students into the process, to help them to participate in the multiple, complicated, shifting, inexact, but powerful readings that constitute the knowledge, the standards and the authority that we create in the community of our discipline. (This account is, then, a belated answer to Betsy's question . . . yes, students can be, and must be, a part of the process; that is our best way of teaching them what our discipline is.)

The fumblings and the inexactitude of our coming to consensus in these sessions can easily be seen as weakness: if we were all good teachers and expert graders, we'd all agree absolutely all the time. Once we abandon that position and see grading papers as another act of reading, as complex and varied as all acts of reading, then we can begin to consider that complicated process of reading papers as part of the knowledge that we must share with beginning teachers and writers, part of the content of our freshman writing classes as well as of our teaching practica.

CONVERSATION TWO: LUCY'S GROUP

"I'd Like to Slit Your Throat," or Words We Might Not Have Heard Spoken

This was a ninety-minute conversation among sixteen experienced writing teachers on 2 December 1991; also present at the meeting were a program administrator and a graduate student observer/recorder. Some of these teachers had taught in the program for more years than any of the program administrators, some had won teaching awards, some had long-established personal and professional relationships with each other; some shared offices, desks, and telephones; most of them shared the rank of adjunct faculty. While adjunct faculty as a group are in many ways marginalized in the department as a whole, their voices were the center of this conversation. And the voices were strong and powerful; they were the voices of teachers with strong personal commitments to teaching writing and, in most cases, a long history of classroom success; the graduate student who observed the group wrote in her notes, "This group seems very self-confident and sure of themselves."

Exactly because of this confidence, however, teachers seemed able to invest freely and heavily in the conversation; they spoke out of their own belief systems, the personal values and standards by which they read/evaluate student writing, and they stood their ground. It is the value of that kind of exchange of views that we point to and interrogate and celebrate here.

First, to place the conversation. In preparation for this meeting, each member of the group had read four portfolios. At the beginning of the meeting, with a show of hands, the group quickly agreed — unanimously — that portfolios one and two were passing and that portfolio four was failing. Portfolio three, discussed earlier in Marjorie's group, was more complicated. While, finally, fourteen people judged it failing, and two judged it passing, the tension over its merits was clear even in the voting process. The observer noted, "While voting, a number of teachers asked for a possible borderline category. They then asked for a few minutes to decide. And while doing so, they conferred among themselves." It's interesting that the impulse to talk about this portfolio was there from the beginning — and so it was about this portfolio that the conversation centered, and in this conversation that one teacher said to another, albeit in jest, "I'd like to slit your throat." (Two of the four papers from Marvin's portfolio appear in the appendix to this chapter.)

What emerges from the transcript of the conversation and from the observer's notes is that teachers who judged the portfolio failing did so for very different reasons. What also emerges is that the groundwork was laid for the sparks to fly as teachers disagreed with each other. One teacher, for example, reflected, "Well, I think that what made me want to fail it finally was thinking, this student's going to have to go to arguments next quarter, and I can't see that he's ready — even though the last paper is the best one. . . . [Argument] is going to require some skills that I just don't think this student has." Another teacher, however, was concerned that the papers weren't long enough, and that became her reason for failing the portfolio. Pat said, "This is just a matter of standards alone. Half the papers in this portfolio aren't even the minimum length requirement." It was Pat's comment that drew the first fount of sparks in the conversation. Interrupting her as she was still working out her thought, another teacher, Jane, bolted in with, "Pat, that's your idea." To which Pat replied, "But I'm saying why I failed [the portfolio]." Jane then wanted to know if the department had a standard length requirement and called on the facilitator of the conversation to arbitrate, and the observer reported that Jane "seemed upset" by Pat's having introduced paper length as a standard of judgment. The transcript shows that the facilitator talked about the importance of uncovering difference, not to force each other to conformity, but to recognize what was real: "what is so interesting . . . is that teachers do have different ideas for doing things and we're not here to sweep them under the rug or to come up with a single voice, but to let come out what some of our differences are so that we can talk about them, so that we can hear what they are and listen to them." Jane allowed as how this was "all right," but in the next breath, and in jest, added, "but I plan to slit [Pat's] throat."

Obviously what this points to is the passion with which teachers claim their reasons for responding to papers as they do. And even more obviously, that teachers — good, solid teachers — don't always agree. The disagreement over this paper opened up in another important way. The issue, not surprisingly, was the importance of superficial correctness. Here are two portions of the transcript that reflect the disagreement and the attempt of the teachers to listen to each other:

> JANE: I think that the least important things [in a student paper] are surface correctness and length. That's the way I feel and that's that.
>
> TOM: What do you mean by surface correctness? Grammatical sentences?
>
> PAT: You mean mechanics?
>
> TOM: You mean syntax? Sentences? Aren't sentences pretty serious? Run-ons?
>
> JANE: No. I mean punctuation of sentences. Not what Bud pointed out before, which is a failure of thought and style. I mean a failure of squiggles.

> AMY: They're forever using any word that looks something like the right word. . . . Any word that sort of starts with the same letter and looks like the same length will do in place of the right word — and I see an awful lot of that.
>
> TOM: Well that's in the liberal view, and that side of the room [here Tom points to the side of the room where Jane is sitting].
>
> AMY: Words have meanings and they don't have any old meaning and not any old word will do.
>
> TOM: I expected somebody to pass this portfolio, but I don't think I would — just because maybe I agree a little more with you, Amy, than I do with Jane on this. But I can see going both ways.

Jane's statements "having drawn fire from across the room" (the observer's words), Jane at this point re-enters the conversation, reclaims her voice and space and continues to make her case on behalf of passing the portfolio, a stance that even Tom thought was possible. What the conversation points to, again, is that people have strong investments in their decision-making about student writing. Superficial correctness, as a concept, means different things to different teachers, and different teachers weigh differently in their judgments. For Jane, it's almost non-issue. For Amy — who in some way deflects the conversation to her issues about language choice and diction — sentence level matters are much more important, and her take, finally, on the paper is, "I do see things that show me that the student doesn't attach any importance to what he's doing."

In some ways, there is no resolution in this kind of conversation, at least not the kind of submissive coming to agreement that we have come to expect in holistic norming sessions. That is, the facilitator does not work toward agreement, and experienced teachers do not fold their hands. What does happen, though, while perhaps harder to see, is in many ways more significant than what does not happen. What does happen is that in a public, safe, and carefully designed space, teachers have the opportunity to articulate for their own sake and for their information of their colleagues, the standards that they invoke and apply in private. Not to name these differences does not mean they don't exist; it simply means that we deny them. To name them, it seems to us, is to name the reality of difference and of diversity that informs, enriches, and enlivens our work.

In addition to naming and arguing on behalf of those standards teachers are committed to, the portfolio conversation also allows teachers to name and to reflect on their uncertainties, the areas that are puzzling to even the most experienced teacher. In this conversation, for example, teachers debated whether or not to pass this portfolio that had two kinds of papers in it, some papers written in "school language" and some in more dialect-inflected prose. One teacher, speaking out of what seemed to be very real frustration, made this passionate statement as part of her argument to pass the student: "We're not doing anything about why the kid . . . went back upon himself, violated his world. I mean, why would he do this? Why did he write two papers in school language and then suddenly decide . . . to write these two papers in the mother dialect? Why? What do we do about it?" The unstated implication is that in spite of the students' serious work, they are caught by conflicting forces and sometimes in impossible situations, and that teachers have to assume at least some of the responsibility for changing that dynamic. So while the initial question was whether to pass or fail a particular portfolio, what emerged was an opportunity for teachers to reflect on ways in which their own standards can evolve and be modified in this process of a portfolio conversation.

From these conversations, teachers also have the opportunity to serve as resources for each other. In this meeting, teachers traded information about the ways they worked with international students and about little known tutoring resources on campus for various student populations. This was a genuine exchange; information was teacher-to-teacher, and resources came with first-hand recommendations. If teachers have much to gain from these conversations, so do students. Surely it is to their advantage to study with a teacher who is more broadly informed as a result of participating in these discussions.

Program administrators also have a great deal to gain from this group-talk. On one level, we learned that in spite of massive amounts of print information, numerous large and small meetings, and pilot programs that ran for a year, some members of the faculty still had major misunderstandings of how we were doing portfolio assessment, and what their role as classroom teachers was. One teacher in this group, for example, thought we were still putting grades on individual papers, rather than deferring grades until the mid-quarter and end-of-quarter. In some ways, these misunderstandings were surprising in that we thought we had saturated teachers with information; in other ways, it wasn't surprising given that ours is a large program, that portfolios were new, and that teachers have different levels of investment in change. Clearly, the major value for program administrators is the opportunity such group-talk provides for hearing what is important to teachers: gripes, desires for change, different approaches to evaluating student text. This kind of conversation is one of the few set-aside spaces where the voices of teachers are central.

CONCLUSION

The portfolio struggles we have been describing are certainly apt for a cultural moment that takes all meaning to be the product of negotiation and construction. The more we study portfolio negotiations, the more information we will have about how we read differently from one another and how we come to change our minds, or to see eventually what at first we did not see. We think of Tom Newkirk's wonderful essay "Looking for Trouble" where students go through several readings of a poem with different colored pencils in hand and then produce the story of their successive readings of a text, and we think that we will need to develop such stories of the reading of students' papers. The portfolio process opens up a range of possibilities for new research on how teachers read and evaluate student writing, and how group discussion in its many manifestations can lead to new interpretations, changed positions, or what one TA cited earlier referred to as "attitude entrenchment." Portfolio negotiations are an ideal site in which to examine how we in composition build consensus and at times resist such consensus and instead challenge authority.

What is powerful about portfolio reading is that it provides us with a place where differences in reading "count"; they produce different consequences. As in Linda Brodkey's work with legal texts, differences of interpretation are here not just matters for idle conversation about "style"; here "readings" have palpable effects, both on the evaluation of individual students' portfolios and on the development of group standards.

In establishing a program-wide portfolio system, especially in a large institution, one wants to set the rules, the structure and procedures, clearly. Yet the actual work is always messy and muddled, a tangle of conflicting claims and concerns that in the old days might be the private psychomachia of the instructor, but in the more public world of the portfolio scoring team has now become an enacted series of pushes and pulls, gives and takes, an articulated duel of competing claims, a committee meeting.

From the perspective of someone directing a program, or leading a portfolio team, there is, as we said, a need to establish the standards, to ensure that the program is accountable to something and that the students in it have equitable treatment. On the other hand (and there is always another hand), there is the danger of coercion, using the pressure of the group, or of the majority, or the authority of the leader, to police judgments in ways that violate individual teachers and their particular styles and ways of reading and teaching. How far can we tolerate the imprecision, or the multiplicity, of our judgments; how comfortable are we with the real differences among us as graders? These questions are the kinds of questions that assault us from every corner of our postmodern lives. Most of us are reconciled to the demise of Truth in its singular, capitalized form. But can we and our students tolerate facing the ultimate indeterminacy, the indeterminacy of the freshman English grade?

To offer one answer to that question is impossible, but we can call attention to the way the portfolio system — in the group form that we've adopted it — allows us to view, and we hope to study, the complexities of our assessment processes. Just as process approaches to writing have allowed us to externalize and make available to observation some of the stages of composition, our continuing work in portfolio teams will allow us to study in more detail the layers of competing claims that struggle in the judgments that we make when we assess student writing.

APPENDIX: TWO PAPERS FROM MARVIN'S PORTFOLIO

Paper One

This essay is a profile of an organization. Students had two weeks to write a rough draft, receive peer and teacher feedback, and revise the essay.

Voices of Youth

There we were, James Lynch and I walking down the deterring sidewalk slowly approaching the enormous Alms Hotel; the home of the infamous Voices of Youth.

We finally reached our destination, yet there was still another obstacle to overcome. There was a huge corroded steel door covered with a thin layer of light-blue paint; nevertheless, a meer attempt to cover the enormous amounts of corrosion on the door. James knocked softly as if he feared that the paint would flack off. The blue door slowly creeped open and we walked in. The radio station WAIF is nothing like I imagined. WAIF is located in the basement of this enormous hotel. When we entered, I first notice this dull brown and white fake leather couch. From just a glance I could see the layers of dust and dirt covering it, and yes, to top it off I seen a mouse on the arm of the couch. James just walked on pass as if not even seeing the mouse. There was a long dark erry hall that we had to go through to get to the equipment room. There was only one red light, and the walk seem endless. When we finally entered the equipment room, and we quickly entered. There was a lot of dirty looking equipment, but it was all clean. There was not a speck of dirt anywhere. That really shows that the members of Voices of Youth took pride in what they were doing. Although there was a lot of old looking things such as: that big silver digital clock which has some numbers that do not light up, and that 1972 Pioneer eight track player, also, an antique recod player. They also had a couple of modern systems.

The thing that I thought was very ironic was that the ten members of this proud orgination ranged from the ages of thirteen to twenty-four and one senior adult. That seems so ironic to me for all the success they have been having for the past seven years. That just shows what hard work and dedication can do.

Voices of Youth is a nonprofit volunteer organization. "The main purpose of our organization is to raise the social consciencesness of our listeners, and to help them become aware of what is going on in our society," said James.

From listening to the topics which were discussed, gave me a sense that an organization of this kind received satisfaction from knowing that they help spread the knowledge that most places are afraid to talk about today. For example, topics such as: The African American Woman, Racisom on Campus, Words from Louis Farrakhan, and knowledge about the success and contributions of African Americans in our history.

All in all, Voices of Youth have proven to me that they are a positive organization striving for awareness, but there is still a need for participation. They feel that they can have more participation because of the vastness of African Americans in our city, yet there isn't a mistory to be solved.

Paper Two

This essay is an evaluation handwritten in class during the last week of the quarter.

Strictly Unorganized

The textbook, Calculus with Analytic Geometry, which is used in the freshman calculus courses, is in need of yet another revision. The present edition, the third edition, inhibits students from learning, it lacks organization and useful appendices.

First, the authors, Robert Ellis and Denny Gulick, have arranged the information in the book poorly. The authors scatter related material throughout the book, instead of building on material covered in previous chapters. Professor Levang, a professor of freshman calculus, expressed his discontent with the textbook by saying, ". . . it looks as though an editor looked over the final copy of the book and handed the authors a list of traditional calculus textbook material. They took it and stuck it in where it doesn't really belong." For instance, the second chapter of the book, "Limits and Continuity," covers the limit process. The students finish the chapter thinking that they know all that they area required to know about the limit process. However, later, in the fourth chapter, the book adds more information about limits in a section entitled "Limits at Infinity".

The material learned in the second chapter is not fresh in the student's mind. Consequently, the professor must waste time going over material that has already been covered. For instance, in most calculus classes chapter two was covered during the second week of the quarter. However, later, during the eighth week of the quarter, the professor was forced to review the material covered in chapter two so that he could teach the seventh section of chapter four, "Limits of Infinity". Moreover, the material following "Limits of Infinity", section 4.8 is entitled "Graphing" and is, at most, remotely related to the limit process. This arrangement of the material only serves to confuse the student. In preparing for class, a student previewing the assigned text would be unable to connect the new material with the old material (from the previous section). In addition to being disorganized, the book contains no helpful appendices to aid the students in quick reference situations. For instance, in reviewing for a test or quiz, a student must search through a lot of pages trying to find a single definition or theorem. This searching is a big waste of time and once the student finds the information, he must deface his book by highlighting. The text does not contain a list of the major theorems, such as the Mean Value Theorem and the Intermediate Value Theorem, which would help the students considerably. Also, it fails to provide a glossary of terms where important words such as "inflection point" and "partition" could be defined.

A number of proofs, definitions, and theorems incorporate the use of Greek letters, but the book lacks a table listing the Greek alphabet. Specifically, in section 2.1 where the authors define a limit: ". . . then a number L is the limit of $f(x)$ as x approaches a if for every number $E > 0$ such that is $0 < [x - a] < E$, then $\{f(x) - L\} < \sigma$." A student cannot begin to ask a question because he does not know what a "E" (epsilon) or a "σ" (delta) is or how to pronounce it.

As a whole, the freshman calculus book is not all bad. One must understand that in order to avoid publishing a calculus book which resembles a telephone book, the author had to omit some old material to make room for the new. Still, rearranging the material is essential.

NOTE

We wish to thank especially Karen Slaper for her assistance in our portfolio program and the following composition teachers who participated in these conversations: Abigail Albert, Alice Bolstridge, Susan Boydston, Tony Chiaviello, Doug Connell, Cynthia Crane, Judy Dehan, Laurie Delaney, Beth Duley, Harriet Edwards, Val Gerstle, Shirley Gibson, Greg Griffith, Jerry Hakes, Patton Hollow, Darrell Hovious, Ron Hundemer, Omar Johnson, Lee Kellogg, Barbara Kuroff, Ellen Lauricella, John Maddux, Lou Marti, Elizabeth McCord, Jim Schiff, Elaine Singleton, Laura Smith, Suqin Song, Taunja Thomson, Jean Timberlake, Rebecca Todd, Lisa Udel, Kevin Walzer, Pam Whissel, Lise Williams, and Bill Zipfel. Teachers' names used in the transcripts are pseudonyms.

WORKS CITED

Austin, J. L. *How to Do Things With Words*. Cambridge, MA: Harvard University Press, 1962, 1975.

Brodkey, Linda. "Hard Cases for Law and Rhetoric." Conference on College Composition and Communication, March 1992, Cincinnati, OH.

———. "Opinion: Transvaluing Difference." *College English* 51 (1989): 597–601.

Elbow, Peter. "Assessing Writing in the 21st Century." In *Composition in the 21st Century: Crisis and Change*. Eds. Lynn Z. Bloom, Donald A. Daiker, and Edward M. White. Southern Illinois UP, 1996. 83–100.

———. "Ranking, Evaluating, and Liking: Sorting Out Three Forms of Judgment." *College English* 55/2 (Feb. 1993): 187–206.

———. "The Uses of Binary Thinking." *Journal of Advanced Composition* 12.1 (Winter 1993): 51–78.

———. "Reflections on Academic Discourses." *College English* 53 (1991): 135–55.

———. "Foreword." *Portfolios: Process and Product*. Eds. Pat Belanoff and Marcia Dickson. Portsmouth, NH: Boynton/Cook, 1991.

———. *What Is English?* New York and Urbana, IL: MLA and NCTE, 1990.

———. "Portfolio Assessment." Workshop delivered at The National Testing Network, Montreal, 1989.

———. *Embracing Contraries*. New York: Oxford UP, 1986.

Newkirk, Thomas. "Looking for Trouble: A Way to Unmask Our Readings." *College English* 46 (Dec. 1984): 755–66.

Roemer, Marjorie, Lucille M. Schultz, and Russel K. Durst. "Portfolios and the Process of Change." *College Composition and Communications* 42.4 (December 1991): 455–469.

14   *Directed Self-Placement: An Attitude of Orientation*

DANIEL J. ROYER AND ROGER GILLES

No particular results then, so far, but only an attitude of orientation, is what the pragmatic method means. *The attitude of looking away from first things, principles, "categories," supposed necessities; and of looking towards last things, fruits, consequences, fact.*
— WILLIAM JAMES (27)

Dan stands at the front of a buzzing lecture hall, a yellow trifold brochure in hand, watching about a sixth of next year's 2400 "seats" find a seat. New students are seats; that's the kind of talk one hears as director of composition at a university that breaks its own enrollment record every year, doubling in size to nearly 16,000 students over the last decade. What Dan has to say to these 400 new seats invites an interesting irony: the administrators love what he's about to say precisely because they think of students as "seats," while Dan is eager to talk because, in Deweyan fashion, he is eager to upset the prevailing student/teacher power relations by presenting the students with an authentic educative choice.

The buzzing subsides, and after brief speeches by the Dean of Students and a counselor from the Financial Aid office, Dan steps forward, holding up the yellow brochure, and introduces himself as the director of composition. "In the next few minutes I'm going to ask you to make the first of many important choices you'll make as a student at this university — so please listen carefully.

"The Admissions people have placed a yellow trifold brochure, like this one, in your folder. Let's take a look at it. It says on the front, *English 098 or 150: Which Course is Right for You?* Before you register for classes this afternoon, you'll need to select one of these two courses to begin with as you begin your freshman year.

"Before I get to the specifics, let me explain why it is we want you to make this decision and why we aren't going to make it for you. At many

From *College Composition and Communication* 50 (1998): 54–70.

schools, in fact at this school until very recently, people like me 'place' you into a writing course by looking at your ACT or SAT score, your high-school GPA, and perhaps by having you step into another room and return to us two hours later with a 'sample' of your writing. But it turns out that this is not a very valid or reliable way to find out which first-year writing course is best for you. Writing ability, at least as we conceive of it, is far too complex to measure so quickly and easily.

"The fact is, we just don't know very much about you as writers. Perhaps the *best* way to measure your writing ability would be for us to sit down with each one of you for an hour or so and talk with you about writing. If I had an hour with each of you, I'd ask you to show me samples of your best writing from high school. I'd ask you to describe your strengths and weaknesses as a writer. I'd ask you to tell me how much you read, and how well you read. If your GPA or standardized test-score didn't look too impressive, I'd ask you if anything much has changed in your image of yourself or in your habits as a student since you started your last year of high school. I know that many students arrive as college freshmen very different people — and become very different students — from what they were just a few months earlier. Some of you here today must know what I mean.

"I'd ask you how motivated you are. I'd ask you how much you like to write. I'd ask you how well you type. I'd ask you many things. I think you get my point: to find out which first-year writing course is really right for you, I would need to know more than a single test score, and I'd need to see more than a single sample of how you write under pressure or even a portfolio of your high school writing — which has probably gotten pretty stale over the summer.

"Instead, I'm going to ask you to make a responsible choice about which course to take. The question you face is: Should I take English 098 or English 150? Let me explain the difference. English 098 is a preparatory course that helps you write more confidently and purposefully, and it helps you develop ways to clarify and edit your writing for a college-level audience. You will get a letter grade in English 098, and it figures into your GPA, but it doesn't count as one of the 120 credits you need to graduate. English 150, on the other hand, is a four-credit course that prepares you for the variety of writing experiences you will have as a university student in the coming years. The focus is on source-based writing in a variety of genres. All students must eventually get a C or better in English 150 in order to satisfy the freshman composition requirement. The decision you face is whether to go ahead and begin with English 150, or to take a two semester sequence by starting with English 098 in the first semester and taking English 150 the second.

"Before you make up your mind too quickly, hear me out. Many schools offer a two-semester sequence of first-year writing anyway, so don't feel that you are going to get behind if you begin with 098. You don't want to enroll in 098 if 150 is best for you, and you don't want to enroll in 150 if 098 is best for you. The university has no interest in making you start with either course — that's why *you* are deciding. What we do have an interest in is your success as a student. There is no advantage to beginning with English 150 if you fail or struggle in the course because it's not the right course for you. People do fail that course, and you don't want that to happen to you.

"Generally speaking, you are well prepared for English 150 if you have done quite a bit of reading and writing in high school. English 150 instructors will assume that you can summarize and analyze published material from magazines, newspapers, books, and scholarly journals. They will also assume that you have written a variety of essays in a variety of forms, including narrative, descriptive, and persuasive writing. Look at the checklist on the center panel inside the brochure. These are some of the characteristics that we faculty look for in solid writing students. Do any of these statements describe you?

I read newspapers and magazines regularly.

In the past year, I have read books for my own enjoyment.

In high school, I wrote several essays per year.

My high school GPA placed me in the top third of my class.

I have used computers for drafting and revising essays.

My ACT-English score was above 20.

I consider myself a good reader and writer.

"Perhaps you do see yourself in at least some of those statements. If many of the statements don't describe you or if you just don't consider yourself a strong reader and writer, you might consider taking English 098. In 098 you will focus on writing in specific ways to reach specific audiences. You will write a lot in order to develop comfort and fluency. You will get lots of practice, including many hours with our Writing Center tutors, and you will work on understanding the conventions of standard written English — spelling, grammar, punctuation, and usage. Let's look at the list of general characteristics that may indicate that English 098 is best for you.

Generally I don't read when I don't have to.

In high school, I did not do much writing.

My high school GPA was about average.

I'm unsure about the rules of writing — commas, apostrophes, and so forth.

I've used computers, but not often for writing and revising.

My ACT-English score was below 20.

I don't think of myself as a strong writer.

"In English 098 you will read successful samples of essays written by professionals and by other students. In a typical class, you will complete five or six short essays — two or three pages each. You may cite some of the essays you have read or people you have interviewed, but generally you will not write research-based essays. Indeed, the purpose of English 098 is to give you the confidence, organization, and command necessary to write the research-based essays demanded in English 150 and beyond. English 098 will get you ready to do well in English 150 the next semester.

"Many of you will see statements that describe you in both lists. Others may clearly see that one or the other course is the right one to begin with. If after thinking about it you still can't decide, I'll be glad to talk with you — even to spend an hour and look at some of your writing as I talked about a minute ago — but I think most of you can make the right choice on your own. You all have advisers, and they can help you as well. You'll be meeting with them later today.

"I said before that we don't know much about you. About all I *do* know is that before you earn a 'C' or better in English 150, you'll become a pretty solid college writer. Today you simply have to decide if that will take you one semester or two.

"You may be wondering if you can squeeze your way through English 150 if you aren't really ready for it. Probably not. We use a portfolio-based grading system that requires each student to submit a folder of final work that is graded by a total of three faculty members from a larger group of English 150 teachers who have met all semester to discuss their own and our university's expectations about college writing. Your final portfolio accounts for the majority of your final course grade, and because we 'team grade,' we're confident that an 'A' in one class matches up pretty well with an 'A' in another. Our grading system is described in more detail in the brochure. For now, I just want you to realize that your decision today should not be taken lightly. You really do have to write well in order to move beyond English 150.

"There's other important information in this brochure. Look at the back page under the heading, 'What to Expect the First Day.' Go ahead and read those paragraphs while you listen to me talk for another minute or so. Notice that in both 098 and 150, on the first day of class your teacher will ask you to write a brief essay. Your teacher will read the essay as a simple indication of your writing abilities and let you know what he or she thinks. During this first week of class, you will have the opportunity to switch from one class to the other if you wish. But remember, the decision is yours, not your teacher's. Note too that the brochure includes information about the Writing Center, the Library Skills program, our junior-level writing requirement, and our Writing Across the Curriculum program. We value writing a lot, and in your time as a student here you'll be doing quite a bit of it, so we want you to be as ready as you can be.

"English 098 and 150 are both very good courses. English 150 is a course you will share in common with every freshman. You will all take it. And many of our very best instructors teach English 098. Believe me, we will have many full sections of 098 and every student in that class with you , if that's the one you take, will be there because he or she chose to take it. Nobody will be in 098 against their will, and for this reason many students find the atmosphere there encouraging and helpful. For many, it is a way to brush up, get some practice, and prepare themselves for the challenge of English 150.

"Finally, before I leave, I'd like to see a show of hands, not to indicate which course you will take, but to indicate whether or not you have made a choice. OK. If you're still not sure which course you should enroll in, please talk with me or your adviser later today. Thanks for your time, and I wish you all the best of luck."

WHY DIRECTED SELF-PLACEMENT?

During the summer of 1996, either Dan or Roger, the previous composition director, gave a version of this ten-minute speech to five other groups — and in the end over 22% of the students placed themselves into ENG 098. What compels 500 students to place themselves in a course that doesn't count as college credit? Are these the same students that we would have placed in ENG 098 had we used our old method of ACT-English score plus writing sample? We don't yet fully know the answers to these questions, but after our second full year of using what we're calling "directed self-placement," we feel that we've found a placement method that works very well for all of us — teachers, students, and administrators alike.

Our decision to give directed self-placement a try originated with widespread frustration over our traditional placement method. We knew of the well-documented limitations of placement tests — the artificiality of direct writing and the questionable reliability and validity of traditional direct assessment (see, for instance, Elbow). And we'd never liked using ACT-English scores, but we'd resorted to them as a preliminary screen when our freshman-orientation groups got so big we had trouble scoring all the essays in the brief turnaround time available to us. The Admissions people who ran orientation didn't like our method much, either; they had to schedule an hour for writing, then wait for the results before they could help the students register.

Our ENG 098 students weren't very fond of the system, either. They started the class with a chip on their shoulder after having been told during orientation that, despite their "B" average in high school, they were *required* to take a no-credit English class. We surveyed our students in the Fall of 1995 and found that only 38% of the ENG 098 students felt they were properly placed in the course. There were quite a few negative comments about both the placement procedure and the course itself.

Finally, the teachers themselves were frustrated. Not only did they have to deal with unhappy students, but they also had to replicate the placement essay during the first week of classes and shift students to the appropriate course, often against the students' will. By January of 1996, it became clear that we were kidding ourselves if we believed that these "supposed necessities" were fair to anyone involved. We decided to rethink our approach.

We first considered trying to improve traditional placement-test procedures. Schools such as the University of Pittsburgh and Washington State have "contextualized" placement decisions by shifting their focus from how student writing matches up against general and fixed criteria to how it fits with the actual curriculum (Huot 553–54). In other words, they place students into *courses* rather than into categories. This alternative does involve some looking away from what William James would call "first things, principles, and 'categories,'" but it seemed to us not to make the full pragmatic turn toward "last things, fruits, consequences, fact." Indeed, we had already been using a version of this method to place our students. But we realized that no matter how site-specific and contextualized we made our reading of placement essays, we might side-step some reliability concerns and finesse our notion of validity, but we would inevitably wind up making decisions based on the inadequate data of a single writing sample. We were beginning to feel that our old placement engine could not, once again, be retuned or rebuilt.

We toyed with the idea of entrance portfolios — which would move us beyond the single piece of writing — but the Admissions directors balked. "This isn't Stanford," they told us. "If we make students put together an entrance portfolio and the next school doesn't, the students will simply pick the next school." Besides, we knew that asking for entrance portfolios would place quite a burden on our already overburdened summer faculty. How would we read over two thousand portfolios? And even if we could do this, we would still be mired in the interrater-reliability fix, even if it was transformed into a question of reliability among those rater/teachers who would be teaching the course. The only real way around this last problem would be to insure that raters taught just those students whose portfolios they assessed, and this would be impossible in the context we faced.

We were stuck. In the meantime, at our administration's prompting, our "institutional analyst" evaluated the placement data and composition grades over the past several years. His conclusion was bleak: statistically speaking, neither of our two placement devices bore much relationship to student success in composition classes, if "success" could be defined as earning credit for the course (earning a "C" or better). High ACT scores did correlate somewhat with *high* grades in our ENG 150 course, but students on all levels of the ACT appeared to have about the same chance of getting a "C" or better. From an administrative point of view, we couldn't very well keep students out of a course they could earn a "B−" or "C+" in.

Of more concern to us within the writing program was the fact that fully one-fifth of our ENG 150 students were either withdrawing or earning below a "C" — that is, failing to earn credit for the course — but according to our analyst these students did not show any particular ACT-score tendencies. That is, ACT scores alone could not predict who would fail or struggle in ENG 150.

Our placement-essay system didn't fare much better, according to the analyst. Over the past few years, enough students had either not taken a placement test or simply ignored our placement decision that he could conclude again that not much relationship existed between "placement" and "success" in composition classes. Students who'd been placed into ENG 150, students who'd skipped the placement test, and even students who'd been placed into ENG 098 but taken ENG 150 instead all had about the same chance of earning credit in our ENG 150 course.

From the students' point of view, they had little to lose in giving ENG 150 a try, for ACT score or placement-essay results had very little predictive value. Statistically, about 80% of them — regardless of test scores — would get a "C" or better. Finally, at a meeting between upper-administration and writing-program administrators, the statistician remarked that, given all the time, effort, and money we put into placing students in composition courses, a random placement would make as much sense and that we might just as well let the students place themselves. At first we chuckled. Then we looked again at our options. In the end, we decided to take the man seriously.

Our statistician had lifted a veil from before our eyes: all of our efforts had been directed toward finding a better way for *us* to place our students — for us to assess our students' writing abilities quickly and effectively, preferably in an hour or two. Before this nudge from the statistician, we lacked what Peter Elbow calls the "utopian or visionary impulse," which kept us "blinded by what seems normal" (83). Normally, the placement universe revolves around teachers; we choose the methods, we score the essays, we tell students what courses to take. Now we began to envision students at the center, and for the first time we turned our attention to the people who knew our students best: the students themselves.

We have not regretted our decision. Our ENG 098 "placement rate" has dropped from 33% to 22%, but for the first time we feel that the right students are taking our developmental writing class. All in all, we believe there are several good reasons to adopt directed self placement.

Directed Self-Placement Feels Right

Directed self-placement possesses what computer programmers call elegance, what philosophers might call the shine of Ockham's razor. It has a pleasing feel about it with influence stretching in every direction: from a simple brochure at the hub, its vectors point to students, local high schools, teachers, and administrators. Its simplicity recommends it over the unreliability of test scores. Its honesty calls out to students and lures them in the right direction. Its focus is on the future and each student's self-determined advance. This alternative placement strategy is a consummate movement toward what Patricia Mann terms "familial unmooring," a concept that Grego and Thompson use to urge compositionists and their academic institutions to break nostalgia's hold on students and their writing and enable students to "remember themselves as whole people (not just a number or a grade)" (74). In this manner, directed self-placement involves the restoration of interpersonal agency — but not without some cost. Grego and Thompson remind us:

> Nostalgic views of student writing would rather hold on to ways of assessing and teaching students writing which make the institution's job predictable and containable, neat and tidy. To do otherwise is to get pretty messy, to engage in the struggle to make sense of the complexities of student writing not "organized" by the traditional assessments and curriculum of a particular academic site. (75)

And it's not just students who are encouraged to change. Directed self-placement is an attitude, James' pragmatic attitude. We feel very differently about our jobs, about students, and about writing after our ten-minute speech, much differently from the way we felt after several hours of reading place-ment essays. Our old concerns about validity and reliability are now replaced with something akin to "rightness." And the rightness of the choice now lies with the student, where we feel it belongs.

We surveyed our Fall 1996 students, and they told an altogether different story from the previous group. Their written comments repeatedly stressed that when the two courses were explained to them at orientation, the students who chose ENG 098 simply felt that it was the course for them. Because of their past experiences with writing, they felt they needed to "brush up" be-fore taking ENG 150. Interestingly, the reasons students cited most frequently for choosing ENG 098 centered on behavior and self-image — not test scores or grades. Our ENG 098 students saw *themselves* as poor readers and writers. In the past, we had done the seeing for them.

We asked students to tell us which of the seven potential indicators most strongly influenced them to take ENG 098. These were the indicators that we faculty had designed as we thought about our own composition classes. The indicators reveal what we saw, and continue to see, as the main prerequisites for success in our first-year composition program: solid reading habits, writ-ing confidence, familiarity with the mechanical aspects of writing, and experi-ence with computers. They are analogous to the "contextualized" placement practices that Huot cites (553–54), but instead of measuring sample student writing against our contextualized expectations, we have asked the students to measure their own perceptions of themselves against our expectations. We added ACT scores and high-school grades to our list primarily as a possible anchor for students not used to assessing their abilities qualitatively.

We were pleasantly surprised by what we found. Of the 230 responses, barely a quarter cited test scores and grades:

1. 24% said "Generally I don't read when I don't have to."

2. 23% said "I don't think of myself as a strong writer."

3. 15% said "My ACT-English score was below 20."

4. 12% said "My high school GPA was about average."

5. 12% said "I'm unsure about the rules of writing."

6. 9% said "In high school, I did not do much writing."

7. 6% said "I've used computers, but not often for writing and revising."

Notice that items 1, 2, and 5 (59%) reflect self-image and self-assessment, items 3 and 4 (27%) reflect external judgments, and items 6 and 7 (15%) reflect high-school or other past educational experience. It seems right to us that our students are selecting ENG 098 because of their own view of themselves. And indeed, we hope that the course will help them change that view and give them confidence as they move on in the curriculum.

In retrospect, we believe that our discomfort with traditional placement methods arose from a uneasy feeling of impropriety. In the space of an hour or two, we had been trying to make a major decision for hundreds of students.

At ten o'clock we didn't know their names, but by noon we "knew" what first-semester course they should take. No matter how careful we tried to be, we felt that any decision would be hasty. The "emergent" placement procedures cited by Huot, which view placement either as "a teaching decision" or as "a screening process," share an assumption that simply doesn't sit well with us — that whatever decision made is to be made by teachers, not students (556).

But what of reliability? Obviously two of the items listed in our brochure, ACT-English scores and high-school GPA, are extremely "reliable" data, even if they are problematic measures of writing ability per se. But we have come to view the other indicators as very reliable as well. First, there is no "interrater-reliability" problem since there is only one rater. More importantly, a student is unlikely to respond to a statement like "I don't read when I don't have to" differently from one week to the next. Leaving aside for a moment the question of validity, we are convinced that student responses to our brochure prompts are very reliable — more reliable, we believe, than summer faculty's holistic responses to anonymous and impromptu student writing.

Directed Self-Placement Works

What does it mean to say that directed self-placement works? First, we might admit failure if *no one* chose our developmental writing course, although even then we might chalk it up as a victory for mainstreaming first-year writing students. Along with those who, with some important cautions, advocate mainstreaming (Elbow and Soliday), we agree that students should not be marginalized, but we think the most practical reconception of remediation does not involve eliminating basic writing courses, but rather thinking very differently about placement. Indeed, conventional notions of "remediation" may not apply to students who in effect *ask* for the extra course. Elbow anticipates this development when he concedes that some students may "*want* to be held apart in a separate and protected situation. . . , so perhaps it would make sense to have a conventional basic writing course for those who want it. But let us ask them and give them a choice instead of deciding for them" (93).

In practice, we observe that many students decide for themselves that they need a basic or conventional writing course, "a sheltered educational pocket" (Soliday 85). For us, reconceiving remediation begins by taking student choice seriously — that is, to heed Elbow's wise concession. Our 22% placement rate has held steady for two years, so we feel that we are reaching a significant population of students. In a sense, our new placement method "works" no matter how many students choose ENG 098; we simply want to make the course available to those who want or need it.

We also might say that self-placement works if it manages to locate the same group of ENG 098 students that our more traditional (and labor-intensive) methods located. In 1995, our method was to screen with ACT-English scores and then to look at a timed writing sample. In 1996 and 1997 we used directed self-placement. We compared two of the most easily measured characteristics of the two populations and found that the groups shared very similar high-school GPAs (just under 3.0, compared to our freshman class's overall average of just over 3.2) and ACT-English scores (17.8 in 1995, 18.6 in 1996 and 1997, compared to our overall average of 22). This suggests that the students took their high-school GPAs and ACT-English scores into account: we didn't need to do it for them. So as a "replacement" of the old system, directed self-placement worked, though as we have begun to discover, there may be good reasons to dismiss these general indicators of academic ability as unable to predict success in writing courses.

We also looked at grades in ENG 098 and ENG 150. The overall GPA in ENG 098 was significantly lower in 1996 (2.56) than it was in 1995 (2.90), but then it jumped back up to 2.82 in 1997. We hesitate to conclude too much from these three years, but one possible explanation for the general drop in GPA in ENG 098 is that directed self-placement did a better job of locating genuinely struggling writers — that is, the very writers we hope to assist in ENG 098 — within the larger group with below-average ACT scores and high-school GPAs. On the other hand, perhaps our grading has simply fluctuated.

If our overall goal is to help students succeed in ENG 150 (so that they can go on and succeed in other classes and in their careers), then perhaps it's too early to say whether our directed self-placement system really works. We do know that about 66% of our 1995 ENG 098 students went on to earn credit for ENG 150 by the end of the next semester, while just 55% of the 1996 group did the same. The difference seemed to be that while in 1995 about 87% of the ENG 098 students went on to take ENG 150 the next semester, in 1996 only 75% of our ENG 098 students took ENG 150 the next semester. There could be several reasons for this, and we're still looking into it. Did they drop out of school? Did they feel overwhelmed by writing and choose to stay away from the next course? Or did they feel well-prepared for their other classes and simply decide to delay ENG 150 until a more convenient time?

Even with questions like these unanswered, we are convinced that directed self-placement is working at our school. We continue to locate hundred of students each year that feel they need additional help with their writing, and we do it very efficiently and on terms the students understand and appreciate.

Directed Self-Placement Pleases Everyone Involved

To analyze numbers is, to some extent, to fall back into the thinking that what's most important about placing students in developmental or regular first-year writing courses is a quantifiable assessment of their writing ability. Teachers assess students' ability at the end of every term, but placement ought to be a student's own choice. Traditional placement procedures, as well as those procedures that Huot calls "emergent writing assessment" (556), assume that students don't know enough about what lies before them to make an intelligent choice. Or perhaps they cynically hold that students don't want to make wise choices and that they want to take as few writing courses as possible. We are careful to address the former assumption with our talk and our brochure. We address the latter concern by assuming ourselves that students will live, for better or for worse, with the choices they make, and by teaching each class at the level described in our brochure and course catalog.

Huot indicates that notions of assessment validity are evolving. Beyond measuring what they purport to measure, valid assessment procedures "must have positive impact and consequences for the teaching and learning of writing" (551). We tell students that their education — and this first decision about ENG 098 or ENG 150 — is their responsibility. We can offer direction, we can outline the purposes and expectations of each course, but we simply can't make the decision as intelligently as they can. It pleases students to know that they are in charge of their learning. It may be the most important message they receive at freshman orientation. It also puts some pressure on them — pressure that rightly belongs to them. When we place students, we take away from them a critical component in their educational lives. If we choose for them, they may think that the right thing is being done, but it is understandable that many take our choosing for them as an excuse to become either angry or defeated. The sense of rightness comes to students who make their own decisions in a matter like this and when they vow to affirm through hard work that the right decision has been made.

Students who appraise their ability too highly have a challenge before them. On the other hand, students who believe that ENG 098 is the best course for them are happy to have the opportunity to improve themselves and pleased to possess the dignity of making such a choice for themselves.

To illustrate this, we'll describe the experiences of two students — not to prove that directed self-placement works in the same way for everyone, but to show how it *can* work for individual students.

Kristen and Jacob were both traditional freshmen, a month or two past their 1997 high-school graduation ceremonies, when they attended summer orientation and selected their first composition courses. Based on sheer numbers (3.68 high-school GPA, ranked in top 12% of her class, ACT-English score of 19), we might have expected Kristen to place herself into ENG 150, but she selected ENG 098. And we might have expected Jacob (3.16 high-school GPA, ranked in the top 46% of his class, ACT-English score of 15) to place himself into ENG 098, but he selected ENG 150.

What went into their decisions? Kristen, who made her decision while looking over the two lists of "characteristics" in the brochure, felt unsure of her ability to step right into college-level writing. "I was just being cautious," she says now. "I was just starting college and didn't know what to expect. I figured that English 098 would get me back into the writing mode. I'd been out of school all summer." Kristen's parents supported her decision, but she told them about it afterwards, after she'd already registered. "I made the decision during orientation," she recalls. "I was on my own."

Jacob, on the other hand, sought advice from others before making his final decision. He registered for ENG 150 during orientation, but then he spoke with his parents and high-school English teacher over the next several days. "When I was back home after orientation, I gave my advanced-comp teacher a call and read the class description of both classes, and both she and I decided that 150 was a good choice." His parents, though, disagreed. "My parents wanted me to take 098 because they didn't want me to screw up my first semester. But I wanted to take 150 to show them I wouldn't screw up."

Both Kristen's caution and Jacob's determination seem to us excellent reasons for selecting the courses they chose. Kristen did well in ENG 098 (she earned a B+) and enjoyed the class. "It was flexible, and everyone wrote at their own pace. It was not very stressful. We mostly wrote on things that interested us." She also says that she improved her writing: "We went to a tutor once a week. During the semester, I learned that there are different ways to write a paper. There are different emotions and audiences that a person must consider. You must also deal with many drafts before a final draft. You have to make enough time to get everything done."

Now that she is in ENG 150, Kristen feels well-prepared and well-situated as a college writer. "ENG 150 is more of an 'on-your-own' class. We use computers, and we do a lot of reading and research. Overall, I think I'm doing pretty well."

Jacob also looks back on his decision as a good one. He says that he took the decision very seriously — more seriously than he might have back in high school: "In high school you're just taking classes, but in college you've got money involved." Like Kristen, he feels that he learned a lot in the course. "My final paper was a work of art compared to my high-school papers. The most important thing I gained from the class was to simply make my paper flow much better than I could before, not jumping from thought to thought."

Jacob earned a "C" in ENG 150, and he feels content with the experience. "Now I feel like I'm writing at a proficient college level. In my opinion, that's the goal of a freshman course."

In the responses of these students, we see a welcome shift in attitude, a merging of our goals and theirs. Where there might have been conflict, there is now cooperation. And we can say that as teachers, we adopt a very different attitude toward students who place themselves in ENG 098 or ENG 150. Teachers in ENG 098 know that the students, by their own admission, are asking for some help to get ready for college writing. No developmental writing teacher begins class with the view that the first order of business is to prove to the student that he or she was indeed placed correctly. Our best students are the ones that ask us to help them learn, and now in no other class on campus can a teacher assume with as much confidence that this is precisely what every student in the ENG 098 class wants. In fact, the ENG 098 class is becoming a favorite choice among writing faculty because of this positive attitude of orientation. This class fulfills no college requirement and doesn't count as credit toward graduation, yet the students are there and this pleases anyone with teaching instincts.

Those of us teaching ENG 150 know that each student has accepted the challenge of the course. The students have another option, but they feel ready to begin the required first-year writing course. Although occasionally the first-day writing sample indicates there is a student or two that might be better off in ENG 098, the teacher now faces a student, not an ACT score or the evidence of a one-shot writing sample. If the student knows what is expected and accepts the challenge, who are we to tell them they can't take this course? If a student fails ENG 150, that student must recur to his or her own self-placement, not a writing sample or the inflated high-school transcript. Teachers are pleased when the placement responsibility lies with the student, for the relationship is thus cleaner, less muddied with the interference of test scores and with predictions for success or failure from everyone *except* the student.

Finally, we have discovered that administrators are also pleased with directed self-placement. Admissions directors don't have to help organize placement exams or explain to students why they need to begin their college career with a not-for-college-credit course. They are pleased to invite potential students to compare the way we and other schools treat their incoming students: we provide options, while other schools take them away. And of course, unlike placement exams, directed self-placement costs nothing.

Like Huot, we want a placement procedure that focuses "inward toward the needs of students, teachers, and programs rather than outward toward standardized norms or generalizable criteria" (555). With directed self-placement we've found a way to place the focus first and foremost on students and their own self-understanding, capabilities, and purposes. Our teachers have been freed from an uncomfortably hasty kind of assessment so that they can focus entirely on the more authentic kinds of assessment that go on over the course of an entire semester. And the integrity of our program has benefited from the honest challenge presented by our promise to stick to our advertised course standards and objectives and to offer help and preparation to those who believe they need it.

A PRAGMATIST THEORY OF WRITING ASSESSMENT

As we've indicated above, we believe that the assumptions and practices that Huot describes as "new, emergent writing assessment" are not yet deeply enough contextualized in the students' own personal and educational lives. The placement method we are advocating has its theoretical roots in John Dewey's democratic and pragmatist philosophy of education. Pragmatist understanding of experience, particularly Dewey's instrumentalism, supplies the soundest theory in support of directed self-placement. Dewey supplies us with these principles of learning: educational growth should be directed; inquiry begins in uncertainty and moves toward transformation; instrumental intelligence requires the freedom and power to choose.

Dewey says that "it is the office of the social medium," which includes schools, "to direct growth through putting powers to the best possible use" (*Democracy* 114). We direct our students' growth in part by establishing and communicating the goals of ENG 150 and the abilities required to succeed in the courses. The *power* that directed self-placement taps is the desire among new college students to get started on the right foot and to finally make some personal choices about their education. Freshmen come to the university hyper-aware of their educational background, their capabilities, and the promise of success. They generally have a good sense of where they stack up in comparison to their peers. Where there is indetermination and uncertainty — uncertainty about preparation, about writing, and about one's ability to fit in to the new discourse community — there is a need for what Dewey calls transformation.

The *instrumental* function involves the way inquiry is used as a tool to intelligently direct one's experience. For Dewey, inquiry "is the controlled or directed transformation of an indeterminate situation into one that is so determinate in its constituent distinctions and relations as to convert the elements of the original situation into a unified whole" ("Pattern" 320). Instrumentalism replaces static understanding ("you are a basic writer") with an emphasis on the dynamic relation between the student and the possibilities waiting in his or her environment ("perhaps I should take a developmental writing course").

Our placement program thus relies on honest student inquiry and interactive participation. Our orientation talk offers direction: it is a critical first moment in four years of communication. We tell students where they need to end up, and they tell us how they want to get there. Dewey writes in *Democracy and Education*: "The communication which insures participation in a common understanding is one which secures similar emotional and intellectual dispositions — like ways of responding to expectations and requirements" (4). Our invitation to satisfy the first-year writing requirement in two semesters or one, by beginning with either ENG 098 or ENG 150, fosters the disposition characteristic of genuine learning and offers an invitation to academic community as opposed to establishing from the get-go that teachers are going to take over control of student learning.

Other theories of assessment define two narrowly what placement is all about. Edward White maintains that essay tests are "perfectly appropriate" if all we seek is "information that will help students enroll in courses for which they are ready" (33). But placement is not about *our* discovery of information; it is about getting a student's higher education started in the best way. If we want to communicate to students the dispositions characteristic of all inquirers, then most decidedly an essay test is *not* perfectly appropriate. To think so is to take on the mindset of administrators, who often view students merely as "seats" in a classroom. Finding the right "seat" for a student is not enough.

A pragmatist theory of assessment situates placement with regard to each student's aims and dispositions. The power relations that are violated by taking away choices are not repaired by mainstreaming, which simply eliminates options, or by updating methods of administering and scoring placement-essays, which continues to tell students that they are not ready to make their own decisions. Dewey remarks that "aims, beliefs, aspirations, knowledge — a common understanding — . . . cannot be passed physically from one to another like bricks" (4). What is required is communication — and every placement method communicates something important to students. Perhaps this is why traditional placement into remedial courses has not proven to equip students to succeed in the regular writing course. Perhaps those students are still waiting for someone to fix what ails them. We hope that we are encouraging in our new students, in pragmatist fashion, an intelligent way of responding to expectations and requirements.

If proper placement is a matter of guiding students into the course that is best suited to their educational background and current writing ability, directed self-placement may be the most *valid* procedure we can use. If the clarity of criteria and their consistent application is the standard of *reliability*, directed self-placement ranks high as long as we use current course goals and standards for success to inform and guide students in their choice.

Directed self-placement is no panacea. It does not address the problem of how to teach, how to bring students in from the margins, or how to deal with all of the politics of institutional change. Soliday, Grego and Thompson, Bartholomae and others address many of these concerns that would take us far beyond the limited scope of placement alternatives. But our placement alternative does lay the ground work for much that these authors recommend.

And so to conclude this essay, we return finally to a practical concern we confronted when we turned an important choice over to students — the risk. The "risk" of directed self-placement is peculiar. We imagined, for example, that, left to make the final decision on their own, no students would enroll in ENG 098. There we would be with 20 empty sections. If this were to happen, who would we blame? How bad would it really be? Who would be hurt? The peculiar feature of directed self-placement is that, in once sense, it can't really fail. If nobody took our developmental writing class, it would be a choice that each student made with his or her eyes open; our brochure and our orientation talk would make sure of that much. And if ill-prepared students take ENG 150, the teacher's complaint about unprepared students would have to be directed back toward the students. If they pass the course, who can blame them for taking the chance? If they fail, they will, we hope, learn that a college education is a serious endeavor and that success often begins with a proper estimation of one's abilities.

Acknowledgments: We would like to thank Peter Elbow for his generous encouragement and for his thoughtful comments on the early drafts of this article. We also want to acknowledge our indebtedness to Thomas Newkirk's "Roots of the Writing Process" for its clear exposition of several key concepts in Dewey's philosophy as they relate to writing instruction.

WORKS CITED

Bartholomae, David. "Inventing the University." *Perspectives on Literacy*. Ed. Eugene R. Kintgen, Barry M. Kroll, and Mike Rose. Carbondale: Southern Illinois UP, 1988. 273–85.
Dewey, John. *Democracy and Education*. 1916. New York: Free P, 1966.
———. "The Pattern of Inquiry." *Logic: The Theory of Inquiry*. New York: Holt, 1938. 101–19. Rpt. in *Pragmatism: The Classic Writings*. Ed. H. S. Thayer, Indianapolis: Hackett, 1982. 316–34.

Elbow, Peter. "Writing Assessment in the Twenty-First Century: A Utopian View." *Composition in the Twenty-First Century: Crisis and Change.* Ed. Lynn Bloom, Donald Daiker, and Edward White. Carbondale: Southern Illinois UP, 1996.

Grego, Rhonda, and Nancy Thompson. "Repositioning Remediation: Renegotiating Composition's Work in the Academy." *CCC* 47 (1996): 62–84.

Huot, Brian. "Toward a New Theory of Writing Assessment." *CCC* 47 (1996): 549–66.

James, William. "What Pragmatism Means." *Pragmatism.* 1907. Cleveland: World, 1955.

Newkirk, Thomas. "Roots of the Writing Process." *More Than Stories: The Range of Children's Writing.* Portsmouth: Heinemann, 1989. 177–208.

Soliday, Mary. "From the Margins to the Mainstream: Reconceiving Remediation." *CCC* 47 (1996): 85–100.

White, Edward M. "An Apologia for the Timed Impromptu Essay Test." *CCC* 46 (1995): 30–45.

15

WAC Assessment and Internal Audiences: A Dialogue

RICHARD HASWELL AND SUSAN McLEOD

I t started in spring (1995). At first, it was a query in passing. "What's up? You know what they want?" But it quickly evolved into a series of sit downs, with caffeine and working papers between us — on the one side, Rich, campus coordinator of writing assessment; on the other side, Susan, associate dean of liberal arts. The last of the dialogue — at least for the time being — was the conversation transcribed later in this article. We knew what we were talking *about* from the beginning: a request from central administration for a status report on our university's rising-junior writing assessment. But what we were *talking* about dawned on us only gradually: the rhetorical nature of writing program assessment within an academic institution. This article uses the report as an example. But our principal topic is the institutional realities of such a report.

THE RHETORIC OF ASSESSMENT

We listed below some assumptions readily made about the rhetorical nature of writing-across-the-curriculum (WAC) assessment. These assumptions are easy to make but, for evaluators, easier to forget than put into practice. First, the need for assessment arises out of both a general and a particular context. The general context is provided by institutions of higher learning, which are large, complex, and thoroughly stratified. The particular context is complex and is also continually changing. It follows that the rhetorical participants in a WAC assessment will be varied. Even when there is only one evaluator (which is rarely the case), there will be multiple readers, multiple stakeholders. Further, each of these participants will have different relationships, purposes, and needs for the evaluation. The two main participants — faculty evaluator and administrative reader — often assume diverse motives and roles. This means that WAC assessment provides ample grounds for commu-

From *Assessing Writing Across the Curriculum: Diverse Approaches and Practices*, ed. Kathleen B. Yancey and Brian Huot (Westport, CT: Ablex, 1997), 217–36.

nicative conflict, clashes that stem from misunderstandings and which can lead to further misunderstandings. In short, the rhetorical nature of WAC evaluation tests all that the evaluator knows about rhetorical purpose, context, kairos, and audience.

This article explores the rhetoric of WAC assessment in a very pragmatic way. It stresses — realistically, we hope — the crucial fact of multiple purpose and multiple audience. WAC directors, for instance, need information from ongoing assessment in order to know how their programs are working and where they might need to fine tune. In such situations, the WAC director herself is the audience, and the purpose is formative. Oftentimes, however, the WAC director is asked to assess the program for some other audience: a central administrator, a board of regents, or a legislator. The purpose in such a case may be summative or outright political, assuring the reader of the program's overall worth. This chapter focuses on situations where readers stand outside the WAC program. We take the perspective of what Michael Patton calls "utilization-focused evaluation" — a perspective that foregrounds the needs of the decision makers who have asked for or will be using the results of the assessment. Our pragmatic approach assumes that all elements of assessment have constitutive links with sociopolitical action, from value-construction (Swidler), validity (Messick), and methodology (Smith), to the evaluator's concerns about personal reputation (Gomm). We agree with these authors that program assessment is a negotiative process among stakeholders, a way of organizing and valuing experience with institutional and personal consequences.

Pragmatically put, our goal is to arrive at some recommendations to help WAC evaluators write reports that will achieve their own goals. Our route is fairly straightforward. We begin by contrasting the typical roles and motives of evaluator and administrator, because these two groups form the rhetorical core of an assessment report, writer and reader, and because clashes between their respective roles and motives lead to some of the most common rhetorical failures in WAC evaluation. We then describe our own particular situation of Spring 1995, in much detail, in order to argue that rhetorically WAC assessment is always particular, always sui generis and always complex. We do so with our dialogue between a WAC coordinator evaluating his own program for an outside audience and an administrator who knows both the program and the outside audience and its needs. The dialogue mode is appropriate because it models the ideal spirit in which we believe program assessment should be undertaken. Dialogue, in a very real sense, is both the nature of WAC evaluation and the solution to its rhetorical problems. From this specific case, we then extract some general ways that evaluators and administrators tend to clash, because we believe that it is often with attention to these conflicting perspectives that functional evaluation arises within an academic institution. We have found that it is out of the specific history of particular WAC assessments on the one hand, and out of general notions of conflicting perspective between evaluator and audience on the other hand, that good rhetorical advice for WAC evaluation emerges.

ROLES OF THE WAC EVALUATOR

Typically, the roles of WAC coordinators who are evaluating their own program arise out of a matrix of professional experience different from that of administrators. This is an obvious but crucial point. WAC coordinator– evaluators are entangled, in a direct and ongoing way, with the very programs and personnel that they are evaluating. They may be teaching one or more of the WAC courses that are being scrutinized. Or they may be managing a testing office responsible for both the cross-campus assessment procedures and the validation of those procedures. They may even have helped design the courses, the assessments, and the validation studies. Certainly they are experiencing daily and front-line encounters with the people who are most immediately affected (and sometimes confused) by WAC programs: students and their relatives, advisors, teachers, department chairs, and clerical staff. They spend more time than they would like in meetings with statisticians, oversight committees, and technology teams from the computing center. And because they are at once teachers and researchers as well as evaluators, they usually persist in the endless task of reading the professional literature, conducting workshops, and writing, presenting, and publishing their own scholarship.

This might seem an impossible melange of experience in which any one individual could find reasonable roles, but in fact out of this primordial soup a certain number of roles emerge for the WAC evaluator. The catalyst is the end of WAC evaluation for the evaluator. That primary motivation — to describe and assess the WAC program in order to better it — synthesizes the variety of drives and impulses into a few overriding motives. It is, of course, these motives that shape and fuel the roles that the evaluator will assume.

What are those basic motives?

- The first is intellectual curiosity, i.e., the simple need to learn the truth. Are teachers really following the procedures recommended by the program and reading drafts of student writing? Do students really appreciate or even understand the principles that govern WAC initiatives? WAC evaluators want to sound out these and other mysteries. Indeed, sounding out stands as a core impulse behind any WAC evaluation.

- A second basic motive, which is sometimes at odds with the first, is self-defense. Evaluators — caught up in the formation and implementation of WAC programs — need to defend their positions. They need to justify both the educational practices in the program they are assessing and the assessment procedures they are using — and in the process to demonstrate their expertise.

- A third motive is to maintain social groups. WAC evaluation may help unify coworkers in the assessment office, bind together a cohort of WAC teachers through self-understanding, or support the self-image of an entire faculty to making programmatic outcomes public. The motivation to further social groups lies behind a spectrum of evaluator actions, from placating oversight boards to gaining budgetary support.

- A final basic motive is to better the educational process. WAC evaluation may satisfy some quite self-serving ends of the evaluator, but it never fully lacks — at least for WAC evaluators it never fully loses — that essential yearning to find a better way for students and teachers.

These motives establish ends to be achieved, and expose the need for evaluators to take on certain roles. Because we will be comparing the roles of the WAC evaluator with those of the academic administrator, we will start with the roles for the WAC evaluator.

1. *Expert*: One who knows what has been done and what can be done in terms of assessment.

2. *Interpreter*: One who serves a constituency outside the program (e.g., administrators) by explaining how things operate and fare from the inside. Or one who serves an internal group (e.g., a WAC seminar or an assessment office) by conveying and explaining the position from outside (e.g., the university budgetary office).

3. *Educator*: One whose final allegiance is the learning and welfare of students.

4. *Scientist-Researcher*: One whose final allegiance is to the truth as far as it can be determined; one who will uphold assessment standards of reliability, validity, and fairness.

5. *Team Worker*: One who will maintain and further the cohesion and viability of a group, be it validation team, testing office, or WAC faculty.

6. *Apologist*: One whose duty it is to defend historically and theoretically an enterprise, be it a validation process, a WAC initiative, or an inter-disciplinary writing workshop.

ROLES OF THE ADMINISTRATOR

It is part of academic culture to grouse about administrators, to classify them as "other," to blame them for the day-to-day inconveniences and stupidities of university life. After all, they set and enforce policies and procedures; ipso facto, they are the focal point for dissatisfaction about such issues. The two of us have done our share of such recreational grousing. However, in order to write an effective assessment of a WAC program, we need to think carefully about administrators as audience — what they do, what they want, and what kind of information they might need from evaluators in order to do their job.

Administrators have different motives than WAC coordinators–evaluators. The primary motive of administrators, unlike evaluators, is to decide where the WAC program fits in the institutional priorities so that decisions can be made about it. Administrators are not devoid of intellectual curiosity and the need to discover the truth, but those motives are always secondary to a primary need: to make decisions about allocation of resources. As the academic equivalent of managers in a corporation, it is their job to maintain the quality of the institution while dealing with budgets (these days ever-shrinking). Administrators are busy people. They work on long-range planning for the institution, articulate and enforce policies, monitor (and worry about) such things as enrollments, faculty hiring and retention, and outside perceptions of the university. Like WAC evaluators, they too have particular roles to play.

1. *Generalist*: One who knows a good deal about several different disciplines by virtue of being in charge of all departmental units, but who is not an expert in any discipline but his or her own, and who is usually not an expert in assessment. The description of administrative knowledge, "a mile wide and an inch deep," is useful to keep in mind.

2. *Mediator–Problem-solver*: One who explains various groups in the university hierarchy to each other, conveying the wishes and needs of those above (trustees, legislators) to those below, and in return representing the needs and desires of those below to those above. Mediation often includes resolving conflicts (for example, between faculty who feel overworked and legislators who think that the number of hours in a faculty teaching load is equivalent to the number of hours in that faculty's work week).

3. *Manager–Team Leader*: One whose final allegiance is to the health and welfare of the institution or the unit which he/she heads.

4. *Steward*: One who is charged with upholding standards and maintaining quality control, of using resources in accordance with institutional priorities.

5. *Entrepreneur*: One who is expected to meet with possible donors to the institution, to be involved in fundraising.

6. *Spokesperson–PR Specialist*: One whose duty it is to publicly defend the institution or a piece of it by highlighting its quality and its success.

In summary, on one side the evaluator tends to operate as an expert researcher and educator with commitments to the truth, to student learning, and to various circumscribed groups within the institution, guiding those groups by interpreting the larger academic community and informing the community by defending theoretically and pragmatically the groups. On the other side, the administrator tends to operate as a steward and manager with commitments outside the institution to efficiency and to public standards, creating and enforcing policy, solving problems, gaining funding, and in the other diplomatic ways mediating between academic groups for the benefit of the whole institution.

Listing their roles helps identify one major conflict in the ways that evaluators and administrators see and utilize assessment. When evaluators assess their own WAC programs, they look toward improvement in the program. But administrators, though not unconcerned about improving WAC programs, are more concerned about the health of the entire institution. They look toward quality assurance, accountability, and public relations. The WAC assessment thus must give administrators *only* the particular data that will fill their needs. An unexpected outcome ripe for further research, for instance — an evaluator's plum — is of no interest to the administrator unless it demonstrates the ongoing health of the program.

Our listing of the different roles suggests many further areas of conflict and potential misunderstanding between evaluator and administrator. Conflicts will arise, however, not simply out of clash between two divergent academic functions, but complexly out of the particular situation at hand. They will depend on the history of the program and the institution, on the current political and economic forces at play, on the organizational channels in operation, on the personnel in place, and on a wealth of other contingencies. By definition, WAC programs are complex, and many of them are youthful and still in development. It is not that some general areas of conflict cannot be extracted; we plan to end this article by doing just that. It is just that the very nature of the conflicts — the fact that they exist *as* dialogue among the participants (or lack of dialogue) — recommends that they be conceived in context. An understanding of misunderstanding between evaluator and administrator requires a look at its local, messy venue.

A Dialogue About Reporting Assessment Results

To illustrate the interaction of all these roles, we present here a dialogue between an administrator, Susan, and an evaluator, Rich. This dialogue will illustrate two things: (a) the potential for misunderstanding which we have just discussed and (b) the advantages when the administrator occupies a middle ground between the intended audience and the WAC program. Susan happens to occupy this middle ground, although she is certainly not unique in this advantage. As we have said, this particular dialogue was occasioned by one particular WAC assessment initiative, dating from Spring 1995. Two years earlier, as part of an ambitious WAC program, upper-division students at Washington State University had begun taking a new writing portfolio examination, our version of a "rising junior" writing assessment instrument (see Haswell, Johnson-Shull, & Wyche-Smith; Haswell & Wyche-Smith 1996). For their University Writing Portfolio of five pieces, all undergraduates had been submitting three pieces of writing from previous courses and then composing two essays under timed conditions. Their completed portfolio, once evaluated, either deemed them as qualified for upper-division writing intensive courses in their major or required that they take further writing instruction.

In 2 years the examination had produced results and data that told us some interesting things about the institution: Besides the rates of "pass" versus "needs work" assigned to the portfolios, we could track which departments assigned a good deal of writing, which teachers within those departments assigned the most writing, and which groups of students (e.g., transfers, biology majors, internationals) received the highest and the lowest evaluations on their portfolios. By the spring, the central administration (that is, the provost, who is the chief academic officer of the university, and the vice provost) indicated that they were looking for a report on these results. What eventually ensued was that the coordinator of writing assessment (Rich Haswell) produced, in fact, not one but four reports: chronologically,

1. A four-page "stopgap" information report issued 5 weeks into the spring semester, directed to the director of general education and sent on to the provost, to whom he reports.

2. A 5-minute oral report, delivered to the board of regents during their annual meeting at commencement, with the vice provost, the provost, and the president in attendance.

3. A six-page "progress" report to the provost and vice provost, via the director of general education, sent a month after the end of the spring semester.

4. A long, formal "internal" report issued at the end of the summer, sent to the director of general education with copies to the chair of the All-University Writing Committee (AUWC) and director of university assessment.

The following dialogue occurred between the two of us in June, after the first two reports had been issued, but while the third, the "progress" report, was still being written. The dialogue is both a reminiscence of the circumstances that occasioned the first two reports and a working session adding finishing details to the third.

Rich Haswell, as the director of writing assessment, was the principal designer, administrator, and now the evaluator of the campus-wide junior Writing Portfolio. Susan McLeod had left her position as director of composition to become the associate dean of the college of liberal arts, and was thus well positioned to know the campus-wide writing program as well as the administrators to which this report will go and the decisions they might make as a result. Both of us had thought a good deal about writing assessment.[1] Here we are, looking at the raw data out of which this third report will be shaped: a list of teachers who have signed off on papers that went into the portfolios and the departments from which the papers came; statistics on how many students fell into which category in the readings ("pass," "pass with distinction," "needs work") and what majors those students have declared; statistics on other populations, such as males and females, transfer students, students who have identified themselves as first-language or ESL writers.

Eventually, out of this data we will create the rest of the reports. The report under construction, the third, has multiple audiences. Besides the usual routing (to the provost and the vice provost via the general education director), other readers may be the AUWC, the dean of the college of liberal arts (in whose area most of the writing courses reside), the president, the board of regents, and the higher education coordinating board (a statewide oversight body which looks at all of higher education in the state). The reports may also come into the hands of a stray legislator or two, as well as a local reporter who thinks of himself as "investigative" and seems convinced that the university is hiding important secrets from the public.[2] Indeed, it was an awareness of the diversity of needs among these readers that led to the splitting of one report into four.

RICH: This January I heard that the central administration was itchy for a formal account of the Portfolio. That caught me by surprise by because the exam is only 2 years old and not yet at full steam. From the start I have sent results of student performance (the percentage of "pass with distinction," "pass," and "needs work") to people who needed them at the moment, such as the AUWC, the director

of general education, the director of assessment, various department chairs, the director of composition, and the student advising
and learning center. Of course I thought that sooner or later there
would be a validation study, but I didn't imagine the kind of accountability report the administrators wanted. Do you know what
lay behind that want?

SUSAN: Yes. I remember that the biennial budget was coming due, and
every time that the university's budget request comes before the legislature, there are questions about accountability: What are we
spending the state's money on, and what kind of bang we are getting for their buck, what's working, what isn't. The administration
needs data, evidence of quality for the budget hearings, to justify the
newest request. I think the other driver was the Higher Education
Coordinating Board. The HEC Board, like its counterparts in other
states, is heavily invested in outcomes assessment statewide.

RICH: My first response was what we are calling the stopgap report. The
name reflects my mood at the time. In it I asked six questions, which
reflect problem areas, and gave whatever statistics or data I had as
answers to these questions. Looking back, would you say this was
wise?

SUSAN: Were they questions or problem areas that you had been asked
about, or were they ones you just saw in the material?

RICH: Both. I saw that I had answers to questions that I was interested in,
and there were questions that had come out in some conversations
that I had with the AUWC. Like this whole issue of performance: at
what rate are we giving out ratings of "needs work" and "pass with
distinction"? The issue of how well transfer students do is a question that the general education director has brought up several
times. Now in the subsequent report to the regents, I took a considerably different approach, highlighting positive outcomes of the
exam and mentioning no areas in need of action. Won't such a radical change of format and content make administrators suspicious?

SUSAN: No, because the two reports have different purposes. Earlier in
the spring the pressure was to give a preliminary report, and it looks
to me that there were some very specific questions that people
wanted to know the answers to — for instance the success of the
transfer students. In fact, one way to approach a report like this is
simply to contact the administrator who requested it and ask, "What
do you want to know?" Then frame the report as you did, using the
questions they want answered. It's a way of getting a quick outline.
Administrators don't have a lot of time to answer questions they are
being asked by their constituencies — they much prefer that the expert craft answers for them. But the presentation to the regents —
well, the regents want to hear that the program is working. They are
here for just one day, and they have a lot to absorb. That doesn't give
us much time for subtleties.

RICH: That brings up the question of what they mean by "working."
Everyone seems to have a different take on the outcomes. For in-

stance, after the director of general education saw the stopgap report, he told me that the figure of 10% of exam takers put into the "needs work" category was low. He said that he thought 20% was more "accurate." On the other hand, the dean of liberal arts thought that 10% was a good sign, showing that undergraduates are writing well here, better than expected.

SUSAN: There will be some readers of all your reports who think that undergraduates write very badly, but that notion is based on some comparison with what they remember as the golden days of their undergraduate years. I think of this as a "Paradise Lost" mindset, and it is perhaps more prevalent than you and me might like to believe. What they think they should see and what the report says may be two different things, and we need to be honest.

RICH: Well *what's honest* has about the same rhetorical status as *what works* — both are equally problematical, though from different sides of the fence. One of the learning moments in all of this was when I first talked with a central administrator about my oral report to the regents. On the phone he said that — he was looking at this "stopgap" report — "you have some good data here, could you give me five minutes at that meeting?" And then he was very careful, and he said, "Vanilla, nothing fancy." So from that I put together some stuff, most of it positive. But at the time I asked him would it be all right to report the poor performance of the transfer ESL students and the comparative performance of colleges, and he hesitated. Then he said, "Yes, if you want to." Then at the meeting itself, I quickly saw that he was giving me good advice about the audience and kairos — what was being reported by other presenters was truly nothing but vanilla.

SUSAN: Right. The regents technically are at the top of the university's organizational chart — the deans and the general education director and the vice provost report to the provost, the provost reports to the president, the president to the regents. The regents are appointed by the governor; they are bright, well-educated people who are deeply concerned about the institution, but they are more of a ceremonial body. They must approve all tenure decisions, for example, but that approval is really a rubber-stamp. This is not to say they are not an important audience — they are in fact influential in the state and quite shrewd, and they have a veto power they are not afraid to use. But they don't have the decision-making power that the provost has at the local level. They are interested in the overall picture. They are like the president — more external, more involved in liaison efforts between the university and the legislature.

RICH: As I was giving this oral report to the regents, there was one piece of data that they reacted to much more than to the others. It was when I said that portfolio papers had been submitted from "880 different teachers in 660 different courses in 63 different departments." That seemed to be very impressive to them. You could hear the intake of breath. Why do you think it was?

SUSAN: You said generally that there was widespread compliance. But when you started talking about actual numbers, I think that makes it real to them. They are thinking, wow, this is a big operation. Until you hear those numbers, you don't realize the sheer size of it. That is precisely the sort of fact that the provost will want to quote in his various public presentations, for good public relations. It gives people an idea of how hard we are working.

RICH: There is also something about the picture that those numbers give of the whole university that was impressive to them, too.

SUSAN: I think so. They probably had the notion, based perhaps on the "why-Johnny-can't-write" articles in the newspaper, that teachers nowadays aren't assigning writing, or not as many as when they went to school (that "Paradise Lost" mindset), and I think that those numbers gave them a different picture of the institution — that there are a lot of conscientious teachers out there who care about writing and are assigning papers to their students. To put it in very simplistic terms, the regents wanted some kind of evidence that WSU was doing something about the literacy crisis, and they got it.

RICH: As I said, at the regents' meeting I saw they were truly getting vanilla. And so as reports of others kept coming in, I kept marking stuff to leave out of mine. I left out that data on transfer ESL students. I did mention that the portfolio was having a good cross-curricular effect, that a number of departments are doing exceptionally well, and I named them. But I did not name the departments that are having trouble.

SUSAN: I think that was a really wise strategy, because you were talking to regents, who want to hear only about what's working. But the provost and vice provost need to have a more complete picture, because they are the chief academic officers of the institution. Quality control is their job.

RICH: So we are back to what's working. What is the vice provost's take?

SUSAN: He is first and foremost interested in academic quality. That is his definition of "working." As vice provost for academic affairs, he is responsible for the day-to-day quality control of academic programs. He is the provost's right hand person and feeds him information. As one of the very first participants in the original WAC seminar I ran in 1986, and as a fine teacher who has always required writing in his anthropology classes, he is very supportive of anything having to do with the writing effort. He has read Boyer's book, *College: The Undergraduate Experience,* and firmly believes that communication skills are the key to a successful undergraduate experience. He will define "working" as "improving the quality of our product" — student writing.

RICH: How will he use the progress reports?

SUSAN: To show the folks above him in the administrative hierarchy who hold him accountable — the provost, the president, the regents, the HEC board, and the legislators — that the university is doing a good job with writing on the undergraduate level.

RICH: So that is why you insist that, even with him, we need to emphasize the positive?

SUSAN: Yes. Not that we don't want to think about how the program can be improved, but things that we can improve ourselves are not his concern.

RICH: What about the provost? Is he different from the vice provost in how he defines what is working?

SUSAN: Yes, but mostly in the way he wants that information given to him. He is a hard scientist—where the vice provost is used to ethnographic studies (because that is how he writes up his own research), the provost wants clean facts, to show quality and cost effectiveness. One of the ways I get at the question of readers is to look at the documents they themselves have produced. And, if you look at what the provost produces for other people in the university to consume, it is a very short amount of text with a series of bullets, one right after another. Like many public figures, that's also the way he talks, in sound bites, giving nuggets of information. One of the things we want to do with this report is to provide something that then he could translate very easily into one of the overhead transparencies that he uses in his presentations to show what the institution is doing.

RICH: Is that why you recommended in the progress report an executive summary of no more than a page?

SUSAN: Yes, and not just because the bullets and executive summary are parts of his own administrative style. That format will help him get the gist of the report quickly, and he will appreciate that because he has so much paper to go through. Administrators are overwhelmed by paper—there's always a stack to be read and translated into action. They don't have much time to ponder and reflect.

RICH: Which of these bullets will most attract his attention?

SUSAN: I think the fact that students are complying with the portfolio requirement in good order, especially with the legislature asking about efficiency and time to graduation. They want to be sure that this new writing requirement isn't holding students back. Also the fact that students are doing writing in all corners of the campus— that teachers as well as students are complying. The numbers will also attract him. He wants data and statistics, and it is not just a characteristic of the provost. Decisions at the university are data driven. Administrators all have to have some kind of data-based justification, not just whim or gut reaction. The bullet giving the ESL data will be particularly interesting because I think there is a general feeling on campus that ESL students have writing difficulties but no one quite knows what to do about the problem. I'm sure you are going to hear about this figure, that 36% of transfer students who identified themselves as ESL received the "needs work" designation. That's going to be pulled out immediately. And this bullet, "By all signs the portfolio examination is entrenched and healthy," ought to be pulled out and put at the very beginning. And this final bullet, "Areas in need of further study and improvement," needs to be changed to "Recommendations." What we want them to do with this report is not just learn about what we are doing, but take some action.

RICH: Now the provost will be the one who finally makes the decision to take action. What kinds of action do you think he will take?

SUSAN: It depends on what the data show, and we need to foreground the data that we think are most suggestive of the action that the provost has the power to take. The data show pretty convincingly that ESL students need support, and at the moment we have no area in the university with the expertise to provide that help. So we may want to recommend that a specialist in ESL be hired to provide us with that expertise. University administrators are problem-solvers; we can help them solve those problems by suggesting solutions.

RICH: Well, because I leave most of the negative information about departments out of this progress report, how is the provost to learn about it? About a month ago, after I had written the stopgap report, we talked and decided that for the "final" product I should in fact write two different accounts, this short progress report and then a longer internal report with the data in full—each college and each department and how well they are doing in terms of their students' performance and of their faculty's compliance with assigning writing in their classes. Your suggestion was that the progress report should go up the administrative line, while the internal report should go to the AUWC, and they should decide what should be done with it. Why do you think that is better than sending negative information directly to the vice provost and the provost?

SUSAN: Because the AUWC has been the body working directly with individual faculty members on writing-in-the-major courses and on issues of faculty compliance with assigning writing in their classes. The provost and vice provost are decision makers, but on a day-to-day basis the university committee structure is the machinery by which we get things done. Rather than forwarding what could be damaging information to the provost and putting the provost in a position of needing to reward or punish departments or colleges through his decisions, it would be much better politically to have the AUWC look at this material and say to the committee's representative from Business, "Your area is not doing well—your faculty are not assigning writing, as far as we can tell from the portfolios, and a larger percentage of your students get the 'needs work' designation, perhaps as a result of the fact that they do not do much writing in your college. What do you suggest we should do about this situation? We don't want to embarrass your college. How could we work with your faculty so that they are in better compliance, and so that your students' writing ability improves?"

RICH: So because the AUWC is representative, their decision to do something about it can be more effective.

SUSAN: They can do something about it in a formative way by working with faculty who are their colleagues, rather than in a punitive way, as the provost might be pressured to do.

RICH: And that would take the heat off of me. And keep people from saying, well, he's from English, and of course he has something against Business, so all he wants to do is humiliate my college and colleagues publicly.

SUSAN: Right.

RICH: Early on you said that we should not discuss anything that had to do with our startup problems in the reports that went up the line to the administration. Why was that?

SUSAN: Because administrators are interested not in startup but bottom-line issues, ones they can do something about. I hear that phrase "bottom line" a lot. Administrators have to make decisions. The issue of startup or pilot difficulties is of interest to those of us who administer the exam; we want to understand, for example, why the percentage of "pass with distinction" ratings was higher during the first year of the portfolio's existence. Was it due to the raters' inexperience, or perhaps our training methods? What we found was that the better writing students, for instance those in the Honors Program, tended to take the exam early. As the less motivated (or less organized) students were brought into the exam, the "pass with distinction" ratings dropped. But administrators are interested only in final implications, not in interesting little blips in the data that intrigue us as researchers.

RICH: So the question is always, what will administrators make of this data, what will they do with it?

SUSAN: Absolutely. Administrators are always under pressure in terms of resources and are always looking for reasons to reallocate those resources. The only reason to give them negative information about the workings of the program is if the program really isn't working over all and should be discontinued, or if we thought they should do something about the problem by allocating more resources. For example, in our ESL situation, we have a clear problem and we can't solve it. The administration can help solve the problem by allocating resources (hiring an expert in this area). But if it is a problem we can correct, they don't need to know about it, or if they do, just enough to know that we are correcting it. Any negative information in an otherwise positive report can be easily misunderstood and misused by those who have their own agendas. What would happen if we said in our report that rater reliability could be improved? Administrators might respond by saying, "OK — then we will discontinue the Portfolio and put in a machine-scored multiple choice test, which will be reliable." Ouch. We have to be honest in the overall picture, of course. If a program is not doing what we thought it would, we need to come clean.

RICH: So it's a matter of including in a report only the information that administrators can use, can show to their constituencies or take particular action that we can't take.

SUSAN: Yes, utilization-focused assessment.

RICH: With the progress report, you recommended showing the various departments that portfolio raters came from. Why did you think this information would be useful to administrators?

SUSAN: I want to make sure that they understood that this is not an English department operation, that it is a broad-based assessment effort involving people from all disciplines on campus. I think that this is important politically.

RICH: You mean as a general perception on campus?

SUSAN: Yes. Because you have been so proactive in getting people from all different disciplines involved in the reading of the portfolios, the word has spread among faculty that this is an effort that includes all who wish to be involved. But administrators tend to be isolated from such general campus understandings. It's hard for them even to attend faculty meetings in the departments with which they are officially affiliated. Administrators have to be careful about their understanding of what is really happening, because so many times they hear only from the squeaky wheels. When things are going well, they tend not to hear about it. Your report then serves as important informational function; you are telling them what the general campus already knows.

RICH: And telling them in a substantive form, with figures, so they can test the information against what they have heard.

SUSAN: Yes, so if Professor Indignant marches in and says, "This is an English department plot against the rest of us!" the administrator can pull out the report and say, "Well that's not what these figures show."

RICH: As I was preparing the stopgap report, there was one area where I began to sense that I had a different concept of this assessment than the central administrators did. I have always thought of the portfolio as instructional, as a diagnostic tool to get students the help they need in order to succeed at the upper-division level. But administrators seem to see the portfolio as a test, a hurdle demonstrating quality control. Two clashing notions of the basic motive behind the portfolio — and a good candidate for misunderstandings.

SUSAN: I think that as long as the people in charge of the portfolio understand that its function is diagnostic rather than punitive, there's no need to explain the niceties of that distinction to the administration. Administrators are involved in two things that may make it better for them to think of this as a test: quality control and public relations. Their job is to let people know that yes, we have standards and we are doing something about student writing. We're testing it. And furthermore, no institution of our size has been able to make this sort of test work but (trumpets, please) we are. I don't think we need to be overly concerned about the distinction between our professional "expert" conception of what we are doing and their more general understanding. The portfolio does finally function, after all, as a quality control device, and also as a way to improve student writing. We're just not doing it in a sheep–goats sort of way.

RICH: So this is one area in which the display of data can get around those conceptual issues.

SUSAN: Yes. And that understanding of the portfolio as a test might even work in their favor — when they are talking to legislators, or potential donors, or to the regents or the HEC board. Some segments of the public have a rather punitive notion of what education is all about, and the notion of a test might fit their schema of an institution with high standards.

RICH: To what degree should I think about any of these reports I have been writing as public?

SUSAN: Once it is out of your hands, it is a public document. Anyone can ask for it, including reporters from the local newspaper. A report that goes to an administrator has the potential for a very long life and many different readers. This is a thought to make even the most reckless person cautious about any information in the reports that could be misinterpreted or misrepresented.

RICH: Let's talk a little about length. You advise that this progress report should be no more than three or four pages. It's now six pages, and I worry that it is too long.

SUSAN: Right — you don't want to include everything. Besides an executive summary, one way to deal with the issue of length is to have a short document with appendices, which readers can refer to if necessary. It is a mistake to send a comprehensive report to an administrator and expect him or her to extract important information from it. Sometimes people think of reports on assessment as analogous to reports sent to granting agencies, who want to know every nuance. That is not the case with administrators, who want to know specific things — as we have said before, quality assurance issues, possible PR opportunities, and information that will help them make decisions about resources. I said earlier that in this progress report instead of a list of "issues for further study," you should have a list of "recommendations." One thing that I always have to remind myself when I'm writing up a report for the administration is that I'm not writing a research report for journal article. The administrators are not necessarily interested in a detailed discussion of methodology; for example — what they want are the results of our study, the answers to particular questions that they might have or that their various constituencies or the people they report to might have.

RICH: One last question: It was my idea to make this progress report the first of a sequence, 1 every 2 years. Does that make sense?

SUSAN: Yes. You have managed to coordinate it with the biennial budget request that the director of general education has to send forward. You want to make sure that if you are asking administrators to do something with the information you give them, then you do it at a time when they have the resources. It's very savvy of you to know what the budget cycle is and coordinate your report and accompanying recommendations with that cycle.

RICH: So 2 more years and another progress report?

SUSAN: The administration will hope so. Administrators are always being held accountable by all of their constituencies — above and below them. The information we give them is information that they want to use. Especially these days when authority of any sort is under fire, they are constantly scrambling to find data that show the university is really doing its job — that professors are not just a bunch of drones and that we are teaching students something useful. They are eager for information, especially when we have programs that are really working and can prove that they are.

CONFLICTS BETWEEN EVALUATOR AND ADMINISTRATOR

As we hope our dialogue shows, there are numerous possibilities for conflicts between WAC evaluators and administrators. Within the arena of WAC programs, there are six common conflicts that warrant isolation. These conflicts may appear to be simplifications and even abstractions, but they have served to help troubleshoot or clarify encounters between WAC evaluators and administrators in the past. An understanding of these conflicts should serve to ameliorate such encounters in the future.

1. *The clash between a vision of a part and a vision of the whole.* Almost by definition, evaluation of a program requires a restricted gaze. An evaluator who studies an upper-division writing-intensive program, for example, is constantly tempted to disregard the relevance of that program to the university as a whole. The attention is given to certain courses, certain teachers and students, and certain outcomes. The nature of empirical testing and inferential statistics further circumscribes that attention, and the evaluator may investigate only a sample of sections and test for a small selection of outcomes. When all is done, it is hard to resist speaking in the time-honored words of many a validation study and refuse to vouch for the implications of the conclusions beyond the few variables measured. But the administrator, however sympathetic, needs to go beyond. Decisions need to be made about the entire program, with constant attention to the ramifications of those decisions in terms of the university as a whole.

2. *The clash between description and action.* Indeed, when administrators rightly complain that the evaluation report lacks clear relevance to the formation of policy or fails to recommend a clear course of action, the evaluator may easily fall back on the researcher's defense that the study is purely descriptive and that others must decide on its implications. Descriptive findings, however, can be more or less useful. The evaluator can measure the number of pages submitted in writing-intensive courses, from which it is difficult to recommend further action, or to assess the value of the writing from the students' and the teachers' point of view, from which point recommendations for change are more readily seen. A wise evaluator will design the need for final recommendations right from the start.

3. *The clash between problem discovery and problem solving.* It is a temptation for program evaluators to think of assessment as a search for problems. Compar-

ison of syllabi from writing-intensive courses across disciplines should show some departments weaker than others in the integration of writing assignments with subject matter. This is a problem for which the administrator will wish the evaluator had included other findings indicating a solution. Of more use to the administrator might be the identification of especially successful teachers and techniques within disciplines, in which case recommendation for improvement is clearer. Again, evaluators could well be aware of the need to shape evaluation toward solutions from the beginning.

4. *The clash between expert and public understanding.* Evaluation of human performance has become a highly technical field in that every part of it has a professional history of unresolved debate. It is easy for knowledgeable evaluators (the more knowledgeable, the easier) to direct their reports to their own kind. Administrators need to send evaluation findings to persons and groups who may have little professional understanding of evaluation and even personal bias against aspects of it such as data collection and statistical analysis.

5. *The clash between the need for truth and the need for usefulness.* By nature and certainly by the creed and procedures of assessment methodology, the evaluator will present all the findings, the whole findings, and nothing but the findings, no matter how negative, discouraging, or confounding. There is even a commitment to report conclusions of the evaluation that suggest the evaluation itself was flawed. It is often very difficult for the administrator to make use of such an approach. Some of the most difficult standoffs between evaluator and administrator occur because of the imperative of one to report negative findings and the need of the other to have findings that are convincing, supportive, or persuasive for a particular constituency.

6. *The clash between abstractions and personalities.* Formal assessment asks that the evaluator move toward objectivity and abstractions whenever possible. The evaluator is looking for generalities that lie underneath the confusion of surface input, and is trying to set the eccentricities and individual agendas of the individuals involved in assessment — students and teachers — aside. The administrator, on the other hand, must deal directly with personalities because they are a means by which and an avenue through which things in a complex organization are accomplished. And the administrator must deal with them on a sui generis basis, knowing that each person is unique and that uniqueness often is the key to successful action through that person.

RECOMMENDATIONS

Having presented our own dialogue, which illustrates some of these clashes, we would like to follow our own advice and close with some recommendations for those asked to produce evaluations of WAC programs.

1. Ask as many questions as you politely can about the needs of your primary audience (who may or may not be the person requesting the assessment report). Who is your most important reader, and why does that person or committee want this evaluation? Is the purpose to find out how well the program works? To find out how cost efficient it is? To justify additional funding for (or slashing of) the program? Then sketch out as much as you can about this

primary audience and their intended utilization of the evaluation report. Your report (or as in our case, reports) will no doubt have multiple audiences, and you should not ignore them, but you should focus on the primary audience, usually central administrators, and the use they will make of the report.

2. Examine the sorts of documents that are consumed and produced by the office to which your report ultimately will go. Use these documents as models.

3. If at all possible, as you draft your report, carry on your own dialogue with an administrator who knows all the stakeholders and is willing to help you think through all the issues we have raised here. This dialogue will work best, we think, if that person is a mid-level administrator, not someone to whom the report will go, but someone who knows the personalities and their motives and who has experience writing similar reports and can help you phrase things where necessary in administrationese.

4. Focus on recommendations and action. Administrators rarely ask for reports so that they can file them — they are decision makers. They need evidence that they have made good decisions and evidence on which to base new ones. Think carefully about what you want to happen as a result of the information that you are presenting. Do the data suggest that you need a bigger budget for the program? Is the program growing at such a rate that you need a new computer to track it? Do you need (as it seems we do) some expertise to provide support for students whose first language is not English? Don't expect administrators to figure out what you need. Tell them the problems your data illuminate and then suggest a solution. For this audience, do not ignore the need for public relations. As members of the academic community, we tend to scorn self-promotion (although of course we can see that vice clearly in some of our colleagues). But public relations are an important part of any administrator's job. It is wise to offer a few choice sound bites to tout your program (if indeed it is toutable).

5. Find out about the budget cycle at your institution and what relationship your report might have to that cycle. Unless we have been involved with administration at the chair's level or above, most of us have little knowledge of how the budget process actually works. If we want resources for our program, we have to tie our evaluations and subsequent recommendations to the budget process.

If we may return to our opening point, writing an assessment of a WAC program tests all that the evaluator knows about rhetoric. We should take the advice we give our students: to figure out who the audience is, what the purpose and situation are, what the audience will do with what we send them; to tailor the format to meet the audience's needs, to use models to guide us, to ask for feedback on our drafts. This is less difficult than it may seem. After all, the distance between evaluator and administrator is not that great. Although we have contrasted their motives and roles, we also think it instructive to remember that both usually started out with the same experiences, as faculty. Where there are commonalties in experience, there are ways to communicate. We have presented our own dialogue as a model of the process, but as we have pointed out, rhetorical contexts for WAC programs differ markedly from institution to institution. Our final products may turn out useful at our university, but probably not at yours. To those WAC evaluators just starting, our final recommendation is to find someone at your institution with whom you can discuss your evaluation and carry out your own dialogue.

NOTES

1. See Richard Haswell and Susan Wyche-Smith, 1994; Haswell, *Gaining Ground*, Ch. 14; Susan McLeod, 1992.

2. A recent headline from this reporter read, "University President Lives Like a King at Taxpayer's Expense." The story had to do with the President's relatively modest budget for entertainment, all of which comes from donations to the institution, not from taxes.

REFERENCES

Gomm, R. (1981). Salvage evaluation. In D. Smetherham (Ed.), *Practising evaluation* (pp. 127–144). Chester, England: Bemrose Press.

Haswell, R. (1991). *Gaining ground in college writing.* Dallas: Southern Methodist University Press.

Haswell, R., Johnson-Shull, L., & Wyche-Smith, S. (1994). Shooting Niagara: Making portfolio assessment serve instruction at a state university. *WPA: Writing Program Administration,* 18, 44–53.

Haswell, R., & Wyche-Smith, S. (1994). Adventuring into writing assessment. *College Composition and Communication* 45(2), 220–236.

Haswell, R., & Wyche-Smith, S. (1996). A two-tiered rating procedure for placement essays. In T. Banta (Ed.), *Assessment strategies that work* (pp. 204–207). San Francisco: Jossey-Bass.

Messick, S. (1989). Meaning and values in test validation: The science and ethics of assessment. *Educational Researcher,* 18(2), 5–11.

Patton, M. (1986). *Utilization-focused evaluation* (2nd ed.). Newbury Park, CA: Sage.

Smith, M. L. (1986). The whole is greater: Combining qualitative and quantitative approaches in evaluation studies. In D. D. Williams (Ed.), *Naturalistic evaluation. New Directions for Program Evaluation* (Vol. 31, pp. 37–54). San Francisco: Jossey-Bass.

Swidler, A. (1986). Culture in action: Symbols and strategies. *American Sociological Review,* 51, 273–286.

16 A Process for Establishing Outcomes-Based Assessment Plans for Writing and Speaking in the Disciplines

MICHAEL CARTER

O utcomes-based assessment is gaining prominence in higher education. Many regional accreditation agencies are either strongly encouraging or requiring that colleges and universities under their purview instate this kind of assessment.[1] Professional accreditation organizations are also moving toward outcomes-based assessment. Perhaps the most dramatic case has been the American Board of Engineering and Technology (ABET), but there are others as well. For example, the National Council for Accreditation of Teacher Education, the Institute of Food Technologists, and the Council on Social Work Education are either considering or have fully established this assessment method for accrediting member institutions.[2] In addition, many colleges and universities, such as mine, have embraced outcomes-based assessment as a way of encouraging continual improvement in academic programs and of demonstrating accountability.

Outcomes-based assessment invites us to view our courses and curricula from a different perspective. We're used to thinking about education primarily in terms of inputs: we designate a particular set of courses for students to take and when the course count is completed we declare them educated and send them on their way. We assume that the inputs we provide for students will lead to certain outcomes, the knowledge, skills, and other attributes we believe graduates should possess. However, an outcomes-based approach to education does not rely only on assumption. By that method, faculty identify the educational outcomes for a program and then evaluate the program according to its effectiveness in enabling students to achieve those outcomes.

The main advantage of this outcomes perspective is that it provides data for closing the educational feedback loop, that is, faculty can use the results of program assessment to further improve their programs. In addition to this general benefit, an outcomes-based model also has potential advantages for writing and speaking professionals working in the disciplines. First, asking faculty in the disciplines to identify writing and speaking outcomes for their programs — either as part of an institution-wide initiative or, on a smaller scale, focusing individually on departments — encourages greater faculty investment in their students'

From *Language and Learning Across the Disciplines* 6.1 (2003): 4–29.

writing and speaking. Because these outcomes reflect the values and goals of the disciplinary faculty, not those of outsiders, the outcomes may possess greater credibility with the faculty in the discipline. The role of the writing and speaking professional, then, is to work with faculty in the disciplines to help them make their insider's knowledge and expectations explicit, to enable them to recognize and define their own expertise in writing and speaking in their disciplines.

Second, asking faculty in the disciplines to assess their students' writing and speaking based on the disciplinary outcomes they themselves have created places the responsibility for writing and speaking in the majors on the program faculty. Writing and speaking become intimately tied to disciplinary ways of thinking and professional discourses of the field. Thus, the quality of students' writing and speaking is also an indicator of students' ability to master the ways of thinking and professional discourses of a discipline. Communication abilities are not outside the discipline, solely the purview of writing teachers, but linked directly to the discipline and are thus the responsibility primarily of faculty in the disciplines. The role of the writing and speaking professional, then, is not to take on the task of teaching students to communicate more effectively but to better enable program faculty to meet their responsibility for their students' writing and speaking.

And third, involving disciplinary faculty in outcomes-based assessment encourages them to take a wider view of writing and speaking in their programs. One of the problems of incorporating writing- or speaking-intensive courses in the disciplines is that faculty tend to see communication as isolated within their programs, something to be taken care of elsewhere, not in their own courses. However, program outcomes lead to a programmatic perspective. Writing and speaking come to be seen as critical throughout the program. Students' failure to meet an identified outcome means that faculty must look at the entire program to identify opportunities to improve students' learning. The role of the writing and speaking professional is to help faculty recognize those opportunities and design instruction that will better enable students to meet the outcome.

Thus, the function of writing and speaking professionals may change in an outcomes-based model of assessment. This paper focuses on the first role mentioned above, helping faculty in the disciplines identify program outcomes and devise assessment procedures for measuring those outcomes. At my university, we have been involved in university-wide outcomes-based assessment for over five years and have developed a procedure for working with program faculty to generate assessment plans. I will present that procedure in detail here as an aid to writing and speaking professionals interested in initiating or in taking a more prominent position in an outcomes-based program on their campuses.

INSTITUTIONAL CONTEXT AT NC STATE

Institutional context is, of course, critically important. The particular history and ethos of a college or university shapes its writing and/or speaking programs in particular ways. In order to provide a better understanding of the NC State program, I will briefly describe its background.

In spring 1997, a university committee submitted a proposal for a rather modest writing-across-the-curriculum program instituting two writing-intensive courses within the majors, ideally one each in the junior and senior years. Much to our surprise, the proposal was rejected by the provost and deans, who asked us instead to design a more ambitious program that would: (1) focus on speaking as well as writing, (2) place primary responsibility for writing and speaking in the majors on the faculty in each department, and (3) hold departments accountable for writing and speaking in their majors through outcomes-based assessment. After a brief period of shock, we set about designing a discipline-specific, outcomes-based writing and speaking program.

It was clear that we could not simply expect the colleges and departments to manage writing and speaking assessment by themselves. Thus, the university created the Campus Writing and Speaking Program (CWSP) to provide guidance to departments for assessment and to offer faculty and course development related to writing and speaking. The CWSP began by creating a plan whereby it would work with each of the nine undergraduate colleges over five years to help departments generate writing and speaking outcomes and procedures for evaluating those outcomes. After this process had begun, the CWSP provided additional support for faculty through an extensive program of faculty development workshops, seminars, and grants.

In the fourth year of the five-year plan, another NC State faculty committee launched a university-wide assessment initiative that mandated all academic programs be reviewed periodically through outcomes-based assessment. This change in program review dove-tailed quite well with the ongoing writing and speaking assessment because we had realized very early in the process that, to a large extent, writing and speaking outcomes are also curricular outcomes: the sophisticated knowledge and skills that faculty expect of their graduates can best be demonstrated (as well as taught) by students' writing and speaking.

The university program review and the CWSP have worked closely with each other toward mutual goals. The program review has taken advantage of the fact that the campus had already been thinking in terms of outcomes-based assessment and so many departments had already generated assessment plans. The CWSP has taken advantage of the university's putting its full weight and resources behind outcomes-based assessment. The CWSP continued to work with departments in creating outcomes-based assessment plans.

NC State's CWSP represents one approach to writing and speaking in the disciplines. There are, however, other ways an outcomes-based model can be applied. For example, it could be used with just one department or college seeking a better focus for its curriculum. It could also be used in conjunction with writing- or speaking-intensive courses to help program faculty to consider students' communication abilities within a wider programmatic framework. The following process, then, may be useful in a variety of institutional contexts.

A PROCESS FOR GENERATING AN OUTCOMES-BASED PROGRAM ASSESSMENT PLAN

Outcomes-based assessment of academic programs typically seeks answers to three questions: (1) What are the outcomes — skills, knowledge, and other attributes — that graduates of the program should attain? (2) To what extent is the program enabling its graduates to attain the outcomes? and (3) How can faculty use what they learn from program assessment to improve their programs so as to better enable graduates to attain the outcomes?

The first question marks the starting point for the process; outcomes-based assessment must begin with outcomes. After identifying outcomes, program faculty answer the second question by assessing the program according to the outcomes, which requires an assessment procedure. The last of the three questions is the most important. The primary purpose of outcomes-based assessment is, as I have said, to provide program faculty the opportunity and the data for improving their programs. Faculty can close the feedback loop of the assessment process by using the data from the program assessment to discern strengths and weaknesses of the program and find ways to build on the strengths and target areas that need improvement.

In this paper, I will address the first two of the three questions, describing a process we have developed at NC State to guide faculty in the disciplines in identifying outcomes and generating assessment procedures to evaluate those outcomes. The following process is designed to meet three criteria. It should be:

1. student centered, i.e., it should place students at the center of the process by focusing on student learning outcomes;

2. faculty driven, i.e., it should encourage broad faculty investment in and responsibility for teaching and assessing program learning outcomes; and

3. meaningful, i.e., it should provide the data and the means for faculty to make valid and appropriate improvements in their programs.

1. *Setting the stage.* The initial goal of the assessment process is to establish a committee of program faculty for the writing and speaking professional as facilitator to work with. But before that can occur, it's important to prepare the way by involving college and departmental administrators in the process. Even though we are seeking a bottom-up engagement in assessment, we cannot ignore the top-down administrative structures of most colleges and universities. Sometimes this can be a time-consuming part of the process, so it's best to begin early.

Our work with each departmental program starts at the college level. The facilitator meets with the associate dean for academic affairs, the second-in-command after the dean, and also with the dean if she would like to be involved. We explain the institutional background of the assessment process, describe its goals, provide examples of assessment plans from other colleges, and then ask for guidance on how to proceed in that college. This latter move is the critical one. It includes the deans as partners in the process, allowing the facilitator to take advantage of their political stature within the college and their understanding of its culture. This usually provides a valuable insider's perspective into the college. Its programs, its needs, its politics, all of which may be useful in working with departments in the college.

Next, the facilitator moves to the level of department heads. We prefer to meet with the college deans and department heads together if such a venue is possible. The facilitator runs through the same topics as above, ending as before by asking the department heads for their suggestions for making the process work in their departments and in the college as a whole. If there is no opportunity for meeting with the heads together, then we set up individual meetings, also including the undergraduate coordinators or associate heads of the department and, perhaps, other critical faculty, such as the chair of the departmental curriculum and instruction committee. In a large university such as ours, we have found that it is the undergraduate coordinators or associate heads who typically become the primary and most valuable contact in the departments.

The last element of setting the stage is to visit faculty meetings of the various departments we will be working with. It is at this point that we begin to involve the faculty directly in developing an assessment plan. The facilitator gives a five-minute overview of the procedure, its goals, the process we will follow, a sample assessment plan from a similar department, and the potential value for the department's programs. After the short presentation, the facilitator takes questions for as long as the meeting's agenda allows, responding as frankly as possible (see Dealing with Resistance below). This is a critical meeting because it is where faculty buy-in must begin.

We have found that this procedure of working down through the administrative ranks works well at a university as large and decentralized as ours. Colleges and universities that are smaller or more centralized may not require such an elaborate operation for setting the stage. Whatever the situation, though, it is helpful for the facilitator to be sensitive to the political structure of the institution and to work effectively within that structure.

2. *Establishing a program assessment committee*. Creating the assessment plan is the task of a committee of program faculty who are assigned or volunteer to work with the facilitator. Usually, the undergraduate coordinator or associate head will appoint faculty to the committee or identify an appropriate standing committee to work with. We generally ask that the committee meet three criteria:

   a. it should be representative, i.e., it should be composed of faculty from the major elements of a department so that the final document produced by this committee reflects the outcomes of the faculty as a whole. For example, a committee from the department of history may consist of faculty from American history, modern European history, ancient and non-Western history, and philosophy of history and historiography.

   b. it should be large enough to be representative but not so large as to be unwieldy. We prefer groups in the range of five to eight faculty.[3]

   c. it should be able to focus its attention on the assessment plan. One of the problems with working with standing committees such as a department's curriculum and instruction committee is that they usually have very full agendas. One such committee kept putting us off for more pressing matters until the time allotted for them had disappeared.

How the facilitator interacts with these committees is also important. It's a good idea, for example, never to chair the committee. Not only would that bur-

den the facilitator with calling the meetings and sending out reminders and trying to work with faculty members' schedules, but it also projects the impression
that it is the facilitator who is in charge, the one who is responsible for the assessment plan, thus sending a mixed message as to her role as facilitator. In conjunction with that, the facilitator should also pay close attention to other aspects of
committee management in order to place authority and responsibility for the
process on the faculty. For example, always let the chair of the committee initiate
the meeting, avoid sitting at the head of a conference table, and defer whenever
possible to the chair when there are disagreements among members or logistical
issues to be decided. It is important to demonstrate that it is the program faculty
who are in charge of the process and that the facilitator is there primarily to make
their job easier.

3. *Explaining the task to the committee.* At the first meeting of the program assessment committee it is necessary to make sure all the members understand the
purpose and goals of the process. The facilitator may quickly restate some of the
material presented during the faculty meeting (if there had been a faculty meeting), place the committee's task within the broader assessment process of the university, and then describe in more detail what it is that the committee will produce
and the recommended process it may follow. The committee's assessment plan
will consist of objectives, outcomes, and a procedure for assessing the outcomes. It
is helpful for the facilitator to define each of these terms.[4]

   a. *Objectives* are broad goals that the program expects to achieve, defining
      in relatively general terms the knowledge and skills the program fac-
      ulty will help the students to attain.

   b. *Outcomes* are operational definitions for each of the objectives. Because
      educational objectives are broadly stated, they do not provide enough
      detail to be teachable and measurable, that is, to guide teaching in the
      curriculum and to be reliably assessed. Thus, they should be written in
      a way that is demonstrable, that is, they should state what it means to
      demonstrate the knowledge and skills named in the objectives.

   c. An *assessment procedure* outlines the methods program faculty will fol-
      low to determine the degree to which the program is enabling students
      to attain the outcomes. It typically identifies for each outcome what
      data will be gathered, what kind of assessment tools will be applied to
      the data, and when assessment will be done.

To help the committee members comprehend and keep up with the overall
process, we give them a checklist of the various tasks of the committee (see Figure
16–1). And to set their minds at ease about the commitment they are taking on, we
make it clear that mainly what we need from them is their time and disciplinary expertise. The work of drafting the assessment plan will be the job of the facilitator.

4. Dealing with resistance. As you can imagine, some faculty members may
be initially resistant to outcomes-based assessment. And this resistance is often expressed in the first meeting of the program assessment committee (also in the faculty meeting). We can certainly appreciate the source of such resistance.
Course-counting has served as our standard of practice for so long it is difficult for
many faculty to see any other way. A significant change in the status quo, and particularly the prospect of being held accountable for program outcomes, may un-
derstandably generate feelings of threat.

FIGURE 16–1   This handout is given to faculty on a program assessment committee. It outlines the initial steps in the outcomes-assessment process.

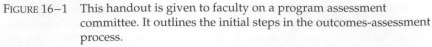

_____ 1. Draft of program objectives (a list of broad goals the program seeks to achieve)

_____ 2. Draft of program outcomes (a list of specific, teachable, and measurable skills, knowledge, and abilities majors are expected to achieve)

_____ 3. Objectives and outcomes approved by program faculty

_____ 4. Draft of program assessment procedure (the data to be gathered and the form of analysis to be used for each outcome)

_____ 5. Program assessment procedure approved by program faculty

_____ 6. Assessment initiated (begin to gather and analyze data)

_____ 7. Preliminary report submitted to college Courses and Curriculum Committee and University Academic Program Review:
- list of approved program objectives
- list of approved program outcomes
- approved program review plan
- results of initial assessment
- description of assessment activities to be carried out in the following year

So after the introductory remarks, the facilitator invites comments and questions about the assessment procedure (often an invitation is not necessary). It's extremely important that faculty be given the opportunity to speak their minds as well as that the facilitator demonstrate that she is open to their concerns and will not dismiss them. Often, we will spend the entire first meeting dealing with resistance. And that's perfectly fine. We know what drives it and do our best not to take it personally. The challenge is to avoid becoming defensive, to listen to faculty concerns and respond with empathy and good humor. In our experience, the overwhelming majority of resistant faculty will energetically engage in generating the assessment plan once they are able to voice their objections and to see that those objections have been heard.

Here are some of the questions and comments faculty may bring up:

- Why do we have to do this?

- Who's behind this, who's making us do this?

- Is there any evidence that this outcomes-based approach actually improves programs?

- Focusing only on measurable outcomes reduces our program only to what is measurable. All the nonmeasurable goals we have will no longer be of value.

- How's this going to be used against us? What kinds of punishment will there be if we don't meet our outcomes? Are we going to have our funding cut?

- We're already way too busy with what we're doing now. How in the world will we be able to find the time to do all this assessment stuff?

- We already give grades to students in our courses. Why can't we just use those grades for assessing our program. If students are passing our courses, that must mean we are doing a good job. Or doesn't the university trust the faculty?

- I think it's unfair to evaluate individual faculty this way.

- This process assumes there are problems with our program. What evidence is there that such problems exist?

- What happens if we don't do assessment?

These are all legitimate issues and deserve a fair response. Often they are the result of misunderstandings that can be easily clarified; sometimes they are only exhibitions of resistance. In all cases, the facilitator should take them seriously and respond as helpfully as possible. (Responses to some of these and other questions may be found at http://www.ncsu.edu/provost/academic_programs/uapr/FAQ/UAPRFAQ.html; see also Patton et al.).

5. *Eliciting information about program objectives and outcomes.* Now it's time to turn to the task of generating objectives and outcomes. We avoid asking the committee directly to identify program outcomes, which can make for a very constricted conversation punctuated by lots of squirming in chairs. Rather, it's best to start indirectly by asking open-ended questions that encourage faculty to talk about their program, particularly its value, what it offers its students, and what opportunities for student learning and performance of learning it provides (see Figure 16–2). Our strategy is to take detailed notes of the conversation generated by the questions, trying to capture as much of the language of the faculty as possible. It usually takes somewhere between forty-five minutes and one-and-a-half hours to get enough information to begin drafting objectives and outcomes.

We have found that it is best not to start this process with any list of departmental goals that may have been previously drawn up. Such goals are generally created by administrators and are not likely to encourage the faculty investment that comes of a process that involves the faculty in defining their own values for teaching and learning. Indeed, the facilitator will likely find that this step is the most enjoyable part of the process. Typically, all resistance disappears because faculty love talking about their programs, especially with a very interested outsider. Also, the experience provides the facilitator a unique opportunity to understand a discipline from an insider's perspective.

6. *Drafting objectives and outcomes.* The next, and perhaps the most challenging, step is to use the notes to draft objectives and outcomes that the program faculty will readily see as reflective of their own program. This means identifying the broader values or goals, which could become objectives, and the detailed information about each of those goals, which could become outcomes.

One way of doing this is to:

  a. type up and print the notes while the conversation is fresh and it is still possible to elaborate where the notes may be sketchy;

  b. read the printed notes several times, at first just to get a sense of the whole and then to search out superordinate ideas or themes: broad

FIGURE 16–2   These are questions the facilitator can use for initiating and guiding the conversation with faculty concerning program objectives and outcomes. They are meant to be heuristic, not to be rigorously covered by the facilitator.

Questions for Brainstorming Objectives and Outcomes

Imagine an ideal graduate from your program. What kinds of skills, knowledge, or other attributes characterize that graduate?

What is it that attracts students to this program?

What value does this program offer a student?

How do you know whether your students possess the kinds of abilities, knowledge, skills, and attributes you expect of them?

What kinds of assignments or other activities do people in this program use to encourage the kinds of abilities, knowledge, and skills you have identified?

What is it that distinguishes this program from related programs in the university?

Is there anything about your program that makes it stand out from other similar programs?

What kinds of research methodologies are people in this field expected to perform?

Oftentimes, disciplines are defined by ways of thinking. What does it mean to think like a person in this discipline?

What kinds of jobs do students in this field generally take?

What kinds of skills are appropriate to jobs in this field?

How do you know whether students possess those skills?

What advantages does a student in this program have on the job?

What sorts of speaking and writing do professionals in this field do on the job?

What sorts of speaking and writing do students do in their classes?

Are there any particular types of communication that people this field are expected to master?

---

concepts that emerge from the conversation, ideas that are repeated, points that faculty members particularly emphasized, key words or phrases that keep coming up, etc.;

c.   mark the themes in the text of the notes and make a list of them, eliminating all but the ones that seem to be most important to the faculty;

    d. rearrange the electronic version of the notes to create a rough thematic outline consisting of the themes and under each theme the subordinate ideas that are attached to it and define it in more concrete terms;

    e. draft formal objectives by starting with a heuristic sentence opener such as, "Graduates of the Department of X should be able to demonstrate that they can: . . ." and rewriting each objective, i.e., each theme, as the completion of the sentence;

    f. draft the outcomes for each objective also by starting with a sentence opener such as, "Specifically, graduates should be able to demonstrate that they can: . . ." and completing the sentence by incorporating, wherever possible, concrete verbs used by the faculty to indicate what students should be able to do — to describe, to analyze, to critique, etc. (when in doubt, Bloom's taxonomy provides a good source for such verbs).

See Figure 16–3 for an example of a final draft of objectives and outcomes.

7. *Reviewing the draft of objectives and outcomes with committee.* The next meeting of the committee is given over to reviewing the draft. At the end of the previous meeting, the facilitator should ask whether or not and in what form the committee members would like to see the draft before the following meeting. The facilitator will likely find, however, that even if they elect to review it, many if not most of the members won't read it ahead of time and often forget to bring the copy to the meeting. So it's helpful to arrive with a few extra copies.

The procedure that seems to work best is to read the draft aloud one objective and outcome at a time and, after each, to stop and give the members time to process the material and to ask questions and suggest revisions. As facilitators, we take great care to distance ourselves from the draft so as to give faculty full rein in criticizing it. We do not want the faculty to think that they are criticizing us personally. We actively invite revisions by asking questions about the draft as we go through it, pointing out areas we're uncertain about, asking for committee members' advice about the phrasing, etc.

This step marks a particularly productive point in the overall process because faculty are seeing their program set forth in black and white, usually in an explicitness that they've never encountered before. The course-counting approach to curriculum typically requires little if any discussion of its goals, keeping those goals safely implicit for each faculty member. However, outcomes make these goals explicit, often prompting useful disagreement among committee members as they discuss, usually for the first time, what it is that defines their programs. Generally speaking, the more abstract the discipline, the more disagreement there is. In many technical programs, there tends to be a broad consensus about the outcomes. But elsewhere, in the social sciences and humanities for example, the revision process can go through as many as six drafts.

It's helpful for the facilitator to encourage the faculty to do the hard work of revising together in the meeting, resisting attempts to put it all off on the facilitator to do it afterward. The outcomes need to reflect their words and their decisions. Use prompts such as: "How can we put that into words?" "What can we do here to make it better?" "How can we restate this so that you would agree with it?"

FIGURE 16–3   This document, created by anthropology faculty at NC State, contains the major elements of an assessment plan, program objectives, outcomes, and an assessment procedure.

Program Review
Department of Sociology and Anthropology
BA in Anthropology

PROGRAM OBJECTIVES
The objectives of the faculty in Anthropology are to:
1. provide instruction to enable students to understand the interrelationships among the social, cultural, and biological bases of human behavior

2. help students achieve competence in understanding, critically assessing, and using major anthropological concepts

3. introduce students to the various theoretical perspectives of anthropology and to encourage an appreciation for the historical development of the discipline as a social science

4. equip students with a knowledge of research methods appropriate to socio-cultural anthropology

5. encourage in students a rich understanding of and appreciation for cultural differences through knowledge of major forms of social organization from a cross-cultural perspective

PROGRAM OUTCOMES
Students should be able to demonstrate:
1. An understanding of the interrelationships among the social, cultural, and biological bases of human behavior. Specifically, students should be able to demonstrate that they:
   a. can describe critical cross-cultural *differences* in human behavior (in evolutionary and/or contemporary contexts) and to account for those differences in terms of the interplay among society, culture, and biology

   b. can describe critical cross-cultural *similarities* in human behavior (in evolutionary and/or contemporary contexts) and to account for those similarities in terms of the interplay among society, culture, and biology

2. Competence in understanding, critically assessing, and using major anthropological concepts. Specifically students should be able to demonstrate that they:
   a. can define major anthropological concepts in such a way that shows a firm grasp of the concepts

b. can apply major anthropological concepts to specific situations, showing that they are able to (1) use the concepts to organize and make sense of what they find in specific situations and (2) use specific situations to exemplify and amplify major anthropological concepts

3. A familiarity with various theoretical perspectives of anthropology and an appreciation for the historical development of the discipline as a social science. Specifically, students should be able to demonstrate that they:
   a. understand the major theoretical perspectives of anthropology

   b. appreciate the contribution of the major theoretical perspectives to the development of anthropology as a discipline

4. A knowledge of research methods appropriate to socio-cultural anthropology. Specifically, students should be able to demonstrate that they can:
   a. identify, define, and give examples of various methods used in anthropological research of contemporary societies

   b. recognize and interpret research methodology in anthropological literature

5. A rich understanding of an appreciation for cultural differences through knowledge of major forms of social organization from a cross-cultural perspective. Specifically, students should be able to demonstrate that they can:
   a. show that they are familiar with the major forms of social organization characteristics of the cultures of at least one non-Western ethnographic area

   b. show a rich appreciation for cross-cultural differences and an understanding of the importance of cultural context

SOURCES OF DATA FOR REVIEWING PROGRAM OUTCOMES

Exit interview question
Faculty survey of students' abilities
Portfolios of student work
- selected exams or other assignments from all 400-level courses except theory (ANT 411) and methods (ANT 416)
- selected assignments for ANT 411
- selected assignments for ANT 416
Student self-assessments
- ten-to-fifteen-minute in-class exercise in which students are asked to identify and comment on two major theoretical perspectives in anthropology
- ten-to-fifteen-minute in-class exercise in which students are asked to identify and comment on two major anthropological research methods

continues

FIGURE 16–3   *continued*

Outcome #1: an understanding of the interrelationships among the social, cultural, and biological bases of human behavior
- Exit interview question to be added to the existing instrument: "Did your program of study help you become aware of cross-cultural similarities and differences among human groups?"

Outcome #2: competence in understanding, critically assessing, and using major anthropological concepts
2a: to demonstrate that majors can define major anthropological concepts in such a way that shows a firm grasp of the concepts
- Faculty survey of students' abilities

2b: to demonstrate that majors can apply major anthropological concepts to specific situations, showing that they are able to (1) use the concepts to organize and make sense of what they find in specific situations and (2) use specific situations to exemplify and amplify major anthropological concepts
- Faculty survey of students' abilities
- Portfolio of selected exams or other assignments from all 400-level courses except theory (ANT 411) and methods (ANT 416)

Outcome #3: a familiarity with various theoretical perspectives of anthropology and an appreciation for the historical development of the discipline as a social science
3a: to demonstrate that majors understand the major theoretical perspectives of anthropology
- Portfolio of selected assignments for ANT 411
- Student self-assessment: ten-to-fifteen-minute in-class exercise in which students are asked to identify and comment on two major theoretical perspectives in anthropology

3b: to demonstrate that majors can appreciate the contribution of the major theoretical perspectives to the development of anthropology as a discipline
- Portfolio of selected assignments for ANT 411

Outcome #4: a knowledge of research methods appropriate to socio-cultural anthropology
4a: to demonstrate that majors can identify, define, and give examples of various methods used in anthropological research of contemporary societies
- Student self-assessment: ten-to-fifteen-minute in-class exercise in which students are asked to identify and comment on two major anthropological research methods

4b: to demonstrate that majors can recognize and interpret research methodology in anthropological literature
- Portfolio of selected assignments for ANT 416

Outcome #5: a rich understanding of and appreciation for cultural differences through knowledge of major forms of social organization from a cross-cultural perspective
• Faculty survey of students' abilities

PROGRAM REVIEW CYCLES
Initial Program Review Cycle

2001/2002: Develop program objectives, outcomes, and assessment plan; initiate assessment of outcomes

August 2002: Preliminary program review report submitted to CHASS Dean and to Committee for Undergraduate Program Review:
- program objectives
- program outcomes
- program review plan
- results of initial assessment
- description of assessment activities to be carried out in the following year

Fall 2002: Continue gathering assessment data and complete assessment of outcomes

Spring 2003: Assessment reports submitted to departmental Curriculum Committee:
- description of process of assessing program outcomes
- results of assessment
- recommendations for changes in curriculum and/or changes in outcomes and assessment plan

Departmental Curriculum Committee considers recommendations and takes them to faculty for discussion and approval

August 2003: Full program review portfolio completed and submitted to College for review and then, with any necessary revisions, to Committee for Undergraduate Program Review

Subsequent Seven-Year Review Cycles for University Program Review

2002–2005: Continue gathering assessment data at appropriate intervals

Fall 2004: Assessment reports submitted to departmental Curriculum Committee:
- description of process of assessing program outcomes
- results of assessment
- recommendations for changes in curriculum and/or changes in outcomes and assessment plan

continues

FIGURE 16-3   *continued*

Spring 2005:	Departmental Curriculum Committee takes recommendations to faculty for discussion and approval
August 2005:	Full program review portfolio completed and submitted to College for review and then, with any necessary revisions, to Committee for Undergraduate Program Review
2005–2008:	Continue gathering assessment data at appropriate intervals for third review cycle
Fall 2007:	Complete assessment of outcomes; assessment reports (including description of assessment process, results, and recommendations for changes in curriculum and changes in outcomes and assessment plan) submitted to Curriculum Committee
Spring 2008:	Curriculum Committee takes recommendations to faculty for discussion and approval
August 2008:	Program review report completed
August 2009:	Reports of both review cycles submitted to Committee for Undergraduate Program Review
Etc.	

8. *Getting full faculty approval for objectives and outcomes.* After the committee members accept a draft of the objectives and outcomes, they then decide how and when to take the draft to the rest of the faculty for discussion and approval. Making the assessment process truly faculty driven requires extending the process to the full program faculty. We recommend doing so at this point because the committee will need to have faculty approval of the objectives and outcomes before it begins to consider the assessment of the outcomes.

In most cases, the committee members will place a discussion of the draft on the agenda of the next scheduled faculty meeting. Of if there is no meeting soon, they may call a special one. But the logistics of bringing the full faculty into the conversation will vary according to the departmental culture. In some cases, committee members prefer to send the draft to their colleagues beforehand; sometimes they choose to handle the entire approval process by e-mail. The facilitator may or may not be asked to attend the meeting. Whatever the means, it has been our experience that objectives and outcomes are almost always accepted by the full faculty with at most a few minor revisions. Even so, it is critical to involve the rest of the faculty at this stage of the process.

9. *Identifying data and research tools for assessment procedure.* Once the program faculty have approved the objectives and outcomes, the next major task of the committee begins — deciding how to assess the outcomes. Even though we all access student learning in our classes, most faculty find it challenging to think in terms of program assessment. It is not assessing students, though it is likely to incorporate some materials produced by students. It is assessment that takes a programmatic perspective; its central question is, "To what extent is the full program enabling students to attain the outcomes designated by program faculty?"

An assessment procedure should identify data to be gathered, how the data are to be evaluated, and when assessment will take place. We have found that it's best to start by giving the committee members a list of possible assessment tools and going over the list to explain the kinds of assessment that are most applicable to the program (see Figure 16–4). This list helps to make program assessment more concrete for faculty and provides a valuable heuristic for talking about assessment. The tool that often arouses the greatest concern among faculty is the portfolio of student work. We tell them that the portfolio need not be longitudinal, collecting individual students' work over time, but is likely to be a best-case portfolio, meaning that faculty would identify the student performance that best represents students' ability related to an outcome, usually from a more advanced class, and collect a sample of that performance, such as a homework assignment, a video-tape of a presentation, a lab report, or a project report. In colleges and universities where assessment already plays an important role, such as through institutional use of portfolios or individual program accreditation, it is useful to link outcomes assessment, where appropriate, to assessment measures already required.

We ask faculty to apply two criteria to their decisions about assessment procedure: it should be valid (i.e., provide a way to measure what they want to measure) and it should be feasible (i.e., can be done with a reasonable outlay of resources). Sometimes there are faculty, particularly in the social sciences, who will cloud the issue by raising abstruse issues of research methodology. We assure them that for this kind of assessment it may not be necessary to meet rigorous research standards. Rather, the point is to gather data that will enable them to make judgments about their program and to use those judgments to guide decisions for improving it.

We begin this part of the process with brainstorming, going through the outcomes one at time and for each one asking how the faculty would know whether or not students were able to achieve the outcome. Then from the list of the means of assessment we have accumulated for each outcome, we identify the ones that best meet the criteria of validity and feasibility. Finally, we consider the timing of assessment, when and how often it is to be done; this may already be determined by college or university policy.

10. *Drafting and reviewing the assessment procedure.* Drafting the assessment procedure is much more straightforward than drafting the objectives and outcomes. During the meeting, the faculty committee has identified the key elements in the procedure. If the committee was not able to get through all the outcomes in one meeting, the facilitator should draft the ones they have done, review these at the beginning of the next meeting, and then finish the rest of the outcomes. The review of the assessment procedure typically runs to no more than two drafts. (See Figure 16–3 for an example of the assessment procedure.)

FIGURE 16-4   This list has been divided into relatively direct and indirect evidence as a way of encouraging faculty not to rely only on the latter. Though not all these assessment tools lend themselves to evaluating writing and speaking, most do.

**Possible Sources of Data for
Program Assessment**

SOURCES OF DATA THAT PROVIDE RELATIVELY DIRECT EVIDENCE

Samples of student work (longitudinal or best-case portfolios), such as:
- Homework assignments
- Essay tests
- Research reports
- Capstone projects
- Project proposals
- Student journals
- Reaction papers
- Literature reviews
- Oral presentations
- Student reflections on projects or other assignments

Formal observations of student behavior
External reviews of student projects
Internship reports
Standardized tests
Performance on national licensure examinations
Student self-assessments/reflections on learning

SOURCES OF DATA THAT PROVIDE RELATIVELY INDIRECT EVIDENCE

Alumni, employer, student surveys
Focus groups with selected students or alumni
Surveys of faculty concerning students' abilities
Discussions at faculty meetings or retreats concerning students' abilities
Senior exit interviews
Percentage of students going to graduate or professional schools
Enrollment and retention patterns
Job placement statistics
Reviews from accreditation agencies
Reports from external review committees

---

11. *Getting full faculty approval for assessment procedure.* This is a similar process to the approval of objectives and outcomes. The committee usually prefers to have the facilitator at the meeting to explain the logistics of some of the assessment procedures to the faculty.

CONCLUSION

An outcomes-based model for writing and speaking in the disciplines can be applied in different circumstances. For example, it can be used in a highly focused way with a single college, department, or even a program within a department. It can be used for a broader, campus-wide writing and speaking program. Or it can be used in conjunction with other outcomes-based initiatives, associated perhaps with university or program accrediting agencies.

In the last case, even though the primary motivation for assessment may not be the improvement of writing and speaking, the potential for such improvement is certainly strong, especially if writing and speaking professionals take an active role in the process. Indeed, writing and speaking professionals have the opportunity to enhance considerably their roles on campus by taking a lead in outcomes-based assessment. Our understanding of assessment, our experience in working with faculty from across the university, and our grasp of a wide variety of disciplines make us valuable players in the process.

Creating assessment plans is only the first step in a longer process. Writing and speaking professionals can also play important roles as the assessment process itself gets under way and faculty must gather data, make judgments based on the data, and devise changes to improve their programs. We can help faculty at each stage of the process through consulting and faculty development workshops. Outcomes-based assessment provides the impetus for continuous improvement of programs. We can play an important role in providing direction and support for that improvement.

Acknowledgment: I would like to recognize my colleagues Chris Anson, Director of NC State's Campus Writing and Speaking Program, and Deanna Dannels, Assistant Director, both of whom have made major contributions to our university's outcomes-based assessment process, placing the CWSP in the forefront of that process.

NOTES

1. For example, the Southern Association of Colleges and Schools sets as a standard that "The institution identifies expected outcomes for its educational programs. . . ; assesses whether it achieves these outcomes; and provides evidence of improvement based on analysis of these results" ("Principles of Accreditation" 11 http://sacscoc.org/accrrevproj.asp).

2. Information about the assessment procedures of these professional organizations may be found at their web sites: ABET at http://abet.org/accreditation; NCATE at http://ncate.org/accred/m_accreditation; IFT at http://ift.org/education/standards; and CSWE at http://cswe.org. Other organizations, such as the Council of Writing Program Administrators, have published national outcomes to encourage greater articulation among institutions and higher or more standardized expectations for student achievement (see http://www.cas.ilstu.edu/english/hesse/outcomes.html).

3. In smaller institutions, the faculty in entire departments may be fewer than the number of representatives mentioned here. Even at our university, we worked with one program with three faculty members, all of whom comprised the program assessment committee. When working with small programs, it is probably best to include all the faculty in creating assessment plans; it is certainly more efficient, and having the full faculty engage in defining their program can be beneficial.

4. Our usage of *objectives* and *outcomes* is derived from the assessment guidelines of ABET and formally designated by our university as common language for all programs. As a land grant university with a strong emphasis on engineering, this choice was appropriate. However, other colleges and universities with different traditions and perhaps even previously accepted assessment vocabulary may find language that is a better fit, goals and objectives or teaching aims and learning demonstrations, for example. We have found that having both general and specific levels for defining outcomes is useful for helping faculty generate assessment plans.

WORKS CITED

"ABET Accreditation." (14 July 2002). n. page. Online. Internet. 19 Oct. 2002. Available http://www.abet.org/accreditation.html.

"NCATE Accreditation Procedures: Accreditation." n. pag. Online. Internet. 19 Oct 2002. Available http://ncate.org/accred/m_accreditation.htm.

"CSWE Accreditation." n. pag. Online. Internet. 19 Oct. 2002. Available http://cswe.org.

Patton, Martha D., Aaron Krawitz, Kay Libbus, Mark Ryan, and Martha A. Townsend. "Dealing with Resistance to WAC in the Natural and Applied Sciences." *Language and Learning Across the Disciplines* 3.1 (October 1998): 64–76.

"Principals of Accreditation." (21 March 2001). 16 pp. Online. Internet. 19 Oct. 2002. Available http://sacscoc.org/accrevproj.asp.

"Undergraduate Education Standards for Degrees in Food Science." n. pag. Online. Internet. 19 Oct. 2002. Available http://www.ift.org/education/standards.shtml. Program Review Goals.

PART THREE

Issues

17 Influences on Evaluators of Expository Essays: Beyond the Text

SARAH WARSHAUER FREEDMAN

This study examines the relative effects on holistic scores given to college students' expository essays of three types of variables — essay variables, reader variables and environment variables. Sixty-four essays by students at four colleges were judged by four readers using a holistic scale and by two readers using a Diederich-type analytic scale. The essays were on eight topics. Readers were trained by two trainers. Of the three types of variables, the essay contributed most significantly to the variance in the holistic scores (p<.001). One of the environment variables, the trainers, contributed next most significantly (p<.01). Another environment variable, the topic, also affected the holistic scores. The readers judged consistently, their traits not affecting the variance in the scores. Finally, a comparison of ratings on the holistic and analytic scales revealed that the only additional information over the holistic score that the analytic scale yielded was a usage score.

In recent years, the student essay has become an increasingly common item on many standardized writing tests (e.g., the College Entrance Examination Board's *English Composition Test*, Educational Testing Service's *English Placement Test* in California and New Jersey, and local proficiency tests around the country such as the *Junior English Proficiency Essay Test* at San Francisco State University). Unlike multiple choice items on paragraph organization, sentence structure, and the like that accompany many of these essays, the essays cannot be scored by machine. Rather, they usually are scored in holistic evaluation sessions by large groups of hand-picked, trained, teacher-readers. Since the essay provides the only direct measure of writing and since the scor-

From *Research in the Teaching of English* 15.3 (1981): 245 – 55.

ing is not objective in the way that scoring a multiple choice item is, exact knowledge about why the essays are scored as they are yields information about how to interpret their very special scores. This study aims to provide information about such essay scoring, in particular about what influences readers to give the scores they do to expository, argumentative essays written as part of a writing test.

Several types of variables can influence the score that this type of essay receives. First of all, variables within the *essay* itself should influence the score — does the essay show sensitivity to the reader's needs by supplying enough background information, is the essay well organized, does the essay adhere to the surface conventions demanded in formal written prose? Second, variables within the *reader* may influence the score — is the reader strict or lenient, does the reader comprehend well, is the reader biased in any way? And finally, variables within the *environment* of the rating may influence the score — is the room well lit, is it morning or afternoon, who is doing the training and how is the training being conducted?

Past research on holistic rating falls into two types. In the first type, the researcher attempts, just as writing testers do, to hold the readers constant. Readers are chosen because they are a homogeneous group of English teachers who can discriminate well between papers with different characteristics and who can be trained to adjust their values with respect to those characteristics and thus rate reliably, that is agree well with one another. Once this homogeneous group of readers, who will probably score reliably, has been selected, the researcher attempts to determine what variables within the essays influence the readers to raise or lower their scores. The following studies take this approach: Page, 1968; Hiller, Marcotte, and Martin, 1969; Slotnick and Knapp, 1971; Thompson, 1976; Nold and Freedman, 1977; Harris, 1977; Freedman, 1979 a, b.

The second type of researcher on holistic rating attempts to study variables within readers. Most important here is the work of Diederich, French and Carlton (1961) who, by studying heterogeneous, untrained readers, proved, as Diederich wrote later, "how commonly and seriously teachers disagree in their judgments" (1974, p. 5). By analyzing the comments of the disagreeing readers Diederich and his colleagues contributed to knowledge about the basis of readers' natural disagreements and provided the field with ideas on how to train readers to lose their biases and to agree better with one another. He also developed an analytic rating scale (Diederich, 1974) which is based largely on the types of comments his readers made. Meyers, McConville, and Coffman (1966) examined how 25 readers rated 25 of the 20-minute essays written for the 1963 *English Composition Test*, observing whether the readers actually rated globally and checking to see whether or not their scores reflected different values about the qualities requisite to good compositions. Meyers et al. found that some raters were more lenient than others but that otherwise their values about the essays seemed to be similar.

Both types of past research only partially answer the fundamental question: why do evaluators award the scores they do to student papers? It should be noted that no one has even begun to examine the effects of the rating environment on raters' scores.

In this study, I explore the relative effects of the three sources of variables — essay, reader, and environment (including essay writer) — on the essay score and the particular effects within the environment that affect the score.

METHOD FOR WRITER AND TOPIC SELECTION

Writers

Four San Francisco Bay Area colleges, providing writers representing a wide range of abilities, participated in the study. According to Cass and Birnbaum's (1972) most recent descriptions of admissions criteria, the schools, in order from most to least selective admissions requirements were: Stanford University, University of Santa Clara, California State University at Hayward, and San Jose City College. A sample of eight students was taken from each of two classes at each institution — 16 students per school, 64 writers in all. The classes were obtained on the recommendation of the department chair who was asked to suggest two "typical" classes taught by different teachers. In order to assess further the typicality of the classes, the investigator also interviewed the teachers. Writers were selected from within the two classes at each school.

Topics

I selected eight essay topics, four asking students to compare and contrast two *quotations* and four asking students to argue their *opinion* on a current controversial issue. The following topics illustrate each type:

1. A Founding Father said: "Get what you can, and what you get hold; 'Tis the Stone that will turn all your Lead into Gold.'"

   A contemporary writer said: "If it feels good, do it."

   What do these two statements say? Explain how they are alike and how they are different.[1]

2. The Supreme Court has ruled that no state may deny a woman an abortion within the first six months of her pregnancy. Do you agree or disagree with this decision? Give reasons for taking your position.

The other eight topics, modelled after those above, can be found in Freedman, 1977.

This study is limited to evaluations of papers on topics in the argumentative mode of discourse so that differences in evaluations caused by mode of discourse would not have to be examined. The argumentative mode was chosen because it is so frequently demanded of college students in test situations.

Procedure for Collecting Essays

Each student in the class received one of the eight topics and wrote during forty-five minutes in his or her class. Only eight essays, one on each topic, were used in the study. Teachers distributed the essay topics in all except one Stanford class in which the investigator administered the essay.

After all essays were collected, the investigator coded them and had them typed to conceal the identity of the writers and to facilitate the evaluation process. Typing also avoided the inevitable effects of handwriting on raters (Markham, 1976). The essays were transcribed exactly, including all errors.

Method for Evaluating Essays

I aimed to examine *how* well-qualified readers judge essays. Therefore, for this first evaluation of the essays, I selected the four most qualified readers available, whom I paid to perform the evaluations. All expected to complete their doctorates in English literature at Stanford in the immediate future; all had taught writing requirement classes for at least three years. Their superiors in the English department at Stanford recommended them as excellent teachers and as able evaluators of college student prose.

Table 17–1 contains the plan for collecting the holistic ratings during four sessions on two mornings. During each of the four sessions on each day, two readers rated one topic while the other two rated a different topic. One pair rated an opinion topic; the other pair rated a quotation topic. Each pair was trained by a different trainer. The pairs of readers changed, rotating in a

TABLE 17–1   Plan for Collecting Ratings

	Day 1	
	X	Y
I	RS-3	TU-8
II	RU-4	TS-2
III	TU-6	RS-5
IV	TS-7	RU-1
	Day 2	
	X	Y
I	TU-5	RS-6
II	TS-1	RU-7
III	RS-8	TU-3
IV	RU-2	TS-4

Key to abbreviations: R, S, T, and U are the four readers; X and Y are the two trainers; the quotation paper topics are 1, 2, 3, and 6; the opinion topics are 4, 5, 7, and 8. I, II, III, and IV refer to the different rating sessions.

balanced way from one session to the next. The balancing insured that both quotation and opinion topics were read first and last, so that the effect on the readers' scores of the order of judging each type of topic could be examined. The balancing also insured that both trainers would train all raters, so that the effect of a particular trainer on a particular rater could be examined. Furthermore, the same readers did not always evaluate together, so that agreement between readers could be determined not to be merely pair specific. No time limits were set for the length of the sessions beforehand so that the evaluators would feel no pressure to rush through their task. Analytic ratings were collected during the afternoons.[2] On the first afternoon, sessions I and II of the morning were repeated; on the second afternoon, sessions III and IV of the first morning were repeated.

The training packets for each topic contained two training essays. Holistic scoring forms were included for training before holistic evaluations; an analytic scale and scoring forms were included for training for the analytic evaluations. In the reading packets several additional training essays preceded the eight experimental student essays. The reading packet always consisted of eleven essays with the potential training essays first and the eight student essays next. The eight student essays for the study were randomized twice for each reader, once for the holistic ratings and once for the analytic ratings.

PROCEDURE FOR EVALUATING ESSAYS

The evaluators judged the original essays on two Saturdays, two weeks apart. Before the evaluations, the readers were informed only that all essays were produced mostly by college students during a 45-minute, in-class session.

On the first morning every reader evaluated four of the eight topics according to the four-point holistic rating scale. The holistic rating sessions lasted approximately one hour each. The analytic scale demanded extra time for rating; the afternoon analytic evaluation sessions lasted about two hours each.

Pairs of readers were trained for each topic before every holistic and analytic rating. Training aimed to establish a realistic context for the rating and to provide opportunity to practice applying the rating scales.

In the end, all four readers judged all eight topics with the holistic scale. Every reader judged the papers on four topics with the analytic scale, two readers judging each topic analytically. So each paper received four holistic and two analytic ratings.

RESULTS

Evaluator Reliability

To establish the readers' reliability, Cronbach's alpha (Cronbach, 1970) was computed. Even with only two readers giving a score to each essay on day one and on day two, the consistency of the differences in the papers proved quite high ($\alpha = .58$ and $\alpha = .62$) while there was little consistent difference between the readers ($\alpha = .0$). After combining the readers' scores across both days so that each paper received four scores, the reliability of the differences in papers was even higher ($\alpha = .84$) and the consistency of differences between readers was extremely low ($\alpha = .20$). Thus, it was concluded that all four of the readers consistently agreed with each other on the scores they gave the student papers, that indeed the group rated homogeneously.

Influences of Essays, Topics, and Evaluation Procedure on Holistic Evaluations

An analysis of variance was performed to determine how parts of the readers' environment during the rating affected differences in scores (Table 17–2). In comparing the effects of the reader, the essays and parts of the environment on the essays' scores, it was found that characteristics of the essays themselves contributed most to the scores ($p < .001$). The only other contributor to the scores proved to be one part of the environment, the trainers. The readers did not contribute significantly to the differences in the scores they gave, an indication of their homogeneity.

Although the different topics and different types of topics did not affect the scores significantly, readers gave higher scores to one of the opinion topics. A further analysis of how the two separate types of topics contributed to

TABLE 17–2   Analysis of Variance for Holistic Scores: Contributions of Parts of the Environment for the Reading

Score	df	MS	F
Reader (R)	3	.45	1.33
Topic (T)	7	2.42	1.81
Type (Ty)	1	3.75	5.95
T (Ty)	6	2.20	1.50
Essays (T(Ty))	56	2.27	6.72***
Sessions	3	.75	2.28
Day	1	.09	.27
Trainer	1	3.28	9.72**
R × T	21	1.34	
R × Ty	3	.63	
R × (T(Ty))	18	1.46	
R × Essays (T(Ty))	163	.37	

F ratio for the sources T, Ty, and (T(Ty)) are based on the corresponding R interactions (i.e., R × T, R × Ty, and R × (T(Ty))).
All other F ratios are based on the main residual, R × Essays (T(Ty)).
**$p < .01$
***$p < .001$

TABLE 17–3   Holistic Evaluations by Topics

			Summed Holistic Scores for Each Topic				
	Quotation				*Opinion*		
63	66	72	70	76	73	90	63

Analysis of Variance for Holistic Scores: Contributions of Topic Types

	df	MS	F1
Readers	3	.45	
Topic Type	1	3.75	
Topic (Q)	3	.51	1.21
Topic (O)	3	3.89	7.66***
Essays (Topic (Q))	28	2.64	6.33***
Essays (Topic (O))	28	1.90	3.75***
Readers × Essays (Topic (Q))	84	.42	
Readers × Essays (Topic (O))	84	.51	

***$p < .001$

the variance between the holistic scores revealed a significant difference between the scores given the different opinion type topics (Table 17–3). Although these similar topics did not call for different scores generally, topics can affect raters' scores.

Relationship Between Holistic and Analytic Rating Scales

Table 17–4 details the Pearson product moment correlations between the holistic score, six categories of the analytic rating scale, and the sum of the scores on the categories of the analytic scale. The correlation matrix reveals high correlations between all scores except the ones for usage.

    Because of the extent of the correlations, a factor analysis was carried out to determine a simpler structure for the rating scales. To examine the categories of the analytic scale with the factor analysis, I created three orthogonal, linear contrast scores from the categories of the scale. Table 17–5 shows how the numerator for each contrast was computed. In forming the first contrast, *content/style*, I hypothesized that three of the categories, voice, development, and organization, should measure most directly the overall content of a composition and that sentence structure, word choice, and usage most likely measure more micro-stylistic aspects of a composition. The first contrast opposed these two subcategories of the analytic scale, content and style. Next I hypothesized that voice was somewhat discrete from development and organization and that usage was somewhat discrete from word choice and sentence structure. Voice should measure the personality behind the prose; development and organization should measure how the writer treated the content in

TABLE 17–4   Pearson Correlations of Different Ratings

	HSC	ASC	V	D	O	SS	WC	US
Holistic Score (HSC)	1.00	.76	.67	.76	.74	.63	.61	.36
Analytic Score (ASC)		1.00	.86	.93	.91	.83	.84	.63
Voice (V)			1.00	.83	.73	.64	.66	.41
Development (D)				1.00	.84	.73	.74	.46
Organization (O)					1.00	.75	.69	.45
Sentence Structure (SS)						1.00	.75	.57
Word Choice (WC)							1.00	.58
Usage (US)								1.00

terms of expanding and ordering it. This contrast was labeled *voice/content*. Usage should measure purely mechanical aspects of standard edited English like punctuation and capitalization. Sentence structure and word choice, on the other hand, should not be dictated completely by matters of convention and thus should have more to do with the writer's actual style. This third contrast was labeled *usage/style*.

A principal component factor analysis with varimax rotation was performed on the correlation matrix of the three linear contrast scores, the holistic score, and the sum of the categories on the analytic scale. The results of the factor analysis, also in Table 17–5, reveal that the five contrast scores represented two discrete, independent qualities of the papers, two factors. The two

TABLE 17–5   Factors from Rating Scales

Linear Contrast Scores from Analytic Scale		
Content/Style = V + D + O − SS − WC − US		
Voice/Content = 2V − D − O		
Usage/Style =		SS + WC − 2US

	Factor Loadings	
	Factor 1	*Factor 2*
HSCORE	.837	.326
ASCORE	.845	.148
CONTENT/STYLE	.259	.782
VOICE/CONTENT	−.255	.011
USAGE/STYLE	−.003	.583

Abbreviations: V = voice; D = development; O = organization; SS = sentence structure; WC = word choice; US = usage; HSCORE = holistic score; ASCORE = analytic score variables loading highest on Factor 1 after rotation were the holistic and summed analytic scores. The variables loading highest on Factor 2 proved to be the content versus stylistic categories and within the stylistic categories usage versus the others. In short, these two factors suggested that holistic and analytic scales measured one trait of compositions, and that a stylistic category can be separated from a content category with usage probably dominating the separation.

DISCUSSION

The unexpected significant effect on the holistic scores caused by the different trainers was disturbing. The investigator and a colleague, who is a known expert on evaluation, conducted the training sessions. Both trainers worked together before the rating sessions to plan and standardize the training. We purposefully aimed to avoid the training effect by selecting training essays on each topic that represented the range of the responses and by agreeing on the scores we thought these training essays deserved. For the training, we planned first to discuss the topic and then to present these essays to the readers.

After finding differences in scoring due to trainers, I reviewed tape recordings of the training sessions, looking for differences in the *actual* training that might have contributed to the effect. I found first that the two trainers approached the discussion of the topics differently. The first trainer simply presented the topic, and the readers discussed its meaning. The second trainer asked the readers to discuss what they would expect from a good essay on the topic. During the discussion, this trainer reminded the readers that the students only had 45 minutes to complete the task. Such a discussion could have lowered the readers' expectations for a good essay and encouraged them to award higher scores. The readers did award higher scores under this trainer.

Interestingly, during the discussion of the training essays, the trainers stuck to their agreed upon scores, but sometimes they differed in how they handled the discussion about the scores. For example, in one case in which the trainers had previously agreed on a 2 for a particular essay, the two readers in each session each gave a 2 and a 1. Both trainers revealed that they had agreed on a 2 for the essay, but the first trainer then continued by saying that the trainers thought the essay represented the low range of the 2's and that they could understand a 1 score. Given the same situation, the second trainer continued by saying that 1's should be saved for worse essays. Again, it was this second trainer who elicited higher scores from the readers.

Although I cannot say why the trainers caused scoring differences, in retrospect I hypothesize that subtle and not such subtle remarks can push readers to score higher or lower, regardless of the training essays. It stands to reason that if readers can be trained to agree, they can also be trained, advertently or inadvertently, to score higher or lower. Since readers have a natural tendency to rate low, to shy away from using the upper end of the scoring range, it is traditional in training sessions for holistic scoring to push readers to raise their scores (see "How the Essay in the CEEB English Composition

Test is Scored: An Introduction to the Reading for Readers," ETS mimeo, 1976, p. 4). But no one has investigated exactly what it takes for a trainer to effect that push, and no one has explored whether or not readers can be pushed too much.

This study establishes the fact that training changes readers' rating behavior. To establish the cause of the trainer effect, I recommend experiments in which carefully described training conditions are varied. I know of no cases in which the differential effect of trainers has been investigated. Usually small research projects employ only one trainer; large scale readings, as for College Board or Educational Testing Service employ many trainers, but all are under the direction of one chief trainer, the question leader. In small scale projects the investigator probably should not train the evaluators. Since trainers affect evaluators and since the investigator knows the results he or she expects, the investigator may help to produce, either intentionally or unintentionally, the hypothesized results with the training. In all projects, the effect of trainers needs to be monitored more precisely; what is it that trainers do and what causes their influence?

Although this study shows that topics generally do not affect readers' scores, it shows that topics can have significant effects. Because in most testing situations the topic must change from one administration to the next in order to insure the security of the test, topics should be pretested carefully enough to establish their equivalence with past topics. Indeed because both topics and trainers usually change with the test administration and because both of these variables can significantly affect essay scores, it becomes impossible to compare test results from one administration to the next; for that matter, it becomes difficult to compare research results which do not account for the effects of topics and trainers.

The high correlation between the holistic scale and all categories of the analytic scale except usage indicates that researchers and testers should not use the more time-consuming analytic scale. They will gain little more from it than from a holistic rating. Techniques for gaining additional information beyond a usage score remain to be discovered. It is possible that the scales showed such high correlations in this study because the design allowed the evaluators to remember the holistic scores they gave, and the raters adjusted their analytic score to match the holistic scores. This seems unlikely, however, because there was a two-week lapse between the holistic and analytic ratings for half of the papers. Also, the raters were instructed that if they remembered their earlier holistic scores, they were not to be concerned about giving different ratings to the same paper because the analytic scoring allowed them extra time to ponder. It was expected that this extra thought would allow them a chance to "correct" any "mistakes" they made during the snap judgment required by the holistic scoring.

In general, the strong relationship between the two scales could be due to the fact that the raters were unable to separate the categories. Descriptions of the categories on analytic scales must be written to remove any inevitable relationship between them. I revised the Diederich and Adler analytic scales so that the categories would be described more discretely. However, my rewriting for some of the categories was probably not extensive enough. For example, the low range under "voice" is described as follows: "The reader gets the sense that the writer has nothing to say on the topic. It is either difficult to tell what this writer is trying to get across, or the thoughts are so silly as to be better left unsaid." It is difficult to imagine a paper fitting this description also to fit under the high range of "development": "A thesis guides this paper; all points clearly relate to it. Each main point proving the thesis is supported concretely, with sound arguments or convincing examples." Such descriptions insure the correlation of the scores for voice and development. However, descriptions of other categories (e.g., organization and sentence structure) appear to allow for discrete ratings. In such cases, the correlation that occurred might have been lessened by training the readers more intensely in the application of the scale. It is still possible that the relationships between these categories stem from the way writers write; a writer who performs well or poorly on one category will do similarly on most of the others and on a holistic scale. In any event, the reasons for these high correlations deserve further investigation.

In spite of the significant effects of trainer and topic on essay scores and in spite of the high correlation between the holistic and analytic rating scale, the essays themselves still contributed most to the different scores ($p<.001$). In another study, I examined the relative effects on readers' scores of four qualities within the essays: development, organization, sentence structure and mechanics. I found the larger discourse categories of development and organization to be most influential (Freedman, 1979 a, b). Finally, the readers themselves and two parts of the rating environment, the session of the rating day did not affect the scores.

In conclusion, the influences on readers' scores are numerous. Although the essay itself contributes most to the score, other influences beyond the text, such as the trainer and the topic, also have their effects.

NOTES

1. This quotation topic was first developed by the California State University and College System for their Freshman English Equivalency Examination.
2. The analytic rating scale was adapted from scales developed by Diederich (1974) and Adler (1971) and can be found in Freedman (1977).

REFERENCES

Adler, R. *An investigation of the factors which affect the quality of essays by advanced placement students.* Unpublished doctoral dissertation, University of Illinois at Urbana-Champaign, 1971.

Cass, J., & Birnbaum, M. *Comparative guide to American colleges* (5th ed). New York: Harper & Row, 1972.

Cronbach, L. *Essentials of psychological testing* (3rd ed.). New York: Harper & Row, 1970.

Diederich, P. *Measuring growth in English.* Urbana, Ill.: National Council of Teachers of English, 1974.

Diederich, P., French, S., & Carlton, S. *Factors in judgments of writing ability* (Research Bulletin 61–15). Princeton, N.J.: Educational Testing Service, 1961.

Freedman, S. *Influences on the evaluators of student writing.* Unpublished doctoral dissertation, Stanford University, 1977.

Freedman, S. How characteristics of student essays influence teachers' evaluations. *Journal of Educational Psychology*, 1979, *71*, 328–338. (a)

Freedman, S. Why teachers give the grades they do. *College Composition and Communication*, 1979, *30*, 161–164. (b)

Harris, W. Teacher response to student writing: A study of the response patterns of high school English teachers to determine the basis for teacher judgment of student writing. *Research in the Teaching of English*, 1977, *11*, 175–185.

Hiller, J., Marcotte, D., & Martin, T. Opinionation, vagueness, and specificity distinctions: Essay traits measured by computer. *American Educational Research Journal*, 1969, *6*, 271–286.

Markham, L. Influences of handwriting quality on teacher evaluation of written work. *American Educational Research Journal*, 1976, *13*, 277–283.

Meyers, A., McConville, C., & Coffman, W. Simplex structure in the grading of essay tests. *Educational and Psychological Measurement*, 1966, *26*, 41–54.

Nold, E., & Freedman, S. An analysis of readers' responses to essays. *Research in the Teaching of English*, 1977, *11*, 164–174.

Page, E. Analyzing student essays by computer. *International Review of Education*, 1968, *14*, 210–225.

Slotnick, H., & Knapp, J. Essay grading by computer: A laboratory phenomenon? *Educational Measurement*, 1971, *9*, 253–263.

Thompson, R. *Predicting writing quality, writing weaknesses that dependably predict holistic evaluations of freshman compositions.* English Studies Collections, Series 1, No. 7, 1976. (Available from Scholarly Publishers, 172 Vincent Drive, East Meadow, New York 11554.)

18   *"Portfolio Scoring": A Contradiction in Terms*

ROBERT L. BROAD

Certainly any theory of aesthetic value must be able to account for continuity, stability, and apparent consensus as well as for drift, shift, and diversity.

— Barbara Herrnstein Smith, "Contingencies of Value" (19)

Suppose we were to take up Barbara Herrnstein Smith's challenge in the specific context of communal portfolio assessment. How might we account meaningfully for both consensus *and* diversity among our evaluations of student writing? How would we have to change our attitudes toward evaluative disagreement in order to make sense of that disagreement?

In the noble tradition of Galileo, let's conduct an imaginary experiment. Subject A walks into a room full of writing-assessment specialists and utters this speech: "When people *agree* in their evaluations of student writing, things are working just as they should. Their agreement constitutes useful information about the text being evaluated and about the group conducting the evaluation." What response does Subject A's speech elicit? Friendly nods, pats on the back.

Now Subject B walks into the same room and pronounces the following: "When people *disagree* in their evaluations of student writing, things are working just as they should. Their disagreement constitutes useful information about the text being evaluated and about the group conducting the evaluation." What reaction might Subject B expect? Cold stares, turned backs.

Disagreement is a fly buzzing crazily around the clean white room of communal writing assessment, and we seem bent on exterminating the insect no matter what precious objects we break and no matter whom we bruise in the process. Dominant voices in our field consistently portray "discrepant" readings as the result of incompetence or ill intent: "Excessively rigid teachers or those who are insecure often have difficulty adopting group standards, and faculty who take pride in their differences with their colleagues may resent the

From *New Directions in Portfolio Assessment*, eds. Laurel Black, Donald A. Diaker, Jeffrey Sommers, and Gail Stygall. (Portsmouth, NH: Boynton/Cook, 1994), 263–76.

entire process" (White, *Teaching* 157). In the name of "fairness" and "science," they exhort us to seek ever higher levels of numerical agreement among scorers, a goal well known to us as "inter-rater reliability."

Edward M. White, for example, *defines* reliability as fairness (*Teaching* 22), and has stated flatly that "A reader who scores differently from everyone else is wrong" ("Portfolios"). We shouldn't be surprised, then, when White censures Peter Elbow's recent suggestion that reliability may not be worth what it costs us. Reviewing Belanoff and Dickson's *Portfolios: Process and Product*, White admonishes Elbow and other skeptics of reliability in ominous tones:

> We do not have to throw away fairness to be honest in our measurement, and we make ourselves irrelevant to serious measurement if we assert that we must . . . Unreliable measures are merely subjective impressions by disparate individuals and we have more than enough of that already . . . (Review 538)[1]

I advocate communal writing assessment precisely because I agree with White that we have "more than enough" teachers grading as "disparate individuals" in isolation from one another. I must, however, protest White's disparagement of disagreement as "subjective impressions" and his appropriation of the weighty terms "fairness," "honesty," and "serious measurement." I want to re-appropriate each of those terms and propose a substantial shift in our theory and practice of communal writing assessment.

We need to transform our notions of consensus and differences in the context of communal writing assessment much as John Trimbur has transformed them in the area of collaborative learning:

> We need to see consensus . . . not as an agreement that reconciles differences through an ideal conversation but rather as the desire of humans to live and work together with differences. The goal of consensus . . . ought to be not the unity of generalizable interests but rather what Iris Marion Young calls "an openness to unassimilated otherness." ("Consensus and Difference in Collaborative Learning" 615)

As the culmination of twenty years' rapid movement toward more and more enlightened evaluation of writing, portfolio assessment cries out for just such "openness to unassimilated otherness"; yet "difference" remains a dirty word in most large-scale evaluation settings. In my view, portfolio assessment both deserves and demands that we reconsider the meanings and merits of evaluative disagreement.

Let me begin with a few critical observations regarding the nearly universal twin practices of scoring portfolios and demanding evaluative consensus. For starters, I propose that quantification and the demand for agreement intertwine theoretically and reinforce one another practically; quantification and statistical reliability make perfect partners. I further suggest that those twin practices not only contradict our best theoretical insights — including those that undergird the very practice of portfolio assessment — but also lead us to deceive our students and to abuse our colleagues and ourselves.

Everything I argue here follows from a single premise: that the construction of textual meaning depends upon social context. While this axiom has so far been much more commonly discussed among literary theorists than among compositionists, I nevertheless understand it to be widely accepted by those in both the literary and the rhetorical subfields of English. In the opening pages of *What is English?*, Peter Elbow recounts as the "main conclusion" of the 1987 English Coalition Conference that " . . . we see the same *constructive and social activity* [of making meaning] as the central process at all levels of the profession of English. . . . At all levels we stressed how this central activity is *deeply social*" (18, emphasis added).

Below, I group my initial premise with several corollaries that follow from it, and illustrate each statement with examples.

Main Premise: *The construction of textual meaning depends upon social context.*

The "OK" gesture, interpreted in U.S. culture to signify cheerful agreement, in Mediterranean cultures is taken as an insult with clear references to aberrant sexual behavior. Similarly, the phrase "make love" encountered in a 17th-century lyric poem likely refers to various acts of courtship (including the composition of love poems), whereas the same phrase found in 20th-century verse likely suggests activity subsequent to courtship (and probably exclusive of literary pursuits).

Corollary #1: *Textual value, being inextricably bound up with textual meaning, also depends upon social context.*

In "Contingencies of Value," Barbara Herrnstein Smith proposes an inquiry that would foreground the link between textual value and social context: "The type of investigation I have in mind . . . would seek to explore the multiple forms and functions of literary evaluation, institutional as well as individual, in relation to the circumstantial constraints and conditions to which they are responsive [including] specific local conditions . . ." (14).

Corollary #2: *We can establish no single, fixed meaning or value for any text.*

Laura Bohannon's "Shakespeare in the Bush" offers an entertaining illustration of the mutability of value and meaning. Recounting the story of *Hamlet* to members of an un-Westernized African culture, she is startled when her listeners not only radically re-interpret the tale, but also correct the "mistakes" Shakespeare made in telling the story and impugn Shakespeare's literary capabilities.

Corollary #3: *Differences of interpretation and evaluation are not only inescapable, they are downright wholesome elements of everyday rhetorical experience*, elements that we do harm to ourselves and our students in trying to conceal or extirpate.

The powerful concept of "interpretive community" is often invoked to explain why evaluators in a given large-scale assessment must agree in their judgments of a given text. If, however, such an "interpretive community" includes — as it often will — rhetoricians, literary types, Africanists, Marxists, feminists, creative writers, technical writers, New Critics, New Historicists, grammarians, expressivists, graduate students, adjuncts, and tenured faculty, then we achieve agreement only by bleaching out the kaleidoscopic quilt of values which comprises the *true* community of many English departments. A bit later, I present the story of "Martha" by way of example.

Working from this theoretical basis, I believe we can and should change our attitudes toward difference in large-scale writing assessment. And nowhere is the need for this change more urgent than in the realm of portfolio assessment.

The peculiarly 20th-century hunger to quantify writing ability and demand interrater agreement has never, in my view, served teachers and students of writing well. In the current context of the portfolio assessment boom, that penchant for quantification and homogenization seems even more questionable. Figure 18–1, "A (Very) Brief History of Large-Scale Evaluation in the Department of English at Miami University," illustrates why.[2]

Compare the striking developments in "evaluative INPUT (what the students do)" to the puzzling stasis of the "evaluative PRODUCT." The changes in the nature of evaluative input from multiple-choice testing to writing portfolios are two-pronged: a surrender of strict control over the writing process and a movement to broaden and enrich the context for composition. We've abandoned the effort to make students' writing the same in favor of letting students make the differences among them into resources for writing. So difference and context are transvalued from "confounding variables" (as in the discourse of psychometrics) into useful, stimulating elements in the process of evaluating writing.[3]

But where are difference and context when it comes to the evaluative product? To what exactly does the number assigned to a writing portfolio refer? How can requiring all readers to produce the same number in response to the same texts account for the differences among raters and their varying responses to the powerful content and context offered by the writing portfolio?

Figure 18–1 illustrates that, while our work in portfolio assessment has made the ground fertile for context, choice, difference, and multiplicity in the area of students' evaluative *input*, we persist in stripping context and quashing difference when it comes to our evaluative *output*. In other words, in equating interrater disagreement with "unfairness," we cling to what are for most of us outmoded and discredited ideologies: foundationalism and scientific positivism.

I am aware that I must handle the term "positivism" with caution. In "The Legacy of Positivism in Empirical Composition Research," Carol Berkenkotter traces the history of that term to illustrate how complex are the positivist and post-positivist traditions within science, and to resist the notion that any attempt by composition researchers to be "scientific" is necessarily positivist. A further restraint against employing the term as a critique of mainstream writing assessment is that the literature of holistic scoring appears res-

FIGURE 18–1 A (Very) Brief History of Large-Scale Evaluation in the Department of English at Miami University

→ → (historical time, 60's through 90's) → → → → → →

	Multiple-Choice	Impromptu Essay	Portfolio
evaluative **DESIGN**	evaluators write all questions and all answers, designating a single right answer to each of their questions	evaluators compose and field-test prompts, making room for a variety of approaches to their topic	evaluators compose formal guidelines, leaving choice of topics, audiences, and approaches to the student
evaluative **INPUT** (what the students do)	select the correct item from among test-makers' answers (to test-makers' questions); strict time limits imposed	actual WRITING (first-draft, single-genre) on a topic of the test-makers' choice; strict time limits imposed	actual WRITING (revised, multiple-genre), featuring choice of topics and audiences, collaboration, revision, and research; writer sets context for her writing using reflective letter; no imposed time limits
evaluative **PROCESS** (what the evaluators do)	feed answer sheets into the scoring machine	actual READING, requiring interpretation and evaluation	actual READING, requiring interpretation and evaluation
evaluative **PRODUCT**	single score quantifying "writing ability"	single score quantifying "writing ability"	single score quantifying "writing ability"

→ → → the evaluative process → → → → → →

olutely social-constructionist, rife with references to Stanley Fish and "interpretive community."

I persist in applying the term to the predominant discourse of writing assessment because it accounts for the otherwise inexplicable circularity, rigidity, and authoritarianism of "interpretive community" as it is practiced in large-scale assessment events. Only if one believes that a given text "has" a certain value and that some people know that "true" value better than others — and only if one believes that *community* and *value-pluralism* are mutually exclusive concepts — does it make sense to demand that a roomful of readers agree in their evaluations of a given text.[4] The story of "Martha and Portfolio 354" will help to illustrate the problems inherent in our single-minded insistence upon evaluative consensus.

Portfolio 354 was chosen to serve as an anchor portfolio in the 1992 Writing Portfolio Program here at Miami University. This means that during our "calibration" discussion, the entire group of forty or so evaluators read this portfolio, discussed its strengths and weaknesses, and scored it. Since interrater reliability was equated with "fairness" throughout, our goal was to see whether we could agree about the value of portfolio 354. For the most part, we did. But what interested me most, and the reason I'm telling this story, was a moment in which one reader offered a notably different reading of portfolio 354.

A friend of mine, whom I'll call Martha, had the job of recording the evaluators' comments on the chalkboard at the front of the room. First we discussed what we saw as the portfolio's strengths, then we discussed its weaknesses. During the first part of the discussion, Martha silently recorded the strengths and didn't speak up until the very last moment, just as the chief reader was getting us ready to talk about weaknesses. I make a point of the timing of her comment because I had two strong impressions about it: first, that it almost went unspoken, and second, that it significantly shifted the group's assessment of this student's writing abilities.

Martha's comment referred specifically to the third piece in the portfolio, an essay about Dr. Martin Luther King, Jr.'s "Letter from Birmingham Jail." In that piece, the student writer first examines King's arguments about the failure of the white church to confront racism and join in the civil rights struggle, and then traces the implications of "Letter from Birmingham Jail" for the present-day church. Everyone in the group-grading session had read that essay, and they had also read the student's "reflective letter," which introduces and sets a context for the other pieces in the portfolio. Among the forty or so readers in that room, however, *only Martha pointed out the connection between the topic of [the] third piece and the audience for which the reflective letter had said the piece was originally written*: the admissions committee at the University of Notre Dame, a Catholic university.

"You could," Martha observed, "call it [the student's selection and handling of the topic for that piece] audience awareness, given that he sent it to Notre Dame."

After Martha spoke there was a brief pause, and then an audible and visceral reaction from the entire group: "Mmmmm!" "Aahhh!" People nodded their heads thoughtfully; others shook their fingers in a gesture I interpreted to mean: "good point!" or "touché!" The chief reader gazed at the ceiling with a mock blank expression, brought his index finger to his forehead, then cried out "Bing!" as the light bulb suddenly switched on. He laughed and said, "Nice, Martha."[5]

Martha had apparently made a strong point in the writer's favor that the other forty readers in that room (including me) had simply overlooked. Since the scoring rubric prominently featured "a clear sense of audience and context" as a criterion for judgment, it seems likely and appropriate that Martha's comment shifted the group's evaluation of the portfolio upward to some degree. The crucial point of the story is that under the ideology that drives mainstream quantitative assessment, in her evaluation of portfolio 354 Martha was "different from everyone else," and therefore, according to Ed White's formulation, "wrong."[6]

Martha's story spotlights how getting people to discuss their evaluations prior to scoring helps to open up the conversation and make room for divergent perspectives that are often squeezed out under the pressure for numerical agreement. Our usual reliance upon *numbers*—as opposed to the positioned readings that "produce" those numbers—and our ardent pursuit of numerical *agreement*—at the expense of conversation about why we do or don't agree—corrupt portfolio assessment and prevent it from being as serious, fair, and honest as it could otherwise be.[7] Thanks to the way that calibration discussion was handled, Martha's story ended happily: her divergent reading carried the day, and that student's portfolio appeared to receive a more favorable—and, if we consider the scoring guide, a more fair—reading as a result.[8] Unfortunately, the ideology that criminalizes discrepant readings is rarely so kind to students and teachers.

In the context of our department's optional "team grading" system (in which instructors evaluate each other's students' papers), I have seen my students become deeply disturbed when their writings received widely discrepant evaluations, and I have asked myself "Why?" Evidently we have taught our students that evaluative disagreement signals sloppiness or malice: if readers' assessments conflict, someone must be wrong. Worse yet, evaluative diversity leads some students to believe that writing assessment is a chaotic, meaningless, arbitrary process. Should we be surprised, then, when students turn cynical about writing assessment, concluding that they have absolutely no control over the reception their writing receives? These are the students whose only interest in the evaluation their work receives is the grade. As teachers of writing we complain bitterly about such students, yet I wonder how seriously we've considered our complicity in "educating" such students into their depressing relationship to writing assessment.

What about us? How does the drive for interrater reliability affect the lives of administrators, instructors, and evaluators involved in large-scale assessments? Participating in and researching holistic scoring sessions at three different institutions over a span of ten years, I have encountered a number of situations that give me reason to worry. Here are a few examples:

- Evaluators complain of a contradiction between their experiences in "calibration" or "norming" sessions and the way administrators represent such sessions. While administrators will usually portray such an event as a *democratic* process articulating the values of the entire group, many evaluators experience it as an *autocratic* process requiring the large group to adopt the evaluations of the leaders. This incongruity leads one participant to label such sessions "a hoax" and another to comment, "I was surprised that 'consensus' was so often imposed on the group. I think discussions (and my sense of calibration) suffered because of it." A third evaluator says she felt "extremely frustrated" during the calibration discussions because the anchor group "had all the answers beforehand."

- Faced with several discrepant scores for a particular portfolio, a chief reader invites the anonymous discrepant readers to take a job other than grading, explaining that their lack of calibration may undermine the group's interrater reliability. One of these discrepant scorers finds this invitation "disconcerting," particularly because he was well "calibrated" in evaluating most of the other portfolios that day and didn't see himself as a defective reader. Another participant — not one of the discrepant readers in this scenario — comments that she "felt frightened" by the chief reader's invitation.

- Administrators monitor individual scorers' rates of discrepancy and compose a list of those who will not be invited to participate in future sessions due to their discrepant tendencies.

- In the course of a norming session ostensibly held for the purpose of "building consensus," and despite principled arguments from the minority for passing a particular portfolio, a chief reader states that the portfolio "absolutely cannot pass."

By no means do I mean to suggest that such painful anecdotes tell the whole story of communal assessment. Scorers often speak of how encouraged and gratified they feel when their evaluations correspond with the majority; being told that you are successfully "normed" can mark a genuinely euphoric moment. The crisis on which I focus here arises from our treatment of the minority. My personal experience and the experiences of many of the scoring-session participants I've interviewed is that incidents like those described above severely undermine instructors' sense of professionalism, dignity, intellectual integrity, and community. Interviewees use words like *oppressed, silenced, intimidated, frustrated, angry, depressed*, and *insulted* to describe such episodes. If these are the feelings of some of the people whom we attempt to draw into our "interpretive community," we might want to begin asking ourselves just what sort of community it is, and whether the rules for belonging are due for a change.

Ultimately, I judge the stupendous energy pumped into achieving statistical reliability in holistic scoring sessions (see Charney; Charles Cooper; Huot, "Reliability, Validity, and Holistic Scoring"; White, *Teaching & Assessing Writing*) to be a waste of precious resources, destructive to our students, to our colleagues, and to our project as teachers of literacy. If we let go of the quantification of writing ability in large-scale assessments, we could also dispense with our fixation on statistical reliability. Rather than allowing a number to be the evaluative output of what is otherwise a rhetorically sophisticated process, we could offer something more useful and more appropriate theoretically: positioned, situated, or located assessment.

In an essay entitled "Traveling Theory," Edward Said warns against transporting theories into new situations without sufficient consideration of the circumstances that gave rise to those theories in the first place. When I argue for positioned or located evaluation, I make a parallel argument: I believe that the circumstances and process of any evaluation are crucial to understanding the outcome of that evaluation and putting that outcome to ethical use. The quantification of writing ability radically simplifies what a reader has said about someone's writing and frees that reader from responsibility for his or her evaluation: "Oh yes, she's a *B writer*." Simplification and freedom from responsibility are the two elements that make quantification both appealing and appalling. Located assessment is more difficult to transport, manipulate, and flatten; from my perspective as a teacher of rhetoric, that is its great strength. In practical terms, then, what would it mean to provide situated, positioned, or located assessments?

First, we could offer *institutional* location. Rather than asking evaluators to provide scores that are later translated by administrators into institutional action, we could restore to evaluators responsibility for making the institutional decision at hand, whether pass/fail, 0–3–6 credits, or otherwise. This shift would represent a gain not only in professionalism (since it would put the decision in the hands of the teacher-experts) but also in accountability, since teachers would need to face the consequences of their evaluations: "I am failing this student," or "I am granting this student an entire year of credit; she may never take another writing course in her life!"[9]

Second, we could offer *axiological* location.[10] Contrary to the irresistible implications of quantification, the evaluation of writing is a critical and creative act carried out by some human beings upon the critical and creative work of others. The key here is that *not everyone's values are the same*. In fact, even in an apparently homogeneous group of evaluators — the infamous "interpretive community" — astonishing differences in interpretation and evaluation sometimes arise. During last summer's portfolio assessment here at Miami University, for example, forty college English instructors gave one portfolio all six possible scores. Foundationalist ideology makes such a circumstance chaotic, meaningless, or corrupt: "What is their problem that they can't get their evaluations *right*?" Constructivist ideology, on the other hand, makes evaluative differences meaningful, instructive, and useful.

In "The Idea of Community in the Study of Writing," Joseph Harris offers a metaphor which helps clarify the contrast between foundationalist and constructivist portraits of "community":

> The metaphor of the city would allow us to view a certain amount of change and struggle within a community not as threats to its coherence but as normal activity . . . We need to find a way to talk about [the workings of communities] without first assuming a consensus that may not be there. (20)

We often hear from people who were as writing students either terrified by or furious about the fact different instructors valued different things in students' compositions. In the "city" of positioned evaluation and constructivist community, differences would be less threatening; they would constitute a crucial part of one's rhetorical education.

What would truly constructivist, post-positivist assessment look like? In *Embracing Contraries* and *What is English?*, Peter Elbow proposes what strikes me as the most moderate (and therefore the most likely) first step: multiple scales of evaluation (*Embracing* 171, *What* 256). From the perspective of valuing context and difference this is an obvious improvement over the single scale, yet multiple quantitative scales still tempt us to "average" them into a single number, as in the notorious example of grade-point averages. The virtue of narrative and qualitative evaluative output, by contrast, is that it can better resist these reductionist temptations.

Brief narratives like those used at Hampshire College, Evergreen College, and the University of California at Santa Cruz can replace grades very successfully in a classroom context. For the purposes of large-scale assessments, however, narratives are nearly impossible to manage. Most of us have experienced how draining the relatively quick and superficial act of marathon scoring can be; those who have tried offering actual commentary along with a number have found that approach to be even more grueling. Yet I've argued here that numbers undermine our purposes. So what's the best option for large-scale assessments? A number of people have experimented with a form for "positioned evaluation." It indicates the institutional decision (pass/fail, 0–3–6 credits, etc.) but also offers a substantial checklist of writing qualities such as "organization," "humor," "detail," "tone," "correctness," and "surprise." Evaluators can check off those qualities that most affect their decisions, and indicate with another quick mark whether that quality figures in as a strength or a weakness. Without adding much time to the old approach of producing a number on a scale, such a checklist proves more informative and professional than scoring. Figure 18–2 shows such a checklist, this one designed by Shannon Wilson for the Miami University English Department's Team Grading process.[11]

To me, the most compelling alternative to quantification is one about which Brian Huot writes in "Reliability, Validity, and Holistic Scoring." Huot describes William Smith and his colleagues at the University of Pittsburgh sitting around a table, reading the writing of incoming students *not* to judge them but to place them. The question ceased to be "How shall we quantify and rank these writings by 'quality' or 'ability'?" and instead became "With which of us four instructors will this writer grow and learn best?" By institutionalizing the fact of evaluative and pedagogical diversity, Smith and his colleagues achieved the most creative, most honest evaluation process I have encountered (or imagined), an approach wholly untainted by what Stephen Jay Gould calls the twin fallacies of reification and ranking.

In my argument for post-positivist methods of writing assessment, I've stuck close to the particular concerns of teachers and students and their lives

FIGURE 18–2

PAPER # _____   GRADE _____
GRADER # _____

The criteria below were derived from the anchoring session responses. Some of the qualities are specific to particular assignments (i.e., discourse analysis and reflective narratives); others are more general.

Check three to five qualities that were key in the grade determination.

+	−
____ asks good questions	____ appropriates research
____ aware of methodological influence on research	____ clichéd
	____ difference denied
____ clear	____ difference not examined
____ challenging topic	____ disjointed
____ complex ideas	____ disorganized
____ contextualizes	____ doesn't fulfill assignment
____ depth	____ doesn't explore issues raised
____ describes method used	____ doesn't consider own location
____ engaging	____ ends where it should begin
____ focused	____ essentializes
____ includes data	____ formulaic
____ incorporates discourse in analysis	____ generalizes
____ in-depth analysis	____ importance of topic unclear
____ interesting topic	____ incompetent mechanical skills
____ interesting use of language	____ location is superficial
____ locates/positions self in relation to social	____ "normal" goes unexamined
	____ not self-reflective
____ mechanical competence	____ overstated conclusions
____ organized	____ passes judgment without considering location
____ provides examples	
____ reflective	____ plagiarism
____ resists generalizations	____ proofreading
____ resists pat ending	____ repetitious
____ specific	____ superficial
____ style	____ surface analysis only
____ takes risks	____ takes on too little
____ thoughtful	____ takes on too much
____ uses humor	____ topic nebulous
____ uses research/data	____ undefined terms
____ uses quotes	____ unfocused
____ voice	____ unorganized
____ well-developed	____ voice
____ other _____	____ weak connections
____ other _____	____ other _____
____ other _____	____ other _____
	____ other _____

within educational institutions. Yet I believe the implications of the conflicts I have traced here go well beyond the classroom or the holistic scoring session; I see these issues as seamlessly bound to questions of culture and politics.

Would it be extreme to say that the discourse of positivism and the exclusionary version of "interpretive community" which guide the drive for statistical reliability are ill-suited to democracy, regardless of how congenial and liberal most of its advocates may be? Would it sound grandiose to claim that narrative, positioned assessment better supports democratic culture, whether in the classroom or across society? Perhaps. Consider, however, this paragraph from Pat Belanoff's "The Myths of Assessment":

> We need to realize that our inability to agree on standards and their applications is not something we need to be ashamed of . . . far from it, [that inability] is a sign of strength, of the life and vitality of words and the exchange of words. For, if we agreed, we could set up hierarchies and fit ourselves and others into then and then all could dictate to those below them and follow the orders of those above them. And in fact, in such a set up there would have to be an autocrat at the top who knows what's best for us and who knows what texts are best. Then someone would know what sort of texts to write and to teach and the variety would leave our profession and along with the variety, the richness. (62)

This tendency toward the devaluation and extermination of difference is what troubles me most in the discourse of mainstream writing assessment. I have proposed that we replace it with the more rhetorical, more theoretically engaged, and more educationally holistic practices of positioning our evaluations and (trans)valuing our differences. We can make our theories and practice — both educational and political — truer to what we as enthusiasts of communal portfolio assessment really believe.

NOTES

1. Although I focus here on Edward M. White as one of the most influential voices in the field, he is not alone in his dim view of evaluative difference; throughout the literature on communal evaluation, disagreement is represented as inherently problematic.

2. I sketch Miami's history of large-scale assessment because it is the institution I know best. The overall historical movement traced in my "Very Brief History" is, however, common to a large majority of the educational institutions of which I am aware.

Two elements of Miami University's Writing Portfolio Assessment Program may insulate it from part of my critique: Miami's is a voluntary program, not one required of all students in the institution, and it awards advanced placement and credit, rather than functioning as a proficiency measure. I accept these as qualifying factors even while I maintain doubts regarding the push for agreement and the quantification of writing ability, both of which are key features of the Miami program.

3. For the concept of "transvaluing difference" I am indebted to Linda Brodkey's editorial.

4. Too late to integrate it more fully into my essay, I discovered Michael M. Williamson's remarkable article, "An Introduction to Holistic Scoring: The Social, Historical, and Theoretical Context for Writing Assessment." Williamson's article serves as the introduction to *Validating Holistic Scoring for Writing Assessment*, a volume he recently co-edited with Brian Huot. In that opening chapter, Williamson traces the historical and theoretical geneology of holistic scoring. He strongly affirms that the mainstream tradition in holistic scoring carries with it assumptions about knowledge and value that he calls "positivist" and "psychometric." Lamenting the "simplistic and dated views" from which specialists in writing assessment often operate, he exhorts us

to develop our practices out of an evolving theory of writing rather than out of a "fossilized" theory of assessment.

5. Details and quotations of this event are taken from videotapes I made of the session for research purposes. I wish to thank participants at two different research sites for opening their portfolio assessment programs to my inquiry even when they knew that I brought to the research a critical point of view.

6. In his keynote address to the Miami University Conference on New Directions in Portfolio Assessment, White told a similar story. Having found his evaluation of an essay on Faulkner's *The Sound and the Fury* discrepant, White realized that his score was discrepant because he had read the novel and knew that the writer was misrepresenting it. Since none of his fellow readers had read the novel, they were quite satisfied with the essay.

7. Fortunately, a number of programs have found ways to open up the conversation and to legitimate evaluative differences. At SUNY Stony Brook, for example, instructors *talk* about portfolios when their evaluations disagree. At Miami University, the aggregate score for a disputed portfolio includes all three evaluators' scores, including that of the "discrepant" evaluator. Unfortunately, during the calibration and norming sessions I've witnessed, discrepancy is still usually treated as failure, as the anecdotes [here] illustrate.

8. The difference between the anchor group's and the calibration group's scores for portfolio 354 supports my hypothesis that Martha's comment boosted our estimation of the portfolio. In the anchor session, "audience awareness" was never mentioned as a strength of this portfolio; most anchor-group members gave portfolio 354 a "3 minus" and one scorer gave it a "2," so the portfolio was rated there as a "low 3." At the conclusion of the calibration discussion in which Martha spoke, most raters gave the portfolio a "3," but more scored it above a "3" than below it. So where "audience awareness" was credited to the portfolio, it ceased to be a "low 3" and became a "solid 3" at least.

9. The leaders of the Miami University Portfolio Program tried this once. In 1991, they replaced their standard scale designating six levels of writing "ability" or "quality" in favor of an institutionally located 0–3–6 scale indicating how many credits the evaluator of a given portfolio felt the writer ought to be awarded.

Unfortunately, the resulting distribution of scores did not allow administrators sufficient flexibility in designating who would place out of first-year English; administrators knew that in order to meet budgetary constraints and keep down class sizes they need to exempt "X" number of students, but the composition instructors' evaluations were telling them to exempt "Y" number. In the name of "economic realities," the six-point scale was reinstated the following year.

10. *Axiology* refers to the study of value judgments.

11. The team running the Miami Portfolio Assessment Program is also experimenting with ways of providing more location of and information about instructors' evaluations, including checklists like this one.

BIBLIOGRAPHY

Belanoff, Pat. "The Myths of Assessment." *Journal of Basic Writing*. 10.1 (1991): 54–66.

Belanoff, Pat, and Marcia Dickson. Eds. *Portfolios: Process and Product*. Portsmouth, NH: Boynton/ Cook, 1991.

Berkenkotter, Carol, Thomas N. Huckin, and Jon Ackerman. "The Legacy of Positivism in Empirical Composition Research." *Journal of Advanced Composition* 9 (1989): 69–82.

Bohannon, Laura. "Shakespeare in the Bush." *Points of Departure*. Ed. James Moffett. New York: Mentor, 1985. 179–89.

Broad, Robert L. "Portfolio Scoring: A Contradiction in Terms." Miami University Conference on New Directions in Portfolio Assessment, Oxford, OH. October 1992.

Brodkey, Linda. "Hard Cases for Law and Rhetoric." Conference on College Composition and Communication, March 1992, Cincinnati, OH.

———. "Opinion: Transvaluing Difference." *College English* 51 (1989): 597–601.

Charney, Davida. "The Validity of Using Holistic Scoring to Evaluate Writing: A Critical Overview." *Research in the Teaching of English* 18 (February 1984): 65–81.

Cooper, Charles R. "Holistic Evaluation of Writing." *Evaluating Writing: Describing, Measuring, Judging*. Eds. Charles R. Cooper and Lee Odell. Urbana, IL: National Council of Teachers of English, 1977. 3–31.

Elbow, Peter. "Assessing Writing in the 21st Century." In *Composition in the 21st Century: Crisis and Change*. Eds. Lynn Z. Bloom, Donald A. Daiker, and Edward M. White. Southern Illinois UP, 1996.

—————. *What is English?* New York and Urbana, IL: MLA and NCTE, 1990.

—————. *Embracing Contraries.* New York: Oxford UP, 1986.

Fish, Stanley. *Is There a Text in This Class?* Cambridge: Harvard UP, 1980.

Gould, Stephan Jay. *The Mismeasure of Man.* New York: Norton, 1981.

Harris, Joseph. "The Idea of Community in the Study of Writing." *College Composition and Communication* 40 (1989): 11–22.

Huot, Brian. "Reliability, Validity, and Holistic Scoring: What We Know and What We Need to Know." *College Composition and Communication* 41.2 (May 1990): 201–13.

Said, Edward W. *The World, the Text, and the Critic.* Cambridge: Harvard UP, 1983.

Smith, Barbara Herrnstein. *Contingencies of Value: Alternative Perspectives for Critical Theory.* Cambridge: Harvard UP, 1988.

Trimbur, John. "Consensus and Difference in Collaborative Learning." *College English* 51 (October 1989): 601–16.

White, Edward M. Rev. of *Portfolios: Process and Product.* Ed. Pat Belanoff and Marcia Dickson. *College Composition and Communication* 43.4 (December 1992): 537–39.

—————. *Teaching and Assessing Writing.* San Francisco: Jossey-Bass, 1985.

—————. "Teaching and Assessing Writing in the Future." Conference on College Composition and Communication, March 1992. Cincinnati, OH.

—————. "Portfolios as an Assessment Concept." Miami University Conference on New Directions in Portfolio Assessment, Oxford Ohio. October 1992.

Williamson, Michael M. "An Introduction to Holistic Scoring: The Social, Historical, and Theoretical Context for Writing Assessment." *Validating Holistic Scoring for Writing Assessment.* Eds. Michael M. Williamson and Brian Huot. Cresskill, NJ: Hampton, 1993.

19 Questioning Assumptions about Portfolio-Based Assessment

LIZ HAMP-LYONS AND WILLIAM CONDON

Interest in and commitment to portfolios for assessing college writing have swelled enormously in the past decade and are still growing. In "Using Portfolios," Pat Belanoff and Peter Elbow wrote extensively about the benefits portfolios brought to the freshman composition program they ran at SUNY-Stony Brook. Anson and Brown have written, in "Large-Scale Portfolio Assessment in the Research University," about the efforts of faculty at the University of Minnesota toward large-scale portfolio collection at entry which, while they ultimately sank under the weight of campus-wide politics, inspired similar efforts at places such as the University of Alaska (Wauters). As the use of portfolios for purposes ranging from entry-level writing assessment (at Miami University: see Daiker) to campus-wide curriculum development (Larsen) becomes common, evaluation by portfolio method is increasingly accepted as an enriched evaluation and thus a better evaluation. Our own experience with portfolios at the University of Michigan (Condon and Hamp-Lyons) confirms that portfolio-based assessment does enrich the process of assessing writing; further, it enriches the process of teaching writing, of developing curriculum and faculty in a writing program, of collecting data about the program's effectiveness, and much, much more. The benefits of portfolio assessment are real, and the indications are that its potential has hardly begun to develop.

We write, then, from the perspective of a commitment to portfolio assessment, but also from the perspective of teacher-researchers who seek to understand all we do, even when it is successful. A great deal is still unknown about what portfolios do and, perhaps even more interestingly, about the nature of the role and activities we, as teachers and readers, engage in during portfolio assessment. In order to explore some of the issues involved in how teacher-evaluators use, perceive, and react to the portfolios they collect in their classes, we conducted a study of how they handle the cognitive task of making what we had initially thought would be a "holistic" judgment of the multiple texts

From *College Composition and Communication 44.2* (1993): 176–90.

in portfolios in one composition program. The insights we gained from viewing the reading of a portfolio from a kind of reader-response perspective caused us to question some of the major assumptions behind most portfolio assessments, including our own, and to find ways of working with portfolios that would take these new insights into account.[1]

The first stage of our work with portfolios, begun in 1987, taught us that what had looked originally like a system that we could put into place was actually a process, iterative in nature and different in each iteration (Condon and Hamp-Lyons), a discovery echoed by Roemer, Schultz and Durst as they worked with portfolios and discovered "processes of change," and doubtless by many colleagues across college writing programs. While the first stage taught us many exciting, challenging, and worthwhile lessons, this second study taught us many new lessons. It led us to the realization that a portfolio-based system of writing assessment must continually be questioned, and must continually grow in response to new discoveries and to new phenomena, phenomena often engendered by the portfolio evaluation process itself. As a result, we realized that we needed to move to another stage of thinking about portfolios within a writing program, a kind of thinking that would prepare us to incorporate the new knowledge we gained from our study while maintaining the carefully wrought strengths of the system we had developed. To achieve this difficult balancing act, the portfolio assessment process itself must provide mechanisms for (1) prompting readers to be aware of the process they are going through, (2) gathering appropriate data about that process, and (3) making the changes or accommodations which each new iteration shows are necessary. Our study of teacher-evaluators' reading and judging of portfolios demonstrated that portfolio assessments require maintenance that may be different in kind from that required for traditional writing assessments, but which at least equals them in intensity. In the remainder of this paper we point out that certain commonly assumed benefits of portfolio assessment — ones which had informed our own adoption and design of this method — are not inherent to portfolio assessment but come only as a result of the same kind of care and attention that allow a holistic assessment to achieve reliability and validity. We continue to assert that portfolio-based assessment is vastly superior to traditional holistic assessment because of the many programmatic benefits it brings with it. But we must also assert that, like all beneficial innovations, its greatest benefits come when it is not entered into lightly or unquestioningly, but when critical eyes are brought to bear on it, demanding enlightenment and thereby helping to ensure excellence.

Setting up a portfolio-based writing assessment requires a great deal of planning and a great deal of work. It is also by its nature a highly contextualized operation, an aspect that we see as a strength rather than a weakness. In the University of Michigan's English Composition Board, approximately twelve percent of entering students receive entry assessment scores which place them in Practicum, scores based on a standard holistic reading of fifty-minute impromptu argumentative essays, which students produce during their orientation sessions. Practicum — an intensive half-term course limited to sixteen students per section, each of whom has a half-hour individual conference with the instructor each week — is an introductory course in academic writing, focusing on argumentation. At the end of this course, students prepare portfolios of the best writing they have done in the course. Each portfolio contains four pieces: two revised essays, one of which must be an argument; one impromptu essay, written in class; a reflective piece, written in class, that deals in some way with the writing in the portfolio (metacognition); plus a table of contents. Students also take a post-test in which they write a fifty-minute impromptu essay that is not part of the portfolio but which may in rare cases of major disagreements figure into the student's exit placement.[2] The outcome of this credit/no credit course, rather than a grade, is a placement: Repeat Practicum, Introductory Composition, or Exempt from Introductory Composition.

The system for arriving at decisions about portfolios at Michigan has been carefully developed, but like those in other portfolio assessment contexts, we found our imponderables in the human dimensions of portfolio assessment (see, for example, Roemer, Schultz and Durst; or Smit, Kolonosky and Seltzer). As we tried to answer our colleagues' questions about "how" they should arrive at a judgment of a portfolio, we discovered that the procedural changes involved in converting from the essay test to the portfolio for assessment are simple compared to the cognitive changes implicated in the conversion from reading single, fifty-minute impromptu arguments from each writer to reading portfolios consisting of several different pieces of writing produced by different writers from different sections of the same course. Portfolio assessment involves a "people-oriented" kind of self-examination. We were satisfied that we understood the needs and responses of the writers to the portfolio approach in these courses: with only 16 students and a one-on-one half-hour conference weekly, all instructors come to know their students well. But we realized we needed to know more about what another key group of people, the portfolio readers, were doing and how what they were doing affected student outcomes. Therefore, we wanted to look as closely as we could at the process of reading a portfolio. At the same time, we did not want to set up an experimental study, or to intrude into the complex process by which a class instructor who has worked with a student throughout a course reads the student's work again from an evaluative perspective. Similarly, we did not want to intrude, if we could avoid it, into the process by which instructors read portfolios from students in other sections of the program.

Therefore, we began by giving copies of five portfolios from past classes to all our faculty/readers, and asking them to read the portfolios and keep a log of their reading so that we might first check our assumptions about some easily definable "problem" areas. We gave readers some general guidelines for what to note and comment on, based on the discussions we had had about portfolios in faculty meetings, but left the activity fairly open. Reading these logs allowed us to see the need to understand more about two areas: the criteria readers used to make their judgments, and the process by which they applied those criteria as they read.

We next asked our faculty to repeat the reading log activity, but this time with a more conscious focus on these two key areas, and with the "live" portfolios they were reading from their own class and a colleague's. As we worked with the data from this second stage, we identified for the faculty several facets of writing that seemed to be especially salient to their reading: evidence of awareness of viewpoints other than the writer's own; recognition of complexity in the issues the writer discusses; coherent presentation of support which accommodates the issues the author raises; adequate transitions; and consistent voice. These facets, of course, grow out of the local values of our program, and we do not suggest that they would be appropriate in a different writing program with different values. Drawing also from the vast quantity of data generated by the first and second stages, we began to see some aspects of the portfolio reading process we should ask readers to examine: whether a portfolio is seen as a unit or as parts which must somehow be weighed; at what point judgment (i.e., scoring) occurs; the differences between reading our own students' portfolios versus those from another class; whether standards are stricter in a portfolio than on a timed post-test.

In the next stage, therefore, we constructed a more formal kind of reading log that at the same time limited the amount of work we asked readers to do — for readers were unanimous that the intense self-reflection we were asking of them was extremely time-consuming. Readers completed this log on selected portfolios during actual portfolio reading sessions. This "Reader Response Questionnaire" attempted to get at such questions as how and when a reader makes the decision about a score on a portfolio, what standards readers feel they are bringing into play, what divergent evidence among texts lead them to a score decision, and so on. We gave the questionnaire to groups of readers on different exit assessment occasions, so that some readers completed several over an academic year, while others completed only one. On different occasions, readers were asked to complete the survey on portfolios from their own class, from another instructor's class, or on a batch of portfolios chosen to be common to them all.

Because our faculty members are well-trained and experienced in formal writing assessment, their expectations of formal characteristics of assessment for the portfolio process were quite high. For them, it was critical that we go as far as possible in establishing criteria and standards for judging the portfolios. Thus, during the year and a half that we were collecting these data, we also began holding standardizing sessions, though the purposes here were somewhat different from the purposes for the traditional standardizing sessions in holistic assessment. Since we found no discussion of standardizing in the literature on portfolio assessment, we needed, in the first place, to find out what standardizing for portfolios should be like, how it differed from that other kind of standardizing session, and what the goals of standardizing should be (e.g., to what extent we should strive for agreement in score levels, how similar our criteria needed to be, how much portfolios can differ and still be generally recognized as fulfilling the requirements of the course). Getting people to read and score portfolios and to talk about their processes for doing so and the standards they were applying made the reading itself a more public activity, exposing each of us to the methods others were using to make their judgments, and the perceptions we shared about portfolio assessment in general and about individual portfolios in particular. These standardizing sessions added enormously to our understanding of the data we were collecting in the various stages of our reader-response study.

IDENTIFYING AND QUESTIONING ASSUMPTIONS ABOUT PORTFOLIOS

As we moved through the stages of reader-response data collection described above, and as we attended to the discussions in standardizing sessions, we became conscious of some of our own assumptions about portfolio-based assessment, assumptions that we seemed to share with our colleagues and with people in other programs that employ portfolio assessment. We identified five areas where our study of readers' responses to portfolios during their reading led us to question those assumptions. In what follows, we first explain each assumption, relating it to the questions raised by our data; then we consider how a portfolio assessment program may respond to these insights.

Assumption One: Because a portfolio contains more texts than a timed essay examination, it provides more evidence and therefore a broader basis for judgment, making decisions easier.

This assumption contradicts the widely held belief that teachers read holistically: a larger number of texts only offers a broader basis for judgment if quality varies from text to text, and readers can only take a variation of quality into account if they read non-holistically. Our surveys of reader behavior suggest that holistic reading, in the case of portfolios, is highly unlikely, if not impossible. Multiple texts, unless texts are so close in kind and quality that they are virtually identical, inevitably force readers to consider one text in the light of another, to weigh one against the other, and to make a decision that, while representing a judgment about the whole portfolio, is grounded in a weighing of the parts, rather than in a dominant impression of the whole. In such cases, decisions become harder, not easier, as the portfolio presents a more complex, more comprehensive "snapshot" of the writer's ability. And even this more comprehensive decision requires that readers make use of all the evidence the portfolio provides, an issue we shall examine at greater length in our discussion of common aspects of Assumptions One and Two.

Assumption Two: A portfolio will contain texts of more than one genre, and multiple genres also lead to a broader basis for judgments, making decisions easier.

Here we can see two underlying assumptions: first, that writing quality will vary from genre to genre, and second, that a portfolio will necessarily contain texts of more than one genre. While we can expect, for example, that writing a personal narrative is different from writing a critical analysis (since those forms make different demands on the writer's skills), it does not necessarily follow that a student will do well on one and poorly on the other. If writing quality does not vary from one genre to another, there is no assessment argument for including multiple genres (though there may be pedagogical reasons), since they do not actually broaden the basis for the decision. And if writing quality *does* vary from one genre to the other, then the decision is harder, and the reader is thrown back into the dilemma of holistic versus non-holistic reading described above. In addition, in a system like ours that leaves the contents of a writer's portfolio in the writer's hands as far as possible, there is no guarantee that genres will vary. We had specified that *one* of the revised essays had to be an argument, and the prompts for in-class essays cued students to write arguments. The genre for the second revised essay was left open, but in practice it was almost uniformly another argument. Introducing the requirement that a student include a reflective piece in the portfolio was in part a reaction against the perception that too many of our students' portfolios contained only one genre, argumentation.

Our data also reveal that, for these readers in this context, the influence of multiple genres, when they occurred, seemed to be minor. There was nothing in any of the reading logs about writing performance on one genre rather than another. Never did a reader say, "This student knows how to present a point of view, but can't handle reporting the views of others," for example, or even, "This student can write an effective narrative, but has a good deal of trouble with more complex forms of discourse." Rather than finding that different genres offered readers different kinds of evidence, we discovered that revised texts seemed to offer different evidence from the impromptu texts, even though those texts were almost always the same genre. Often, we saw in the readers' logs occasions where readers had to backtrack and reread a revised piece in the light of what they were seeing in the impromptu. And when readers did comment on weighing the evidence of one text against another, it seemed to be that the different kinds of evidence, rather than anything else, caused them problems. As far as we could see, knowing more made the decision harder, not easier.

But behind all this, and behind Assumption One, is an assumption that readers will attend to all the text they see; that is, if readers are given more text to read, they will read it all as intensely as they would the limited text generated during a single essay-test session. We have found again and again in portfolios of different kinds, at different times, from different readers, a clear suggestion that readers do not attend equally to the entire portfolio. Although the portfolios in our study contain four texts from a course of instruction, each of which has the potential to offer conflicting evidence to the other three, readers' self-reports indicate that readers arrived at a score during their reading of the first paper. A few readers reached a tentative score after the first or second paragraph of the first piece of text. Some readers postponed any decision until the second piece, but moved to a score rather soon within it. Readers seemed to go through a process of seeking a "center of gravity" and then read for confirmation or contradiction of that sense. The following reading log extract shows a process that is typical:

> *What is the first thing you read in full?*
> The cover sheet.
>
> *Where do you go from there?*
> I read in page order.
>
> *At what point does a possible score occur to you?*
> Pretty much in the middle of paper 1, but I try to keep an open mind . . .
>
> *Do you revise the score you first thought of?*
> I move more toward a "2-" on the impromptu.
>
> *At what point do you become certain of the score?*
> After the impromptu, but I look at the third paper briefly.

These data question the assumption that portfolios provide a broader basis upon which readers can make judgments. On the basis of the reader-response questionnaires, for example, perhaps four pieces are not needed in the portfolio, and some other configuration (perhaps an impromptu and a revised piece with all its prior drafts) might be more constructive. These insights have also led us to advise instructors to tell their students to organize the pieces they put in their portfolio in descending order of quality, i.e., to put what they think is their best piece first. Students who use the technique of saving the best for last and bracketing their worst in the middle may lose out in the reading process.

Perhaps discovering that some of our assumptions were unfounded should have led us to abandon the notion of portfolio-based assessment — but there are many reasons for moving to portfolio assessment, many of which we have discussed at length elsewhere (Condon and Hamp-Lyons). Our response was not to abandon the approach, but to give serious thought to what we wanted from exit assessments, and how we could achieve those results.

Clearly, if we are interested in whether the quality of a student's writing varies from genre to genre, we need to ensure that each portfolio contains multiple genres, a move that would simply mean redesigning the instructions to students about the contents of the portfolio. However, even the seemingly simple and unambiguous step of requiring multiple genres has far-reaching implications for the ethos of a writing program, since it requires teachers to redesign their goals to fit the portfolio expectations — in our case, for example, to value other written genres in addition to argumentation. Making such a pedagogical decision is a matter for the whole writing faculty, and indeed is likely to go beyond the writing program. In our case, for example, the focus on argumentation was established as the result of several research studies which highlighted the importance of the genre within the specific University of Michigan context (Keller-Cohen and Wolfe; Hamp-Lyons and Reed).

Studying our reader-response data, then, made us more aware of the values upon which the writing program was built.

And if the change to multiple genres occurs, the question whether different genres necessarily result in evidence of different writing qualities or competencies remains. Even if it is true that a portfolio contains more than one genre, we must doubt whether this will indeed provide a broader basis for a decision. Our data show that many readers are not conscious of genre as a factor, or are unconsciously compensating for variation due to genre. If we wanted to hold to Assumption Two, then, we would need to provide explicit response criteria that differ from genre to genre, and require faculty to use these criteria while reading (not to mention while teaching). This in turn means that writers would have to state the genre of each of their texts in the cover sheets of their portfolios. This seems to us an unlikely scenario. But we reiterate our questioning of the assumption that having a broader basis for evaluation will make evaluation easier; we have become convinced that it is likely to make decisions more complex and difficult.

A problem with many of the suggestions we have sketched out above for both Assumptions One and Two is that the response sheets — and the processes expected of readers — would be extremely complex and time-consuming. Readers do not normally follow the procedures set out for them using the predicted processes when they read evaluatively (Huot; Cooper and Hamp-Lyons; Hamp-Lyons). Our studies have already suggested that readers tend to reduce the cognitive — and time — load in portfolio reading by finding short cuts to decisions; indeed, it is often these short-cut strategies that raise the issues we are seeking to resolve. We believe this is a human trait and not unique or idiosyncratic to our situation or our readers, who are professional and well-trained in assessment reading. It is impracticable to seek to solve a problem with a solution more cumbersome than the original plan. But what we have learned about our inability to validate Assumptions One and Two raises the specter of readers not reading the whole portfolio — of this wonderful mechanism, this excellent pedagogical tool, losing some of its assessment value because readers are missing some portion of what is there. The superiority of portfolios as an assessment tool is dependent on readers reading, judging, and valuing *all* the texts. Hence, we believe we should be able to resolve our problems with Assumptions One and Two together, since they are so closely related. We have considered three possibilities.

Perhaps a practical solution would be to require readers to answer a couple of questions on each portfolio, designed to place subsequent texts in the context of the first piece in the portfolio, e.g., "Specify the strengths present in this text which make it better than the first text"; "Specify the characteristics of this text that make it less competent than the first piece in the portfolio"; "Specify the ways in which this text appears to be of the same quality as the first." An alternative might require the readers to generate some kind of feedback that demands commenting intelligently on the portfolio as a whole, which could at least ensure that readers pay more careful attention to all the pieces in the portfolio, attention which would probably translate into different scoring behaviors as well. Finally, if we adopt the assumption that readers read a portfolio holistically — which, so far at least, would be no more than a convenient fiction — we might combine these approaches and design criteria that force readers to make judgments about whether the quality of the pieces in the portfolio was consistently or inconsistently high (or low, or medium), and provide a means for generic feedback tied to those criteria. A different kind of solution addresses our finding that readers attend to differences between revised and impromptu texts; portfolios could contain fewer texts and more stages. Would readers pay more attention to multiple versions of one text than they do to multiple separate texts? We don't know at this stage, but, again, removing one of the two revised texts in exchange for a draft or two of the other, which means trading one type of evidence for another, is a solution that could be simply accomplished, but which raises complex questions of curriculum and values. Such a solution requires, at least, the participation of the faculty as a whole, and if the decision is to be an informed one, it will require more information than we have at present. It seems that, in order to ensure that readers read the student's whole text, responses must go beyond merely putting a score down on a piece of paper. We hope that the next stage of our investigation of portfolio reading will begin to answer questions concerning which if any of these proposed strategies may be successful.

Assumption Three: Portfolios will make process easier to see in a student's writing and enable instructors to reward evidence of the ability to bring one's own text significantly forward in quality.

As soon as we articulated this assumption — before we looked at any data — it was obvious to us that this assumption necessitates that drafts (i.e., evidence of the writing processes prior to the product) be included in the portfolio. A system requiring multiple texts is not inherently based on multiple passes at any of those texts, and if it is not, process will not be "easy to see." We had expected to find (given the earlier assumptions about what readers do) that instructors would reward evidence of the student's ability to bring her or his own text significantly forward in quality. But as we studied the reading logs we realized that inferring process from the contrast between formal, finished papers and impromptu writing is too restrictive to enable readers to see and reward effective applications of processes and clear improvement in texts. In fact, we found several instances where readers' perceptions of greater competence in the revised texts than in the impromptu led them to place greater emphasis on the lack of skill in the impromptu. It seemed from readers' self-reflections that they were aware of the part they had played *as instructors* in improving *their own* students' texts, and that this led them to be suspicious when they saw significantly better revised texts than impromptu writing in portfolios from other classes. Perhaps this means that the readers were seeing the improvement as the instructor's work rather than the student's. Some readers' self-reports, in fact, indicated this very belief. A reader might say something like: "The two revised essays look very competent but I know how hard we [NB: "we"] worked on them; I think the impromptu shows more accurately the kinds of problems this student has." Thus, a reader might place the student "Repeat Practicum" while accepting that two of the four papers are at a level that warrants placement into Introductory Composition. This problem would, we believe, have been considerably lessened if the portfolios had contained multiple drafts of at least one of the revised papers. If readers have only product data to evaluate, and if the instructional context does not necessarily require students to write more than one draft, portfolios cannot support process pedagogy.

Assumption Three, then, is rather easy to validate: we need to encourage, even require, students to include drafts in their portfolios. Nothing else can happen here if readers don't have drafts to respond to. We stress drafting, conferencing, and multiple revision in our courses, but currently our portfolios fail to reflect our pedagogical values in this vital respect. Thus, while our "taught" curriculum emphasizes revision and process, our "tested" curriculum explicitly requires only product, leaving students free to ignore what their teachers tell them about process. Given the full context of the Practicum course, with its class meetings, regular weekly conferences, and so forth, avoiding revision would not be easy, but the portfolio, in theory, allows students to complete the course without having to revise, and some students have done so. Expanding the portfolio to include drafts is the first and most important change the second stage of our study has resulted in. Future studies will explore whether and how readers use the information provided by the inclusion of process evidence in a student's portfolio.

Assumption Four: Portfolio assessment allows pedagogical and curricular values to be taken into account.

Assumption Four posits, first, that possessing contextual knowledge helps the reader to make decisions, and second, that decisions made in light of that knowledge are better decisions. In this way, Assumption Four represents the common argument that portfolios somehow automatically represent a closer connection with curricular values. Here, too, we have come to believe that this can only be true if the connection between curriculum and portfolio is carefully and consistently built. The mere existence of a portfolio method of assessment does not assure it. Through the creation of portfolio reading teams, the requirement of sharing assignments among members of a team, the meetings of portfolio readers in small teams, and the general portfolio standardization for all faculty, we have striven to ensure that our portfolio system represents our pedagogical values.

Portfolio assessment allows pedagogical and curricular values to be taken into account when a teaching program provides ways for faculty to interact. The interactions must extend beyond coming together for portfolio standardizing sessions; they must run deep enough for every member of the community to feel that s/he completely understands the values and teaching goals of the program, and to feel that s/he can influence what happens and how it happens. This level of interaction will be easiest when programs provide a close working environment and plenty of informal opportunities for interaction; a carefully constructed and monitored portfolio assessment system with portfolio groups, calibrating sessions, etc.; and a well-developed professional structure where faculty meet to consider both pedagogy and research on a regular basis. In making decisions about individual portfolios, faculty must have strong input, not only though the scores they give but through an internal appeal procedure. In the program we studied, instructors are notified of the proposed outcome for every student in their sections and have an opportunity to request a change, explaining why and producing additional evidence. These are the minimum requirements if a program is to ensure that the portfolios the students prepare and the scores the faculty give actually reflect the pedagogical and curricular values of that program and, more importantly, that those pedagogical and curricular values are subject to revision as a result of the evidence the portfolios present. To the extent that a program does not have these attributes, it must either develop them or develop other mechanisms for assuring that its pedagogical and curricular values will be expressed in the portfolios; such expression will not occur without careful program-wide attention.

Assumption Five: Portfolio assessment aids in building consensus in assessment and in instruction.

Assumption Five suggests that more information, more data, will lead a group of faculty more easily to consensus. To the extent that faculty are aware of their values and willing to take them out in public and look at them, portfolio assessment can aid in building consensus about instruction. We believe we have gone further in this direction than most, but we can't say we've produced consensus and clarity about instructional goals and methods. We have found some instances where discussions over portfolios have revealed differences among faculty over pedagogical goals, differences that discussion in the small portfolio teams that meet regularly during the semester could not resolve. Our experience, our close investigation, has shown us that to make portfolio assessment aid in building consensus in assessment and instruction, we have to go much further than we first thought. Yes, portfolios do build community and consensus more effectively and dynamically than impromptu writing assessments, but even here there are no easy outcomes. A community is not a group of people who all agree with each other. Communities have to work continually to find their grounds for agreement and to find ways to compromise on areas where they disagree. Some of our faculty, for example, privilege "academic writing" more than others; some define argument quite narrowly, others rather widely; some are more troubled by final drafts with errors in traditional grammar than others are. We have learned that maintaining a strong portfolio-based assessment program requires us to (a) seek out issues that demand consensus and (b) provide forums for building consensus. The process doesn't stop with the first consensus-building stage. If a portfolio evaluation is introduced but not maintained, no matter how thoughtfully it was established, consensus will disappear and the community will find itself with more discord than under less pervasive methods of assessment.

THE NEED FOR CRITERIA

We hadn't made many passes through the portfolio assessment process before we realized that portfolio reading requires as much of an evaluative stance as a traditional essay-test reading does, despite the portfolio reading's contextualized nature. Readers still had to make decisions, and we still expected that we would be able to identify and, ultimately, define a standard for a passing portfolio and for an outstanding one. Indeed, this quest to establish external, written criteria provided the impetus for what became our inquiry into readers' responses to portfolios, which turned into our analysis of common assumptions about portfolio assessment, above. Our readers have told us over and over that they feel the need for criteria and standards against which to measure portfolios, both those from other classes and from their own. This need is real, yet it is a difficult need to address, for it confronts one of the differences between traditional, holistic essay assessment (a proficiency test) and portfolio assessment (an achievement test): the relationship of criteria to the reading and scoring process. In essay assessment, the criteria are external to the goals of a writing program's curriculum. The context within which the writer produces the essay is essentially separate from the criteria by which the essay will be judged. For such an entry assessment, criteria are based on expectations of the academy as a whole. Thus, explicit, written criteria are important to the holistic scoring process; training readers, establishing reliability and validity, standing up to public scrutiny — all would be impossible without these explicit, external criteria.

On the other hand, in the portfolio exit assessment context of which we write, the criteria are grounded in the curriculum of the course in which the portfolio is produced. As students move through the course, they discover important features of writing and the writing process. In other words, what students learn in the class, among many other things, is a gradual revealing of the criteria, and that knowledge in turn informs the student's preparation of the portfolio. And because the scoring criteria are implicit in the whole system of writing instruction that leads up to the completion of the portfolio, the instructor's contextual knowledge of that system guides her/his process of reading and scoring the portfolios. In such a situation, the absence of external standards and external criteria for portfolios makes standardizing sessions central to the portfolio judgment process. In these sessions, all the faculty have worked together to search out the criteria we should apply to portfolios and the language we could best use to talk about them, continually discovering new kinds of portfolios and new kinds of problems and continually needing to redefine and re-draw our expectations about portfolios and how we respond to them. In other words, as the context for making a judgment changes, so do the implicit criteria for making the judgment, and the standardizing sessions become the locus for identifying those changes and "fixing" them for the duration of the current reading. Such a system of continually developing criteria appeals to the romantic side of human nature, yielding criteria that remind us of Tennyson's Camelot:

> For an ye heard a music, like enow
> They are building still, seeing the city is built
> To music, therefore never built at all,
> And therefore built for ever. (33)

Yet the classical side of us yearns for hard and fast criteria, for permanence, for "rules" readers as teachers can point to and say, "Here. Look at this. This is why you need to continue in Practicum." Furthermore, our classical side tells us that in order for a program to be fully accountable for its decisions, it must have explicable, sharable, consistent criteria. To date, portfolio assessments have relied on common values, on a shared sense of what competence is and what excellence is. Developing explicit criteria would require codifying our common values, while probably setting aside the individual emphases which have on occasion brought two readers to an impasse. Making values external also makes them less subject to change as the goals of a writing program change. We must search for an approach that permits criteria that are constantly open to negotiation, open to the changes that a recursive process of teaching and reading portfolios must involve. At the same time, perhaps there is strength in formalizing a method that would reflect the best of what readers already do, seeking to guide all toward those "good reader" processes. We perceive that the issues we have to resolve center on our emerging understanding that using portfolios to make exit decisions from our courses calls for an evaluative stance, as does traditional direct writing assessment, but that the evaluative stance it calls forth is of a different kind. We see a difficult balancing act ahead, but one that will become necessary to all portfolio assessment programs as they grow toward maturity.

CONCLUSION

Like the portfolio-based assessment we established, this article has undergone many transformations. It began as a project that would help our faculty reach consensus about what they meant by argumentation, a necessary step considering that two of the four items in our portfolios are arguments. Out of that project grew an effort to define criteria for assessing portfolios, a project that led us to ask readers to describe their practice of coming to a decision about portfolios. In the process, we came up hard against the assumptions we have examined in this article, assumptions which we found were common to portfolio-based assessments. Like most writing programs, we shifted to portfolios because we thought they provided a more accurate assessment of writing. After examining our assumptions, however, we have found that increased accuracy is not an inherent virtue of portfolio assessment; while it stands to reason that including more writing and a wider variety of writing as the basis for a judgment would make that judgment more accurate, our research indicates that these improvements come not as a result of using portfolios, but as a result of how a faculty or a program approaches the task of portfolio assessment. Over the last five years, we have discovered that portfolio assessment brings many benefits to a writing program: it promotes communication among faculty; it promotes faculty training and development as a natural outgrowth of the teaching experience; it democratizes a faculty, allowing the grizzled veterans of the composition wars to learn from the raw recruits, as well as allowing the inexperienced access to the advice, support, and knowledge of our most experienced faculty; it promotes consensus and collaboration; the list could go on and on. Ironically, the reason we adopted portfolio assessment in the first place is the one reason our research calls into question: the assessment reason. Further research into the problems we have encountered with these common assumptions will help establish whether portfolio assessment is better *qua* assessment; its other benefits, in our experience, make it a worthwhile endeavor, even if we are never able to prove that it is a better *assessment* than a timed writing holistically scored.

We have tried to show in our study both our commitment to portfolio assessment and our determination to question it closely and use what we learn to make the weak stronger and the good even better. We believe this can only happen when we confront our own assumptions. For us, this is neither the beginning nor the end, but a stage in a continuing process of learning and growth as we try to find ways of affirming what our students can do with writing.

NOTES

1. We must offer our appreciation to all the colleagues who participated in the portfolio assessment and in particular in the reader-response study during this period: Jan Armon, Cheryl Cassidy, Francelia Clark, George Cooper, Kathy Dixon, Louise Freyman, Helen Isaacson, Emily Jessup, Martina Kohl, Phyllis Lassner, Mark McPhail, Eleanor McKenna, Barbra Morris, Kenn Pierson, Sharon Quiroz, Martin Rosenberg, Bill Shea, Kim Silfven, and Maureen Taylor.

2. At the time this study was conducted, the post-test was still administered and scored; the success of the portfolio-based exit assessment has since allowed us to discontinue the post-test.

WORKS CITED

Anson, Chris, and Robert L. Brown. "Large-Scale Portfolio Assessment in the Research University: Stories of Problems and Success." *Notes from the National Testing Network in Writing* 19 (Mar. 1990): 8–9.

Belanoff, Pat, and Peter Elbow. "Using Portfolios to Increase Collaboration and Community in a Writing Program." *Journal of Writing Program Administration* 9 (Spring 1986): 27–39.

Condon, William, and Liz Hamp-Lyons. "Introducing a Portfolio-Based Writing Assessment: Progress through Problems." *Portfolios: Process and Product.* Ed. Pat Belanoff and Marcia Dickson. Portsmouth: Boynton/Cook, 1991. 231–47.

Cooper, George, and Liz Hamp-Lyons. *Looking in on Essay Readers.* Ann Arbor: English Composition Board, 1988.

Daiker, Donald A., Jeffrey Sommers, Gail Stygall, and Laurel Black. *The Best of Miami's Portfolios.* Oxford: Miami U, 1990.

Hamp-Lyons, Liz. "Reconstructing Academic Writing Proficiency." *Assessing Second Language Writing in Academic Settings.* Ed. Liz Hamp-Lyons. Norwood: Ablex, 1991. 127–53.

Hamp-Lyons, Liz, and Rebecca Reed. *Development of the New Michigan Writing Assessment: Report to the College of LS and A.* Ann Arbor: English Composition Board, 1990.

Huot, Brian. "Reliability, Validity, and Holistic Scoring: What We Know and What We Need to Know." *College Composition and Communication* 41 (Feb. 1990): 201–13.

Keller-Cohen, Deborah, and Arthur Wolfe. *Extended Writing in the College of Literature, Science, and the Arts: Report on a Faculty Survey.* Ann Arbor: English Composition Board, 1987.

Larsen, Richard L. "Using Portfolios in the Assessment of Writing in the Academic Disciplines." *Portfolios: Process and Product.* Ed. Pat Belanoff and Marcia Dickson. Portsmouth: Boynton/Cook, 1991. 137–50.

Roemer, Marjorie, Lucille M. Schultz, and Russel K. Durst. "Portfolios and the Process of Change." *College Composition and Communication* 42 (Dec. 1991): 455–69.

Smit, David, Patricia Kolonosky, and Kathryn Selzer. "Implementing a Portfolio System." *Portfolios: Process and Product.* Ed. Pat Belanoff and Marcia Dickson. Portsmouth: Boynton/Cook, 1991. 46–56.

Tennyson, Lord Alfred. *Idylls of the King.* New York: New American Library, 1961.

Wauters, Joan K. "Evaluation for Empowerment: A Portfolio Proposal for Alaska." *Portfolios: Process and Product.* Ed. Pat Belanoff and Marcia Dickson. Portsmouth: Boynton/Cook, 1991. 57–68.

20 Rethinking Portfolios for Evaluating Writing: Issues of Assessment and Power

BRIAN HUOT AND MICHAEL M. WILLIAMSON

INTRODUCTION

Issues in writing assessment have traditionally revolved around our ability to construct procedures that represent the ways students write and at the same [time] adhere to the guidelines set down by theories of educational measurement. Moss asserts that this tension between theoretical constraints of literacy education and assessment has been productive in promoting the many new and improved methods for assessing student writing (see Camp 1993a for a discussion of the relationship between the teaching and testing communities in creating writing assessment procedures). Moss also warns, however, that "Proposed solutions often reflect compromises between competing criteria rather than the fundamental rethinking that might push both fields forward" (Moss 1994b, 110). We concur with Moss's admonition about relying solely upon compromises between teaching and testing. While these compromises have been a necessary part of the development of writing assessment, they are also responsible for much of the dissatisfaction educators feel about the continuing importance of interrater reliability and test-type conditions which constrain our ability to develop assessment practices sensitive to the ways people read and write.

To meet Moss's challenge to "rethink" solutions that are more than compromises, we focus in this chapter on portfolios because they are, perhaps, the most popular form of writing assessment ever.[1] As well, portfolios and other forms of performance assessment provide the most rigorous challenges to traditional notions of educational assessment (Moss 1992). Our "rethinking" demands broadening the discussion beyond a consideration of just assessment and pedagogy to include important but often forgotten issues of power.

From *Situating Portfolios: Four Perspectives*, eds. Kathleen B. Yancey and Irwin Weiser. (Logan, UT: Utah State University Press, 1997), 43–56.

Moss's tension between competing criteria is framed in theoretical terms. We contend that oftentimes issues of power rather than theory drive important assessment decisions. While Moss cites tension between the two disciplines of literacy education and educational measurement, we believe that power is a third, important determinant in crucial decisions about how students will be tested and what impact this testing will have on student learning. To control testing is to control education, to control what will be valued and taught within the schools. Crucial decisions concerning assessment are often made by regulatory agencies and political and educational policymakers based on practical and political concerns of cost, efficiency, and public opinion.

This chapter discusses the relationship between assessment procedures and the underlying power structures which dictate and profit from their use. Examining the various theoretical and political pressures which influence what measurements are chosen and how they are implemented allows us to conceive of assessment procedures as instruments of power and control, revealing so-called theoretical concerns as practical and political. We challenge the notion that concepts like validity and reliability are unquestionable and theoretically necessary. In other words, the need to standardize assessment procedures to achieve reliability, validity, or some common standard can also be seen as a move to impose particular standards on large numbers of teachers and students. Our reconception of the tension Moss describes focuses on who will control assessment and curriculum.

We fear that unless we make explicit the importance of power relationships in assessment, portfolios will fail to live up to their promise to create important connections between teaching, learning, and assessing.

ISSUES OF ASSESSMENT

Newer approaches to writing assessment, such as writing portfolios, continue to be subjected to the routine scrutiny of the various theoretical approaches and political pressures all procedures undergo in the fight for control over writing assessment in American schools and colleges (Messick 1989; Moss 1992). No matter what form assessment takes, tradition and accountability dictate a need for standardization. "Standardization refers to the extent to which tasks, working conditions, and scoring criteria are the same for all students" (Moss 1994b, 110). Primarily, standardization is used to compare different educational programs or institutions in terms of their relative effectiveness in student achievement (Moss 1994a).

In writing assessment the need for standardization has been central to its development. The scoring of essays was so unreliable (inconsistent) that writing ability was commonly tested indirectly through the use of multiple choice tests of usage and mechanics.[2] Although the debate between the implementation of direct and indirect measures of assessing writing was often cast in terms of the tension between the teaching and testing communities (White 1993), in fact this debate was always within the field of measurement since it involved the achievement of the psychometric concept of reliability. In direct writing assessment, consistency in scoring is achieved through a set of procedures developed explicitly to ensure agreement of independent raters on the same papers. These procedures which ensure rater consistency in scoring include having students write to common topics in a controlled environment. Readers are trained to agree with one another on scoring guidelines they may or may not have any control over. An acceptable rate of reliability in scoring is crucial because traditionally testing theory dictates it.

Moss (Moss 1994a) challenges the traditional notion that assessment has to be reliable in order to be valid. For Moss, the very concept of reliability as a consistent interchangeable series of judgments on discrete skills or test items privileges standardization, thus limiting the power of local, contextual, performative, and holistic forms of measurement and the curriculum they inform and justify. Moss advocates local, contextual reading of portfolios or other assessment instruments. She offers the example of the procedures commonly used to decide upon the best candidate in a job search, where a committee of colleagues convene and discuss their understanding of each candidate's qualifications based on a full dossier of material. Moss suggests that this discursive, communal, interpretive search for value and meaning makes more sense for performance measures like portfolios. She acknowledges the inability of the psychometric theory of traditional testing to support such procedures but advocates instead the theoretical umbrella of hermeneutics in which the shared search for knowledge and judgment are often considered appropriate. Moss calls for a shift from one conceptual framework to another in order to create practices that are more firmly based on theoretical grounds which support the activity of reading and responding to literate activities. Delandshere and Petrosky invoke a similar switch from psychometrics to poststructuralism in the creation of assessment procedures for teacher performance and certification. Both Moss (Moss 1994a) and Delandshere and Petrosky contend that psychometric theory stipulates a limiting and inaccurate framework for interpretive and judgmental decision-making about complex human behavior.

In current psychometric theories of testing, individual achievement is decontextual and standardized, so that testers can draw generalized inferences about individual performances and compare particular students and groups based upon performance on a particular test. These types of comparisons delete the context of individual learning environments and student populations and assume that the ability to write is a universal, identifiable human trait that can be measured accurately and consistently. The emphasis is on the technical rigor of testing procedures and statistical operations and explanations rather than the complexity of student performance and judgments about that performance. The goal of large group and/or standardized assessment procedures is typically to assess substantial numbers of students and to provide a single numerical index that can be used to compare different groups of students within and among particular settings, assuming that the assigned numbers depict an adequate picture of student achievement and teacher effectiveness across various social, cultural, historical, and geographical contexts.

The losers in the high stakes assessment[3] game made possible by psychometrics are the students and teacher. (See Moss 1994b, "Validity in High Stakes" for a review of the literature on the deleterious effects of large-scale, high stakes testing on students' ability to learn.) Moss notes that large group, standardized assessment procedures present an inherent validity problem (Moss 1994a). Current theories of validity privilege the concept of construct validity in which a test must contain an adequate representation of the ability to be tested and the influence of this test on the teaching and learning of those who take it (Cronbach 1989; Messick 1989). Large-scale, high stakes testing requires standardization and tends to reduce the curriculum to what can be measured. At best, test scores obtained under these conditions are a very poor indicator of the range of learning fostered by a school curriculum. The value of these scores is often affected by the number of students tested and the diversity inherent in such large populations of students. Furthermore, when tests are used for comparisons among students, the procedures have to be standardized. Moss's critique of standardized assessment procedures is that they sacrifice validity for the objectivity of reliability, often resulting in a trivialization of the goals of assessment itself (Moss 1994a). Wiggins contends that this focus on standardization is really a confounding of standards with standardization:

> Standards are never the result of imposed standardization ... Standards, like good assessment, are contextual. The standards at Harvard have little to do with standards at St. John's College or Julliard; the standards at all our best independent schools and colleges are determined by each faculty, not by policy-maker mandate. (Wiggins 1993a, 282)

Although we recognize the inevitability of assessment driving delivery of curricular goals, we do not see assessment as an inherent evil. If assessment procedures are developed from specific curricular goals, then the assessment will tend to influence teachers and students toward mastering those goals. If, however, the assessment is based upon only those goals that are easily measured, then curriculum will be limited to its assessment procedures (Berlak 1992; Moss 1994b). The crucial element in all these "ifs" and in the ability of assessment to be a positive influence on teaching and learning revolves around the degree of power local stakeholders like principals, teachers, parents, and students have over the many aspects of an evaluation program. Many assessment programs, including those associated with reform movements which advocate site-based decision-making (see Callahan for a good review of portfolios and educational reform), mandate certain assessment procedures or euphemistically titled "conceptual frameworks" school districts, principals, and teachers are obliged to implement (Murphy, 1997).

The particular form of assessment creates much of what is considered relevant, valuable, and worthwhile by teachers, students, and parents; assessment is never separate from curriculum. Whether curriculum can drive assessment or whether assessment always drives curriculum is a matter for debate (also an issue upon which we, the authors of this chapter, do not agree). Murphy's recent review of various portfolio programs illustrates that there can be an interactive relationship between assessment and curriculum in which they exist as a dialectic, limiting, affecting, and informing each other (Murphy 1994b). Traditionally, high stakes writing assessment has been handed down, reducing the amount of interaction and creating a situation where, indeed, assessment not only drives curriculum, it "subsumes" it (Elbow and Yancey 1994).

Much has been made about the diverse and individual nature of portfolios to best represent literate behavior in a school setting (Belanoff 1994; Berlin 1994; Graves and Sustein 1992; and others). However, the move to standardize portfolios is an important aspect of the tradition in educational measurement since assessment instruments have always been standardized in some sense or another. This sets up a conflict, relative to Moss's notion of competing criteria of two disciplines. In fact, the deck is slightly stacked on the side of standardization, for as Moss points out, "we are considerably less knowledgeable about how to design and evaluate nonstandardized assessments and about how to incorporate them into our ongoing assessment practices" (Moss 1994b, 124). What do we do with portfolios as assessment instruments is a legitimate and perplexing question. The problems occur, we believe, when we succumb to the knee-jerk answer "standardize them!" Moss and others would have us look beyond psychometrics to hermeneutics or poststructuralism for theoretical answers to address the tension between the disciplines involved with literacy education and those who assess that education (Moss 1994a). Nonetheless, we think it necessary to also consider issues of power which often appear to exist outside or be invisible within this tension. In fact, issues of control and political expediency ultimately often supply much of the pressure to standardize portfolios and other performance assessments.

Power

If recent history in writing assessment has taught us anything, it has demonstrated that decisions about assessment ultimately involve decisions about where to locate power in educational and political institutions. For instance, the aspects of a writing curriculum that are chosen for evaluation through an assessment program and the procedures of the assessment itself control students' learning and teachers' instruction. The simple truth of educational assessment is that what we choose to evaluate in our students' performances will determine what they attend to in their approach to learning. For example, Resnick and Resnick point to the need to evaluate students' abilities to do independent and self-chosen tasks because they contend that what is not assessed often disappears from the curriculum (Resnick and Resnick 1992). Those aspects of the curriculum for which we are held accountable will determine what we emphasize in our teaching. Furthermore, our approach to assessment can lead to some unexpected learning on the part of our students when we design an assessment that inadvertently cues them to attend to some aspect of our classroom that we had not intended.

The effects of testing are pervasive and at times surprising. In some instances, poor test results are better than strong ones because this might mean more funding to shore up the valiant but failing efforts of the schools who are seen to be struggling against the inherent problems that certain members of the community bring with them to school. In other instances, notably strong achievement test results can increase the value of property in a specific school district, information which is routinely used by realtors to sell homes to prospective buyers. Test scores can give a school or district the right to claim that it is winning the fight against educational sloth. Clearly, test results can carry with them strong and persuasive outcomes beyond the intended function of the tests themselves.

Another powerful influence of testing on our schools is that assessment often functions as a form of surveillance[4] (Berlak 1992): a way for administrators or other powerful stakeholders to assume and wield their power and influence. Testing in the public schools, for example, allows principals to check up on teachers, who are in turn watched by superintendents and school boards, who are checked up on by state agencies, who are ultimately responsible to the federal government.[5] Linn, in examining the influence of performance assessment instruments on testing practices notes that in the mid-90s we have entered an era of increased testing. Unlike past initiatives, however, "the role of the federal government is much greater than with previous test-based accountability and reform efforts" (Linn 1994, 4). This increased role of the federal government in assessment can also be seen at the postsecondary level in the form of the proposed National Assessment of College Student Learning (NASCL)[6] which will give the federal government more influence over higher education.

Kentucky, which is in the midst of massive and ambitious school reform, provides a good example of the many issues surrounding power, assessment, and portfolios as it moves toward a new statewide curriculum that calls for activity-based instruction and interactive classroom environments. In the Kentucky system, students attend ungraded primary classrooms their first three years in school and are given increased instruction and exposure to computers, and much of the curriculum centers on problem solving and group projects. Also, individual schools have some say over the actual form and rate of change. However, another aspect of the reform is that all fourth, eighth, and twelfth graders are to submit learning portfolios in math and composition to be graded according to the same rubric and anchors generated by the state department of education.

Although there have been efforts by the state to involve teachers in the construction of the assessment program, the program itself has been mandated by the state, and the scores of the portfolios are used to make high stakes decisions. In an ethnographic study of one high school in Kentucky during the second year of the state's mandated assessment program, Callahan (1994) observes that the use of portfolios increased both the amount of writing students do and the attention teachers give writing in the classroom. "However, since 'portfolio' and 'test' have become synonymous it [will be] difficult for Kentucky teachers to use portfolios for any other purpose . . . [because] they perceive the creation of a portfolio as a stressful activity performed only in response to an external set of demands."

Even though we may use portfolios to assess student writing performance, standardizing their contents and scoring works to locate the power centrally in the hands of the very few who control other sorts of power and decision-making. For example, in the case of portfolio assessment in Vermont, the low interrater reliability coefficients have been enough to raise the call for increased standardizing of the contents of portfolios, even though portfolios are already being viewed as having many positive, though immeasurable, effects on teaching and learning (Koretz et al. 1993). This move to standardize portfolios is based on traditional notions of reliability which claim it "a necessary but insufficient condition for validity" (Cherry and Meyer 1992; and others). In other words, if a measurement system doesn't produce consistent judgments among independent raters, then it cannot be valid. Within the measurement community, however, there is no consensus about the absolute necessity for interchangeable judgments from independent raters. New, emerging theories of assessment point to the problems with rigid and simple conceptions of reliability for measures which include sophisticated judgments about complex activity like that exhibited in a portfolio of student writing. A whole range of assessment specialists are in the process of developing alternative forms of assessment which conceive of reliability as a "critical standard" or "confirmation" (Berlak 1992; Guba and Lincoln 1989; Johnston 1989; Moss 1992, 1994b; and others). At the very least, current conceptions of validity require a consideration of the importance of a test's consequences (Cronbach 1989; Messick 1989). However, these appeals to less rigid notions of reliability and the positive consequences of portfolio assessment in Vermont are not part of the decision to further standardize writing portfolios to achieve higher interrater reliability coefficients (Koretz 1994). In other words, decisions about portfolios in Vermont are not being based upon the theoretical developments which inform performative assessment procedures like portfolios. If the decision to standardize portfolios in Vermont is being based upon theory, we need to ask whose theory is being used and why?

It is not difficult to see where the power for assessment is located when portfolios or any other measurement instrument is mandated and standardized by a state department of education. The fact that students are compiling portfolios or writing in their classes with their teachers' and classmates' help is secondary. The ultimate authority in these situations has nothing to do with the activity in the classroom which produces the portfolios themselves. Instead, they are being used to generate scores which can support the reform movement. Like all such massive changes, the ones in Kentucky and Vermont require a huge investment from its citizens and politicians, and all of them want some proof that the effort is worth it. While all of this is understandable, we have no assurance that portfolios can encourage a learning environment in which the teachers and students have no say in how they are used, compiled, and scored. In these instances, it appears that the use of portfolios in high stakes assessment scenarios are predicated on political rather than educational rationale. While it is hoped that the wide-scale use of portfolios like that in Kentucky and Vermont can improve student writing ability, surely we increase the chances of this happening when we base decision-making upon educational rather than political premises.

This interweaving and confounding of politics and education is an ongoing dilemma in American schools. Part of the problem stems from the fact that in a very real sense schools are "agents of government to be administered by hierarchical decision-making and controls" (Darling-Hammond 1989, 63). This mixture of political policy and educational theory often creates an odd and ineffective marriage. For example, Berlak talks of how the educational policies of the Reagan and Bush era were contradictory and incoherent because on the one hand they called for increased local control while at the same time they advocated increased use of standardized assessment for increased accountability. According to Berlak, schools cannot attain autonomy when there is an emphasis on standardized assessment which takes the power for curriculum, accountability, and finances away from localities and invests it in centrally located sites controlled by those without knowledge or investment in local contexts.

Alternatives to locating power centrally already exist. In the job search scenario we referred to earlier, Moss offers an example of the way hiring decisions are made at the college level. In her example, the power for judgment rests within the committee itself and the local community from which it is constituted and to which it is responsible. This type of arrangement is considered appropriate for making important decisions about hiring university personnel, and as Wiggins argues, similar localized procedures are used in private and independent institutions to make decisions about students. In discounting traditional notions of reliability as interchangeable consistency, Moss calls for a critical standard by which student performance can be assessed on a local level which honors the importance of contextual and community values necessary for students and teachers to perform at their best within a specific environment (Moss 1994a). Moss's position is similar to Wiggins's, who maintains, "Standards are not fixed or generic. They vary with a performer's aspirations and purpose ... It is true we use the word standard as if there were a single excellence. But that hides the fact that different criteria and contexts lead to different single excellences" (Wiggins 1993a, 283–284). Citing Sizer, Wiggins maintains that the correct question is not "'Which Standards?' but 'Whose Standards?'" (Wiggins 1993a, 283), similar in effect to our question about whose theory.

As we see it, ultimately, decisions and discussions about standardization or reliability are political since they are about where to locate the power in an assessment program. Traditionally we have disguised the political character of such issues by referring to the sanctity of technical terms like reliability or validity even though there is little consensus in the measurement community not only about what such terms mean but about their value as meaningful representations. In fact, there have been several calls for dismantling the very notion of validity itself (Berlak 1992; Guba and Lincoln 1989; Johnston 1989).

One way to approach the dilemma we have raised about rethinking the tension between the assessment and educational communities is to "rethink" the notion of accountability. Most initiatives to assess student ability and educational programs are based upon the need for administrators and teachers to be accountable for their programs, practices, and the performances of their students. While we wholeheartedly endorse the importance of education striving for, achieving, and documenting excellence, we wonder how teachers and site-based administrators can be accountable to individuals and organizations who have little understanding of local problems and conditions. The problem, as we see it, is that the concept of accountability often assumes unequal power relations in an inverse relationship to the knowledge and understanding of the salient difficulties in providing a quality education. In other words, the least knowledgeable people often make the most important decisions, many times based upon assessment schemes that are so pared down by standardization that they produce information that has little meaning and importance for local contexts. Programs like those in Kentucky which advocate site-based councils recognize this inherent flaw in the power relationships of accountability. However, as we have already demonstrated, to control curriculum and other important factors in education, you must also control the assessment instruments.

Our "rethinking" of accountability is to replace it with the concept of responsibility. At first glance, there appears little difference between being accountable and being responsible. Like accountability, responsibility also involves providing evidence that local teaching and administrative decisions are based upon the ability of schools to provide quality educational experiences for their students. The difference lies in the relationship of power. Being responsible does not assume that local authorities have to account to higher authorities. The use of assessment for surveillance and other hierarchical functions diminishes as local assessment instruments focus on local programs and actually assist teachers and administrators in being responsible for the spending of public money, the design of educational program, and the education of its students. Changing the power relationships opens up a much more productive set of possibilities for assessment practices.[7]

IN CONCLUSION: CONSIDERING PORTFOLIOS

As portfolios are continually defined in terms of both their pedagogical value and measurement properties, it is important to remember that an assessment technique itself is not always of primary importance. Although we have some good examples of how portfolios can function in the classroom (see for example Belanoff and Dickson 1991; Paulson, Paulson and Meyer 1991; Yancey 1992a, 1992b), how portfolios are defined by the assessment procedures and how they are used and received by educational regulatory agencies, administrators, teachers, students, and parents will determine their ultimate role in enabling or disabling teaching and learning in writing classrooms.

Although we have no commonly agreed upon definition of portfolios, certain characteristics seem constant. Portfolios contain not only a collection of student work but also the process of how the writing got to be included in the portfolio. Ideally, students learn to make decisions about their writing in terms of what to include and how to improve what they choose to work on. Portfolios can also contain the reflective work students do as they prepare a body of their work not only to be evaluated but to represent them as writers. In this sense each portfolio can be an individual record of a student's journey to understand herself as a writer. Efforts to standardize such a record cut into its ability to help the individual student make sense of herself as a literate person struggling not only to make meaning but to create a context within which she learns to read and write.

As Moss notes, there is an obvious tension between standardized assessment and the highly contextualized, individual nature of communication (Moss 1994b). The power struggle over portfolios is a result of this tension. Any form of assessment which is so individualized as to let students choose their own tasks will be extremely difficult to standardize, unless their individual and self-directed nature is controlled by outside criteria. To do this is to risk reducing portfolios to a specific number of papers on specified topics to enable scoring reliability and standardization that would permit comparisons among different schools. Furthermore, as we have demonstrated, this tension results from the pressure to locate power in a central regulatory agency such as the state education department rather than in the schools and school districts themselves. To preserve the integrity of portfolios and to harness their ability to truly alter the power relationships in assessment, it is necessary to maintain their localized character and to resist any attempts to centrally evaluate them. "Compromises" like statewide scoring guidelines and training sessions are merely disguises to enable standardization.

Many of the initial arguments for portfolio assessment were made in opposition to the standardization required for the reliable scoring of essays. Portfolios are an important juncture in the struggle between educational assessment and political forces. They represent a crossroads, of sorts, at which we need to decide if we will continue along current and traditional lines and standardize their use, so that regulatory agencies can maintain their grip on educational practices. It is important to recognize that this decision is not just about theoretical soundness but about political pressures. We can choose to serve political expedience and create portfolio systems that produce numerical indices and allow for comparability. Or, we can resist such pressures, citing and importance of local control and the power of context in the creation of effective communication.[8] Our position in calling for a reassessment of the way power is located in assessment, especially in the use of writing portfolios, can be viewed, perhaps, as somewhat utopian, unrealistic, or unobtainable. However, there are ways to use portfolios and other assessments which allow them to retain their local character and allow for the kind of assessment which provides rich feedback to inform and enrich teaching and learning. These are already emerging (see Berlak 1992; Johnston 1989; Moss 1994b; and Murphy

1994b for a discussion of such methods). For example, instead of having portfolios compiled by students at various levels and having them read and scored according to mandated guidelines, portfolios could be read by a local board comprised of the teachers themselves, parents, school administrators, and students, who would decide what criteria most relates to their students and school. These portfolios would be discussed and the criteria could change from year to year as student populations and local concerns evolved.[9] Instead of complicated numerical scores, we might think of judging portfolios on the basis of whether a student is on track, ahead of the game, or needs additional help. These numbers could be used to report student progress to the school district or department of education. A central board composed from local constituents would look at a small number of student portfolios either randomly or at particular segments of the school's population, depending upon the purpose. It might be possible, because of the much smaller numbers, to look at portfolios from several grades each year. In terms of the positive effect of assessment on curriculum, this scheme dictates that students compile portfolios every year, and that they are locally read with the potential of being sampled beyond the school. Portfolios have the potential to be more than just what "you do" in certain grades for assessment. Instead, they have the ability to assume a positive role in influencing the curriculum and culture of the school.

Such examples do not, by themselves, provide the necessary reconceptualization we are suggesting; they do, however, acknowledge the critical importance of schools retaining power over their ability to assess and teach. Of course, there are no easy answers to this struggle between locating power for assessment within or outside the schools. Compromises in this struggle have traditionally been resolved in favor of standardization and central authorities, often in the guise of being theoretically sound. It is important that we begin to devise new schemes for assessment which recognize the power relationships within our decisions for assessment and acknowledge the importance of context. It is also vital that individual teachers recognize the power struggles they and their students find themselves in as they attempt to use assessment instruments like portfolios to teach their students.

NOTES

1. We base our contention about the popularity of portfolios on the impressive number of volumes (more in the last five years than on all of writing assessment in the last two decades) and the four national conferences held between 1992 and 1994.

2. By the way, these indirect tests are still quite common. In a recent survey on placement practices of colleges and universities, half of the respondents report using indirect measures to place students (Huot 1994).

3. By "high stakes" we borrow a definition from Moss, to include any assessment used for "informing consequential decisions about individuals and programs" (Moss 1994b, 110).

4. There is a long standing concern for government agencies and policies assuming "big brother" roles. See Foucault for an historical review and critical discussion.

5. Although most testing for regulation takes place in the public schools, there is increasing pressure to extend this type of assessment to postsecondary institutions as part of the emerging National Assessment of College Student Learning (NACSL). For a review of the NACSL and its relationship to writing assessment, see Witte and Flach 1994.

6. See Witte and Flach, 1994 for a discussion of the NASCL and its influence on the assessment of writing at the postsecondary level.

7. We are indebted to Patricia F. Carini for discussing with us the differences between accountability and responsibility and their importance in education and educational assessment.

8. The importance of context in language use is arguably the most significant development to come out of the great changes in linguistics, rhetoric, and education during the last three decades. See Witte and Flach, 1994 for a review of the literature on context in communication and its importance to the construction of adequate measures of literacy.

9. Murphy (Murphy 1994b) describes such procedures already in use in her review of school districts and portfolios across the country.

WORKS CITED

Belanoff, Pat. 1994. *Portfolios and Literacy: Why? New Directions in Portfolio Assessment: Reflective Practice, Critical Theory, and Large-Scale Scoring*, ed. Laurel Black, Donald A. Daiker, Jeffrey Sommers, and Gail Stygall. Portsmouth, NH: Boynton/Cook, Heinemann: 13–24.

———, and Marcia Dickson, ed. 1991. *Portfolios: Process and Product*. Portsmouth, NH: Boynton/Cook.

Berlak, Howard. 1992. Toward the Development of a New Science of Educational Testing and Assessment. *Toward a New Science of Educational Testing and Assessment*, ed. Howard Berlak et al. Albany, NY: SUNY Press.

Berlin, James. 1994. The Subversions of the Portfolio. *New Directions in Portfolio Assessment: Reflective Practice, Critical Theory, and Large-Scale Scoring*, ed. Laurel Black, Donald A. Daiker, Jeffrey Sommers, and Gail Stygall. Portsmouth, NH: Boynton/Cook, Heinemann: 56–67.

Callahan, Susan. 1994. "Trying to Dance in the Glass Slipper: Portfolios and Accountability." Paper presented at the Conference on College Composition and Communication. Nashville, TN.

———. 1995. Portfolio Expectations: Possibilities and Limits. *Assessing Writing* 2: 117–152.

Camp, Roberta. 1993a. Changing the Model for the Direct Assessment of Writing. *Validating Holistic Scoring for Writing Assessment: Theoretical and Empirical Foundations*, ed. Michael M. Williamson and Brian Huot. Cresskill, NJ: Hampton.

Cherry, Roger, and Paul Meyer. 1993. Reliability Issues in Holistic Assessment. *Validating Holistic Scoring for Writing Assessment: Theoretical and Empirical Foundations*, ed. Michael M. Williamson and Brian Huot. Cresskill, NJ: Hampton.

Cronbach, Lee J. 1989. Five Perspectives on Validity Argument. *Test Validity*, ed. Harold Wainer. Hillside, NJ: Lawrence Erlbaum.

Darling-Hammond, Linda. 1989. Accountability for Professional Practice. *Teacher's College Record* 91: 59–80.

Elbow, Peter, and Kathleen Blake Yancey. 1994. On the Nature of Holistic Scoring: An Inquiry Composed on Email. *Assessing Writing* 1: 91–108.

Foucault, Michel. 1977. *Discipline and Punish*. NY: Vintage Books.

Graves, Donald H., and Sunstein, Bonnie, eds. 1992. *Portfolio Portraits*. Portsmouth, NH: Heinemann.

Guba, Egon, and Yvonna Lincoln. 1989. *Fourth Generation Evaluation*. Newbury Park, CA: Sage.

Huot, Brian. 1994. A Survey of College and University Placement Practices. *Writing Program Administration* 17: 49–67.

Johnston, Peter. 1989. Constructive Evaluation and the Improvement of Teaching and Learning. *Teachers College Record* 90: 509–528.

Koretz, Daniel. 1994. *The Vermont Portfolio Assessment Program: Findings and Implications*. Washington, DC: RAND.

Koretz, Daniel M., B. Stecher, and E. Deibert. 1993. The Reliability of Scores from the 1992 Vermont Portfolio Assessment Program (Technical Report No. 355). Los Angeles: University of California, Center for the Study of Evaluation.

Linn, Robert L. 1994. Performance Assessment: Policy Promises and Technical Measurement Standards. *Educational Researcher* 23.9: 4–14.

Messick, Samuel. 1989. Meaning and Values in Test Validation: The Science and Ethics of Assessment. *Educational Researcher* 18.2: 5–11.

Moss, Pamela A. 1992. Shifting Conceptions of Validity in Educational Measurement: Implications for Performance Assessment. *Review of Educational Research* 62: 229–258.

———. 1994a. Can There Be Validity Without Reliability? *Educational Researcher* 23.2: 5–12.

————. 1994b. Validity in High Stakes Writing Assessment: Problems and Possibilities. *Assessing Writing* 1: 109–128.

Murphy, Sandra. 1994b. Portfolios and Curriculum Reform: Patterns in Practice. *Assessing Writing* 1.2: 175–206.

Murphy, Sandra. Teachers and Students: Reclaiming Assessment via Portfolios. *Situating Portfolios: Four Perspectives*, ed. Kathleen Blake Yancey and Irwin Weiser. Logan, UT: Utah State Press, 1997. 72–88.

Paulson, F. Leon, Pearl R. Paulson, and Carol A. Meyer. 1991. What Makes a Portfolio a Portfolio? *Educational Leadership* 48.5: 60–63.

Resnick, Lauren B., and David Resnick. 1992. Assessing the Thinking Curriculum: New Tools for Educational Reform. *Changing Assessments: Alternative Views of Aptitude, Achievement and In-struction*, ed. Byron R. Gifford and Mary C. O'Connor. Boston: Klewer.

White, Edward M. 1993. Holistic Scoring: Past Triumphs and Future Challenges. *Validating Holistic Scoring for Writing Assessment: Theoretical and Empirical Foundations*, ed. Michael M. Williamson and Brian Huot. Cresskill, NJ: Hampton.

Wiggins, Grant. 1993a. *Assessing Student Performance*. San Francisco: Jossey-Bass.

Witte, Stephen. P., and Jennifer Flach. 1994. Notes Toward an Assessment of Advanced Students Ability to Communicate. *Assessing Writing* 2.1: 207–246.

Yancey, Kathleen Blake, ed. 1992a. *Portfolios in the Writing Classroom: An Introduction*. Urbana, IL: NCTE.

————. 1992b. Portfolios in the Writing Classroom: A Final Reflection. *Portfolios in the Writing Classroom: An Introduction*, ed. Kathleen Blake Yancey. Urbana: NCTE: 102–116.

21

The Challenges of Second-Language Writing Assessment

LIZ HAMP-LYONS

T he language minority population (not including international students) makes up about ten percent of the school-age population nationally, yet nowhere in President Bush's (now President Clinton's) America 2000 report, the spur for the current intense activity in the development of models and proposals for national competency testing in literacy, was there any mention of that ten percent. Those of us who are concerned about the well-being of nonnative English-speaking citizens and residents of this country see the development of tests that are responsive to the special needs of this large group as essential to its equitable access to education at all levels and thus essential to the integration into our society of nonnative English speakers as fully functioning citizens. In this paper I look closely at the assessment of second-language writing and describe some of its best practices and some of the challenges it poses. I conclude by reasserting the need to find assessment methods and measures whose fairness to language minority test takers can be shown.

THE CONTEXT

The multiplicity of terms used for nonnative speakers and writers of English is potentially confusing and blurs an important distinction between two groups. The first group consists of overseas visitors from non-English-speaking countries who come to the United States to attend college (often as graduate students in technical subjects) and then return to their home countries. The second, much larger group is composed of the various immigrant groups that have entered and continue to enter the United States. Students in this group are often called bilingual, but many of them came here as children or have been in this country for many years, and many are the second or third generation of their family to be born here. Thus, they may not be literate in the

From *Assessment of Writing: Politics, Policies, and Practices*, eds. Edward M. White, William D. Lutz, and Sandra Kamusikiri. (NY: MLA, 1996), 271–83.

language of their heritage. Furthermore, their social circumstances coupled with the inadequate attention they receive in schools may cause them to graduate from high school with poor English literacy skills. Overseas visitors, in contrast, usually arrive with strong literacy skills in their first language and a strong orientation to the values of formal education. They take the ESL courses they need, pursue their degrees, usually successfully, and return home. The challenges of second-language writing instruction and assessment, then, are not from the first group but from the second.

The United States government refers to the students of the second group in K-12 education as "limited English proficient," or LEP, a term that has been found objectionable by many educators and students. In this paper I prefer to use the more neutral ESL (English as a second language) or to describe such a student as NNS (nonnative speaker, the opposite of which is NS, native speaker) or as a second-language or first-language writer. There is astonishingly little attention paid to writing assessment for NNS citizens and NNS future citizens; states and school districts are generally satisfied to base their decisions for tracking and special provision on standardized tests. Colleges and universities are usually satisfied to apply the TOEFL (Test of English as a Foreign Language), another standardized test, to international students. Educational Testing Service's TOEFL Program developed the Test of Written English (TWE) and introduced it in 1986, but we still do not know how many schools consider TWE scores when making acceptance decisions or assigning students to language courses. Furthermore, because of privacy laws, students not holding overseas-student visas are not identified as potentially having special needs. The larger and more needy group of nonnative writers I describe above, then, are unidentified, or they are identified as underachieving without attention to the cause of their underachievement.

At the college level, some international students go through an English language institute and then into required mainstream composition courses; some have high enough TOEFL scores to go straight into the composition sequence. Few "bilingual," that is, resident-status, students go through English language institutes, though there is increasing provision for these students in special programs at colleges. But typically our writing programs find, in the lowest levels, a disproportionately high number of students for whom English is not a first language. Most composition teachers have no training in teaching second-language writing; most of them learn to be sensitive to their second-language writers through trial and error, which is not the best way when the errors are mistakes made in individual students' lives.

THE CHALLENGES

I have argued elsewhere ("Basic Concepts") that the assessment of second-language writing shares many problems with the assessment of first-language writing but adds some new ones. In the field of writing assessment generally, we accept that if assessment is to have positive effects, its instruments must be well designed and sensitive to the contexts of the learners to be tested and of their teachers, and its users must be conscious of the social environment that has engendered the demand for assessment. The purpose of the assessment, the objectives to be tested, the test format, question types, and so on must all be clear to those affected by the test — test takers, their families, teachers, school administrators, and the people and agencies who will receive scores. Because the anecdotal evidence for "curricular alignment" (changes in what is taught made in conscious or subconscious response to what is tested) is strong, the test developers must know what the curricular consequences of their test instruments are likely to be. In addition to taking such general considerations into account, second-language writing assessments must respond to the diversity of the test population. But there are many special considerations that developers of writing assessments must be aware of as they design instruments for writers for whom English is a second language.

Probably the first thing that the untrained reader of NNS writing notices is the prevalence of certain linguistic features. Until fluency in English is quite advanced, second-language writers may not master features such as agreement of subjects and verbs, correct choice of prepositions, correct use of definite or indefinite articles, or maintenance of proper time relations. Studies by Terry Santos; by Roberta Vann, Frederick Lorenz, and Daisy Meyer; and by Michael Janopoulos have shown that college faculty members are generally more tolerant of NNS errors in writing than they are of NS errors. Nevertheless, the existence of persistent linguistic errors in nonnative writing may result in miscommunication between student and reader and from that lead to lowered grades on subject-area papers. Having to spend extra time and effort reading papers may negatively affect professors' judgments of their NNS students. Vann, Lorenz, and Meyer find that the less exposure faculty members have to NNS writing, the more affected they are by grammatical errors in that writing. In all three studies, errors found to be most serious include incorrect word order and incorrect relative clause structure, while errors such as incorrect article and preposition usage are treated more tolerantly. Janopoulos questions whether nonnative speakers who have been allowed to pass through composition courses with lower standards of language accuracy in coursework will suffer when they find themselves in test settings where they are judged by the same standards as NS writers. In large-scale testing where NS and NNS writers are tested together, NNS writers may be disadvantaged by readers' paying excessive attention to the multiple occurrences of fossilized local errors in their writing. Robert Carlisle and Eleanor McKenna found that readers at the University of Michigan could ignore surface errors and attend to the quality of ideas and argument in NNS students' essays, even when NNS and NS essays were mingled together in a reading day. However, these were well-trained readers using a multiple-trait scale that emphasized ideas and coherence over correctness, and they were supported by reading leaders with strong backgrounds in second-language writing instruction. It is not known whether this finding would transfer to other contexts. Nor is it known how much more readers could be influenced by global language errors (errors that affect sentence and text comprehension rather than merely obtrude momentarily at the phrase level), such as incorrect relative clause construction and inappropriate word choice, on a large-scale test of the writing of mixed NS and NNS writers. While our current tendency is to place greater weight on the command of ideas, the ability to form and develop an argument, and other higher-order text-making skills than on sentence grammar and surface accuracy, it is not clear how much weight should be placed on the various aspects of writing competence. It is perhaps worth noting that the current trend in writing assessment and in the teaching of writing is in the opposite direction to the current trend in educational politics; before long we may find ourselves obliged to pay more attention to external accountability for accuracy in writing. If so, the question of accuracy versus expression of ideas and knowledge will become more problematic for teachers and testers of second-language writing than it is at present.

Another element that potentially intrudes, though more subtly, into essay readers' judgments of second-language writing is the question of rhetorical structure and rhetorical style. Teachers of second-language writing generally accept that those who are literate in their own language bring to writing in English a set of writing habits, patterns, and perceptions that affect the way they structure their texts in English: we call the study of such differences "contrastive rhetoric." Spanish-speaking and Spanish-influenced students, for example, have been found by Rosario Montano-Harmon to rely more on "additive, explicative, or resultative relationships between ideas," whereas Anglo students in the same study rely more on deductive and enumerative relations (254). Paul Lux finds that essays by Anglo-American students have significantly fewer supporting points than do those by Latin American students but that in the Anglo-American essays there is more detail for each point. His findings echo those of earlier studies, which show that students of Spanish-speaking background prefer a style that privileges long sentences with heavy subordination, whereas students of English background prefer a style that privileges "efficiency" (96). Phillip Elliott finds that writers of Spanish background and writers of English background even seem to prefer different approaches to an essay prompt (topic). Cross-cultural differences in handling essay prompts and in constructing text can importantly influence raters' judgments of essays. Examining the writing subtest of the British Council's English Language Testing Service, I found that raters' judgments were affected by the rhetorical choices made by writers and that, depending on the rater's background and knowledge, the rhetorical choices transferred from some languages might be more favored than those transferred from others. Japanese patterns were favored by raters who had taught in Japan and disfavored by those who had not; Greek patterns were generally favored and Arabic patterns generally disfavored ("Raters Respond"). Terry Santos describes some key differences between the educational cultures of first-language composition teachers and second-language writing teachers. She points out that rhetorical modes are still commonly taught in ESL composition courses, that the focus is still on form, and that discussion of rhetorical differences between English writing and writing in other languages is very common (2). In the philosophy and practice of basic writing courses, emphasis is more likely to be placed on fluency and confidence of self-expression. Because rhetorical structure is so closely allied with coherence, a key criterion for strong writing in English, international students may have an advantage over bilingual immigrant and ESD (English as a second dialect) students, who have not been overtly taught the conventional expectations of formal English text and who do not have an alternative set of recognizable conventions that they can apply instead. This point is discussed by Miriam Chaplin, who found that the writing of black students was often recognizable to essay raters because it had many features of oral style. Chaplin recommended that black students be specifically taught the conventions of formal academic writing style. Perhaps a similar strategy could usefully be applied to students from immigrant backgrounds.

The two aspects of ESL writing discussed so far require attention in testing and teaching contexts equally; I turn now to issues specifically applicable to testing contexts. The first issue is task, that is, prompt development. Good essay prompts are difficult to develop, and this difficulty is compounded, in tests for a diverse population, by the problem of avoiding culture bias. Probably the most important component of culture bias is the assumption of shared background knowledge. The Test of Written English (TWE), testing the writing of a quarter of a million international students annually, necessarily puts great emphasis on avoiding topics that assume certain kinds of cultural background or information that will not be shared by all the test takers, who come from hundreds of countries. Even though the TWE uses a panel of composition experts to develop prompts, it accepts for pretesting only about one of every eight prompts prepared, and of every three or four prompts accepted perhaps one pretests successfully. There are always surprises, as when the term *theater* was interpreted by a number of students as "operating theater." Avoiding problems of background knowledge is vital on an essay test because an essay test is usually a one- or two-item test. Students who happen to know a lot about the topic are lucky, and while variations in background knowledge can never be completely avoided, a lack of knowledge is especially problematic for ESL and bilingual writers who are being treated as basic NS writers and given the kinds of questions found on typical composition-program placement tests. The solution to this problem is likely to look like that used by the TWE and the Michigan English Language Assessment Battery (MELAB): anodyne prompts that are of limited interest and stimulation to all students. Although the jury is still out on the benefits versus the disadvantages of offering students a choice of prompt (Hamp-Lyons, "Second Language Writing"), many composition programs have decided that they must offer a choice in order to try to combat the bias likely to result when only a single prompt is offered to their diverse student populations.

Another challenge for ESL writing assessment is the training of readers to rate ESL student essays. There has been no serious investigation of the question whether NNS writing needs to be evaluated by raters who are specially trained in ESL writing or have experience teaching ESL students. The faculty studies cited above (Santos; Janopoulos; Vann, Lorenz, and Meyer) suggest that familiarity brings tolerance. Is the opposite true? At the moment we don't know. Some researchers found that, in the context of the TWE, scores given by an ESL-trained rater and a composition-trained rater correlated as strongly as scores given by two raters of the same cultural background. Yet looking in depth at raters' reasons for assigning scores, I found that familiarity with the writing of some cultures affected raters' judgments ("Raters Respond"). Rosemary Hake found that the race, the gender, and the language background of raters could predict their scoring behaviors; according to Hake, black raters were harsher than white, women harsher than men, and southerners harsher than northerners.

The search for appropriate scoring methods also poses special problems in second-language writing assessment. As Davida Charney points out, holistic scoring, because it has single-score outcomes and is not designed to offer correction, feedback, or diagnosis, is problematic in ESL writing assessment contexts. Diagnostic feedback and correction, while useful to every student, is especially valuable for NNS writers. First, many overseas ESL students have had only limited exposure to instruction in English and are only partway through their individual process of mastering the language. If they are given the right guidance, continued growth in writing is a real possibility for most of these learners. Second, many immigrant NNS students have been allowed to move through school with little opportunity to write, and teachers' expectations of their writing, when such students do write, have been low. If the students then find themselves in a program that places high value on writing, whether in a secondary or postsecondary institution, they will need a great deal of support. A single score does not provide sufficient information for either kind of student, for the teacher, or for the administrator who must decide on the optimal use of courses as curricular options and must set up special services like tutoring, conferencing, or workshops. Such services can be especially helpful to both international and immigrant ESL students. Further, a second-language writer often acquires the different components of written control at different rates. Every teacher of ESL writing has seen students who have fluency without accuracy and students who have accuracy but little fluency. Some writers will have a wide vocabulary but markedly less syntactic control, some will have syntactic control but little rhetorical control, and so on. From second-language writers who already have some mastery of a specialized discipline, it is common to encounter texts that show very strong content while their grammatical and textual competence lags far behind.

A better choice of scoring method for such students might be primary-trait scoring, where a single trait is defined and the writer's performance on that trait carefully described. When a student is given several primary-trait tasks, the several scores that result can provide a rich diagnostic picture of where that student's strengths and weaknesses lie, information that is very useful to teachers and administrators as well as to the students themselves. But primary-trait assessments are expensive and so have generally been used only in extremely large-scale assessments such as the National Assessment of Educational Progress.

In my view, the best option for assessing ESL writing and the writing of all minority students is the multiple-trait method. A multiple-trait assessment instrument builds up a scoring guide that permits a reader to respond to the salient features of the writing whether they are all at the same quality level or not. The essential characteristics of the multiple-trait instrument are its grounding in judgments and discussions of essays in the context where decisions will be made; the selection of salient features of writing quality within that context, which selection in turn focuses the reader's attention on contextually salient features in future assessments; and the provision of scores on each of these features for use in such decision making as acceptance into a program or placement within a program or for use in the instructor's diagnosis of specific writing problems. When proponents of holistic scoring object to methods that give separate scores for various traits in an essay, they are usually reacting against the analytic scoring used in the 1960s and 1970s, which focused on relatively trivial features of text (grammar, spelling, handwriting) and which did indeed reduce writing to an activity apparently composed of countable units strung together — hence the label "analytic," which came to have a derogatory connotation in writing assessment. What I am calling multiple-trait procedures are quite different from the old analytic scoring (Hamp-Lyons, "Scoring Procedures"). Measures very like multiple-trait assessment have been used for over a decade now to assess the writing of second-language English writers (see Jacobs, Zinkgraf, Wormuth, Hartfiel, and Hughey; Weir; Purves; Hamp-Lyons, *Assessment Guide*). Like primary-trait scoring, a multiple-trait procedure is an approach to the whole writing assessment process, not only to the scoring. Reader training is the norm in all writing assessment these days, but a multiple-trait procedure goes beyond other procedures by including reader involvement as a vital component in instrument development. Like primary-trait instruments, multiple-trait instruments are grounded in the context of their use; they are therefore developed on-site for a specific purpose, for a specific group of writers, and with the involvement of the readers who will make judgments in that context. Each is also developed as a response to actual writing on a single, carefully specified topic type. Containing no content specifications, they can be applied to a range of prompts, as long as those prompts fulfill the initial design criteria and as long as the context remains essentially unchanged. It is therefore easy for small but committed groups of teachers to use, develop, pilot, and monitor them in the teachers' own context, adding new prompts and making sure that the new prompts pursue the same writing goals as the original prompts. Of course, multiple-trait instruments can be developed that do include content specifications, but the amount of work to develop such instruments and to train readers for their scoring is much greater.

Multiple-trait scoring also helps ensure that scores reflect the salient facets of ESL writing in a balanced way. As we saw above, NNS writing typically contains significantly more language errors than does NS writing, and the danger is that a reader might respond negatively to the large number of grammatical errors found in the second-language text and not reward the strength of ideas and experiences the writer discusses. Holistic scoring obscures a pattern of consistent overemphasis or underemphasis on basic language control, but a multiple-trait instrument, in which language control is a trait to be judged together with other traits found salient in the context, and in which the reader is free to attend to the multidimensionality of ESL writing, is likelier to facilitate a balanced response to the strengths and weaknesses of the writer's text.

All this careful test development and reader training would ultimately go to waste without profile score reporting. This is the reporting of all the separate trait scores rather than, or in some contexts in addition to, a composite score. Scores exist not simply to assign decisions but also to communicate useful information that can be shared with the writers, their academic advisers, and other concerned parties. As I have argued above, detailed information is especially useful for second-language writers. When the writing in any one sample looks similar from different perspectives and has no noticeable peaks or troughs of skill, I call the resulting set of multiple-trait scores a flat profile. Such writing performance may reasonably be expressed as, for example, a single score of six on a nine-point scale without significant loss of information. But sometimes — and often with ESL writers, for the reasons discussed above — the writing quality looks different from different perspectives. I call the set of scores that show this unevenness a marked profile. By looking at the score profile, the writer, the class teacher, and the program administrator can make informed decisions about which course offering or other kind of service will most help the individual writer make progress. And when a writer has generally sound writing skills but a weakness in just one area, a single-number score will almost certainly fail to reflect the extremely marked aspect of the writing performance, whereas multiple-trait scores will reveal it. While the overall score may not indicate that the writer needs any special help, program administrators, college counselors, the teacher, and the writer as well can see the unusual pattern and decide whether to take action about it. Second-language users of English are particularly likely to be in this category.

The need to design better contextualized and more informative measures of NNS writing has led to multiple-trait assessments. At the same time, innovations in measurement theory have begun to liberate us from some of the constraints of classical testing practices, which have been problematic in first-language writing assessment but even more so in second-language writing assessment. Instead of classical measures, generalizability theory can be applied to estimate the effect of multiple sources of error. Using g-theory, we can begin to assess the effect of all sources of error rather than express error variance merely as an estimate of interrater reliability, as though the rater were the only source of error. With the development of item response theory and particularly with the recent introduction of multi-faceted Rasch analysis, we can account statistically for the effect of different raters, topics, and other factors and place all students' performances on the same relative metric. These procedures will eventually enable us to identify topics that are especially problematic for NNS writers (or any other special group) within an assessment of a mixed population, raters who are unduly harsh or lenient toward ESL writers, and other kinds of special factors that need to be accommodated. Multiple-trait analysis will be more useful in writing assessment than are the existing differential item functioning (DIF) procedures presently used to attempt to identify test items that are functioning differently for members of specifiable groups (by gender, race, ethnicity), and it will avoid test bias by eliminating such items. These procedures require a large number of existing items to act as criterion measures for making the decisions. In writing assessment, of course, we rarely have large numbers of items that have been administered to comparable populations.

PORTFOLIO ASSESSMENT FOR ESL WRITERS

Portfolio assessment has become the assessment of choice in many fields, but it has yet to be widely accepted in second-language writing classes. In part I think this is because the influence of language testing on ESL instruction has been much greater than the influence of educational measurement on first language writing instruction (the ESL community's flagship journal, *TESOL Quarterly*, regularly publishes serious articles on language testing and other quantitative research). In part too I think the lack of acceptance of portfolio assessment relates to the different, more conservative paradigm Santos describes ESL-writing teachers as inhabiting (the first-language writing community's flagship journal, *College Composition and Communication*, where post-modernism is the flavor of the decade, seems quite far from the concerns of most ESL teachers). Whatever the reasons, this relative lack of use of and research on portfolios in the ESL-writing context seems to me a matter for regret.

Portfolios are thought to be especially suitable for use with NNS students because they provide a broader measure of what those students can do and because of the elimination of the timed-writing context, which has long been claimed to be particularly discriminatory against nonnative writers. There is some evidence for this view. When I was at the University of Michigan, we found that after we introduced portfolios, more ESL students tested out of Practicum (the lowest-level mainstream writing class) the first time. There seem to be two reasons for this: first, students have time to revise. They don't have to turn in papers that are full of fossilized errors that pop out when time pressures are on; they can take the time to find and correct their errors, to go to the writing center and get tutorial help with problems of expression, to write in the computer and use a spell-checker programs, and so on. These are all strategies that any writer is free to use in normal writing environments but is denied in the setting of a timed impromptu exam. The portfolio method of evaluation is more realistic, and in its realism it appears not to penalize ESL students relative to other students as much as timed writing tests do. A second reason may be that ESL students are encouraged to do more than zip out a quick, short text and work on getting its language correct. They know that papers may come around again and that any paper may be one they choose to put in a portfolio to represent them to outside readers. They can see the paper in layers and work on different layers at different times. It is often the need to focus on competing textual needs simultaneously that overwhelms uncertain writers, NNS or NS, in timed situations. In the portfolio assessment context, ESL writers can be convinced that concentrating on ideas, content, support, text structure, and so on is worthwhile because they don't have to fear that such concentration will be at the cost of attention to technically correct language — which most of them have been conditioned to believe that teachers value most.

Although I have rarely heard the issue discussed, it seems to me that portfolios can reveal the differences between novice and skilled writers. In narrow writing contexts, novice writers always have the excuse of time pressure to account for their single-draft writing approach, for sticking to simple ideas and simple sentences, for editing instead of revising: all those features of novice writing that have been identified by Sondra Perl ("Composing Processes"), Janet Emig (*Composing Processes*), and others in the first language and confirmed by Vivian Zamel, Ann Raimes, and others in the second language. Such an excuse isn't possible in a portfolio assessment. Novice writers, or experienced ESL writers who have chosen novice strategies for their ESL-writing survival, have time to see that their teachers expect more and that those expectations are reasonable given the time available. Thus, when we find a portfolio that displays novice writing skills, we know that the writer is truly there, at that point in growth toward writing excellence, rather than driven there by time and context pressures. For long-term residents even more than for international students the portfolio, once they understand it, provides a motivation, or at least a prod, they haven't had before. These students often need to be motivated; they often have figured out ways to survive in the society, in jobs, and even in most courses in college, with very poor writing skills. But faced with a portfolio assessment, they begin to realize they will have to become skilled, for this assessment mode does not allow them to pump out the same old, barely acceptable, formulaic, extremely short writing that has got them through high school. Teachers' expectations are higher; they dig more deeply; there are no excuses for weak writing, no "Well, it isn't that bad, he is ESL after all." Failure to work, failure to listen to peer input and revise to meet it, failure to put the teacher's comments into practice in the revision, failure to go to the writing center and get special help when the teacher asks — all these failures are not hidden, not washed away in a quick test at the end. Questions such as "Did the writer follow through?" and "Did the writing really get better?" play an important part in deciding pass/fail and/or grades. Improvement, the ability to act on input, can be expected of every writer however weak she or he is at the outset. In this way portfolios are a tougher form of assessment. That many ESL writers do better on portfolio assessment tells me that most of them are indeed motivated and will still learn even after years in this country.

When we began to introduce portfolios at the University of Colorado, Denver, we had a lot of discussion about what type of portfolio we should use. Some teachers wanted everything to be in the portfolio; others wanted a limited set of texts, as at the University of Michigan or the State University of New York, Stony Brook. My experience made me suggest that to read all the writing of another class of students could be too time-consuming, and I convinced my colleagues to go with a limited portfolio, which we called the show portfolio by analogy with an artist's portfolio. But nearly half the teachers require a full portfolio as well, which they use to confer with students on their future writing needs, to discuss grades with them as the semester's end approaches, and sometimes to have them critique their portfolio and propose their own grade. Students are amazed when they see their whole portfolio, all that writing gathered together and presented neatly; they can't believe how much they've accomplished and how far they've moved. Even students who have to be told that they haven't moved far enough to reach the level where they can move on are impressed and encouraged by their visible development, so that they are less unhappy about repeating the level. They are likelier to accept the argument, which we think an honest one, that they are making progress but need more time and more professionally guided, intensive practice and that another semester of such progress will benefit them. Since we introduced portfolios as the exit assessment from our composition classes, issues of ESL writing have repeatedly come up and have had to be centrally addressed. In two major meetings to discuss portfolio criteria and standards, a serious topic of discussion for many teachers was what skills ESL students should show to pass a level, what skills they can be expected to gain in a single semester, and whether expectations for regular students and ESL students should be different. The consensus seemed to be that expectations should be the same but that certain perceptions need to be revised. For example, teachers may respond to fossilized linguistic errors in portfolios as negatively as they do to them in timed essays. When teachers discuss the ESL writers in their own classes in the general portfolio meetings and in the meetings of their portfolio teams, opportunities arise to talk about how significant those ESL writers' problems are in comparison to the level of their ideas, the level of their ability to provide appropriate support for ideas, the level of their macrostructural control, and so on. Useful discussion about portfolios necessitates sharing a good deal of contextual information such as the kinds of assignments given, the writing skills taught and practiced, the role of reading in the course, and the challenges posed as stimulus to writing. Teachers, thinking at length about the special needs and problems of ESL students, strengthen one another's skills in looking at ESL writing. In most composition programs, where there are a small number of ESL students and only maybe three or four ESL-trained teachers out of thirty, that sharing of skills and knowledge is important.

In portfolio assessment, the advantages of multiple-trait methods in traditional writing assessment are taken further: contextualization, teacher involvement, meeting over texts, and opportunities to provide detailed feedback that can inform not only pass-fail and placement decisions but also the availability and variety of support services. Not all the potential advantages of portfolio assessment have yet been implemented: portfolio readings typically result in single-score and single-element decisions rather than in diagnostic information, for example. Some classroom teachers have begun exploring the tremendous possibilities of student self-assessment, which is a logical corollary of portfolio practices (see, e.g., Ballard), but self-assessment has yet to make its way into large-scale assessments.

Sandra Murphy and Barbara Grant (1996) describe positivist and constructivist approaches to portfolio assessment, seeing them as oppositional. I consider it essential that we reconcile these apparently unreconcilable views rather than choose one over the other. The portfolio is a concept rather than an entity, and its chameleon nature, although confusing to some, is for me its greatest strength. For each context we need to understand the purpose for which we are using a portfolio and to decide the type of portfolio that best meets the needs of that context.

We must also remember that evidence for the benefits of portfolios for NNS writers is more rational and anecdotal than empirical. There is an urgent need for empirical investigation of how portfolio assessment affects differently the measured writing performances of NNS students and NS students. Using portfolios does not necessarily mean that ESL and other minority populations will suddenly find themselves on a level playing field. Robert Linn, Eva Baker, and Stephen Dunbar see no reason why issues of fairness and bias should not loom as large for performance assessments as for traditional testing; they remind us that "results from the NAEP indicate that the difference in average achievement between Black and White students is of essentially the same size in writing (assessed by open-ended essays) as in reading (assessed primarily, albeit not exclusively, by multiple-choice questions)." Gaps in performance among groups exist, they say, "because of [the influence of] difference in familiarity, exposure, and motivation on the tasks of interest" as well as because of unfair assessments (18). Rebecca Zwick has referred to evidence of bias in high-stakes portfolio assessment. Daniel Koretz has pointed out that scores on portfolios cluster and therefore do not discriminate, obscuring actual differences between strong and weak writers: not only does that lack of discrimination jeopardize classical reliability, it also means that strong and weak writers may receive the same scores. The advantage to weaker writers — among them, perhaps, ESL writers — may entail disadvantaging stronger writers. We must ask ourselves how equitable that would be and also what empirical evidence will be necessary before we know for sure whether portfolios allow readers to see the best of what ESL writers can do or whether portfolios simply depress real differences.

Second-language writing assessment, along with first-language writing assessment, has developed in several exciting ways in the last twenty years. But we still have a long way to go. Beyond the assessment methods themselves, we need better programs for identifying non-international students whose first or dominant language is not English; we need greater acknowledgment at federal, state, and local levels of the existence of these students; and we need funding for their educational support beyond initial language-survival programs, including funding at the college level. We also need, in our training programs for writing teachers, much more attention paid to the special needs of ESL (and, indeed, other minority) students. Above all, we need to remember, and to remind the politicians, that although the decisions we make about testing practices are highly political, a good test is not necessarily good politics. And assessments were never meant to be instruments of social engineering. I believe that those who look to assessments to solve social problems, even relatively benevolent assessments like portfolio assessment, are misguided. Turning to writing tests as the big stick to beat the nation into universal literacy is more than dangerously naive: it is disastrous. We develop improved assessments to better reflect what students are learning, with the minimum intrusion into the teaching-learning miracle. We are still learning how to do that well.

NOTE

This paper was written while the author was an associate professor at the University of Colorado, Denver.

WORKS CITED

Ballard, Leslie. "Portfolios and Self-Assessment." *English Journal* 81 (1992): 46–48.
Carlisle, Robert, and Eleanor McKenna. "Placement of ESL/EFL Undergraduate Writers in College-Level Writing Programs." Hamp-Lyons, *Assessing* 197–214.
Chaplin, Miriam T. *A Comparative Analysis of Writing Features Used by Selected Black and White Students in the National Assessment of Educational Progress and the New Jersey High School Proficiency Test*. Research report 88–42. Princeton: Educ. Testing Service, 1988.
Charney, Davida. "The Validity of Using Holistic Scoring to Evaluate Writing: A Critical Overview." *Research in the Teaching of English* 18 (1984): 65–81.
Elliott, Phillip. "Spanish and English Opinion Essays: A Study in Contrastive Rhetoric." Unpublished paper.
Emig, Janet. *The Composing Processes of Twelfth Graders*. Research report 13. Urbana: NCTE, 1971.
Hake, Rosemary. "Composition Theory in Identifying and Evaluating Essay Theory." Diss. U of Chicago, 1973.
Hamp-Lyons, Liz, ed. *Assessment Guide for ELTS M2 Writing*. London: English Lang. Testing Service of the British Council, 1987.
———. "Basic Concepts." Hamp-Lyons, *Assessing* 5–18
———. "Raters Respond to Rhetoric in Writing." *Interlingual Processes*. Ed. Hans Dechert and Gunther Raupach. Tubingen: Narr, 1989. 229–44
———. "Scoring Procedures for ESL Contexts." Hamp-Lyons, *Assessing* 241–78.
———. "Second Language Writing: Assessment Issues." *Second Language Writing: Research Insights for the Classroom*. Ed. Barbara Kroll. New York: Cambridge UP, 1990. 69–87.
Jacobs, Holly L., Stephen A. Zinkgraf, Deanna Wormuth, V. Faye Hartfiel, and J. B. Hughey. *Testing ESL Composition: A Practical Approach*. Rowley: Newbury, 1981.
Janopoulos, Michael. "University Faculty Tolerance of NS and NSS Writing Errors." *Journal of Second Language Writing* 1.2 (1991): 109–22.
Koretz, Daniel. "The Evaluation of the Vermont Portfolio Assessment Programs: Interpretations and Implications of Initial Findings." Meeting of the Natl. Council on Measurement in Educ. Atlanta. 1993.

Linn, Robert L., Eva I. Baker, and Stephen B. Dunbar. "Complex, Performance-Based Assessment: Expectations and Validation Criteria." *Educational Researcher* 20.8 (1991): 5–21.

Lux, Paul. "Discourse Styles of Anglo and Latin American College Student Writers." Diss. Arizona State U, 1991.

Montano-Harmon, Rosario. "Discourse Features in the Compositions of Mexican English as a Second Language, Mexican-American Chicano, and Anglo High School Students: Considerations for the Formulation of Educational Policy." Diss. U of Southern California, 1988.

Murphy, Sandra and Barbara Grant. Portfolio Approaches to Assessment: Breakthroughs or more of the same? *Assessment of Writing: Politics, Policies, Practices.* Eds. Edward M. White, William D. Lutz, and Sandra Kamusikiri. New York: Modern Language Association, 1996. 284–300.

Perl, Sondra. "The Composing Processes of Unskilled College Writers." *Research in the Teaching of English* 13 (1979): 317–36.

Purves, Alan. "Reflections on Research and Assessment in Written Composition." *Research in the Teaching of English* 26 (1992): 108–22.

Raimes, Ann. "What Unskilled ESL Students Do As They Write." *TESOL Quarterly* 19 (1985): 229–58.

Santos, Terry. "Ideology in Composition: L1 and ESL." *Journal of Second Language Writing* 1 (1991): 1–16.

Vann, Roberta J., Frederick O. Lorenz, and Daisy M. Meyer. "Error Gravity: Faculty Response to Errors in the Written Discourse of Nonnative Speakers of English." Hamp-Lyons, *Assessing* 181–96.

Weir, Cyril. "The Specification, Realisation and Validation of an English Language Proficiency Test." *Testing English for University Study.* Ed. Arthur Hughes. ELT Documents 127. Oxford: Modern English, 1988.

Zamel, Vivian. "The Composing Processes of Advanced ESL Students: Six Case Studies." *TESOL Quarterly* 17 (1983): 165–88.

Zwick, Rebecca. "The Technical Requirements of High-Stakes Performance Assessments: Answers to Your Questions." Panel discussion at the Annual Meeting of the Natl. Council on Measurement in Educ. Atlanta. Apr. 1993.

22

Expanding the Dialogue on Culture as a Critical Component When Assessing Writing

ARNETHA F. BALL

This article reports on the findings of a study that illustrates the value of including the voices of teachers from diverse backgrounds in discussions concerning writing assessment. The inclusion of such voices can help, not only to inform, but to re-shape current assessment practices, research priorities, and policy debates that focus on finding solutions to problems of assessment, particularly as they relate to diverse populations. In Part one of the article, I review the findings of an investigation in which four European-American teachers assess students' written texts. These teachers rated essays written by ethnically diverse fifth- and sixth-grade students using an array of rhetorical and linguistic measures—including overall quality, coherence, sentence-level mechanics, and use of an organizational structure. In Part two, I describe a replication of this investigation in which four African-American teachers assessed the writings of the same students' written essays using the same rhetorical and linguistic measures. Findings suggest that European-American and African-American teachers hold some consistently different views about the assessment of diverse students' written texts. Motivated by these observed differences and a desire to expand the dialogue on culture as a critical component in assessing writing, I present in the third and final section of the article the voices of the African-American teachers who participated in this study. Through candid and reflective comments, these teachers share deep felt concerns and specific suggestions concerning writing assessment. In this section, I also discuss how the voices of teachers from diverse backgrounds can be useful for broadening debates about the reform of writing assessment in general, and the assessment of writing for culturally and linguistically diverse students in particular.

The publication of *The Silenced Dialogue: Power and Pedagogy in Educating Other People's Children* by Delpit (1988; 1995) created a substantial amount of controversy centering around the debate over how to best meet the educational

From *Assessing Writing* 4.2 (1997): 169–202.

needs of African-American and poor students. Delpit, an anthropologist and educator, used the debate over process-oriented versus skills-oriented writing instruction to stimulate a dialogue about the complex rules of power that influence the education of African-American and poor students in this society. According to Delpit, process-oriented writing instruction focused energy on fluency and creative expression, rather than on "correctness," in getting students to put their ideas onto paper. Skills-oriented writing instruction, on the other hand, focused energy on teaching students the technical skills of writing academic mainstream prose; teaching useful and usable knowledge which contributes to a student's ability to communicate effectively in standard, generally acceptable literary forms (Delpit, 1986). Of primary interest to us in this article was Delpit's (1988) discussion concerning assumptions that underlie educational practices and the "silenced" dialogue between progressive White educators and educators of color who speak of being left out of the dialogue about how best to educate children of color. She explained how, when individuals come from different cultures (as do low socioeconomic African-American students and the majority of their teachers who come from middle-class backgrounds), they may have different rules for participating in a power culture. When teachers insist that students practice the rules of mainstream institutions, miscommunications often occur based on different educational and behavioral expectations, communication strategies, and presentations of self. Delpit's article concluded that the most troubling aspect of the dilemma did not really reside in the debate over instructional methodology, but rather in communicating across cultures and in addressing the more fundamental issue of whose voice gets to be heard in determining what is best for poor children and children of color. In addition to this work by Delpit, it has been more than two decades since Whiteman (1976) conducted her early research on dialect influence and the writing differences between African-American and European-American students. Since that time, scholars such as Hoover and Politzer (1981) and Robinson (1980) have raised questions about cultural influence and assessing the writing of students who are speakers of non-prestige varieties of English. Still others in the scholarly community have suggested that language operates within a culture of power in our schools and that some voices are privileged while others are denied or silenced within our educational institutions (Bizzell, 1991; Huot & Williamson, 1997; Schaafsma, 1993).

In this article, I also propose that writing assessment is a part of the power culture that exists in educational institutions and that there is a need to include the voices of more teachers from diverse backgrounds in discussions concerning writing assessment. Indeed, this is not a new proposal, however, the implications of this notion for certain populations have not received sufficient discussion in the literature. This article re-visits the issue of the importance of including culture as a critical component in discussions on writing assessment. Through a study that contrasts the assessment practices of two groups of teachers, it becomes more evident that culture is a critical component in writing assessment. And through the shared reflections of the African-American teachers who participated in this study, this article illustrates how including the voices of teachers from diverse backgrounds can help to broaden the discussion concerning assessment and can perhaps also help to re-shape assessment practices, research priorities, and policy debates on the topic.

Background

Almost ten years after the publication of articles similar to those written by Hoover and Politzer (1981), Robinson (1980) and Delpit (1988), programs such as the National Writing Project still consist of populations that are still predominantly European American while the student populations in our nation's large city and urban schools are predominantly non-European American. With changing demographics in many schools and research indicating that African-American and Hispanic-American students' writing achievement levels are generally lower than European-American students' (Applebee, Langer, & Mullis, 1986; Applebee, Langer, Mullis, Latham, & Gentile, 1994), it seems an appropriate time to review Delpit's argument, revisit the issue of writing assessment with students of color, and revitalize the dialogue on culture as a critical component in such assessments.

A high percentage of today's college-educated, traditionally underrepresented people of color are choosing to work in fields other than education. While urban and inner-city classrooms are being filled by African Americans, Hispanic Americans, and recent immigrants from Southeast Asia, Central America, and the Caribbean, teachers in these classrooms are characterized as being predominantly middle-class European Americans, and often educated in predominantly European-American institutions of higher education (Gomez, 1993; Grant & Secada, 1990). Products of their up-bringing and educational experiences, teachers with more than 15 years of experience show a greater tendency toward conservatism in their teaching and assessment practices while younger teachers, at least those who have had a more diversified experience with regard to curriculum and peer exposure, show a higher tendency toward liberalism in their teaching practices and philosophies. In the case of middle-class teachers, many consider themselves to be "liberals" (defined by Delpit as those whose beliefs include striving for a society based upon maximum individual freedom and autonomy). Often such teachers assume that to have very high expectations that are made explicit to students through instructional and assessment practices is to act against liberal principles, limiting the freedom and autonomy of the students subjected to the explicitness. According to Bizzell (1991), many writing professionals "want to serve the common good with the power we possess by virtue of our position as teachers, and yet we are deeply suspicious of any exercise of power in the classroom" (p. 54). Although in positions of power in the classroom, both categories of teachers also have difficulty assessing African-American students' writing because of their acknowledged lack of knowledge about the cultural and linguistic differences in patterns of expression between African American vernacular English (AAVE) and academic English and lack of confidence about how to approach the assessment of these students' written texts (Heath, 1983; Ball, 1998). In their efforts to de-emphasize grades, these teachers often move toward indirect communications concerning expectations and writing assessment in their classrooms. Teachers often do not give explicit instructions or clear criteria for grading, and the directions they do give to students often lack precise details. As a result, students are not clear about what is expected of them or how they will be evaluated. The resulting grades are sometimes partly motivated by the teacher's uneasiness about the extent of cultural influence represented in students' texts versus those features that should be considered incorrect usage. For example, if an AAVE speaking student writes "He be on time," using the habitual "be" marker used in AAVE to distinguish something that happens on an on-going basis from something that does not, should this be considered an error or a culturally influenced variation in this students' writing style (Ball, 1998)? Such questions arise for teachers who are unaware of the subtle features that characterize AAVE as a distinct linguistic system. Because of this lack of familiarity on teachers' parts, problems often occur for low socioeconomic students from diverse backgrounds who come from homes and communities that depend on schools to provide instruction and information about expected performances in academic settings. These students receive mixed messages from both groups of teachers because teachers are often unaware of, unable or unwilling to acknowledge the existence of conflicting cultures. In addition, teachers generally do not explicitly explain the rules of participation for the culture of power in which they participate. This situation contributes to students' failure in classrooms that require them to demonstrate their knowledge through writing. Improving this situation depends a great deal on improving cross-cultural communication and understandings — which can be accomplished through the study of attitudes, techniques, and assessment practices of those teachers who work effectively with culturally and linguistically diverse students and by acknowledging and including the voices of more teachers from diverse backgrounds in conversations on assessment. Through a contrastive analysis of assessment practices by two groups of teachers — one European-American and one African-American — the research that follows begins to accomplish this goal.

THE INITIAL STUDY

This initial study was designed to investigate the rhetorical and linguistic features that contribute to holistic assessments of the overall quality of students' written expository texts by European-American teachers.

Method

Participants

Four experienced English teachers volunteered to serve as raters in the initial study. The teachers were enrolled in a masters and teacher certification program at a highly regarded private university. They were all European-

American speakers of academic American English with teaching experiences that ranged from one to four years.

Materials

Texts collected from six culturally and linguistically diverse students from lower- and working-class backgrounds served as materials for the study. Six students served as subjects for this case study, including three males and three females who came from three 5/6th grade classrooms. Two of the 5/6th grade classes were located at the same inner-city, predominantly African-American and Hispanic public intermediate school in a lower-working-class community. The third 5/6th grade classroom was located in an ethnically mixed, parochial school in a middle-working-class community. These classrooms were selected in an effort to secure student writers from varying ethnic backgrounds. The three African-American students who provided texts for this study came from the predominantly African-American and Hispanic public school and spoke both African American vernacular English (AAVE) and mainstream American English. The two U.S. born Hispanic-American students came from the same public school, spoke both Spanish and English and were fluent in English. The European-American student came from the ethnically mixed, parochial school and was a monolingual, mainstream American English speaker. All six students came from working-class homes. Within this group, all participants were considered to be good academic students: two were classified academically as high achievers, two hi-average achievers, and two were mid-average achievers. The academic classifications of the students were determined by calculating students' total grade point average over the school year and classifying those above the 85th percentile (3.4–4.0) as high achievers; those between the 65th and 84th percentile (2.6–3.4) as hi-average achievers; those between the 55th and 64th percentile (2.2–2.6) as mid-average achievers; and those between the 45th and 54th percentile (1.8–2.2) as low-average achievers. African-American and non-African-American students were matched according to their levels of academic achievement. One African-American and one non-African student fell into each category. Thus, two high achievers, two hi-average achievers, and two mid-average achievers participated in this study.

I organized a four week voluntary after-school writing club to provide a setting for collecting informal oral and written data. Girls and boys met separately to ensure a freer flow of interactive communication. During these sessions, the writing club participants played games, ate snacks, and enjoyed talking to other students without censure on the tape recorder about topics they themselves had generated. All students were given journal notebooks and asked to make daily entries over the four week period. The six students that participated in this study were members of the after-school writing club. All students were asked to write on topics like African-American history, sports, music, friends, self, and community issues. The informal writing samples that were used in this study came from these journals and from other informal letters shared with the researcher. The formal academic written samples that were used in this study came from the reports and essays these six students produced for their classes during the school year. A total of 23 formal and informal written texts on a variety of topics were collected for analyses in this study. Of those 23 texts, six were formal academic texts written by African-American students, five were informal journals, letters, or essays written by the same African-American students, four were formal academic texts written by Hispanic-American students, four were informal journals, letters, or essays written by these same Hispanic-American students, two were formal academic texts written by the European-American student, and two were informal journals, letters, or essays written by the same European-American student.

Procedures

This study adapted Bamberg's (1984) and Durst, Laine, Schultz, and Vilter's (1990) framework for analyses to investigate preferences for uses of organizational patterns by students from different ethnic backgrounds, the types of organizational patterns students used in their writing, their variation from organizational patterns rewarded by raters and rating scales, and their impact on raters' holistic judgments about the overall quality of the essays (Ball, 1991). To examine both global and local aspects of content and organization, Durst et al. developed an array of analyses, including the holistic quality, mechanics, and coherence rubrics used in this study. I adapted their organizational rubric to more closely investigate issues concerning the ways students organize their written texts and the impact of organizational patterns used on teachers' assessments of texts. A detailed description of each scoring rubric appears in Appendix A.

A six-point holistic rubric was used to reflect the teachers' overall impression of students' texts and four point scales were used to reflect the teachers' impressions of text coherence, organization, and sentence boundaries, agreement, and spelling conventions. After the teachers were trained on the scoring system, approximately one half of the texts were scored during a one half-day-long rating session. Teachers scored the remaining texts on their own time and returned them to the researcher. I then tallied the scores assigned to each text by each rater and calculated a mean score for each rubric on each text. I also calculated the descriptive statistics for all scores assigned to each text and averaged the six teachers' ratings for each rubric to attain an "overall mean" holistic, organization, coherence, and mechanics score for each text.

Results

Table 22–1 shows that the overall mean holistic scores given to the European-American student by the European-American teachers were higher than those given to African-American or Hispanic-American students.

Table 22–1 also shows that the mean organization, coherence, and mechanics scores given to the European-American student by the European-American teachers were higher than those given to African-American or Hispanic-American students.

TABLE 22–1   European-American Teachers' Mean Score Ratings
by Student Ethnicity

Teachers	Teachers' Mean Holistic Ratings (6 pt scale)	Teachers' Mean Organization Ratings (4 pt scale)	Teachers' Mean Coherence Ratings (4 pt scale)	Teachers' Mean Mechanics Ratings (4 pt scale)	Total Number of Texts
European-American Student(s)					
Teacher #1	6.00	4.00	4.00	3.75	
Teacher #2	4.75	3.50	3.25	3.25	
Teacher #3	5.25	3.75	3.50	3.75	
Teacher #4	4.25	3.50	3.50	3.75	
Overall mean	5.06	3.69	3.56	3.63	(N=4)
African-American Student(s)					
Teacher #1	4.46	3.18	3.64	2.46	
Teacher #2	3.82	3.00	3.09	3.00	
Teacher #3	4.27	2.91	3.18	2.64	
Teacher #4	3.36	2.73	2.91	3.18	
Overall mean	3.98	2.96	3.21	2.82	(N=11)
Hispanic-American Student(s)					
Teacher #1	3.38	2.63	3.13	1.88	
Teacher #2	3.00	2.25	2.88	2.75	
Teacher #3	3.00	2.63	2.88	2.25	
Teacher #4	2.50	2.00	2.25	2.00	
Overall mean	2.97	2.38	2.79	2.22	(N=8)

THE REPLICATION STUDY

In 1996, following the completion and analysis of the above study, I conducted a replication of that study with the primary objective of investigating how the same rhetorical and linguistic features contributed to holistic assessments of the overall quality of students' written texts when the assessments were completed by African-American, rather than European-American, teachers. In this study I gave special attention to the careful replication of procedures and analyses used in the original study.

Method

Participants

Four experienced teachers of English and social studies volunteered to serve as raters in this replication study. These teachers were enrolled in masters and/or teacher certification programs at a highly regarded public university. All four of the teachers were African-American speakers of mainstream American English; however, all four teachers considered themselves to be bidialectal speakers of African American vernacular English as well.

Materials

The same 23 texts collected from six culturally and linguistically diverse students from lower- and working-class backgrounds that were used in the initial study served as materials for this study as well.

Procedures

After these teachers were trained by the same researcher as the prior teachers on the same scoring system using the same training procedures, more than half of the texts were scored during a one half-day-long rating session. Raters scored the remaining texts on their own time and returned the texts to the researcher. I then tallied the scores assigned to each text by each rater and calculated a mean score for each rubric on each text. I calculated the descriptive statistics for all scores assigned to each text and averaged these four teachers' ratings for each rubric to attain an "overall mean" holistic, organization, coherence, and mechanics score for each text.

Results

Table 22–2 shows that the overall mean scores assigned to European-American, African-American, and Hispanic-American students by these African-American teachers were quite similar across student ethnic groups.

When comparing the results of the assessment ratings assigned by this group of European-American teachers with the African-American teachers, it was noted that two interesting trends emerged. One, that all teachers, regardless of ethnic background, rated texts that were written in academically oriented organizational patterns higher than those written in non-academic, orally-based patterns. Two, that the overall mean scores given by European-American teachers were noticeably more hierarchically assigned to students from different ethnic backgrounds than those scores assigned by African-American teachers. Scores assigned by African-American teachers were also noticeably lower for each group than those assigned by European-American teachers.

In their ratings of these texts, both European-American and African-American teachers consistently gave their highest ratings to the texts written by the European-American student, moderate ratings to African-American students, and their lowest rating to Hispanic-American student writers — even though teachers had been given no prior details concerning the demographics of the sample population, other than the fact that the student writers were 5/6th graders from diverse backgrounds. Along these same lines, while the European-American student organized her texts only in standard academic organizational patterns, including the topical net and matrix patterns, the African-American and Hispanic-American students structured their texts in a wide variety of organizational patterns, including not only the topical net academic oriented pattern, but also the narrative interspersion and circumlocution patterns identified in Ball (1991; 1992) as orally-based. These results, indicating that teachers give higher ratings to students who organize their

TABLE 22–2   African-American Teachers' Mean Score Ratings
by Student Ethnicity

	Teachers	Teachers' Mean Holistic Ratings (6 pt scale)	Teachers' Mean Organization Ratings (4 pt scale)	Teachers' Mean Coherence Ratings (4 pt scale)	Teachers' Mean Mechanics Ratings (4 pt scale)	Total Number of Texts
European-American Student(s)	Teacher #5	3.25	2.50	2.50	2.25	
	Teacher #6	3.50	2.00	2.50	1.75	
	Teacher #7	3.50	2.50	2.50	2.25	
	Teacher #8	3.00	3.00	3.00	2.50	
	Overall mean	3.31	2.50	2.63	2.19	(N=4)
African-American Student(s)	Teacher #5	3.64	2.36	2.55	2.36	
	Teacher #6	3.55	2.55	2.91	2.09	
	Teacher #7	3.46	2.73	2.73	2.55	
	Teacher #8	2.73	3.00	3.00	2.36	
	Overall mean	3.35	2.66	2.80	2.34	(N=11)
Hispanic-American Student(s)	Teacher #5	3.00	1.88	2.38	2.25	
	Teacher #6	3.00	2.38	2.63	1.75	
	Teacher #7	3.13	2.25	2.25	1.88	
	Teacher #8	2.25	2.63	2.63	2.25	
	Overall mean	2.85	2.29	2.47	2.03	(N=8)

texts in standard academic organizational patterns, including the topical net and matrix patterns, support the findings of Ball (1991) which concluded that:

> teachers seem to prefer that students write exposition in academic, literacy-based organizational patterns. This preference is reflected in their ratings of formal and informal written texts . . . Teachers scored texts written in oral-based patterns (narrative interspersion and circumlocution) lower than those written in mainstream American academic literacy-based patterns (topical net and matrix). This evaluation trend is generally in keeping with a bias displayed in our society. DiPardo (1990) posits that many composition instructors feel that one of their primary tasks in promoting academic success involves teaching objective expository prose . . . A negative assumption is that oral-based literacy is impoverished compared to objectified exposition . . . This philosophy has been adopted and reinforced in our society's academic culture and reflects a bias against students preferring orally-based patterns . . . [p. 188]

While the European-American teachers gave noticeably higher scores to the texts written by the European-American writer, moderate scores to the texts written by the African-American writers, and lowest scores to texts written by Hispanic-American writers, the African-American teachers gave consistently moderate ratings to texts written by all students, regardless of their ethnic or linguistic backgrounds. Even though all these teachers came from similar educational backgrounds and received the same training on the same rubrics from the same trainer, resulting assessments by African-American teachers were consistently lower for all students from all backgrounds (Allen, Frick, & Yancey, 1997). European-American teachers' overall mean scores for texts written by the European-American student ranged from 5.06 to 3.56. These same teachers' overall mean scores for texts written by the academically matched African-American students ranged from 4.5 to 3.19. Comparatively, African-American teachers' overall mean scores for texts written by the European-American student ranged from 3.31 to 2.19 while their overall mean scores for texts written by the academically matched African-American students ranged from 3.69 to 2.50. Table 22–3 below illustrates that the European-American teachers were more impressed with the texts written by the high achieving European-American student while the African-American teachers were more impressed with the texts written by the high achieving African-American student. The comments shared by the African-American teachers in the section that follows, further clarifies these teachers' feelings about assessing writing as well as their feeling that all of these students should be functioning at higher levels of writing performance.

DISCUSSION

Because teachers are often unaware of the instructional and assessment practices of their fellow colleagues on individual students' assignments, discrepancies generally go unnoticed. However, when Delpit (1988) published her article — which pointed out the need to open the dialogue on these issues — published responses varied from indignation and resentment to skepticism. Some felt that process-oriented instruction doomed poor and minority students to failure; others were doubtful that a change in educators' attitudes would have much effect on students' plight in society in general; still others

TABLE 22–3   European-American and African-American Teachers' Mean Score Ratings Given to the High Achieving Students in the Study

	European-American Teachers		African-American Teachers	
	Scores for European-Am High Achiever	Scores for African-American High Achiever	Scores for European-Am High Achiever	Scores for African-American High Achiever
Holistic	5.06	4.5	3.31	3.69
Organ	3.69	3.56	2.5	2.5
Coher	3.56	3.56	2.63	2.88
Mech	3.63	3.19	2.19	2.69

condemned existing reform programs that failed to impact instructional or assessment practices:

> ... process-oriented programs doom poor and minority children to subservient roles because they inadvertently deny these children access to the "power code" spoken and written by affluent whites. . . . teachers have an obligation to help students learn how to read and write in that code. (Pearson, 1989)

> Reform of regular education is moving towards use of less explicit, more developmental approaches — [this is] a renewed prescription for failure of many students with disabilities and those already at risk for failure. (Kauffman & Hallahan, 1990)

> It is impossible to create a model for the good teacher without taking issues of culture and community context into account. (Lucas, Henze & Donato, 1990)

Almost ten years after Delpit received these comments in response to her article, the African-American teachers who participated in this study voiced opinions that were reminiscent of the outcries from earlier years. Following the rating sessions in which the four African-American teachers scored the texts written by the six students in this study, I sensed a desire on the part of these teachers to discuss the experience further. I sensed this desire because, unlike the European-American teachers in the earlier study, these teachers lingered around, making small talk and comments related to the experience, well after the rating session had ended. We therefore gathered into a round table discussion in which the teachers offered comments on how they felt about the quality of the students' writing and their reactions to the usefulness of having a rubric to guide them in the grading of students' papers. Rich reflective comments emerged during this impromptu session — comments that I wanted to capture for the purposes of this study. I therefore approached the teachers again several days following the discussion and asked them to respond to five questions that I created based on their earlier comments. At this point, I informed these teachers that three of the students in the study were African American, two were Latino, and one was European American. I also provided the teachers with these students' grade point averages and asked them — after having the opportunity to read over these students' texts and after having their own teaching experiences with students of color — to respond to the following questions:

1. If you were involved in a debate about assessing writing in general, what would the main thesis of your message be?

2. If you were involved in a debate about assessing the writing of African-American students or students of color specifically, what would the main thesis of your message be?

3. What changes do you recommend or comments do you have to offer concerning current writing assessments of African-American students and students of color in most classrooms?

4. Specifically, what kinds or types of research do you think needs to be done to improve assessment practices of African-American students' writing or the writing of students of color?

5. If you were talking to a group of policy makers, what suggestions would you have a) concerning writing assessments in classrooms and b) concerning school-wide or district-wide writing assessments (in general, and for students of color in particular)?

In response to these questions, the African-American teachers who participated in this study voiced a sense of outrage and despair over the state of education for poor and minority students who are at-risk for educational failure. This feeling of despair was summarized by one of the African-American teachers in the study. This writer was a male, middle school teacher who had three years of classroom teaching experience. He wrote, "I think that these students should be further ahead in their development as writers. At the very least, these students need to learn a few writing strategies before they are promoted to the next grade level." Another one of these writers, a female African-American high school teacher who had four years of teaching experience, went into much more detail when she offered the following comments:

> These compositions further add to my frustration and the sense of an overwhelming task that lies before us to teach logical, thoughtful writing skills to the modern student. I am quite disappointed to find evidence of this deficient writing at such young ages. This finding only upsets me more because I know at what level their knowledge of good writing practices will be in a few years. For the past two years, I have struggled with the lack of knowledge of good writing practices expressed by my ninth and eleventh grade English students. And I struggled with this same dilemma with my seventh grade language arts students. At each of these grade levels, I had to teach the basics of writing, imparting the same information despite the difference in grades. Yet, the majority of all of the students said they had never in their scholastic literacy experiences been acquainted with this information. I find this situation deplorable, and I see no chance of these fifth and sixth grade students ever learning how to write logically nor thoughtfully except for by luck and prayer. I mean, how realistic is it to expect that all of these students are going to cross the path of a patient, determined, and knowledgeable teacher who is expertly skilled in teaching writing? Not very realistic at all . . . Personally, I think that kids can write as well as they are expected to. I think their writing merely reflects the efforts of their teachers. I must add that a few of these compositions demonstrated great potential. I just hope their teachers recognize that potential and push them to really excel.

Still another teacher, an African-American female who had two years of experience teaching at the elementary and middle school levels, shared the following:

> I think that the majority of these students were writing at about the same level. I was not particularly impressed by many of the essays, and was a bit dismayed at the quality of some. They were, in the majority, very short and did not explore themes or analysis in particular depth. Based

on my experience with teaching 5, 6, 7, and 8 graders I am afraid that this quality of writing may be the norm, but I do not think that this makes it desirable or acceptable. I think that students need practice and more exposure to writing in order to feel that it is a meaningful event, task, or undertaking.

The final teacher, an African-American female who had three years of teaching experience at the elementary school level, added the following insights concerning her feelings:

> I must say that I am disappointed that at this grade level, these students haven't yet mastered concepts related to basic punctuation and grammar. As a sixth grade teacher in an "inner-city" public school, and a mother of two school-age children (3rd and 1st grade respectively), I do know when these concepts are introduced in schools. In addition, having lived in a variety of cities and having had the opportunity to visit schools in those areas, I know that schools are covering material at about the same time. I find it hard to believe that these students were never "taught" how to write a good sentence. I do understand that the whole process of writing is a controversial subject, and again, having been a teacher, I do have first-hand experience with trying to teach students "how to write." However, I never understood how students advance to the next grade without a basic understanding of how to write a sentence.

These comments come from four experienced teachers from African-American backgrounds who have worked with African-American and other students of color in their own classrooms. Each of these teachers express disappointment at the students' level of writing achievement and a concern that these students, and many others like them, will not receive the explicit instruction they need to develop to their full potential as writers. Implicit in these comments is a belief that all of these students do have the ability to perform at higher levels. Although the voices of these teachers, and others from diverse backgrounds, are seldom represented in national dialogues about writing assessment, they have much to say that can be useful for broadening debates about the reform of writing assessment in general, and the assessment of writing for culturally and linguistically diverse students in particular.

Based on the low to moderate scores assigned to all texts by these African-American teachers, it appears that these teachers hold very high standards for all of their students. In the African-American culture, it is often felt that teachers who have low expectations for their students are denying them opportunities to learn how to participate and survive in the real world. As illustrated in the work of Foster (1987), many African-American teachers feel that low expectations and lack of explicitness in assessment are ill-affordable luxuries within the current social and economic climate that stigmatizes those who are non-standard varieties of English. In the African-American culture, a culture in which apprenticeship is a predominant form of instruction, teachers are expected to share their expertise with their students, holding high standards for performance (Ball, 1995). Historically and in present-day contexts, African-American educators have supported assessment practices that provide credibility, predictability and support for their students, even in light of the criticism they receive from their European-American counterparts who say that "Black teachers seem to be so authoritarian, so focused on skills, and so teacher directed" (Delpit, 1988). Many successful African-American educators have remained connected to their students' cultural experiences — either by themselves being members of the same community or by integrating cultural references of connectedness into their instructional practices. Within the context of this cultural connectedness, the four African-American teachers in this study have responded to the five questions that are listed above. Their responses include specific recommendations concerning writing assessment as well as some related recommendations concerning pedagogy, research priorities, and policies that need to be considered. The reflective comments that follow demonstrate that these African-American teachers were not limited by the prompts that were presented to them. Not only did they comment on the specific points raised in the five questions, these teachers commented on additional issues that concerned them. Their comments generally fell into three overarching categories concerning issues of assessment and pedagogy, research needed on assessment and policy. These teachers also added comments on issues of personal concern or passion.

Concerning Assessment and Pedagogy

All four teachers contributed comments concerning writing assessments and writing pedagogy for students in general, and for students of color in particular. Following are excerpts from comments offered by teacher #1, the African-American female who had three years of teaching experience at the elementary school level. She voices a concern, not only for tailoring instruction and assessment to meet the individual needs of students, but for helping students to understand the importance of accuracy because their writing will remain under continual scrutiny. This teacher urges us to find ways to assess for accuracy without losing sight of the importance of honoring the essence of what the student is really trying to say.

> **Teacher #1:** Certainly as a teacher I am always concerned about "accuracy." By that I mean, spelling, grammar, punctuation, etc. As an African-American teacher this notion of accuracy becomes particularly important when I am working with African-American students. We (and I include myself in this because I understand the standard by which my own writing is assessed despite my educational achievement) as African Americans have had to contend with the fact that our handling of the English language is, and I suspect always will be, under constant scrutiny. So, pragmatically, I think we do our students a disservice if we don't in some way assess for accuracy and have them understand that assessment in terms of accuracy.
>
> Having said all that, I think it is very important when assessing, that assessment be done in stages. That is, that students' work should be as-

sessed in the context of that individual's own progression or growth through the attainment of literacy skills. I don't think that we can assume that at a particular point in his/her academic career, a student will have mastered skill A and therefore we access his/her writing based on that criteria alone . . . Therefore, in my teaching, I had to tailor my lessons and my assessment of students' work to the student's individual levels of achievement and their individual needs.

I think, also, that it is very important that we assess for content. By content I mean, what is the student trying to say? I had a number of students who were struggling with punctuation and other mechanical aspects of writing who had a lot to say. On paper, it sometimes didn't make sense, but if I asked them what they were trying to write, they were able to express to me wonderful and profound ideas. My job then was to help them make sense of the mechanics. It was very hard because I didn't want to lose the essence of what they were trying to express. I often found written language a terribly inadequate vehicle for expressing the often profound thoughts of my students.

In her comments on assessment and pedagogy, teacher #2, the African-American female high school teacher who had four years of teaching experience, recommends that we need to be careful to assess students only on material they have had the opportunity to learn and that we balance negative comments with positive ones so we do not discourage students or stifle their growth.

Teacher #2: . . . [A]ssessment should be tailored to the population; teachers should only assess what students have been taught, not what they should have been taught. Comments on students' papers should always accompany a score; and negative comments should always be countered with positive ones. African-American students do have the ability to write cohesive, organized, content-rich compositions that employ "standard" language practices; however, it is unfair to assess the writing of African-American students with the criteria that is not reflective of what they have been taught . . . For example, a student should not receive a failing grade on a paper for incorrect verb usage if he hasn't been taught correct verb usage; perhaps, he could lose a few points and get an explanation of that loss . . . but he should not have his academic future jeopardized because his teachers (yes, many teachers do not speak "standard" English even on the job), family, friends, and community have failed him in ensuring that he uses the "right" language at the right time . . . Assessment is often unfair because it does not encourage, but rather discourages. When assessing the writing of African-American students, efforts should be made to validate the evidence of cultural practices in their work. Their writing should be praised, encouraged, and refined. Their voices and motivation to learn and write should not be stifled.

In her comments, teacher #3, an African-American female who had two years of experience teaching at the elementary and middle school levels, recommends that we focus assessment on issues of students' ability to use writing in functional, realistic and practical ways.

> **Teacher #3:** The teaching and assessment of writing should not be reduced to how to form perfect letters, where to place capital letters, periods, commas, etc. The point of being able to write is for students to be able to do things with the writing—not just to write. In considering assessment, then, I think that the real issue is that students' work should be evaluated on their ability to functionally use writing in a realistic and practical way.

The following comments on assessment and pedagogy come from teacher #4, the African-American male middle school teacher who had three years of classroom teaching experience. This teacher expresses his feelings that teachers' expectations need to change in positive ways. These changes would involve implementing instruction and assessments that are culturally relevant to the students. As these changes occur, then teachers will work closer with students of color and become more sensitive to their needs as learners.

> **Teacher #4:** If there are going to be some changes made in assessment . . . they have to start with the TEACHING of writing. What I mean is that African Americans and people of color do not need any special assessment, but they do need more exposure to a variety of texts . . . and they need to be taught how to write for different audiences in different situations. The change needs to occur with having more culturally relevant curriculum where the students see themselves in the lessons, engage in the learning, and feel as though they have an invested interest in understanding the knowledge being provided. The change has to occur with the teachers' expectations of the students by working closer with students of color and being sensitive to their needs as a learner; not sensitive to them being a person of color.

Reading across these comments, some important notions arise that are not very different from many current discussions on writing assessment and pedagogy. First, like most other teachers in this country, these teachers recognize the importance of teaching accuracy and mechanics to students of color because they realize that all students will be held accountable for demonstrating their abilities to use spelling, grammar and punctuation in conventional ways. They also state that African-American students need to have the ability to write cohesive, organized, content-rich compositions that employ "standard" language practices, and they need to be able to use the "right" language at the right time. They even go so far as to say that we do our students a disservice if we don't provide them with access to conventional accuracy and provide them with an understanding that assessment is often defined in terms of conventions of accuracy. These teachers, however, go on to state that, although important, surface level errors should not be the primary focus of writing assessment. Rather, the primary focus should be on the wonderful and profound ideas that the students are trying to express, on using writing in realistic, functional and practical ways, and on providing praise, encouragement and sensitivity to the needs of the individual learner.

Concerning Assessment and Research

In response to the question, what types of research do you think needs to be done to improve assessment practices of African-American students' writing or the writing of students of color, these teachers provided a range of responses. Following are responses that represent the gist of their suggestions:

> **Teacher #2:** Research is needed on classrooms that produce effective Black writers to see what types of assessments occur there. Research is needed on the beliefs and attitudes of teachers towards Black students' writing, and research is needed on the assessment practices of writing teachers of Black students.

> **Teacher #1:** I think more work like that of Carol Lee's (1993) on scaffolding needs to be done. Her work was important because it helped to validate the skills that kids already had and showed them a different way to use them. I think we need to empower kids more, and we could do that with the help of more research like this.

> **Teacher #4:** More research needs to be done on using alternative forms, or non-traditional forms of writing in the classroom . . . a lot of teachers are set in doing things the old fashioned way; take out a book, read the chapter, and answer questions at the end. So in terms of research, researchers need to take a more active role in making connections with teachers to do action research; find out what is going on in the classroom, and the two components should work together to conduct the research.

> **Teacher #3:** Honestly, I think that the research has already been done. There is a lot of information, generated by research, about how to improve writing assessment practices in ways that would increase the writing success of African Americans and other students of color as well as provide them with feedback that would enhance the learning process. What is needed, then, is more implementation rather than more research.

Although teacher #3 voiced the opinion that sufficient research has already been done and what we need to focus on at this time is more implementation rather than more research, the other teachers felt that there is a need for further research. Specifically, these teachers recommend that research be done in classrooms where non-traditional, innovative approaches are being implemented and in classrooms that produce effective African-American writers to see what types of assessments occur in those classrooms. These teachers also recognize the importance of conducting research on the beliefs and attitudes of teachers toward the writing of African-American students. In our discussions they expressed the concern that until the issues of teachers' beliefs and attitudes are better understood and addressed, it is unlikely that the current experiences of underachieving students will change.

Concerning Assessment and Policy Making

In response to the question, if you were talking to a group of policy makers what suggestions would you have concerning writing assessments for students in general and for students of color in particular, these teachers' responses generally focused on two areas: the need for policies that will help to close the gap between the performance of students of color and European-American students and the need for policies that encourage the development of students who are skilled at expressing their ideas in a wide range of forums and genres rather than privileging a narrow range of specific forms. Following are two representative responses:

> **Teacher #4:** I think that writing assessment should be the same for all students as long as everyone is on the same page . . . I believe that the key component here is that students need to learn how to write in a variety of ways, for different contexts, in different voices. This is where the problem occurs because a lot of students of color, particularly African Americans, are restricted in their writing skills because they only know how to write in one or two styles which, most of the time, are not standard English. Other students, like European-American students, are exposed to a variety of texts growing up and are usually better at writing standard English. By middle school this gap is growing because standard English is what is being required of the students and any variation is considered wrong.

> **Teacher #1:** I would end my statements by saying to policy makers that the idea of one writing style being better than another must be dealt with before dealing with the issue of assessment. As long as society privileges one type of writing over another, then the assessments will always be biased. If standard English were put on the same level and not above other forms of communication — like a foreign language, home writing, and, yes, even Ebonics — then the evaluation of students would not produce this drastic achievement gap between students of color and European-American students. Therefore, if we endorse the implementation of teaching strategies that produce thinkers in our society, using writing as a tool, and keep the student as the focal point of our motivation to improve the teaching and learning of students, then aren't we all doing our jobs — teachers, researchers, and policy makers — as educators?

In an earlier reflection, teacher #4 made the comment that African Americans and people of color were not in need of any special assessment, however, if change is to occur then it must occur in the areas of teachers' expectations of their students and in developing teachers' abilities to work closer with students of color: being sensitive to their needs as learners rather than sensitive to them being people of color. This comment has far reaching implications for policy issues. Along the same lines, the two comments above are suggesting that policy makers enact procedures that support students of color writing in a variety of ways, for different contexts, in different voices, just as European-American students are exposed to a variety of texts in their homes and communities. They further recommend that we can begin to see decreases in the achievement gap as we acknowledge the value of diverse writing styles, because, as teacher #1 states, as long as society privileges one type of writing over another, then assessments will always be biased.

Many of the comments and suggestions given above are not too different from the comments and suggestions that are currently voiced in mainstream and national dialogues concerning writing assessment. The following comments, however, have the potential to bring some very different perspectives to the discussion. The first teacher below raises an important question for us to consider: "What should be judged first?" Should it be mechanics, content, form, effort, originality, or what? Teacher #1 writes:

> **Teacher #1:** I think we need to understand the complexity of thought that African-American students have. I think that this often goes unnoticed because they don't use "correct" syntax or grammar. I think we also need to consider the fact that written language is often an inadequate vehicle to express all the nuances of what African-American students have to say. It's like jazz music. Jazz musicians will tell you that the European system of music notation cannot capture the essence of what, for example, Charlie Parker played on his saxophone. Even among African-American writers who write in the vernacular, they cannot capture the true essence of folk expressions in any other written form. That's not to say that form and "accuracy" are not important, because they are. The question becomes "what should be judged first?"

This teacher argues that it is the complexity of the thoughts that the students express — like jazz — that so often go un-noticed. However, it is the expression of these complex thoughts that should be the primary focus of our initial judgments. Perhaps we need to design assessments that encourage and reward students for expressing these wonderful and profound ideas. Designing assessments that attend to accuracy and mechanics while privileging the importance of the essence of what students are trying to express remains a challenge. To this comment, teacher #3 adds concerns about the challenge of making assessment relevant and meaningful to students:

> **Teacher #3:** I think that current assessments of Black students' writing in most classrooms is ineffective and irrelevant because they are assessments of how students use abstract and isolated language conventions (often of a secondary discourse) without giving students any purpose or desire to buy into the idea that written language is important, relevant to their lives, or even interesting. So, I suggest that in order to make writing assessment meaningful for these students, assessors must keep in mind the practices of proficient written language users and should evaluate students on their ability to do these things. Only in such a context are comments about the effectiveness of one's syntax, discourse, or writing style relevant . . .
>
> It seems to me that African Americans, and other students of color, suffer the most from disembodied curriculum and assessment. When I say

disembodied I mean that it is instruction or assessment that is not grounded in purpose or meaning in the ways discussed above. If the purpose of the writing assignment is to present an opinion or argument, and students are then graded on their use of correct spelling, punctuation and syntax, such students will become disengaged. Rather than being challenged to master these grammatical conventions, they will lose interest in writing entirely . . .

For students whose environments may not provide an implicit value for written language, writing tasks must be designed to foster such value and assessment must work cooperatively with developing the understanding of "why write." Students often ask the question, "Why write it down when I could just say it?" For these students, the value of writing has to be adopted, then they can begin to ask the question of "How can I write better so that I can have meaning?" Only then do they begin to care about where to put that comma, so that the meaning of what I WANT TO SAY is not lost — then it becomes important to them. If writing assessments are just given to evaluate students' use of grammar and the like, then who cares? Most of the students in this population have not, do not, and will not care until writing and writing assessments are made meaningful to them.

In the comments above, teacher #3 critiques current assessments used with students of color as being ineffective, irrelevant and lacking meaningful purpose from the students' perspective. This teacher introduces the concept of "disembodied" curriculum and assessment. She explains what the concept is — assessment that has no purposeful meaning for the students being assessed — and then goes on to make some suggestions about improving the situation. This teacher recommends that we design writing tasks that have some relevance to the students and design assessments that work cooperatively with students to develop an understanding of why it is important to write things down when they could just as easily have been spoken. According to this teacher, we must design assessments that reflect concepts and contexts that are valued by this population.

In the statement that follows, teacher #2 also visits the issues of relevance and purposes for writing as important factors when assessing the writing of students of color. This teacher proposes that we should focus on four primary goals in our assessments, namely, students' writing abilities in the areas of communicating, documenting, creating and exploring. She further points out that the idiosyncratic conventions of writing mechanics can be worked out within the process of writing:

Teacher #2: . . . For example if you are writing an essay about a personal experience, the point may be to communicate with others or to simply explore your current understanding of the experience and how it has affected you. If that is the case, then the standardness of your language use seems amazingly irrelevant. So I guess, my main point in such a discussion would be that writing assessment should be designed to evaluate either the effectiveness of students' writing at communicating, documenting, creating or exploring — whichever meets the goal set by the teacher in giving the assignment. The idiosyncratic conventions of writing mechanics can be worked on in the process of writing. However, that should not be the primary focal point of either writing instruction or assessment.

The final reflection below questions the entire process and concept of assessment, stating that "we really don't need to assess writing" because assessment has generally been geared toward using the results to penalize students, teachers, and institutions when they fail to do what society expects.

> **Teacher #1:** I guess that what I am coming to, is the opinion that we really don't need to assess writing. I do understand that as a society there seems to be a need for assessment of everything. In a way, I see it as a filtering process. I guess my experiences as an unwilling participant in assessment, both as a student and a teacher, have not been positive. But it seems that assessment is not necessarily diagnostic in the sense that they (assessments) are generally not used to help students progress. Rather, they're used to penalize and stratify students. As a teacher, I tested my students because I had to. I had to have something tangible to prove to my principal, the parents, and the superintendent that I was actually teaching and that my students were learning. In a way, the tests helped me to readjust my teaching for students who didn't "get it" the first time; however, unfortunately, for those who didn't "get it," assessment often served only to remind them of how "stupid" they were. Despite my creative efforts to let students retake tests, for students who had not done well throughout their academic careers, retaking the test was just another opportunity to fail. I know that they were saying, "Why go through it?" Additionally, the district and state "achievement" tests are often used to penalize teachers (i.e., not granting tenure or raises) for "not teaching," and students (i.e., grade retention, not admitted in to "magnet schools," not allowed to graduate from high school, etc.) for "not learning," and school districts (i.e., state funds cut-off, loss of control to state board of education, and public ridicule) for whatever it is they are supposed to do. And so, too often I also find myself asking the question, "Why go through it?"

This teacher's reflection ends with a statement of personal passion and identification with the experiences of students of color. She also ends with a challenge for us to reassess our reasons for continuing to assess students.

The voices of these teachers — and others like them — can help us as we attempt to move toward a theory that supports effective teaching and learning environments for all students. These voices challenge us to reassess our purposes for assessing students, they challenge us to question "What should be judged first," and they tell us that writing assessments in effective environments must focus on the complex, wonderful and profound ideas that students are trying to express rather than on surface level variations. They also recommend that we judge students on their abilities to write in a variety of ways, for different contexts and in different voices, and that we reward students for developing abilities to use writing in realistic, functional and practical ways. They caution us that writing assessments must also reinforce the students' cultural expectations for learning, provide validation and value for the students' cultural resources, provide opportunities for students to contribute their expertise, and structure high expectations into the assessment experience. Such assessments must also reflect the fact that African-American youths can and do respond positively to high expectations and high standards of performance when given adequate opportunities and resources to master the materials and succeed (Lee, 1993).

The problem, however, according to Huot (1996) is that "for the most part, writing assessment has been developed, constructed, and privatized by the measurement community as a technological apparatus whose inner workings are known only to those with specialized knowledge" (p. 549). The teachers' voices and the students' needs are left out of discussions on assessment, and quite often teachers have been made to feel inadequate and their hands have been tied by mandates that require them to focus on skills they see as less important, such as mechanics or surface level issues. Many teachers become skeptical of assessment practices that do not reflect the values that are important to an understanding of how people learn to read, write and apply information to their everyday lives. Too often, those teachers who do feel some level of confidence about the assessment of students of color, have been shut out of the conversation. Their voices have been silenced by bureaucratic procedures, lack of inclusion, and lack of acknowledgment for the resources they can bring to the discussion. In order to remedy this situation, not only must we "learn how to better privilege the voices and interpretations from teachers most knowledgeable about the context of students' assessment" (Huot, 1996), but we must learn how to better privilege the voices and interpretations from teachers most knowledgeable about the *cultural* context of students' assessment. Unless we accomplish this task, writing achievement for underachieving students will, quite likely, continue to decline.

In the past, issues of cultural context have been quieted, and certainly have not been adequately attended to. The absence of dialogue on cultural context in traditional writing assessment procedures contributes to the lack of progress being made in assisting students from diverse backgrounds. For example, as Huot (1996) points out, the traditional response to rater's ability to agree has been to impose an artificial context, consisting of scoring guidelines and rater training in an attempt to "calibrate" human judges as one might adjust a mechanical tool, instrument or machine (p. 557). However, Pula and Huot's (1993) study of the influence of teacher experience, training, and personal background on raters points out the existence of two discourse communities in a holistic scoring session; one the immediate group of raters and the other a community whose membership depends upon disciplinary, experiential, and social ties (p. 558). Realizing this, it would be most productive to begin to find ways to privilege interpretations from readers who are most knowledgeable about the disciplinary, experiential, social, and cultural contexts of the assessment and find ways to privilege the interpretations of those who are most connected to the culture of those students being assessed, rather than spending time focusing exclusively on calibrating human judges.

When trying to understand the differences in scores assigned to students from different cultural and linguistic backgrounds, the comments of one of the teachers in this study shed some unexpected new light that relates to the important role that culture plays in the assessment process. This reaction, voiced by an African-American teacher when assessing the paper of an African-American student, is one that is seldom recorded in the literature:

> I found that some reactions I had as a reader were difficult to qualify on the rubric, for instance some of the essays "caught" me right off, and I found that I cared (for lack of a better word) about them. With these essays, I found that I was more interested in what the writer was trying to say and less likely to feel that these students' mechanical errors had interrupted my reading or my understanding of a text.

Making students aware of the presence of writing styles and expressions that some of their teachers find appealing may serve to make writing and its assessment a more engaging and enjoyable experience for students. For the last two to three decades writing pedagogy has moved toward process-oriented, culturally sensitive, and content-specific approaches that focus on students' individual cognitive energies and their socially positioned identity as members of culturally bound groups. On the contrary, writing assessment has remained a contextless activity that emphasizes standardization and an ideal version of writing quality. As Huot (1996, p. 561) discusses these issues, his comments are in synchrony with the teachers who participated in this study. He emphasizes the notion that perhaps we need to "begin thinking of writing evaluation in new ways, not so much as the ability to judge accurately a piece of writing or a particular writer but to be able to describe the promise and limitations of a writer working within a particular social, rhetorical, and linguistic" — and might I add cultural — context (p. 564).

CONCLUSIONS AND IMPLICATIONS

Today's multicultural society continues to challenge writing professionals to re-conceptualize assessment as part of a broad-based ongoing school reform movement that is taking place. As we approach the year 2000, we realize that larger proportions of our students are poor, minority, and at-risk (Hodgkinson, 1985; Scott, 1992; Orfield, Eaton, & The Harvard Project on School Desegregation, 1996). For large numbers of that population, writing and experiences with writing assessment have not been successful. Because of these and other school-related frustrations, drop-out rates are high, academic achievement levels are low, and college-going rates are significantly below high school graduation rates. To break this cycle of school failure for a growing segment of the school population, progressive and responsive institutions are challenged to seek information that will enable them to understand students' sociocultural perspectives in the design and management of successful learning and assessment environments. In these efforts, we can turn to teachers from diverse backgrounds who have historically been left out of the dialogue on important cultural components that impact writing assessments. We can look again at issues of differences in teacher expectations and attitudes that often result in breakdowns in communication among teachers and students and among teachers themselves. We can begin to take a proactive stance toward including the voices of diverse teachers in dialogues concerning writing assessment.

According to Huot (1996), "the door is open for real and lasting changes in writing assessment procedures" by inviting others, not only to become active in the dialogue on assessment issues, but to become "active developers of new, emergent practices" (p. 564). Opening the door, however, to real and lasting changes in writing assessment procedures that will have lasting implications for students of color, must also entail opening the door to dialogue on the *cultural* components in writing assessments, learning how to better privilege the voices and interpretations of teachers most knowledgeable about the *cultural* context of students' assessment, and looking anew at some difficult issues (e.g., differences in teacher expectations and teacher attitudes that often result in breakdowns in communication). In the past, dialogues on writing assessment were largely carried on by predominantly European-American teachers and other testing entities that were insensitive to issues of culture. It is time to include the voices of teachers from diverse backgrounds in discussions concerning writing assessment. And as we do so, we will find that these voices have much to add that can not only inform, but re-shape current assessment practices, research priorities, and policy debates that focus on finding solutions to the challenges that face us as we try to improve writing assessment for a diverse population.

Acknowledgments: I would like to thank each teacher and the students who generously donated their time to this research.

APPENDIX A

**A Detailed Description of Each Holistic Quality Scoring Rubric
Durst, Laine, Schultz, & Vilter, 1990**

A.1 — The Holistic Quality Scoring Rubric
6 score: The "**six**" essay is characterized by consistent control of the rhetorical situation. The complexity of the issues is addressed, and the essay shows a

consistent awareness of a larger world. As the position is developed, sophisticated language and complex sentence structure are employed. The response to the topic is effectively organized and the points are supported with complex illustrations or explanations. Grammar, punctuation, and spelling do not interfere with the reading of the text.

5 score: The **"five"** essay is generally characterized by control of the rhetorical situation. The complexity of the issues involved is usually recognized and the essay shows an awareness of a larger world. As the position is developed, sophisticated language and/or complex sentence structure may be attempted, sometimes resulting in awkwardness. Usually the response to the topic is effectively organized, and the points are supported with illustrations or explanations. Grammar, punctuation, and spelling do not significantly interfere with the reading of the text.

4 score: The **"four"** essay is characterized by some control of the rhetorical situation. The complexity of the issues may be acknowledged but not necessarily addressed, and the perspective goes beyond the personal context. The language is effective but not necessarily sophisticated; the sentence structure is clear but not necessarily complex. Although the response to the topic may be formulaic and/or there may be occasional digressions in the development of the position, the points themselves are reasonable and have some support. Grammar, punctuation, and spelling do not significantly interfere with the reading of the text.

3 score: The **"three"** essay is characterized by an attempt to respond to the topic that generally shows an awareness of the rhetorical situation. The perspective might not go beyond a strictly personal context. It may lack a coherent pattern of organization; on the other hand, it may be organized but lack substance. The development of its position is usually thin and relies on platitudes, assertions, and clichés. Language and/or syntax are often rudimentary and lacking in variety. The essay may have recurring problems with grammar, punctuation, and/or spelling of common words which interfere somewhat with the reading of the text.

2 score: The **"two"** essay is characterized by a seriously limited awareness of the rhetorical situation. The arguments are oversimplified; often the perspective does not go beyond a strictly personal context. Its organization may be like that of a "three" essay, but examples and illustrations are often confused or missing. Often, the syntax is tangled and the language is ineffective or inappropriate. Errors in grammar, punctuation, and spelling occur which interfere with the reading of the text.

1 score: The **"one"** essay is characterized by little or no awareness of the rhetorical situation. It usually suffers from general incoherence and has no discernible pattern of organization. The use of language is ineffective and inappropriate. Although the essay may address the topic, it might be so brief or incomplete that giving it a higher score is not possible. The frequency of errors in punctuation, spelling, and grammar often frustrate the reader.

A.2 — The Coherence Scoring Rubric

4 — Fully Coherent
- Writer clearly states main points of the paper in the introduction
- Writer organizes points according to a discernible plan that is sustained through the essay
- Writer presents points that are logical and consistent
- Writer skillfully uses cohesive ties such as transition sentences, conjunctions, and topically related words and phrases to link sentences and/or paragraphs together
- Writer often concludes with a statement that gives the reader a definite sense of closure
- Discourse flows smoothly — few or no grammatical and/or mechanical errors interrupt the reading process

3 — Partially Coherent
- Writer may identify or allude to but not clearly state main points of the paper in the introduction
- Writer organizes points according to a plan, but they may be only loosely or implicitly related, or the plan may not be sustained throughout
- Writer presents points which generally make sense, but which may overlook certain important points or not be fully consistent with one another
- Writer uses some cohesive ties to link sentences and/or paragraphs together
- Writer does not usually conclude with a statement that creates a sense of closure
- Discourse generally flows smoothly, although occasional grammatical and/or mechanical errors may interrupt the reading process

2 — Not Coherent
Some of the following problems prevent the reader from integrating the text into a coherent whole:

- Writer does not identify main points of the paper
- Writer does not organize the paper according to an identifiable plan throughout most of the text
- Writer employs a number of weak, specious, or inconsistent analytical points
- Writer uses few cohesive ties to link sentences and/or paragraphs together
- Writer creates little or no sense of closure
- Discourse flow is irregular or rough because mechanical and/or grammatical errors frequently interrupt the reading process

1 — Nearly Incomprehensible
Many of the following problems prevent the reader from making sense of the text:

- Main points of the paper cannot be identified
- Text is not organized into any kind of recognizable structure
- Analysis is extremely weak or nonexistent
- Writer creates no sense of closure
- Writer uses very few cohesive ties linking sentences and/or paragraphs together
- Discourse flow is very rough or irregular because writer makes numerous grammatical and/or mechanical errors that continually interrupt the reading process

A.3 — The Sentence Boundary, Agreement, and Spelling Rubric

1 — Sentence Boundary Errors. Looked at three constructions that contain errors: the fused sentence, the comma splice, and the incorrect fragment.

> *Fused sentence.* A sentence that contains two or more independent clauses with no conjunction or punctuation separating them. Example: "A United Dairy Farmers was located near the party the students went into the store in groups of ten, gagged the cashier, and stole large amounts of items."

> *Comma splice.* A sentence that contains two or more independent clauses joined by a comma rather than a semicolon or coordinating conjunction. Example: "Not all young people are problems, we are not all irresponsible or reckless drivers."

> *Incorrect sentence fragment.* Any word group, other than an independent clause, that is written and punctuated like a sentence (for other than stylistic reasons) is an incorrect sentence fragment. Example: "Something to relieve our tension from school work."

2 — Agreement. Looked for occurrences of several kinds of agreement errors:

> Lack of agreement between a pronoun and its antecedent. Example: "At our school these problems are very few and not much is said about it."

> Lack of agreement between a subject and a verb. Example: "There has been a few problems."

> Lack of agreement between a noun and a demonstrative adjective. Example: "No one under 18 years of age should be out at this times."

> Lack of clear referent for the pronoun. Example: "More officers on duty would get very costly, and it wouldn't always work anyhow."

3 — Spelling. In addition to any obvious misspellings, counted the following as spelling errors:

> Groups of letters that do not make legitimate words ("gret")

> Two words that are made into one ("alot") or one word that is made into two ("how ever")

> Clear cases of homonym confusion ("to" for "too")

Plurals that are not formed ("The parent stand on their legal rights.")

Plurals that are formed incorrectly ("communitys")

Wrong word divisions that occur at the end of a line ("delinqu-ency")

Mechanics Scoring

4   Few or no grammatical and/or mechanical errors interrupt the reading process

3   Occasional grammatical and/or mechanical errors may interrupt the reading process

2   Mechanical and/or grammatical errors frequently interrupt the reading process

1   Writer makes numerous grammatical and/or mechanical errors that continually interrupt the reading process

Note: Teacher raters assigned each text a score for each rubric, including holistic (1–6), coherence (1–4), organization (1–4), and mechanics (1–4).

A.4 — Adapted Version of the Organizational Scoring Rubric Adapted for Use in Ball (1991)

4 — Strong Use of Good Organizational Pattern

These writers demonstrate a good understanding of the format for the organization of a theme. They present thesis statements and organizational plans in their first paragraphs. Then, the writers try to follow their plans with several paragraphs. These paragraphs have topic sentences and some development. At the end of these essays, the writers establish closure of some sort.

3 — Moderate Use of Good Organization Pattern

These writers seem to understand the conventions of organizing a theme. In the introductions to their essays, they may present thesis statements, often followed by some superfluous materials or by an abbreviated plan. They then try to support their thesis statements with several paragraphs over which they demonstrate only moderate control. Often, there is no sense of closure to these essays.

2 — Some Use of Adequate Organization Pattern

These writers know that their ideas should be presented in an organized fashion. These writers create a thesis statement. They then support their ideas with text that is organized in an acceptable manner so ideas can flow.

1 — No Use of Organization Pattern

These writers have not used an adequate plan of organization for presenting their ideas. Ideas may seem to ramble.

REFERENCES

Allen, M., Frick, J., & Yancey, K. (1997). Outside review of writing portfolios: On-line evaluation. *WPA, 20*(3).

Applebee, A., Langer, J., & Mullis, I. (1986). *The writing report card: Writing achievement in American schools*, pp. 6–7, 16. Princeton, NJ: NAEP.

Applebee, A., Langer, J., Mullis, I., Latham, A., & Gentile, C. (1994). *NAEP 1992 writing report card*, Report No. 23–W01, pp. 101–105. Washington, DC: Office of Educational Research and Improvement.

Ball, A. F. (1991). *Organizational patterns in the oral and written expository writing of African-American adolescents*. Unpublished doctoral dissertation, Stanford University.

Ball, A. F. (1992). Cultural preference and the expository writing of African-American adolescents. *Written Communication, 9*(4), 501–532.

Ball, A. F. (1995). Community-based learning in urban settings as a model for educational reform. *Applied Behavioral Science Review, 3*(2), 127–146.

Ball, A. F. (1998). Assessing the writing of culturally and linguistically diverse students: The case of the African American student. In C. R. Cooper & L. Odell (Eds.), *Evaluating writing*, 2nd ed. Urbana, IL: NCTE Press.

Bamberg, B. (1984). Assessing coherence: A reanalysis of essays written for the National Assessment of Educational Progress, 1969–1979. *Research in the Teaching of English, 18*, 305–319.

Bizzell, P. (1991). Power, authority, and critical pedagogy. *Journal of Basic Writing, 10*(2), 54–70.

Delpit, L. (1986). Skills and other dilemmas of a progressive Black educator. *Harvard Educational Review, 56*(4), 379–385.

Delpit, L. (1988). The silenced dialogue: Power and pedagogy in educating other people's children. *Harvard Educational Review, 58*(3), 280–298.

Delpit, L. (1995). *Other people's children: Cultural conflict in the classroom*. New York: The New York Press.

DiPardo, A. (1990). Narrative knowers, expository knowledge: Discourse as a dialectic. *Written Communication, 7*, 59–95.

Durst, R., Laine, C., Schultz, L., & Vilter, W. (1990). Appealing texts: The persuasive writing of high school students. *Written Communication, 7*(2), 232–255.

Foster, M. (1987). *It's cookin now: An ethnographic study of the teaching style of a successful Black teacher in a White community college*. Unpublished doctoral dissertation, Harvard University.

Gomez, M. L. (1993). Prospective teachers' perspectives on teaching diverse children: A review with implications for teacher education and practice. *Journal of Negro Education, 62*(4), 459–474.

Grant, C. A. & Secada, W. G. (1990). Preparing teachers for diversity. In W. R. Houston (Eds.), *Handbook of research on teacher education* (pp. 403–422). New York: Macmillan.

Heath, S. B. (1983). *Ways with words: Language, life, and work in communities and classrooms*. Cambridge: Cambridge University Press.

Hodgkinson, H. L. (1985). The changing face of tomorrow's student. *Change, 19*(3).

Hoover, M. R. & Politzer, R. L. (1981). Bias in composition tests with suggestions for a culturally appropriate assessment technique. In M. F. Whiteman (Ed.), *Variation in writing: Functional and linguistic-cultural differences*. Hillsdale, NJ: Lawrence Erlbaum Associates.

Huot, B. (1996). Toward a new theory of writing assessment. *College Composition and Communication, 47*(4), 549–565.

Huot, B. & Williamson, M. M. (1997). Rethinking portfolios for evaluating writing: Issues of assessment and power. In K. B. Yancey & I. Weiser (Eds.), *Situating portfolios: Four perspectives* (pp. 43–56). Logan, UT: Utah State University Press.

Kauffman, J. M. & Hallahan, D. P. (1990). What we want for children: A rejoinder to REI proponents. *Journal of Special Education, 24*(3), 340–344.

Lee, C. (1993). *Signifying as a scaffold for literary interpretation: The pedagogical implications of an African American discourse genre*. Urbana, IL: NCTE.

Lucas, T., Henze, R., & Donato, R. (1990). Promoting the success of Latino language-minority students: An exploratory study of six high schools. *Harvard Educational Review, 60*(3), 315–340.

Orfield, G., Eaton, S. E., & The Harvard Project on School Desegregation. (1996). *Dismantling desegregation*. New York: The New York Press.

Pearson, D. P. (1989). Commentary: Reading the whole-language movement. *The Elementary School Journal, 90*(2), 230–241.

Pula, J. & Huot, B. (1993). A model of background influences on holistic raters. In M. M. Williamson & B. Huot (Eds.), *Validating holistic scoring for writing assessment: Theoretical and empirical foundations*. Cresskill, NJ: Hampton Press.

Robinson, J. L. (1980). The wall of Babel; Or, up against the language barrier. In Jay L. Robinson (Ed.), *Conversations on the written word: Essays on language and literacy* (53–91). Portsmouth, NH: Boynton/Cook Heinemann.

Schaafsma, D. (1993). *Eating on the street: Teaching literacy in a multicultural society*. Pittsburgh, PA: University of Pittsburgh Press.

Scott, M. S. (1992). One-on-one: The great defender Marian Wright Edleman. *Black Enterprise*, 22(10), 67–69.

Whiteman, M. F. (1976). *Dialect influence and the writing of black working class Americans*. Ph.D. Dissertation, Georgetown University.

23 Gender Bias and Critique of Student Writing

RICHARD H. HASWELL AND
JANIS TEDESCO HASWELL

The main purpose of this empirical investigation into gender and writing instruction is to locate ways that the critique of readers may be affected by their foreknowledge of the student writer's sex. Thirty-two teachers and 32 students evaluated and diagnosed two student essays, neither overtly marked as to the sex of the writer. Independent variables controlled for were sex of reader, sex of the interviewer who prompted response during the taped session, professional status of participant (student or teacher), and knowledge of author's biological sex by participant (prior knowledge or no prior knowledge). Statistical analysis found gender interacting with all these variables. Among other associations, readers spontaneously constructed the author's sex even when they had not been informed of it; they rated the essays lower when they knew the writer was of their own sex, as measured by holistic rating and percentage of positive critique; they showed an anti-male bias as measured by holistic rating, and an anti-feminine bias as measured by attribution of agency to the writing; and they tended to suppress gender, as measured by the amount of agency that they passivized or made neutral. In sum, the study found evidence for the active presence of gender effects, especially via polarized gender stereotypes, as students and teachers appraise student writing.

In 1968 Phillip Goldberg published what seemed clear evidence of an anti-female bias in readers evaluating a piece of writing. His college-student participants rated five of six articles authored by a "John T. McKay" more favorably than the identical articles authored by a "Joan T. McKay" (Goldberg, 1968). The clarity of Goldberg's finding did not last, however, at least not among serious investigators of gender and language. There have been over 100 replications of Goldberg's design, where language performance is held constant and the evaluator's conception of the sex of the performer is

From *Assessing Writing* 3 (1996): 31–84.

changed systematically. Findings vary depending on context. For instance, when the authors' names included the honorific "Dr." and the subject field was dietetics, women college students rated articles marked as female-authored *higher* than the same articles marked as male-authored (Isaacs, 1981). In another instance, female college students preferred poems labeled as male-authored while male students preferred the same poems labeled as female-authored, but only during individual rating sessions; in mixed-sex groups, the female-labeled poems were preferred by both women and men (Starer & Denmark, 1974). Overall, in Goldberg-type replications with different participants, language targets, and rating situations, evaluative bias against women can be minute or absent, and sometimes women authors are favored over men (Swim, Borgida, Maruyama, & Myers, 1989; Top, 1991).

Not that these replications question either the basic premise that "Sex and gender as informational systems serve as a major means to evaluate others" (Unger, 1990, p. 121) or its particular corollary that gender affects the way writing is judged. The history of Goldberg's findings just argues that the influence of gender upon language evaluation is more subtle, complex, and contextual than was first thought. In natural social contexts, gender does not emerge in evaluation as a single main effect — say, inferred sex of the author upon the evaluation — but rather as an interaction among many factors. The importance of context is highlighted by all recent reviews of the literature — in the areas of performance evaluation (Top, 1991), role behavior (Unger, 1988), physical competence and causal attribution (Wallston & O'Leary, 1987), speech communication (Aries, 1987), nonverbal communication (Hall, 1987), and stereotyping (Ruble & Ruble, 1982).

Our multilfactorial study looks for interactive effects of gender upon a particular kind of language-performance evaluation: critique of student writing. By "critique" we mean the activity of composition teachers and students as they determine the quality of drafts of student writing and offer recommendations for revision. We start with two basic assumptions, that such critique is liable to be influenced by gender, and that such effects will emerge not for a single factor but for a number of interactive factors, such as sex-associated traits in the written text, individual sex typing of the reader, and culture-wide gender stereotyping and gender role construction.

CONTEXTUAL FACTORS AND PRIOR KNOWLEDGE OF THE WRITER'S SEX

Within the restricted area of gender and writing critique, research has been slow to study the possible presence of interactive factors. Most work has concentrated on a search for differences in the way men and women write — usually in style (e.g., R. Haswell, 1986; Hiatt, 1977; Keene, 1986; Key, 1975; Peterson, 1986; Rubin & Greene, 1992; Warshay, 1972), less frequently in habits of composing or choice of mode, argument, or topic (e.g., Cayton, 1990; Emig, 1971; Engelhard, Gordon, & Gabrielson, 1991; Hunter, Pearce, Lee, Goldsmith, Feldman, & Weaver, 1988; Keroes, 1990; Pianko, 1979; Sirc, 1989). These descriptive studies, however, do not look directly at the way such sex-preferred language traits may affect the act of evaluation. Only a few studies have investigated the possible presence of gender bias in evaluative situations: in reading of portfolios (Black, Daiker, Sommers, & Stygall, 1994), in holistic scoring (Johnson & Roen, 1992; Roen, 1992), in teacher critique of impromptu writing (R. Haswell, 1991), in student written response to feminism (D. Rubin, 1993; Wolff, 1991), in manner of complimenting during peer critique (Roen & Johnson, 1992), in conferencing (Green, 1990), in teaching strategy (Kramarae & Treichler, 1990), and in written comments by teachers (Barnes, 1990). And only a few of these investigations adopt a multilfactorial design. As a possible interactive effect on evaluation, D. Rubin (1993) explores reader's sex and mode of instruction, Rubin and Greene (1992) writer's sex and gender-role orientation, Rubin and Greene (1991) interviewer's sex and age, R. Haswell (1991) writer's sex and personal development.

Prior Knowledge of the Writer's Sex

Paucity of knowledge about interaction among gender, evaluation, and other factors undercuts efforts to put research findings into practice. For just one example, Purves (1992) describes an attempt to establish an international method for evaluation of writing. Raters claimed they often could tell the sex of the writer from handwriting, but since researchers did not verify the claims, the finding that females aged 10 to 19 outperformed male cohorts remains moot: according to Purves, "whether this was a result of the presumed knowledge by the raters of the gender of the writer cannot be determined" (p. 117). This instance shows that one important variable interactive with other factors, yet still largely problematic, is the reader-critic's prior inference of the sex of the student writer from anonymous writing.

Rubin and Green (1992) identify sex differences in mode and syntax of college female and male epistolary writing, but, as they note, they cannot tell whether such gender-typical stylistic features "generalize to classroom evaluation" (p. 36); male and female teachers may or may not be aware of the features and may or may not be influenced by them. Stygall, Black, Daiker, and Sommers (1994) describe the traits readers found in student portfolios that encouraged them to guess the sex of the author, but do not systematically connect that interpretation with either the sex of the reader or the evaluation of the portfolios. In the other direction, D. Rubin (1993) investigates gender differences in male and female teachers' critiques of four anonymous essays, yet leaves unexplored possible gender differences in the inferences the readers made about the sex of the writer and the cultural stereotypes they attached to those inferences (p. 48).

Construction of the sex of the writer probably depends on both external and internal factors, both on sex-associated traits of the writing ("gender-linked language effect," Mulac & Lundell, 1980) and on gendered presuppositions biologically, psychologically, or socially lodged in the evaluator. Since the present study explores this sociopsychological context, it will be useful to identify the main variables that current gender/evaluation research suspects is operating on subsequent acts of language evaluation. Listed roughly in the order that the variables have emerged historically in gender studies, they are: biological sex and sex typing of the judge (Bem, 1981); gendered image of the occupational field under scrutiny (Kramarae, 1981; Ruble & Ruble, 1982); social status of both the evaluators and the target person, including experience, age, and authority (Hall, 1987; Hare-Mustin & Marecek, 1990; Ortner & Whitehead, 1981; Shields, 1987; Top, 1991); causal attribution or assumed purpose and outcomes of the evaluation (Ruble & Ruble, 1982); dynamics of the evaluating group, including the sex, intimacy, and power relationships of the participants (Kramarae, 1981; O'Barr & Atkins, 1980; Top, 1991; Unger, 1990); the evaluator's interpretation of the evaluation scenario socially (Hall, 1987; Hare-Mustin & Marecek, 1990; Top, 1991); and presence of an interviewer (Etaugh, Houtler, & Ptasnik, 1988; Rubin & Greene, 1991).

These contingencies raise questions about the evaluation of writing in an educational setting, questions that our research hopes to start answering:

- How often do readers create a picture of the writer's sex even when the author's name is withheld?

- Is this mental picturing different for men and women, adolescents and adults, students and teachers?

- In this act of inferring the sex of the writer from text, on what kind of clues and presuppositions — linguistic, psychological, cultural — do readers rely?

- Will different groups respond differently to writing when they already know the sex of the writer, as typically during the writing course, than when they do not know, as typically during formal assessment of essays?

- Do gender stereotypes affect different parts of the critical act: the summative rating of the essay (as in a grade), the identification of rhetorical problems, the amount of positive feedback, the recommendations for revision?

- Is the reading of student critics more gender-biased than that of teachers, or biased in different ways and associated differently with diagnosis and advice for revision?

These questions apply directly to the few standard practices with which the composition profession currently handles the supposed influence of gender upon evaluation. Names of authors are hidden during normed rating of student essays, for placement, proficiency, and research — but to what purpose if large numbers of readers form a notion of a writer's sex anyway? Since in a classroom setting composition teachers usually know the sex of the student writer, they are advised to find ways to suppress potential anti-female bias in grading and in assignments, perhaps to take care that they value emotional content or narrative organization — but what if instruction in composition happens to be one of those cultural milieux where bias is not anti-female, or even is anti-male? Or a third case; student writers are taught ways to neutralize gender messages (e.g., to initialize the given names of cited authors) — but what if gender neutralization itself influences critique?

THE PRESENT STUDY

Our investigation broached such questions by means of a contrast between two conditions, when readers critically judge a piece of student writing before knowing the sex of the writer and when they judge a piece already knowing it. To capture this contrast, we designed a moderately complex simulation of the familiar pedagogical event in which a teacher or peer student recommends revision on submitted drafts. We activated, controlled, and measured a number of the factors that theorists have hypothesized as both influential and understudied in gendered acts of language evaluation. We made the hypothesized evaluation scene naturalistic, a "critique session" with reader-critics discussing pieces of actual student writing (Hall, 1987; Hare-Mustin & Marecek, 1980; Unger, 1990). We had each participant judge both a male and a female authored essay in order to produce opposing attitudes "within" single individuals (within-reader contrasts), where evidence for gender bias often appears most naturally and saliently (Olian, Schwab, & Haberfeld, 1988). We contrasted older professional judges (composition teachers) with younger novice judges (first-semester college students), defined a clear purpose and outcome for the evaluation, and asked readers to discuss concretely how their evaluation should subsequently affect the writer (causal attributions) (Hare-Mustin & Marecek, 1990; Ruble & Ruble, 1982; Top, 1991). We accounted for sex of the interviewer, a contextual factor that has been routinely disregarded in gender/evaluation research (Top, 1991, p. 101). Most importantly, we studied a crucial phenomenon with little research history (Paludi & Strayer, 1985), the incidence and success of readers in inferring the sex of an author when they are reading an anonymous piece in a natural, unforced manner.

Research Questions and Hypotheses

Expectations for Goldberg-type effects in the critique of student writing arise from an array of theories about adult gender bias. Psychoanalysis might look for the sway of parental identification (e.g., Chodorow, 1978), psycholinguistics for an unconscious linkage with sex-associated language (e.g., Lakoff, 1975), developmental psychology for the affirmation of self-categorization (e.g., Kohlberg, 1966), radical feminism for the oppressive power of patriarchal language constructions (e.g., Penelope, 1990), strategic feminism for the plans and tactics for goal achievement (e.g., Kramarae, 1981), social learning theory for the conditioning of cultural stereotypes (e.g., Cameron & Coates, 1988), information processing for the fulfillment of gender schemas (e.g., Bem, 1984), and social constructivism for the sway of group cohesion (e.g., Unger, 1990). We do not subscribe exclusively to any one of these theories. Instead, we presume some mixture of explanatory causes, agreeing with Top that in evaluation of human performance "any particular form of stereotyping or prejudice is in all likelihood multiply determined by cognitive, motivational, and social learning processes" (1991, p. 78).

We did expect to find, however, a few components basic to acts of language evaluation in general. Those components are a prior set of beliefs, an observation of performance, an assignment of value to the performance, an explanatory matrix for the quality of the performance, and a projection of consequences of the evaluation (modified from Ruble & Ruble, 1982, p. 211–212). In our experiment, we took the participants' reading of the essays as the observation of performance, their rating of the essays and allotment of positive and negative commentary as the assignment of value, their critique of the essays and their identification of gender signals in the texts as the explanatory matrix, and their recommendations for revision as the projection of consequences. We interpreted their prior set of beliefs from the inferences they made about writers of the texts.

The breadth of our protocol and the rather full response elicited by it (over 800 typed pages) allowed us to hope for answers to a linked series of research questions:

1. As our readers read an anonymous essay, would they construct a picture of the sex of the author, and how often would that image prove correct? We hypothesized that the majority of readers would automatically generate a gendered image of the writer (gender is "our culture's pet category," Bem, 1987, p. 266). To our knowledge, only four investigations have studied how readers of nameless student essays determine a writer's sex, but all found the presence of gender stereotyping (J. Haswell, 1990, 1992; Roen, 1992; Rose, 1991; Stygall, et al., 1994). Since in a preliminary study of gender inference (J. Haswell, 1991), the two target essays used in the present study were misidentified as to author's sex 75% of the time, we also predicted that our readers would be mistaken with both pieces more often than not.

2. Of course, a reader's picture of a writer's sex, right or wrong, may not relate to that reader's evaluation of the writing. Would our readers' inference about the writer's sex prove associated with their holistic rating of the writing, and would that association interact with their own biological sex, with their status as student or teacher, or with the sex of the interviewer? Given the findings elsewhere of gender bias in evaluations of language performance, we predicted that associations would emerge.

3. Of course, a reader's summative evaluation of a piece of writing, such as grade or a holistic score, may poorly reflect that reader's critical reaction sentence by sentence. Swim et al. warn that gender-stereotyped global evaluations may dilute with "individuating evidence" (1989, p. 424). Would our readers' ratio of positive to negative critique, as measured proposition by proposition, prove systematically related to their inference about the writer's sex, to their own biological sex, to their status as student or teacher, or to the sex of the interviewer? We predicted that effects would emerge, given previous findings of sex differences in the distribution of positive and negative evaluation (Johnson & Roen, 1992; McMahan, 1991).

4. Of course, readers need not attribute their critique, positive or negative, to a gendered writer or to a writer at all. They can always attribute it to the text alone. A reader can say about a woman's essay, "She needs to organize this paragraph better," which allows agency to the writer as a woman. Or the reader can say, "This paragraph needs more structure," which elides the writer both as an

agent of the text and as a sexual being. Would our readers' assignment of agency to the writing prove systematically related to their inference about the writers' sex, to their own biological sex, to their status as student or teacher, or to the sex of the interviewer? Denying women agency of their own acts is a well-explored aspect of anti-female discrimination, the generic "mankind" being only the linguistic *locus classicus* for a multitude of social ploys (Penelope, 1990; Russ, 1983, p. 20–38), and we expected bias effects to emerge.

5. Of course, as Butler (1990) emphasizes, a discriminatory attribution of agency is less verifiable than action based upon that discrimination: "Gender ought not to be construed as a stable identity or locus of agency; rather, gender is an identity tenuously constituted in time, instituted in an exterior space through a stylized repetition of acts" (p 140). In other words, the readers' allocation of agency to the text under review may not necessarily connect with the rhetorical values expressed in their critique, which includes recommendations for revision. The two critique propositions, "She needs to organize this paragraph better" and "This paragraph needs more structure," construe agency differently, but both rely on the same critical center of value and its projected consequences — in this case on the need of the writer to meet textual conventions (obvious paragraph organization). The propositions could rely on another center of value, say, the need to express inner convictions. Would our readers' preference for certain rhetorical centers of value for critique prove systematically related to their inference about the writer's sex, to their own biological sex, to their status as student or teacher, or to the sex of the interviewer? On the basis of scattered evidence that sex of writer influences classroom critique (Barnes, 1990; Green, 1990; Roen, 1992), and of wider evidence that students and teachers show different patterns of critique (e.g., Newkirk, 1984), we assumed effects would emerge.

All five of these hypotheses assume the probability of interactions among sex of writer, reader, and interviewer, and status of reader. Admittedly, our five research questions are broad. But such breadth of target seems appropriate given the scanty and ill-defined nature of our current understanding of gender effects in the critique of student writing. Loose and exploratory as our hypotheses are, they still put into sharp question some standard practices of the field, for instance, the assumption by writers of textbooks that rhetorical axioms and practice stand independent of the sex of the writer (an "organized" paragraph is good, regardless of who wrote it), or the assignment by teachers of student essays indiscriminately to single-sex and mixed-sex peer groups, or the masking by assessment professionals of the student author's name with the hope that readers will evaluate essays free of gender bias.

Design of the Study

Thirty-two college composition instructors (16 female and 16 male) and 32 college first-year students (16 female and 16 male) each read and responded to two student essays, one written by a female, and other by a male (see the Appendix for texts of the two essays). During the 30-minute taped session, one participant was alone with one interviewer in the interviewer's faculty office. As their main task, participants were asked to offer advice for revision to two students, each of whom had submitted the first draft of an essay. Participants did not know the sex of the author of the first essay until after they had finished their critique, but they were told the sex of the author of the second piece before they started reading it (see Figure 23–1 for a schematic of the protocol). Systematic rotation allowed control of four independent variables; prior knowledge of the sex of the writer (known and not known); status of the reader (student or teacher), sex of the reader, and sex of the interviewer. Analysis of the readers' responses produced six dependent variables (see below).

Evaluation Target. The two target essays were written impromptu during the fifth week of a semester beginning-composition class. The topic was gender-neutral. One essay was written by a female (Victoria), the other by a male (Kevin). We selected them for study because their length is comparable. More important, the markers they provide as to the author's sex are ambiguous, according to a previous study in which the true sex of both writers was misinferred by readers 75% of the time. (J. Haswell, 1991). Following Goldberg's design, we varied the prior understanding of the author's sex while keeping the writing performance the same. Many researchers, including Goldberg himself, have achieved this design by labeling the same writing with opposite-sex author names, a method that may introduce unknown artificial effects. More natural, we believed, would be a contrast in prior understanding achieved by the reader's own unprompted inferences. The essays were typed exactly as written, without the author's name.

Participants (n = 64). Half of the reader-critics were first-year students at a mid-sized land-grant university in the western United States. Aged 17–22 (median age 18), half of them female (*n* = 16) and half male (*n* = 16); they

FIGURE 23–1   Schematic of Research Design, Showing the Two Contrasting Protocols

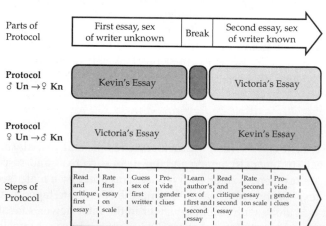

were randomly chosen from two sections of beginning composition taught by the same instructor. They were not paid for their work, only promised that the results of the experiment would be presented to them later. The other half of the readers were instructors teaching composition at the same university. Half were novices, aged 22–47 (median age 27), who had been teaching in college only for two months, half were more experienced, aged 30–56 (median age 35), having taught college writing from two to eight years. Half of the teachers were female ($n = 16$) and half male ($n = 16$). All but one of the students and all of the teachers who were originally asked to participate did so.

Protocol. (See Figure 23–1.) The interviewer told participants to imagine themselves in a teaching or peer editing situation, wherein they would offer critical advice to the two writers. For each of the essays, the readers were asked, in this order, (a) to read and critique the essay, (b) to offer suggestions for revision, (c) to summarize the good and bad qualities of the writing, (d) to rate the essay on a scale of 1 (low) to 5 (high) with 3 defined as "average" first-year student writing under the circumstances, (e) to identify the one most important aspect the writer should work on in revision, (f) to identify clues to the sex of the author, (g) to discuss whether they felt knowledge of a student writer's sex should influence a teacher's evaluation of the writing, and (h) to say how familiar they were with feminism. With the first essay, whose author's sex was withheld, participants were asked before they undertook step (f) whether they pictured the writer as male or female and then to guess the writer's sex. The protocol took approximately 30 minutes to administer. Interviews were taped and later transcribed for analysis.

Midpoint in the interview, when participants had finished with the first essay but before they had seen the second essay, they were told the correct sex of the author of the first and then of the second. For our look into the effects of prior knowledge about the author's sex upon subsequent critique, this within-reader comparison would be the most telling. Every reader-critic evaluated the first essay *without* prior knowledge of the writer's sex, and evaluated the second essay *with* prior knowledge. Systematic rotation of the two essays resulted in two contrasting situations:

Protocol ♂ Un → ♀ Kn: Kevin's essay read and interpreted first, sex unknown; Victoria's essay read and interpreted second, sex known.

Protocol ♀ Un → ♂ Kn: Victoria's essay read and interpreted first, sex unknown; Kevin's essay read and interpreted second, sex known.

This contrast enabled us to compare responses under different reader presuppositions: when readers knew that the male essay had been written by a male *versus* when they did not know; when readers knew that the female essay had been written by a female *versus* when they did not know; when readers *inferred* that a male or female essay had been written by a male or female *versus* when they *knew* that it had been.

Further rotation of participants and interviewers resulted in eight basic research groups, composed of four females (two students and two teachers) and four males (two students and two teachers) undergoing one of the two protocols and administered by either the female or the male interviewer (see Table 23–1). This rotation allowed statistical testing for interactions among the four independent variables: Sex of Reader, Sex of Interviewer, Status of Reader, and Prior Knowledge.

Independent variables:

1. Sex of Reader (female, male).

2. Status of Reader (student, teacher).

3. Sex of Interviewer (female, male).

4. Prior Knowledge, or the order of essays as presented to the participant: Protocol ♂ Un → ♀ Kn or Protocol ♀ Un → ♂ Kn.

Analysis of Elicited Response.   The transcripts of the interviews were coded for analysis, as follows:

1. *Unspoken assumption of the author's sex.* In the response of most participants to the first essay, with the author's sex unknown, there were clear indications — usually pronouns — that the reader had assumed the writer to be male or fe-

TABLE 23–1   Rotation of Independent Variables Producing Eight Basic Research Groups

Group	Sex of Reader	Prior Knowledge	Status of Reader	Sex of Interviewer
1.	4 females/ 4 males	Protocol ♂ Un → ♀ Kn	student	female interviewer
2.	4 females/ 4 males	Protocol ♂ Un → ♀ Kn	student	male interviewer
3.	4 females/ 4 males	Protocol ♂ Un → ♀ Kn	teachers	female interviewer
4.	4 females/ 4 males	Protocol ♂ Un → ♀ Kn	teachers	male interviewer
5.	4 females/ 4 males	Protocol ♀ Un → ♂ Kn	student	female interviewer
6.	4 females/ 4 males	Protocol ♀ Un → ♂ Kn	student	male interviewer
7.	4 females/ 4 males	Protocol ♀ Un → ♂ Kn	teachers	female interviewer
8.	4 females/ 4 males	Protocol ♀ Un → ♂ Kn	teachers	male interviewer

male. This assumption, or lack of evidence indicating an assumption, was recorded for each reader.

2. *Inference of the author's sex.* The answer of readers, when asked to review the text and make a best guess as to the sex of the author, was recorded as "male," "female," or "unable." This answer sometimes differed from the unspoken assumption.

3. *Rating on the evaluative scale.* The point that readers marked on the line scaled 1 through 5 was converted to a number score, to the nearest tenth. Since participants placed their mark anywhere on the line from 1 to 5, the data were treated as continuous, not categorical.

4. *Classification of critique propositions.* We define "critique proposition" as any assertion that attaches value to a portion of writing. Where participants discussed the good and bad qualities of the essay and recommended revision, we reduced the commentary to monoclause propositions (see Newkirk), each reflecting a value statement about the essay or the writer. For example, the comment, "The beginning of this paragraph is good, but I think they need to provide more of a transition," was reduced to two critique propositions: *The beginning of this paragraph [three] is good* and *They need to provide more of a transition at the beginning of paragraph [three].* When a participant reiterated the content of a critique proposition, only one instance was enumerated for that reader. In this reduced format, each proposition was then classified four different ways:

   A. According to a five-category system of written discourse centers of value modified from Fulkerson (1979, 1990), who classified commentary on writing by four "axiologies" or "what is valued in writing."

      (1) *mimetic*: success of the writer in conveying objective reality truthfully or logically.

      (2) *formalist*: success in creating a conventionally correct or stylistically approved text.

      (3) *expressive*: success in expressing psychological constructs of the author, such as openness, sincerity, or authenticity.

      (4) *rhetorical/situational*: success in conveying the writer's purpose to an audience and in handling the pragmatic situation that prompted the writing. The distinction between *rhetorical* and *situational*, not in Fulkerson, was maintained in the original analysis but merged for the present study.

      (5) *unattached*: success not explicitly connected to any of the above five centers of value ("Good ideas").

   B. According to whether the proposition was expressed *positively* ("Mature word choice") or *negatively* ("Inappropriate diction here").

   C. According to whether the proposition referred to the accomplished *text* ("The beginning of this paragraph is good") or to a projected *revision* of the text ("They need to provide more of a transition").

   D. According to *authorial agency*, that is, according to the proposition's assumption about what agent had produced the accomplished text or would produce the revised text:

(1) *female*: human agent identified as female ("Her conclusion is redundant").

(2) *male*: human agent identified as male ("He ought to work on his sentences").

(3) *first person*: human agent imaged as the reader-critic ("I wouldn't start this paragraph with 'For example'").

(4) *sex-neutral*: human agent with sex indeterminate ("The writer [he/she, they, you] will need to rethink the whole subject").

(5) *non-human*: assertion of human agency avoided, by either passives ("The conclusion is well written"); statives ("The essay has some surface problems"); or personification of the text, in which the text appears to act as its own agent ("The paragraph makes some false statements").

Table 23–2 provides illustrative examples of these four classifications of critique propositions (A, B, C, and D).

5. *Classification of gender clue propositions.* By "gender clue" we mean essentially "gender marker" as defined by McConnell-Ginet (1985): an association people make between linguistic units and gender phenomena. Many people, for instance, associate expletives with males. We call our markers "clues," however, because our readers were identifying them as evidence for the sex of the writer—that is, doing so consciously—whereas according to McConnell-Ginet people often react to gender markers unconsciously (p. 81). In order to measure gender-clue propositions, we first reduced the commentary where participants explained how they determined the sex of the author from the essay to a set of non-repeated propositions, similar to but distinct from the set of critique propositions. We classified the gender-clue propositions in two basic ways:

A. According to Showalter's categorization of the four ways people rationalize gender differences (1982). We deemed Showalter's classification appropriate for our study because it analyzes "models of gender difference" that are expressed through discursive texts:

(1) *biological*: arguments following the "textuality as anatomy" line of reasoning that the biological sex manifests itself directly in the text.

(2) *linguistic*: arguments assuming men and women use language differently, as seen in their choice of words, topics, and style.

(3) *psychoanalytic*: arguments drawing on differences in the intellectual/emotional make-up of men and women, assuming that an author's "self" exists separable from the social context that prompted the text.

(4) *cultural*: arguments allowing that textual gender features may be shaped by the social context.

B. According to whether gender traits are expressed as feminine or masculine. The reader's task of identifying the sex of an author through written clues must rely, of course, on an interpretive scheme of gender differences. Even where that scheme is dichotomous (e.g., women are more or-

TABLE 23–2   Classifications of Critique and Gender-Clue Propositions

Critique Propositions

Critique Proposition	Axiology	Positive/ Negative	Text/ Revision	Agent
"She considers different perspectives"	mimetic	positive	text	female
"He needs to provide more examples"	formalist	negative	revision	male
"I would expand the conclusion"	formalist	negative	revision	first-person
"They are sure of what they want to say"	expressive	positive	text	sex-neutral
"The introduction is not easy to follow"	rhetorical	negative	text	non-human
"The essay should answer the question"	situational	negative	revision	non-human
"You have a good essay started"	unattached	positive	text	sex-neutral

Gender-Clue Propositions

Proposition	Argument	Attribution
"Women have a different tie into their emotions"	biological	feminine
"This reflects the testosterone in my blood"	biological	masculine
"Women can express themselves more easily"	linguistic	feminine
"A man would write, 'feeding me a load of bull'"	linguistic	masculine
"Women look inside for truth"	psychoanalytic	feminine
"Men are self-reliant"	psychoanalytic	masculine
"Women accept people's advice and apply it to what they think"	cultural	feminine
"Men are trained to separate things more logically"	cultural	masculine

ganized and men less organized), participants almost always dealt with a clue as if it pertained to only one sex or as if it had its positive center in one sex. A clue such as "Girls find it easier to organize ideas" would then be classified as *feminine*.

Table 23–2 illustrates the two classifications of the gender-clue propositions.

Dependent Variables. We reduced the above analysis of the transcripts to six dependent variables. Most of these dependent variables are expressed as percentages in order to standardize the variance in quantity of propositions produced by participants. We preferred this method to using word-length of the transcript as a co-variant (e.g., Rubin & Greene, 1992) because participants varied widely in the degree to which they repeated critique propositions and gender clues.

All dependent variables aggregate the responses of an individual participant to *both* essays. With the scaled rating, for instance, the basic unit of measurement for statistical analysis is a participant's rating of Kevin's essay subtracted from the same participant's rating of Victoria's essay, regardless of which protocol is involved.

It is crucial to understand the necessity for this procedure, since it appears to confound the independent variable of Prior Knowledge. We aggregate data across the two halves of the protocol because the two responses were not independent. How readers rated the first essay must have influenced their reading and rating of the second essay. Say Reader$_F$ (a female) first gave Victoria's essay a scale rate of "4" and then Kevin's a rate of "3," and Reader$_M$ (a male) first rated Victoria's essay "3" and then Kevin's "2." Reporting the first and second readings as independent would make it appear that Reader$_F$ rated a known male essay more highly (score of "3") than did Reader$_M$ (score of "2"). But such data would disregard well known rater errors, effects due to order, or primacy and proximity that occur in judgments of value when performances are sequential. An essay judged first may affect judgment on subsequent essays (error of primacy) and more strongly on those closest (error of proximity) (Guilford, 1954). Subtracting the rating of Kevin's piece from the rating of Victoria's piece (performing the calculation in the opposite direction would have no effect on the statistical results) helps standardize data. In this instance, our method of calculation would make the two raters' holistic rating of the two essays appear identical: both would record a data point of +1 (4 less 3 for Rater$_F$; 3 less 2 for Rater$_M$). This method loses the information about how each rater rated each essay absolutely on the holistic scale, but it retains the information that both raters saw Kevin's essay as worse than Victoria's. It is this relative evaluative distance between the two essays that we feel is a more accurate measure of critical difference. Other dependent variables (e.g., discourse center-of-value, gender clues) are also susceptible to order effects. A reader who spends a proportionately large amount of time attending to formalist features — say, paragraph organization — in the first essay may be primed to notice or discuss the same features in the second essay.

Note that aggregating results for the two halves of the protocol to generate this unit actually does not erase the effects of prior knowledge. If Reader$_F$ under Protocol ♀ Un → ♂ Kn first gave Victoria's essay a scale rate of "4" and then Kevin's a rate of "3," and Reader$_M$ under Protocol ♂ Un → ♀ Kn first rated Kevin's essay "2" and then Victoria's "4," then our variable for holistic rating would record a difference for the two readers (Reader$_F$ = +1, Reader$_M$ = +2) and we would have a piece of evidence that prior knowledge of Victoria's sex may have boosted the value of her essay more than prior knowledge of Kevin's sex boosted his.

In sum, our basic phenomenological unit is not the difference between two essays read in isolation but rather two essays read in sequence — an appropriate unit, we believe, since in instructional and assessment situations essays are almost always read and judged in a series. Our main statistical evidence for the influence of prior knowledge of the author's sex, then, will emerge with significant group contrasts in *relative* differences in evaluation, for instance, the difference between the judgment on a male essay (author unknown) read first and the judgment on a female essay (author known) read second (Protocol ♂ Un → ♀ Kn) compared to the difference between the judgment on the same female essay (author now unknown) read first and the judgment on the male essay (author now known) read second (Protocol ♀ Un → ♂ Kn). We will report the aggregated data first in the "Findings" section below. For post-hoc analysis, however, in the "Discussion" section that follows, we will break down results for the two halves of the protocol. Only such analysis can show how differences in critical distinctions were achieved. In our second hypothetical instance, for example, the two raters rated Victoria's essay the same (Reader$_F$ = "4," Reader$_M$ = "4") and Kevin's differently (Reader$_F$ = "3," Reader$_M$ = "2"). It is possible that they could have recorded the same difference in critical distance in the opposite way, rating Kevin's essay the same (Reader$_F$ = "2," Reader$_M$ = "2") and Victoria's differently (Reader$_F$ = "3," Reader$_M$ = "4").

It should be also noted that we sometimes disregarded or collapsed dependent variables in order to maintain a reasonable ratio of number of participants and variables tested. For instance, our variable of Prior Knowledge disregards the inferences of readers about the writer's sex in the first half of the protocol — an important factor in their prior knowledge, which we must reserve for post-hoc discussion. Critique propositions collapse the distinction between evaluation of text and recommendation for revision, and gender-clue propositions collapse the distinction between feminine and masculine. We discuss some of these subcomponents elsewhere (Haswell & Haswell, 1995).

We ended with five dependent variables:

1. *Essay rating.* The participant's scale rating of Kevin's essay subtracted from the participant's rating of Victoria's essay.

2. *Positive critique.* The portion of all of a reader's critique propositions that are positive (as opposed to negative) for Kevin's essay, subtracted from the portion of the readers critique propositions that are positive (as opposed to negative) for Victoria's essay.

3. *Authorial agency cluster.* To avoid singularity effects (see "Statistical Analysis," below), this cluster of variables excludes *First-person* references and therefore does not include all critique propositions. Each subvariable aggregates critique on both essays.

    a. *Male-agent critique.* Percentage of all of a reader's critique propositions that assume a human male as agent of the writing.

    b. *Female-agent critique.* Percentage of a reader's critique propositions that assume female as agent of the writing.

    c. *Sex-neutral critique*. Percentage of a reader's critique propositions that assume a human as agent of the writing but do not identify the agent's sex.

    d. *Non-human critique*. Percentage of a reader's critique propositions that assume no human agent to the text.

4. *Discourse center-of-value cluster*. To avoid singularity, this cluster of variables omits the *Unattached* category. Each sub-variable aggregates critique on both essays.

    a. *Mimeticist critique*. Percentage of all of a reader's critique propositions that fall into the mimetic category.

    b. *Formalist critique*. Percentage of a reader's critique propositions that fall into the formalist category.

    c. *Expressive critique*. Percentage of a reader's critique propositions that fall into the expressive category.

    d. *Rhetorical/Situational critique*. Percentage of a reader's critique propositions that fall into the rhetorical or situational categories.

5. *Gender-clue cluster*. To avoid singularity, this cluster of variables omits *Biological* clues. Each sub-variable aggregates critique on both essays.

    a. *Linguistic gender clues*. Percentage of all of a reader's gender-clue propositions that assert an argument from the arena of language use.

    b. *Psychological gender clues*. Percentage of a reader's gender-clue propositions that assert an argument from the arena of the author's self.

    c. *Cultural gender clues*. Percentage of a reader's gender-clue propositions that assert an argument from the arena of social context.

Interrater Reliability. We classified the critique and gender-clue propositions, first independently and then in collaboration to resolve differences. To allow a test of reliability on this subjective process, two experienced college English teachers — one female, one male, both unfamiliar with the study and working at another institution — repeated our procedure on propositions whose interpretation did not require consultation of the transcript context. They classified 213 randomly chosen critique propositions (about a quarter of the total) and 184 randomly chosen gender-clue propositions (about half). They applied only the Fulkerson and Showalter classifications, since we deemed the other classifications too forthright to require a test of rater reliability.

Statistical Analysis

The first two dependent variables — the essay rating and the percentage of positive critique — were tested by a 2 × 2 × 2 × 2 fixed effects analysis of variance. This fully factorial model nests participants ($n = 64$) in four independent variable factors of two levels each: Sex of Reader (female, male), Status of Reader (student, teacher), Prior Knowledge or order of essays as presented to the reader (Protocol ♂ Un → ♀ Kn, Protocol ♀ Un → ♂ Kn), and Sex of the Interviewer (female, male). Data observations were the adjusted measurement of the two researchers. The next three variables were treated in clusters by multiple analysis of variance. The design of the MANOVA was the same for all three clusters, a 2 × 2 × 2 × 2 factorial with the same independent variables of the previous ANOVAs but with the categories of classification forming the dependent variables. Since the variables were percentages, one category of the complete classification was omitted from the cluster to avoid a singularity effect (Bock, 1975). For all MANOVAs, Wilks's likelihood ratio criterion (λ) provided the inference testing to determine whether the multiple effect would be further explored through univariate analysis.

Findings

Interrater Reliability. In the six-category classification of the sample of 213 discourse center-of-value propositions, the adjusted category assignment of the two independent raters matched the adjusted assignment of the two researchers 202 times (94.8%). In the four-category classification of the sample of 184 discourse gender-clue propositions, the adjusted category assignment of the two independent raters matched the adjusted assignment of the two researchers 157 times (85.3%).

Assumption and Inference of the Author's Sex. On evidence from the 64 reader's comments, 41 (64%) had assumed and spontaneously formed a gendered image of the author of the first, anonymous essay by the time they had finished analyzing it. Half of the images (20) were correct and half (21) incorrect. The rate of spontaneous gender-image formation was the same with Kevin's essay (63%) as with Victoria's (65%), but more readers were correct with Kevin (41%) than with Victoria (22%). There were no obvious differences in performance of female and male readers or students and teachers. As for the readers' explicit inference of the author's sex, which they determined on conscious review of the text, 21 were correct (33%), 41 incorrect (64%), and 2 refused to say. Teachers appeared no better at this than the students, females no better than males. Kevin's piece fared the same (31% correct) as Victoria's (34% correct).

Essay Rating. (See Table 23–3.) The measurement was the difference of the reader's rating of Kevin's essay subtracted from the reader's rating of Victoria's essay on the five-point scale. Across all 64 participants, Victoria's essay was rated consistently better than Kevin's (scale mean for Victoria = 3.67, SD .59; scale mean for Kevin = 2.78, SD .72). Regardless of protocol, only eight of the 64 readers rated Kevin's essay equal or better than Victoria's. Of those eight, seven were female — an apparent anomaly that subsequent findings will explain.

TABLE 23–3   Subgroup Means on Essay Rating (Variable 1)

	Victoria		Kevin		Protocol ♂ Un → ♀ Kn		Protocol ♀ Un → ♂ Kn	
	Sex Unknown	Sex Known	Sex Unknown	Sex Known	Variable 1*	(SD)	Variable 1*	(SD)
Students (cell n = 16)	3.39	3.62	2.58	2.83	1.04	(0.85)	0.56	(1.05)
Female (cell n = 8)	3.31	3.49	2.58	3.29	0.91	(0.34)	0.02	(1.22)
Male (cell n = 8)	3.47	3.76	2.58	2.38	1.18	(1.18)	1.09	(0.49)
Teachers (cell n = 16)	3.86	3.88	2.93	2.78	0.95	(0.84)	1.08	(0.61)
Female (cell n = 8)	4.02	3.47	2.88	2.85	0.59	(0.85)	1.17	(0.70)
Male (cell n = 8)	3.71	4.28	2.98	2.72	1.31	(0.70)	0.99	(0.53)

*With Protocol ♂ Un → ♀ Kn, Variable 1 is the scale rating on Kevin (sex unknown) subtracted from the scale rating on Victoria (sex known); with Protocol ♀ Un → ♂ Kn, Variable 1 is the scale rating on Kevin (sex known) subtracted from the scale rating on Victoria (sex unknown).

There was a significant main effect for Sex of Reader, $F(1,48)$ = 5.45, $p < .05$. Males recorded nearly twice the difference than did females (mean difference with males = +1.14; with females = +0.67). The contrast derives from the fact that, compared to the females, the males rated Kevin lower (male mean rate = 2.67; female = 2.90) and Victoria higher (male mean rate = 3.80; female = 3.57). (This effect can be seen in Figure 23–2.) There was also a main effect for Sex of Interviewer, $F(1,48)$ = 5.34, $p < .05$. Readers with the female interviewer recorded nearly twice the difference in scale points than with the male interviewer. Victoria's essay was rated much the same with the female interviewer (mean rate 3.64) as with the male interviewer (3.74) but Kevin's was lower with the female interviewer (2.50) than with the male (3.06). Finally there was a three-way interaction among Prior Knowledge, Sex of Reader, and Status of Reader, $F(1,48)$ = 4.49, $p < .05$. As Figure 23–2 graphs, among readers who had prior knowledge of Kevin's sex (Protocol ♀ Un → ♂ Kn), the eight female students raise his essay relative to Victoria's, contrary to the other reader groups (male students, female and male teachers), who lower it; and among readers who had prior knowledge of Victoria's sex (Protocol ♀ Un → ♂ Kn), the eight female teachers lower Victoria's essay relative to Kevin's, contrary to the other reader groups, who raise it.

Positive Critique.   (See Table 23–4.) There was a significant main effect for Prior Knowledge, $F(1,48)$ = 4.60, $p < .05$. The difference in percentage of positive critique propositions (as opposed to negative) is greater when readers judged Kevin's essay first, with sex of author unknown (25.2% positive), and Victoria's second, with sex of author known (42.7%), than when they read Victoria's essay first (32.6%) and Kevin's second (25.7%). Knowledge of Kevin's sex had no effect on positive critique, but knowledge of Victoria's sex increased positive critique. There was also a sizable interaction effect for Prior

FIGURE 23–2   Knowledge of Writer's Sex and Scale Rating

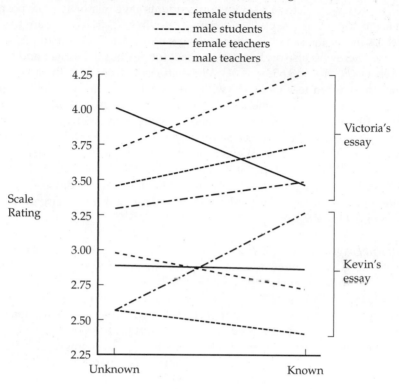

Knowledge of Writer's Sex

TABLE 23–4   Subgroup Means on Positive Critique (Variable 2)

	Victoria		Kevin		Protocol		Protocol	
	Sex	Sex	Sex	Sex	♂ Un → ♀ Kn		♀ Un → ♂ Kn	
	Unknown	*Known*	*Unknown*	*Known*	*Variable 2**	*(SD)*	*Variable 2**	*(SD)*
Students (cell *n* = 16)	27.0%	47.9%	23.0%	29.5%	24.9%	(23.7)	−2.4%	(16.9)
Female (cell *n* = 8)	29.0%	46.0%	29.6%	36.5%	16.5%	(23.3)	−7.5%	(19.8)
Male (cell *n* = 8)	25.1%	49.7%	16.4%	22.4%	33.4%	(22.2)	2.6%	(12.9)
Teachers (cell *n* = 16)	38.1%	37.6%	27.4%	21.9%	10.2%	(26.3)	16.3%	(19.8)
Female (cell *n* = 8)	33.2%	36.7%	21.7%	23.8%	15.0%	(16.5)	9.4%	(16.7)
Male (cell *n* = 8)	43.1%	38.4%	33.1%	19.9%	5.4%	(34.0)	23.2%	(21.3)

*With Protocol ♂ Un → ♀ Kn, Variable 2 is the percent of critique that is positive on Kevin (sex unknown) subtracted from the percent of critique that is positive on Victoria (sex known); with Protocol ♀ Un → ♂ Kn, Variable 2 is the percent of critique that is positive on Kevin (sex known) subtracted from the percent of critique that is positive on Victoria (sex unknown).

Knowledge and Status of Reader, $F(1.48) = 11.40, p < .01$. Under Protocol ♂ Un → ♀ Kn, with Victoria's sex known, students gave relatively more positive advice to Victoria's essay (47.9%) than to Kevin's (23.0%), compared to the teachers under the same situation (who gave 37.6% to Victoria and 27.4% to Kevin). There was also an interaction effect for Sex of Interviewer and Status of Reader ($F(1,48) = 8.65, p < .01$). When students were with the male interviewer and when teachers were with the female interviewer, they assigned portions of positive critique equally to the two essays, but when students were with the female interviewer and teachers were with the male interviewer, they gave almost twice as much positive critique to Victoria's essay than to Kevin's. Finally, there was a significant three-way interaction involving Sex of Interviewer, Status of Reader, and Prior Knowledge ($F(1,48) = 5.73$, $p < .05$). The prominent effect indicates that the just described two-way interaction between interviewer and status of reader took place largely during Protocol ♂ Un → ♀ Kn.

Authorial Agency. (See Table 23–5.) The four dependent variables in this cluster were percentages of male-agent, female-agent, sex-neutral, and non-human critique propositions. MANOVA discovered a main effect for Prior Knowledge ($\lambda(4,45) = .323, p < .001$). Subsequent univariate F tests found a strong main effect on male agency ($F(1,48) = 25.28, p < .001$). Participants in Protocol ♂ Un → ♀ Kn averaged 5.9% male-agent propositions for the two essays; participants in the reverse Protocol ♀ Un → ♂ Kn averaged 27.4% male-agent propositions for the two essays. There was a parallel but even larger main effect on female agency ($F(1,48) = 60.32, p < .001$). In Protocol ♂ Un → ♀ Kn, they averaged 20.8% female-agent propositions for the two essays; in Protocol ♀ Un → ♂ Kn, they averaged 1.4%.

MANOVA also discovered a main effect for Sex of Reader ($\lambda(4,45) = .685$, $p < .05$). Subsequent univariate tests found a strong main effect for female agency ($F(1,48) = 14.24, p < .001$). Females overall, regardless of protocol or status, cast 15.8% of their critique in terms of female agency, males 6.4%. MANOVA also discovered a main effect for Status of Reader ($\lambda(4,45) = .723$, $p < .05$). Univariate tests located an effect on male agency ($F(1,48) = 4.11$, $p < .05$), where students devoted 21.0% of their critique to male-agent propositions, teachers only 12.3%. There was a related effect on sex-neutral agency ($F(1,48) = 17.11, p < .01$), where students made 26.1% of their critique human but gender-neutral, while teachers made 45.5% of theirs so.

MANOVA found the interaction of Prior Knowledge with Sex of Reader significant ($\lambda(4,45) = .814, p < .05$). A univariate test on female agency recorded a significant effect ($F(1,48) = 9.17, p < .01$): in Protocol ♂ Un → ♀ Kn, females expressed 29.4% of their critique as female-agented, males only 12.3%; in the reverse Protocol ♀ Un → ♂ Kn, females expressed 2.3% of their critique as female-agented, males 0.4%. There was also a multivariate finding of significance with the interaction of Status of Reader and Sex of Interviewer ($\lambda(4,45) = .766, p < .05$). Univariate F tests located an effect on male agency ($F(1,48) = 8.34, p < .01$). Students interviewed by the male researcher cast

TABLE 23–5   Subgroup Means on Authorial Agency (Variable 3)

	Victoria		Kevin		Protocol ♂ Un → ♀ Kn		Protocol ♀ Un → ♂ Kn	
	Sex Unknown	Sex Known	Sex Unknown	Sex Known	Variable 3*	(SD)	Variable 3*	(SD)
Male Agency								
Students (cell n = 16)	23.3%	0.9%	17.5%	43.1%	8.6%	(13.2)	33.4%	(29.3)
Female (cell n = 8)	6.7%	0.0%	16.1%	30.0%	7.2%	(15.3)	17.4%	(23.4)
Male (cell n = 8)	39.8%	1.8%	18.9%	56.2%	10.1%	(11.7)	49.4%	(26.5)
Teachers (cell n = 16)	4.9%	3.0%	3.3%	39.5%	3.2%	(9.7)	21.5%	(18.6)
Female (cell n = 8)	3.4%	0.0%	2.5%	45.7%	1.3%	(3.5)	25.2%	(20.5)
Male (cell n = 8)	6.4%	6.0%	4.2%	33.3%	5.2%	(13.4)	17.7%	(17.0)
Female Agency								
Students (cell n = 16)	4.0%	30.8%	12.1%	0.0%	24.8%	(16.5)	2.1%	(8.3)
Female (cell n = 8)	8.1%	34.1%	22.3%	0.0%	35.1%	(8.9)	4.2%	(11.8)
Male (cell n = 8)	0.0%	27.5%	1.9%	0.0%	14.5%	(16.2)	0.0%	(0.0)
Teachers (cell n = 16)	1.2%	31.7%	2.3%	0.0%	16.9%	(16.0)	0.7%	(1.9)
Female (cell n = 8)	1.0%	45.5%	0.0%	0.0%	23.7%	(18.4)	0.4%	(1.3)
Male (cell n = 8)	1.4%	17.8%	4.5%	0.0%	10.2%	(10.2)	0.9%	(2.5)
First Person Agency								
Students (cell n = 16)	4.6%	5.3%	1.1%	5.1%	2.3%	(6.1)	4.8%	(5.1)
Female (cell n = 8)	2.2%	10.7%	1.0%	5.5%	4.0%	(8.3)	4.0%	(5.1)
Male (cell n = 8)	7.0%	0.0%	1.3%	4.7%	0.5%	(1.5)	5.6%	(5.3)
Teachers (cell n = 16)	2.3%	2.9%	0.0%	3.6%	1.6%	(4.9)	2.7%	(5.0)
Female (cell n = 8)	3.1%	0.9%	0.0%	2.3%	0.4%	(1.1)	2.5%	(5.0)
Male (cell n = 8)	1.6%	4.8%	0.0%	4.9%	2.8%	(6.8)	2.9%	(5.4)
Sex Neutral Agency								
Students (cell n = 16)	32.9%	19.4%	36.3%	19.1%	26.7%	(17.4)	25.5%	(21.6)
Female (cell n = 8)	45.5%	24.4%	34.5%	23.2%	25.4%	(14.1)	33.7%	(24.4)
Male (cell n = 8)	20.2%	14.3%	38.2%	14.9%	28.1%	(21.2)	17.2%	(15.6)
Teachers (cell n = 16)	54.8%	26.6%	66.5%	35.2%	45.7%	(14.1)	45.2%	(21.2)
Female (cell n = 8)	65.5%	19.9%	72.1%	39.3%	45.1%	(12.5)	51.9%	(25.2)
Male (cell n = 8)	44.2%	33.3%	60.9%	31.1%	16.5%	(14.9)	38.6%	(15.0)
Non-human Agency								
Students (cell n = 16)	35.2%	43.6%	33.0%	32.7%	37.6%	(20.5)	34.3%	(17.0)
Female (cell n = 8)	37.5%	30.7%	26.2%	41.3%	28.3%	(10.9)	40.8%	(15.8)
Male (cell n = 8)	32.9%	56.4%	39.8%	24.1%	46.9%	(24.2)	27.8%	(16.4)
Teachers (cell n = 16)	36.8%	35.9%	27.9%	21.7%	32.5%	(17.9)	29.9%	(19.7)
Female (cell n = 8)	27.1%	33.7%	25.4%	12.7%	29.6%	(21.1)	20.0%	(14.1)
Male (cell n = 8)	46.5%	38.1%	30.4%	30.6%	35.5%	(14.9)	39.9%	(20.2)

*With Protocol ♂ Un → ♀ Kn, Variable 3 measures the percent of particular critique propositions on Kevin (sex unknown) combined with that on Victoria (sex known); with Protocol ♀ Un → ♂ Kn, Variable 3 measures the percent of particular critique propositions on Kevin (sex known) combined with that on Victoria (sex unknown).

28.5% of their critique as male-agent propositions, teachers 7.4%; students interviewed by the female researcher generated only 13.5% male-agent propositions, teachers 17.2%. There was also a parallel effect on female agency ($F(1,48) = 7.93$, $p < .01$). Students interviewed by the male researcher cast 17.2% of their critique as female-agent propositions, teachers 5.5%; students interviewed by the female researcher 9.6%, teachers 12.1%. Finally, there was a clearly related effect on non-human critique ($F(1,148) = 5.48$, $P < .05$). Students interviewed by the male researcher expressed 33.2% of their propositions as having no explicit human agent, teachers 38.8%; students interviewed by the female researcher 38.8%, teachers 23.7%.

MANOVA identified one three-way interaction as a significant effect: Prior Knowledge with Sex of Reader with Status of Reader ($\lambda(4,45) = .811$, $p < .05$). Univariate tests found the interaction on male agency ($F(1,48) = 5.62$, $p < .05$). The regularities in this interaction are the tendency of students to express more male-agent propositions than did teachers regardless of order, and the tendency of males to provide more male-agent propositions than did females. The contrasts are the eight female teachers under Protocol ♀ Un → ♂ Kn, who provide nearly 10% more male-agent propositions than did the male teachers or the female students under the same protocol, and the eight male students under this protocol, who provide twice as many male-agent propositions as did any other group there. There was also a univariate interaction on non-human critique ($F(1,48) = 6.58$, $p < .05$). The basic pattern here is for readers to express more of their critique without human agency when the known sex of the author is opposite to their own sex. This pattern holds for three of the four groups: male teachers, male students, and female students. The anomaly is the group of eight female teachers, who reverse the pattern.

Discourse Center of Value.   (See Table 23–6.) The four independent variables in this cluster were percentage of critique devoted to mimetic, formalist, expressive, and a combination of rhetorical and situational values. MANOVA discovered a significant effect for Status of Reader ($\lambda(4,45) = .751$, $p < .05$). Subsequent univariate F tests found a strong main effect on the formalist variable ($F(1,48) = 11.12$, $p < .01$). Students cast 66.8% of their critique propositions into a formalist or text-valued mode, compared to 54.8% for teachers. There was also a strong main effect on rhetorical/situational propositions ($F(1,48) = 15.41$, $p < .001$). Students put only 17.8% of their critique into that discursive value system, teachers 28.0%. MANOVA also discovered a significant interaction between Prior Knowledge and Sex of Reader ($\lambda(4,45) = .800$, $p < .05$). Univariate testing found a significant effect on expressive critique ($F(1,48) = 11.52$, $p < .01$). With expressive values in writing, there appears an inverse relationship between sex of reader and knowledge of the writer's sex. Under Protocol ♂ Un → ♀ Kn, with Victoria's sex known, female readers averaged 5.7% expressive critique, male readers 2.6%. Under Protocol ♀ Un → ♂ Kn, with Kevin's sex known, female readers averaged 2.9% expressive critique, male readers 5.9%.

TABLE 23–6   Subgroup Means on Discourse Center of Value (Variable 4)

	Victoria		Kevin		Protocol ♂ Un → ♀ Kn		Protocol ♀ Un → ♂ Kn	
	Sex Unknown	Sex Known	Sex Unknown	Sex Known	Variable 4*	(SD)	Variable 4*	(SD)
Mimeticist Center								
Students (cell *n* = 16)	5.3%	4.6%	4.8%	6.0%	5.0%	(4.5)	5.7%	(4.2)
Female (cell *n* = 8)	3.0%	3.9%	5.4%	5.3%	4.6%	(5.1)	4.3%	(4.4)
Male (cell *n* = 8)	7.6%	5.4%	4.2%	6.7%	5.4%	(4.0)	7.1%	(3.7)
Teachers (cell *n* = 16)	7.9%	4.9%	8.9%	3.2%	6.7%	(5.3)	5.7%	(6.7)
Female (cell *n* = 8)	8.8%	3.9%	4.7%	2.5%	4.1%	(4.9)	5.7%	(4.9)
Male (cell *n* = 8)	7.0%	5.9%	13.1%	3.9%	9.2%	(4.6)	5.6%	(8.5)
Formalist Center								
Students (cell *n* = 16)	68.8%	70.0%	63.9%	63.1%	66.6%	(10.7)	65.7%	(13.2)
Female (cell *n* = 8)	69.0%	69.8%	58.9%	59.0%	65.1%	(8.2)	63.6%	(14.7)
Male (cell *n* = 8)	68.7%	70.2%	68.8%	67.1%	68.1%	(13.2)	67.8%	(12.2)
Teachers (cell *n* = 16)	58.5%	59.7%	53.2%	47.8%	56.7%	(9.5)	53.4%	(16.0)
Female (cell *n* = 8)	60.1%	55.7%	54.8%	46.8%	55.0%	(11.3)	53.5%	(13.4)
Male (cell *n* = 8)	56.9%	63.7%	51.7%	48.8%	58.4%	(7.6)	53.2%	(19.2)
Expressive Center								
Students (cell *n* = 16)	3.2%	5.5%	2.2%	5.6%	4.1%	(2.9)	4.7%	(5.0)
Female (cell *n* = 8)	1.4%	10.1%	1.6%	2.8%	5.9%	(1.9)	2.3%	(3.4)
Male (cell *n* = 8)	5.0%	1.0%	2.9%	8.5%	2.4%	(2.6)	7.1%	(5.4)
Teachers (cell *n* = 16)	4.4%	3.0%	6.2%	5.4%	4.7%	(4.0)	4.9%	(5.6)
Female (cell *n* = 8)	3.7%	5.6%	7.6%	3.3%	6.7%	(2.9)	3.6%	(6.0)
Male (cell *n* = 8)	5.1%	0.5%	4.7%	7.4%	2.8%	(4.2)	6.3%	(5.2)
Rhetorical/Situational Center								
Students (cell *n* = 16)	14.8%	12.8%	23.0%	18.1%	17.9%	(6.8)	17.0%	(8.0)
Female (cell *n* = 8)	18.7%	9.8%	24.1%	21.3%	16.5%	(7.8)	21.0%	(8.8)
Male (cell *n* = 8)	10.8%	15.7%	21.7%	14.8%	19.3%	(5.8)	13.0%	(14.0)
Teachers (cell *n* = 16)	23.4%	23.0%	28.4%	37.8%	25.6%	(8.0)	30.2%	(14.2)
Female (cell *n* = 8)	22.6%	29.4%	30.4%	41.9%	30.4%	(7.3)	32.0%	(13.8)
Male (cell *n* = 8)	24.3%	16.5%	25.4%	33.7%	20.7%	(5.5)	28.5%	(15.3)

*With Protocol ♂ Un → ♀ Kn, Variable 4 measures the percent of particular critique propositions on Kevin (sex unknown) combined with that on Victoria (sex known); with Protocol ♀ Un → ♂ Kn, Variable 4 measures the percent of particular critique propositions on Kevin (sex known) combined with that on Victoria (sex known).

Gender Clues.   (See Table 23–7.) Subjected to multivariate analysis here was the cluster of linguistic, psychological, and cultural clues, expressed in percentages of all clues. MANOVA found a significant effect for Sex of Reader ($\lambda(3.44) = 7.48$, $p < .01$). Univariate tests located a strong effect on cultural clues ($F(1,46) = 12.49$, $p < .01$). Females relied on cultural evidence in support of a supposition of author's sex 24.7% of the time, males only 7.6%. Since the distribution for cultural percentages were skewed, due to a large number of

TABLE 23–7   Subgroup Means on Gender Clues (Variable 5)

	Victoria		Kevin		Protocol ♂ Un → ♀ Kn		Protocol ♀ Un → ♂ Kn	
	Sex Unknown	Sex Known	Sex Unknown	Sex Known	Variable 5*	(SD)	Variable 5*	(SD)
Linguistic								
Students (cell $n = 16$)	60.3%	51.0%	48.7%	56.6%	53.3%	(32.6)	60.4%	(35.3)
Female (cell $n = 8$)	59.5%	32.9%	43.8%	53.3%	44.1%	(38.8)	53.7%	(37.5)
Male (cell $n = 8$)	61.1%	72.2%	54.3%	61.1%	63.8%	(22.0)	67.1%	(34.1)
Teachers (cell $n = 16$)	35.3%	56.4%	23.9%	21.5%	36.2%	(27.0)	32.9%	(23.6)
Female (cell $n = 8$)	27.5%	42.9%	21.1%	26.7%	36.5%	(32.2)	29.6%	(26.5)
Male (cell $n = 8$)	44.2%	72.2%	26.6%	17.8%	35.9%	(22.2)	36.1%	(21.7)
Psychoanalytic								
Students (cell $n = 16$)	25.9%	35.9%	39.7%	24.8%	35.4%	(24.5)	24.4%	(26.7)
Female (cell $n = 8$)	21.9%	52.4%	34.4%	24.0%	39.9%	(29.8)	25.0%	(26.0)
Male (cell $n = 8$)	30.6%	16.7%	45.7%	25.8%	30.2%	(17.5)	23.9%	(29.2)
Teachers (cell $n = 16$)	45.2%	37.0%	53.1%	43.6%	45.7%	(28.3)	41.9%	(27.1)
Female (cell $n = 8$)	47.1%	44.8%	42.6%	22.0%	35.4%	(27.5)	37.0%	(20.8)
Male (cell $n = 8$)	43.0%	27.8%	63.7%	59.0%	57.4%	(26.2)	46.8%	(32.9)
Cultural								
Students (cell $n = 16$)	13.8%	11.8%	11.7%	18.6%	10.8%	(17.8)	15.2%	(21.9)
Female (cell $n = 8$)	18.6%	14.8%	21.9%	22.7%	16.0%	(20.7)	21.4%	(27.0)
Male (cell $n = 8$)	8.3%	8.3%	0.0%	13.1%	4.8%	(12.6)	9.1%	(14.6)
Teachers (cell $n = 14$)	18.9%	6.6%	23.0%	25.4%	18.1%	(24.8)	21.4%	(22.3)
Female (cell $n = 7$)	25.4%	12.3%	36.3%	51.3%	28.1%	(30.5)	33.4%	(21.3)
Male (cell $n = 7$)	11.4%	0.0%	9.7%	6.9%	6.7%	(8.6)	9.3%	(16.8)

*With Protocol ♂ Un → ♀ Kn, Variable 5 measures the percent of particular gender clues in Kevin (sex unknown) combined with that in Victoria (sex known); with Protocol ♀ Un → ♂ Kn, Variable 5 measures the percent of particular gender clues in Kevin (sex known) combined with that in Victoria (sex unknown).

zero responses, the data were re-tested by chi-square analysis on proportion of the two groups (males and females) that used cultural clues at all in their analysis. This test supported the ANOVA (Pearson $\chi^2 = 9.00$, df 1, $p < .01$). About 69% of the females used the cultural category for clues at least once, compared to only 31% of the males.

MANOVA also found a significant effect for Status of Reader ($\lambda(3,44) = .826, p < .05$). Univariate testing located an effect on linguistic clues ($F(1,46) = 8.15, p < .01$). MANOVA found no two-way interactive effects, but one three-way effect: Prior Knowledge, Status of Reader, and Sex of Interviewer ($\lambda(3.44) = .804, p < .05$). Univariate testing located an effect on cultural clues ($F(1,46) = 10.10, p < .01$). Essentially, the cultural category was used the least often when students analyzed essays with sex of Victoria *known* and Kevin *unknown* in the presence of the male interviewer, and when they analyzed essays with sex of Victoria *unknown* and Kevin *known* in the presence of the female interviewer; under these same interviewing conditions, with teachers the cultural category was used most often. Due to the skewed distribution of the cultural percentages, we consider this finding suspect, although it makes intuitive sense.

Discussion

Influence of Interviewer.   Any conclusions drawn from the sex of the two interviewers would be highly tenuous. The presence of the interviewers obviously introduced rather directly into the experiment a number of uncontrolled factors. As with Etaugh, Houtler, and Ptasnik (1988), only two interviewers were used, permitting personality contrasts to enter in, as well as other differences such as age, appearance, authority, and even office decor. Little that is known about interviewer influence in gender/evaluation studies helps interpret our findings. Even a short list of empirically supported factors influencing gender bias in evaluation indicates the problems in making plausible interpretations; distance and medium of interview (e.g., by telephone or in person), transiency of group (e.g., ad hoc research group or semester class), sex ratio of group (e.g., mixed, same-sex, isolated sex), publicness (e.g., confidential interview or group session), size of group, age differential of interviewer and participant, authority of interviewer (Etaugh, Houtler, & Ptasnik, 1988; Rubin & Greene, 1991; Top, 1991; Unger 1900; Wallston & O'Leary, 1987). Our one clear conclusion is that future studies of gender bias in evaluation must systematically rotate third parties (as we did), and whether they serve as interviewer, proctor, or facilitator in the experiment. To leave discussion of our findings of interviewer effects at this point is not, however, to say that they are unimportant. They support current awareness among researchers that writing evaluation is subject to group and role interactions of some complexity and magnitude.

Reader's Assumption and Inference about the Writer's Sex.   The two student essays selected as targets in this study contain no explicit assertions of the author's sex, so readers analyzing the first essay given them must have based their notion of the author's sex indirectly on style and content. At that point in the protocol they had no inkling that sex of the author was an issue up for discussion. Still, about two-thirds of the readers spontaneously formed a gender image of the author, supporting our first hypothesis. The finding has considerable import for any project for unbiased appraisal of student writing, although it is not surprising, given the propensity of most people to assign gender to people and their behavior (Bem, 1984). Certainly the finding questions the validity of gender research designs that presume that presenting participants with anonymous writing will isolate, in their responses, sex-linked language traits, as distinguished from psychological sex-role stereotypes (Mulac, Incontro, & James, 1985; Roulis, 1990). Of equal importance is the fact that our readers' spontaneous gendering was wrong about half the time. Further, their subsequent conscious inference of the writer's sex was wrong about two-thirds of the time. Originally we selected the two pieces as gender-ambiguous, and we do not argue they are typical. But they are not unusual. In an earlier study, we found that four highly experienced teachers of college writing misinferred the author's sex with between 24% to 28% of the full run of 63 typed in-class essays, despite the fact that 22% of the essays gave away the sex of the author (J. Haswell, 1991). Stygall et al. (1994) found readers misidentifying the author's sex of portfolio sets 27% of the time (the figure may be inflated since it confounds essays that explicitly gave the author's sex away with those that did not, and essays that were identified quickly were read more often than essays that were not). Other investigators have found readers guessing the author's sex of typed, anonymous essays at no better than chance (Mulac, Incontro, & James, 1985; Mulac, Studley, & Blau, 1990; Roen, 1992). Individually, however, some authors succeed in conveying their sex much more often than others. In Roen's study of high school teachers, correct assignment of the writer's sex for the four target essays was 21, 26, 70, and 86%. It is likely that in a typical run of nameless but otherwise undoctored student writing (as in a placement reading), readers on their own will automatically ascribe sex to the writer much of the time and show a large variance of correctness in their inferences.

Scale Rating.   The readers' holistic rating is our first evidence that their construction of gender may have influenced their evaluation of the essays. This rating came after they had read and verbally analyzed each essay in terms of good and bad rhetorical qualities, so the judgment was not thin or hastily considered. The most informative evidence for influence of gender on the rating appears in the three-way interaction among Prior Knowledge, Sex of Reader, and Status of Reader. This complex interaction is exposed with breakdown of the ratings by halves of the protocol and by subgroups — that is, by female students, male students, female teachers, male teachers (see Table 23–3). With Victoria's essay, all subgroups except the female teachers rated it higher when they knew it was written by a woman than when they did not know. With Kevin's piece, all subgroups except the female students rated it lower when they knew it was written by a man. Figure 23–2 diagrams the two countertendencies. Figure 23–2 also illustrates two general findings of gender bias in the critique of college writing. First, female student writing, compared to male student writing, is elevated. Second, this sex-of-writer bias is partially countered by a status-of-reader bias. Here female teachers show a nontypical harshness with Victoria's essay when they find it has been written by a woman student, and the female students a nontypical approval of Kevin's essay when it is known to have been written by a male peer.

The main effect for Sex of Reader on the rating scale indicates that these two trends are complicated by a third. Readers as a whole treat same-sex student writing relatively more harshly than opposite-sex (see Figure 23–3). "Relatively" is a key word, and Figure 23–3 also shows the way that both sexes judged Kevin's essay as worse written than Victoria's. The female ratings for Kevin averaged 2.90, the male 2.67; the female for Victoria 3.57, the male 3.80. Figure 23–3 also presents evidence that this trend of same-sex

FIGURE 23-3   Scale Rating When the Rater Knows the Sex of the Writer (Second
Half of Protocol) and When the Rater Must Infer the Sex of the
Writer (First Half)

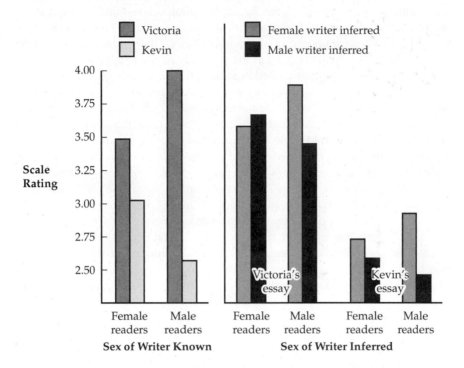

depreciation transcends the chance effect of a contrast in writing quality between two particular essays. Male readers, it can be argued, may simply be
more intolerant of writing judged poorer (Kevin's), females more intolerant of
writing judged better (Victoria's). In fact, response to the two essays during
the first part of the protocol shows that same-sex depreciation still emerges
before readers had a chance to compare essays and when readers were misas-
cribing the sex of the author at least half the time. Across groups, male raters
judge essays (whether Kevin's or Victoria's) higher than do female raters
when both sexes attribute them to a female author; and male raters judge essays (whether Kevin's or Victoria's) Lower than do female raters when both
sexes attribute them to a male author. Within rater groups, however, same-
sex-depreciation is stronger with the males, and not apparent with the females, as Figure 23–3 shows. Our findings support Etaugh, Houtler, and
Ptasnik (1988), whose male college students rated job applications for a variety of fields low when they were coded as male-authored and high when
coded as female-authored. Our findings do not support Roen (1992), whose
male high school teachers preferred male-authored writing and female teachers preferred female-authored.

That women are more competent than men in language use is, or course, one of the most venerable of gender stereotypes in currency. It is a common belief that females learn to talk earlier, talk more, speak and write more correctly, communicate better socially, learn foreign languages faster and better, and so on. The notion of women's verbal superiority, however, is contextual, as is illustrated by Goldberg's finding of anti-female bias in the evaluation of professional writing. In formal speaking at the college level, there is a core of research that finds female performance rated higher than male (reviewed by McMahan, 1991). The stereotype that college-age women are better writers than their male peers, however, has not been systematically researched. But the report, for instance, that male-female student dyads tended to elect the man to give the speech and the woman to write it (Wanzenried, Franks, & Powell, 1989) only documents the intuitive experience of many college teachers. It certainly matches the gender-clue analysis of our participants, whose most common tactic for identification of writer's sex was reasoning that if the piece was well written it probably was female-authored. Our finding of pro-female bias in college writing is also supported by the most common reversal of Goldberg's anti-feminine finding, that when the field under evaluation is judged feminine, then raters often favor female performance (Top, 1991). Students as well as teachers may be unconsciously sex-typing student writing as a woman's province.

This anti-male bias is countered by one group of raters, the female students. It is a finding without close parallel in the research literature. In Protocol ♀ Un → ♂ Kn, when Kevin's sex was known to the female students, the familiar gender polarities depreciating male writing are mostly absent from their transcripts, where in fact they appreciate qualities that stereotypically are assigned to females, such as open expression of feelings (see Haswell & Haswell, 1995). Perhaps it is not surprising to find a certain attraction to male students of their own age. Less unexpected is that the female teachers who had prior knowledge of Victoria's sex should show an equally strong bias countering the general trend in favor of her (see Figure 23–2). Feminist research, of course, has compiled a lengthy record of women devaluing their own sex, and since Goldberg's language performance studies have uncovered negative bias against female writing on the part of female evaluators fairly regularly (reviewed by Paludi & Bauer, 1983). A related factor may be the way Victoria's essay suggested masculine authorship to many of our female teachers; Victoria was "plodding to the man's world too much," according to one of them. The teachers were much more knowledgeable of feminism than were the female students, and may have reacted negatively to a piece of writing they saw had masculine academic traits. Generally, evaluators show a negative bias when they perceive a performance as gender-switched, where they imagine one sex showing sex-typed traits of the other sex, in language, dress, mannerism, or status (Cameron, 1985, Ruble & Ruble, 1982).

Positive Critique.   Across all groups, men and women in our study gave nearly identical amounts of positive critique: 31%, a figure that supports the well known fact that typically, in critique of student writing, negative response far outweighs positive (Harris, 1977; Zak, 1990). Roughly, our readers meted out positive commentary in proportion to their holistic appraisal of the two essays, making positive around 38% of their reaction to Victoria's essay and around 25% to Kevin's (see Table 23–4). As for gender effects, our primary finding is that, as with the holistic rating, knowledge of the author's sex is associated with departures from this value ranking. Definite knowledge of Victoria's sex raised the percentage of praise for her textual accomplishments by about 10%. As the group breakdown in Table 23–4 shows, the students are mainly responsible for this increase. When sex of writer was unknown, the students were less decisive than were the teachers about the distinctive merits of the two essays, the students awarding only 5% more praise to Victoria than to Kevin, the teachers 11%. When sex of writer was known, teachers show little change with Victoria's essay, but students record a remarkable increase of positive remarks, from 27% to 48%. This finding adds to the research record of college students awarding more praise to classroom language performance of females than of males (McMahan, 1991; reviewed by Pearson, 1985).

Figure 23–4 illustrates another parallel with the holistic rating. The amount of positive critique complicates this pro-female bias with same-sex

FIGURE 23–4 Percent of Positive Critique When the Rater Knows the Sex of the Writer (Second Half of Protocol) and When the Rater Must Infer the Sex of the Writer (First Half)

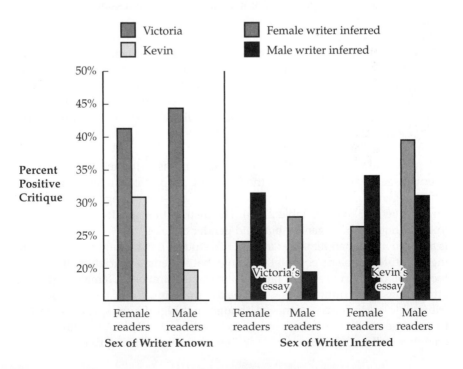

depreciation. Male readers tended to give Victoria more and Kevin less praise than did female readers. Although this is a non-significant trend ($F(1,48) = 2.48$, $p = .12$), it is strongly supported — as was the holistic rating — by the performance of readers during the first half of the protocol when they were relying on their own often incorrect inferences of the writer's sex. In a pattern parallel to and even more pronounced than the holistic rating (compare Figure 23–3), male raters praise either essay more than do female raters if they guess it was written by a woman, while female raters praise either essay more than do male raters if they guess it was written by a man. Behind these effects may lie the common belief that women need more positive support in evaluations (McMahan, 1991). Overall, our findings do not support the admittedly tentative findings of Barnes (1990) that, in marginal commentary of college writing teachers, men tend to praise male-authored writing, women female-authored.

Authorial Agency.   The gender effects in global evaluation and in positive commentary extend to the content of that commentary. Assignment of agency, which we will consider first, truly is an element of content. Of course, it can be made to appear otherwise by grammatical constructions peculiar to the language — for instance passivizations, the generic "he," or the singular "they." The statements "This essay ends well," "The student ends their essay well," and "She ends her essay well" seem to convey the same content. Psycholinguists, however, have argued otherwise (e.g., Bodine, 1975; Stanley [Penelope], 1975; Switzer, 1990). These different expressions convey different choices — frequently conscious choices — made by the speakers. For instance, the first expression appears to circumnavigate the issue of author's sex by erasing the issue of authorship altogether. But if the speaker knows the piece was written by a female, then the content includes a statement to the effect that it would be better to suppress the fact that a woman was responsible and deserves credit for crafting the excellent ending. If the speaker does not know the sex of the writer, then the utterance may still express gender bias in avoiding reference to any human agency, since all human acts are inherently gendered. Our findings show that some of the strongest effects of gender upon critique of student writing may be found in the arena of agency attribution.

Across all participants and protocol conditions, critique propositions attributed agency to the writing in the following proportions: male agent 16.7%, female agent 11.1%, first-person agent 2.8%, sex-neutral agent 35.8%, non-human agent 33.6% (see Table 23–5). The distribution speaks to the presence in the critique of both gender bias and gender counter-bias. That male agency is allowed more than female stands as this study's most straightforward finding of anti-feminine discrimination. Note that systematic variation of the protocol would otherwise have elicited an equal number of female and male attributions. The counter-bias is that nearly three-fourths of the critique is attributed to a genderless agency. Although that high figure speaks in part to the critique conditions, where essays were anonymous half of the time, and in part to a well known tendency of judges of student writing to consider text and not author, still the commentary of the readers provides ample evidence that they did not want to appear "prejudiced," "sexist," or "chauvinist." Even in the second half of the protocol, when the writer's sex had been announced before readers began discussing the essay, all subgroups except one (the male students with Kevin's essay) refer to the author in ways that avoid sex attributes the majority of the time — more than 65% of the time by the male teachers with Victoria's essay (Table 23–5). Nearly every transcript provides instances of the reader struggling to avoid mentioning the agent by sex, even when the author's sex is known. The most common tactic is the singular "they," which, as researchers have noted, has become the singular generic pronoun of choice in the speech of both students and teachers (Bate, 1979; Meyers, 1990).

Nevertheless, gender effects still emerge. The main effect of Prior Knowledge upon proportion of male or female agents, of course, speaks largely to the success of the protocol design, where all readers used more female-agent propositions when Victoria's sex was known and more male-agent propositions when Kevin's sex was known. But while the writing stimulus was gender-balanced, due to rotation of essays, the critique of the readers is gender-asymmetrical. There emerges a highly regular but multilayered pattern of gender bias, most precisely expressed by the three-way interaction among Prior Knowledge, Sex of Reader, and Status of Reader, and partially shown in the main effects of Sex of Reader and of Status of Reader. In sum, across sex, the male readers' preference for male agency outweighs the female readers' preference for female agency; within sex, participants attribute more human agency to their own sex; and across experience, students allow more gendered agency than do teachers.

The breakdown in Table 23–5 shows that male readers are mainly responsible for the overall higher incidence of male-agent attributions. Males allow male agency in 44.8% of their propositions when they know Kevin is the author of his essay and allow female agency in 22.7% when they know Victoria was the author of hers; for female readers the comparable proportions are 37.9% for Kevin and 39.8% for Victoria. That female students and female teachers tolerantly attribute male agency in Kevin's piece to the same degree they attribute female agency in Victoria's supports evidence that women are more gender-inclusive in their language than men are (Rubin & Greene, 1991; Hiatt, 1977). Once told the sex of a writer, the females not once attribute the writing to the other sex, whereas males referred to Victoria's essay as male-authored in 4% of their propositions in Protocol ♀ Un → ♂ Kn. In the first half of the protocol, with sex of author unknown, male readers average 17.3% male agency and 2.0% female agency, female readers 7.2% male agency and 7.9% female agency. It is important to see that these tendencies can be found in the first half of the protocols, because it shows gender bias emerging from the readers' unforced inferences about the sex of the writer, not from the interviewer's explicit raising of the question. For instance, when the men inferred female authorship to Kevin's and Victoria's essays, they still described the agent behind the words as male 13% of the time, as female only 2%. Operating under the same inference, the women describe the agent as male 0% of the time and as female 15%. With Kevin's essay alone, men produced 4% female-agent propositions when they thought it was female-authored, women 18%. It is largely our male readers, then, who show signs of a masculinized culture where male agency is unconsciously assumed before female.

This asymmetrical bias is entwined with a symmetrical one. Both sexes preferred agency of their own sex. With Victoria's sex known, females allowed female agency 39.8% of the time, males 22.7%; with Kevin's sex known, males allowed male agency 44.8% of the time, females 37.9%. (As the main effect for Sex of Reader suggests, this pattern appears most consistently with female agency.) The complement of this pattern can seen in the sex-neutral and non-human attribution rates. Strategies there — passivizing the author as a person out of explicit being and personifying the text into a self-acting being — appear related inversely to knowledge of the writer's sex: readers use them more when they know that the essay under consideration has been written by a member of the other sex. This finding suggests a mild form of gender bias, not where critic-readers demonstrate animosity or depreciation toward the opposite sex but where they seem to have difficulty entering into its perspective or life experiences (compare the similar pattern with expressive discourse, discussed below).

Status emerges as a strong factor in these gender effects, suggesting that attribution of agency in terms of sex is in part a developmental or learned practice. Students are more prone to refer to the author in a sex-specific way. They express a male agent 21.0% of the time, the teachers 13.5%; they express a female agent 13.5% of the time, the teachers 8.8%. The difference is made up not in first-person or non-human attributions but in sex-neutral. The students construct 26.1% and the teachers 45.5% of their critique with "he/she" constructions, the singular "they," or gender-neutral terms such as "the student" or "the writer." The difference is especially pronounced during the first half of the protocol when the sex of the author was not known. Then the students often create gender-definite language that, with an anonymous essay, might be deemed inappropriate, referring to the writer as "he" 20.4% of the time. The teachers do so only 4.1%. The teachers are much better at following the profession's nonsexist guidelines — a reflection perhaps of their greater practice in talking about authorship, their deeper understanding of gender issues, or their conscious sense of professional duty to supply critique apart from gender. The findings support recent studies showing teachers much more conscious of nonsexist-language principles than are their students (Rubin & Greene, 1991; Wolff, 1991).

The two three-way interactions on agency identify two groups as occupying extremes — the male students and the female teachers. The male students averaged 29.4% male agency for their critique during the first half of the protocol, compared to 6.6% for the other subgroups, identifying them as arguably the most sexist of the participants. By contrast, the female teachers allowed only 2.9% male agency in the first half of the protocol. At the same time, they recognized Kevin when his authorship was known to them with male-agent propositions one-third more than did the male teachers and more even than did the female students, who we have seen as especially sympathetic to Kevin. The female teachers show a combination of sensitivity to sexist language when an author's sex is unknown and willingness to acknowledge gendered agency to the author when it is known. It is worth noting, incidentally, that these women, along with the female students, do not use the first-person more than do the men, contrary to findings elsewhere (Barnes, 1990; Johnson & Roen, 1992; Peterson, 1986; Rubin & Greene, 1991). In part this may be because we measured a specialized use of it, where the critic assumes the role of the writer (e.g., "I would switch these two paragraphs around").

Discourse Centers of Value. Across the board, the readers devoted 4.6% of their critique to expressive values, 5.8% to mimetic, 7.8% to rhetorical, 14.9% to situational, and 60.6% to formalist; 6.3% were unattached (Table 23–6). These proportions add to the perpetually current finding that both teachers and students remain firmly text-centered in their analysis of discourse (e.g., Connors & Lunsford, 1993; Kucer, 1989). With our participants, these proportions show little association with gender factors. The exception lies in the expressive category. Our finding, however, does not exactly support other evaluation studies, which tend to confirm the classic gender polarity of men as instrumental and women as expressive. Generally in the literature, female evaluators value emotion more than do male (reviewed by Shields, 1987). In critique of student writing, Barnes (1990) found male-teacher written commentary more intolerant of emotional writing. Roen and Johnson (1992) found women graduate students putting more weight on personal involvement as a successful rhetorical tactic in peer-critique memoranda. Our male and female participants, however, devote exactly the same amount of their critique to expressive concerns; 4.6%. The difference surfaces when readers had prior knowledge of the writer's sex. Then one sex increases the percentage of expressive critique propositions in their commentary on the same-sex essay over that on the other-sex essay. To Kevin males offer 8.0% expressive commentary, to Victoria less than 0.8%; to Victoria females offer 7.9%, to Kevin 3.1%. The situation we find is close to that described by Green (1990), who taped a male teacher in conference encouraging a female student to master the rules and a female teacher encouraging her to find her voice — except that our expansion of the context would not be surprised to find Green's female teacher encouraging a male student to master the rules and her male teacher encouraging the male student to find his voice. This is to say that, just as with the non-human agency attributions, the evidence does not support the essentialist position on sexual characteristics, that males (including male critics) do not value expressiveness and females do, but rather the position that definitive knowledge of same-sex authorship releases critical intuitions having to so with same-sex inner life.

The other significant factor with the discourse centers of value is Status of Reader. Two highly consistent contrasts appear between the students and teachers. Students produce more formalist analysis (66.2%) than do the teachers (55.1%), and teachers produce more rhetorical/situational critique (27.9%) than do the students (17.5%). Together, the differences bespeak of well known changes a few years make in the way undergraduates and composition teachers — even young teachers — deal with text. Whether it is theorized that the changes stem from a growth in expertise or educational experience (e.g., Haas & Flower, 1988) or a progression in psychosocial development (e.g., Labouvie-Vief, 1984), compared to students, teachers tend less to grasp the text as a self-contained verbal production and more to understand it as an interpersonal, situational event.

Gender Clues.   Except in interaction with the interviewer, types of clues used to identify the author's sex were not systematically related to prior knowledge of it. This is to say that the kinds of evidence participants selected did not differ whether they were backing up an inference of author's sex that they had made on their own or identifying clues to back up the interviewer's assertion of the writer's sex. Since in the first condition readers were searching essays that they had misascribed more often than not, the system of gender identification that they brought to the text, it seems, stands somewhat independent of sex-linked language effects in the text itself. Of course, textual features certainly helped prompt gender deductions, as Roen (1992) found with high school teachers, and certain items stand as more salient gender markers than others. Contrary to the findings of Stygall et al. (1994), who worked with fifth-year education majors and Master of Arts in Teaching graduate students, we did not find that word-choice clues were marked for females and unmarked for males; in our two essays, "gut instinct," "load of bull," and "variable" were identified as male language. Actually, our readers were able to find ample "feminine" or "masculine" clues from either essay (see the Appendix). Assuming that, historically, observed linguistic sex-role behavior helps form gender schema (Anastasi, 1984), our transcripts suggest a certain lag between schema and current social realities. A case in point might be the fact that 62 out of 64 of our readers made no recourse to the biological category of gender clues. Historically it is a recent feminist category, and although most of the teachers said they were familiar with feminism (most of the students said they were not), as yet they seem not to have internalized the interpretive frame. Another case is the phrase "load of bull" from Victoria's essay, which a large number of readers cited as evidence that the piece was male-authored. Expletives are still widely regarded as male-marked (see Rasmussen and Moely, 1986), yet in a post-experiment interview Victoria herself selected the phrase as reflective of her femininity (Haswell & Haswell, 1995), and de Klerk (1991) has shown that "stereotypical expectations of coy, non-swearing females" are not upheld in verbal practice among late-teen students.

A more persuasive case in point is the shared gendered logic that all participants, student and teacher, brought to the task of identifying author's sex. Pervasive was the schema of bipolar opposites that researchers have found little changed in American culture for the last forty years (Broverman, Vogel,

Broverman, Clarkson, & Rosenkrantz, 1972; D. Rubin, 1993; Ruble & Ruble, 1982; Spence, 1984; Stygall et al., 1994); females are emotional and males are distanced, females are social-minded and males aloof, females are accepting and males skeptical, females write well and males don't, and so on. This interpretive schema is wide-ranging, and our readers used it to argue that both Victoria's and Kevin's essay were either female- or male-authored. The amount of actual text cited to derive support for author's sex was substantial — over half of both essays. The simple finding questions the common opinion among the readers that gender and critique of writing are not linked, and the opinion of compositionists at large that gender and evaluation of text interface only marginally. (The Appendix identifies the parts of their texts that were gender-marked for our readers.)

There is, however, a difference in the gendered identification systems according to Sex of Reader and Status of Reader. Combined, readers showed the following distribution of gender-clue categories: biological 1.2%, cultural 16.4%, psychoanalytic 36.7%, linguistic 45.7% (Table 23–6). Females and males differed significantly in one category, the cultural, to which females devoted more attention (24.7%) and males much less (7.6%). Clues, based on the cultural, focus on social or interpersonal situations. They rely on contextual generalizations such as women accepting people's advice or men breaking laws just for the sake of breaking them. It has been a consistent finding in gender studies that the female in American culture is more attuned to the interpersonal and social, both as an observed behavioral trait and as a gender stereotype. In a recent study of students from kindergarten through college, Biernant (1991) found males distinguishing themselves from females physically, females distinguishing themselves from males behaviorally. The contrast in Status of Reader found students relying on the linguistic category 57.0% of the time, teachers 34.5%. Table 23–7 shows that teachers make up the difference in both the psychoanalytic and cultural categories. College students only slowly sharpen their sense of a human presence lying behind words (Haas, 1994), only gradually develop away from adolescent literal-mindedness toward a more mature sense of language as constructed, not given (Cavanaugh, Kramer, Sinnott, Camp, & Markley, 1985; Labouvie-Vief, 1984). In a sense, students seem to analyze the issue of author's sex much as composition research did ten years ago, with a focus on language-trait sex differences and a disregard of social and psychological differences. To be fair, we ought to point out that the teachers relied as much as did the students on the familiar bipolar stereotypes. Still, students rely much more on linguistic polarizations (e.g., female writing is smooth, male rough) — in tune with their heavy use of the textual discourse center of value.

SUMMARY OF DISCUSSION

As review of recent gender studies predicts, inclusion of contextual factors into research design produced findings that break down simplistic notions of both gender bias and the gender schemas that help create bias. Our exploration, unlike most studies of gender and writing, is also multicriterial. We tested for gender bias not via one evaluative dimension — for instance, sexist language (Rubin & Greene, 1991) or complimenting (Johnson & Roen, 1992) — but rather via a series of criteria; inference of author's sex, holistic rating, positive critique, authorial agency, discursive center of value, gender clues. The result strongly suggests that any explanation for the effects of gender on writing evaluation will be complex. As Holland and Skinner found in their study of college-student courtship stereotypes, we found gender bias interacting with critique in ways that cannot be reduced to "dictionary-type definitions of gender" (1987, p. 79), for instance to stereotypical notions of gender bipolarities or to one-way sexist discrimination. A multi-componential picture fits better (Biernant, 1991; Six & Eckes, 1991), or more exactly Holland and Skinner's blend of previously learned stereotypes and expected behavioral patterns played out in context-specific "scenarios."

Each act of criticism that we studied implies its own characteristic explanatory gendered motive or cluster of motives. The mere act of reading an anonymous piece of writing activates an automatic impulse to assign gender to unmarked human products. The request to deduce the author's sex for a piece of writing encourages reliance on the culture-honored panoply of sterotypical, bipolar gender traits. The need to label an essay with a single, nom-referenced holistic rate tends to trigger the stereotype that women write better in college. Critically analyzing an essay, with the specific injunction to look for good and bad qualities, may activate the belief that women deserve or require more praise than men do. With the need at nearly every point in critique to identify a creative source for the writing, readers indulge in same-sex attribution or find ways to bypass the issue with gender-erasing maneuvers (which is gender bias in another guise). In choosing regions of the discursive act to value, readers avoid the province of the author's inner feelings, beliefs, and motives if the author is member of the other sex. Cutting across these specialized acts are more pervasive motives for bias: same-sex depreciation, antipathy toward writing perceived as code-switched, and reluctance to intuit the inner life of the opposite sex. And complicating these acts are proclivities of one sex or the other: attraction of the female students to male peers, distrust of the women teachers in a female piece that sounds masculine-academic, sensitivity of the women teachers to nonsexist language, anti-feminine sexism of the men students, awareness of social-contextual issues with the women.

These effects are more sizable than those found in many evaluation-bias studies (Top, 1991). Nearly two-thirds of our participants form a gendered image of the author spontaneously with essays lacking explicit references to the sex of the author. Half of these images are incorrect. Nearly two-thirds of our readers, in making careful inferences about the sex of the author, are incorrect. Female teachers lower their rating of an essay by more than a tenth of a holistic scale when they discover it was written by a woman. Female students raise their rating of an essay by a sixth of the scale when they know it was written by a male peer. Students increase their proportion of positive critique by 20% when they understand an essay is written by a woman. Male readers acknowledge females as the agent of writing 10% less often than female readers do. With an essay known to have been written by a woman, male readers acknowledge female agency two times for every five times female readers do. Teachers neutralize the author's sex twice as often as students do. Seventy percent of female readers use clues from the cultural arena to determine the sex of an author, whereas only 30% of male readers do.

Reasons for the unusual size of these gender associations may be attributed in part to the fact that for each participant the protocol set an essay written by one sex for evaluation against an essay written by the other sex. We also used essays that must have given many readers a gender shock in the second half of the protocol on finding the sex of the first author different than they had inferred. What evaluators perceive as "cross-dress," the gendered form of code-switched, has proved a fertile source for evaluative bias in gender studies (Hartman, Griffith, Crino, & Harris, 1991; Kramarae, 1981; Penelope, 1990; Ruble & Ruble, 1982; Stygall et al., 1994). In other key ways, our study duplicated recent research designs that have elicited unusually strong gender effects: comparison of students and professionals, creating of a naturalistic setting, and requirement that readers consider the pragmatic effects of their evaluation (Top, 1991). The main conclusion to draw from our study is that, in the research condition that we set, there occur plentiful, varied, and complex gender effects upon critique. Only time will tell whether our particular research environment artificially inflated similar effects as they occur naturally. We suspect that it did not, that traditional gender research has probably underestimated the presence of gender bias in compositional settings.

Implications for Teachers and Assessors

The basic critical activities of the present experiment, including the reading of essays in sequence and the evaluation of essays seen as mildly code-switched, occur weekly in the lives of composition teachers. If the extent of gender effects found here seems surprising, one reasonable conclusion may be that gender bias exerts more sway in everyday critique of student writing than has been assumed. Gender bias in the teaching of composition, of course, has been assumed and detected empirically in a number of different instructional situations, from classroom lecturing (Kramarae & Treichler, 1990) to written response (Sperling & Freedman, 1987) to peer review (Roen & Johnson, 1992) to portfolio evaluation (Black et al., 1994). Our findings indicate that similar biases are present in that fundamental act of pedagogical critique, when assessor, teacher, or student scrutinizes a submitted piece of writing in order to evaluate it and recommend revision.

We do not contend, of course, that compositional critique will always betray exactly the same configuration and extent of bias that we report here. Our findings should be interpreted and applied with no less caution than is due any empirical experiment. With different target essays (perceived as cross-dress or otherwise), new readers of varying status, and other interviewers working under different protocols, the resulting gender effects on critique will vary from our own. In natural compositional settings, critique is applied in a bewildering variety of ways in an endless variety of circumstances — from assigning grades under the pressure of an unstated departmental aegis to responding with unconscious body language to a student suggesting a library paper topic in an office conference. The profession will have to see much more investigation into gender and evaluative practices before we will be able to discern the customary parameters of bias with any confidence. A second caution is that despite our efforts to interview reader-participants in as natural a setting as possible, there was still some degree of artificiality in the process. Above all, when we asked readers to identify textual features that suggested the sex of the writer, some seemed to have so much difficulty that their selections may have been forced, perhaps exaggerating the bipolar configuration of their gender clues.

Nevertheless, despite these cautions, we believe educators can trust that our investigation tapped into some commonalities of gender and critique extending beyond the merely local. A number of the outcomes here are supported with strong confidence levels statistically, with parallel findings in sociological gender research, and with the intuitive experience of practitioners. "There are no social activities that escape gendering," writes Harding (1986, p. 57). Within the activity of composition critique, our most salient conclusions about gender offer implications to which assessors and teachers may well attend.

Assessment. This study questions some entrenched practices of formal writing assessment. Most obviously, it warns that even experienced composition teachers — who constitute the majority of readers engaged in formal assessment of writing around the country — may often unconsciously allow stereotypical preconceptions about male and female writing abilities to affect their holistic judgment of individual essays. Technically, they are prone to a gendered form of the "logical rating error," where judges give similar ratings to traits that are artificially connected in their minds. (The error was first named by Newcomb, 1931, who found that the appraisal of certain behavioral traits of schoolboys intercorrelated at .49 within the ratings of evaluators, while independent observational records of the same traits intercorrelated at .14.) If raters logically associate advanced skill in writing, rhetorical appeals based on feelings, and female authorship — and many of our readers did — then they will tend to award an essay organized around feelings and signed with a female name a higher holistic score than it might deserve otherwise. Further, in what might be called the "logical-disrupted rating error," a portion of our raters reacted negatively when traits pre-associated in their minds were contradicted by an essay, as in a piece perceived as cross-dressed where affective content co-occurs with male authorship.

The traditional method of countering gender bias in raters is to mask writers' names, as in formal holistic evaluation of student essays or in local placement tests or national advanced placement examinations. Our evidence concurs with that of Stygall et al. (1994), namely that blocking out of names is largely unsuccessful in blocking the entrance of gender biases. A certain portion of student writers voluntarily divulge their sex in their essays, even when the topic does not directly connect with gender issues: 22% of them in J. Haswell (1990). And with essays where the authors have avoided explicit mention of their sex, a majority of raters form a mental image of it spontaneously: 64% in the present study. Consider what may happen with a group of teachers, many of whom hold the gender stereotype that female students write better than male students. The teachers serve as readers in a holistic evaluation of student writing for placement or for a research project. The names of writers are masked but 20% identify their sex anyway. Of the remaining 80%, half of the time (a conservative estimate) readers still construct the author's sex and get it right half of the time.

Writers give the information about their sex away	20%
Readers construct the writer's sex correctly	20%
Readers construct the writer's sex incorrectly	20%
Readers form no image of the writer's sex	40%
	100%

There is then 40% of the essays where the rater images or imagines the sex of the writer correctly. This is easily a situation where, despite masking of names, rater presuppositions about the superior writing ability of women could bias the results and generate, for instance, the 5–8% edge that holistic assessments in the past have awarded to first-year female writers over their male peers (e.g., Meyer, 1982). Such assessments, of course, help entrench the original stereotype.

There are two other concerns when authors' names are withheld. In our study, half of the time readers were incorrect in the image of the writer's sex they had spontaneously formed. This would mean that, in the above hypothetical situation, around 20% of the students would have their essays read under false presumptions about their sex, with unknown effects upon the evaluation of their writing. Will such presuppositions increase misinterpretation of content? Will readers react negatively to subliminal dissonances in gender messages? The second concern challenges more directly the orthodox practice of withholding writers' names, yet has more support for it from gender research. What about students whose essays prompt no image of author's sex, as in 40% above? Such an outcome would seem the goal of name-masking, yet in our analysis of the commentary generated during the first half of the protocol, the 23 readers who formed no image of the author's sex evaluated the essay (either Victoria's or Kevin's) more harshly than did the other 41 who had imaged the writer as either female or male (Haswell & Haswell, 1995). This provocative finding concurs with a scattering of language-evaluation studies that find gender-neutral performance often rated more negatively than gender-marked performance (Illich, 1982; Kramarae, 1981; Paludi & Strayer, 1985; Rajecki, de Graaf-Kaser, & Rasmussen, 1992). This bias itself would be neutralized were all raters able to neutralize the sex of all writers in a formal assessment, but the evidence is that such mental control is unlikely to happen, regardless of rater training.

With name-masking in formal writing assessment, it seems to be a case of biased if you do, biased if you don't. Should names of writers be withheld, making students indirectly vulnerable to inferences and misinferences and neutralization, or should names be provided, making students directly vulnerable to gender stereotyping? Until more is known about gender effects during rating sessions, perhaps the solution is to train raters in the dangers of whichever system is to be used. If writers' names are to be masked, raters can be alerted to the inevitable imaging of the author's sex in most cases, to the rate at which those images will be incorrect, to the temptations and unfairness of gender stereotypes, to the negative bias of gender suppression. If writers' names are to be provided, training can center on gender stereotyping, with special emphasis on the common negative reaction to writing that is perceived as code-switched. All in all, given the variety of complex interpretive strategies that readers engage in when names are masked, it seems easier for raters and fairer to students if essays be presented for assessment readings with names attached.

Teaching.   It is worth emphasizing that the current study investigates reader response, not student writing styles. We draw no conclusions and therefore will not consider any implications having to do with the way Victoria or Kevin chose to write their essays. We have called them "cross-dressed" not because we have any evidence that they depart from expected norms of student writing — we don't — nor because we know the authors' intentions, feelings, or sexual orientation — we don't — but simply because of the gendered way that readers interpreted the essays. In short, nothing can be inferred from this study about how students ought to write. Faced with the response situation our study pictures, should students strive toward a genderless style, or toward a more openly gendered style, or toward an androgynous style, or toward the normative style of their own sex, or toward the gendered expectations of their audience? Teachers must make up their own minds about how to help students answer such questions. But our investigation does provide evidence about the complexly gendered conditions of response to student writing in typical reader groups. It does offer, then, implications about how both teachers and students might better deal with those conditions.

The most pressing implication for writing teachers has to do with the presence of polarized gender stereotypes observed here with both students and teachers. So long as these persist, they will perpetuate themselves. Teachers, for instance, will expect female students to prefer interpersonal topics such as friendship and family ties; most students will respond in kind because they are alert to what teachers want and because their culture has taught them the same expectations (Keroes, 1990; Sirc, 1989; Ware, 1991); and then teachers will find their expectations confirmed. To escape this evaluative circle, teachers and (with the help of teachers) students can become better aware of their own gendered reactions to writing, and of their position within groups with histories of biased response: female teachers who tend to devalue masculinized writing, male teachers who tend to elevate female student writing, female students who perhaps tend to romanticize male peer writing, male students who perhaps tend to compete with and devalue male peer writing. And everyone might well become especially sensitive to the plight of students whom readers imagine are writing in a cross-dressed gendered style. Our evidence shows Victoria writing in an approved masculine vein and then being disapproved for it because she is a woman, a double bind well investigated by feminists of the last decade. We also found support for a similar bind experienced by Kevin, who receives negative criticism because he writes about his interest in friends and family ties.

For teachers, this study has special implications in connection with the formation, training, and conducting of peer critique groups. The evidence is that the popular peer editing sessions can be a two-edged sword. On the one hand, fellow students may likely extend to writers more positive comments and allow more authorial agency than does the teacher. Like our female students in response to Kevin's writing, peers may also validate textual features that the teacher overlooks. On the other hand, peers seem to indulge in more sexism and to treat gender content superficially as an isolated stylist feature of text and not as a mode of cultural being. Students also seem more resistant to writers who violate stereotyped gender codes, such as our male students critiquing Kevin's essay with his sex known. Using peer editing and peer evaluation in writing classrooms without alerting students to possible pitfalls in their responses to each other might further perpetuate gender stereotypes as well as exert punitive consequences, regardless of the quality of the writing.

A more general implication of our study questions the professional tenet that rhetorical critique and gender should be separated. The credo appeared frequently in the commentary of our participants: "Good writing is good writing, regardless of who wrote it." It also appears in the current routines of the profession. The masking of names on assessment essays is only one manifestation. Others include the gender-random assignment of students to teachers, the disregard for the sex of participants in the formation of peer-editing groups, and the analysis of text as if the sex of the writer has nothing to do with its rhetorical value in standard rhetorics and textbooks. It is not surprising that teachers may yearn to deal with rhetorical problems separate from the disturbing and messy realities of gender, class, and ethnicity (Brodkey, 1989). Our findings, of course, offer multiple evidence that gender and critique are never separate, with either students or teachers. It might be argued that since our factor of Prior Knowledge of author's sex showed no systematic connections with the readers' assignment of discourse values (Dependent Variable 4), then the operating framework of rhetorical value in critique of student writing actually does resist gender, that teachers and student peers do offer critical advice uncolored by knowledge of the writer's sex. But our statistical analysis leaves unexplored the critical activity taking place within those over-arching discursive value categories. Readers may devote the same portion of textual analysis to an essay whether they know it is female- or male-authored, but what happens within that portion? A bottom-up subcategory analysis, reported elsewhere (Haswell & Haswell, 1995), again finds active the presence of gendering — in tone, degree of agency neutralization, circularity of gender stereotypes and critique, and differential recommendations for revision.

Teachers are left with an important question: if gender cannot be untangled from the work of critique, then what is to be done with the situation? Rose (1991) found that writing teachers often deny the presence of gender effects or try to suppress them, a method not absent in our own corps of readers. This solution has its problems, as we have shown, in part because such suppression is associated with an especially harsh critical response. Again, as with the problems in erasing gendered response from holistic assessments, teachers might better become more aware of gender effects in reader response than teach as if those effects do not exist. And they might teach that response, in all of its complexity, as part of the content of their writing courses. If gender response is a reality, then it is a rhetorical reality that young writers will do well to study as they consider their audience. They can be taught that it is customary for good writers to seize control of the gendering of their readers' response by gendering their own voice, by shaping that audience response with the projection of a gendered image of themselves as author — what we have called "gender voice" or "gendership" (Haswell & Haswell, 1991, 1995) and perhaps what Stygall et al. call "rhetorical gender" (1994, p. 262).

A final implication for teachers, perhaps the most far-reaching, arises from the fact that most of the gender effects uncovered by our investigation are interactive. The relationship between critique and prior knowledge of the author's sex emerges in diverse, disguised, and complex ways. The situation we found supports the theory of Ochs (1993): "the relation between language and gender is not a simple straightforward mapping of linguistic form to social meaning of gender. Rather the relation of language to gender is constituted and mediated by the relation of language to stance, social acts, social activities, and other social constructs" (p. 146). Our findings, along with the majority of findings in the last decade of research into gender and evaluation, recommend that teachers, in their watchfulness for gender effects, make what Ochs calls "local expectations" (p. 146). They may expect prior knowledge or inferences about the author's sex to affect the evaluation of a piece of student writing, but they should also expect them to do so in no across-the-board manner — as with simple anti-female bias — but rather depending upon the sex and educational status of the evaluator, upon the critical task assumed by the evaluator, upon the presence of other evaluators, upon the contiguity of other pieces read before, and no doubt upon many other factors and contexts. Gender will often be active during the critique of student writing, but not in the generalized manner once suggested by Goldberg's study. Consequently, advice for student writers must go beyond simple solutions, such as adherence to nonsexist language. Assessors, teachers, and students must question their own assumptions and practices, read with a new awareness, talk with each other, and be open to a situation that is too complex to accommodate universal claims.

REFERENCES

Anastasi, A. (1984). Reciprocal relations between cognitive and affective development — with implications for sex differences. In T. B. Sonderegger (Ed.), *Psychology and gender: Nebraska symposium on motivation, 1984* (pp. 1–35). Lincoln: University of Nebraska Press.

Aries, E. (1987). Gender and communication. In P. Shaver & C. Hendrick (Eds.), *Sex and Gender, Review of personality and social psychology: Vol. 7* (pp. 149–176). Newbury Park, CA: Sage.

Barnes, L. L. (1990). Gender bias in teachers' written comments. In S. L. Gabriel & I. Smithson (Eds.), *Gender in the classroom: Power and pedagogy* (pp. 140–159). Urbana: University of Illinois Press.

Bate, B. (1979). Nonsexist language in transition. *Journal of Communication, 28*, 139–149.

Bem, S. L. (1981). Gender schema theory: A cognitive account of sex typing. *Psychological Review, 88*, 354–363.

Bem, S. L. (1984). Androgyny and gender schema theory: A conceptual and empirical integration. In T. B. Sonderegger (Ed.), *Psychology and gender: Nebraska symposium on motivation. 1984* (pp. 179–226). Lincoln: University of Nebraska Press.

Bem, S. L. (1987). Gender schema theory and the romantic tradition. In P. Shaver & C. Hendrick (Eds.), *Sex and gender. Review of personality and social psychology: Vol. 7* (pp. 251–271). Newbury Park, CA: Sage.

Biernant, M. (1991). A multicomponent, developmental analysis of sex typing. *Sex Roles, 24*, 567–586.

Black, L., Daiker, D. A., Sommers, J., & Stygall, G. (1994). Writing like a woman and being rewarded for it: Gender, assessment, and reflective letters from Miami University's student portfolios. In L. Black, D. A. Daiker, J. Sommers, & G. Sommers (Eds.), *New Directions in Portfolio Assessment* (pp. 235–247). Portsmouth, NH: Boynton/Cook.

Bock, R. D. (1975). *Multivariate statistical methods in behavioral research*. New York: McGraw-Hill.

Bodine, A. (1975). Androcentricism in prescriptive grammar: Singular "they," sex-indefinite "he," and "he or she." *Language in Society, 4*, 129–146.

Brodkey, L. (1989). On the subject of class and gender. *College English, 51*(2), 125–141.

Broverman, J. K., Vogel, S. R., Broverman, D. M., Clarkson, F. E., & Rosenkrantz, P. S. (1972). Sexrole stereotypes: A current appraisal. *Journal of Social Issues, 28*, 59–78.

Butler, J. (1990). *Gender trouble: Feminism and the subversion of identity*. New York: Routledge.

Cameron, D. J. (1985). *Feminism and linguistic theory*. New York: Macmillan.

Cameron, D. J., & Coates, J. (1988). *Women in their speech communities: New perspectives on language and sex*. New York: Longman Group.

Cavanaugh, J. C., Kramer, D. A., Sinnott, J. D., Camp, D. J., & Markley, R. P. (1985). On missing links and such: Interface between cognitive research and everyday problem-solving. *Human Development, 28*, 146–168.

Cayton, M. K. (1990). What happens when things go wrong: Women and writing blocks. *Journal of Advanced Composition, 10*, 321–337.

Chodorow, N. (1978). *The reproduction of mothering: Psychoanalysis and the sociology of gender*. Berkeley: University of California Press.

Connors, J., & Lunsford, A. (1993). Teachers' rhetorical comments on student papers: Ma and Pa Kettle visit the topics of commentary. *College Composition and Communication, 44*, 200–223.

de Klerk, V. (1991). Expletives: Men only? *Communication Monographs, 58*, 156–159.

Emig, J. (1971). *The composing process of twelfth graders*. (NCTE Research Report No. 13.) Urbana, IL: National Council of Teachers of English.

Engelhard, G., Jr., Gordon, B., & Gabrielson, S. (1991). The influence of mode of discourse, experiential demand, and gender on the quality of writing. *Research in the Teaching of English, 26*, 315–336.

Etaugh, C. B., Houtler, D., & Ptasnik, P. (1988). Evaluating competence of women and men: Effects of experimenter gender and group gender composition. *Psychology of Women Quarterly, 12*, 191–200.

Fulkerson, R. (1979). Four philosophies of composition. *College Composition and Communication, 30*, 343–348.

Fulkerson, R. (1990). Composition theory in the eighties: Axiological consensus and paradigmatic diversity. *College Composition and Communication, 41*, 409–429.

Goldberg, P. (1968). Are women prejudiced against women? *Transition, 5*(5), 28–30.

Green, L. (1990). *Gender-based role perceptions in conference settings.* Paper presented at the American Educational Research Association Conference, Boston.

Guilford, J. P. (1954). *Psychometric methods* (2nd ed.). New York: McGraw-Hill.

Haas, C. (1994). Learning to read biology: One student's rhetorical development in college. *Written Communication, 11,* 43–84.

Haas, C., & Flower, L. (1988). Rhetorical reading strategies and the construction of meaning. *College Composition and Communication, 39,* 167–183.

Hall, J. A. (1987). On explaining gender differences: The case of nonverbal communication. In P. Shaver & C. Hendrick (Eds.), *Sex and gender. Review of personality and social psychology: Vol. 7* (pp. 177–200). Newbury Park, CA: Sage.

Harding, S. (1986). *The science question in feminism.* Ithaca, NY: Cornell University Press.

Hare-Mustin, R. T., & Marecek, J. (1990). Gender and the meaning of difference: Postmodernism and psychology. In R. T. Hare-Mustin & J. Marecek (Eds.), *Making a difference: Psychology and the construction of gender* (pp. 22–64). New Haven: Yale University Press.

Harris, W. H. (1977). Teacher response to student writing. *Research in the Teaching of English, 11,* 175–185.

Hartman, S. J., Griffith, R. W., Crino, M. D., & Harris, J. (1991). Gender-based influences: The promotion recommendation. *Sex Roles, 25,* 285–300.

Haswell, J. E. [Tedesco]. (1990). Applying the Perry and Belenky developmental schemes to English 101 students. Paper presented at the Wyoming Conference on English, Laramie.

Haswell, J. E. [Tedesco]. (1991). Ascribing gender to anonymous student writing. Unpublished paper.

Haswell, J. E. [Tedesco]. (1992). Read-aloud protocols and gender markers. Unpublished paper.

Haswell, J. E., & Haswell, R. H. (1995). Gendership and the miswriting of students. *College Composition and Communication, 46,* 223–254.

Haswell, R. H. (1986). *Change in undergraduate and post-graduate writing performance (part I): Quantified findings.* (ERIC Document Reproduction Service No. ED 269 780.)

Haswell, R. H. (1991). *Gaining ground in college writing: Tales of development and interpretation.* Dallas: Southern Methodist University Press.

Haswell, R. H., & Haswell, J. E. [Tedesco]. (1991). Gender and the evaluation of writing. (ERIC Document Reproduction Service No. ED 343 141.) Paper presented at the annual meeting of National Council of Teachers of English, Seattle, WA.

Hiatt, M. (1977). *The way women write.* New York: Teachers College Press.

Holland, D., & Skinner, D. (1987). Prestige and intimacy: The cultural models behind Americans' talk about gender types. In D. Holland & N. Quinn (Eds.), *Cultural models in language and thought* (pp. 78–111). Cambridge: Cambridge University Press.

Hunter, P., Pearce, N., Lee, S., Goldsmith, S., Feldman, P., & Weaver, H. (1988). Competing epistemologies and female basic writers. *Journal of Basic Writing, 7,* 73–81.

Illich, I. (1982). *Gender.* New York: Pantheon.

Isaacs, M. B. (1981). Sex role stereotyping and the evaluation of performance of women: Changing trends. *Psychology of Women Quarterly, 6,* 187–195.

Johnson, D. M., & Roen, D. H. (1992). Complimenting and involvement in peer reviews: Gender variation. *Language in Society, 21,* 27–57.

Keene, N. A. (1986). Male/female language: A stylistic analysis of freshman compositions. *Dissertation Abstracts International, 47,* 09A.

Keroes, J. (1990). But what do they say? Gender and the content of student writing. *Discourse Processes, 13,* 243–257.

Key, M. R. (1975). *Male/female language.* Metuchen, NJ: Scarecrow Press.

Kohlberg, L. (1966). A cognitive-developmental analysis of children's sex-role concepts and attitudes. In E. E. Maccoby (Ed.), *The development of sex differences.* Stanford: Stanford University Press.

Kramarae, C. (1981). *Women and men speaking: Frameworks for analysis.* Rowley, MA: Newbury House.

Kramarae, C., & Treichler, P. A. W. (1990). Power relationships in the classroom. In S. L. Gabriel & I. Smithson (Eds.), *Gender in the classroom: Power and pedagogy* (pp. 41–59). Urbana, IL: University of Illinois Press.

Kucer, S. B. (1989). Reading a text: Does the author make a difference? In B. Lawson, S. S. Ryan, & W. R. Winterowd (Eds.), *Encountering student texts: Interpretive issues in reading student writing* (pp. 159–168). Urbana, IL: National Council of Teachers of English.

Labouvie-Vief, G. (1984). Culture, language, and mature rationality. In K. A. McCluskey & H. W. Reese, *Life-span developmental psychology: Historical and generational effects* (pp. 109–128). Orlando, FL: Academic Press.

Lakoff, R. (1975). *Language and woman's place*. New York: Harper and Row.

McConnell-Ginet, S. (1985). Language and gender. In F. J. Newmeyer (Ed.), *Language: The socio-cultural context. Linguistics: The Cambridge survey, Vol. 4*: Cambridge: Cambridge University Press.

McMahan, C. R. (1991). Evaluation and reinforcement: What do males and females really want to hear? *Sex Roles, 24*, 711–783.

Meyer, P. R. (1982). *A study of sex differences in the freshman composition course at the University of Texas at Austin*. (EDRS No.ED214167).

Meyers, M. W. (1990). Current generic pronoun usage: An empirical study. *American Speech, 65*, 228–235.

Mulac, A., & Lundell, R. (1980). Differences in perception created by syntactic-sematic productions of male and female speakers. *Communication Monographs, 47*, 111–118.

Mulac, A., Incontro, C., & James, M. (1985). Comparison of the gender-linked effect and sex role stereotypes. *Journal of Personality and Social Psychology, 49*, 1098–1109.

Mulac, A., Studley, L., & Blau, S. (1990). The gender-linked language effect in primary and secondary students' impromptu essays. *Sex Roles, 23*, 439–469.

Newcomb, T. (1931). An experiment designed to test the validity of a rating technique. *Journal of Educational Psychology, 22*, 279–289.

Newkirk, T. (1984). How students read student papers. *Written Communication, 1*, 283–305.

O'Barr, W., & Atkins, B. K. (1980). "Women's language" or "powerless language?" In R. Borker, N. Furman, & S. McConnell-Ginet (Eds.), *Women and language in literature and society* (pp. 93–110). New York: Praeger.

Ochs, E. (1993). "Indexing Gender." In B. D. Miller (Ed.), *Sex and gender hierarchies* (pp. 146–169). Cambridge: Cambridge University Press.

Olian, J. D., Schwab, D. P., & Haberfeld, Y. (1988). The impact of applicant gender compared to qualifications on hiring recommendations: A meta-analysis of experimental studies. *Organizational Behavior and Human Decision Processes, 41*, 180–195.

Ortner, S. B., & Whitehead, H. (1981). Introduction: Accounting for sexual meanings. In S. B. Ortner & H. Whitehead (Eds.), *Sexual meanings: The cultural construction of gender and sexuality* (pp. 1–27). Cambridge: Cambridge University Press.

Paludi, M. A., & Bauer, W. D. (1983). Goldberg revisited: What's in an author's name? *Sex Roles, 9*, 387–390.

Paludi, M. A., & Strayer, L. A. (1985). What's in an author's name: Differential evaluations of performance as a function of author's name. *Sex Roles, 12*, 353–361.

Pearson, J. C. (1985). *Gender and communication*. Dubuque, IA: Brown.

Penelope, J. (1990). *Speaking freely: Unlearning the lies of the fathers' tongues*. New York: Pergamon.

Peterson, S. L. (1986). Sex-based differences in English argumentative writing: A tagmemic sociolinguistic approach. *Dissertation Abstracts International, 47*, 2146-A.

Pianko, S. (1979). A description of the composing processes of college freshman writers. *Research in the Teaching of English, 13*, 5–22.

Purves, A. C. (1992). Reflections on research and assessment in written composition. *Research in the Teaching of English, 26*, 108–122.

Rajecki, D. W., de Graaf-Kaser, R., & Rasmussen, J. L. (1992). New impressions and more discriminations: Effects of individuation on gender-label stereotypes. *Sex Roles, 27*, 171–185.

Rasmussen, J. L., & Moely, B. E. (1986). Impression formation as a function of the sex role appropriateness of linguistic behavior. *Sex Roles, 14*, 149–161.

Roen, D. H. (1992). Gender and teacher response to student writing. In N. McCracken & B. Appleby (Eds.), *Gender issues in the teaching of writing* (pp. 126–141). Portsmouth, NH: Boynton/Cook.

Roen, D. H., & Johnson, D. M. (1992). Perceiving the effectiveness of written discourse through gender lenses: The contribution of complimenting. *Written Communication, 9*, 435–464.

Rose, S. K. (1991). *Developing literacy/developing gender: Constructing college freshmen*. Paper presented at the National Council of Teachers of English annual convention, Seattle.

Roulis, E. (1990). *The relative effect of a gender-linked language effect and a sex role stereotype effect on readers' responses to male and female argumentative-persuasive writing*. Unpublished doctoral dissertation, University of Minnesota.

Rubin, D. L., & Greene, K. (1991). Effects of biological and psychological gender, age cohort, and interviewer gender on attitudes toward gender inclusive/exclusive language. *Sex Roles, 24*, 391–412.

Rubin, D. L., & Greene, K. (1992). Gender-typical style in written language. *Research in the Teaching of English, 26*, 7–20.

Rubin, D. (1993). *Gender influences: Reading student texts.* Carbondale: Southern Illinois University Press.

Ruble, D. N., & Ruble, T. L. (1982). Sex stereotypes. In A. G. Miller (Ed.). *In the eye of the beholder: contemporary issues in stereotyping* (pp. 188–253). New York: Praeger.

Russ, J. (1983). *How to suppress women's writing.* Austin: University of Texas Press.

Shields, S. (1987). Women, men, and the dilemma of emotion. In P. Shaver & C. Hendrick (Eds.), *Sex and gender. Review of personality and social psychology: Vol. 7* (pp. 229–250). Newbury Park, CA: Sage.

Showalter, E. (1982). Feminist criticism in the wilderness. In E. Abel (Ed.), *Writing and sexual difference.* Chicago: University of Chicago Press.

Sirc, G. (1989). Gender and "writing formations" in first-year narratives. *Freshman English News, 18,* 4–11.

Six, B., & Eckes, T. (1991). A closer look at the complex structure of gender stereotypes. *Sex Roles, 24,* 57–71.

Spence, J. T. (1984). Gender identity and its implications for the concepts of masculinity and femininity. In T. B. Sonderegger (Ed.), *Psychology and gender: Nebraska symposium on motivation, 1984* (pp. 59–95). Lincoln: University of Nebraska Press.

Sperling, M., & Freedman, S. (1987). A good girl writes like a good girl: Written responses to student writing. *Written Communication, 4,* 343–369.

Stanley [Penelope], J. P. (1975). Passive motivation. *Foundations of Language, 13,* 25–39.

Starer, R., & Denmark, F. (1974). Discrimination against aspiring women. *International Journal of Group Tensions, 4,* 65–70.

Stygall, G., Black, L., Daiker, D. A., & Sommers, J. (1994). Gendered textuality: Assigning gender to portfolios. In L. Black, D. A. Daiker, J., Sommers, & G. Sommers (Eds.), *New directions in portfolio assessment* (pp. 248–262). Portsmouth, NH: Boynton/Cook.

Swim, J., Borgida, E., Maruyama, G., & Myers, D. G. (1989). Joan McKay versus John McKay: Do gender stereotypes bias evaluations? *Psychological Bulletin, 105,* 409–429.

Switzer, J. Y. (1990). The impact of generic word choices; An empirical investigation of age- and sex-related differences. *Sex Roles, 22,* 69–82.

Top, J. T. (1991). Sex bias in the evaluation of performance in the scientific, artistic, and literary professions: A review. *Sex Roles, 24,* 73–106.

Unger, R. K. (1988). Psychological, feminist, and personal epistemology: Transcending contradiction. In M. M. Gergen (Ed.), *Feminist thought and the structure of knowledge* (pp. 124–141). New York: New York University Press.

Unger, R. K. (1990). Imperfect reflections of reality: Psychology constructs gender. In R. T. Hare-Mustin and J. Marecek (Eds.), *Making a difference: Psychology and the construction of gender* (pp. 102–149). New Haven: Yale University Press.

Wallston, B. S., & O'Leary, V. E. (1987). Sex makes a difference: Differential perceptions of women and men. In P. Shaver & C. Hendrick (Eds.), *Sex and gender. Review of personality and social psychology, Vol. 7* (pp. 9–41). Newbury Park, CA: Sage.

Wanzenried, J., Franks, L. J., & Powell, F. C. (1989). *He speaks, she writes: An experimental study of gender and choice of communication mode.* Paper presented at the Conference of the Organization for the Study of Communication, Language and Gender, Cincinnati.

Ware, A. E. (1991). A discourses analysis of gender differences in the persuasive writing of eleventh-graders. *Dissertation Abstracts International, 51,* 10A.

Warshay, D. W. (1972). Sex differences in language style. In C. Safilios-Rothschild (Ed.), *Toward a sociology of women* (pp. 3–9). Lexington, MA: Xerox.

Wolff, J. M. (1991). Writing passionately: Student resistance to feminist readings. *College Composition and Communication, 42,* 484–492.

Zak, F. (1990). Exclusively positive responses to student writing, *Journal of Basic Writing, 9,* 40–53.

APPENDIX

Topic and Target Essays

When Plato describes a person's "search for truth," he uses the "Allegory of the Cave." How would you describe your "search for truth" and the process you use to pursue it?

Victoria's Essay*

The process *by which* I search for "truth" is dependent upon what kind of an answer I am looking for.

For example, if I were looking for the answer to a *question of morality, I would look within myself*. I believe that *only I can know if what I am doing or what I am saying is "good" or "bad." I use myself and my own personal values to determine the difference between right and wrong*. I use the beliefs I hold strongly to act as a kind of guide to help me through some more complex *moral decisions*. For instance, *I believe in obeying the law* but I realize that the law is only as perfect as those who made it. Thus, *if an occasion arises where someone is in danger or is hurt and helping them would conflict with* the law, *I would tend to ignore that specific law*.

If I were searching for an answer to *a question involving knowledge, I would first look to myself* and see how much I know about the particular subject or question I am contemplating. I then will take what knowledge I have an *compare it to what other people (or other resources) know*. This process also involves a *gut instinct*, for *I'm the only one who can decide if a source or a person* is giving me a qualified answer. In other words, *it's up to me to figure out if somebody/source* is feeding me a load of bull. Once I have the chance to gather as much information that I can, *I will try to make as accurate answer as possible*. It should be noted that on some occasions I choose not to us other people/sources *to find the truth*. Sometimes I am able to *find* the answers without the help of anyone else.

In conclusion I would like to say that, while these methods for finding my own kind of truth *seem* to work *fairly* well, I realize that *there are drawbacks. One involves emotion. Sometimes, in cases where there is a lot of emotion going on, I am apt to make decisions that are too hasty. Another drawback* is the amount of time I have to make these decisions. In cases such as these, *I just go with what I know definitely and my instinct*. Also, like any other person, I don't like to be proven wrong, but *I guess* it's something I've learned to live with.

Kevin's Essay*

When Plato describes a person's "search for truth," he was the "allegory of the cave." How would you describe your "search for truth" and the process you use to pursue it?

When I find myself searching for truth I usually try *to find it in friends and my family*. I also find it through my own self, because *I have to take in the information my friends and parents give me* and decide *what I want to believe it real*. So I basically decide what is real *through my own self and my own beliefs*, but I get most of the information from other people outside myself.

To find truth is something that comes naturally to me I guess. When *I take in information that my friends or my family is telling me* I have to take in all the good, truthful information and through out all the bad information. Something that they believe is truthful may not be truthful to me. I am my own person and I like to make my own decisions so when I get the information I take all the variables that go along with it to make sure my decision will be right. There are so many things that could influence my decision, but the biggest thing is whether I trust the source I am getting my information from. That is, why when people I do not know try to give me information I really don't pay attention. I mean I pay attention because I am interested, but I am not going to take what they are saying as truthful. *Only if I thought that it could be truthful would I then go to a friend or family and ask them to elaborate on the subject* that I brought up. So, to me, *all truth is something that I have to find myself through others. To know if somebody's information is really true or false is my own decision. I have to think whether I believe the information is real or true.* In this part of the decision making, *everything comes down on my own decision.* This is the hardest part, trying to decide what is true and what is false. *I see it as what I believe in and what I want to see is real, is real.* Even if everybody else sees the same thing as false and *I want to believe it is real, it will be real.* This is the one problem with my decision making process on what is real and what isn't real because if it happens that the information that I believe is real is not real, by definition, then I go all through my life believing it is real. This is why I have to take so much caution and time to make the right decision on what is real, who do I get the information from, and making the final decision.

The information that I get from other people than myself is when I get the information to decide what is real and what is the truth. Making the right decision I encounter lots of variables, but I have to make the right choice because it stays with me my whole life. *The information comes from the outside by the truth comes from my inside.*

NOTE

Text used by readers to argue that the author is female is italicized; text used by readers to argue that the author is male is underscored.

24

Validity of Automated Scoring: Prologue for a Continuing Discussion of Machine Scoring Student Writing

MICHAEL M. WILLIAMSON

Writing assessment has developed along two separate lines, one centered in professional organizations for writing teachers and the other centered in professional organizations for the broader assessment community. As the controversy about automated scoring continues to develop, it is important for writing teachers and researchers to become fluent in the discourse of the broader assessment community. Continuing to label the work of the broader assessment community as positivist and continuing to ignore it will only result in a continuing sense of defeat as automated assessment is adopted more widely. On the other hand, an examination of the literature on educational assessment will reveal that the theoretical base for assessment is quite consistent with the principles adopted by the writing assessment community.

Grading essays by computer seems to have entered an explosive new phase, and I hope that, by the end of this talk, you folks will be excited, too, about all the changes this may mean for testing. After all, essay grading has been done for perhaps 4 thousand years. But now we seem to face a brand-new opportunity: Not simply to help in human essay grading, but to firm it up with actual objective data, of the kind never really used.

— ELLIS BATTEN PAGE (1995)

INTRODUCTION

Anson (2003), reflecting on developments in artificial intelligence (AI), suggests it has provided little to serve any useful purpose in the English classroom because software has not been sufficiently sophisticated. Earlier, Herrington and Moran (2001) examined an emerging application of AI in

From *Journal of Writing Assessment 1.2* (2003): 85–104.

English Studies, automated scoring, the use of computer algorithms to simulate holistic ratings of student writing. Although they are concerned about the adequacy of the feedback provided by such programs, the greater concern is the implications for students' learning when computers are the basis for grades. However, automated scoring technologies are finding wider acceptance among educators. The Commonwealth of Pennsylvania recently made a commitment to the use of *Intellimetric,* the scoring engine reviewed by Herrington and Moran (2001). Some reports suggest that this engine was to be used in 2003 to score the writing of students on the mandatory Pennsylvania state achievement examinations (*Indiana Gazette,* 2003). Other states and individual school districts are either implementing or exploring implementation of one of the available engines.

This obvious conflict suggests that some may see valid applications for automated scoring, whereas others see none, suggesting that a deeper examination of the available inquiry about the validity of automated scoring is necessary. English teacher responses to automated scoring has been limited and such response (Anson, 2003; Herrington & Moran, 2001) does not refer to any of the evidence presented by the developers of automated scoring programs. There remains a need to examine the claims made by test developers about the validity of automated scoring and to determine whether any possible objections have been addressed.

Initially, I hoped to write an article that picked between the various arguments and claims and contended for a certain use of automated scoring in writing assessment. Unfortunately, my reading of the literature around this issue left me feeling that other precursor work needed to be done before the two camps, what Moss (1998) first labeled college writing assessment and educational measurement, could productively learn to talk to each other about automated scoring. In this article, I explore various beliefs and assumptions held by each side. Looking at the history of test development in general and writing assessment in particular, I examine the drive toward more reliable and efficient ways to measure educational achievement and writing ability. Additionally, I consider the various epistemological orientations of those who work in social science and the humanities, noting how each disciplinary area has changed over the last several years with the influence of postmodern theories of knowing and making meaning. I hope that this article can establish a common ground for future scholarship and discussion. At the very least, automated scoring is an incredible research opportunity through which we can explore the many different ways student writing can be read, valued, and sanctioned.

Automated scoring is not new. It first appeared in 1966, in the work of Ellis Page (1995). The response to this early work from the English-teaching community was similar to current responses. Reviewed in *Research in the Teaching of English,* Page's original work drew a response similar to Anson and Herrington and Moran from Macrorie (1969). On the other hand, Coombs (1969) was skeptical, but not entirely dismissive of the potential demonstrated in Project Essay Grade. However, automated scoring does not seem to have been wholeheartedly embraced by anyone in English Studies publishing in typical outlets, such as *College English* or *Research in the Teaching of English*.

On the other hand, a recently burgeoning literature on automated scoring has appeared in the literature typically examined by the broader assessment community, much of it suggesting that automated scoring does have valid applications for the assessing of writing.

AUTOMATED SCORING AS WRITING ASSESSMENT

Although it has a new face, the controversy over automated scoring reflects the constant struggle over writing assessment and the apparent stasis in achieving a resolution (Williamson, 1993). Until recently, the controversy focused on movement from indirect to direct measurement of writing (Williamson, 1993), as reflected in Yancey's (1999) history of the last 50 years of writing assessment. Currently, writing assessment seems to be caught in a three-way tug of war involving the introduction of portfolio assessment in the teaching and assessing of writing. Yancey suggests a shift in focus from reliability in the dispute over direct and indirect assessment, to validity, a dispute over how much writing is necessary to make a valid judgment about students' writing. From the beginning, there has been an explicit concern about the effects of particular approaches to assessment on the teaching and learning of writing, in effect, a question about the validity of assessment. Yancey's view reflects a trend in the literature by and for writing teachers and researchers to respond primarily to the challenges posed by systems developed to ensure the reliable scoring of student writing. The proposal to replace essay examinations with objective examinations, based in multiple-choice technologies began the controversy.

> The most recurrent criticism of essay tests, and the one about which the most has been written, concerns the unreliability of evaluating essay answers. If a test is to be worth while [sic] as a measuring instrument, it must measure what it purports to measure consistently and dependably. (Stalnaker, 1951, p. 498)

As Yancey points out, the response to objective testing was the development of direct assessment approaches using writing, justified in terms of their reliability, just as the justification for indirect assessment, using multiple-choice items, was grounded in its reliability compared to the earlier use of writing as a tool for assessment. Although the battleground itself was seen as reliability, the larger struggle was about validity, though it was focused at the time in terms of reliability.

> All educational measurements are generally intended to elicit information regarding the structure, dynamics, and functioning of the student's mental life as it has been modified by a particular set of learning experiences. The special problem in the case of the achievement test is to obtain information which is reliable and pertinent, and to do so efficiently. (Stalnaker, 1951, p. 496)

These concerns evolved into the traditional claim that a test had to measure what it purports to measure and that reliability is a necessary but insufficient claim for validity.

> Validity has two aspects, which may be termed relevance and reliability. "Relevance" concerns the closeness of agreement between what the test measures and the function that it is used to measure. "Reliability" concerns the accuracy and consistency with which it measures whatever it does measure in the group with which it is used. To be valid — that is, to serve its purpose adequately — a test must measure something with reasonably high reliability, and that something must be fairly closely related to the function it is used to perform. (Cureton, 1951, p. 622)

Although some developers have made claims about potential pedagogical uses of automated scoring programs, I only focus on their validity as it pertains to writing assessment. The larger, and perhaps more important issue of their pedagogical value is another question, one that does not seem of immediate relevance for writing assessment. I begin with Herrington and Moran's (2001) exploration because it reflects my own examination of particular programs. There is, however, a paucity of research beyond such informal examinations. Second, for the most part, feedback to students is based on boilerplate rubrics, some quite complex and sophisticated. Rubric-based feedback in any kind of scoring may not address the particular reason an essay was placed in a score category (Broad, 2003; Huot, 1993; Pula & Huot, 1993; Smith, 1993). The qualities and bases for human judgment of complex performances cannot be explained by a rubric. Two things are certain. One, automated scoring programs can replicate scores for a particular reading of student writing, and this technology is reliable, efficient, fast, and cheap. Two, automated scoring has been and will continue to be used in various large-scale assessments of student writing.

VALIDITY

As early as 1951, validity was defined by Edward Cureton in the first edition of what would become a periodic definition of the state of the art in educational measurement, *Educational Measurement*.

> The essential question of test validity is how well a test does the job it is employed to do. The same test may be used for several different purposes, and its validity may be high for one, moderate for another, and low for a third. (p. 621)

An important and forward-looking aspect of this definition is that it is grounded in the use of a test, not in the test itself. The definition of validity evolved with both formal and informal meanings, as can be noted in Cronbach's (1971) leading text on the theory and practice of educational measurement.

> We defined validity as the extent to which any measuring instrument measures what it is intended to measure. However, as we pointed out in

Chapter 1, strictly speaking, "One validates, not a test, but *an interpretation of data arising from a specified procedure.*" (p. 447)

While conforming with this general definition, Anastasi (1976) presents three primary forms of validity, each defined by the procedures used to determine them.

> Fundamentally, all procedures for determining test validity are concerned with the relationships between performance on the test and other independently observable facts about the behavior characteristics of under consideration. (p. 134)

She also provides a separate treatment of validity as an issue for interpreting test results through the use of decision theory, a further coupling of validity with particular uses of a test.

In one of the seminal works on writing assessment produced by writing researchers, Cooper and Odell (1977) define validity with a slightly different focus, one that may ultimately be responsible for spreading the informal definition of validity as the dominant meaning in writing assessment.

> If a measure or measurement scheme is valid, it is doing what we say it is doing. We want to insist on a careful distinction between *predictive validity* and other kinds of *validity*, content and *construct validity*. (p. xi)

This definition reflects what I am labeling the *informal definition of validity*. Later definitions of validity tend to adopt this informal definition, for instance,

> Although validity is a complex concept—colleges offer advanced courses in it—one simple concept lies behind the complexity: honesty. Validity in measurement means that you are measuring what you say you are measuring, not something else, and that you have really thought through the importance of your measurement in considerable detail, (White, 1994, p. 10)

White's definition of validity is metaphorical, and although metaphor is not unknown in social sciences research, the redefining of validity in this case moves two fundamentally different definitions of the same concept further apart.

The essential, crucial difference between these two definitions lies in the distinction between defining validity as procedure and validity as a property of a test. This distinction emerges from the difference between understanding the mathematical basis for assessment and the application of assessment in what Stalnaker (1951) labels achievement testing. Tests like statistical operations are conducted to make informed educational judgments. The simplicity of distinction between a procedural and conceptual understanding of validity is not always as clear and separate as it might seem. The fundamental nature of validity can be rendered confusing by educational researchers themselves.

> While the definition of validity seems simple and straightforward, there are several different types of validity that are relevant in the social

sciences. Each of these types of validity takes a somewhat different approach in assessing the extent to which a measure measures what it purports to. (Carmines & Zeller, 1980, p. 17)

Broad (2003) labels one stance in writing assessment "positivist," a stance that can be traced to Berlin's (1984) history of writing instruction. Positivism as a theoretical approach to the philosophy of science certainly characterizes early psychometric theory and its attempt to define psychology and educational and psychological assessment as a science. Guilford (1954) traces the emergence of statistical investigation in psychology and grounds his approach to the field in mathematics, as well as statistical inquiry, "The progress and maturity of a science are often judged by the extent to which it has succeeded in the use of mathematics" (p. 1). Gulliksen (1950) specifically limits his description of mental testing to those defined by quantitative methods, while specifically noting the difference between statistics and mathematics. In Guilford's terms, mathematics is a "universal language that any discipline may use with power and convenience" (p. 1). That this movement toward the use of mathematics and quantification may be positivist is one that deserves larger exploration in the literature of the field. However, there is an interesting contrast to what may be perceived as the problem of quantification in writing assessment.

As early as the 1950s, at least, such issues as validity were seen less as defined by the results of a statistical test than as a matter of disciplinary disputation, the assembling of evidence, not the simple results of a statistical test (Cureton, 1951). In a related example, in discussing educational evaluation, one of the primary applications of educational measurement, Cooley and Lohnes (1976), both eventually to become president of the American Educational Research Association, suggest that the scrutiny of the field and not objectivity is the issue. Moss (1998) calls her response essay to a study of writing assessment validation, "The Test of the Test." For Moss, validation is a practice in turning the gaze toward the construct of the assessment itself. It is a form of reflective practice, or as Ellen Schendel (1999) claims, "social action."

> What tends to keep researchers honest is the publicly available record of what they did and what they found, and not a godlike objectivity which some people seem to feel those doing evaluations should exhibit. Scientists doing basic research know that if their work is to have any value whatsoever, it will be closely read and critically examined by their colleagues in the field. (Cooley & Lohnes, 1976, p. 2)

These and other perspectives of validity are rooted in the ideas of Cronbach (1988, 1989) and Messick (1989). Cronbach (1989) characterizes validity as a form of disciplinary argumentation, one that is never finished and that evolves with each new use of an assessment in a new locale: "Validation is a lengthy, even endless process" (p. 151). Such a definition is supported by Cureton (1951) and Anastasi (1976) as well. It is this definition that leads Huot (2002) to characterize assessment as a continuing form of research. Thus, writing assessment should be viewed as a continuing examination of the available tools for assessment, as they are used for making new decisions. New developments will inevitably bring new tools, all of them requiring validity inquiry of their own.

Smith (1993) is probably the first researcher in writing assessment who fully reflects the complexity of validity inquiry. Although his work is some of the first substantive research that looks at the validity and not reliability of a writing assessment (Huot, 1994), ironically, he eschewed the word *validity* because he wanted to avoid any baggage associated with such a term. He used *accuracy of placement* as the goal for his placement testing program at the University of Pittsburgh. With collaborators, he designed a series of studies on the procedures that structure the way teachers make decisions based upon their reading of placement essays. Each of the studies led to a modification of the procedures that allowed a stronger claim to the validity of the assessment, the accuracy of placement of students in the writing program. This not only demonstrates more accurate placement of students over time, but it also led to a modification of the scoring procedures themselves. The end result was a less costly system because the reading and decision making were rooted in the context about which the teachers were expert.

The notion of validity as argument and the nature of professional judgment is related to Bleich's (1975) view of interpretive communities and Kuhn's (1996) view of the way that science changes through changes in the worldview of the members of the discipline. The meaning of a text, be it a poem or a validity inquiry, lies with the community of readers in the field and their intertextual experiences with the field. Such a position reflects a more postmodern view than the positivism cited as the basis for psychometric theory.

An additional consideration for validity is the impact of the assessment (Messick, 1989). The consequences of decisions made on behalf of a test is a core concern for validity inquiry because the uses of a test may impact what is learned and how that learning takes place. This concern for the impact of a test is one of the ethical bases for validity theory. Thus, validity inquiry must examine how learning changes as a result of the implementation of an assessment. Although this sounds like an ethical way to proceed, English professionals might question the existence of studies of the consequences of high-stakes testing on individual students taking high-stakes tests. Interaction among various fields is important if we are to understand complex phenomena. In particular, measurement theory in education and psychology has to respond to developments in psychology and education if the field is to remain viable. The impact of theoretical changes is not universally distributed in a field (Kuhn, 1996). If there are specialists in educational measurement still working with a variety of validities, there are still writing teachers and researchers who pursue grammar study as a prescriptive methodology in the teaching of writing. If validity theory has not coalesced into a univocal stance in measurement, the meaning of error is equally problematic for many teachers who are not able to grasp or who are unfamiliar with the complexity of disciplinary discourses on error.

After all, members of any academic field are part of both the paradigm that is disappearing and the new paradigm that provides a new synthesis for the field (Kuhn, 1996). That some may quote the contemporary definition and unwittingly include older definitions is not surprising. An interpretive community does not need to be, indeed is unlikely to be, univocal about any reading of any text. Importantly, if early theories of assessment were deterministic in the positivist sense that they were seen as objective explanations of reality, the postmodern influence in assessment publicly acknowledges the debate that always existed, and provides a new understanding of the meaning of such debate.

The core of my concern in the different representations of validity has to do with the difference between English Studies and educational measurement, the difference between social science and humanistic disciplines. A science depends on a clearly defined methodology as the basis for disciplinary disputation. Although English Studies depends largely on a hermeneutic form of inquiry, one based in close reading, assessment depends on evidence defined by the procedures that are used to collect it. For instance, the heart of the definition provided by Carmines and Zeller (1980) highlights the defining of each of the various types of validity as a procedure, despite the fact that it misses the more important concern that validity is contextualized.

Two conflicting views of research methodology are the primary problem for humanists as they attempt to represent their views outside of English Studies because any argument about validity will have to face the need to address the basic procedural issues of social science. Furthermore, if validity is seen as a unitary construct that involves the consequences of the test's use in context, validity can be seen as a situated construct, one that must observe the same situatedness that literacy theorists have been articulating for some time.

As a student of English Studies, I am concerned by the claims of Herrington and Moran (2001). As any good scholars in the field, they read the text of the automated scoring engine and see the rhetorical implications of its use in English classrooms. However, as a student of educational assessment, I know that their review of automated assessment does not provide the kind of structured inquiry necessary to convince a member of the community of readers in assessment. It is easy to adopt the stance that all psychometricians are positivists if one does not understand the fundamental role of scientific procedure in defining inquiry. However, the label itself has no meaning outside of English Studies because any form of quantification is labeled positivist. The label itself is, therefore, one that does not make the case against claims by psychometricians about the validity of particular approaches to assessment. In fact, most first-year composition texts would probably characterize such an argument as ad homenim.

PRINCIPLES GUIDING THE EXAMINATION OF THE VALIDITY OF AUTOMATED SCORING

All of the following statements are derived from the literature on education assessment and follow from my characterization of validity as it is defined by the following

1. The validity of an assessment lies in the decision that is made on the basis of the test, not the test itself.

2. Validity is a form of scholarly argumentation, based on research, which subjects the assessment to open discussion about both its substance and its meaning.

3. Validity is not a substantial or concrete set of claims, the argument is open to question with each use of the assessment and as developments in various theories, both within and outside of assessment provide new perspectives on assessment, what is being assessed, and how the assessment is being used.

4. Validation research is never a closed circle. Each use of an assessment, whether in the same or different contexts, must be examined to ascertain and revalidate the validity argument for the assessment, its uses, and the meaning of its uses.

5. In addition to examining the adequacy of the assessment for the decisions that are to be made from its use, assessment developers and users also have an ethical responsibility to examine the consequences of an assessment, to examine the effects of the assessment on both immediate contexts and broader cultural contexts.

Notice that each of these statements contains a procedural definition of validity. I argue that the definitions of validity that are common in English Studies are static, indeed, are positivist in the sense that they suggest we can know that a test is valid in objective terms, because we can know it is doing what we say it is doing. In other words, because many in English Studies ascribe to an older notion of validity (White, 1994; Yancey, 1999), they are unwittingly missing an opportunity to apply postmodern theories to validity inquiry and are, instead, promoting a rigid, decontextualized "positivist" concept of validity for writing assessment.

Artificial Intelligence

Automated scoring is based in the technology of AI, and claims to bring the relative efficiency of automation to scoring essays. These two concepts need to be defined as part of the process of validity inquiry. AI is a research paradigm built around several sciences. The primary goal of the emergent paradigm has been the simulation of human intelligence and behavior in the electronic system of a computer. Developments in each of these sciences, from linguistics to psychology and mathematics to computer science, have allowed a nearly continuous development of demonstrations of intelligent machines. The emergent technologies have resulted in a variety of applications that both enhance and simulate human performance in a variety of fields. Thus, it seems that the use of such technologies would inevitably lead to their application in English Studies. The first such application — Project Essay Grade — was seen by its developers as a method of relieving writing teachers of the burden of grading, leading also to more objective grades (Ajay, Tillett, & Page, 1973; Page, 1966, 1967a, 1967b, 1995; Page & Fisher, 1968). After an initial ambiguous response (Coombs, 1969; Macrorie, 1969), the concept of computer grading seems to have had little attention from researchers in composition and rhetoric for some time (Huot, 1996).

The development of the personal computer in the 1980s led to an outburst of enthusiasm for the use of computers in the writing classroom. The cutting edge of the field of computers and composition was initially defined by the seminal work of Hugh Burns (1979) with rhetorical invention and the rapid growth of word processing, among other business and personal applications. Burns' work reflected the early applications of artificial intelligence to English Studies. His work demonstrated the programming theories of artificial intelligence pioneered by Joseph Weizenbaum in the development of *Eliza*, a computer program designed to simulate the psychotherapeutic interviews of Carl Rogers. *Eliza* was considered to be a failure because the program did not meet Turing's criterion for a computing machine simulating human behavior, a primary consideration in judging the validity of computer programs that "artificially" simulate human intelligence.

Alan Turing was one of the pioneers of digital computing at Bletchley Park in England during World War II. As a very early theorist in computing, he suggested that a successful demonstration of human intelligence by a computer would be indistinguishable from the performance of an actual human. In other words, *Eliza* would be successful if the program were able to provide counseling to a human client without the client being able to determine whether the advice came from a machine or another human. Neither *Eliza* nor Burns' invention programs meet the criterion because they were unable to respond coherently to aberrant statements. The result of aberrant statements or questions about questions from the human use resulted in meaningless responses from the programs. Although the programming had a rudimentary syntactic parser, enabling it to extract relevant words from the input, it had no means of examining the meaning of any of the input. Therefore, it was easily "fooled" into giving unintelligible or meaningless responses. Subsequently, demonstrations of AI have been based on successively sophisticated approximations of human intelligence. Most of these early demonstrations were intended only to model what was possible, not necessarily to meet Turing's criterion.

Since the early demonstrations of machine intelligence, researchers working in the multidisciplinary field of natural language processing were busy with both basic research into computer simulation of language and immediate applications of this technology. With each new demonstration of the emerging technology, more sophisticated responses to human language were possible, as were more sophisticated applications. The accessibility of computers to those outside of computer sciences owes as much to the developments in AI as to the developments in the electronics side of computing.

Automation

Automated scoring — the use of computers to simulate holistic ratings of English essays — is quite accurately described as automation in the original sense of the word — the use of technology to relieve humans of repetitive work, work that taxes the limits of our abilities. It is, simply, the performance of tasks by machines, tasks that were originally performed by skilled humans, made skilled humans more productive, or created less skilled work from more complex work. Early automation is represented by the agricultural machines that first improved tilling the soil and subsequently harvesting. The original Luddites of 1811–1812 were weavers in England, members of a craft guild who attempted to destroy the newly invented machinery that left fewer jobs for unskilled workers. Mechanical developments in automation began to skyrocket with the introduction of computer technology. Today, labor unions representing the interests of workers have been watching the emergence of automation with considerable concern because industrial, production line workers have been replaced by electronically operated machines that perform repetitive tasks with greater precision and accuracy than humans, at least in the view of industries that have adopted this technology. The motivation underlying electronic automation, even as it was in the planning, viewed constant repetition as a weakness in humans. Industrial automation was motivated by efficiency. To the extent that computers can make any task more efficient, they will be of interest in industry. Although workers in AI may not perceive the impact of their work, much of the research and development for applications of the emergent theories in AI have been funded by governments and industry looking for ways to operate more efficiently, even if only to get beyond errors and other problems that reflect the limits of human performance.

In the case of automation, the concern for a computer's performance is not on whether it meets Turing's criterion. Instead, the question is whether the task itself is *computable*. According to Johnson-Laird (1977), computability depends on being able to specify a task with sufficient precision to develop a programming algorithm, based in the computational structure of computer software. For instance, welding an exact spot on a car body involves only a question of space and time — the movement of the machine to the location of the weld and the length of the welding time. Although the relative quality of human labor and automation is certainly one issue, the real question lies with the sufficiency of the performance of the machine. If sufficient quality can be achieved by a computer program or robot, operating at greater speed and less cost, clearly, the programming is successful. The cost reduction and increased efficiency of machine operation, when seen only in terms of the costs of production and profit margins, are clearly a business issue.

Can Holistic Scoring Be Automated?

In an earlier essay, I discussed in some detail the underpinning of much assessment practice in the "Worship of Efficiency" (Williamson, 1994). Further demonstration of the role of efficiency in assessment is provided by some of the sources cited earlier in this text (Cureton, 1951; Stalnaker, 1951). The question of validity for automated scoring turns, in this circumstance, on whether automated scoring can provide results at least as trustworthy as human raters with greater efficiency and less cost. From this perspective, the question of validity for automated scoring can be answered in the same way that questions of quality are determined for other forms of automation. Although cost accounting may be more relevant to business, the mathematical apparatus of assessment theory is employed in demonstrating the quality and validity of automated assessment as it compares to holistic raters. For others, the question of any automation of the work of writing teachers and assessors is a question of the computability of human language in the first place. In other words, can a computer using AI *read*?

Validity, as it is related to the comparability of holistic rating, is considerably more limited than some of the larger questions that have been raised about holistic scoring itself, such as the adequacy of the criterion definition of writing represented by a single essay and the adequacy of the criterion definition of reading represented in standardized rating sessions. The distinction between these two views of validity inquiry about automated scoring has important consequences for how specific investigations into its validity will be understood.

For example, the key issue for those creating automated scoring is whether the program can predict holistic ratings of more than six raters (Burstein, 2003), many more than the number typically employed in a holistic scoring session. To support their claim, automated scoring needs to demonstrate that it is more efficient and costs considerably less than rating sessions.

However, the discussion, within English Studies, seems to be dominated by a very different definition of the activity of holistic rating. The criterion that Herrington and Moran (2001), as well as Anson (2003) appear to be using is whether a computer can *read*. At least three studies (Huot, 1993; Huot & Pula, 1993; Wolfe, 1997) established that holistic scoring is a limited form of reading. In the Huot and Pula and Huot studies, holistic raters made rapid decisions about the placement of students reflected in the writing, and then spent time responding to other aspects of the writing. Wolfe found that raters who agree at a high rate with each other have a more focused reading process.

For a social scientist, the immediate question is whether the procedures used by automated scoring engines simulate the scoring process of human raters. This question is more difficult to answer because holistic rating is not reading as is usually defined in literacy research where the goal is to produce various readings; the push for writing assessment has been toward a single reading (Elbow & Yancey, 1994). Holistic scoring, by definition, limits the features of a text that the rater attends to. The scoring process also limits the purposes for which a text is read. Such convergent reading is not what is typically represented as fluent adult reading, an act of making meaning that typically leads to divergent views of a text.

Is Holistic Scoring Valid?

There have been two large studies of the validity of holistic scoring, as applied to individual essays (Gottshalk, Swineford, & Coffman, 1966) and to multiple essays from the same writers, intended as a form of portfolio assessment (Breland, Camp, Jones, Morris, & Rock, 1987). The earlier study suggested that multiple-choice tests of grammar predict a student writer's performance more accurately than an essay when it is scored using a holistic procedure by two or three raters. Consequently, the relatively cheaper and more efficient indirect approach was justified because it could predict an individual's score on a criterion with the greater precision and accuracy than a writing sample. The claim for the validity of indirect assessment is based on a form of criterion validity known as concurrent validity that compares an examinee's performance on two different valued measures. Veal and Hudson (1983) dispute that result in another study of the use of holistic scoring using state assessment data from Georgia in which students' performances on multiple-choice tests of usage and grammar do match well with a holistic score.

Breland et al. (1987), stipulating that direct writing assessment is more efficient and less costly, demonstrated that one essay read two or three times could attain the reliability of indirect measures. Their criterion definition of writing was six essays from each writer. They conclude that the best approach to writing assessment is a combination of both direct and indirect assessment because the two work together to provide both a broader and more reliable picture.

Although psychometric theory clearly supports the need for studying validity in particular applications of a test, in practice multiple-choice tests were considered adequate when used "off the shelf" by educational institutions. Thus, although the theory was suggesting the need for more study of assessment procedures in particular applications, conventional wisdom allowed for their use as readymade instruments for student, teacher, and program evaluation. This was equally true in the use of holistic scoring. For the most part, writing assessments used holistic scoring without much examination of the validity of its actual use, because the understanding of assessment theory prevalent in the field was that a test using writing is more valid on its face and in its content than any form of indirect test (Yancey, 1999).

White (1994) recounted the political struggles involved with the adoption of direct assessment. However, the extant theory in measurement could have been used to support the argument against indirect assessments had more writing assessment developers, like Veal and Hudson (1983), used the theory to argue their position. Hence, with greater fluency in the theory that was used, writing teachers and researchers would likely have been able to develop assessments that could be demonstrated to have the same kinds of properties that were valued in the validation of indirect assessment. One good example is the study by Breland et al. (1987), which suggests that holistic scoring of a writing portfolio leads to more accurate predictions than the score of any single essay in the portfolio. As early as Terman's 1916 book on the measurement of intelligence, statistical procedures were well defined for an examination of the contributions of test length to overall test reliability. Item validity was really the only focal concern, because as Gulliksen (1950) points out:

> We see that the validity coefficient is the square root of that for the reliability coefficient. . . . Since the validity coefficient is usually considerably smaller than the test reliability, this usually means that changing the

length of the test can be expected to have a very slight effect on the validity of the test. (p. 90)

Thus, the ultimate focus in measurement theory is on reliability to the extent that it is defined statistically. A test reliability of 0.9 will provide a test validity of 0.3, for instance. Little wonder that the traditional debate over holistic scoring confuses reliability and validity.

If, as I have argued, validity is seen as existing in a particular use of a test, in a particular context, at a particular time, validity reflects the situatedness of literacy as most researchers and teachers of writing have been claiming. Thus, validity does not lie in statistical procedures alone. However, test developers themselves rarely study the validation of decisions. Furthermore, the kind of study undertaken by Smith (1993) is costly and lengthy, and requires both experience and training in empirical research. Because efficiency is valued in applications of assessment theory (Williamson, 1994) and not very many involved with writing assessment have training in empirical research (White 1994), it is not surprising that there is very little validation research available for particular uses of writing assessment. Exceptions are seen in the work of Blakesley (2003) with *Directed Self-Placement* and Herrington on the use of technology using Smith's (1993) and Haswell's (2001) approach to scoring.

Validation Studies of Automated Scoring

There is really only a single automated scoring engine that has a consistent record of validation research, *eRater* as it is used to score essays for the Graduate Management Aptitude test. Until recently, the essay portion of the test was read by a group of holistic raters, trained by Educational Testing Service (ETS), the test developer and vendor. The scores are used by graduate programs in business to determine admission to their programs. Like the SAT and the Graduate Record Examination (GRE), the scores are used as one indication of performance in a program of study, along with other indicators, such as class rank, grade-point average (GPA), and the school graduating the applicant. However, the responsibility of the actual validation of each of those examinations lies with the institutions that use them to make decisions about admissions. ETS cannot provide validation data for any of those examinations because they do not have relevant local data to determine the suitability of each examination for the decision to admit or deny admission to an applicant to a particular program. Validation data, such as national norms and performance of students with self-reported characteristics such as GPA are frequently part of these examinations. But, the only place to determine the validity of admissions decisions is within the institution using the scores. In the case of the SAT, most admissions departments use the scores in formulas to predict such things as first-year GPA. Similarly, ETS reports the success of similar predictions for a number of schools as part of their validation research.

The GRE is now scored by one human rater and *eRater*. For the most part, ETS has been examining the accuracy of *eRater* in predicting holistic scores from human raters. Their research suggests that *eRater* is able to predict the scores of six raters with greater accuracy than two human raters. The question, then, is, are the *eRater* scores any more or less accurate than the scores provided by the two human raters typically used? If the criterion is the more raters the better, then the answer is obviously, yes. The science of psychometrics depends on the sheer magnitude of numbers in order to statistically prove anything. A traditional direct writing assessment like holistic scoring generates a single score, technically a one item test. Because reliability is greatly improved by the number of scores, it is easy to see how subtly and quickly the question can turn to reliability. In the case of Smith's (1993) accuracy of placement, accuracy focuses on the decision and the underlying principle that all decisions are not equal. *eRater*, however, focuses on the predictive power of one set of procedures compared to another. For validity, the real question for *eRater* is whether the scores help make better decisions about students than the current procedures used by a particular college or university.

For those of us who use traditional holistic scoring procedures, the answer is likely to be that they do, because *eRater* is going to provide more stable scores than two holistic raters. However, the real test of the validity of *eRater* may lie in a comparison with procedures like Smith's that focus on the expert knowledge of teachers who determine whether the student who wrote the essay belongs in their course or the one above or below it. In this case, it is not clear that one procedure has an advantage over the other because there has never been an attempt to examine the relative value of *eRater* compared to the expert placement model defined by Smith.

Because the immediate question of the validity of automated scoring turns on reliability, as Huot (2002) asserts, reliability has always been the focus of the debate about writing assessment. Thus, the question of which assessment provides the best judgment of a student's placement into a writing program has still not been answered. As various new assessments have been created (Broad, 2003; Haswell, 2001; Murphy & Underwood, 1998; Royer & Gilles, 2003, etc.), there has been a pressing need to document that these assessments promote valid and reliable educational decisions about students, teachers, and programs. Unfortunately, systematic and rigorous attention is not always given to things like consequences for various participants in the assessment.

For placement, the study of the validity of writing assessment should be focused, like Smith's, on the decision about the best course for a student to enter the writing program at a particular college. Writing exit examination validation research should be focused on a decision about a student's mastery of the curriculum, for both college and school students. Furthermore, there is little reporting of validation research in the assessment literature, in part, I suspect, because writing assessment is a field marginalized by most writing teachers and researchers. Most teachers, with good reason, fear any use of assessment, because assessment has become highly politicized by federal and state government, as well as by local school boards and administrators.

CAN COMPUTERS REPLACE ENGLISH TEACHERS?

Ultimately, one question that may cause an implicit fear is the unspoken potential for the role of automation in education as a whole, not just assessment. Does the future suggest that teachers can be replaced by computers or some evolutionary mutation of them or that one teacher via distance education technology can instruct innumerable students at various locations? One primary question I am attempting to examine is whether automated assessment should be seen as a potential threat or benefit. This fear has been the root of response to automation because automation has typically reduced the workforce in any industry. The curriculum research of the 1970s and the 1980s is best summarized as an attempt to find the holy grail of education, a curriculum that is teacher proof, in the sense that the training and experience of a teacher are irrelevant to its success. The tepid results of that search are probably the reason experimental comparison of curriculums disappeared. The most valuable lesson that emerged is the importance of the teacher. Trained, experienced, and motivated teachers are the heart of successful education, despite the public furor over teachers' qualifications. Darling-Hammond and Youngs (2002) examine hundreds of studies about educational progress of various kinds of students and found that the overriding variable, more than ethnicity or income, that predicted student success was the teacher.

Many futurists, both utopian and dystopian, have seen the future filled with intelligent machines. At this stage, Anson's (2003) suggestion may be the best view, there is little that AI can offer a writing teacher. However, our real concern should be how AI might augment the teaching of writing in the future. Explicit views of the future are not of much value, particularly because the likelihood of automation replacing some aspects of teaching writing is already evident, as we have been seeing, the continuing use of electronic technology to compliment or replace some of the work of teachers. As we have also experienced, there will be those who claim that computers allow for greater efficiency, justifying increasing the numbers of students working with individual teachers. It seems clear that computers are here to stay in English Studies, even if only as word processors to make the production of paper text easier and as communication devices to connect writers to one another for responding. We have to expect that the future will also hold some developments that can help us and some that can be hurtful. Some developments will be faddish, oversold by developers and producers of the technology, whereas others will enter our toolbox with the potential to help students learn if used properly.

My answer to the problem of automated assessment is precisely the last point. Its potential suggests that it *might* have some value in writing classrooms, but it is not clear what that may be. Second, if it does have value, it will take continuing study to understand the consequences and to establish the value through validity inquiry.

I am suggesting a stance on automated assessment that can best be characterized as carefully directed critique toward the developers of automated assessment. Because Pennsylvania has adopted automated assessment and the results of that automation will be used to determine funding for school districts, there is no question it is being used in regulatory ways. Why should we expect anything different? Assessment has been used as a gate keeper for as long as assessment has resulted in excluding some and including others in schooling.

Out-of-hand or outright rejection of automated assessment, a blanket condemnation, can only be self-serving. More importantly, we need to examine the use of automated scoring as we would any other assessment, according to the criteria of the most current theories on validating educational assessment. Arguing that theories of literacy do not justify the use of automated assessment, is similar to earlier arguments that indirect assessment does not have content validity. This argument is not going to be compelling with an educational measurement audience, not to mention policymakers and regular citizens. Furthermore, without an understanding of the common language of assessment as it is grounded in the social sciences research methodology, we will find that our righteous indignation, our hermeneutic arguments about the meaning of new types of assessment, are met by a wondering stare, at best, and a dismissive glare, at worst.

What I am arguing we do is to study automated assessment in order to explicate the potential value for teaching and learning, as well as the potential harm. The theory of the developers can itself be used as a ground for validity arguments. However, we have to be willing to look outside our field to understand the theory of another, a theory that has clearly been at the heart of assessment practices in our culture for more than a century, and an industry that has become embedded in education in America over the last 50 years. The practices are accepted by most Americans as valid for use in education. If educators have not been successful in opposing those practices, it may be that we have not been able to understand what drives them and to be able to offer critiques that have been seen as questioning that validity.

CONCLUSION

Writing assessment in American education has two professional groups with developed bodies of theory and practice. The first group, whose primary interest is assessment, is the membership of the two professional organizations, the American Education Research Association (AERA) and the American Psychological Association (APA). They far outnumber the members of the second group, the membership of the National Council of Teachers of English and College Composition and Communication. For a number of years, APA and AERA were loosely allied through members with dual memberships. More recently, recognizing their common concerns and shared field, they began to work together. The result is a clearly defined statement of definitions and standards for test development and validation (Standards, 1999). Although the measurement community is not inherently hostile to the concerns of writing teachers, its members will be looking for the kinds of evidence articulated in the standards, applying the technology of validation research to the discussion of implementing automated scoring. Furthermore, their direct involvement with public education, as the primary source for assessment tools, lends them a strong voice in the federal, state, and local politics of assessment.

The contrasts between English Studies and educational assessment are many, running beyond concepts or methodology. The common ground is also quite large. One important point of comparison lies in the question of what constitutes important research in the two fields. In English, researchers are typically expected to demonstrate their mastery of the field in publications that are authored by a single individual. In assessment, as in most scientific fields, important research can only be conducted by a team of people, each contributing to the conceptualization and execution of the study. If it is time to examine the research methodology or social sciences as it impinges on assessment, it may also be time to explore the potential for collaborative research, not just within either a social science or humanistic tradition (see Huot, 2002, for a discussion of a unified field of writing assessment). If we continue to espouse outmoded views of assessment, to fail to understand the complexity of validity theory, for instance, we are going to be frustrated at every turn. If for no other reason, as Sun Tsu (1994) observed, one has to know the enemy to defeat him. In this case, I hope knowing one's enemy might lead to a productive alliance.

A student of mine was attempting to articulate a complex problem for her dissertation project, one involving the value of historical study of the field. She finally told me that she recognized she was approaching the project with the wrong attitude. She said that she had forgotten a couple of the basic things she tries to teach her students: Who is the audience and what kinds of rhetorical practices are expected?

Who is our audience for our critique of automated scoring? If it is ourselves, we can continue to confront assessment developers with the challenge that their work does not conform to contemporary theories of literacy. However, when they suggest that contemporary theories of literacy are at the basis of their work, our best critique lies in a close examination of the theory, as opposed to an examination of the practice itself. Surely, well-directed critique is more successful than blanket condemnation. But, such critique emerges from the study of assessment theory, validity theory in particular. Such a critique is supported by those theories, if we take the time to use our own research skills, interpretive reading of culture icons, such as the texts of the field.

I will leave you with a story that has guided my work in the use of technology in my classroom and the suggestions that I give to others: In graduate school, I shared an apartment with a fellow student. At the time, he was working as a welder for a local company building automobile transport trailers. One day, he come from work telling me that he had been let go. His schedule was flexible, built around his class schedule at the university. His boss had told him that the computer was not able to work with his schedule, so he had to either work full time or leave. He left and went on to accomplish some fine work in our field. However, I have adopted as a basic principle of working with computer analysts and programmers, "If your program does not do what we need it to do, you have done a poor job, go back and fix it!" The goals of people must drive the development of automation, not the automation itself. We have to find the right way to say, "Fix it!" The real trick is to get the right people to listen. As inheritors of the tradition of rhetoric, writing teachers should know more about how to speak to their audiences.

REFERENCES

Ajay, H. B., Tillett, P. I., & Page, E. B. (1973). *Analysis of essays by computer (AEC-II).* Final report to the National Center for Educational Research and Development (Project No. 80101), p. 231.

Anastasi, A. (1976). *Psychological testing* (4th ed.). New York: Macmillan.

Anson, C. R. (2003). Responding to and assessing student writing: The uses and limits of technology. In P. Takayoshi & B. Huot (Eds.), *Teaching writing with computers* (pp. 234–246). Boston: Houghton Mifflin.

Berlin, J. A. (1984). *Writing instruction in nineteenth-century American colleges.* Carbondale: Southern Illinois University.

Blakesley, D. (2003). Directed self-placement in the university. In D. Royer & R. Gilles (Eds.), *Directed self-placement: Principles and practices* (pp. 31–48). Cresskill, NJ: Hampton Press.

Bleich, D. (1975). *Readings and feelings: An introduction to subjective criticism.* Urbana, IL: National Council of Teachers of English.

Breland, H. M., Camp, R.., Jones, R. J., Morris, M. M., & Rock, D. A. (1987). *Assessing writing skill. College Entrance Examination Board Research Report No. 11.* Princeton, NJ: Educational Testing Service.

Broad, B. (2003). *What we really value: Beyond rubrics in teaching and assessing writing.* Logan: Utah State University Press.

Burns, H. L. (1979). Stimulating rhetorical invention in English composition through computer-assisted instruction. *Dissertation Abstracts International,* DAI-A 40/70, p. 3734, January 1980, DAI Order number AAT 7928268.

Burstein, J. C. (2003). The E-rater® Scoring Engine: Automated essay scoring with natural language processing. In M. D. Shermis & J. C. Burstein (Eds.), *Automated essay scoring: A cross-disciplinary perspective* (pp. 113–121). Mahwah, NJ: Erlbaum.

Carmines, E. G. & Zeller, R. A. (1980). *Reliability and validity assessment.* Beverly Hills, CA: Sage Publications.

Cooley, W. W., & Lohnes, P. R. (1976). *Evaluation research in education: Theory, principles, and practice.* New York: Irvington.

Coombs, D. H. (1969). Review of *The Analysis of Essays by Computer,* by Ellis B. Page and Dieter H. Paulus. *Research in the Teaching of English, 3,* 222–228.

Cooper, C. R., & Odell, L. (1977). *Evaluating writing: Describing, measuring, judging.* Urbana, IL: NCTE.

Cronbach, L. J. (1971). Test validation. In R. L. Thorndike (Ed.), *Educational measurement* (2nd ed., pp. 443–507). Washington, DC: American Council on Education.

Cronbach, L. J. (1988). Five perspectives on test validity argument. In H. Wainer (Ed.), *Test validity* (pp. 3–17). Hillsdale, NJ: Erlbaum.

Cronbach, L. J. (1989). Validity after thirty years. In R. Linn (Ed.), *Intelligence: Measurement theory and public policy* (pp. 147–171). Urbana: University of Illinois Press.

Cureton, E. (1951). Validity. In E. F. Lindquist (Ed.), *Educational measurement* (pp. 621–694). Washington, DC: American Council on Education.

Darling-Hammond, L., & Youngs, P. (2002). Defining "highly qualified teachers": What does "scientifically-based research" actually tell us? *Educational Researcher, 31*(9), 13–25.

Elbow, P., & Yancey, K. B. (1994). On the nature of holistic scoring: An inquiry composed on email. *Assessing Writing, 1,* 91–108.

Gottshalk, F. I., Swineford, F., & Coffman, W. (1966). *The measurement of writing ability. College Entrance Examination Board Research Monograph N. 6.* Princeton, NJ: Educational Testing Service.

Guilford, J. P. (1954). *Psychometric methods.* New York: McGraw-Hill.

Gulliksen, H. (1950). *Theory of mental tests.* New York: Wiley.

Haswell, R. (Ed.). (2001). *Beyond outcomes: Assessment and instruction in a university writing program.* Westport, CT: Ablex.

Herrington, A., & Moran, C. (2001). What happens when machines read our students' writing? *College English, 63*, 480–499.

Huot, B. (1993). The influence of holistic scoring procedures on reading and rating student essays. In M. M. Williamson & B. A. Huot (Eds.), *Validating holistic scoring for writing assessment* (pp. 206–236). Cresskill, NJ: Hampton Press.

Huot, B. (1996). Computers and assessment: Understanding two technologies. *Computers and Composition, 13*, 231–244.

Huot, B. (2002). *(Re)Articulating writing assessment for teaching and learning*. Logan: Utah State University Press.

Johnson-Laird, P. N. (1977). *Mental models: Towards a cognitive science of language, inference, and consciousness*. Cambridge, MA: Harvard University Press.

Kuhn, T. S. (1996). *Structure of scientific revolutions* (3rd ed.). Chicago: University of Chicago Press.

Macrorie, K. (1969). Review of *The Analysis of Essays by Computer*, by Ellis B. Page and Dieter H. Paulus. *Research in the Teaching of English, 3*, 228–236.

Messick, S. (1989). Test validity. In R. Linn (Ed.), *Educational measurement* (3rd ed., pp. 13–103). Washington, DC: American Educational Research Association and National Council on Measurement in Education.

Moss, P. (1998). The role of consequences in validity theory. *Educational Measurement: Issues and Practices, 17*(2), 6–12.

Murphy, S., & Underwood, T. (1998). Interrater reliability in a California middle school English/language arts portfolio assessment program. *Assessing Writing, 5*(2), 201–230.

Page, E. B. (1966, January). The imminence of grading essays by computer. *Phi Delta Kappan*, 238–243.

Page, E. B. (1967a). Grading essays by computer: Progress report. *Proceedings of the 1966 Invitational Conference on Testing* (pp. 87–100). Princeton, NJ: Educational Testing Service.

Page, E. B. (1967b). Statistical and linguistic strategies in the computer grading of essays. *Proceedings of the Second International Conference on Computational Linguistics*. Grenoble, France. August 24, 1967. No. 34.

Page, E. B. (1985). Computer grading of student essays. In T. Husen & Postlethwaite (Eds.), *International Encyclopedia of Educational Research* (pp. 944–946). Oxford, England: Pergamon.

Page, E. B. (1993, January). *New computer grading of student prose, using a powerful grammar checker*. Paper presented at the annual meeting of the North Carolina Association for Research in Education, Greensboro, NC.

Page, E. B. (1995, April). *Computer grading of essays: A different kind of testing?* Invited address sponsored by the American Psychological Association, Divisions 5, 7, 15, 16).

Page, E. B., Fisher, G. A., & Fisher, M. A. (1968). Project Essay Grade: A FORTRAN program for statistical analysis of prose. *British Journal of Mathematical and Statistical Psychology, 21*, 139. (Abstract)

Page, E. B., Tillett, P. I., & Ajay, H. B. (1989). Computer measurement of subject-matter essay tests: Past research and future promise. *Proceedings of the First Annual Meeting of the American Psychological Society*, Alexandria, VA.

Pula, J., & Huot, B. (1993). A model of background influences on holistic raters. In M. M. Williamson & B. A. Huot (Eds.), *Validating holistic scoring for writing assessment* (pp. 237–265). Cresskill, NJ: Hampton Press.

Royer, D., & Gilles, R. (2003). *Directed self-placement: Principles and practices*. Cresskill, NJ: Hampton Press.

Schendel, E. (1999). Exploring the theories and consequences of self-assessment through ethical inquiry. *Assessing Writing, 6*(2), 199–227.

Smith, W. L. (1993). Assessing the reliability and adequacy of using holistic scoring of essays as a college composition placement technique. In M. M. Williamson & B. A. Huot (Eds.), *Validating holistic scoring for writing assessment* (pp. 142–205). Cresskill, NJ: Hampton Press.

Stalnaker J. M. E. (1951). The essay type of examination. In E. F. Lindquist (Ed.), *Educational measurement* (pp. 495–532). Washington, DC: American Council on Education.

Standards for Educational and Psychological Testing (1999). Washington, DC: American Education Research Association, American Psychological Association, and the National Council on Measurement in Education.

Sun Tsu. (1994). *The art of war*. Boulder, CO: Westview. (Original work published circa 300 BCE)

Terman, L. M. (1916). *The measurement of intelligence*. New York: Houghton Mifflin.

Veal, R. A., & Hudson, S. A. (1983). Direct and indirect measures for the large-scale evaluation of writing. *Research in the Teaching of English, 17*, 285–296.

White, E. M. (1994). *Teaching and assessing writing: Recent advances in understanding, evaluating and improving student performance*. San Francisco: Jossey-Bass.

Williamson, M. M. (1993). An introduction to holistic scoring: The social, theoretical, and historical context for writing assessment. In M. M. Williamson & B. A. Huot (Eds.), *Validating holistic scoring for writing assessment* (pp. 1–43). Cresskill, NJ: Hampton Press.

Williamson, M. M. (1994). The worship of efficiency: Untangling theoretical and practical consideration in writing assessment. *Assessing Writing, 1,* 147–174.

Wolfe, E. W. (1997). The relationship between essay reading style and scoring proficiency in a psychometric coring system. *Assessing Writing, 4*(1), 83–106.

Yancey, K. B. (1999). Looking back as we look forward: Historicizing writing assessment. *College Composition and Communication, 50,* 483–503.

ADDITIONAL READINGS[1]

FOUNDATIONS

Aiken, Lewis R., and Gary Groth-Marnat. *Psychological Testing and Assessment.* Boston: Allyn & Bacon, 2006.

Applebee, Arthur N. "English Language Arts Assessment: Lessons from the Past." *English Journal 84.4* (1994): 40–46.

Camp, Roberta. "Changing the Model for the Direct Assessment of Writing." *Validating Holistic Scoring for Writing Assessment: Theoretical and Empirical Foundations.* Eds. Michael M. Williamson and Brian Huot. Cresskill, NJ: Hampton, 1993. 45–78.

Cooper, Charles R. "Holistic Evaluation of Writing." *Evaluating Writing: Describing, Measuring and Judging.* Eds. Charles R. Cooper and Lee Odell. Urbana, IL: NCTE, 1977.

Cooper, P. *The Assessment of Writing Ability: A Review of Research.* Princeton, NJ: Educational Testing Service, 1984. GREB No. 82–15R.

Davis, Barbara Gross, Michael Scriven, and Susan Thomas. *The Evaluation of Composition Instruction.* New York: Teachers College P, 1987.

Diederich, Paul B. *Measuring Growth in English.* Urbana, IL: NCTE, 1974.

Eldridge, Richard. "Grading in the 70s: How We Changed." *College English 43.1* (1981): 64–8.

---

[1]This bibliography of readings, which is a selection from a more comprehensive one that includes classroom-based sources, began with Brian Huot's reading list for a graduate seminar in writing assessment many years ago. It has been updated and revised over the years, including by Ellen Schendel of Grand Valley State in 2000. More recently, Dayna Goldstein and Emily Dillon of Kent State conducted a substantive revision. Several of these citations are annotated in the first three volumes of *The Journal of Writing Assessment.*

Elliot, Norbert. *On a Scale: A Social History of Writing Assessment in America.* New York: Peter Lang, 2005.

Fuess, Claude. *The College Board: Its First Fifty Years.* New York: College Entrance Examination Board, 1967.

Godshalk, Fred I., Frances Swineford, and William E. Coffman. *The Measurement of Writing Ability.* Princeton, NJ: Educational Testing Service, 1966. CEEB RM No. 6.

Greenberg, Karen L., Harvey S. Wiener, and Richard A. Donovan, eds. *Writing Assessment: Issues and Strategies.* New York: Longman, 1986.

Hanson, F. Allan. *Testing Testing: Social Consequences of the Examined Life.* Berkeley: U of California P, 1993.

Huot, Brian. "Introduction to Assessing Writing." *Assessing Writing 1* (1994): 1–9.

———. "The Literature of Direct Writing Assessment: Major Concerns and Prevailing Trends." *Review of Educational Research 60* (1990): 237–63.

———. *(Re)Articulating Writing Assessment for Teaching and Learning.* Logan:, Utah State UP, 2002.

Huot, Brian, and Michael Neal. "Writing Assessment: A Techno-History." *Handbook of Writing Research.* Eds. Charles A. MacArthur, Steve Graham, and Jill Fitzgerald. New York: Guilford Press, 2006. 417–32.

Lemann, Nicholas. *The Big Test: The Secret History of the American Meritocracy.* New York: Farrar, Straus, and Giroux, 1999.

Lloyd-Jones, Richard. "Primary Trait Scoring." *Evaluating Writing: Describing, Measuring and Judging.* Eds. Charles R. Cooper and Lee Odell. Urbana, IL: NCTE, 1977.

Madaus, G. F. "A Technical and Historical Consideration of Equity Issues Associated with Proposals to Change the Nation's Testing Policy." *Harvard Educational Review 64.1* (1994): 76–94.

Palmer, Orville. "Sixty Years of English Testing." *College Board 42* (1960): 8–14.

Spandel, Vicki, and Richard J. Stiggins. *Direct Measures of Writing Skills: Issues and Applications.* Portland, OR: Northwest Regional Educational Laboratory, 1981.

Starch, D., and E. C. Elliott. "Reliability of the Grading of High School Work in English." *School Review 20* (1912): 442–57.

Trachsel, Mary. *Institutionalizing Literacy: The Historical Role of College Entrance Examinations.* Carbondale: Southern Illinois UP, 1992. 21–74.

Valentine. J. A. *The College Board and the School Curriculum: A History of the College Board's Influence on the Substance and Standards of American Education 1900–1980.* New York: College Entrance Examination Board, 1987.

White, Edward M. "Holistic Scoring: Past Triumphs and Future Challenges." *Validating Holistic Scoring for Writing Assessment: Theoretical and Empirical Foundations*. Eds. Michael M. Williamson and Brian Huot. Cresskill, NJ: Hampton, 1993.

————. *Teaching and Assessing Writing*, 2nd Edition. San Francisco: Jossey-Bass, 1994.

Williamson, Michael M. "An Introduction to Holistic Scoring: The Social, Historical, and Theoretical Context for Writing Assessment." *Validating Holistic Scoring for Writing Assessment: Theoretical and Empirical Foundations*. Eds. Michael M. Williamson and Brian Huot. Cresskill, NJ: Hampton, 1993. 1–43.

Wolcott, Willa, and Sue M. Legg. *An Overview of Writing Assessment: Theory, Research, and Practice*. Urbana, IL: National Council of Teachers of English, 1998.

Yancey, Kathleen Blake. "Looking Back as We Look Forward: Historicizing Writing Assessment." *College Composition and Communication 50* (1999): 483–503.

Validity and Reliability

Aiken, Lewis R., and Gary Groth-Marnat. *Psychological Testing and Assessment*. Boston: Allyn & Bacon, 2006.

American Educational Research Association, American Psychological Association, & National Council on Measurement in Education. *Standards for Educational and Psychological Testing*. Washington, DC: American Educational Research Association. 1999.

Bachman, L. F. "Alternative Interpretations of Alternative Assessments: Some Validity Issues in Educational Performance Assessments." *Educational Measurement: Issues and Practices 21.3* (2002): 5–19.

Berlak, Harold. "Toward the Development of a New Science of Educational Testing and Assessment." *Toward a Science of Educational Testing and Assessment*. Eds. Harold Berlak et al. Albany: State U of New York P, 1992. 181–234.

Brown, Gavin T. L., Kath Glasswell, and Don Harland. "Accuracy in the Scoring of Writing: Studies of Reliability and Validity Using a New Zealand Writing Assessment System." *Assessing Writing 94.2* (2004): 105–21.

Chapman, Carmen. "Authentic Writing Assessment." *Practical Assessment, Research & Evaluation 2.7* (1990).

Charney, Davida. "The Validity of Using Holistic Scoring to Evaluate Writing: A Critical Overview." *Research in the Teaching of English 18.1* (1984): 65–81.

Cherry, R., and P. Meyer. "Reliability Issues in Holistic Assessment." *Validating Holistic Scoring for Writing Assessment: Theoretical and Empirical*

Foundations. Eds. Michael Williamson and Brian Huot. Cresskill, NJ: Hampton, 1993. 109–41.

Cherryholmes, Cleo. *Power and Criticism: Poststructural Investigations in Education.* New York: Teachers College P, 1998.

Crocker, L., ed. [Special Issue]. *Educational Measurement: Issues and Practices* 16.2 (1997).

Cronbach, Lee J. "Construct Validation after Thirty Years." *Intelligence Measurement, Theory, and Public Policy: Proceedings of a Symposium in Honor of L. G. Humphreys.* Ed. R. L. Linn. Urbana and Chicago: U of Illinois P, 1989. 147–71.

———. "Five Perspectives on Validity Argument." *Test Validity.* Eds. H. Wainer and H. I. Braun. Hillsdale, NJ: Lawrence Erlbaum, 1988. 3–17.

Greenberg, K. "Validity and Reliability Issues in the Direct Assessment of Writing." *WPA: Writing Program Administration 16* (1992): 7–22.

Haswell, Richard H. "Multiple Inquiry in the Validation of Writing Tests." *Assessing Writing 5* (1998): 89–109.

Hayes, John R., and Jill A. Hatch. "Issues in Measuring Reliability: Correlation versus Percentage of Agreement." *Written Communication 16* (1999): 354–67.

Herman, Joan L., Maryl Gearhart, and Eva L. Baker. "Assessing Writing Portfolios: Issues in the Validity and Meaning of Scores." *Educational Assessment 1.3* (1993): 201–24.

Huot, Brian A. "Reliability, Validity, and Holistic Scoring: What We Know and What We Need to Know." *College Composition and Communication 41*(1990): 201–13.

Huot, Brian, and Ellen Schendel. "Reflecting on Assessment: Validity Inquiry as Ethical Inquiry." *Journal of Teaching Writing 17* (2001): 37–55.

James, Cindy L. "Validating a Computerized Scoring System for Assessing Writing and Placing Students in Composition Courses." *Assessing Writing 11.3* (2006): 167–78.

Kuncel, Nathan R., Marcus Crede, and Lisa L. Thomas. "The Validity of Self-Reported Grade Point Averages, Class Ranks, and Test Scores: A Meta-Analysis and Review of the Literature." *Review of Educational Research 75.1* (2005): 63–82.

Messick, Samuel. "Meaning and Values in Test Validation: The Science and Ethics of Assessment." *Educational Researcher 18.2* (1989): 5–11.

———. "The Standards of Validity and the Validity of Standards in Performance Assessment." *Educational Measurement: Issues and Practice 14.4* (1995): 5–8.

Moss, Pamela A. "Can There Be Validity Without Reliability?" *Educational Researcher 23.4* (1994): 5–2.

———. "Shifting Conceptions of Validity in Educational Measurement: Implications for Performance Assessment." *Review of Educational Research 62.3* (1992): 229–58.

———. "Testing the Test of a Test: A Response to the Multiple Inquiry in the Validation of Writing Tests." *Assessing Writing 5* (1998): 111–22.

———. "Themes and Variations in Validity Theory." *Educational Measurement: Issues and Practice 14.2* (1995): 5–13.

Powers, D. E., J. C. Burstein, M. S. Chodorow, M. E. Fowles, and K. Kukich. "Comparing the Validity of Automated and Human Scoring of Essays." *Journal of Educational Computing Research 26.4* (2002): 407–25.

Powers, Donald E., Mary Fowles, and Ann Willard. "Direct Assessment, Direct Validation? An Example from the Assessment of Writing." *Educational Assessment 2.1* (1994): 89–100.

Quellmalz, Edys. "Designing Writing Assessments: Balancing Fairness, Utility, and Cost." *Educational Evaluation and Policy Analysis 6.1* (1984): 63–72.

Reynolds, Cecil R., Ron Livingston, and Victor Willson. *Measurement and Assessment in Education*. Boston: Allyn & Bacon, 2006.

Scharton, Maurice. "The Politics of Validity." *Assessment of Writing: Politics, Policies, Practices*. Eds. Edward M. White, William D. Lutz, and Sandra Kamusikiri. New York: Modern Language Association, 1996. 52–75.

Shaftel, Julia, Xiangdong Yang, Douglas Glasnapp, and John Poggio. "Improving Assessment Validity for Students with Disabilities in Large-Scale Assessment Programs." *Educational Assessment 10.4* (2005): 357–75.

Shepard, Lorrie A. "The Centrality of Test Use and Consequences for Test Validity." *Educational Measurement: Issues and Practice 16.2* (1997): 5–24.

———. "Evaluating Test Validity." *Review of Educational Research in Education 19* (1993): 405–50.

Slomp, David H., and Jim Fuite. "Following Phaedrus: Alternate Choices in Surmounting the Reliability/Validity Dilemma." *Assessing Writing 9.3* (2004): 190–207.

Smith, William L., ed. "Special Issue: Validation and Writing Assessment." *Assessing Writing 5.1* (1998).

Wiggins, Grant. "The Constant Danger of Sacrificing Validity to Reliability: Making Writing Assessment Serve Writers." *Assessing Writing 1* (1993): 129–39.

Williamson, Michael M. "The Worship of Efficiency: Untangling Theoretical and Practical Considerations in Writing Assessment." *Assessing Writing 1* (1994): 147–74.

MODELS

Portfolios

Baker, Nancy W. "The Effects of Portfolio-Based Instruction on Composition Students' Final Examination Scores, Course Grades, and Attitudes Toward Writing." *Research in the Teaching of English 27* (1993): 155–74.

Belanoff, Pat. "Portfolios and Literacy: Why?" *New Directions in Portfolio Assessment*. Eds. Laurel Black et al. Portsmouth, NH: Boynton/Cook, 1994.

Belanoff, Pat, and Marcia Dickson. *Portfolios: Process and Product*. Portsmouth, NH: Boynton/Cook, 1991.

Berlin, James. "The Subversions of the Portfolio." *New Directions in Portfolio Assessment*. Eds. Laurel Black et al. Portsmouth, NH: Boynton/Cook, 1994.

Black, Laurel, Donald Daiker, Jeffrey Sommers, and Gail Stygall. *New Directions in Portfolio Assessment: Reflective Practice, Critical Theory and Large-Scale Scoring*. Portsmouth, NH: Boynton/Cook, 1994.

Calfee, Robert, and Pam Perfumo, eds. *Writing Portfolios in the Classroom*. Mahwah, NJ: Lawrence Erlbaum, 1996.

Callahan, Susan. "All Done With the Best of Intentions: One Kentucky High School after Six Years of Portfolio Tests." *Assessing Writing 6* (1999): 5–40.

———. "Kentucky's State-Mandated Writing Portfolios and Teacher Accountability. *Situating Portfolios: Four Perspectives*. Eds. Kathleen Yancey and Irwin Weiser. Logan: Utah State UP, 1997. 57–71.

———. "Portfolio Expectations: Possibilities and Limits." *Assessing Writing 2* (1995): 117–52.

———. "Tests Worth Taking?: Using Portfolios for Accountability in Kentucky." *Research in the Teaching of English 31* (1997): 295–336.

Camp, Roberta. "The Writing Folder in Post-Secondary Assessment." *Directions and Misdirections in English Evaluation*. Ed. Peter J. A. Evans. Ottawa: The Canadian Council of Teachers of English, 1985. 91–99.

Camp, Roberta, and Denise S. Levine. "Background and Variations in Sixth-through Twelfth-Grade Classrooms." *Portfolios: Process and Product*. Eds. Pat Belanoff and Marcia Dickson. Portsmouth, NH: Boynton/Cook, 1991.

Hamp-Lyons, Liz, and William Condon. *Assessing the Portfolio: Principles for Practice, Theory, and Research*. Cresskill, NJ: Hampton, 2000.

———. "Questioning Assumptions about Portfolio-Based Assessment." *College Composition and Communication 44* (1993): 176–90.

Herman, Joan L., Maryl Gearhart, and Eva L. Baker. "Assessing Writing Portfolios: Issues in the Validity and Meaning of Scores." *Educational Assessment 1.3* (1993): 201–24.

Herter, Roberta J. "Research and Practice: Writing Portfolios: Alternatives to Testing." *English Journal 80.1* (1991): 90–91.

Hirvela, Alan, and Yuerong Liu Sweetland. "Two Case Studies of L2 Writers' Experiences across Learning-Directed Portfolio Contexts." *Assessing Writing 10.3* (2005): 192–213.

Huot, Brian, and Michael M. Williamson. "Rethinking Portfolios for Evaluating Writing: Issues of Assessment and Power." *Situating Portfolios: Four Perspectives.* Eds. Kathleen B. Yancey and Irwin Weiser. Logan: Utah State UP, 1997. 43–56.

Larson, Richard L. "Portfolios in the Assessment of Writing: A Political Perspective." *Assessment of Writing: Politics, Policies, and Practices.* Eds. Edward M. White, William D. Lutz, and Kamusikiri. New York: Modern Language Association, 1996. 271–83.

Mathieu, Paul G., Drew H. Gitomer, and JoAnne Eresh. "Portfolios in Large-Scale Assessment: Difficult But Not Impossible." *Educational Measurement: Issues and Practices 14.3* (1995): 11–28.

Murphy, Sandra. "Teachers and Students: Reclaiming Assessment via Portfolios." *Situating Portfolios: Four Perspectives.* Eds. Kathleen B. Yancey and Irwin Weiser. Logan: Utah State UP, 1997. 72–88.

———. "Portfolios and Curriculum Reform: Patterns in Practice." *Assessing Writing 1* (1994): 175–206.

Murphy, Sandra, and Barbara Grant. "Portfolio Approaches to Assessment: Breakthrough or More of the Same." *Assessment of Writing: Politics, Policies, Practices.* Eds. Edward M. White, William D. Lutz, and Sandra Kamusikiri. New York: Modern Language Association, 1996. 284–300.

Murphy, Sandra, and Terry Underwood. *Portfolio Practices: Lessons from Schools, Districts and States.* Norwood, MA: Christopher Gordon, 2000.

Nystrand, Martin, Allan S. Cohen, and Norca M. Dowling. "Addressing Reliability Problems in the Portfolio Assessment of College Writing." *Educational Assessment 1.1* (1993): 53–70.

Ostheimer, Martha W., and Edward M. White. "Portfolio Assessment in an American Engineering College." *Assessing Writing 10.1* (2005): 61–73.

Popham, W. James. *Classroom Assessment: What Teachers Need to Know.* Boston: Allyn & Bacon, 2008.

Richardon, Susan. "Students' Conditioned Response to Teacher Response: Portfolio Proponents Take Note." *Assessing Writing 7* (2000): 117–41.

Scott, Tony. "Creating the Subject of Portfolios: Reflective Writing and the Conveyance of Institutional Prerogatives" *Written Communication 22* (2005): 3–35.

Smith, Cheryl A. "Writing Without Testing." *Portfolios: Process and Product.* Eds. Pat Belanoff and Marcia Dickson. Portsmouth, NH: Boynton/Cook, 1991.

Thelin, William H. "The Connection Between Response Styles and Portfolio Assessment: Three Case Studies of Student Revision." *New Directions in Portfolio Assessment.* Eds. Laurel Black et al. Portsmouth, NH: Boynton/Cook, 1994.

White, Edward M. "The Scoring of Writing Portfolios: Phase 2." *College Composition and Communication 56.4* (2005): 581–600.

Yancey, Kathleen Blake. *Portfolios in the Writing Classroom: An Introduction.* Urbana, IL: NCTE, 1992.

———. "Postmodernism, Palimpsest, and Portfolios: Theoretical Issues in the Representation of Student Work." *College Composition and Communication 55.4* (2004): 738–61.

Yancey Kathleen, and Irwin Weiser. *Situating Portfolios: Four Perspectives.* Logan: Utah State UP, 1997.

Program Assessment Theory and Practice

Brady, Laura. "A Case for Writing Program Evaluation." *WPA: Writing Program Administration* 28.1–2 (2004): 79–94.

Carson, Stanton, Patricia Wojahn, John Hayes, and Thomas Marshall. "Design, Results, and Analysis of Assessment Components in a Nine-Course CAC Program." *Language and Learning Across the Disciplines 6.1* (2003): 30–61.

Condon, William, and Diane Kelly-Riley. "Assessing and Teaching What We Value: The Relationship between College-Level Writing and Critical Thinking Abilities." *Assessing Writing 9.1* (2004): 56–75.

Harrington, Susanmarie. "Learning to Ride the Waves: Making Decisions about Placement Testing." *WPA: Writing Program Administration 28.3* (Spring 2005): 9–29.

Harrington, Susanmarie, Keith Rhodes, Ruth Overman Fischer, and Rita Malenczyk, eds. *The Outcomes Book: Debate and Consensus after the WPA Outcomes Statement.* Logan: Utah State UP, 2005.

Haswell, Richard, ed. *Beyond Outcomes: Assessment and Instruction Within a University Writing Program.* Greenwich, CT: Ablex, 2001.

Haswell, Richard, and Susan McLeod. "WAC Assessment and Internal Audiences: A Dialogue. *Assessing Writing Across the Curriculum: Diverse Approaches and Practices.* Eds. Kathleen B. Yancey and Brian Huot. Greenwich, CT: Ablex, 1997. 217–36.

Huit, C. "Assessment Topics: The Importance of the Rhetorical Frame." *WPA: Writing Program Administration Journal 10* (1987): 19–28.

Huot, Brian, and Ellen Schendel. "A Working Methodology of Assessment for Writing Program Administrators." *The Allyn & Bacon Sourcebook for Writing Program Administrators.* Eds. Irene Ward and William J. Carpenter. New York: Longman, 2002. 207–27.

Martin, Wanda. "Outcomes Assessment Research as a Teaching Tool." *The Writing Program Administrator as Researcher: Inquiry in Action and Reflection.* Eds. Shirley K. Rose and Irwin Weiser. Portsmouth, NH: Boynton/Cook, 1999.

Rubin, Donnalee. "Evaluating Freshman Writers: What Do Students Really Learn?" *College English 45* (1983): 373–79.

Selfe, Cynthia L. "Contextual Evaluation in WAC Programs: Theories, Issues, and Strategies for Teachers." *Assessing Writing Across the Curriculum: Diverse Approaches and Practices.* Eds. Kathleen B. Yancey and Brian Huot. Greenwich, CT: Ablex, 1997. 51–68.

Slevin, James F. "Engaging Intellectual Work: The Faculty's Role in Assessment." *College English 63.3* (2001): 288–305.

White, Edward M. "The Rhetorical Problem of Program Evaluation and the WPA." *Resituating Writing: Constructing and Administrating Writing Programs.* Eds. Joseph Janangeklo and Kristine Hansen. Portsmouth, NH: Boynton/Cook, 1995.

Williamson, Michael M. "Pragmatism, Positivism and Program Evaluation." *Assessing Writing Across the Curriculum: Diverse Approaches and Practices.* Eds. Kathleen B. Yancey and Brian Huot. Greenwich, CT: Ablex, 1997. 327–58.

Yancey, Kathleen, and Brian Huot, eds. *Assessing Writing Across the Curriculum: Diverse Approaches and Practices.* Greenwich, CT: Ablex, 1997.

Placement and Proficiency

Anson, Chris M. "Assessing Writing in Cross-Curricular Programs: Determining the Locus of Activity." *Assessing Writing 11.2* (2006): 100–12.

Bedore, Pamela, and Deborah F. Rossen-Knill. "Informed Self-Placement: Is a Choice Offered a Choice Received?" *WPA: Writing Program Administration 28.1–2* (2004): 55–78.

Carter, Michael. "A Process for Establishing Outcomes-Based Assessment Plans for Writing and Speaking in the Disciplines." *Language and Learning Across the Disciplines 6.1* (2003): 4–29.

Durst, Russel K., and Marjorie Roemer and Lucille Schultz. "Portfolio Negotiations: Acts in Speech." *New Directions in Portfolio Assessment.* Eds. Laurel Black et al. Portsmouth, NH: Boynton/Cook, 1994. 286–300.

Hansen, Kristine, Jennifer Gonzalez, Suzanne Reeve, Patricia Esplin, Richard Sudweeks, William S. Bradshaw, and Gary L. Hatch. "An Argument for Changing Institutional Policy on Granting AP Credit in English: An Empirical Study of College Sophomores' Writing." *WPA: Writing Program Administration* 28.1–2 (2004): 29–54.

Haswell, Richard, ed. *Beyond Outcomes: Assessment and Instruction Within a University Writing.* Greenwich, CT: Ablex, 2001.

Haswell, Richard, and Susan Wyche-Smith. "Adventuring into Writing Assessment." *College Composition and Communication 45* (1994): 220–36.

Lowe, Teresa J., and Brian Huot. "Using KIRIS Writing Portfolios to Place Students in First-Year Composition at the University of Louisville." *Kentucky English Bulletin 46.2* (1997): 46–64.

Martin, Deb, and Diane Penrod. "Coming to Know Criteria: The Value of an Evaluating Writing Course for Undergraduates." *Assessing Writing 11.1* (2006): 66–73.

McLeod, Susan, Heather Horn, and Richard H. Haswell. "Accelerated Classes and the Writers at the Bottom: A Local Assessment Story." *College Composition and Communication 56.4* (2005): 556–80.

Moran, Charles, and Anne Herrington. "Program Review, Program Renewal." *Assessing Writing Across the Curriculum: Diverse Approaches and Practices.* Eds. Kathleen B. Yancey and Brian Huot. Greenwich, CT: Ablex, 1997. 185–216.

Ostheimer, Martha W., and Edward M. White. "Portfolio Assessment in an American Engineering College." *Assessing Writing 10.1* (2005): 61–73.

Powers, D. E., and M. E. Fowles. "Balancing Test User Needs and Responsible Professional Practice: A Case Study Involving the Assessment of Graduate-Level Writing Skills." *Applied Measurement in Education 15* (2002): 217–47.

Prior, Paul, et al. "Research and WAC Evaluation: An In Progress Reflection." *Assessing Writing Across the Curriculum: Diverse Approaches and Practices.* Eds. Kathleen B. Yancey and Brian Huot. Greenwich, CT: Ablex, 1997. 185–216.

Royer, Daniel J., and Roger Giles, eds. "Directed Self-Placement: An Attitude of Orientation." *College Composition and Communication 50* (1998): 54–70.

———. *Directed Self-Placement: Principles and Practices.* Cresskill, NJ: Hampton, 2003.

Rutz, Carol, and Jacqulyn Lauer-Glebov. "Assessment and Innovation: One Darn Thing Leads to Another." *Assessing Writing 10.2* (2005): 80–99.

Shay, Suellen Butler. "The Assessment of Complex Performance: A Socially Situated Interpretive Act." *Harvard Educational Review 75.2* (2004).

Smith, William L. "Assessing the Reliability and Adequacy of Using Holistic Scoring of Essays as a College Composition Placement Program Technique."

Validating Holistic Scoring for Writing Assessment: Theoretical and Empirical Foundations. Eds. Michael M. Williamson and Brian Huot. Cresskill, NJ: Hampton, 1993.

Yancey, Kathleen, and Brian Huot, eds. *Assessing Writing Across the Curriculum: Diverse Approaches and Practices.* Greenwich, CT: Ablex, 1997.

Yancey, Kathleen B., and Brian Huot. "Introduction — Assumptions about Assessing WAC Programs: Some Axioms, Some Observations, Some Context." *Assessing Writing Across the Curriculum: Diverse Approaches and Practices.* Eds. Kathleen B. Yancey and Brian Huot. Greenwich, CT: Ablex, 1997. 7–14.

ISSUES

Abedi, Jamal, Carolyn Huie Hofstetter, and Carol Lord. "Assessment Accommodations for English Language Learners: Implications for Policy-Based Empirical Research." *Review of Educational Research 74.1* (2004): 1–28.

Belanoff, Pat. "The Myths of Assessment." *Journal of Basic Writing 10* (1991): 54–66.

Berlak, Harold. "Toward the Development of a New Science of Educational Testing and Assessment." *Toward a New Science of Educational Testing and Assessment.* Eds. Harold Berlak et al. Albany: State U of New York P, 1992.

Bernstein, Susan Naomi. "Teaching and Learning in Texas: Accountability Testing, Language, Race, and Place." *Journal of Basic Writing 23.1* (2004): 4–24.

Black, Laurel, Edwina Helton, and Jeffrey Sommers. "Connecting Current Research on Authentic and Performance Assessment through Portfolios." *Assessing Writing 1* (1994): 247–66.

Boudett, Kathryn Parker, Elizabeth A. City, and Richard J. Murnane, eds. *Data Wise: A Step-by-Step Guide to Using Assessment Results to Improve Teaching and Learning.* Cambridge, MA: Harvard Education P, 2005.

Broad, Bob. *What We Really Value: Beyond Rubrics in Teaching and Assessing Writing.* Logan, UT: Utah State UP, 2003.

Brown, Richard S., and David T. Conley. "Comparing State High School Assessments to Standards for Success in Entry-Level University Courses." *Educational Assessment 12.2* (2007): 137–60.

Carini, Patricia F. "Dear Sister Bess: An Essay on Standards, Judgment and Writing." *Assessing Writing 1* (1994): 29–66.

———. *Starting Strong: A Different Look at Children's Schools and Standards.* New York: Teachers College P, 2001.

Cherryholmes, Cleo H. "Construct Validity and the Discourses of Research." *Power and Criticism: Poststructural Investigations in Education.* New York: Teachers College P, 1998. 99–129.

Cheville, Julie. "Automated Scoring Technologies and the Rising Influence of Error." *English Journal 93.4* (2004).

Christenbury, Leila, Anne Ruggles Gere, and Kelly Sassi. *Writing on Demand: Best Practices and Strategies for Success.* Portsmouth, NH: Heinemann, 2005.

Crotteau, Michelle. "Honoring Dialect and Culture: Pathways to Student Success on High-Stakes Writing Assessments." *English Journal 96.4* (2007).

Darling-Hammond, Linda. "Accountability for Professional Practice." *Teacher's College Record 91* (1989): 59–80.

———. "No Child Left Behind and High School Reform." *Harvard Educational Review 76.4* (2005).

———. "Performance-Based Assessment and Educational Equity." *Harvard Educational Review 64* (1994): 5–30.

Delandshere, Ginette, and Anthony J. Petrosky. "Assessment of Complex Performances: Limitations of Key Measurement Assumptions." *Educational Researcher* (1998): 14–25.

———. "Capturing Teachers' Knowledge: Performance Assessment, a) and Post-Structuralist Epistemology, b) from a Post-Structuralist Perspective, c) and Post-Structuralism, d) None of the Above." *Educational Researcher 23.5* (1994): 11–18.

Duke, Charles R., and Rebecca Sanchez. "Giving Students Control over Writing Assessment." *English Journal 83.4* (1994): 47–53.

Garcia, George E., and P. David Pearson. "Assessment and Diversity." *Review of Research in Education 20* (1994): 337–91.

Gere, Anne Ruggles. "Written Composition: Toward a Theory of Evaluation." *College English 42.1* (1980): 44, 48, 53–8.

Greenberg, Karen L. "Competency Testing: What Role Should Teachers of Composition Play?" *College Composition and Communication 33* (1982): 366–76.

———. "Writing Tests and Their Contexts." *College English 43.7* (1981): 743–44.

Guba, Egon, and Yvonna Lincoln. *Fourth Generation Evaluation.* Newbury Park, CA: Sage, 1989.

Hamp-Lyons, Liz. "Rating Nonnative Writing: The Trouble with Holistic Scoring." *TESOL Quarterly 29.4* (1995): 759–62.

Harley, Kay, and Sally I. Cannon. "Failure: The Student's or the Assessment's?" *Journal of Basic Writing 15.1* (1996): 70–87.

Hawkey, Roger, and Fiona Barker. "Developing a Common Scale for the Assessment of Writing." *Assessing Writing 9.2* (2004): 122–59.

Heck, Ronald H., and Marian Crislip. "Direct and Indirect Writing Assessments: Examining Issues of Equity and Utility." *Educational Evaluation and Policy Analysis 23.1* (2001): 19–36.

Howe, Kenneth R. "Standards, Assessment, and Equality of Educational Opportunity." *Educational Researcher 23.8* (1994): 27–36.

Huot, Brian. *(Re)Articulating Writing Assessment for Teaching and Learning*. Logan: Utah State UP, 2002.

———. "Toward a New Theory of Writing Assessment." *College Composition and Communication 47* (1996): 549–66.

Huot, Brian, and Ellen Schendel. "Reflecting on Assessment: Validity Inquiry as Ethical Inquiry." *Journal of Teaching Writing 17* (2001): 37–55.

Johnston, Peter. "Constructive Evaluation and the Improvement of Teaching and Learning." *Teachers College Record 90* (1989): 509–28.

Kixmiller, Lori A. "Standards without Sacrifice: The Case for Authentic Writing." *English Journal 94.1* (2004).

Kraemer, Don J. "Fighting Forward: Why Studying Standardized Tests with Our Students Is Important." *English Journal 94.4* (2005).

Lederman, Marie Jean. "Why Test?" *Writing Assessment: Issues and Strategies*. Eds. Karen L. Greenberg, Harvey S. Wiener, and Richard A. Donovan. New York: Longman, 1986. 35–43.

Lindblom, Kenneth. "Teaching English in the World: Obstacles to Authentic Reading: The USA Patriot Act and High-Stakes Testing." *English Journal 93.5* (2004).

Linn, Robert. "Performance Assessment: Policy, Promises and Technical Measurement Standards." *Educational Researcher 23.9* (1994): 4–14.

Lloyd-Jones, Richard. "Skepticism about Test Scores." *Notes from the National Testing Network in Writing* (1982): 3, 9.

Luce-Kapler, Rebecca, and Don Klinger. "Uneasy Writing: The Defining Moments of High-Stakes Literacy Testing." *Assessing Writing 10.3* (2005): 157–73.

Lynne, Patricia. *Coming to Terms: A Theory of Writing Assessment*. Logan: Utah State UP, 2004.

Madhaus, George. "A National Testing System: Manna From Above." *Educational Assessment 1* (1993): 9–26.

Maxwell, John C. "National Assessment of Writing: Useless and Uninteresting?" *English Journal 62.9* (1973): 1254–57.

Moss, Pamela A. "Enlarging the Dialogue in Educational Measurement: Voices from Interpretive Research Traditions." *Educational Researcher 25.1* (1996): 20–28.

————. "Validity in High Stakes Writing Assessment." *Assessing Writing 1* (1994): 109–28.

O'Brien, Charlotte W. "A Large-Scale Assessment to Support the Process Paradigm." *English Journal 81.2* (1992): 28–33.

O'Neill, Peggy, Ellen Schendel, Michael Williamson, and Brian Huot. "Assessment as Labor and the Labor of Assessment." *Labor, Writing Technologies, and the Shaping of Composition in the Academy.* Eds. Pamela Takayoshi and Patricia Sullivan. Creskill, NJ: Hampton, 2007. 75–96.

Peckham, Irvin. "Statewide Direct Writing Assessment." *English Journal 76.8* (1987): 30–3.

Quellmalz, Edys, and Richard Stiggins. "Problems and Pitfalls in Writing Assessment." *Notes from the National Testing Network in Writing* (1985): 4.

Schendel, Ellen, and Peggy O'Neill. "Exploring the Theories and Consequences of Self-Assessment through Ethical Inquiry." *Assessing Writing 6* (1999): 199–227.

Scott, Mary. "Student Writing, Assessment, and the Motivated Sign: Finding a Theory for the Times." *Assessment and Evaluation in Higher Education 30.3* (2005): 297–305.

Shohamy, Elana. *The Power of Tests: A Critical Perspective on the Uses of Language Tests.* London: Pearson Education, 2001.

Sleeter, Christine E. *Facing Accountability in Education: Democracy and Equity at Risk.* New York: Teachers College P, 2007.

Spellmeyer, Kurt. "Response: Testing as Surveillance." *Assessment of Writing: Politics, Policies, Practices.* Eds. Edward M. White, William D. Lutz, and Sandra Kamusikiri. New York: Modern Language Association, 1996. 52–75.

Sudol, Ronald A., and Alice Horning, Eds. *The Literacy Standard.* Cresskill, NJ: Hampton, 2006.

Sunderman, Gail, James S. Kim, and Gary Orfield. *NCLB Meets School Realities.* Thousand Oaks, CA: Corwin, 2005.

Todd, Richard Watson, Patteera Thienpermpool, and Snthida Keyuravong. "Measuring the Coherence of Writing Using Topic-Based Analysis." *Assessing Writing 9.2* (2004): 85–104.

Valenzuela, Angela. *Leaving Children Behind: How "Texas-Style" Accountability Fails Latino Youth.* Albany: State U of New York P, 2005.

Warne, Bonnie Mary. "Teaching Conventions in a State-Mandated Testing Context." *English Journal 95.5* (2006).

Wiggins, Grant. *Assessing Student Performance.* San Francisco: Jossey-Bass, 1993.

———. "A True Test: Toward More Authentic and Equitable Assessment." *Phi Delta Kappan* 70 (1989): 703–13.

Williamson, Michael M., and Brian Huot. "Literacy, Equality, and Competence: Ethics in Writing Assessment." *The Ethics of Writing Instruction: Issues in Theory and Practice*. Ed. Michael Pemberton, Greenwich, CT: Ablex, 2000. 191–210.

Williard-Traub, Margaret K. "Writing Assessment and the Labor of 'Reform' in the Academy." *Labor, Writing Technologies, and the Shaping of Composition in the Academy*. Eds. Pamela Takayoshi and Patricia Sullivan. Cresskill, NJ: Hampton, 2007. 287–304.

Wilson, Maja. *Rethinking Rubrics in Writing Assessment*. Portsmouth, NH: Heinemann, 2006.

Assessment and Technology

Allen, Michael. "Valuing Differences: Portnet's First Year." *Assessing Writing 2* (1995): 67–90.

Allen, Michael, Jane Frick, Jeff Sommers, and Kathleen Yancey. "Outside Review of Writing Portfolios: An On-line Evaluation." *WPA: Writing Program Administration 20* (1997): 66–90.

Anson, Chris M. "Responding to and Assessing Student Writing: The Uses and Limits of Technology." *Teaching Writing with Computers: An Introduction*. Eds. Pamela Takayoshi and Brian Huot. Boston: Houghton Mifflin, 2002. 234–46.

Breland, Hunter M. "Computer-Assisted Writing Assessment: The Politics of Science versus the Humanities." *Assessing of Writing: Politics, Policies, and Practices*. Eds. Edward M. White, William D. Lutz, and Sandra Kamusikiri. New York: Modern Language Association, 1996. 249–56.

Cheville, Julie. "Automated Scoring Technologies and the Rising Influence of Error." *English Journal 93.4* (2004).

Ericsson, Patricia Freitag, and Richard Haswell, eds. *The Machine Scoring of Student Writing: Truth and Consequences*. Logan: Utah State UP, 2006.

Goodfellow, Robin, Michael Morgan, Mary R. Lea, and John Petit. "Students' Writing in the Virtual University: An Investigation into the Relation between Online Discussion and Writing for Assessment." *Doing Literacy Online: Teaching, Learning, and Playing in an Electronic World*. Eds. Ilana Snyder and Catherine Beavis. Cresskill, NJ: Hampton, 2004. 25–44.

Hawisher, Gail E., and Cynthia L. Selfe. "Wedding the Technologies of Writing Portfolios and Computers: The Challenges of Electronic Classrooms." *Situating Portfolios: Four Perspectives*. Eds. Kathleen B. Yancey and Irwin Weiser. Logan, UT: Utah State UP, 1997. 305–21.

Herrington, Anne, and Charles Moran. "What Happens When Machines Read Our Students' Writing?" *College English 63* (2001): 480–99.

Huot, Brian. "Computers and Assessment: Understanding Two Technologies." *Computers and Composition 13* (1996): 231–44.

James, Cindy L. "Validating a Computerized Scoring System for Assessing Writing and Placing Students in Composition Courses." *Assessing Writing 11.3* (2006): 167–78.

Krucli, Thomas E. "Making Assessment Matter: Using the Computer to Create Interactive Feedback." *English Journal 94.1* (2004).

Lee, H. K. "A Comparative Study of ESL Writers' Performance in a Paper-Based and a Computer-Delivered Writing Test." *Assessing Writing 9.1* (2004): 4–26.

Li, Jiang. "The Mediation of Technology in ESL Writing and Its Implications for Writing Assessment." *Assessing Writing 11.1* (2006): 5–21.

Madhaus, George F. "A Technological and Historical Consideration of Equity Issues Associated With Proposals to Change the Nation's Testing Policy." *Harvard Educational Review 64* (1994): 76–95

Moran, Charles, and Anne Herrington. "Evaluating Academic Hypertexts." *Teaching Writing with Computers: An Introduction*. Eds. Pamela Takayoshi and Brian Huot. Boston: Houghton Mifflin, 2002. 247–57.

Penrod, Diane. *Composition in Convergence: The Impact of New Media on Writing Assessment*. Mahwah, NJ: Lawrence Erlbaum, 2005.

Takayoshi, Pamela. "The Shape of Electronic Writing: Evaluating and Assessing Computer-Assisted Writing Processes and Products." *Computers and Composition 13* (1996): 245–58.

Whithaus, Carl. *Teaching and Evaluating Writing in the Age of Computers and High Stakes Testing*. Mahwah, NJ: Lawrence Erlbaum, 2005.

Williamson, Michael M. "Validity of Automated Scoring: Prologue for a Continuing Discussion of Machine Scoring Student Writing." *Journal of Writing Assessment 1* (2003): 85–104.

Wolfe, Edward M., et al. "The Influence of Student Experience with Word Processors on the Quality of Essays Written for a Direct Writing Assessment." *Assessing Writing 3* (1996): 123–46.

ABOUT THE EDITORS

Brian Huot has been working in writing assessment for nearly 20 years, publishing extensively in assessment theory and practice. His work has appeared in a range of journals, including *College Composition and Communication, College English*, and *Review of Educational Research*, as well as numerous edited collections. Huot is one of the founding editors of the journal *Assessing Writing* and more recently the *Journal of Writing Assessment*, which he continues to edit. He has coedited several scholarly books and in 2002 published *(Re)Articulating Writing Assessment for Teaching and Learning*. He is currently at work on the *Handbook of College Writing Assessment*, coauthored with Peggy O'Neill and Cindy Moore. Huot is professor of English and coordinator of the writing program at Kent State University.

Peggy O'Neill's scholarship focuses on writing assessment theory and practice as well as writing program administration and the disciplinarity of composition and rhetoric. Her work has appeared in such journals as *College Composition and Communication, Composition Studies*, and the *Journal of Writing Assessment* as well as several edited collections. She has edited or coedited three books and is currently coauthoring the *Handbook of College Writing Assessment* with Brian Huot and Cindy Moore. O'Neill serves as coeditor of the Hampton Press scholarly book series, "Research and Teaching in Rhetoric and Composition" and on the editorial board of several journals. She is an associate professor and director of composition in the writing department at Loyola College in Maryland.

Edward M. White, "Holisticism." Originally published in *College Composition and Communication* 35.4 (1984): 400–9.

Michael Williamson, "The Worship of Efficiency: Untangling Theoretical and Practical Considerations in Writing Assessment." Reprinted from *Assessing Writing*, Vol. 1 (2), pp. 147–73. Copyright © 1994, with permission from Elsevier.

Michael M. Williamson, "Validity of Automated Scoring: Prologue for a Continuing Discussion of Machine Scoring Student Writing." From *Journal of Writing Assessment*, Vol. 1 (2), 2003. Reprinted with permission of Hampton Press, Inc.

Kathleen Blake Yancey, "Looking Back as We Look Forward: Historicizing Writing Assessment." Originally published in *College Composition and Communication* 50.3 (1999): 483–503.

INDEX

AAVE. *See* African American vernacular English

accountability in education, 77, 88, 92
  curriculum determined by what is evaluated, 334
  educational communities versus standardized assessment, 338–40
  narrative evaluation of students, 81–83
  reporting to multiple audiences, 256
  versus responsibility, 338–40
  teachers as evaluators, 309

ACT-English scores, 237–38, 241, 242

administration of public schools
  assessment, historical changes in, 63–64
  craft workshop approach, 75–79
  models of schooling, 59–63
  roles of WAC administrator, 252–54
  taxpayer funding, 62
  universal education, 64–65

administration of testing, 22–23, 32, 264–65, 308

Advanced Placement Program (AP), 22, 137

"Adventuring into Writing Assessment" (Haswell and Wyche-Smith), 203–17

AERA. *See* American Educational Research Association

African Americans. *See also* "Expanding the Dialogue on Culture as a Critical Component When Assessing Writing" (Ball)
  accuracy of mechanics in writing, 370–71
  achievement, 354

integration, 62
issues in testing, 359–380
policy making and its effects, 373–79
writing programs, 372

African American vernacular English (AAVE), 359–61, 374

AI. *See* artificial intelligence

Allen, Michael, 140, 142, 164–65, 169, 172, 366

American Board of Engineering and Technology (ABET), 268

American education
  administration of public schools, 59–63, 75–79, 252–54
  assessment, growth and changes in, 61, 63–64, 67–70
  basic skills controversy, 59
  common school movement, 57
  demographic changes, 58, 133
  efficiency, 57–58, 65, 75, 78
  ethnic diversity, 77–78
  fairness in, as a goal, 62–63, 69, 75, 78
  grading standards, national, 133
  integration, 62
  literacy issues, 59, 76–77
  meritocracy in, 58, 61–62
  models of schooling, 56–63
  National Assessment of Educational Progress (NAEP), 160–61, 354
  political pressures on assessment, 331–40
  Reagan and Bush administration policies, 337
  socioeconomic factors in, 359–84
  Spanish-speaking students, increase in, 77